Advance Praise for Cyberlibel: Information Warfare in the 21st Century?

"Cyberlibel is in a state of flux. I found Mr. Potts' interpretation of disclosure of the identities of anonymous parties during the course of libel proceedings invaluable because it covered every aspect of it and provided access to innumerable sites of which I was completely unaware. I think in order to follow cyberlibel you have to think laterally and Mr. Potts' text offers shrewd comments and provides necessary cautions to litigators who wish to plunge into the internet with Statements of Claim blazing."

— *Julian Porter, Q.C.*

"David Potts has produced an authoritative and insightful study of cyberlibel which needs to be on the bookshelf of every media lawyer and author. His analysis of this emerging area of global law is first class."

— *Bruce Sanford, Baker & Hostetler LLP, Washington DC,*
Author of Libel and Privacy, *2d ed. (New York: Aspen Publishers, 2010)*

"The internet is a soapbox like no other we've known before. Defamation actions were always difficult at best and now cyberlibel has muddied the waters even further. This book is the perfect tool to help clear those waters."

— *Gavin May, Legal Counsel, OPP Association*

"This book will surely be required reading for those who become involved in defamation proceedings involving statements disseminated over the Internet. There can be little doubt that the Internet has become one of the most powerful means of disseminating information ever invented, and that when misused the Internet can become an instrument of oppression. Regrettably, cyberlibel has become increasingly prevalent and pernicious. Through years of study and analysis, David Potts has assembled a wealth of valuable information concerning the manner in which cyberlibel has been dealt with by courts and legislatures in different jurisdictions, including Canada. I predict that this book will be relied upon quite heavily in the years to come by those who seek guidance in this rapidly evolving area, including litigators, litigants and the courts."

— *Kent Thomson, Davies Ward Phillips & Vineberg*

"Potts has written a practical how-to (and why-to) book on an omnipresent yet generally unexplored subject. His book is more than just a text on the subject. He has identified the touchstones of the topic and has de-mystified them in a readable yet comprehensive manner. The useful Q & A chapter provides straightforward exploration of common events, actions and alternatives while directing the reader to more detailed and cited sections of the book for support and substantiation. A must have for all those who publish (or who are published about) on the Internet as well as their counsel."

— Tony Sutcliffe, Sr. Vice President, General Counsel, Ricoh Canada Inc.

"David Potts has created a thorough and practical work, aimed squarely at assisting Canadian lawyers and judges to navigate the developing area of cyberlibel. The author uses an array of tools, including descriptions of the general applicable legal principles, existing case-law, surveys of the Internet technology central to the nature of cyberlibel and a strong analysis and breakdown of the relevant substantive and procedural issues, to carefully demonstrate the link between traditional libel law and emerging online issues that will be unfamiliar to many legal professionals. Mr. Potts' division of the text into distinct chapters addressing different aspects of the topic, as well as the inclusion of case-law and materials from relevant foreign jurisdictions, makes this book a solid, succinct reference tool that will be indispensable to lawyers and judges dealing with cyberlibel issues."

— Mark S. Hayes, Hayes | eLaw LLP

"David Potts, who has made a significant contribution over time to the inventory of scholarly materials relating to the law of defamation, has devoted his most recent publication to the highly contemporary subject of cyberlibel.

His book deals with this important subject in all its aspects, including the substantive law of defamation as developed in traditional common law jurisdictions, in actions for defamation relating in particular to intermediaries and users of the Internet. The text is comprehensive, covering causes of action, remedies, defences, damages, jurisdictional issues and the unique problems associated with cyberlibel examined in the light of traditional principles in the law of defamation.

Furthermore, the text, which is developed in a pragmatic format, is organized with a view to providing an effective research tool and an instrument for problem-solving. As such, it provides an extremely thorough and useful inventory of contemporary jurisprudence and related legal analysis devoted to this rapidly developing area of the law."

— David Scott, Borden, Ladner, Gervais, Ottawa

"This new book by David Potts will be helpful to a broad cross-section of the bench and bar. Mr. Potts provides helpful information as to the characteristics of the Internet and web protocol and procedures. He explains how cyberlibel differs from libel claims involving off-line media. Mr. Potts then frames his discussion of the legal issues by relating how the unique aspects of cyberlibel present different issues and demand different solutions.

Mr. Potts draws on leading cases and authorities from the United States, England, Australia and elsewhere in addressing important and challenging issues such as jurisdiction, damages, the availability of injunction relief and the enforcement of judgments. This is a great asset for the many readers who would not otherwise have ready access to these materials. The format is user friendly. Charts are provided which, for example, allow for efficient review of case law concerning general, aggravated and punitive damages. The book also features a helpful section of Frequently Asked Questions.

This book will be extremely helpful to counsel considering whether and where to litigate and in providing realistic advice to their clients as to damages. This book will also provide excellent guidance to government and corporate counsel facing the challenge of advising clients who are posting content on the web how to limit exposure and manage risk in an interconnected and interactive world."

— The Honourable Mr. Justice John Sproat
Ontario Superior Court of Justice, Brampton

"David Potts has produced a superb guide to the complex matrix of legal issues surrounding cyberlibel in the global information age, artfully navigating the myriad issues of procedure and substance, practical judgments, legal doctrines, and theoretical policy issues with which lawyers and jurists world-wide must contend in meeting the challenges posed by libel litigation arising from Internet communication."

— Rodney A. Smolla, President, Furman University, South Carolina,
Author of The Law of Defamation, 2d ed. (Egan, MN:Thomson West, 2010)

"In this compelling and highly readable book, David Potts vividly describes the ways in which defamation disputes involving the new media differ from those involving the old. Full of practical and tech-savvy advice, it will quickly earn a place on the bookshelves of practitioners, Internet publishers and those whose reputations are attacked online. "

— Dr. Matthew Collins, Barrister, Melbourne, Australia
Author of The Law of Defamation and The Internet, 2d ed.
(Oxford: Oxford University Press 2010)

"In a world where the medium is the message, new media constantly creates innovative threats and forms of cyberlibel attack. Potts has provided us with a complete and essential work that definitively guides us through the dangerous nuances of the vital defences that are available to us."

— *Duncan Cornell Card, B.A., LL.B., LL.M.*
Partner and Co-Chair, Technology Practice, Bennett Jones LLP

"This book will be extremely useful to legal practitioners. It is well indexed and, because of the way it is set out and extensively quotes from relevant judgments, provides a search resource of considerable value. The reader obtains a real insight into relevant defamation law and also to how judges have applied it in the developing area of cyberlibel."

— *Alasdair Pepper, Partner, Carter-Ruck Solicitors, UK*

CYBERLIBEL: INFORMATION WARFARE IN THE 21ST CENTURY?

Cyberlibel

INFORMATION WARFARE IN
THE 21ST CENTURY?

David A. Potts

B.A., LL.B., LL.M., BARRISTER, BAR OF ONTARIO

Dedicated to the memory of Frederick L. Miller, Q.C.

Cyberlibel: Information Warfare in the 21st Century?
© Irwin Law Inc., 2011

Published in 2011 by
Irwin Law Inc.
Suite 206, 14 Duncan Street
Toronto, ON
M5H 3G8

www.irwinlaw.com

ISBN: 978-1-55221-203-5

Cataloguing in Publication data available from Library and Archives Canada

The publisher acknowledges the financial support of the Government of Canada through the Book Publishing Industry Development Program (BPIDP) for its publishing activities.

We acknowledge the assistance of the OMDC Book Fund, an initiative of Ontario Media Development Corporation.

Printed and bound in Canada.

1 2 3 4 5   15 14 13 12 11

SUMMARY TABLE OF CONTENTS

DETAILED TABLE OF CONTENTS

CHAPTER 4:

SUMMARY OF THE LAW OF DEFAMATION AND ITS APPLICATION TO CYBERLIBEL   *23*

CHAPTER 10:

DISCLOSURE OF THE IDENTITY OF AN ANONYMOUS AUTHOR   *135*

Part III: Remedies   *177*

CHAPTER 22:

SEARCH ENGINES

CHAPTER 23:

USER-GENERATED CONTENT —WEB 2.0 AND ONLINE SOCIAL NETWORKS

Part VIII: Reference Material   407

FOREWORD

David Potts has written a timely and necessary book on one of the most elusive areas of the law. Internet defamation, or "cyberlibel," is easy to commit and complex to combat. In the print and television world, the publisher has control and responsibility: it owns the means of publication, is usually insured, and is certainly visible. In the Internet world, the defamer has control: he is invisible and anonymous; his postings cost nothing and are immediately available to a world-wide audience. Responsibility for the posting is another issue. Power without responsibility is a dangerous mixture. It may take weeks or months to find out who the defamer is and much longer to get his posting removed, unless the site is a monitored one. In the Internet world, where libel spreads with the speed of light, and anonymity paradoxically can enhance the apparent truth of what is written, damage to the victim can swiftly become so severe as to demand legal action to remove the posting.

This, and indeed, all other legal problems in cyberlibel, are greatly exacerbated by the Internet's utter indifference to national boundaries. If an American travelling in Libya uses a computer in a British-owned hotel to post a defamatory statement on a website whose server is in India, and the Russian victim reads it in Canada, whose courts can hear the lawsuit? David Potts has tackled this very real issue with thoroughness and insight and the result is greatly helpful.

An inescapable fact is that the shape of the Internet is constantly evolving, most recently led by applications such as Skype, Facebook, Twitter, and Apple's emerging i-world. It is not yet clear whether this trend is likely to further fragment the Internet and complicate the task of obtaining legal remedies, or lead to closed proprietary profit-making networks which might bear some structural resemblance to the print world and make things easier. The one certainty about the Internet is change. But, whatever the outcome, it is most unlikely that defamatory postings will disappear. Cyberlibel appears likely to prove to be a growth industry.

David Potts has spent his professional lifetime in the defamation field. His insights are invaluable and he has pursued case law on cyberlibel from around the world to create a work that is a necessary tool for every lawyer seeking to understand and work in this challenging field.

Hon. Dennis Lane QC

SUPERIOR COURT, ONTARIO, 1989–2007

SEPTEMBER 2010

ACKNOWLEDGEMENTS

A book of this size and complexity can only be completed with the assistance and work of a very competent team. This book is no different. First, I would like to thank the assistance I received from the individuals in our office. Leandra Delgado began simply typing my drafts. She blossomed into an "air traffic controller" who has organized, coordinated, and made decisions on a wide range of issues in the book, and without whose assistance this book could have never been completed. A great deal of help in typing was received from a number of individuals. Linda Haney, as usual, has kept us all on track and allowed us to continue with this project without the other aspects of the law firm collapsing.

Outside the office, I received enormous assistance from Irwin Law. In particular, Jeff Miller has been more than merely a publisher; he has been a sounding board, advisor, and in many cases a friend in the production of this book. Dan Wiley, our editor, has gone far beyond the duties of an editor. He has tackled this topic with real enthusiasm, and has contributed enormous expertise through his own skills and graduate work in communications. His impact is evident throughout the book, in particular in the Search Engines, Hyperlinks and Social Networking Sites sections.

I have known Dennis Lane for nearly twenty-five years. When he was senior counsel at Oslers, he spent a full day with me discussing and trying to unravel some of the obscure aspects of libel practice for my first book, *Canadian Libel Practice*. As a judge in the Ontario Superior Court of Justice, he has written some of the leading defamation decisions in Canada: *Magnotta Winery Ltd. v. Ziraldo* on pleadings;[1] *Lubarevich v. Nurgitz* on absolute privilege;[2]

---

1   *Magnotta Winery Ltd. v. Ziraldo*, 1995 CanLII 7122 (ON S.C.),
2   *Lubarevich v. Nurgitz*, [1996] O.J. No. 1457 (Gen. Div.)

and *Hodgson v. Canadian Newspapers Co.*,[3] an extremely important decision in a libel action against the *Globe and Mail*. Aside from generously writing the Foreword, he has suggested to me the concepts of transmogrification, the judicial glossary, and provided insights about the recent changes on the Internet. His comments about the complicated subject of hyperlinks and publications helped crystallize and clarify my thinking. Finally, his enthusiasm for libel in general, and cyberlibel in particular, is infectious. I always leave a conversation with him full of ideas and energy.

I would like to thank Duncan Card, Matt Collins, Mark Hayes, Gavin May, Alasdair Pepper, Julian Porter Q.C., Bruce Sanford, David Scott Q.C., Rod Smolla, Honourable Mr. Justice John Sproat, Tony Sutcliffe, and Kent Thomson, for undertaking the dreary task of reviewing all or parts of the manuscript, a task they most cheerfully agreed to do and squeezed into their enormously busy schedules.

I am also in great debt to other writers of text books and blogs on the Internet. First and foremost, Matt Collins' book, *The Law of Defamation and the Internet*, is an indispensable book. His insights have been invaluable. It was the first book that really examined many of the questions of cyberlibel. My only complaint with the book is its binding—since I use it so much I have had to tape it together with hockey tape. Professor Brown's encyclopædic multi-volume treatise of *The Law of Defamation in Canada* was an enormous help.

Various online commentaries have been very helpful. I do not want to single out anyone. It would be invidious and unfair as I have benefited from many of them. The growth and proliferation of online resources has enabled me to write this book in a much more economical and expeditious way. I regularly used CanLII, BaiLII, AustLII, and SafLII as well as Google Scholar for American cases. Great thanks as well to Brian O'Leary for providing me with a sanctuary which enabled me to recharge my batteries periodically and helped me to realize there is more to the world than hyperlinks, search engines, and Internet intermediaries.

I have dedicated the book to Fred Miller Q.C. For nearly fifty years, while in general practice, Mr. Miller did the prepublication review work for the *St. Catharines Standard*. He became in-house counsel at in his seventies. Mr. Miller retained me to advise him on libel issues after attending a lecture I gave on libel law. His decision to do so reflects more on his generosity of spirit than on my competence as I only had been called to the bar seven years

---

3   *Hodgson v. Canadian Newspapers Co.*, 1998 CanLII 14820 (ON S.C.) affirmed in part 2000 CanLII 14715 (ON C.A.).

before. My lunches with him at the St. Catharines Club were an education in themselves. He was a wonderful raconteur with a self-deprecating sense of humour. His stories ranged from his experiences in World War II, practising law, and politics. I always left these lunches with many insights from a truly wise man. I know he would have embraced the internet and cyberlibel with great enthusiasm.

Finally, I thank Cheryl, Jason, Stuart and Taylor. The advantages of children who have never known a world without Internet is invaluable. They provide a perspective and a sense of balance as they view the Internet with all the excitement and romance of TV, indoor plumbing and central heating. If they look at this book in the future they will likely wonder how primitive my observations were at this time.

As is customary, I assume responsibility for all errors.

David Potts
Halloween 2010
Toronto

PART I: Introduction

CHAPTER 1: Summary of My Personal Observations about Cyberlibel

1. Cyberlibel is a form of and part of the law of defamation.
2. The common law is adaptable enough to resolve many of the questions that arise.
3. The introduction of Internet-specific rules should be primarily introduced through the legislature.
4. While cyberlibel is a form of defamation, I believe it should be considered and examined separately for several reasons:
   a. It has its own distinctive, if not unique, characteristics. Many of these will be discussed in this book.
   b. An understanding of the technology is essential to properly apply the legal principles. For example, in hyperlinks cases it is critical to understand the difference between user-activated hyperlinks and automatic or imbedded hyperlinks. When looking at intermediaries it is important to understand that different functions will lead to different liabilities and different exemptions. When dealing with search engines, it is important to understand that they will retrieve defamatory statements published online, but also will reproduce, in any case, the original defamatory statement in a search engine results page format which typically includes a hyperlink and a "snippet." The search engine results pages are critical in deciding whether to institute proceedings and in assessing the impact of a defamatory statement on a person's character.
   c. Important changes in the dynamics of information distribution have occurred. It is likely the end of the monopoly, if not the dominance, of the centralized institutional media. No longer is information controlled and edited entirely by organizations who dictate what we watch/

read, when we watch/read it, and how we receive our information.[1] Despite these changes there is certainly nothing preordained about the nature of the Internet. In fact, the openness of the Internet itself is now in question: "About 15 years after its manifestation as a global unifying network it has entered its second phase: it appears to be balkanizing, torn apart by three separate related forces."[2] These forces are government, large information technology companies, and network owners. "The trend to more closed systems is undeniable."[3]

d. There are different interests and different conflicts between these interests at different times in cyberlibel. The conventional conflict in libel proceedings involves the clash between reputation and freedom of speech, including freedom of press. While this conflict applies to cyberlibel proceedings, there are a number of other conflicts that are quite different, such as that (i) among reputation, privacy, and freedom of speech; (ii) between reputation and privacy; (iii) among reputation, freedom of speech, and electronic commerce; and (iv) between electronic commerce and freedom of speech.

e. The different characteristics of cyberlibel actions, which require different objectives, strategies, and tactics, will be referred to throughout this book. As the subtitle implies, I believe that cyberlibel should be viewed in a framework of informational warfare, guerilla warfare, and cyberwar. Strategies and tactics that work in offline libel are often ineffective, counterproductive, and even disastrous in cyberlibel proceedings. To survive, let alone succeed, in cyberlibel litigation will require lawyers to analyze and resolve cyberlibel litigation differently, on behalf of both plaintiffs and defendants. As libel lawyers we have not even scratched the surface of an examination — let alone a resolution — of these questions.

5. Finally, some humility should be exercised when approaching Internet defamation problems. We are not the first generation of lawyers and judges to confront and grapple with the legal implications of a global tele-

---

1   See Ken Auletta, *Googled: The End of the World As We Know It* (New York: Penguin, 2010) for discussions about the future of the conventional media in comparison with David Halberstam, *The Powers That Be* (New York: Knopf, 1979) written at probably the apogee of the institutional print and electronic network media in 1979.

2   "The Future of the Internet: A Virtual Counter-Revolution," *The Economist* (4 September 2010) at 75. See also Jonathan Zittrain, *The Future of The Internet* (New Haven, CT: Yale University Press, 2008) and Tim Wu, *the Master Switch: The Rise and Fall of Information Empires* (New York: Knopf, 2010).

3   *Ibid.* at 76.

communications technology. Lawyers and judges in the Victorian and Edwardian eras faced perplexing defamation questions with the emergence of the telegraph. Their job was arguably more difficult than ours. They were the real pioneers in global telecommunications defamation law. We at least have had the opportunity to examine, analyze, and apply decisions involving the telegraph, telephone, and television. See the following telegraph cases:

- *Grisham v. Western Union Telegraph Co.* 238 Mo. 480, 142 S.W. 271 (1911)
- *Moran v. O'Regan* (1907), 38 N.B.R. 189 (C.A.)
- *Puterbaugh v. Gold Medal Furniture Manufacturing Co.* (1904), 7 O.L.R. 582 (C.A.)
- *Nye v. Western Union Telegraph Co.*, 104 Fed. 628 at 631 (D. Minn. 1900)
- *Robinson v. Robinson* (1897), 13 T.L.R. 564
- *Smith v. Crocker* (1889), 5 T.L.R. 441
- *Dominion Telegraph Co. v. Silver* (1882), 10 S.C. R. 238
- Brett J. in *Williamson v. Freer* (1874), L.R. 9 C.P. 393 at 395
- *Whitfield v. S.E. Ry. Co.*, (1858), E.B. & E. 115

See a direct application of a telegraph defamation case to a cyberlibel case in *Lunney v. Prodigy Services Co.*, 94 N.Y.2d 242 (1999).

The trial judge in *Dow Jones and Company Inc. v. Gutnick*, [2002] HCA 56; 210 CLR 575; 194 ALR 433; 77 ALJR 255, Hedigan J., showed that the courts have dealt with questions similar to those arising from earlier technology. See para. 198 of Callinan J.'s reasons for the High Court of Australia:

> As Hedigan J held, the torts of libel and slander are committed when and where comprehension of the defamatory matter occurs. The rules have been universally applied to publications by spoken word, in writing, on television, by radio transmission, over the telephone or over the Internet. In *Browne v Dunn* the House of Lords held that there was no publication of a defamatory petition to a person (Mrs Cook) who had signed but not read the petition. [Footnotes omitted.]

The Internet seems to be the quintessential millennial technological creation. In fact, the Internet and the telegraph, developed in the nineteenth century, are surprisingly similar, as argued so clearly by Tom Standage in his book *The Victorian Internet*:

> The similarities between the telegraph and the Internet — both in their technical underpinnings and their social impact — are striking. But the story of

the telegraph contains a deeper lesson. Because of its ability to link distant peoples, the telegraph was the first technology to be seized upon as a panacea. Given its potential to change the world, the telegraph was soon being hailed as a means of solving the world's problems. It failed to do so, of course — but we have been pinning the same hope on other new technologies ever since.[4]

. . .

The optimistic claims now being made about the internet are merely the most recent examples in a tradition of technological utopianism that goes back to the first transatlantic telegraph cables, 150 years ago.[5]

. . .

That the telegraph was so widely seen as a panacea is perhaps understandable. The fact that we are still making the same mistake today is less so. The irony is that even though it failed to live up to the utopian claims made about it, the telegraph really did transform the world. It also redefined forever our attitudes toward new technologies. In both respects, we are still living in the new world it inaugurated.[6]

The epilogue of this insightful book deserves to be considered.[7] It adds a tincture of perspective to the frequent trumpeting about the uniqueness of the Internet:

The hype, skepticism and bewilderment associated with the Internet — concerns about new forms of crime, adjustments in social mores, and redefinitions of business practices — mirror the hopes, fears, and misunderstandings inspired by the telegraph. Indeed, they are only to be expected. They are the direct consequences of human nature, rather than technology.

Given a new invention, there will always be some people who see only its potential to do good, while other[s] see new opportunities to commit crime or make money. We can expect exactly the same reactions to whatever new inventions appear in the twenty-first century.

Such reactions are amplified by what might be termed chronocentricity — the egotism that one's own generation is poised on the very cusp of

---

4   Tom Standage, *The Victorian Internet* (New York: Walker, 2007) at 210–11.
5   *Ibid.* at 211.
6   *Ibid.*
7   See also Mark Sableman, "Link Law Revisited: Internet Linking Law at Five Years" (2001) 16:3 *Berkeley Technology Law Journal* 1273 on the approach to technological problems.
        See also the High Court of Australia's comments about the notion of "ubiquity of the internet" at para. 186 of *Dow Jones and Company Inc v. Gutnick*, [2002] HCA 56; 210 CLR 575; 194 ALR 433; 77 ALJR 255.

history. Today, we are repeatedly told that we are in the midst of a communications revolution. But the electric telegraph was, in many ways, far more disconcerting for the inhabitants of the time than today's advances are for us. If any generation has the right to claim that it bore the full bewildering, world-shrinking brunt of such revolution, it is not us — it is our nineteenth century forbears.

Time-travelling Victorians arriving in the late twentieth century would, no doubt, be unimpressed by the Internet. They would surely find space flight and routine intercontinental air travel far more impressive technological achievements than our much-trumpeted global communications network. Heavier-than-air flying machines were after all, thought by the Victorians to be totally impossible. But as for the Internet — well, they had one of their own.[8]

---

8   Tom Standage, *The Victorian Internet* (New York: Walker, 2007) at 212–13.

CHAPTER 2: How to Use this Book

A. WHAT THIS BOOK IS

This book is not designed to be read cover to cover. Rather, it is designed to provide judges and lawyers, faced with a problem or number of problems arising from cyberlibel, a source of pertinent information as needed.

B. CHARACTERISTICS OF THIS BOOK

The following features have been introduced to facilitate the book's use:

1. The body of the text has largely been written in a factum-style format.
2. There are a series of Frequently Asked Questions (FAQs) in Chapter 3 covering a variety of issues, which can be consulted as a starting point.
3. My personal observations are identified as personal observations. This has been done so that you can ignore them if you wish and so there will be no confusion with the statements of law that are contained throughout the book. Where there are comments on certain cases, I have distinguished between my opinion and statements of law.
4. The chapters are designed as much as possible to be self-contained. This has, in my view, both a central benefit and a central drawback. The benefit is that tiresome scampering back and forth between chapters for required information by the reader will be reduced. The drawback is duplication of aspects of the law among certain chapters.
5. The book contains large caselaw extracts from certain decisions, especially from the Supreme Court of Canada, House of Lords, the US Supreme Court, the High Court of Australia, and other appellate courts. The large extracts are inserted in several situations, more specifically:

a. When they are the most authoritative statements of the law either because of the level of the court or because of the content of the decision.

b. When there is absolutely nothing else (i.e., no other law) available. Consequently, it is not only the authoritative statement, it is the only statement of law.

c. When there are useful pieces of practical advice for lawyers contained in the decisions, such as cross-examinations or discussions of the use of expert evidence.

d. When the summaries of the arguments of counsel are included, particularly when the issues have not yet been decided by the courts in Canada.

6. The judicial decisions covered are not limited to Canada, but include Australia, New Zealand, South Africa, the UK, and the US. This is essential in a field that is international, where many of the issues are very similar, and there are no or a limited number of Canadian cases in certain areas. See, for example, the treatment of intermediaries, the role and liability of search engines, abuse of process arguments, and take down notices.

7. A glossary of judicially defined terms is included. This is not a glossary or dictionary of Internet terms, which can be found in a number of different resources such as:

   • Matthew Collins, *The Law of Defamation and the Internet*, 2d ed. (Oxford: Oxford University Press, 2005)

   • Douglas Downing, *et al.*, eds., *Dictionary of Computer and Internet Terms* (Hauppage, NY: Barron's Educational Series, 2009)

   • Darrel Ince, *A Dictionary of the Internet* (Oxford: Oxford University Press, 2009) (Also available online, as are numerous other Internet glossaries). See online: www.webopedia.com

   • Barry Sookman, *Computer, Internet and Electronic Commerce Terms: Judicial, Legislative and Technical Definitions* (Toronto: Carswell, 2001)

   However, it contains terms, such as "Internet," "hyperlinks," "intermediaries," "facebook," "blogs," and "search engines." Many of these terms are defined differently by different courts in different jurisdictions at different times. The concepts are fluid and dynamic. Consequently, I felt it was necessary to provide counsel and judges with a variety of explanations, should they want to use them or, at least, be aware of them. This form of glossary makes the actual text less cumbersome, as I have only included a few definitions or explanations in the body of the text.

8. Finally, there are charts for damages, injunctions, and jurisdictional motions to provide an accessible form of reference to cases. The law is stated

as of 1 August 2010. These charts will be regularly updated in the electronic version.

Here is an example of how you can use the book: Imagine you want to determine how to obtain the identities of anonymous defendants.

1. Go to the FAQ section. There will not be an FAQ for every issue, but there will be for many of the most common issues.
2. Turn to the relevant chapter and examine the different remedies.
3. If you want further information, you can see what remedies are available in the book for Australia, the UK, or the US.

C. WHAT THIS BOOK IS NOT

This book is not a text or even a primer on defamation. It is a text about cyberlibel. The basic principles of defamation, as stated by the Supreme Court of Canada, are included. I have also referred to other texts for further information, including, but not limited to:

- Julian Porter and David A. Potts, *Canadian Libel Practice* (Toronto: Butterworths, 1986)
- Roger D. McConchie and David A. Potts, *Canadian Libel & Slander Actions* (Toronto: Irwin Law, 2004)

Consequently, there is no discussion about certain areas of libel law if there are no cyberlibel cases on that topic. There is no need to duplicate such areas of law that have been substantively treated elsewhere. Furthermore, there are several areas of law, such as the discussion and analysis of UK legislation relating to intermediaries, that I have not covered in detail. This book is written primarily for Canadian lawyers and judges and therefore areas of law where no Canadian legislation exists or is yet in place have been intentionally omitted. References to the other legislation are included, because I believe it is important that Canadian lawyers are aware of it, as are extracts of judicial discussions of the legislation. There is an excellent comprehensive analysis, and commentary of such legislation in Matthew Collins, *The Law of Defamation and the Internet*, 2d ed. (Oxford: Oxford University Press, 2005).

When there are areas of law that I do not pursue, I will refer the reader to this text and others rather than re-examining what other writers have ably discussed previously.

CHAPTER 3: Frequently Asked Questions

A. CAN I OBTAIN AN INTERLOCUTORY INJUNCTION TO REMOVE A DEFAMATORY PUBLICATION FROM THE INTERNET?

Answer: Interlocutory injunctions are not readily granted in libel actions, including cyberlibel.

1. The test for the issuance of an interlocutory injunction is much more stringent in cyberlibel and libel actions than in other proceedings because there is a concern for the restriction of freedom of speech prior to trial.
   - See *Canadian Human Rights Commission v. Canadian Liberty Net*, [1998] 1 S.C.R. 626
   - *Rapp v. McClelland & Stewart Ltd.* (1981), 34 O.R. (2d) 452 (H.C.J.)
   - *Canada Metal Ltd. v. C.B.C.* (1975), 55 D.L.R. (3d) 42 (Ont. Div. Ct.)
2. The test for granting interlocutory injunctions in libel proceedings in Canada was articulated by Griffith J. of the Ontario Court of Justice in *Rapp v. McClelland & Stewart Ltd.* (1981), 34 O.R. (2d) 452 at 455–56 (H.C.J.):

> In my view, however, the test for determining whether the interim injunction should issue involves not only a consideration of the likelihood of the defendant proving justification at trial, but also whether a jury will inevitably come to the conclusion that the words however false are also defamatory of the plaintiff.
>
> The guiding principle then is, that the injunction should only issue where the words complained of are so manifestly defamatory that any jury verdict to the contrary would be considered perverse by the Court of Appeal. To put it another way where it is impossible to say that a reasonable jury must inevitably find the words defamatory the injunction should not issue.

In this case, I am not prepared to predict at this stage that a jury will, inevitably, find the words here complained of defamatory of the plaintiff. The English Court of Appeal has recently held in *Herbage v. Times Newspapers*, May 1981 (not yet reported) that the decision of the House of Lords in *American Cyanamid Co. v. Ethicon Ltd.*, [1975] A.C. 396, has not affected the well-established principle in cases of libel that an interim injunction should not be granted unless the jury would inevitably come to the conclusion that the words were defamatory.

In my view as well, the principle should be preserved in libel cases that, except in a case of manifest libel, the interim injunction should not issue where the wrong suffered by the plaintiff may be adequately compensated for in damages. There is early authority for this in the decision of *Monson v. Tussauds Ltd.*, [1894] 1 Q.B. 671.

Coltsfoot Publishing Ltd. v. Harris (1999), 43 C.P.C (4th) 282 at para. 26 (N.S.S.C.)
Canadian Human Rights Commission v. Canadian Liberty Net, [1998] 1 S.C.R. 626
Daishowa Inc. v. Friends of the Lubicon 1995 CanLII 7298 (ON S.C.)
Maritime Telegraph & Telephone Co. v. C'Nara, [1989] N.S.J. No. 281 (S.C.)

3. Interlocutory injunctions in libel proceedings will not be granted if the defendant pleads a *prima facie* legitimate defence, particularly the defence of justification or truth.

Holley v. Smyth, [1998] All E.R. 853 at 861
Khashoggi v. IDC Magazines Ltd., [1986] 3 All E.R. 577 at 581
Herbage v. Pressdram Ltd., [1984] 2 All E.R. 769 at 771

4. Permanent injunctions have been granted in the following cyberlibel actions.

Newman et al. v. Halstead et al., 2006 BCSC 65 (CanLII)
Barrick Gold Corp v. Lopehandia (2004), 71 O.R. (3d) 416 (C.A.)
Henry v. Stockhouse Media Corp., [1999] B.C.J. No. 3202 (*ex parte* injunctions granted against anonymous publisher)

5. There are complications with cyberlibel injunctions that should be considered including:
   a. Migration of the defamatory statements to other jurisdictions outside of Canada.
   b. Coverage by the media both offline and in online websites, chat rooms, and blogs.
   c. Difficulties in enforcing orders (see *Barrick Gold Corp v. Lopehandia* (2004), 71 O.R. (3d) 416 (C.A.).
   d. Exposure to further mockery by the author.

B. WHAT ARE THE DAMAGES I CAN EXPECT TO OBTAIN IN A CYBERLIBEL ACTION?

Answer: As in other libel actions, the size of the award will differ on the individual facts of the case. A decision of the Ontario Court of Appeal states that publication of defamatory statements on the Internet may aggravate damages (see *Barrick Gold Corp. v. Lopehandia* (2004), 71 O.R. (3d) 416 at paras. 34–44 (C.A.)). See the charts on damages in Chapter 25.

C. WHAT OTHER CAUSES OF ACTION ARE AVAILABLE ASIDE FROM DEFAMATION FOR REPUTATIONAL ATTACKS ON THE INTERNET?

Answer: Invasion of privacy (statutory and common law), negligent misstatement, malicious falsehood, negligence, data protection, legislation, and misleading and deceptive conduct.

Competition Act, R.S.C. 1985, c. C-34
Trade-Marks Act, R.S.C. 1985, c. T-13

D. WHAT PROBLEMS PECULIAR TO CYBERLIBEL SHOULD I CONSIDER BEFORE STARTING A CYBERLIBEL ACTION?

Answer: Aside from ensuring there is no defence to the action you should consider at least the following issues:

1. If any of the defendants are anonymous you will have to attempt to obtain their identity from the Internet Service Provider (ISP). You may have to resort to court proceedings to compel the ISP to disclose the identity of the author of the defamatory statement.
2. If the defendant resides outside of Canada, you will probably face a motion to stay the action on jurisdictional grounds.
3. Equally important, you may not be able to enforce a Canadian judgment in the jurisdiction where the defendant resides.
4. The defendant may not defend the action for numerous reasons, but may continue to post defamatory statements on other websites located outside of Canada.
5. By launching a cyberlibel action you may attract more attention to the libel by igniting re-publication by other persons to more active websites, or the offline media throughout the world.

6. An offline media outlet usually has standards to which they are accountable. In contrast, many online publishers view rules and standards with an anarchistic sense of contempt.

7. In offline libel actions lawyers are advisors, while in cyberlibel lawyers are often targets of attack.

E. DO I NEED TO SERVE A NOTICE UNDER THE ONTARIO *LIBEL AND SLANDER ACT* OR OTHER PROVINCIAL DEFAMATION ACTS?

Answer:

1. The Ontario Court of Appeal has held that it is necessary for the plaintiff to serve a notice under the *Libel and Slander Act*, R.S.O. 1990, c. L.12 relating to an online publication of a newspaper or a radio broadcast.

   Jonssen-Ortho Inc. v. Amgen Inc., [2005] O.J. No. 2265
   Weiss v. Sawyer (2002), 61 O.R. (3d) 526 (C.A.)

2. Both non-media and media-based defendants have to be served with notice.

   Watson v. Southam Inc. (2002), 189 D.L.R. (4th) 695
   Siddiqu v. C.B.C., 2000 CanLII 1690 (ON C.A.)

3. Failure to serve a notice is a complete bar to the action.

   MCF Capital Inc. v. CBC, [2003] M.J. No. 324 (Q.B.)
   Gallant v. Moncton Publishing Co. (1994), 146 N.B.R. (2d) 241 (C.A.)
   Grossman v. CFTO TV Ltd. (1982), 39 O.R. (2d) 498 at 501 (C.A.)

4. The law is unclear and unsettled as to whether you need to serve a notice for a defamatory statement on a website that is not connected to a newspaper or a radio station located in Ontario.

   Bahlieda v. Santa, 2003 CanLII 2883 (ON C.A.)

F. IS US LIBEL LAW DIFFERENT FROM ANGLO-CANADIAN LIBEL LAW?

Answer: Canadian libel law imposes the burden of proof of the truth of what was published upon the publisher (the defendant). In contrast, US libel law, at least in the case of a plaintiff who is a "public figure," imposes the burden on the plaintiff to prove falsity and actual malice on the part of the publisher. There is, therefore, a judicial disadvantage for a plaintiff compelled to sue in the US.

Barrick Gold Corp. v. Blanchard & Company [2003] O.J. No. 5817 at paras. 35–36 and 66 (S.C.J.)

See similar statements in the following cases:

Black v. Breeden, 2009 CanLII 14041 (ON S.C.) affirmed, 2010 ONCA 547 (CanLII)

Research in Motion Ltd. v. Visto Corp., [2008] O.J. No. 3671 at para. 107, Gordon J. (S.C.J.)

Burke v. New York Post Holdings Inc., [2005] B.C.J. No. 1993 at para. 37

Trizec Properties Inc. v. Citigroup Global Markets Inc., [2004] O.J. No. 323 at paras. 43–45

Imagis Technologies v. Red Herring Communications Inc., [2003] B.C.J. No. 533 at paras. 25–26, Pitfield J. (S.C.)

Pindling v. NBC, [1984] O.J. No. 3417 at para. 36

The Supreme Court of Canada has rejected importing the US First Amendment standards into Canadian defamation law as stated in *Hill v. Church of Scientology of Toronto*, [1995] 2 S.C.R. 1130 at para. 137 by Cory J.:

> The *New York Times v. Sullivan* decision has been criticized by judges and academic writers in the United States and elsewhere. It has not been followed in the United Kingdom or Australia. I can see no reason for adopting it in Canada in an action between private litigants. The law of defamation is essentially aimed at the prohibition of the publication of injurious false statements. It is the means by which the individual may protect his or her reputation which may well be the most distinguishing feature of his or her character, personality and, perhaps, identity. I simply cannot see that the law of defamation is unduly restrictive or inhibiting. Surely it is not requiring too much of individuals that they ascertain the truth of the allegations they publish. The law of defamation provides for the defences of fair comment and of qualified privilege in appropriate cases. Those who publish statements should assume a reasonable level of responsibility.

See also similar statements in the following cases:

Research in Motion Ltd. v. Visto Corp., [2008] O.J. No. 3671 at para. 107, Gordon J. (S.C.J.)

Burke v. New York Post Holdings Inc., [2005] B.C.J. No. 1993 (S.C.)

Trizec Properties Inc. v. Citigroup Global Markets Inc., [2004] O.J. No. 323 at para. 44 (S.C.J.)

Barrick Gold Corp. v. Blanchard & Company, [2003] O.J. No. 5817 (S.C.J.)

G. DO THE DIFFERENCES REALLY MATTER?

Answer: The differences do matter. At risk of oversimplification, some of the differences are as follows:

1. A plaintiff in a libel action generally has more difficulty succeeding in the US than in Australia, Canada, or the UK.
2. An American defendant will generally seek to stay cyberlibel proceedings brought in Canada on grounds that the Ontario court has no jurisdiction or that Ontario is not the most convenient forum to try the case.
3. An ISP based in the US will be afforded absolute immunity by section 230 of the *Communications Decency Act of 1996.*

Novak v. Overture Services, Inc, 209 F. Supp. 2d 446 (E.D. N.Y. 2004)

Green v. America Online, 318 F.3d 465 (3d Cir. 2003)

Noah v. AOL Time Warner, Inc., 261 F. Supp. 2d 532 (E.D. Va. 2003)

Patentwizard, Inc. v. Kinko's Inc., 163 F. Supp. 2d 1069 (D. S.D. 2001)

Schneider v. Amazon.com Inc., 3 P.3d 37 (C.A. Wa. 2001)

Doe v. Oliver, 755 A.2d 1000 (S.C. Conn. 2000)

Weinstein, and Company Inc. v. America Online, Inc., 206 F.3d 980 (10th Cir. 2000)

Blumenthal v. Drudge, 992 F. Supp. 44 (D. D.C. 1998)

Zeran v. America Online Inc., 958 F. Supp. 1124 (E.D. Va. 1997)

Zeran v. America Online Inc., 129 F.3d 327 (4th Cir. 1997)

H. WHAT SHOULD MY CLIENT DO WHEN HE IS SUED?

Answer: After assessing whether there are any defences available, it is often wise to consider offering to publish an apology or retraction in exchange for a complete release and a dismissal without costs. Most plaintiffs simply want an apology and a retraction. Many libel actions can be averted with the publication of an apology or a retraction.

I. WHAT DEFENCES ARE AVAILABLE TO DEFENDANTS WHO ARE SUED FOR CYBERLIBEL?

Answer: The usual defences in libel apply to cyberlibel.
- Literal truth
- Substantial truth, or substantial justification
- Justification based on multiple allegations
- *Polly-Peck/Pizza Pizza* defence — allows the defendant to plead her own meaning and then plead that that meaning is true
- Absolute privilege
- Qualified privilege
- Statutory report privilege
- Public interest privilege
- Fair comment

- Consent
- Potential defence of the right to reply
- Innocent dissemination

J. SHOULD "CEASE AND DESIST" LETTERS BE SENT?

Answer: A "cease and desist" letter or a "demand" letter has the advantage of informing the potential defendant of the plaintiff's concerns. It should be written on a "with prejudice" basis and sent in conjunction with the notice of libel if required by provincial legislation. A cease and desist letter should not be sent without some reflection since they can backfire if the potential defendant resides outside of your jurisdiction. She may post your letter on her website, accompanied by a mocking commentary that subjects your client to further ridicule in cyberspace.

K. DOES THE NEW DEFENCE OF RESPONSIBLE COMMUNICATIONS AS A MATTER OF PUBLIC INTEREST APPLY TO STATEMENTS MADE ONLINE? BY BLOGGERS? OR PEOPLE ON FACEBOOK?

Answer: Yes, it does. The Supreme Court of Canada has specifically and expressly indicated that the defence is not restricted to the media and does apply to online statements. See the statement of the Court at para. 97 in *Grant v. Torstar Corp.*, 2009 SCC 61:

> A review of recent defamation case law suggests that many actions now concern blog postings and other online media which are potentially both more ephemeral and more ubiquitous than traditional print media. While established journalistic standards provide a useful guide by which to evaluate the conduct of journalists and non-journalists alike, the applicable standards will necessarily evolve to keep pace with the norms of new communications media. For this reason, it is more accurate to refer to the new defence as responsible communication on matters of public interest.

L. WHAT ARE THE ELEMENTS OF THE DEFENCE OF RESPONSIBLE COMMUNICATIONS?

Answer: They are succinctly summarized at paras. 98 and 126 in *Grant v. Torstar Corp.*, 2009 SCC 61:

This brings us to the substance of the test for responsible communication. In *Quan*, Sharpe J.A. held that the defence has two essential elements: public interest and responsibility. I agree, and would formulate the test as follows. First, the publication must be on a matter of public interest. Second, the defendant must show that publication was responsible, in that he or she was diligent in trying to verify the allegation(s), having regard to all the relevant circumstances.

. . .

Summary of the Required Elements
The defence of public interest responsible communication is assessed with reference to the broad thrust of the publication in question. It will apply where:

A. The publication is on a matter of public interest; and
B. The publisher was diligent in trying to verify the allegation, having regard to:
   (a) the seriousness of the allegation;
   (b) the public importance of the matter;
   (c) the urgency of the matter;
   (d) the status and reliability of the source;
   (e) whether the plaintiff's side of the story was sought and accurately reported;
   (f) whether the inclusion of the defamatory statement was justifiable;
   (g) whether the defamatory statement's public interest lay in the fact that it was made rather than its truth ("reportage"); and
   (h) any other relevant circumstances.

M. WHAT TESTS APPLY FOR INJUNCTIONS IF THE ONLINE STATEMENTS ARE DEFAMATORY? CONSTITUTE AN INVASION OF PRIVACY? OR CONSTITUTE INJURIOUS FALSEHOOD?

Answer: The tests for obtaining injunctions in those three forms of actions are different. In summary, it is more difficult to obtain an injunction for defamation, as it involves a prior restraint of freedom of speech.

See *Rapp v. McLelland & Stewart Ltd.* (1981), 34 O.R. (2d) 452.

An injunction for privacy and injurious falsehood can be obtained by the less rigorous test.

See *RJR-Macdonald Inc. v. Canada (Attorney-General)*, 1994 CanLII 117 (S.C.C.)

N. WHAT TYPES OF HYPERLINKS ARE THERE?

Answer: There are virtual, absolute, and relative. There is also the difference between deep-linking and shallow-linking. The terms are defined in the glossary. However, probably the most important distinction for libel lawyers is whether the hyperlink is automatic or whether the link is user-activated.

Any page on a website may contain one or more hyperlinks to pages on the same or other wesbsites, located on the same or different servers from the one that hosts the linking site. The files at the other site normally are under the control of another entity. However, hyperlinks may be made either with or without a business relationship with the owners of the sites to which links are made.

Hyperlinks can be automatic links or user-activated. A link is automatic when a code is embedded in the webpage that instructs the browser, upon obtaining access to the first site, to automatically download a file from the second site. The information from the second site is pulled without the need for further action on the part of the user. A link is user-activated when the user must click the mouse button over the hyperlink in order to obtain access to the information from the second site. If the linked files are located on another server, the user's browser makes a direct connection to the second server. The user-activated hyperlink may be made to the home page or a sub-page located on the second site, in which case, the end-user may have to take further action to access a particular file at that site. The link may also be made directly to a specific file, in which case the user will receive the content represented by that file without the need for further action.

See the decision of the Copyright Board of Canada, October 27. 1999. online: www. cb-cda.gc.ca/decisions/1999/19991027-m-b.pdf.

This distinction is discussed in some detail in Chapter 15.

O. ARE THE LIMITATION PERIODS AFFECTED BY THE INTERNET?

Answer: The British Columbia Court of Appeal has ruled in a specific case where a defamatory statement has been on the Internet beyond the general statute of limitations and held that the limitation period did not apply and that what is called the "multiple publication rule" applies.

See *Carter v. B.C. Federation of Foster Parents Assn.*, 2005 BCCA 398 (CanLII)

However, this issue has not been resolved in other provinces throughout the country.

P. ARE INTERNET SERVICE PROVIDERS LIABLE FOR DEFAMATION?

Answer: It depends on the jurisdiction. In the US there is virtually an absolute immunity pursuant to section 230 of the *Communications Decency Act*. In Australia and the UK the law is less clear as there are some statutory protections. In Canada there is no legislation and consequently, you have to rely upon the common law to determine: (1) whether there has been publication, and (2) if there has been publication, whether the defence of innocent dissemination applies.

The functions of the ISP must be examined. However, liability will, in effect, depend on the function that they are engaged in at the particular occasion in question. See the treatment of ISPs by the Copyright Board of Canada in its decision of 29 October 1999 at 11–12, online: www.cb-cda.gc.ca/decisions/1999/19991027-m-b.pdf:

> First, they provide the communication service. This service, in turn, involves two main activities: providing and servicing the "backbone" infrastructure and providing connectivity to subscribers. Providing communication services may involve other ancillary activities, such as allocating IP addresses or domain names, or developing and supplying products that implement protocols used for Internet transmissions.
>
> Witnesses before the Board used different terminology to describe the persons involved in providing the Internet communication service. In this decision, ISP (Internet Service Provider) refers to an entity that provides any Internet communication service, including connectivity to subscribers. This is further divided into IAP (Internet Access Provider) for entities that provide connectivity to subscribers, and BSP (Backbone Service Provider) for entities that operate infrastructure components of the Internet.
>
> Providing connectivity involves providing subscribers with an IP address, supplying and operating equipment and software to allow the subscriber to connect to the Internet, making arrangements with other ISPs to connect to the remainder of the Internet, and operating the routers and other equipment to forward information.
>
> Second, persons involved in the Internet provide applications or high level services, including the World Wide Web, Internet e-mail and newsgroups

which are described in greater detail below. Since many of these applications involve making information of any kind available to users, those who provide such information are commonly referred to as "content providers."

See also the treatment of ISPs by the Court in *Society of Composers, Authors and Music Publishers of Canada v. Canadian Assn. of Internet Providers*, 2004 SCC 45, [2004] 2 S.C.R. 427 at paras. 99–102:

> While lack of knowledge of the infringing nature of a work is not a defence to copyright actions generally (J. S. McKeown, *Fox on Canadian Law of Copyright and Industrial Designs* (4th ed. (loose-leaf)), at pp. 21-4 and 21-5), nevertheless the presence of such knowledge would be a factor in the evaluation of the "conduit" status of an Internet Service Provider, as discussed below.
>
> The Internet Service Provider, acting as an intermediary, does not charge a particular fee to its clients for music downloading (although clearly the availability of "free music" is a significant business incentive).
>
> I conclude that the *Copyright Act*, as a matter of legislative policy established by Parliament, does not impose liability for infringement on intermediaries who supply software and hardware to facilitate use of the Internet. The attributes of such a "conduit", as found by the Board, include a lack of actual knowledge of the infringing contents, and the impracticality (both technical and economic) of monitoring the vast amount of material moving through the Internet, which is prodigious. We are told that a large on-line service provider like America Online delivers in the order of 11 million transmissions a day.
>
> Of course an Internet Service Provider in Canada can play a number of roles. In addition to its function as an intermediary, it may as well act as a content provider, or create embedded links which automatically precipitate a telecommunication of copyrighted music from another source. In such cases, copyright liability may attach to the added functions. The protection provided by s. 2.4(1)(*b*) relates to a protected function, not to *all* of the activities of a particular Internet Service Provider.

Functions are analyzed in the following ways:

1. As publishers, distributors, and carriers.
2. Through statutes in South Africa and the UK, as hosts, caches, and mere conduits.

These issues are discussed in more detail in Chapter 21.

Q. ARE SEARCH ENGINES LIABLE FOR DEFAMATORY STATEMENTS IN CANADA AND THE UK?

Answer: At present, there is one case in the UK that has held that search engines are not liable as publishers prior to notification: *Metropolitan International Schools Ltd. (t/a Skillstrain and/or Train2game) v. Designtechnica Corp (t/a Digital Trends) & Ors*, [2009] EWHC 1765 (QB). The law is less clear as to whether search engines are liable after notification by the plaintiff of the defamatory statements.

R. WHAT ARE THE DEFENCES FOR INTERNET SERVICE PROVIDERS?

Answer: In Canada there is just the common law, which means there are two questions: (1) Are they a publisher? and (2) If they are, does the defence of innocent dissemination apply? Different issues may apply before and after notice and has been given. These defences are in addition to the defences available to the author, such as truth, fair comment, and privilege.

S. DO LAWS OF DEFAMATION APPLY TO FACEBOOK IN CANADA?

Answer: Probably. There is one defamation case in the UK in which damages were awarded.

See *Applause and Firsht v. Raphael*, [2008] EWHC 1781 (QB)

There have been some cases in the US where the courts have held that Facebook is an ISP and therefore protected by section 230 of the *Communications Decency Act*.

T. ARE BLOGS COVERED BY THE SAME LAW OF LIBEL OR DEFAMATION AS STATEMENTS OFFLINE? DO THEY HAVE SOME OTHER PROTECTION?

Answer: Generally speaking, they are subject to the same laws as offline statements. There have been several libel actions against blogs, which have been successful. See the charts provided in Chapter 25.

CHAPTER 4: Summary of the Law of Defamation and its Application to Cyberlibel

A. THE LAW AS STATED BY THE SUPREME COURT OF CANADA IN *GRANT v. TORSTAR CORP.*

The Supreme Court of Canada in *Grant v. Torstar Corp.*, 2009 SCC 61 , succinctly and authoritatively, summarized the claim and the defences of the law of defamation in Canada at paras. 28–37:

> A plaintiff in a defamation action is required to prove three things to obtain judgment and an award of damages: (1) that the impugned words were defamatory, in the sense that they would tend to lower the plaintiff's reputation in the eyes of a reasonable person; (2) that the words in fact referred to the plaintiff; and (3) that the words were published, meaning that they were communicated to at least one person other than the plaintiff. If these elements are established on a balance of probabilities, falsity and damage are presumed, though this rule has been subject to strong criticism: see, e.g., R. A. Smolla, "Balancing Freedom of Expression and Protection of Reputation Under Canada's *Charter of Rights and Freedoms*," in D. Schneiderman, ed., *Freedom of Expression and the Charter* (1991), 272, at p. 282. (The only exception is that slander requires proof of special damages, unless the impugned words were slanderous *per se*: R. E. Brown, *The Law of Defamation in Canada* (2nd ed. (loose-leaf)), vol. 3, at pp. 25-2 and 25-3.) The plaintiff is not required to show that the defendant intended to do harm, or even that the defendant was careless. The tort is thus one of strict liability.
>
> If the plaintiff proves the required elements, the onus then shifts to the defendant to advance a defence in order to escape liability.
>
> Both statements of opinion and statements of fact may attract the defence of privilege, depending on the occasion on which they were made.

Some "occasions," like Parliamentary and legal proceedings, are absolutely privileged. Others, like reference letters or credit reports, enjoy "qualified" privilege, meaning that the privilege can be defeated by proof that the defendant acted with malice: see *Horrocks v. Lowe*, [1975] A.C. 135 (H.L.). The defences of absolute and qualified privilege reflect the fact that "common convenience and welfare of society" sometimes requires untrammelled communications: *Toogood v. Spyring* (1834), 1 C.M. & R. 181, 149 E.R. 1044, at p. 1050, *per* Parke B. The law acknowledges through recognition of privileged occasions that false and defamatory expression may sometimes contribute to desirable social ends.

In addition to privilege, statements of opinion, a category which includes any "deduction, inference, conclusion, criticism, judgment, remark or observation which is generally incapable of proof" (*Ross v. New Brunswick Teachers' Assn.*, 2001 NBCA 62, 2001 NBCA 62, 201 D.L.R. (4th) 75, at para. 56, cited in *WIC Radio*, at para. 26), may attract the defence of fair comment. As reformulated in *WIC Radio*, at para. 28, a defendant claiming fair comment must satisfy the following test: (a) the comment must be on a matter of public interest; (b) the comment must be based on fact; (c) the comment, though it can include inferences of fact, must be recognisable as comment; (d) the comment must satisfy the following objective test: could any person honestly express that opinion on the proved facts?; and (e) even though the comment satisfies the objective test the defence can be defeated if the plaintiff proves that the defendant was actuated by express malice. *WIC Radio* expanded the fair comment defence by changing the traditional requirement that the opinion be one that a "fairminded" person could honestly hold, to a requirement that it be one that "anyone could honestly have expressed" (paras. 49–51), which allows for robust debate. As Binnie J. put it, "[w]e live in a free country where people have as much right to express outrageous and ridiculous opinions as moderate ones" (para. 4).

Where statements of fact are at issue, usually only two defences are available: the defence that the statement was substantially true (justification); and the defence that the statement was made in a protected context (privilege). The issue in this case is whether the defences to actions for defamatory statements of fact should be expanded, as has been done for statements of opinion, in recognition of the importance of freedom of expression in a free society.

To succeed on the defence of justification, a defendant must adduce evidence showing that the statement was substantially true. This may be difficult to do. A journalist who has checked sources and is satisfied that a statement is substantially true may nevertheless have difficulty proving this in court, perhaps years after the event. The practical result of the gap between responsible verification and the ability to prove truth in a court of law on some date far in the future, is that the defence of justification is often of little utility to journalists and those who publish their stories.

If the defence of justification fails, generally the only way a publisher can escape liability for an untrue defamatory statement of fact is by establishing that the statement was made on a privileged occasion. However, the defence of qualified privilege has seldom assisted media organizations. One reason is that qualified privilege has traditionally been grounded in special relationships characterized by a "duty" to communicate the information and a reciprocal "interest" in receiving it. The press communicates information not to identified individuals with whom it has a personal relationship, but to the public at large. Another reason is the conservative stance of early decisions, which struck a balance that preferred reputation over freedom of expression. In a series of judgments written by Cartwright J. (as he then was), this Court refused to grant the communications media any special status that might have afforded them greater access to the privilege: *Douglas v. Tucker*, 1951 CanLII 54 (S.C.C.), [1952] 1 S.C.R. 275; *Globe and Mail Ltd. v. Boland*, 1960 CanLII 2 (S.C.C.), [1960] S.C.R. 203; *Banks v. Globe and Mail Ltd.*, 1961 CanLII 6 (S.C.C.), [1961] S.C.R. 474; *Jones v. Bennett*, 1968 CanLII 126 (S.C.C.), [1969] S.C.R. 277.

In recent decades courts have begun to moderate the strictures of qualified privilege, albeit in an *ad hoc* and incremental way. When a strong duty and interest seemed to warrant it, they have on occasion applied the privilege to publications to the world at large. For example, in suits against politicians expressing concerns to the electorate about the conduct of other public figures, courts have sometimes recognized that a politician's "duty to ventilate" matters of concern to the public could give rise to qualified privilege: *Parlett v. Robinson* 1986 CanLII 929 (BC C.A.), (1986), 5 B.C.L.R. (2d) 26 (C.A.), at p. 39.

In the last decade, this recognition has sometimes been extended to media defendants. For example, in *Grenier v. Southam Inc.*, [1997] O.J. No. 2193 (QL), the Ontario Court of Appeal (in a brief endorsement) upheld a trial judge's finding that the defendant media corporation had a "social and moral duty" to publish the article in question. Other cases have adopted the view that qualified privilege is available to media defendants, provided that they can show a social or moral duty to publish the information and a corresponding public interest in receiving it: *Leenen v. Canadian Broadcasting Corp.*, 2000 CanLII 22380 (ON S.C.), (2000), 48 O.R. (3d) 656 (S.C.J.), at p.695, aff'd 2001 CanLII 4997 (ON C.A.), (2001), 54 O.R. (3d) 612 (C.A.), and

Young v. Toronto Star Newspapers Ltd., 2003 CanLII 64296 (ON S.C.), (2003), 66 O.R. (3d) 170 (S.C.J.), aff'd 2005 CanLII 35775 (ON C.A.), (2005), 77 O.R. (3d) 680 (C.A.).

Despite these tentative forays, the threshold for privilege remains high and the criteria for reciprocal duty and interest required to establish it unclear. It remains uncertain when, if ever, a media outlet can avail itself of the defence of qualified privilege.

For further authoritative statements of the law of defamation in Canada, see also:
Leenen v. Canadian Broadcasting Corp., 2001 CanLII 4997 (ON C.A.)
Hodgson v. Canadian Newspapers Co. Ltd., 2000 CanLII 14715 (ON C.A.)
Hill v. Church of Scientology of Toronto, 1993 CanLII 1348 (S.C.C.)

This book, as explained in the Chapter 2, only discusses areas of defamation law where there have been cases involving cyberlibel. Consequently, it covers the plaintiff's claim and defences as follows.

B. THE PLAINTIFF'S CLAIM

1. Publication: see Chapter 15.
2. Defamatory meaning: see Chapter 16.
3. Reference to the plaintiff and defences: see Chapters 17 and 18.

C. DEFENCES

1. The defence of justification was raised in the following cyberlibel cases without any discussion of cyberlibel:

   Hunter Dickinson Inc. v. Butler, 2010 BCSC 939
   Fuda v. Conn, 2009 CanLII 1140 (ON S.C.)
   McQuaig v. Harbour Financial Inc., 2009 ABQB 678
   Griffin v. Sullivan, 2008 BCSC 827
   Mudford v. Smith, 2009 CanLII 55718 (ON S.C.)
   Newman et al. v. Halstead et al., 2006 BCSC 65
   Sanjh Savera Weekly v. Ajit Newspaper Advertising, 2006 CanLII 20852 (ON S.C.)
   WeGo Kayaking Ltd. et al. v. Sewid et al., 2006 BCSC 334

2. The defence of fair comment was raised in the following cyberlibel cases but without any discussion of cyberlibel:

   Hunter Dickinson Inc. v. Butler, 2010 BCSC 939
   McQuaig v. Harbour Financial Inc., 2009 ABQB 678
   Mudford v. Smith, 2009 CanLII 55718 (ON S.C.)
   Griffin v. Sullivan, 2008 BCSC 827

Lee v. Ng, 2007 BCSC 1947

WeGo Kayaking Ltd. et al. v. Sewid, et al., 2007 BCSC 49

Newman et al. v. Halstead et al., 2006 BCSC 65

Sanjh Savera Weekly v. Ajit Newspaper Advertising, 2006 CanLII 20852 (ON S.C.)

WeGo Kayaking Ltd. et al. v. Sewid et al., 2006 BCSC 334

Ager v. Canjex Publishing d.b.a. Canada Stockwatch, 2005 BCCA 467

3. The defence of qualified privilege is discussed in Chapter 19.

4. Absolute privilege and its application to an Internet publication is discussed briefly in the decision *Milne v. Ontario Securities Commission*, 2006 CanLII 12428 (ON S.C.).

5. Report privilege: there are presently no Canadian cases discussing this defence. An Australian decision *Sands v. Channel Seven Adelaide Pty Anor Ltd.*, [2009] SASC 215 held at para. 350 that:

> The statutory defence available to the ABC in respect of its news broadcasts is an absolute privilege and is not defeated by malice. The same cannot be said of the website publication. That only attracts the qualified common law privilege of fair and accurate report.

In this case the defence applied. See paras. 351–71 of the *Sands* case for a discussion of the defence.

6. The defence of responsible communication on a matter of public interest is discussed in Chapter 20.

CHAPTER 5: Characteristics of the Internet

A. INTRODUCTION

A succinct description of the Internet and how it operates was provided by Binnie J. of the Supreme Court of Canada in *Society of Composers, Authors and Music Publishers of Canada v. Canadian Assn. of Internet Providers*, 2004 SCC 45, [2004] 2 S.C.R. 427 at paras. 8–10:

> The Internet is a huge communications facility which consists of a world-wide network of computer networks deployed to communicate information. A "content provider" uploads his or her data, usually in the form of a website, to a host server. The content is then forwarded to a destination computer (the end user). End users and content providers can connect to the Internet with a modem under contract with an Internet Service Provider.
>
> An Internet transmission is generally made in response to a request sent over the Internet from the end user (referred to as a "pull"). The host server provider transmits content (usually in accordance with its contractual obligation to the content provider). The content at issue here is the copyrighted musical works in SOCAN's repertoire.
>
> In its decision dated October 27, 1999 ((1999), 1 C.P.R. (4th) 417, at p. 441), the Copyright Board provided a succinct description of an Internet transmission:
>
> > First, the file is incorporated to an Internet-accessible server. Second, upon request and at a time chosen by the recipient, the file is broken down into packets and transmitted from the host server to the recipient's server, via one or more routers. Third, the recipient, usually using a computer, can reconstitute and open the file upon reception

or save it to open it later; either action involves a reproduction of the
file, again as that term is commonly understood.

Further judicial discussion of the Internet and its operations can be found in
the Judicial Glossary of Selected Internet Terms.

Whether the Internet has ushered in a communications revolution or
simply accelerated the changes introduced by the telegraph, telephone, radio,
movies, and television is beyond the scope of this book. Regardless, the Internet is, indisputably, an entity with characteristics that are completely novel
and distinct from previous methods of communication.

One of the more comprehensive discussions of the distinctive characteristics of the Internet and cyberlibel is found in the Ontario Court of Appeal
decision of *Barrick Gold Corp. v. Lopehandia*, 2004 CanLII 12938 at paras.
28–31 (ON C.A.):

> Is there something about defamation on the Internet — "cyber libel," as it
> is sometimes called — that distinguishes it, for purposes of damages, from
> defamation in another medium? My response to that question is "Yes."
>
> The standard factors to consider in determining damages for defama-
> tion are summarized by Cory J. in *Hill* at p. 1203. They include the plaintiff's
> position and standing, the nature and seriousness of the defamatory state-
> ments, the mode and extent of publication, the absence or refusal of any
> retraction or apology, the whole conduct and motive of the defendant from
> publication through judgment, and any evidence of aggravating or mitigat-
> ing circumstances.
>
> In the Internet context, these factors must be examined in the light of
> what one judge has characterized as the "ubiquity, universality and utility"
> of that medium. In *Dow Jones & Company Inc. v. Gutnick* [2002] HCA 56
> (10 December 2002), that same judge — Kirby J., of the High Court of Aus-
> tralia — portrayed the Internet in these terms, at para. 80:
>
>> The Internet is essentially a decentralized, self-maintained telecom-
>> munications network. It is made up of inter-linking small networks
>> from all parts of the world. *It is ubiquitous, borderless, global and
>> ambient in its nature. Hence the term "cyberspace." This is a word
>> that recognizes that the interrelationships created by the Internet exist
>> outside conventional geographic boundaries and comprise a single
>> interconnected body of data, potentially amounting to a single body
>> of knowledge.* The Internet is accessible in virtually all places on
>> Earth where access can be obtained either by wire connection or by

wireless (including satellite) links. *Effectively, the only constraint on access to the Internet is possession of the means of securing connection to a telecommunications system and possession of the basic hardware* [emphasis added].

Thus, of the criteria mentioned above, the mode and extent of publication is particularly relevant in the Internet context, and must be considered carefully. Communication via the Internet is instantaneous, seamless, interactive, blunt, borderless, and far-reaching. It is also impersonal, and the anonymous nature of such communications may itself create a greater risk that the defamatory remarks are believed: see *Vaquero Energy Ltd. v. Weir*, [2004] A.J. No. 84 (Q.B.) at paragraph 17.

According to the US Federal Court of Appeals at para. 81 in *ACLU v. Reno*, 929 F. Supp 825 (E.D. PA 1996), aff'd by *Reno v. ACLU*, 521 US 844 (1997), there are several features that make the Internet "a unique and wholly new medium of worldwide human communication." The Court stated at paras. 79–80:

> Because of the different forms of Internet communication, a user of the Internet may speak or listen interchangeably blurring the distinction between "speakers" and "listeners" on the Internet. Chat rooms, e-mail and newsgroups are interactive forms of communication providing the user with the opportunity both to speak and to listen.
>
> It follows that unlike a traditional media, the barriers to entry as a speaker on the Internet do not differ significantly from the barriers to entry as a listener. Once one has entered cyberspace, one may engage in a dialogue that occurs there. In the argot of the medium, the receiver can and does become the content provider and vice-versa.
>
> The Internet is therefore a unique and wholly new medium of worldwide human communication.

B. WHAT ARE THE CHARACTERISTICS OF THE INTERNET?

The characteristics of the Internet that are clearly of importance in cyberlibel proceedings are:

- its global nature
- interactivity
- its potential to shift the balance of power in the offline world
- accessibility

- anonymity
- its facilitation of republication
- the prominence of intermediaries
- its reliance on hyperlinks/hypertext
- its long-term impact — the use of permanent archives
- its multimedia character
- its temporal indeterminacy

1) Global Nature

The first feature of the Internet is its truly global nature. Presently, more than 1.9 billion people in more than 190 countries are linked through this massive interconnected web of computer networks.[1]

1. This feature immediately raises several interesting conflicts of law questions for the libel lawyer, such as:
   a. In which jurisdiction did the publication of the defamation occur?
      » Theoretically, every time a third party accesses a defamatory posting on the Internet, publication has occurred.
   b. In what jurisdiction should the plaintiff sue?
      » Where the plaintiff resides?
      » Where the defendant resides?
      » Wherever publication has occurred?
      » Defamation laws vary from country to country and in countries such as Australia, Canada, and the US, it can vary from province to province and state to state. Therefore, plaintiffs may have the luxury of "forum shopping" or choosing the jurisdiction in which the laws are most favourable.

Dow Jones and Company Inc. v. Gutnick, [2002] HCA 56, 210 CLR 575, 194 ALR 433, 77 ALJR 255

The High Court of Australia heard a defamation claim instituted by a plaintiff, who was a resident of the State of Victoria in Australia, against Dow Jones, an American corporation, for allegedly defamatory statements made in articles published by Dow Jones on its website, which was maintained on servers located in the State of New Jersey, USA. Dow Jones brought a motion to have service of the claim set aside or the action permanently stayed on the basis that the courts in Australia did not

---

1   Statistics accurate as of August 2010. See online: www.internetworldstats.com.

have jurisdiction. The High Court of Australia rejected that argument and allowed the action to proceed. The majority of the High Court said at para. 44:

> In defamation, the same considerations that require rejection of locating the tort by reference only to the publisher's conduct, lead to the conclusion that, ordinarily, defamation is to be located at the place where the damage to reputation occurs. Ordinarily that will be where the material which is alleged to be defamatory is available in comprehensible form assuming, of course, that the person defamed has in that place a reputation which is thereby damaged. It is only when the material is in comprehensible form that the damage to reputation is done and it is damage to reputation which is the principal focus of defamation, not any quality of the defendant's conduct. In the case of material on the World Wide Web (web), it is not available in comprehensible form until downloaded on to the computer of a person who has used a web browser to pull the material from the web server. It is where that person downloads the material that the damage to reputation may be done. Ordinarily then, that will be the place where the tort of defamation is committed.

   c. Whose laws should apply?
- » For example, should the First Amendment protection and the public figure defence available in the US apply? Or should the common law of the commonwealth apply? Or the civil law?[2]

   d. Will it be possible to enforce any judgment obtained?
- » Currently, despite legislation allowing reciprocal enforcement of civil judgments, some courts in the US are unwilling to enforce defamation judgments from other jurisdictions because of First Amendment protection of freedom of expression.

   e. What is the quantum of damages?
- » Theoretically, damages could be very large as a publication on the Internet potentially reaches millions of people. In practice, however, it is unlikely that millions of people will actually view each particular publication. In any event, publication on the Internet will generally be larger than in all but the largest print or broadcast media outlets.

2. The global nature of the Internet also raises some interesting procedural questions for the libel lawyer. In traditional libel law, there are three different types of defamatory statements:

---

2   See P.F. Carter-Ruck, *Carter-Ruck on Libel and Slander*, 4th ed. (London: Butterworths, 1992).

a. A statement that is defamatory on its face and which is obviously defamatory.

b. A statement which contains false innuendo. False innuendo is a defamatory statement that has an inferential meaning, therefore only persons with the necessary contextual knowledge appreciate that the statement is defamatory. Since statements on the Internet are published globally, their inferential meanings may vary depending on the geographic or cultural location of the reader or the newsgroups or the Usenet group involved.

c. A statement of legal innuendo. While not defamatory on their face, these statements are defamatory when viewed together with extrinsic circumstances. Once again, contextual knowledge may render a statement defamatory in one jurisdiction but not in another.[3]

The geographical indeterminancy of the technology of the Internet collides regularly with the stark reality of the geographical determinacy of defamation actions. This reality is above and beyond the conflicts of law questions that bedevil all international litigation. It is an example of a larger problem facing other areas of the law and the Internet, as stated by Binnie J. in the Supreme Court of Canada decisions of *Society of Composers, Authors and Music Publishers of Canada v. Canadian Assn. of Internet Providers,* 2004 SCC 45, [2004] 2 S.C.R. 427 at para. 41:

> The issue of the proper balance in matters of copyright plays out *against the much larger conundrum of trying to apply national laws to a fast-evolving technology that in essence respects no national boundaries.* Thus in *Citron v. Zundel* (2002), 41 C.H.R.R. D/274, the Canadian Human Rights Tribunal wrestled with jurisdiction over an alleged hate Web site supplied with content from Toronto but posted from a host server in California. *In Reference re Earth Future Lottery,* 2003 SCC 10 (CanLII), [2003] 1 S.C.R. 123, 2003 SCC 10, the issue was whether sales of tickets from an Internet lottery in Prince Edward Island constituted gambling "in the province" when almost all of the targeted on-line purchasers resided elsewhere. *The "cyber libel" cases multiply.* In *Braintech, Inc. v. Kostiuk* 1999 BCCA 169 (CanLII), (1999), 171 D.L.R. (4th) 46, the British Columbia Court of Appeal refused to enforce a Texas judgment for Internet defamation against a B.C. resident where the B.C. resident's only connection with Texas was "passive posting on an electronic bulletin board" (para. 66). There was no proof that anyone in Texas

---

3   See Julian Porter and David A. Potts, *Canadian Libel Practice* (Markham, ON: Butterworths 1986) at 46–51.

had actually looked at it. On the other hand, in *Dow Jones & Co. v. Gutnick* (2002), 194 A.L.R. 433, [2002] HCA 56, the High Court of Australia accepted jurisdiction over a defamation action in respect of material uploaded onto the defendant's server in New Jersey and downloaded by end users in the State of Victoria. The issue of global forum shopping for actions for Internet torts has scarcely been addressed. The availability of child pornography on the Internet is a matter of serious concern. E-commerce is growing. *Internet liability is thus a vast field where the legal harvest is only beginning to ripen.* It is with an eye to this broader context that the relatively precise questions raised by the Copyright Board must be considered. [Emphasis added].

Emphasis on reputation and freedom of speech varies greatly even within the English-speaking common law world.[4] Jurisdictions such as the UK provide remedies for defamation but, until recently, only limited recourses for invasion of privacy,[5] while the converse is true in other jurisdictions such as France.

The use of legal innuendos, community standards for defamatory meaning, local procedural rules, and jurisdiction arguments accentuate the geographical determinacy of defamation law. This clash has several consequences, for example:

---

4   See *Dow Jones and Company Inc. v. Gutnick*, [2002] HCA 56; 210 CLR 575; 194 ALR 433; 77 ALJR 255 at paras. 188–90:

> Australian defamation law, and, for that matter, English defamation law also, and the policy underlying them are different from those of the United States. There is no doubt that the latter leans heavily, some might say far too heavily, in favour of defendants. Nor has the metaphor for free speech developed by Holmes J in a series of cases and beginning with his dissenting judgment in *Abrams v United States*, a marketplace of ideas, escaped criticism in the United States. Writing in *The New Criterion*, Robert H. Bork pointed out:
>
> > "The market for ideas has few of the selfcorrecting features of the market for goods and services."
>
> Later he added:
>
> > "In a word, what the Constitution says, as interpreted by today's Court, is that one idea *is* as good as another so far as the law is concerned; only the omnipotent individual may judge." (original emphasis)
>
> Quite deliberately, and in my opinion rightly so, Australian law places real value on reputation, and views with scepticism claims that it unduly inhibits freedom of discourse. In my opinion the law with respect to privilege in this country, now and historically, provides an appropriate balance which does justice to both a publisher and the subject of a publication. [Footnotes omitted].

5   *Jameel v. Wall Street Journal*, [2006] UKHL 44, at para. 36 (Lord Hoffmann).

- jurisdictional disputes are a common feature of cyberlibel cases,
- there are limited extraterritorial applications for injunctions against cyberlibel statements published globally (see *Barrick Gold Corp. v. Lopehandia*, 2004 CanLII 12938 (ON C.A.));
- abuse of process motions based on limited publications in the jurisdiction are used in UK cases (see "abuse of process," below Chapter 9, section F; Chapter 11, sections E, F, and G; and Chapter 15, section C (2)); and
- a very uneven "landscape" for the liability or immunity of intermediaries. Section 230 of the *Communications Decency Act of 1996*, 47 U.S.C.A. (*CDA*) provides complete immunity for the Internet Service Provider (ISP). No legislative protection exists for the ISP in defamation claims in Canada.

2) Interactivity

The interactive character of the Internet utterly changes the libel playing field. It is completely different from the Industrial Age paradigm where newspapers and television stations had dominant if not monopolistic relationships with readers and viewers.

> See David Halberstam, *The Powers that Be* (Urbana: University of Illinois Press, 1975)

Someone who is damaged by the press has limited remedies. In the Internet Age a person whose reputation is attacked now has a wide range of offensive and defensive remedies, including juridical, technological, and public relations options. In many cases, the scope of re-publication is as wide or can even be wider than the original publication.

The ease with which users of the Internet can access bulletin boards and Usenets and communicate with each other has engendered in its users a false sense of freedom in their communications. This is exemplified by the prevalence of activities such as "spamming"[6] and "flaming"[7] in Internet communications. As a result, the Internet is qualitatively different from any other

---

6   "'Spamming' is defined as follows: a form of computer based aggression that involves bombarding someone with uninvited, copious information that they must page through before proceeding ... in Usenet 'spamming' is synonymous with 'carpet bombing' — the pelting of dozens, hundreds or even thousands of newsgroups with unwanted messages." Quoted in Bryan Pfaffenberger, *Internet in Plain English* (New York: MIS Press, 1994) 369.

7   "A 'flame' is defined as: in Usenet and electronic mail, an ill considered highly emotional message that in the extreme can be filled with foul language and personal attacks." Quoted in Pfaffenberger, *Internet in Plain English, ibid.* at 170.

medium. Consequently, Mike Godwin, counsel for the Electronic Frontier Foundation, says that "the public figure defence" should apply to statements made on the Internet. The ability to reply, he claims, is much more gratifying, immediate, and potent than launching a libel action.[8]

Some American commentators[9] have proposed that when a libel plaintiff has been defamed by a message posted on an electronic bulletin board and she has access to the bulletin board to post a reply, the First Amendment requires that the plaintiff prove that the defendant acted with "actual malice" in defaming the plaintiff.[10] They argue that "Libel Plaintiffs who have been defamed by bulletin board speech and who have both access to the bulletin board on which the defamatory material appeared and a history of participation on the bulletin board are functionally equivalent to public figures."[11] This proposal raises numerous questions such as:

- Should the conceptual basis of this defence be the First Amendment or the technological ease of reply on the Internet?
- What will be the reactions of courts outside the US to a defence based on the First Amendment?
- Should the elements of such a defence include:
  » access to the Internet?
  » access to the Internet and a particular bulletin board system where the defamatory statement was published?
  » participation in the discussion?
  » a previous history of participation and discussions in that particular bulletin board system?
- More broadly, counsel must consider:
  » what subject matters should be covered?
  » how to define issues of public interest on a global medium of communication?

---

8 Mike Godwin, "Libel Law: Let It Die" *Wired Magazine* (March 1996) 116.

9 Jeremy Weber, "Defining Cyberlibel: A First Amendment Limit for Libel Suits Against Individuals Arising From Computer Bulletin Board Speech" (1995) 46 *Case Western Law Review* 235.

10 See Thomas D. Brooks, "Catching Jellyfish in the Internet; The Public Figure Doctrine and Defamation on Computer Bulletin Boards" (1995) 21 *Rutgers Computers and Tech. L.J.* 461; Iris Ferosi, "Don't Shoot the Messenger: Protecting Free Speech on Editorially Controlled Bulletin Board Services by Applying Sullivan Malice" (1996) 14 *J. Marshall J. Computer and Info. L.J.* 347.

11 Weber, "Defining Cyberlibel: A First Amendment Limit for Libel Suits Against Individuals Arising From Computer Bulletin Board Speech," above note 9 at 237.

- Is this defence only available to the operators of bulletin board systems or to the original publishers as well?
- What test of malice should apply? Should it be the test set out by *The New York Times v. Sullivan* (376 U.S. 254 (1964)) or the tests set out at common law?
- Should this concept be a defence or simply a mitigation of damages?

These issues have not yet been decided by the courts, but they need to be addressed as the Internet does provide a unique means of a quick and responsive reply to an attack on a person's reputation.

See criticisms of this concept in Graham J. Smith, ed., *Internet Law and Regulation* 4th ed. (London: Sweet & Maxwell, 2007) at 345–46.

3) Shifting the Balance of Power in the Offline World[12]

In some situations the Internet can actually change the balance of power that exists normally in the offline world. Any enterprise that has been the target of a concerted cyber-attack comes to realize that the terms of the debate are not what it is accustomed to, where, for example it is able to gain favourable attention for its press releases. On the contrary, the attackers are the persons with the power. The ferocity, ubiquity, and tenacity of cyblerlibel attacks often stun their targets. The power of the Internet to cause instantaneous and irreparable damage was graphically described by the Ontario Court of Appeal in *Barrick Gold Corp. v. Lopehandia*, [2004] CanLII 12938 at paras. 44–45 (ON C.A.):

> Secondly, the motions judge failed to appreciate, and in my opinion misjudged, the true extent of Mr. Lopehandia's target audience and the nature of the potential impact of the libel in the context of the Internet. She was alive to the fact that Mr. Lopehandia "[had] the ability, through the Internet, to spread his message around the world to those who take the time to search out and read what he posts" and indeed that he had "posted messages on many, many occasions." However, her decision not to take the defamation seriously led her to cease her analysis of the Internet factor at that point. She failed to take into account the distinctive capacity of the Internet to cause instantaneous, and irreparable, damage to the business reputation of an individual or corporation by reason of its interactive and globally all-pervasive

---

12   The Hon. Dennis Lane, QC deserves credit for this observation. Mr. Lane was a Judge of the Superior Court of Justice for eighteen years and wrote several influential decisions on the law of libel.

nature and the characteristics of Internet communications outlined in paragraphs 28–33 above.

Had the motions judge taken these characteristics of the Internet more fully into account, she might well have recognized Barrick's exposure to substantial damages to its reputation by reason of the medium through which the Lopehandia message was conveyed.

See also paras. 39–43 of *Barrick Gold Corp. v. Lopehandia* decision.

4) Accessibility

Accessibility is another feature of the Internet which distinguishes it from traditional print or broadcast media. The relatively low cost of connecting to the Internet and even of establishing one's own website means that the opportunity for defamation has increased exponentially. Now, on the Internet, everyone can be a publisher and can be sued as a publisher.

5) Anonymity

Internet users do not have to reveal their true identity in order to send email or post messages on bulletin boards. Users are able to communicate and make such postings anonymously or under assumed names. This feature, fused both with the ability to access the Internet in the privacy of one's own home or office and the interactive, responsive nature of communications on the Internet, has resulted in users being far less inhibited about the contents of their messages. This feature has spawned a body of law in the Australia, Canada, the UK, and the US that discusses when plaintiffs are entitled to the names and addresses of anonymous defendants.

6) Re-publication

The Internet allows statements to be easily re-published on numerous occasions to an unlimited audience. The ease of re-publication raises questions of when the original publisher is liable for re-publication, when the original publisher can avoid a limit liability for re-publication, and when a subsequent person is liable for re-publication of a statement that did not originate from them.

See Matthew Collins, *The Law of Defamation and the Internet,* 2d ed. (New York: Oxford University Press, 2005) at 36–37

7) Intermediaries

". . . Intermediaries are involved in every Internet publication."

See Matthew Collins, *The Law of Defamation and the Internet*, 2d ed. (New York: Oxford University Press, 2005) at 34

Intermediaries occupy pivotal roles on the Internet. The function of intermediaries and their liabilities has been analyzed as categories by the legislation. The various categories of intermediaries both at common law and statute law are examined below in Chapters 18, 21, and 22.

A useful description of the types of Internet intermediaries, and their importance to economical and social development can be found in Karine Perset, "The Economic and Social Role of Internet Intermediaries," *OECD Digital Economy Papers*, No. 171 (2010), online: www.oecd.org/dataoecd/49/4/44949023.pdf.

8) Hyperlinks

a) Overview

The US Court of Appeals in *ACLU v. Reno*, 929 F. Supp 825 (E.D. PA 1996), aff'd by *Reno v. ACLU*, 521 US 844 (1997) clearly explained the role of hyperlinks at para. 77:

> The ease of communication through the Internet is facilitated by the use of hypertext mark-up language (HTML) which allows for the creation of "hyperlinks" or "links." HTML enables a user to jump from one source or other related sources by clicking on the link. A link may take the user from website to website or to other files within a particular website. Similarly, by typing a request into a search engine, a user can retrieve many different sources of content related to the search of the creators of the engine have collected.

As outlined in Philip M. Parker *Hyperlink: Webster's Timeline History, 1965–2007* (London: Icon Group International, 2010) at 5.:

> The term "hyperlink" was coined in 1965 (or possibly 1964) by Theodore Nelson at the start of Project Xanadu. Nelson had been inspired by "As We May Think," a popular essay by Vannevar Bush. In the essay, Bush described a microfilm-based machine in which one could link any two pages of information into a "trail" of related information, and then scroll back and forth among pages in a trail as if they were on a single microfilm reel. The closest contemporary analogy would be to build a list of bookmarks to topically

related Web pages and then allow the user to scroll forward and backward through the list.

Hyperlinks are links created within webpages, typically using HTML, to allow a user to navigate easily, by the click of a mouse, to other content located internally within the website, or externally on another website.[13] The markup language is used to create a tag within the webpage, usually signified by underlined and alternatively coloured text, though icons or images may be tagged as well — this tagged material is known as the link. This link points to the location on the web of other desired material that the webpage designer wants to direct the user's attention to — this other material is known as the target.[14] Links are composed of two parts in HTML: the reference to the target and the descriptor. The reference to the target consists of the Uniform Resource Locator (URL), commonly known as the web address. The descriptor is whatever text the webpage designer chooses to indicate the link.[15] That is, it is the descriptor that appears as hyperlinked to the user (the reference to the target, on the other hand, will not be visible).

b) Hyperlinks and the Web

Hyperlinks are an extremely important, if not dominant, mechanism through which users navigate the web and find information online.[16] As such, hyperlinking is a widely accepted practice[17] that facilitates both usability and the propagation of the web's interconnections.

c) Types of Hyperlinks

There are two main types of hyperlinks: absolute and relative. From the user's perspective they both work in exactly the same way, the difference, however, is in their construction and functionality. Simply put, absolute links rely on the entire URL, which typically consists of a protocol, server name, domain name, directory name, and file name, as the reference to the target. These links are termed "absolute" because they are not dependent on where the document in

---

13   Jon Duckett, *Beginning HTML, XHTML, CSS, and Javascript* (Indianapolis: Wiley, 2010), c. 2.

14   Steven M. Schafer, *HTML, xHTML and CSS Bible*, 4th ed. (Indianapolis: Wiley, 2008), c. 8.

15   *Ibid.*

16   Eszther Hargittai, "The Role of Expertise in Navigating Links of Influence," in Joseph Turow and Lokman Tsui, eds., *Hyperlinked Society: Questioning Connections in the Digital Age* (Ann Arbor, MI: University of Michigan Press, 2008) 86–88.

17   Sylvia Mercado-Kierkegaard, "Clearing the Legal Barriers — Danish Court Upholds 'Deep Linking' in *Home v. Ofir*" (2006) 22 *Computer Law & Security Report* 326.

which they appear is stored; they always remain the same. In contrast, relative hyperlinks do not use the complete URL as the reference to the target. Rather, the address of the target is treated as relative to the location of file in which the link appears. Therefore, only the file name, or in some cases a directory and/ or subdirectory and file name is given as the reference to the target. Such relative hyperlinks are often favoured by web designers because they are simple to maintain and ease the development and management of website hyperlinks, yet they can only be used to facilitate navigation *within* a website. In order to link to information outside the originating website a full URL target reference must be given to direct the link appropriately.[18]

d) Deep Linking

The action of hyperlinking, specifically "deep linking," has come under scrutiny in recent years for a variety of reasons. Deep linking refers to the practice of creating a hyperlink to a webpage or pages on a third party's website that lie deeper within that website's architecture than the homepage. Therefore, through deep linking, the homepage of the target website is bypassed and the user is sent directly to the desired content. Both website designers and, in particular, search engines (with the assistance of automated crawling programs) employ deep linking, allowing users to avoid extraneous information and arrive at the requested information easily.[19] Deep linking has been the subject of some debate in recent years. It is argued, for example, that deep linking creates situations of copyright or trademark infringement. Additionally, the complaint is made that by driving users away from website homepages users also skip much website advertising, a main revenue stream for companies with an online presence.[20]

Hyperlinks will have an impact on every aspect of defamation law including notices, limitation periods, elements of a claim, defences, and damages. Hyperlinks are discussed in conjunction with publication in Chapter 15.

9) Long-Term Impact — Permanent Archives

Another distinctive feature of the Internet is that information can be stored in perpetuity and yet made accessible as though the events are contemporary through a few clicks of the mouse. Instead of the concept of "skeletons in the

---

18   *Ibid.* See also, Duckett, *Beginning HTML, XHTML, CSS, and Javascript*, above note 13, c. 2.

19   *Ibid.*

20   *Ibid.*

closet," the skeletons are now "on the door step." The danger of libel lurking in the background to emerge in the future has been discussed and has been an important factor in damage awards in libel actions.

Compensatory damages are not confined in their scope to pecuniary losses. See Julian Porter and David Potts, *Canadian Libel Practice* (Toronto: Butterworths, 1986) at 609:

> [Defamation] actions involve a money award which may put the plaintiff in a purely financial sense in a much stronger position than he was before the wrong. Not merely can he recover the estimated sum of his past and future losses, but, in case the libel, driven underground, emerges from its lurking place at some future date, he must be able to point to a sum awarded by a jury sufficient to convince a bystander of the baselessness of the charge.

Broome v. Cassell & Co., [1972] 1 All E.R. 801 at 824 (H.L.), cited with approval in *Vogel v. C.B.C.* (1982), 21 C.C.L.T. 105 at 206 (B.C.S.C.):

> The jury should also take into account, as stated by Radcliffe L.J. in *Associated Newspapers v. Dingle*, [1962] 2 All E.R. 737 at 747 "the sad truth that no apology, retraction or withdrawal can ever be guaranteed completely to undo the harm it has done or the hurt it has caused."

See also *Ley v. Hamilton* (1935), 153 L.T. 384 at 386 (H.L.), quoted by Diplock L.J. in *Broome v. Cassell & Co.*, [1972] A.C. 1027 at 1125 (G.C.): "It is impossible to track the scandal to know what quarters the poison may reach."

The long-term impact of cyberlibel on reputations has been very clearly described in two UK cases and a law review article. Justice Tugendhat in *Clarke t/a Elumina Iberica UK v. Bain and Anor*, [2008] EWHC 2636 at paras. 54–55 stated:

> In addressing issues of proportionality, the following must be borne in mind. Defamation actions are not primarily about recovering money damages, but about vindication of a claimant's reputation. If a successful libel claimant recovers, say, £30,000, that figure does not represent the measure of his success. In many cases, after paying his irrecoverable costs, he will be out of pocket if he recovers that amount as damages. That does not mean the litigation is not worthwhile. A claimant wrongly accused of some serious fault, such as malpractice or dishonesty in business, may well suffer very large unquantifiable loss if he does not recover his reputation. The value of the verdict in his favour is expected to consist substantially in the future loss that it is hoped will be avoided by the vindication. Where, as here, the publication complained of

is on an internet news service, a verdict in his favour may provide him with a means of persuading the publishers of an archive to edit it.

The long term effect of a libel has commonly been be expressed in metaphorical terms, such as "the propensity to percolate through underground passages and contaminate hidden springs" (e.g., *Slipper v. BBC*, [1991] 1 QB 283, 300). The position today can be expressed more strongly, as it was in an article published in *The Guardian* (by Siobhain Butterworth, on 20 October 2008):

> The consequences of putting information . . . into the public domain are more far-reaching in a world where things you say are linked to, easily passed around and can pop up if [the subject's] name is put into a search engine by, for example, a prospective employer. The web makes a lie of the old cliché that today's newspaper pages are tomorrow's fish and chip wrapping. Nowadays . . . the things . . . in a newspaper are more like tattoos — they can be extremely difficult to get rid of.
>
> The web is an easily searchable repository of everything published online, which makes it a very unforgiving medium. The problem is not that things can't be removed easily, but that news organisations are inherently resistant to un-publishing. Should a newspaper website agree to un-publish on request? The answer to that question depends on what you think a newspaper's archive is for, and whether you think it matters if there are holes where articles used to be.
>
> The established view is that a newspaper's online archive is a historical record and that there is therefore a strong public interest in maintaining its wholeness, unless deletions or amendments are strictly necessary.
>
> Saying yes to all requests for the removal of material that causes the people concerned distress or hinders their employment prospects would be easier, but it's a solution that, over time, will leave a patchy and unreliable record of what was published. It also means abandoning conventional thinking about the importance of the integrity of the archive.
>
> A less extreme solution . . . . is to replace a real name with a pseudonym and add a footnote explaining that the change has been made. It's not ideal, but it's preferable to re-writing history completely by deleting an article, blog post or letter and pretending that it didn't exist.

The same judge made similar remarks in *Flood v. Times Newspapers Ltd.*, [2009] EWHC 2375 at para. 233 (QB):

Whether or not the scale of a website publication, and any resulting damage, is likely to be modest compared with that of the original publication, will depend on the facts of each case. But the judgment in *Loutchansky* was delivered eight years ago, in 2001. Since then the use of the internet, and in particular of internet search engines, has increased. What has also increased is the amount of material on the internet. In 2001 there were relatively few years of back numbers of newspapers available on the internet. Since then each year's publications have been added. In most cases, as time passes, the original print publication will become increasingly difficult to access, and would be forgotten. But the website publication will remain, and in some cases (where the fame of a person has increased) it may even be viewed with increasing frequency. So a person's reputation may be "damaged forever" in the words of Lord Nicholls in *Reynolds* at p201 cited in para 207 above. As I remarked in another case, quoting from an article by a well known media lawyer, what is to be found on the internet may become like a tattoo (*Clarke (t/a Elumina Iberica UK) v. Bain & Anor*, [2008] EWHC 2636 (QB), para. 55). Some actual and prospective employers, and teachers, make checks on people by carrying out internet searches. An old defamatory publication may permanently blight a person's prospects. This may be so, even in those cases where the allegation has been authoritatively refuted, but the refutation is either not on the internet, or, where it is on the internet, its authority is not apparent, or is not credited, on the footing that there is no smoke without fire.

The reality of an indelible reputational stain in cyberspace even when the individuals were completely exonerated was graphically sketched by Richard Peltz in "Fifteen Minutes of Infamy: Privileged Reporting and the Problem of Perpetual Reputational Harm" (2008) 34 *Ohio Northern University Law Review* 717 at 718–19. Peltz examined the case of the defendants Finnerty and Seligmann, Duke University varsity lacrosse players, who were charged with rape, but the charges were dismissed before trial:

> A review of the top-ten Google results in the Finnerty-Seligmann search does indicate that something is amiss. The eighth search result in the list reports, "Nifong jailed," and Finnerty and Seligmann "declared innocent earlier this year by state prosecutors." But that outcome is not indicated by any of the other nine of top-ten search results, one of which invites users to play, "You're the Jury — Guilty or Not Guilty?" News of the exoneration — while it can be found by follow-up searches on the web sites of Dilby, Findlaw, and Fox — is not indicated anywhere on the top three web pages responsive to the search.

Imagine you are a harried hiring coordinator working for Big X Corporation. Before you sits a stack of 600 resumes, and your job today is to winnow the field by eliminating persons of dubious character. Your tool is Google, today "a commonplace part of hiring (and firing)." A candidate apparently under indictment for rape, sexual assault, and kidnapping is unlikely to make the cut. Applicants Finnerty and Seligmann will probably not get the benefit of careful reading and follow-up searches concerning their charges. Maybe they will get the benefit of your general knowledge about the news. But another applicant, a later-exonerated defendant who once made small-time news for a charge reported from the police blotter, will not have the advantage of your general knowledge.

Finnerty and Seligmann, then, have been injured in their reputations as well as in their persons through wrongful detention. They will continue to be injured in untold ways; they will not even be cognizant of the ways in which they likely will be injured. Revelation of the prosecutor's misconduct in their extraordinary case has rendered the City of Durham vulnerable to a liability claim; at the time of this writing, Evans, Finnerty, and Seligmann have sued the City for $30 million. But the men have not sued the news media, Dilby, Findlaw, Fox, or any other outlet, for perpetuating recitation of the charges and the injuries that follow.

Meanwhile the reputational injuries to these men are perpetuated and compounded by unusual properties of new technology, such as longevity. Where yesterday's news, before the Internet, faded into obscurity on archival tapes and yellowing paper, the Internet never forgets. The news of 2006 remains at the fingertips of the user of 2008, of 2009, and of 2020. Will the top three responsive web pages to a search in 2048 again reveal only the breaking news of Finnerty's and Seligmann's arrests, or will news of their later exoneration rise to the top? Distressingly, the marvelous flexibility that makes the Internet a medium superior to paper — e.g., the ease of hyperlinking to related content and the ability to correct and update content virtually instantaneously at nominal cost — is not apparently being exploited now. Whereas a newspaper morgue search would readily cross-reference the initial charge and later exoneration of a criminal defendant before the electronic era, the broad range of sources available online are not so readily indexed and cross-referenced.

10) Multimedia

The digital electronic technology of the Internet allows statements and images that defame people to emerge rapidly in various different forms. These defamatory statements can transmogrify from one medium to another either completely or partially, and with various levels of intensification or dilution in relation to the original instance. For example, digital technology allows for the simple generation of a picture of a well-known individual that has their head superimposed on Hitler, Stalin, or Osama Bin Laden's body. In a second photo, the individual's picture may not be superimposed on the body of one of these individuals completely, but it may have some references to them and their ruthless acts.

Recently, the South African Supreme Court of Appeal in *Le Roux & Others v. Dey*, [2010] ZASCA 41 at paras. 2–3 described a multimedia online defamation. The appeal related to a claim for damages by a vice-principal of a secondary school in Pretoria, South Africa. The defendants were three students at the school.

> The claims arose from these facts: the first defendant, who then was fifteen and a half and in grade 9, one evening searched the internet for pictures of gay bodybuilders. He found one. It showed two of them, both naked and their legs astride, sitting next to each other in a rather compromising position — a leg of the one was over a leg of the other — and the position of their hands was indicative of sexual activity or stimulation. He manipulated the photograph by pasting a photo of the plaintiff's face on the face of the one bodybuilder and the face of the principal of the school onto the other. He also covered the genitals of each with pictures of the school's badge.
>
> He sent the manipulated photo to a friend who, in turn, sent it by cell phone to the second defendant, who was in grade 11 and 17 years old. The picture spread like fire amongst the scholars. A few days later the second defendant showed the picture to a female teacher during class and later decided to print the photo in colour and showed it around on the playground. At his behest and because he did not have the necessary 'guts' the third defendant, who was in the same grade and of the same age, placed the photograph prominently on the school's notice board. A teacher saw it quite soon and removed it.

11) Temporal Indeterminacy

There is a tension between static concepts of existing libel law, where the past and the present are distinct, from the dynamic and fluid world of the Internet where past and present appear to merge. This is important for any issue upon which timing is based, specifically:

1. notice under the *Libel and Slander Act*, R.S.O. 1990, c. L.12;

2. limitation periods;
3. issues of reference to the plaintiff; and
4. evidence of fair comment, evidence of honest belief, and also issues of contemporaneity in the statutory privileges.

Section 4 of the *Libel and Slander Act* discusses publications of reports of proceedings in court in a newspaper or broadcast contemporaneously with such proceedings.

Section 5 states that no action for libel in a newspaper and a broadcast lies unless the plaintiff has given notice in writing within six weeks of the alleged libel.

Section 6 states that an action for libel in a newspaper and a broadcast shall be commenced within three months after the libel has come to the knowledge of the person defamed.

In the common law of libel there are further examples. The defences of fair comment and qualified privilege refer to evidence at the time of the comment or evidence of the honest belief at the time of the statement.

The difficulty with online libel is that instantaneous retrieval blurs the real distinction between past and present — they are merged. If information was posted on the Internet five, ten, or fifteen years ago it can be retrieved at the same time as an item that was posted on the Internet five minutes ago.

CHAPTER 6: Differences and Consequences in Cyberlibel Litigation and Offline Libel Litigation

A. DIFFERENCES

There are a number of differences between offline libel and cyberlibel litigation.

1) Jurisdiction

In offline libel there is one institution, such as a traditional press or media outlet that is situated in one location and one jurisdiction. In cyberlibel, however, the defendants can be located in numerous jurisdictions.

2) Media

The medium that is used in offline libel is typically one of television, radio, or print. An online libel, in contrast can be digitally iterated in print, radio, television, or any combination thereof.

3) Identifying the Defendant

In offline libel and traditional media libel actions, there is usually an institution such as a media outlet, whereas in online libel there are often a range of networked individuals or simply individuals. In offline libel the original publisher is usually the primary defendant. In online libel there can be numerous different types of defendants, including the original author, the website host, the Internet Service Provider (ISP) and in some cases the search engine. Each of these different defendants will, depending on their characterization, have different liabilities and different defences. In offline libel, the defendants will generally be identifiable. In online libel, quite frequently they will not be identifiable. The plaintiff will have to bring a motion to compel one of the intermediaries, such as the ISP, to disclose the identities of the individuals.

4) Standards

Generally speaking, offline media outlets maintain institutional or industry standards. In online libel, standards may exist in some cases while in others they do not. The proliferation of the Internet as a dominant mode of communication has led to the convergence of traditionally offline media outlets with online technology. For example, most nationally and regionally significant newspapers and broadcast stations now maintain websites as a significant component of their business. Such sites typically adhere to industry standards in their online practices as they do in their offline ones. Even online newspaper sites that encourage user participation through discussion boards or live chats will maintain a gatekeeping function over the content that appears in these sections of its site by editing or removing posted content as they deem it appropriate and requiring users who wish to create content to register, particularly in the case of national publications.[1] However, the web and its related tools, such as blogs, wikis, and myriad other mechanisms, allow for affordable, non-institutional publication of material that can potentially be widely distributed by individuals as has never before been possible. This increases the probability of the publication of libellous material, particularly in the absence of editors or other safeguards to ensure accuracy, credibility, and balance, among other journalistic standards. As has been pointed out *ad nauseam* in the literature, much of what actually gets published on the Internet through blogs or other web-based mechanisms is self-indulgent, poorly researched, unfocused, biased, and often patently inaccurate.[2] Thus the traditional standards employed by the institutional media may appear completely antithetical in some cases when contrasted with the publication practices of non-institutional web publishers. However, despite the lack of institutional standards for publication in much online material it

---

1   Cassandra Imfeld & Glen W. Scott, "Under Construction: Measures of Community Building at Newspaper Web Sites" in Michael B. Salwen, Bruce Garrison, & Paul D. Driscoll, eds., *Online News and the Public* (Mahwah, NJ: Lawrence Erlbaum Associates, 2005), c. 8 at 216–17.

2   See, for example, Terje Rasmussen, "The Internet and the Differentiation of the Political Public Sphere" (2008) 29:2 *Nordicom Review* 73 at 76, online: www.nordicom.gu.se/common/publ_pdf/269_rasmussen.pdf; Dan Gillmor, *We the Media: Grassroots Journalism by the People, for the People* (Sebastopol, CA: O'Reilly, 2006) at 139, referring, in particular, to blogs.

is argued that a number of factors function generally to ensure, for the most part, that such communications avoid transgression. First, because Internet communication is widely differentiated, containing both the best and worst of interpersonal communication and everything in between, and the sheer volume of online content outstrips anything previously experienced by users of more traditional mass media, many services, such as search engines like Google, blog-specific engines like Technorati, and RSS feeds, exist to help users sort through the clutter and target the information they want.[3] Search engines in particular, no matter the type, often rely on links created by users to a given page to help evaluate its prestige, utility, and overall value as a source of information. Therefore, if users do not link to given content, it is an indication that the information is not useful or is untrustworthy and therefore its distribution will automatically be inhibited through the poor ranking it receives from the search engine's algorithm.

Additionally, ". . . moderators, filters and other software systems, [and] the norms of social movements and organisations . . . all serve to normalize communication [on the Internet] in one way or another."[4] Journalist and blogger Dan Gillmor, in his lauded book on citizen journalism, also points to the practice of collaborative publication (such as through wikis); examples of mass background and fact-checking enabled by technology and enacted by online communities to examine online content; and the use of everyday common sense as essential factors to be applied either in creating or consuming online content to ensure its journalistic value.[5] The common denominator here is that, with online material, the responsibility for upholding journalistic standards has shifted from institutions' formalized procedures to ensure compliance to individual producers and consumers, who may or may not employ available mechanisms with which to influence an informal type of compliance with mutually accepted norms.

The CBC includes balance as part of their principles under their Journalistic Standards and Policies, online: www.cbc.radio-canada.ca/docs/policies/journalistic/balance.shtml:

> Canadian Broadcasting Corporation/Radio-Canada programs dealing with matters of public interest on which differing views are held must supplement the exposition of one point of view with an equitable treatment of other rel-

---

3　See Rasmussen, *ibid.* at 78 and Gillmor, *ibid.* 168–69 and c. 9.

4　Rasmussen, *ibid.*

5　Dan Gillmor, *We the Media: Grassroots Journalism by the People, for the People* (Sebastopol, CA: O'Reilly, 2006), c. 9.

evant points of view. Equitable in this context means fair and reasonable, taking into consideration the weight of opinion behind a point of view, as well as its significance or potential significance.

There are two sources of balance and fairness in information programming, one provided by the journalist and the other provided by CBC/Radio-Canada as a journalistic organization.

Journalists will have opinions of their own, but they must not yield to bias or prejudice. For journalists to be professional is not to be without opinions, but to be aware of those opinions and make allowances for them, so that their reporting is, and appears to be, judicious and fair.

When an appropriate representative of one side of the story cannot be reached, the journalist or producer should make every effort to find someone who can represent that point of view and, if unable to do so, should announce the fact in a simple and direct manner.

On the other hand, CBC/Radio-Canada, as a journalistic organization, must ensure that its programming is fair and balanced. Program balance should be achieved, where appropriate, within a single program or otherwise within an identifiable series of programs.

Balance is not to be confused with the concept of right of reply. CBC/Radio-Canada must itself be responsible for determining when a significant imbalance has occurred, and what remedial action must be taken.

The institutional media are not always paragons of balanced reporting. See, for example,

- *Leenen v. Canadian Broadcasting Corp.*, 2000 CanLII 22380 (ON S.C.)
- *Hodgson v. Canadian Newspaper Ltd.* (1998), 39 O.R. (3d) 235
- *Walker v. CFTO Ltd.*, 1987 CanLII 126 (ON C.A.)
- *Munro v. Toronto Sun Publishing Corp.* (1982), 39 O.R. (2d) 100
- *Vogel v. Canadian Broadcasting Corporation*, 1982 CanLII 801 (BC S.C.)

Technological development not only continues to bring people closer together through the easy connections it allows people to make with one another, it also continues to provide enhanced tools to individuals with which to create, publish, and distribute material online. It is these tools that allow for a more interactive and participative society, yet they also allow for a potentially more libellous one. As such, the law that developed to address libel in an age of more traditional mass media needs to adapt to the new conditions of a dynamic digital environment and the communicative power it confers on individuals that now exists.

5) Assets

In offline libel, the defendants usually have some assets that are attachable. In online libel, many of the individuals will have no assets or, if they do, they will be in jurisdictions where the judgments will not be able to be enforced.

6) Counsel

In offline libel, the lawyers are advisors that act for the parties. There are well-established rules both of procedural and professional conduct that the parties adhere to in libel litigation. In contrast, lawyers in online libel are often the targets of attack.

7) Remedies

The remedies in offline libel are usually confined to damages, injunctions, or apologies. In online libel these remedies also exist. However, the primary objective of most plaintiffs is removal of defamatory statements as quickly as possible. The other remedies are often of quite secondary concern. In offline libel litigation, legal remedies predominate. In online libel litigation, legal remedies are only a part of a multidisciplinary arsenal.

8) Action and Reaction

In offline libel actions, action must be taken. Parties are rewarded for taking quick and decisive action. In online libel, precipitous and aggressive action can easily transform a problem into a crisis. The law of unintended consequences applies with particular rigor in cyberlibel litigation.

9) Dynamism

In offline libel, the technology is relatively static, typically consisting of newsprint or other forms of newspaper, magazines, books, television, movies, or radio. In online libel, the technology is breathtakingly dynamic and can require a completely different approach depending on the technology and the defences. That is not to say that there are different laws. There are just different applications of those laws and different approaches that must be taken depending on whether the defamatory statement was published by emails, blogs, threads on bulletin boards, private or public chartrooms, Facebook, or Youtube, and now Twitter.

In offline libel, the law has developed around a number of different elements of the case of action and the defences. Strikingly, while this has also occurred in online libel, the dynamism of web technology has meant that cases have been aggregating around different forms of the technology itself. This is probably apparent in the amount of space that is devoted to particular areas and the lack of space devoted to others. For example, there is a great deal of law relating to publication and re-publication and the role of intermediaries and their characterization and liability before and after notice, both at common law and at statute regulation. The laws vary among different jurisdictions considerably. The role of search engines, hyperlinks, and social networking sites will likely generate widespread litigation and discussion by the courts.

10) Conventional Versus Guerrilla/Information Warfare

Finally, it is probably apparent that if litigation is a form of warfare, cyberlibel is guerrilla/information warfare. This is an enormously complex subject requiring an understanding of the principles of guerrilla warfare, information warfare, information technology, strategic studies, and their applicability to cyberlibel litigation. An annotated list of reference materials about guerrilla warfare, other information warfare, crisis management, risk management, and other topics can be found below in the Selected Bibliography.

B. CONSEQUENCES OF THE DIFFERENCES BETWEEN OFFLINE LIBEL AND CYBERLIBEL LITIGATION

1. It is especially important to consider the objectives and the remedies that are being sought. Usually, in cyberlibel cases the most important objective is removal of the defamatory statement as quickly as possible.
2. The sequence of the proceedings against various defendants is often as important as the action taken. For example, in most libel actions, proceedings are usually taken against all defendants simultaneously or generally concurrently. However, in cyberlibel proceedings it may be wise to proceed against parties sequentially if that facilitates removal of the defamatory statements in a more cost-effective manner.
3. Cyberlibel proceedings are often a series of skirmishes with different defendants, similar to guerrilla warfare. Your adversaries may suddenly proliferate then evaporate or mutate into other forms or migrate to other locations in cyberspace. They often will be anonymous and sometimes unreachable. Victories may necessarily go unpublicized.
4. It is usually unwise to launch proceedings precipitously without first engaging in damage control. You may transform a problem into a disas-

ter. A cost-benefit analysis should also be conducted before any action is taken.

5. Optics are of critical importance in cyberlibel actions, as they are in all libel proceedings.

6. The differences in cyberlibel proceedings are as follows:

   - The action may arouse further sympathy-based attacks throughout the Internet. They may arise in different jurisdictions, demanding further response.

   - The reaction throughout the Internet may be wider than the original defamatory statement.

CHAPTER 7: Should Internet-specific Principles of Law Be Adopted?

A. INTRODUCTION

"Like Wyatt Earp arriving in Dodge City, law and order has come to cyberspace."

W. John Moore, "Taming Cyberspace" (1992) 24 Nat'l J. 745 at 746

"Maybe libel law is obsolete. Maybe it always was. But in the world of Net communications, it is hard to see why anyone should weep if libel lawsuits disappeared altogether."

Mike Godwin, "Libel Law: Let it Die," *Wired* (March, 1996) at 116

"To say that libel and slander are rampant on the Internet would be an understatement."

R. Timothy Muth, "Old Doctrines on a New Frontier: Defamation and Jurisdiction in Cyberspace," *The* [Wisconsin] *Courier* (September, 1995)

As the above quotations demonstrate, cyberlibel has generated controversy for many years. Justice Kirby in *Dow Jones and Company Inc. v. Gutnick*, [2002] HCA 56 at para. 66 stated:

> KIRBY J. : Lord Bingham of Cornhill recently wrote that, in its impact on the law of defamation, the Internet will require "almost every concept and rule in the field ... to be reconsidered in the light of this unique medium of instant worldwide communication." This appeal enlivens such a reconsideration. [Footnote omitted.]

Courts around the world have recognized the distinctive features of the Internet and the necessity of trying to apply the rules of defamation law to the Internet.

- *A.B. v. Bragg Communications Inc.,* 2010 NSSC 215, discussing Facebook and privacy issues.
- *Black v. Breeden,* 2010 ONCA 547, on jurisdictional questions involving cyberlibel.
- *Le Roux and Others v. Dey (44/2009),* [2010] ZASCA 41, 2010 (4) SA 210 (SCA), on defamatory meaning arising out of the multimedia nature of the Internet.
- *Crookes v. Newton,* 2009 BCCA 392, discussing publication and hyperlinks.
- *Metropolitan International Schools Ltd. (t/a Skillstrain and/or Train-2game) v. Designtechnica Corp (t/a Digital Trends) & Ors,* [2009] EWHC 1765 (QB), on search engine liability.
- *Applause Store Productions Ltd. & Anor v. Raphael,* [2008] EWHC 1781 (QB), discussing Facebook.
- *Grant v. Torstar Corporation,* 2008 ONCA 796, discussing the application of a new defence of possible communication in matters of the public interest.
- *Bunt v. Tilley & Ors,* [2006] EWHC 407 (QB), discussing the liability of passive intermediaries.
- *Bangoura v. Washington Post,* 2005 CanLII 32906 (ON C.A.), *Barrick Gold Corp. v. Lopehandia,* 2004 CanLII 12938 (ON C.A.), on questions of damages and impact and extra-territorial application of injunctions.
- *Dow Jones & Co. Inc. v. Gutnick,* [2002] HCA 56, discussing the single publication rule.

Frequently parties raise arguments that Internet-specific rules or principles should be adopted in their particular case. The courts have thoroughly considered and discussed the competing arguments about the development and applications of Internet-specific rules.

> See, for example: *Black v. Breeden,* 2010 ONCA 547
> *Metropolitan International Schools Ltd. (t/a Skillstrain and/or Train2game) v.*
>   *Designtechnica Corp (t/a Digital Trends) & Ors,* [2009] EWHC 1765 (QB)
> *Bangoura v. Washington Post,* 2005 CanLII 32906 (ON C.A.)
> *Carter v. B.C. Federation of Foster Parents Assn.,* 2005 BCCA 398
> *Lewis & Ors v. King,* [2004] EWCA Civ 1329
> *Dow Jones & Co. Inc. v. Gutnick,* [2002] HCA 56
> *Loutchansky v. Times Newspapers Ltd* [2001] EWCA Civ 536

The High Court of Australia rejected an argument by Dow Jones in *Dow Jones & Co. Inc. v. Gutnick,* [2002] HCA 56. The Court determined that, because of the characteristics of the Internet, the Court should not apply the existing multiple publication rule but should adopt an Internet-specific single publication rule. The judges in three separate judgments held that the single publication rule should apply and Internet-specific rules should not apply.

> See *Dow Jones & Co. Inc. v. Gutnick*, [2002] HCA 56, Gleeson, McHugh, Gummow, and Hayne J.J. at p. 11–14; Guadron J. at para. 30; Kirby J. at paras. 72–92.
> Similar arguments were made and rejected by the BC Court of Appeal in *Carter v. B.C. Federation of Foster Parents Assn.*, 2005 BCCA 398
> See also the decision in *Loutchansky v. Times Newspaper Ltd.*, [2001] EWCA Civ 536

B. *DOW JONES & CO. INC. v. GUTNICK* DISCUSSION OF INTERNET-SPECIFIC PRINCIPLES

One of the most comprehensive examinations of the important subject of Internet-specific rules is found in the judgment of Kirby J. in the Australian High Court decision of *Dow Jones & Co. Inc. v. Gutnik*, [2002] HCA 56. Justice Kirby's analysis of the question of Internet-specific rules and his reasons for rejecting Internet-specific solutions with the supporting references is included for several reasons:

1. Due to the comprehensive review of the arguments in for and against Internet-specific rules.
2. Due to the recognition and discussion of the complexity of attempting to apply Internet-specific rules to questions of defamation law.
3. His reasons illustrate the need to be cautious about indulging in what might be called "technological exceptionalism" — a tendency to believe that a certain technology is so exceptional that:
   - existing rules no longer apply;
   - new rules have to be developed immediately;
   - rules have to be developed around the technology;
   - exceptions must be created based on the technology; or
   - existing legal principles are dismissed as archaic fossils incapable of application in contemporary society.
4. Justice Kirby's reasons recognize the inherent limits of appellate decision-making and acknowledge the role of the legislature. Despite the impact of these decisions beyond the parties, and the valuable role played by interveners, these decisions must primarily resolve a dispute between specific parties on a specific set of facts.
5. Finally, it is useful to recognize that the existing rules are often a product of particular cultural values and that national interests are sometimes involved. For example, the arguments in favour of the single rule were

viewed by Callinan, J. at para. 186 as an attempt to impose "American legal hegemony in relation to Internet publications":

> I agree with the respondent's submission that what the appellant seeks to do, is to impose upon Australian residents for the purposes of this and many other cases, an American legal hegemony in relation to Internet publications. The consequence, if the appellant's submission were to be accepted would be to confer upon one country, and one notably more benevolent to the commercial and other media than this one, an effective domain over the law of defamation, to the financial advantage of publishers in the United States, and the serious disadvantage of those unfortunate enough to be reputationally damaged outside the United States. A further consequence might be to place commercial publishers in this country at a disadvantage to commercial publishers in the United States.

Future arguments will certainly be raised about the development of an application of Internet-specific rules. At a minimum, these arguments will be raised about defamatory meanings, fair comment, qualified privilege and liabilities of search engines, and liabilities on social networking sites. Technologically specific approaches already exist, as seen in articles about link law, search engine law, and social networking law. Guidance provided by judges like Kirby J. will provide an invaluable context and foundation for the discussion and resolution of future Internet-specific rules.

To assist the reader in determining whether to read Kirby J.'s complete reasons on this subject, I have provided a summary of the arguments in favour of Internet-specific rules and Kirby J.'s reasons for declining to adopt Internet-specific rules.

C. SUMMARY OF THE ARGUMENTS IN *DOW JONES & CO. INC. v. GUTNICK* IN FAVOUR OF INTERNET-SPECIFIC RULES

Justice Kirby summarized the arguments in favour of adopting Internet-specific rules in *Dow Jones & Co. Inc. v. Gutnick*, [2002] HCA 56:

1. The Internet is a novel development and new rules are needed for a unique technology (see paras. 111–13 and 118).
2. A simple, effective legal rule is needed to help determine jurisdiction (see paras. 118–19).
3. There is a need for a readily ascertainable single rule to govern publication of the statements on the Internet (see paras. 116–17).
4. The problem is too urgent to wait for consideration and resolution by the legislature (paras. 119–20).

5. The present state of the laws leads to problems, including the enforceability of the libel judgments of Australia in the US (paras. 121–22).

D. FULL TEXT OF JUSTICE KIRBY'S ARGUMENT IN FAVOUR OF INTERNET-SPECIFIC RULES

The full text of Kirby J.'s summary of the arguments in favour of Internet-specific rules, found at paras. 111–21 of the case, is as follows:

> *A novel development*: The fundamental premise of the appellant's arguments concerning the reformulation of the applicable rules of defamation depended on the technological features of the Internet. According to the appellant, those features were sufficiently different from pre-existing technology to demand a substantial reconsideration of the relevant law that had been stated in a different context in earlier times. If a more general revision were thought inappropriate or unnecessary, the task should at least be undertaken for any allegedly defamatory imputations published on the Internet.
>
> I accept that a number of arguments support this proposition. Involved in responding to it are important questions of legal principle and policy. The proposition cannot be answered by an enquiry limited to expressions of past law. When a radically new situation is presented to the law it is sometimes necessary to think outside the square. In the present case, this involves a reflection upon the features of the Internet that are said to require a new and distinctive legal approach.
>
> First, the Internet is global. As such, it knows no geographic boundaries. Its basic lack of locality suggests the need for a formulation of new legal rules to address the absence of congruence between cyberspace and the boundaries and laws of any given jurisdiction. There are precedents for development of such new legal rules. The Law Merchant (*lex mercatoria*) arose in medieval times out of the general custom of the merchants of many nations in Europe. It emerged to respond to the growth of transnational trade. The rules of the common law of England adapted to the Law Merchant. They did so out of necessity and commonsense.
>
> *Effective legal responses*: The general principle of public international law obliging comity in legal dealings between states suggests that arguably, with respect to the legal consequences of the Internet, no jurisdiction should ordinarily impose its laws on the conduct of persons in other jurisdictions in preference to the laws that would ordinarily govern such conduct where it occurs. At least this should be so unless the former jurisdiction can demonstrate that it has a stronger interest in the resolution of the dispute in

question than the latter. In conformity with this approach, the advent of the Internet suggests a need to adopt new principles, or to strengthen old ones, in responding to questions of forum or choice of law that identify, by reference to the conduct that is to be influenced, the place that has the strongest connection with, or is in the best position to control or regulate, such conduct. Normally, the laws of such a place are those most likely to be effective in securing the objectives of law, such as here, the protection of the right to free expression and access to information and the defence of reputation.

Effectiveness of remedies: Any suggestion that there can be no effective remedy for the tort of defamation (or other civil wrongs) committed by the use of the Internet (or that such wrongs must simply be tolerated as the price to be paid for the advantages of the medium) is self-evidently unacceptable. Instruments of international human rights law recognise the right of "[e]veryone . . . to hold opinions without interference" and to enjoy "the right to freedom of expression . . . [including] freedom to seek, receive and impart information and ideas of all kinds, regardless of frontiers . . . through any . . . media of his choice." However, such instruments also recognise that those rights carry "duties and responsibilities." They may therefore "be subject to certain restrictions, but these shall only be such as are provided by law and are necessary . . . [f]or respect of the rights or reputations of others."

The International Covenant of Civil and Political Rights also provides that "[n]o one shall be subjected to arbitrary or unlawful interference with his privacy, family, home or correspondence, nor to unlawful attacks on his honour and reputation." And that "[e]veryone has the right to the protection of the law against such interference or attacks." Accordingly, any development of the common law of Australia, consistent with such principles, should provide effective legal protection for the honour, reputation and personal privacy of individuals. To the extent that our law does not do so, Australia, like other nations so obliged, is rendered accountable to the relevant treaty body for such default.

The law in different jurisdictions, reflecting local legal and cultural norms, commonly strikes different balances between rights to information and expression and the protection of individual reputation, honour and privacy. These disparities suggest the need for a clear and single rule to govern the conduct in question according to pre-established norms. If it is to be effective, such a rule must be readily ascertainable. To tell a person uploading potentially defamatory material onto a website that such conduct will render that person potentially liable to proceedings in courts of every legal jurisdiction where the subject enjoys a reputation, may have undesirable consequences. Depending on the publisher and the place of its assets, it might freeze publication or censor it or try to restrict access to it in certain countries so as to comply with the most restrictive defamation laws that could apply. Or it could result in the adoption of locational stratagems in an attempt to avoid liability.

A new rule for a unique technology: In response to the suggestion that similar questions have existed at least since telegraph and international shortwave radio and that such potential liability is a commonplace in the world of global television distributed by satellite, the appellant pointed to the peculiarities of Internet publication. Viewed in one way, the Internet is not simply an extension of past communications technology. It is a new means of creating continuous relationships in a manner that could not previously have been contemplated. According to this view, the Internet is too flexible a structure to be controlled by a myriad of national laws, purportedly applied with no more justification than is provided by the content of such laws, usually devised long before the Internet arrived. For stored information, accessible in cyberspace, the new technology was said to demand a new approach. This would be true as much for the law of taxation, commercial transactions and other areas, as for the law of defamation.

The urgency of a new rule: To wait for legislatures or multilateral international agreement to provide solutions to the legal problems presented by the Internet would abandon those problems to "agonizingly slow" processes of lawmaking. Accordingly, courts throughout the world are urged to address the immediate need to piece together gradually a coherent transnational law appropriate to the "digital millennium." The alternative, in practice, could be an institutional failure to provide effective laws in harmony, as the Internet itself is, with contemporary civil society — national and international. The new laws would need to respect the entitlement of each legal regime not to enforce foreign legal rules contrary to binding local law or important elements of local public policy. But within such constraints, the common law would adapt itself to the central features of the Internet, namely its global, ubiquitous and reactive characteristics. In the face of such characteristics, simply to apply old rules, created on the assumptions of geographical boundaries, would encourage an inappropriate and usually ineffective grab for extra-territorial jurisdiction.

The adoption of a single publication rule, expressed in terms of the place of uploading of material on the Internet might, in this case, favour the jurisdiction of the courts and the law of the United States. However, it would not always be so. Thus, if the liability propounded concerned an Australian who had uploaded material on the Internet within Australia, had taken pains to conform to Australian defamation law but was sued for defamation in some other jurisdiction whose defamation laws were more restrictive than Australia's, respect for the single global publication rule, if it became internationally accepted, could help reduce the risks of legal uncertainty and the excessive assertion of national laws.

Enforceability of judgments: Any rule adopted with respect to publication of defamatory matter on the Internet must eventually face the practical question concerning the enforceability of a judgment recovered in such proceedings. The balance that is struck between freedom of expression and access to information and protection of individual reputation, honour and privacy tends to be a subject about which divergent views exist in the laws of different countries. Sometimes such laws are reinforced by domestic constitutional provisions. A judgment of a country's courts, recovered in defamation proceedings, may be enforced against any property of a foreign judgment debtor that exists within the jurisdiction. But if it is necessary to enforce the judgment in another jurisdiction, the difficulty or impossibility of such enforcement may amount to a practical reason for providing relief to the objecting foreign party on one or more of the grounds of objection raised in this case.

By reference to these and like considerations, the appellant submitted that this Court should look afresh at the common law of defamation. It argued that we, as one of the first final courts asked to consider this problem, should adjust previously stated law to the new technological and legal realities. The adoption of a simple universal rule apt to the new medium, to the effectiveness of law as an influence upon publishing conduct and realistic about the prospects of recovery upon judgments against foreign defendants, was the approach that the appellant invited this Court to take. [Footnotes omitted.]

E. SUMMARY OF THE ARGUMENTS OPPOSED TO INTERNET-SPECIFIC RULES

Justice Kirby presented the following reasons in *Dow Jones & Co. Inc. v. Gutnick*, [2002] HCA 56 for declining to adopt Internet-specific rules:

1. There are limits to judicial innovation and the change proposed exceeds the judicial function (see paras. 123–124 and 137–38).
2. Rules should be technologically neutral (see para. 125).
3. This is a matter that requires legislative reform (see paras. 126–32).
4. If the place of uploading were adopted as the place of publication, which also governs the choice of applicable law, the consequence would often be,

effectively, that the law would assign the place of the wrong for the tort of defamation to the US. Since the location of many of the webservers are in the US, the result might be that the reputations of Australians in Australia would be governed by US law (see paras. 133–36).

F. FULL TEXT OF REASONS FOR DECLINING THE ADOPTION OF INTERNET-SPECIFIC RULES

The full text of Kirby. J's reasons for declining the adoption of Internet-specific rules, found at paras. 123–38 of the case, is as follows.

> *Limits to judicial innovation*: The foregoing considerations present a persuasive argument for the formulation of a new rule of the common law that is particular to the publication of allegedly defamatory matter on the Internet. For myself, I do not regard them as mere slogans. They present a serious legal issue for decision. Judges have adapted the common law to new technology in the past. The rules of private international law have emerged as a result of, and remain alive to, changes in the means of trans-border communication between people. The Internet's potential impact on human affairs continues to expand and is already enormous. Later judges, in a position to do so, can sometimes reformulate the law in order to keep it relevant and just. Specifically they may re-express judge-made rules that suit earlier times and different technologies. For a number of reasons I have concluded that this Court would not be justified to change the rules of the Australian common law as would be necessary in this case to respond to the submissions of the appellant.
>
> First, a starting point for the consideration of the submission must be an acceptance that the principles of defamation law invoked by the respondent are settled and of long standing. Those principles are: (1) that damage to reputation is essential for the existence of the tort of defamation; (2) that mere composition and writing of words is not enough to constitute the tort; those words must be communicated to a third party who comprehends them; (3) that each time there is such a communication, the plaintiff has a new cause of action; and (4) that a publisher is liable for publication in a particular jurisdiction where that is the intended or natural and probable consequence of its acts. Where rules such as these are deeply entrenched in the common law and relate to the basic features of the cause of action propounded, their alteration risks taking the judge beyond the proper limits of the judicial function.
>
> *Rules should be technology-neutral*: Whilst the Internet does indeed present many novel technological features, it also shares many character-

istics with earlier technologies that have rapidly expanded the speed and quantity of information distribution throughout the world. I refer to newspapers distributed (and sometimes printed) internationally; syndicated telegraph and wire reports of news and opinion; newsreels and film distributed internationally; newspaper articles and photographs reproduced instantaneously by international telefacsimile; radio, including shortwave radio; syndicated television programmes; motion pictures; videos and digitalised images; television transmission; and cable television and satellite broadcasting. Generally speaking, it is undesirable to express a rule of the common law in terms of a particular technology. Doing so presents problems where that technology is itself overtaken by fresh developments. It can scarcely be supposed that the full potential of the Internet has yet been realised. The next phase in the global distribution of information cannot be predicted. A legal rule expressed in terms of the Internet might very soon be out of date.

The need for legislative reform: There are special difficulties in achieving judicial reform of the multiple publication rule in Australian law, even if one were convinced that it should be reformed to meet the technological characteristics of the Internet. Legislation in at least one Australian State is expressed in terms that assume the existence of the multiple publication rule.

In *Australian Broadcasting Corporation v. Waterhouse*, Samuels JA stated his opinion that a single publication rule could only be introduced throughout Australia by statute. Whilst that remark was not essential to his Honour's reasoning, was made before the particular features of the Internet were known and does not bind this Court, it reflects the recognition of a judge with much experience in defamation law of the limits that exist on judicial alteration of basic principles to fit the apparent needs of a new technology. Because of such limits other means have been adopted within Australia to reduce the inconvenience of the multiple publication rule. Some, or all, of these would be available in the case of an Internet publication to reduce the suggested inconvenience of that rule.

The defects of the multiple publication rule have been considered by the Australian Law Reform Commission ("ALRC"). In successive reports, the ALRC has proposed different solutions to the problem. In its report on defamation law, the ALRC recommended legislation to abrogate the rule. However, its recommendations have not so far been enacted. Whilst this is not necessarily a reason for this Court to stay its hand, it is appropriate to recall that in a parliamentary democracy such as that established by the Australian Constitution, this is a reason for caution in judicial alteration of basic and long held legal rules. Such caution is reinforced by the consideration that recently, when invited to do so, the House of Lords rejected the global theory of defamation liability. One of the reasons of the majority was that any such change would be incompatible with the long established principle in the *Duke of Brunswick's Case* which, by inference, their Lordships felt to be beyond judicial repair.

There are a number of difficulties that would have to be ironed out before the settled rules of defamation law that I have mentioned could be modified in respect of publication of allegedly defamatory material on the Internet.

Take for example the suggestion that, before proof of damage or comprehension by anyone (apart from the author), the place and law of "publication" was fixed by the jurisdiction in which the text was first uploaded (as the appellant proposed) or in which the publisher last exercised control over dissemination (as the interveners proposed). The respondent complained that either of these rules, if substituted for the present law, would lead to "chaos." Even allowing for an advocate's overstatement, there are indeed difficulties. Publishers could easily locate the uploading of harmful data in a chosen place in an attempt to insulate themselves from defamation liability. They might choose places with defamation laws favourable to publishing interests. Just as books are now frequently printed in developing countries, the place of uploading of materials onto the Internet might bear little or no relationship to the place where the communication was composed, edited or had its major impact.

As if to recognise this problem, the appellant postulated various exceptions to its criterion of the place of uploading. These included exceptions for "adventitious or opportunistic" conduct; or conduct that "targeted" a particular place; or which existed where the website was "promoted." Apart from raising the question of whether the appellant's own publications would, in this case, fall within exceptions of the latter kind, it will be observed that we are already involved in overthrowing established legal rules for new ones that would require great precision in the formulation of detailed exceptions if a satisfactory judicial reformulation were to be achieved.

The uploading approach would also oblige a plaintiff to discover matters of conduct normally exclusively within the knowledge of the persons involved in processing the data. The plaintiff would have to find such facts in advance of the commencement of the proceedings. There are many similar practical problems. However, I have said enough to show that the propounded reformulation presents many complex questions. They are not appropriate for solution in judicial proceedings addressed to deciding a controversy between particular parties mainly or only interested in the outcome of their own dispute.

Attractions of alternative formulations: A connected issue demands consideration. If the place of uploading were adopted as the place of publication which also governs the choice of applicable law, the consequence would often be, effectively, that the law would assign the place of the wrong for the tort of defamation to the United States. Because of the vastly disproportionate location of webservers in the United States when compared to virtually all other countries (including Australia) this would necessarily have the result, in many cases, of extending the application of a law of the United States (and possibly the jurisdiction and forum of its courts) to defamation proceedings brought by Australian and other foreign citizens in respect of local damage to their reputations by publication on the Internet. Because the purpose of the tort of defamation (as much in the United States as in Australia) is to provide vindication to redress the injury done to a person's reputation, it would be small comfort to the person wronged to subject him or her to the law (and possibly the jurisdiction of the courts) of a place of uploading, when any decision so made would depend upon a law reflecting different values and applied in courts unable to afford vindication in the place where it matters most.

At least in the case of the publication of materials potentially damaging to the reputation and honour of an individual, it does not seem unreasonable, in principle, to oblige a publisher to consider the law of the jurisdiction of that person's habitual residence. In its review of this subject, the ALRC expressed the opinion that "[i]n the case of defamation of a natural person, the law to be applied would normally be that of the place where the person was ordinarily resident." In its subsequent report on choice of law, the ALRC concluded that "residence is the best option for a choice of law rule for defamation." The ALRC went on to recommend that it was "unnecessary to qualify residence as 'usual' or 'habitual' for the purposes of this rule, since to do so might take the rule further away from the place of loss of reputation."

In his reasons in *Australian Broadcasting Corporation v. Waterhouse*, proposing the need for legislative reform of defamation law within Australia, Samuels JA suggested much the same. He said that the criterion of the habitual residence of the subject of the publication would present an objective criterion. It would discourage forum shopping. It would also give "effect to the expectations of the parties" on the basis that the place of residence would be where "[a] plaintiff will generally suffer most harm." His Honour's analysis shows how deeply embedded in the concept of the tort of defamation are the ideas of proof of damage to reputation; comprehension of the matter complained of; and acknowledgment that the sting is felt each time a publication is repeated.

When this point is reached it is natural, and proper, for a court such as this to refuse the invitation to re-express the common law, even if persuasive criticism of the present law has been advanced, as I think it has. Although the ALRC's reports proposing relevant reforms have not been implemented, it is not true to suggest that the parliaments of Australia have neglected regulation of liability for particular aspects of Internet content. Further, while the recommendations of the ALRC may provide guidance to the identification of the place of the tort of defamation for choice of law purposes in light of this Court's decisions in *Pfeiffer* and *Zhang*, they do not assist the argument of the appellant. International developments, involving multilateral negotiations, must also be considered if there is to be any chance of the adoption of a uniform approach suitable to the world-wide technology, as the appellant urged. In other sensitive areas of the law requiring international agreement, the Australian Parliament has recently moved with proper speed to implement the emerging international consensus.

Change exceeds the judicial function: Although, therefore, the appellant (and interveners) have established real defects in the current Australian law of defamation as it applies to publications on the Internet, their respective solutions for altering the elements of the tort and expressing it in terms of conduct substantially in the control of the publisher or its agents (and out of the control of the plaintiff whose reputation is alleged to have been damaged) are too simplistic.

It would exceed the judicial function to re-express the common law on such a subject in such ways. This is a subject of law reform requiring the evaluation of many interests and considerations that a court could not be sure to cover. Subject to what follows, I, like the other members of this Court, do not think that a single publication rule should be adopted in terms of the place of uploading as the place of publication of allegedly defamatory material on the Internet, which would also govern the choice of applicable law. [Footnotes omitted].

G. INTERNET-SPECIFIC ARGUMENTS RAISED BY THE DEFENDANTS IN *BLACK v. BREEDEN*

The Ontario Court of Appeal in *Black v. Breeden*, 2010 ONCA 547 examined and rejected two Internet-specific arguments raised by the defendants in a motion to stay libel proceedings on jurisdictional grounds. The defendants raised two Internet-specific arguments in the Court of Appeal that were rejected by the Court. The first, as discussed at paras. 34–38, was "targeting analysis":

The defendants submit that the statements in question were all made in the United States, primarily in New York; although Black pleads republication in Ontario, the republication was not made by the defendants. They take the position that the alleged tort was not committed in Ontario and American libel law would apply.

The defendants submit that treating the *lex loci delicti* as the place in which allegedly defamatory statements were accessed is inappropriate in the context of Internet libel. An approach that looks to where the statements were accessed, they argue, is contrary to the principles of order and fairness, leads to libel tourism and the prospect of unlimited liability and has a chilling effect on freedom of speech.

The defendants advocate a different approach to a claim for libel originating on the Internet. They suggest that the focus of the analysis of where the tort of Internet libel is committed should be on *whether the defendant targeted the statements to the forum rather than where they were downloaded and read.*

In support of the "targeting analysis" advocated, the defendants cite M. Geist, "Is There a There There? Toward Greater Certainty for Internet Jurisdiction" (2001), 16 Berkeley Tec. L.J. 1345, at 1380 and the case of *Young v. New Haven Advocate*, 315 F.3d 256, at 262–63 (4th Cir. 2002). In *Young*, the United States Court of Appeals for the 4th Circuit concluded that two Connecticut newspapers did not subject themselves to the jurisdiction of Virginia courts by posting on the Internet news articles that allegedly defamed the warden of a Virginia prison. The court explained at p. 263: "Something more than posting and accessibility is needed to 'indicate that the [newspapers] purposefully (albeit electronically) directed [their] activity in a substantial way to the forum state', Virginia. The newspapers must, through the Internet postings, manifest intent to target and focus on Virginia readers" (citations omitted).

The defendants do not point to any Canadian authority for such a targeting approach. In *Bangoura v. Washington Post* 2005 CanLII 32906 (ON C.A.), (2005), 258 D.L.R. (4th) 341 (Ont. C.A.), at para. 48, leave to appeal to S.C.C. refused, [2005] S.C.C.A. No. 497, the interveners representing the Media Coalition proposed such an alternative approach to the issue of publication on the Internet and jurisdiction; however, the court did not find it necessary to determine the issue. Similarly, this issue need not be resolved on the facts of this case.

In any event, the Court of Appeal was satisfied at paras. 39–40 that there was evidence that the defendants did target and direct their statements to this jurisdiction:

I am satisfied on this record that there is evidence that the defendants did target and direct their statements to this jurisdiction. The press releases posted on the Internet specifically provide contact information for Canadian media, as well as U.S. and U.K. media. The press releases concluded with the heading "Contacts" for "US/Canada Media" followed by a name and contact information, as well as for "UK Media" with a different name and contact information. The contact information for Canadian media clearly anticipated that the statements would be read by a Canadian audience and invited Canadian media to respond.

For these reasons, I conclude that the motion judge did not err in finding the alleged defamation was committed in Ontario.

The second Internet-specific argument was summarized and dealt with as follows at para. 41:

> Alternatively, the defendants submit that in the context of the Internet, downloading was merely the 'completion' of the tort, suggesting that the tort could be committed in more than one jurisdiction. They suggest that where a tort can be committed in more than one jurisdiction, this court create an exception to the presumption of real and substantial connection. However, in my view, it is unnecessary to create a new exception in order to address principles of fairness and order or jurisdictional restraint.

H. INTERNET-SPECIFIC ARGUMENTS RAISED AND REJECTED BY THE COURTS IN THE UK

Arguments that Internet-specific rules or exceptions should be introduced in Internet libel cases have also been raised and rejected in the UK. The Court of Appeal for England and Wales discussed and reviewed these arguments in *Lewis & Ors v. King*, [2004] EWCA Civ 1329 at paras. 28–32:

> The third strand in the learning to which we would draw attention was initially prompted by what Lord Steyn in *Berezovsky* called "trans-national" libels, thus including libels perpetrated on the Internet. The present case is of course an example. Such libels have generated a good deal of academic discussion, and have been passed on by the High Court of Australia in *Gutnick v Dow Jones*. Mr. Price sought to persuade us to adopt a special rule for Internet libels, and we must deal with that. First, in *Berezovsky* Lord Steyn said this:
>
> > . . . counsel put forward the global theory on a reformulated basis. He said that when the court, having been satisfied that it has juris-

diction, has to decide under Order 11 whether England is the most appropriate forum 'the correct approach is to treat the entire publication — whether by international newspaper circulation, trans-border or satellite broadcast or Internet posting — *as if* it gives rise to one cause of action and to ask whether it has been clearly proved that *this action* is best tried in England.' If counsel was submitting that in respect of trans-national libels the court exercising its discretion must consider the global picture, his proposition would be uncontroversial. Counsel was, however, advancing a more ambitious proposition. He submitted that in respect of trans-national libels the principles enunciated by the House in the *Spiliada* case ... should be recast to proceed on assumption that there is in truth one cause of action. The result of such a principle, if adopted, will usually be to favour a trial in the home courts of the foreign publisher because the bulk of the publication will have taken place there.

This "more ambitious" proposition was rejected by Lord Steyn. But we consider with respect that his reference to the court's need, in the case of trans-national libels, to "consider the global picture" is something more than a passing aside. What is "the global picture"? Where there is publication, say in two jurisdictions only, it remains relatively confined, and the *Albaforth* starting-point may remain very meaningful. But in relation to Internet libel, bearing in mind the rule in *Duke of Brunswick v Harmer* that each publication constitutes a separate tort, a defendant who publishes on the Web may at least in theory find himself vulnerable to multiple actions in different jurisdictions. The place where the tort is committed ceases to be a potent limiting factor.

In *Gutnick v Dow Jones* the High Court of Australia firmly rejected a challenge, in the context of Internet libel, to the applicability of such established principles as that vouchsafed in *Duke of Brunswick*. In doing so the court made certain observations about Internet publication which with respect, we think we may usefully bear in mind:

> 39. It was suggested that the World Wide Web was different from radio and television because the radio or television broadcaster could decide how far the signal was to be broadcast. It must be recognised, however, that satellite broadcasting now permits very wide dissemination of radio and television and it may, therefore, be doubted that it is right to say that the World Wide Web has a uniquely broad reach. It is no more or less ubiquitous than some television services. In the end, pointing to the breadth or depth of reach of particular forms of

communication may tend to obscure one basic fact. However broad may be the reach of any particular means of communication, those who post information on the World Wide Web do so knowing that the information they make available is available to all and sundry without any geographic restriction.

181. A publisher, particularly one carrying on the business of publishing, does not act to put matter on the Internet in order for it to reach a small target. It is its ubiquity which is one of the main attractions to users of it. And any person who gains access to the Internet does so by taking an initiative to gain access to it in a manner analogous to the purchase or other acquisition of a newspaper, in order to read it.

192. . . . Comparisons can, as I have already exemplified, readily be made. If a publisher publishes in a multiplicity of jurisdictions it should understand, and must accept, that it runs the risk of liability in those jurisdictions in which the publication is not lawful and inflicts damage.

So far, then, the *Duke of Brunswick* has well survived the Internet, certainly in the High Court of Australia. And the court's vindication of traditional principles relating to publication and jurisdiction in defamation cases marches with Lord Steyn's rejection, in *Berezovsky*, of counsel's "more ambitious proposition . . . in respect of trans-national libels."

. . . But the court's rejection of sweeping submissions that would have done away with *Duke of Brunswick* in favour of the "single publication rule" known in many states of the USA, alongside the *dicta* in *Gutnick* which emphasise the Internet publisher's very choice of a ubiquitous medium, at least suggests a robust approach to the question of *forum*: a global publisher should not be too fastidious as to the part of the globe where he is made a libel defendant.

We should notice, though we do so only in passing, that the Law Commission were perhaps rather more troubled about the effects of global publication. In *DEFAMATION AND THE INTERNET: A Preliminary Investigation* they stated:

> Although we have some sympathy with the concerns expressed about the levels of 'global risk,' any solution would require an international treaty, accompanied by greater harmonisation of the substantive law of defamation. We do not think that the problem can be solved within the short or medium term. We do not therefore recommend reform in this area at the present time. [Footnotes omitted].

PART II: Preliminary Questions

CHAPTER 8: Notice and Limitation Periods

A. INTRODUCTION

In the libel and slander statutes of many provinces, notice must be given when the offending statement is contained either in a newspaper or in a broadcast. For example, section 5.1 of the Ontario *Libel and Slander Act*, R.S.O. 1990, c. L.12 states as follows:

> No action for libel in a newspaper or in a broadcast lies unless the plaintiff has, within six weeks after the alleged libel has come to the plaintiff's knowledge, given to the defendant notice in writing, specifying the matter complained of, which shall be served in the same manner as a statement of claim or by delivering it to a grown-up person at the chief office of the defendant.
>
> Every jurisdiction in Canada except Ontario, BC, and Saskatchewan requires that a libel notice must be served within three months of the matter. Saskatchewan requires that a notice of intention to sue for libel be given five days before filing a lawsuit against a daily newspaper, and fourteen days before filing a lawsuit against a weekly. There is no requirement relating to broadcasts.

British Columbia does not require service of a notice of intention to sue for defamation. A plaintiff is merely obliged to let one clear day pass between publication of the libel in a newspaper or broadcast and the commencement of litigation.

Libel and Slander Act, R.S.B.C. 1996, c. 263, s. 5

Alberta's *Defamation Act*, R.S.A. 2000, c. D-7, stipulates that a statutory notice of intended action must be served within three months. Section 13 states:

(1) No action lies unless the plaintiff has, within 3 months after the publication of the defamatory matter has come to the plaintiff's notice or knowledge, given to the defendant, in the case of a daily newspaper, 7, and in the case of any other newspaper or when the defamatory matter was broadcast, 14 days' notice in writing of the plaintiff's intention to bring an action, specifying the defamatory matter complained of.

(2) The notice shall be served in the same manner as a statement of claim.

The defamation statutes of Manitoba, New Brunswick, Newfoundland and Labrador, the Northwest Territories, Nova Scotia, Prince Edward Island, and the Yukon Territory contain notice provisions similar to Alberta's.

Manitoba, *Defamation Act*, C.C.S.M., c. D20, ss. 14(1)–(2)
New Brunswick, *Defamation Act*, R.S.N.B. 1973, c. D-5
Newfoundland and Labrador, *Defamation Act*, R.S.N.L. 1990, c. D-3, ss. 16(1)–(2)
Northwest Territories, *Defamation Act*, R.S.N.W.T. 1988, c. D-1, ss. 15(1)–(2)
Nova Scotia, *Defamation Act*, R.S.N.S. 1989, c. 122, ss. 18(1)–(2)
Prince Edward Island, *Defamation Act*, R.S.P.E.I. 1988, c. D-5, ss. 14(1)–(2)
Yukon Territory, *Defamation Act*, R.S.Y. 2002, c. 52, ss. 14(1)–(2)

B. GENERAL PRINCIPLES

1. The notice requirements are intended to give the newspaper, broadcaster, or other person responsible for the libel an opportunity to correct, retract, or apologize for the defamatory statements. In this way, the defendant may avoid or reduce the damages otherwise payable for the publication of the libel.

   Grossman v. CFTO TV (1982), 39 O.R. (2d) 498

2. Failure to serve a notice within the requirements of the act is an absolute bar to the action where notice is required.

   M.E.C. Capital Inc. v. CBC Broadcasting, [2003] M.J. No. 324
   Merling v. Southam Inc. (C.O.B. Hamilton Spectator) (2001), 83 D.L.R. (4th) 748
   Watson v. Southam Inc. (C.O.B. Hamilton Spectator) (2001), 89 D.L.R. (4th) 695 at para. 50
   Grossman v. CFTO TV (1982), 39 O.R. (2d) 498 to 501 (C.A.)

3. While the defamation statutes of each province and territory (except the Yukon Territory) require the plaintiff to give notice of the intended action by "specifying the defamatory matter complained of," no particular form of notice is required.

In a decision of the Ontario Court of Appeal in *Grossman v. CFTO TV* (1982), 39 O.R. (2d) 498 at 501, Cory J.A., as he then was, articulated a test of sufficiency at 505:

> Does the notice identify the plaintiff and fairly bring home to the publisher the matter complained of. Since the Act prescribes no particular form, the Court in answering this question can consider all the relevant circumstances.
>
> The longer and more frequent the broadcasts are, the greater the particularity that may be required of the notice. Similarly the more numerous the possible heads of complaint are, the more detailed the notice must be. The pleadings in a libel action are technical and they provide a wide variety of defences to a publisher. So long as the broadcaster is made clearly aware of the matter of which the plaintiff complains, then there is no reason why the case, as defined by the pleadings, should not be determined on the merits.

4. All defendants involved in the publication of a defamatory statement in the newspaper or broadcast are entitled to the statutory notice under the *Libel and Slander Act*, R.S.O. 1990, c. L.12.

    Weiss v. Sawyer, [2002] O.J. No 357 (C.A.)

    Merling v. Southam Inc. (C.O.B. Hamilton Spectator) (2001), 83 D.L.R. (4th) 748 (Ont. C.A.)

    Watson v. Southam Inc. (C.O.B. Hamilton Spectator) (2001), 89 D.L.R. (4th) 695 at paras. 50–55 (Ont. C.A.)

5. Both media and non-media defendants are entitled to notice under the *Libel and Slander Act*, R.S.O. 1990, c. L.12.

    Watson v. Southam Inc. (C.O.B. Hamilton Spectator) (2001), 89 D.L.R. (4th) 695 at paras. 50–55

    See Chapter 6 of Roger D. McConchie and David A. Potts, *Canadian Libel and Slander Actions* (Toronto: Irwin Law, 2004) for detailed discussion of the law surrounding libel notices.

C. APPLICATION TO CYBERLIBEL ACTIONS

1) Notice to Online Editions of Newspapers

Notice must be given to the online editions of newspapers. See *Weiss v. Sawyer*, 2002 CanLII 45064 at paras. 23–25 (ON C.A.), Armstrong J.A.:

> There is conflicting evidence as to whether the Sawyer letter was published on the Realms Magazine's website. Like Justice Lax I am prepared to assume the most favourable position to the appellant, i.e. there was an online pub-

lication of the letter. This then raises the issue of whether the respondent, Sawyer, is entitled to the benefit of the notice provision in s. 5 (1) of the *Act* in regard to the publication on the internet. As already stated, s. 5 (1) only applies to the publication of a libel in a newspaper or in a broadcast as defined in the *Act*. Is the website of Realms a newspaper, a broadcast, or both?

The *Act* defines a newspaper in part as a "paper" containing certain categories of information for distribution to the public. I think the word "paper" is broad enough to encompass a newspaper which is published on the internet.

If I am wrong in my conclusion and the word "paper" is to be given a more restrictive meaning i.e. the substance upon which a newspaper is ordinarily printed, then arguably s. 5 (1) is not available to the defendant. However, such a result would clearly be absurd. It would mean that if an action was commenced against a newspaper, without serving a s. 5 (1) notice, it would be barred in relation to the newsprint publication but not so barred in relation to the online publication, unless of course it fell within the definition of "broadcast." The ordinary meaning rule of statutory interpretation articulated by Ruth Sullivan, in *Driedger on the Construction of Statutes*, 3rd. ed. (Toronto: Butterworths Canada, 1994) at p. 7 is helpful . . . .

2) Notice to Online Radio Broadcasts

Notice must be given to the online versions of radio broadcasts. See *Janssen-Ortho Inc. v. Amgen Canada Inc.*, 2005 CanLII 19660 at para. 41 (ON C.A.):

> Sections 7 and 8 of the Act limit the application of the notice requirement in s. 5(1) to newspapers printed in and broadcasts made from Ontario. Janssen submits that the motions judge did not make the necessary findings of fact to support the application of s. 5(1) to the March broadcasts. In relation to the CFTR broadcast, there was no need for the motions judge to make any finding of fact as the statement of claim pleads the CFTR broadcast was from a station in Ontario. Insofar as the Warren broadcast is concerned, again, there was no need for her to make any finding of fact because the May 15 notice purportedly given pursuant to s. 5(1) indicates that one of the radio stations making the broadcast is in Ontario. The fact that the broadcast was also made from other stations outside Ontario does not matter: *Weiss, supra*. The decision in *Weiss* also answers the submission that an Internet broadcast is not a broadcast within the meaning of the Act. In *Weiss, supra*, at paragraphs 24–26, the court held that the word "paper" was broad enough to include a newspaper published on the Internet but left the issue until another evidentiary record would allow the court to make a more informed decision. Simi-

larly, the definition of broadcasting is broad enough to include a broadcast over the Internet. In *Weiss*, the original newspaper was published in Ontario. The court did not discuss whether or not the online version was published in Ontario. However, the court held that a s. 5(1) notice was required. Thus, it seems the court inferred the online version was also published in Ontario. I would make the same inference here. The same station that initiated the radio waves also initiated the radio broadcast so it is a logical inference that the Internet broadcast was also in Ontario.

3) Is Notice Required when Statements are Published on Non-Media Connected Websites?

The law is unsettled on the question of whether notice must be given when the statement published on the Internet is on a website that is distinct from an online version of a newspaper or an online version of a television or radio broadcast. See *Weiss v. Sawyer*, 2002 CanLII 45064 (ON C.A.) at para. 26:

> Based upon the above conclusion it is not necessary to consider whether the online publication of the Sawyer letter constitutes a "broadcast" within the meaning of the *Act*. There is also good reason to decline to decide this issue in the case at bar. There is simply no evidence on the record that the online publication of the Sawyer letter falls within the statutory definition of broadcast:
>
> > "Broadcasting" means the dissemination of writing, signs, signals, pictures and sounds of all kinds, intended to be received by the public either directly or through the medium of relay stations, by means of,
> >
> > (a) any form of wireless radioelectric communication utilizing Hertzian waves, including radiotelegraph and radio telephone, or
> >
> > (b) cables, wires, fibre-optic linkages or laser beams, and "broadcast" has a corresponding meaning;

In *Bahlieda v. Santa*, 2003 CanLII 2883 (ON C.A.) the Court stated at para. 6:

> In our view, the motions judge erred in several respects in finding that there was no genuine issue for trial. Section 7 of the Act provides that subsection 5(1) and section 6 apply only to "broadcasts from a station in Ontario." She makes no findings of fact, including no finding as to the essential question of whether the broadcasts were from a station in Ontario. On that basis alone, in our view, the application should have been dismissed. In addition, however, we note that the experts' opinions conflicted on a number of issues, including whether the word "dissemination" can properly apply to informa-

tion distributed by internet and whether internet publication is immediate and/or transient. Summary judgment applications are not a substitute for trial and thus will seldom prove suitable for resolving conflicts in expert testimony particularly those involving difficult, complex policy issues with broad social ramifications.

In *Warman v. Fromm*, [2007] O.J. No. 4754 (S.C.J.) at paras. 81–83 and 86–90 the Court found:

> The argument in *Jansen-Ortho* does not assist us here, as these are Internet postings, e-mails or faxes, however, no newspaper or radio broadcast is involved.
>
> The 2004 Supreme Court of Canada in *Society of Composers, Authors and Music Publishers of Canada v. Canadian Assn. of Internet Providers*, [2004] 2 S.C.R. 427 ["*Socan*"] dealt with copyright issues and the Internet. The Supreme Court dealt specifically with whether an Internet communication occurs in Canada. The comments on the technology of the Internet and the choice of end user, host server, or content provider may serve as guideposts in the future. This court, however, would have required evidence on some of these points and none was proferred in this simplified procedure trial.
>
> In *Jansen-Ortho, supra*, no reference was made to *Socan* by the Ontario Court of Appeal.
>
> . . .
>
> It remains accurate to say that the meaning of "broadcast" has not been conclusively determined in the case law as was enunciated by the Ontario Court of Appeal in *Romano v. D'Onofrio* (2005), 77 O.R. (3d) 583, while disposing of an appeal from a summary judgment motion.
>
> I conclude that the definition of broadcast must be left for a case where the evidentiary record is sufficient to permit the court to make an informed decision. However, in my view, this court can go on to examine the law as it pertains to the requirement that this "broadcast," if it is one, be "in Ontario."
>
> The only evidence before the court is that the main server is located in the United States. There was no evidence led, or submissions made, to the contrary.
>
> Accordingly, whatever "broadcast" in the Act means, there is no evidence that the "Ontario" requirement has been met. Since both elements must be proven, I find that s. 5(1) does not apply. Notice is therefore not required with respect to the five relevant postings in this case.
>
> I further rely on *Weiss v. Sawyer* (2002), 61 O.R. (3d) 526, where the Court of Appeal held that the benefit of s. 5(1) inures to the defendant only if the alleged libel is in a newspaper or a broadcast. No notice is required for faxes, nor for e-mail transmissions.

At this time, an extremely broad application of the Notice provision of the Act's original purpose might not serve the legislation. The original purpose was to allow a newspaper to mitigate its damages by retracting or apologizing for words published as a mistake made in good faith.

Extending the Act's application to a medium where words can be instantaneously disseminated around the entire globe repeatedly and with no viable possibility of effective complete retraction requires further judicial examination.

The Court stated in *Warman v. Grosvenor*, 2008 CanLII 57728 at para. 41 (ON S.C.):

> With respect to the issue of "broadcast," I agree with the reasoning of Métivier J. in *Warman v. Fromm*, where Internet postings and emails were also involved. I am also guided by the decision of the Ontario Court of Appeal in *Weiss v. Sawyer* 2002 CanLII 45064 (ON C.A.), (2002), 61 O.R. (3d) 526 at paras. 23–27 (referred to in *Warman v. Fromm*, at para. 88).

4) Procedure

In *Bahlieda v. Santa*, 2003 CanLII 2883 at para. 6 (ON C.A.) the Court found:

> ... Summary judgment applications are not a substitute for trial and thus will seldom prove suitable for resolving conflicts in expert testimony particularly those involving difficult, complex policy issues with broad social ramifications.

See *Warman v. Grosvenor*, 2008 CanLII 57728 (ON S.C.)
See also *Weiss v. Sawyer*, 2002 CanLII 45064 at para. 26 (ON C.A.)

5) Discoverability Principle

The modern judicial approach to limitations periods prescribed by the former *Limitations Act*, R.S.O. 1990, suggested that the two-year limitation period under the Ontario statute for slander is subject to the "discoverability rule" which indicates that a limitation period begins to run when the material facts upon which the cause of action exists have or ought to have been discovered by the exercise of reasonable diligence. This discoverability rule has been held to apply to defamation actions and to delay the running of time in Ontario for an action for slander.

Strong v. M.M.P., [1997] O.J. No. 2557, at paras. 80–82, Granger J. (Gen. Div.)
Larche v. Middleton (1989), 69 O.R. (2d) 400 at 404–5, Granger J. (H.C.J.)

See Roger D. McConchie and David A. Potts, *Canadian Libel and Slander Actions* (Toronto: Irwin Law, 2004) at 63–65:

> The phrase "after the libel has come to the plaintiff's knowledge" in s. 5 has been interpreted as having an objective component. The six-week limitation period therefore starts to run when the plaintiff could have known of the libel with the exercise of reasonable diligence. It is therefore not necessary that a defendant seeking to rely on the six-week limitation period for notice prove actual knowledge of the libel by the plaintiff. Constructive knowledge is adequate.
>
> *Bhaduria v. Persaud* (1998), 40 O.R. (3d) 140 (Gen. Div.)

> The six-week period for giving notice is therefore subject to the concept of "discoverability," which is an important and well-established extension of the law relating to limitation periods. In *Misir v. Toronto Star Newspapers Limited* (1997), 105 O.A.C. 270 at paras. 14–15 (C.A.) Laskin J.A. stated:
>
> > Section 5(1), however, includes the element of discoverability. The six-week period for giving notice does not commence until the alleged libel has come to the point of knowledge . . . The material before the Motions Judge does not disclose when Misir and Metro Orthopedic became aware of the publication of the May articles. On that ground alone the alleged libels in the May articles cannot be held to be barred by section 5(1) of the *Act*.
> >
> > Moreover, even if the Plaintiff had knowledge of the May articles when they were published, still they would not give effect to the limitation period . . . Section 5(1) requires that the Plaintiff have knowledge of the alleged libel in May. Misir and Metro Orthopedic may have knowledge of the publication of the May article, but not of the libel. The May articles may have been defamatory, but they were not reasonably capable of defaming these plaintiffs until they were named in the September 30th article. Accordingly, the six week notice period for the May articles would not begin before the publication of the September 30th article.
> >
> > Where the plaintiff is clearly identifiable in each of a series of twenty-three articles, there is no issue of discoverability relating to the fact she was not specifically named.
>
> *Merling v. Southam Inc. (c.o.b. Hamilton Spectator)* (2000), 183 D.L.R. (4th) 748 at para. 26, McMurtry C.J.O. (Ont. C.A.).

In *Misir v. Toronto Star Newspapers Limited* (1997), 105 O.A.C. 270 at para. 16 (C.A.) Laskin J.A. stated:

> Indeed, had the plaintiffs given notice within six weeks of the publication of the May articles and issued their statement of claim before September 30, 1995, the defendants undoubtedly would have moved to dismiss the action because the articles did not refer to the plaintiffs. Thus, it seems to me that the trier of fact can look at the September 30 article to see to whom the previous eleven articles referred. A newspaper cannot avoid an action for libel by publishing a series of defamatory articles but only linking the plaintiffs to the defamation by identifying them in the last article. The English Court of Appeal came to a similar conclusion in *Hayward v. Thompson*, [1982] 1 Q.B. 47.
>
> Applying these principles, the Ontario Court of Appeal held in *Misir v. Toronto Star Newspapers Limited* at para. 5 that the trier of fact would be entitled to find that the May articles were defamatory of the plaintiffs because of the publication of the September article.

6) Interaction of Cyberlibel with Limitation Periods

The BC Court of Appeal in *Carter v. B.C. Federation of Foster Parents Assn.*, 2005 BCCA 398, had the opportunity to determine the interaction of cyberlibel with limitation periods. The trial judge found that if the plaintiff knew, for more than two years prior to the amendment of the statement of claim, of the existence of the defamatory comment, she could not rely on the continued presence of the item on the Internet forum in the spring of 2002 as a foundation for advancing her claim against the defendants. The trial judge said at para. 84 of his reasons:

> If the plaintiff is correct in terms of a republication occurring each time a user accesses the forum and such a user was able to read the Dberlane comment, quite apart from the myriad of other innocent postings, then a site provider (as opposed to a service provider such as Blue Frogg) such as the Federation could never avail itself of any limitation period defence.

The lower court relied upon what is known as the single publication rule. This rule has been adopted by a number of American states. The appellate decision in *Carter v. B.C. Federation of Foster Parents Assn.* states as follows in para. 14:

> I turn now to a consideration of the trial judge's decision to dismiss the appellant's action against the Federation based on the Dberlane comment. That comment was found on the forum under the control of the Federation and

maintained by the service provider Blue Frogg. The substantial basis relied upon by the trial judge in dismissing this particular claim was that it was out of time. The judge also went on to hold that in any event the publication was innocent and unintentional. The time bar argument based on the expiry of a limitation period was founded upon what is sometimes referred to as the "single publication rule." This appears to be a rule adopted by a number of American states, particularly New York State, but it is not a universal rule.

In particular, the trial judge relied on and followed a decision of the New York Court of Appeal, *Firth v. State of New York*, 775 NE 2d 463 (Court App 2002). The BC Court of Appeal in *Carter v. B.C. Federation of Foster Parents Assn.* overturned the decision of the trial judge in part because the trial judge relied upon the American single publication rule (see paras. 20–22).

Ultimately, the question of whether the Commonwealth or American approach is preferable has a considerable element of policy inherent in it. Recently, in *Gilles E. Néron Communication Marketing Inc. v. Chambre des notaires du Québec*, 2004 SCC 53 (CanLII), [2004] 3 S.C.R. 95, 2004 SCC 53, a defamation case brought against the CBC by a communications consultant employed by the Chambre des notaires, LeBel J. for the majority remarked on the balancing courts must undertake in defamation actions (at paras. 52 and 54):

> Despite its undoubted importance, freedom of expression is not absolute. As this Court noted in *Prud'homme* [*v. Prud'homme*, 2002 SCC 85 (CanLII), [2002] 4 S.C.R. 663, 2002 SCC 85], at para. 43, freedom of expression can be limited by the requirements imposed by other people's right to the protection of their reputation. Cory J. observed in *Hill* [*v. Scientology*, 1995 CanLII 59 (S.C.C.), [1995] 2 S.C.R. 1130], at para. 108, that reputation, as an aspect of personality, is equally worthy of protection in a democratic society concerned about respect for the individual:
>
>> Democracy has always recognized and cherished the fundamental importance of an individual. That importance must, in turn, be based upon the good repute of a person. It is that good repute which enhances an individual's sense of worth and value. False allegations can so very quickly and completely destroy a good reputation. A reputation tarnished by libel can seldom regain its former lustre. *A democratic society, therefore, has an interest in ensuring that its members can enjoy and protect their good reputation so long as it is merited.*

* * *

> In an action for defamation the two fundamental values of free-
> dom of expression and the right to respect for one's reputation must
> be weighed against each other to find the necessary equilibrium . . . .
>   [emphasis of LeBel J.]

If defamatory comments are available in cyberspace to harm the reputation of an individual, it seems appropriate that the individual ought to have a remedy. In the instant case, the offending comment remained available on the internet because the defendant respondent did not take effective steps to have the offensive material removed in a timely way. Although, for the reasons noted by the trial judge, legislatures may have to come to grips with publication issues thrown up by the new development of widespread internet publication, to date the issue has not been legislatively addressed and in default of that, I do not consider that it would be appropriate for this Court to adopt the American rule over the rule that seems to be generally accepted throughout the Commonwealth; namely, that each publication of a libel gives a fresh cause of action. I consider that the trial judge fell into error when he held that the action of the plaintiff was out of time because she had not commenced her action within two years of first learning of the existence of the Dberlane comment. If Ms. Carter can establish that there occurred publications of the offending comment subsequent to the first publication in February of 2000, then her cause of action would not be time barred. I would observe that there seems to be some uncertainty as to exactly what the evidence does disclose about subsequent publication but I do not consider that the plaintiff should be prevented from seeking to establish, if she can, that there was subsequent publication to others which would found a cause of action.

In the result, I would allow the appeal concerning the Dberlane comment and remit that matter for decision to the trial court. As I observed, it may be that the plaintiff will have difficulty in establishing the fact of publication to a third party subsequent to her originally learning about the existence of the comment in the year 2000, but I do not consider that she should be prevented from tendering evidence that there was such publication. I would allow the appeal to that extent.

7) What Is the Single Publication Rule?

See *Carter v. B.C. Federation of Foster Parents Assn.*, 2005 BCCA 398 at para. 15, where Hall J. states as follows:

> At para. 64 of [*Loutchansky v. Times Newspapers Ltd.*, [2002] Q.B. 783 (C.A.)], the Court of Appeal set forth the substance of the single publication rule:

Some time was taken during the appeal in exploring, with the help of American authorities, the nature of the "single publication rule" in the United States. We take the following clear statement of that rule from the judgment of District Judge Holtzoff sitting in the United States District Court for the District of Columbia in *Ogden v Association of the United States Army* (1959) 177 F Supp 498, 502:

> "From the foregoing discussion the conclusion is inescapable that the modern American law of libel has adopted the so-called 'single publication' rule; and, therefore, this principle must be deemed a part of the common law of the District of Columbia. In other words, it is the prevailing American doctrine that the publication of a book, periodical or newspaper containing defamatory matter gives rise to but one cause of action for libel, which accrues at the time of the original publication, and that the statute of limitations runs from that date. It is no longer the law that every sale or delivery of a copy of the publication creates a new cause of action."

American courts have held that the single publication rule is applicable to statements published on the Internet.

Nationwide Bi-Weekly Admin v. Belo Corp., 512 F.3d 137 (C.A. 5, Dec. 21, 2007)
OJA v. United States Army Corps of Engineers, 440 F.3d 1122, 1127 (9th Cir. 2006)
McCandliss v. Cox Enterprises, 595 S.E.2d 856 (Ga. Ct. App. 2004)
The Traditional Cat Association v. Gilbreath, 118 Cal. App. 4th 392 (2004)
Firth v. State of New York, 775 N.E.2d 463 (Court App 2002)

The lower court in *Carter v. B.C. Federation of Foster Parents Assn.*, 2005 BCCA 398, explained the rationale for the single publication rule at para. 16:

Taylor J. found that since the appellant knew more than two years prior to the amendment of her statement of claim of the existence of the Dberlane comment, she could not rely on the continued presence of the item on the forum in the spring of 2002 as a foundation for advancing her claim against the Federation. The judge said this at para. 84 of his reasons:

> If the plaintiff is correct in terms of a republication occurring each time a user accesses the forum and such a user was able to read the Dberlane comment, quite apart from the myriad of other innocent postings, then a site provider (as opposed to a service provider such as Blue Frogg) such as the Federation could never avail itself of any limitation period defence.

A similar argument was advanced unsuccessfully in the *Loutchansky v. Times Newspapers Ltd.*, [2002] Q.B. 783 (C.A.) case where the court observed at para. 66:

> In *Berezovsky v. Michaels* [1999] EMLR 278 in the Court of Appeal the defendants sought to persuade the court to approach the case as if it involved a single global cause of action to be pursued in whatever jurisdiction was the most appropriate. The single publication rule was invoked by way of analogy. This argument was not advanced in the House of Lords and Lord Steyn observed [2000] I WLR 1004, 1012 that it was "contrary to the long established principle in England libel law that each publication is a separate tort". In the present case the defendants do not suggest that the English courts should apply the single publication rule where a libel has been disseminated in more than one jurisdiction. They contend, however, that the rule should be applied when the issue is one of limitation in relation to an action commenced in this jurisdiction.

At para. 76 of *Loutchansky v. Times Newspapers Ltd.*, the Court rejected the defendants' contention that the single publication rule should be used in England:

> The change in the law of defamation for which the defendants contend is a radical one. In our judgment they have failed to make out their case that such a change is required. The Internet single publication appeal is therefore dismissed.

8) The Single Publication Rule Has Been Expressly Rejected in Australia, the UK, and Canada

a) Australia

In *Dow Jones v. Gutnick*, [2002] HCA 56 the Australian High Court also expressly rejected the application of the single publication rule with respect to Internet libels. At para. 197, Cowen J. held that each publication under current law gives rise to a separate cause of action. This is entrenched in Australian and English Law. The Court also found that a single publication rule can only be introduced in Australia by statute.

b) United Kingdom

A similar argument was advanced unsuccessfully in *Loutchansky v. Times Newspapers Ltd.*, [2002] Q.B. 783 at para. 66 (C.A.) (see above).

c) Canada

The BC Court of Appeal in *Carter v. B.C. Federation of Foster Parents Assn.*, 2005 BCCA 398, stated as follows at para. 18:

> ... Although it is difficult to find an express statement in the Canadian cases about the single publication rule, the clear tendency of the authorities in my view is in favour of the English and Australian position and not in favour of the American position. For instance, in the case of *Lambert v. Roberts Drug Stores Ltd.* (1933), 41 Man. R. 322 (C.A.), Trueman J.A. speaking for the court states at 324:
>
> > It is elementary that every sale or delivery of a written or printed copy of a libel is a fresh publication, for which an action lies, unless the defendant can satisfy the jury that he was ignorant of its contents and had no reason to suspect they were libellous. See *Emmens v. Pottle* (1886) 16 Q.B.D. 354, 55 L.J.Q.B. 51; and *Vizetelly v. Mudie's Select Library* [1900] 2 Q.B. 170, 69 L.J.Q.B. 6456.

(It is to be noted that the English cases he refers to in that passage address the issue of innocent dissemination as opposed to a publication issue.) Similarly, in *Basse v. Toronto Star Newspapers Ltd.* (1983), 44 O.R. (2d) 164 at 165, 4 D.L.R. (4th) 381 (H.C.), Montgomery J. held, "[e]very republication of a libel is a new libel." The Supreme Court of Canada referred to the *Brunswick* case in *McNicholl v. Grandy*, [1931] S.C.R. 696 at 699, [1932] 1 D.L.R. 225, but merely used the case as an example of the low standard required for publication to be found.

Justice Hall stated at para. 20 of *Carter v. B.C. Federation of Foster Parents Assn.*, 2005 BCCA 398, where the Court of Appeal overturned the decision of the trial judge based upon the single publication rule:

> I consider that the trial judge fell into error when he held that the action of the plaintiff was out of time because she had not commenced her action within two years of first learning of the existence of the Dberlane comment. If Ms. Carter can establish that there occurred publications of the offending comment subsequent to the first publication in February of 2000, then her cause of action would not be time barred. I would observe that there seems to be some obscurity as to exactly what the evidence does disclose about subsequent publication but I do not consider that the plaintiff should be prevented from seeking to establish, if she can, that there was subsequent publication to others which would found a cause of action.

D. REMEDIES FOR POTENTIAL INJUSTICE

A potential injustice clearly exists if a plaintiff is allowed to mount a series of lawsuits based on a single article. But the courts in Australia, Canada, and the UK have the power to deal with such courses of action using their abuse of process jurisdiction.

1) Australia

A plaintiff must obtain leave of the court if she wishes to bring more than one cause of action for multiple publications.

See *Defamation Act 1974* (NSW), s. 9(3)

In *Maple v. Davis Symes & Company*, [1975] 1 NSWLR 97 (Comm.) an abuse of process was held for a plaintiff residing in the state of Victoria who brought an action for defamation in New South Wales when an action had already been commenced in Victoria involving the same article. The newspaper was published in Melbourne, had a wide circulation in Victoria, and had only a small circulation in New South Wales (cited in Raymond E. Brown, *The Law of Defamation in Canada*, 2d ed., looseleaf (Scarborough, ON: Carswell, 1994), vol. 2 at 7-87 at note 395).

2) Canada

In *Thompson v. Lambert*, [1938] S.C.R. 253, the Supreme Court of Canada (see *Carter v. B.C. Federation of Foster Parents Assn.*, 2005 BCCA 398 at para. 19) held that successive actions could not be brought against an editor and publisher on the grounds of separate publication where a successful suit had already been brought against the distributors and vendors of the publication. It was held that all those who participated or were responsible for the original publication and its distribution must be joined as jointfeasors in the original cause of action. Justice Hall in the *Carter v. B.C. Federation of Foster Parents Assn.* case held: "There can be a potential injustice if a plaintiff is allowed to mount a series of lawsuits based upon a single article, but the courts have the power using their abuse of process jurisdiction to deal with such a course of action . . . ."

3) The UK

A similar approach to that in Canada was taken by the English Court of Appeal in the recent case of *Jameel v. Dow Jones & Co. Inc.*, [2005] 2 W.L.R. 1614 (H.L.), where the Court said at para. 56:

We do not believe that *Duke of Brunswick v. Harmer*, 14 Q.B. 185 could today have survived an application to strike out for abuse of process. The Duke himself procured the republication to his agent of an article published many years before for the sole purpose of bringing legal proceedings that would not be met by a plea of limitation. If his agent read the article he is unlikely to have thought the Duke much, if any, the worse for it and, to the extent that he did, the Duke brought this on his own head. He acquired a technical cause of action but we would today condemn the entire exercise as an abuse of process.

The abuse of process argument has been recently developed and applied to English libel cases both offline and online:

> *Baturina v. Times Newspapers Ltd.*, [2010] EWHC 696 (QB)
> *Budu v. The British Broadcasting Corporation*, [2010] EWHC 616 (QB)
> *Ewing v. Times Newspapers Ltd.*, [2010] NIQB 7
> *Kaschke v. Gray & Anor*, [2010] EWHC 1907 (QB)
> *Kaschke v. Osler*, [2010] EWHC 1075 (QB)
> *Khader v. Aziz & Ors*, [2010] EWCA Civ 716
> *Smith v. ADVFN Plc & Ors*, [2010] EWCA Civ 657
> *Carrie v. Tolkien*, [2009] EWHC 29 (QB)
> *Lonzim Plc & Ors v. Sprague*, [2009] EWHC 2838 (QB)
> *Atlantis World Group of Companies NV & Anor v. Gruppo Editoriale L'Espresso*
>   *SPA*, [2008] EWHC 1323 (QB)
> *Ewing v. News International Ltd & Ors*, [2008] EWHC 1390 (QB)
> *Mardas v. New York Times Company & Anor*, [2008] EWHC 3135 (QB)
> *Nigel Smith v. M*, [2008] EWHC 1250 (QB)
> *P & Ors v. Quigley*, [2008] EWHC 1051 (QB)
> *Smith v. ADVFN Plc & Ors*, [2008] EWHC 1797 (QB)
> *Amoudi v. Brisard & Anor*, [2006] EWHC 1062 (QB)
> *Bin Mahfouz & Ors v. Ehrenfeld & Anor*, [2005] EWHC 1156 (QB)
> *Bunt v. Tilley & Ors*, [2006] EWHC 407 (QB)
> *Carroll v. Kynaston*, [2005] EWHC 927 (QB)
> *Miller v. Associated Newspapers Ltd.*, [2005] EWHC 557 (QB)
> *Steinberg v. Englefield & Anor*, [2005] EWCA Civ 824

The abuse of process argument is discussed in more detail in Chapter 11.

E. NOTICE TO INTERNET INTERMEDIARIES

1) Introduction

At present, in Canada there is no statutory or caselaw governing
- whether any notice must be given to intermediaries;
- whether notice is mandatory;

- the content of the notices; and
- the consequences of
  - » complying with the notices; and
  - » not complying with the notices.

Fortunately, some guidance to these questions can be found in the legislation and caselaw governing take down notices in legislation in the UK and South Africa and notices under the Canadian provincial Defamation Acts.

2) Contents of the Notice

a) Legislation in the UK

Under legislation in the UK concerning notice for the purposes of actual knowledge, the terms of section 19 of the *Electronic Commerce (EC Directive) Regulations 2002*, SI 2002/2013, in so far as it is relevant, are as follows:

> Where an information society service is provided which consists of the storage of information provided by a recipient of the service, the service provider (if he otherwise would) shall not be liable for damages or for any other pecuniary remedy or for any criminal sanction as a result of that storage where —
>
> (a) the service provider —
>
> > (i) does not have actual knowledge of unlawful activity or information and, where a claim for damages is made, is not aware of facts or circumstances from which it would have been apparent to the service provider that the activity or information was unlawful; or
> >
> > (ii) upon obtaining such knowledge or awareness, acts expeditiously to remove or to disable access to the information, and
> >
> (b) the recipient of the service was not acting under the authority or the control of the service provider.

Attention is also drawn in this context to the terms of r. 6(1)(c):

> 6(1) A person providing an information society service shall make available to the recipient of the service and any relevant enforcement authority, in a form and manner which is easily, directly and permanently accessible, the following information—
>
> . . .
>
> (c) the details of the service provider, including his electronic mail address, which make it possible to contact him rapidly and communicate with him in a direct and effective manner; . . .

Additionally, rule 22 of the *Electronic Commerce Directives* reads as follows:

22. In determining whether a service provider has actual knowledge for the purposes of regulations 18(b)(v) and 19(a)(i), a court shall take into account all matters which appear to it in the particular circumstances to be relevant and, among other things, shall have regard to —

(a) whether a service provider has received a notice through a means of contact made available in accordance with regulation 6(1)(c), and

(b) the extent to which any notice includes —

(i)   the full name and address of the sender of the notice;

(ii) details of the location of the information in question; and

(iii) details of the unlawful nature of the activity or information in question.

See also section 1 (Notice) of the *Defamation Act 1996* of the UK.

b) Legislation in South Africa

The South African take down notification section in the *Electronic Communications and Transactions Act 2002*, No. 25 of 2002, section 77 states:

(1) For the purposes of this Chapter, a notification of unlawful activity must be in writing, must be addressed by the complainant to the service provider or its designated agent and must include —

(a) the full names and address of the complainant;

(b) the written or electronic signature of the complainant;

(c) identification of the right that has allegedly been infringed;

(d) identification of the material or activity that is claimed to be the subject of unlawful activity;

(e) the remedial action required to be taken by the service provider in respect of the complaint;

(f) telephonic and electronic contact details, if any, of the complainant;

(g) a statement that the complainant is acting in good faith;

(h) a statement by the complainant that the information in the take-down notification is to his or her knowledge true and correct; and

(2) Any person who lodges a notification of unlawful activity with a service provider knowing that it materially misrepresents the facts is liable for damages for wrongful take-down.

(3) A service provider is not liable for wrongful take-down in response to a notification.

3) Notice to Intermediaries

Notice does not appear to be mandatory in England or South Africa.

4) Judicial Discussion about the Sufficiency of Notice to Intermediaries in *Bunt v. Tilley & Ors*

The decision of *Bunt v. Tilley & Ors*, [2006] EWHC 407, [2007] 1 W.L.R. 1243 (QB) considered the question of whether notices to intermediaries were sufficient, both under section 1 of the *Defamation Act* and under the *Electronic Commerce (EC Directive) Regulations 2002*. The Court viewed the three different ISPs and the notices for each of them.

a) AOL

See, *Bunt v. Tilley & Ors*, [2006] EWHC 407 at paras. 26–29.

Notice was considered to be insufficient when the defendant (AOL) was only made aware of the plaintiff's case in the statement of claim.

A similar finding regarding a notice under the *Libel and Slander Act*, R.S.O. 1990, c. L.12, was made in *Stuarts Furniture & Appliances v. No Frills Appliances & T.V. Ltd.* (1982), 40 O.R. (2d) 52.

The Court in *Bunt v. Tilley & Ors* concluded that notice had not been sufficiently given to AOL for the following reasons:

1. There was no record of notice.
2. The first time when they received any notice was when they received the claim.
3. There was no request by the plaintiff to remove anything.
4. There was no defamation on the face of the statement (see para. 28).

The Court held that *Bunt v. Tilley & Ors* was distinguishable from *Godfrey v. Demon Internet Limited*, [1999] EWHC QB 244, see paras. 30–31. The Court held that the amended particulars did not constitute notice (see paras. 60–61).

b) Tiscali UK Limited

The second ISP, Tiscali UK Limited, did not receive proper notice. Tiscali only became aware of the complaint upon receipt of the claim and then they immediately removed the statements complained of.

Bunt v. Tilley & Ors, [2006] EWHC 407, [2007] 1 W.L.R. 1243 at para. 32 (QB)

c) British Telecom

British Telecom, the third ISP, had no reason to know because they only became aware when they received the written particulars.

> *Bunt v. Tilley & Ors,* [2006] EWHC 407, [2007] 1 W.L.R. 1243 at paras. 33–35 and
> 67–74 (QB)

5) Provincial Libel Notices

A detailed discussion of the law on provincial libel notices can be found in Chapter 6 of Roger D. McConchie and David A. Potts, *Canadian Libel and Slander Actions* (Toronto: Irwin Law, 2004) as well as in Chapter 3, section E of this book.

CHAPTER 9: Jurisdiction

A. INTRODUCTION AND CAVEAT

Jurisdictional motions are relatively common in cyberlibel actions because many cyberlibels cover several jurisdictions. While some of the principles and authorities relating to libel have been discussed elsewhere, they are included in this chapter as well to reduce "chapter-hopping." A chart listing the Canadian cases disposing of jurisdictional motions involving libel actions has also been prepared.

However, an important caveat must be made about this chapter. The law in Canada on jurisdictional motions in general, including jurisdictional motions involving libel proceedings, is rather unsettled at this time of writing this text. On 2 February 2010, The Ontario Court of Appeal in *Van Breda et al. v. Village Resorts Limited*, 2010 ONCA 84 (CanLII) (*Van Breda*), modified the principles for the analysis on jurisdictional motions as set forth in a previous decision of the Ontario Court of Appeal, known as *"Muscutt* quintet" in *Muscatt v. Courcelles* (2002), 60 O.R. (3d) 20 (see: *Leufkens v. Alba Tours International Inc.*, 2002 CanLII 44958 (ON C.A.), (2002), 213 D.L.R. (4th) 614 (Ont. C.A.); *Lemmex v. Bernard*, 2002 CanLII 44962 (ON C.A.), (2002), 213 D.L.R. (4th) 627 (Ont. C.A.); *Sinclair v. Cracker Barrel Old Country Store Inc.*, 2002 CanLII 44955 (ON C.A.), (2002), 213 D.L.R. (4th) 643 (Ont. C.A.); and *Gajraj v. DeBernardo*, 2002 CanLII 44959 (ON C.A.), (2002), 213 D.L.R. (4th) 651 (Ont. C.A.)). On 8 July 2010 the Supreme Court of Canada granted leave to appeal the decision of the Ontario Court of Appeal in *Van Breda et al. v. Village Resorts Limited*.

Faced with two rather unpalatable options — saying nothing about jurisdiction until the law is settled by the Supreme Court of Canada likely in 2011, or proceeding as if nothing had happened — the following approach has been adopted.

1. I have retained the factors as stated in *Muscutt* for both jurisdiction and forum convenience for lawyers practising outside of Ontario.
2. The *Van Breda* rules and references have been inserted where required.
3. Authorities under the *Muscutt* rules have been inserted.
4. I have provided extracts of reasons to fully understand the precise reasoning of the judges in the actions in which motions for stay have been dismissed, and in actions in the situations where motions for stay has been granted.
5. Decisions from Australia and UK have been included, while recognizing the differences in approach to jurisdictional motions. For further information see Graham Smith, *Internet Law and Regulations*, 4th edition, (London: Thomson Sweet and Maxwell, 2001) at 451–528; Patrick Milmo QC, W.V.H. Rogers, Richard Parkes QC, Professor Clive Walker, and Godwin Busuttil, eds., *Gatley on Libel and Slander*, 11th edition, (London: Sweet & Maxwell 2008) at 901–21; and Matthew Collins, *The Law of Defamation and the Internet* (Oxford: Oxford University Press, 2006), cc. 25–29.
6. As much as possible, the jurisprudence that is cited involves defamation cases designed to be of use and guidance to lawyers faced with jurisdictional motions prior to the release of the decision of the Supreme Court of Canada in *Van Breda*.

It is impossible to know now whether these different principles will survive, and if so, in what form, or what weight will be placed upon them.

B. THE ONTARIO COURT OF APPEAL DECISION IN *VAN BREDA* REFINES THE PRINCIPLES TO BE APPLIED IN JURISDICTIONAL MOTIONS

The Court of Appeal in *Van Breda v. Village Resorts Limited*, 2010 ONCA 84 held as follows at paras. 46–47:

> In *Muscutt*, it was against this background that, at paras 75–76, we concluded as follows:
>
> > It is apparent from *Morguard*, *Hunt* and subsequent case law that it is not possible to reduce the real and substantial connection test to a fixed formula. A considerable measure of judgment is required in as-

sessing whether the real and substantial connection test has been met on the facts of a given case. Flexibility is therefore important.

But clarity and certainty are also important. As such, it is useful to identify the factors emerging from the case law that are relevant in assessing whether a court should assume jurisdiction against an out-of-province defendant on the basis of damage sustained in Ontario as a result of a tort committed elsewhere. No factor is determinative. Rather, all relevant factors should be considered and weighed together.

We then laid down the now familiar eight factors to be used to determine whether there was a real and substantial connection sufficient to support the assumption of jurisdiction in such cases:

1) The connection between the forum and plaintiff's claim;
2) The connection between the forum and defendant;
3) Unfairness to the defendant in assuming jurisdiction;
4) Unfairness to the plaintiff in not assuming jurisdiction;
5) The involvement of other parties to the suit;
6) The court's willingness to recognize and enforce an extra-provincial judgment rendered on the same jurisdictional basis;
7) Whether the case is interprovincial or international in nature; and
8) Comity and the standards of jurisdiction, recognition and enforcement prevailing elsewhere.

The importance of distinguishing the real and substantial connection test from the convenience doctrine was stressed at para. 48:

> We pointed out, at paras. 42–43, the importance of distinguishing the real and substantial connection test from the *forum non conveniens* doctrine:
>
> > While the real and substantial connection test is a legal rule, the *forum non conveniens* test is discretionary. The real and substantial connection test involves a fact-specific inquiry, but the test ultimately rests upon legal principles of general application. The question is whether the forum can assume jurisdiction over the claims of plaintiffs in general against defendants in general given the sort of relationship between the case, the parties and the forum. By contrast, the *forum non conveniens* test is a discretionary test that focuses upon the particular facts of the parties and the case. The question is whether the forum should assert jurisdiction at the suit of this particular plaintiff against this particular defendant.

The Court then described the list of factors used to assess a claim for non-convenience at para. 49:

> At para. 41, we described the different list of factors used to assess a claim of *forum non conveniens*:
>
>> Courts have developed a list of several factors that may be considered in determining the most appropriate forum for the action, including the following:
>> - the location of the majority of the parties
>> - the location of key witnesses and evidence
>> - contractual provisions that specify applicable law or accord jurisdiction
>> - the avoidance of a multiplicity of proceedings
>> - the applicable law and its weight in comparison to the factual questions to be decided
>> - geographical factors suggesting the natural forum
>> - whether declining jurisdiction would deprive the plaintiff of a legitimate juridical advantage available in the domestic court

1)   *Van Breda* Principles

As a result of eight years of jurisprudence and considerable academic commentary, the Court of Appeal decided to refine and simplify the *Muscutt* test. See the discussion at para. 83 reformulating *Muscutt*:

> With the experience gained from the substantial volume of case law applying *Muscutt*, with the perspective offered by the extensive body of scholarly writing on the *Muscutt* test, and with the benefit of the very thorough arguments we have heard in these appeals, it is now possible and appropriate to refine and to simplify the test. I recognize that one of the shortcomings of the *Muscutt* test is that it provided little or no guidance on the relationship between the eight factors or as to the relative weight or significance each factor should bear. I think that it is now possible to simplify the test and to provide for more clarity and ease in its application. I will do this by reviewing each of the eight *Muscutt* factors, not to reinforce their continued application, but to explain the manner in which I would elaborate a new refined test.

The Court of Appeal summarized their previous discussions at para. 109 and stated that the *Muscutt* test should be clarified and reformulated as follows:

- First, the court should determine whether the claim falls under rule 17.02 (excepting subrules (h) and (o)) to determine whether a real and substantial connection with Ontario is presumed to exist. The presence or absence of a presumption will frame the second stage of the analysis. If one of the connections identified in rule 17.02 (excepting subrules (h) and (o)) is made out, the defendant bears the burden of showing that a real and substantial connection does not exist. If one of those connections is not made out, the burden falls on the plaintiff to demonstrate that, in the particular circumstances of the case, the real and substantial connection test is met.[1]

- At the second stage, the core of the analysis rests upon the connection between Ontario and the plaintiff's claim and the defendant, respectively.

- The remaining considerations should not be treated as independent factors having more or less equal weight when determining whether there is a real and substantial connection but as general legal principles that bear upon the analysis.

- Consideration of the fairness of assuming or refusing jurisdiction is a necessary tool in assessing the strengths of the connections between the forum and the plaintiff's claim and the defendant. However, fairness is not a free-standing factor capable of trumping weak connections, subject only to the forum of necessity exception.

- Consideration of jurisdiction *simpliciter* and the real and substantial connection test should not anticipate, incorporate or replicate consideration of the matters that pertain to *forum non conveniens* test.

- The involvement of other parties to the suit is only relevant in cases where that is asserted as a possible connecting factor and in relation to avoiding a multiplicity of proceedings under *forum non conveniens.*

- The willingness to recognize and enforce an extra-provincial judgment rendered on the same jurisdictional basis is as an overarching principle that disciplines the exercise of jurisdiction against extra-provincial defendants. This principle provides perspective and is intended to prevent a judicial tendency to overreach to assume jurisdiction when the plaintiff is

---

1   The presumptive factors are derived from the procedural rules for service of originating process outside Ontario, with two key exceptions. First, Ontario courts will not be presumed to have jurisdiction in cases where the plaintiff has sustained damages in Ontario. Second, there is no presumption of jurisdiction in respect of persons who are necessary and proper parties to proceedings properly brought against persons served in Ontario. The Court impliedly criticized earlier cases where this factor had been used, for example, to justify taking jurisdiction over the foreign parent company of a resident defendant.

an Ontario resident. If the court would not be prepared to recognize and enforce an extra-provincial judgment against an Ontario defendant rendered on the same jurisdictional basis, it should not assume jurisdiction against the extra-provincial defendant.

- Whether the case is interprovincial or international in nature, and comity and the standards of jurisdiction, recognition and enforcement prevailing elsewhere are relevant considerations, not as independent factors having more or less equal weight with the others, but as general principles of private international law that bear upon the interpretation and application of the real and substantial connection test.

- The factors to be considered for jurisdiction *simpliciter* are different and distinct from those to be considered for *forum non conveniens*. The *forum non conveniens* factors have no bearing on real and substantial connection and, therefore, should only be considered after it has been determined that there is a real and substantial connection and that jurisdiction *simpliciter* has been established.

- Where there is no other forum in which the plaintiff can reasonably seek relief, there is a residual discretion to assume jurisdiction. [Footnote added].

C. SOME PRINCIPLES OF LAW TO BE CONSIDERED IN JURISDICTIONAL MOTIONS INVOLVING DEFAMATION ACTIONS

The following principles of law may be considered in jurisdictional motions involving defamation actions.

1) Taking the Claim at Face Value

On an application to stay an action for reasons related to jurisdiction, the court is not to look at the merits of the case, but rather to take the claim at face value. This principle is not restricted to defamation claims. See, *Incorporated Broadcasters Ltd. v. Canwest Global Communications Corp.*, [2003] O.J. No. 560 at para. 57 (C.A.), Rosenberg. J.A.

> *In any event, as I have said, it is my view that the court should not decide the merits of the claim for the purposes of determining jurisdiction or convenient forum. I will therefore apply the convenient forum test, taking the appellants' claim at face value* [emphasis added].

King v. Lewis & Ors, [2004] EWHC 168 at para. 21
Pearl v. Sovereign Management Group Inc., [2003] O.J. No. 2161 at para. 10 (S.C.J.)

1248671 Ontario Inc. (c.o.b. Macartney Farms) v. Michael Foods Inc., [2000] O.J. No.
   4349 at para. 41 (S.C.J.)

Berezovsky v. Michael, [2000] U.K.H.L. 25 at 9

Berezovsky v. Forbes, [1998] E.W.C.A. 1791 at paras. 10–11 and 17

2) Elements of a Libel Claim

A defamatory statement is one which has a tendency to injure the reputation of the person to whom it refers, a statement which tends to lower that
person in the estimation of right-thinking members of society generally and,
in particular, to cause the person to be regarded with feelings of hatred, contempt, ridicule, fear, dislike, or disesteem. The very essence of a defamatory
statement is its tendency to injure reputation, which is to say all aspects of a
person's standing in the community.

To show defamation, the onus is on the plaintiff to prove three elements:

1. that the words complained of were published;
2. that the words complained of refer to the plaintiff; and
3. that the words complained of, in their natural and ordinary meaning, or
   in some pleaded extended meaning, are defamatory of the plaintiff.

Leenen v. Canadian Broadcasting Corp. (2000), 48 O.R. (3d) 656 at paras. 40–41, 50
   C.C.L.T. (2d) 213 (S.C.J.), aff'd (2001), 54 O.R. (3d) 612 (C.A.)

3) Publication

Publication occurs where the defamatory words are published in the sense
of being heard, read, or downloaded. See *Dow Jones & Co. Inc. v. Gutnick*,
[2002] HCA 56 at paras. 25–27 and 184, Gleeson. C.J., Gummow and Hayne
J.J.:

> *The tort of defamation, at least as understood in Australia, focuses upon*
> *publications causing damage to reputation. It is a tort of strict liability, in*
> *the sense that a defendant may be liable even though no injury to reputation*
> *was intended and the defendant acted with reasonable care.* Yet a publica-
> tion made in the ordinary course of a business such as that of bookseller
> or news vendor, which the defendant shows to have been made in circum-
> stances where the defendant did not know or suspect and, using reasonable
> diligence, would not have known or suspected was defamatory, will be held
> not to amount to publication of a libel. There is, nonetheless, obvious force
> in pointing to the need for the publisher to be able to identify, in advance,
> by what law of defamation the publication may be judged. But it is a tort

concerned with damage to reputation and it is that damage which founds the cause of action. Perhaps, as Pollock said in 1887, the law went "wrong from the beginning in making the damage and not the insult the cause of action" for slander but it is now too late to deny that damage by publication is the focus of the law. *"It is the publication, not the composition of a libel, which is the actionable wrong"* [emphasis added].

Harm to reputation is done when a defamatory publication is comprehended by the reader, the listener, or the observer. Until then, no harm is done by it. This being so it would be wrong to treat publication as if it were a unilateral act on the part of the publisher alone. It is not. It is a bilateral act — in which the publisher makes it available and a third party has it available for his or her comprehension [emphasis added].

The bilateral nature of publication underpins the long-established common law rule that every communication of defamatory matter founds a separate cause of action. That rule has found reflection from time to time in various ways in State legislation and it would be a large step now to depart from it.

   . . . .

The most important event so far as defamation is concerned is the infliction of the damage, and that occurs at the place (or the places) where the defamation is comprehended [emphasis added].

See also *Imagis Technologies v. Red Herring Communications Inc.*, 2003 BCSC 366 at para. 16.

The British Columbia Supreme Court found in *Imagis Technologies v. Red Herring Communications Inc.*, 2003 BCSC 366 at paras. 22–24:

The cause of action on which Imagis sues arose in British Columbia. "Red Herring" was distributed and sold in British Columbia. The allegedly defamatory statements therein were repeated and republished by the *Vancouver Sun* newspaper, a Vancouver publication known as *Stockwatch*, and by the *National Post*, another Canadian newspaper circulated in British Columbia. *The fact of publication in British Columbia means that if the published statements were defamatory, there is a cause of action on which to proceed in British Columbia, notwithstanding that separate causes of action may have arisen in other jurisdictions by virtue of publication in those jurisdictions.*

If the statements were defamatory, Imagis may have sustained loss or damage in British Columbia, a factor that favours an action being pursued in this court. The evidence on this application indicates that Imagis has a reputation with customers as well as regulatory and financial institutions in the province. While it may also have a reputation with customers and financial or regulatory institutions in other jurisdictions, there is no evidence to suggest that such other reputations are disproportionately more significant than its reputation in British Columbia.

> *The fact of publication in British Columbia and the claim that Imagis suffered damage here favour British Columbia* as the *forum conveniens* [emphasis added].

The Ontario court found as follows in *Barrick Gold Corp v. Blanchard and Company*, [2003] O.J. No. 5817 at paras. 41 and 63:

> In my view, the plaintiff has established that there is a real and substantial connection between its claim and Ontario. While the allegedly libellous statements were made in many places, they were clearly made in Ontario. *If the tort of defamation consists both of the making and the receipt of a libellous statement, and I conclude that it does, then the tort was committed in Ontario.* As admitted by the defendants, the press releases were published in Ontario. I am satisfied on the evidence before me that the notices were sent to persons in Ontario. *The websites are accessible in Ontario* and, as I shall discuss further below, *the damage to reputation only occurs when the offending material is downloaded from the website onto a computer in Ontario and then read by a person in Ontario. Lastly, there were re-publications of the allegedly defamatory statements in Ontario. All of this occurs in the context of a plaintiff which is resident in Ontario and its reputation, if it was libelled, would be damaged in Ontario* [emphasis added].
>
> . . . .
>
> In this case, of course, factors (i) and (ii) must be read as the location where the tort occurred and the law applicable to the tort. For the reasons I have already *enunciated above, I believe that, if the tort of defamation occurred, in the circumstances of this case it occurred in Ontario.* The law applicable to the determination of whether the tort occurred is therefore the law of Ontario. These factors therefore favour Ontario [emphasis added].

In the UK, the court in *Lewis & Ors v. King*, [2004] EWCA Civ 1329, found the following at para. 2:

> The libels alleged consist in two texts stored on websites based in California. In the ordinary way they can be, and have been, downloaded here. *It is common ground that by the law of England the tort of libel is committed where publication takes place, and each publication generates a separate cause of action. The parties also accept that a text on the Internet is published at the*

*place where it is downloaded. Accordingly there is no contest but that subject
to any defences on the merits the respondent has been libeled in this jurisdiction* [emphasis added].

In *Burke v. NYP Holdings Inc.*, 2005 BCSC 1287, the court found at paras.
18–20 and 29:

[18] It is well established that public comments originating in another jurisdiction are actionable in a jurisdiction where the comments are published
and where the reputation of a plaintiff is said to have been damaged: *Jenner v. Sun Oil Co. Ltd. et al,* [1952] 2 D.L.R. 526 (Ont. S.C.); *Chinese Centre
of Vancouver et al v. Holt et al* (1978), 87 C.L.R. (3d) 744 (B.C.S.C.); *Pindling v. National Broadcasting Corp. et al* (1985), 49 O.R. (2d) 58 (Ont. H.C.J.);
and *Barrick Gold Corporation v. Lopehandia* 2004 CanLII 12938 (ON C.A.),
(2005), 71 O.R. (3d) 416 (Ont. C.A.). There has been a steady expansion of
that general principle regarding publication and republication as technology
moves from radio broadcasts to television broadcasts to internet broadcasts
to website broadcasts.

[19] *Jenner, supra,* dealt with an Ontario defamation action against New
York State defendants for alleged defamatory material broadcast by radio in
New York with the broadcast being heard in Ontario. In holding that the ac-
tion could be maintained in Ontario, McRuer C.J.H.C. stated:

This is a case where it is necessary for Judges and lawyers to realize that statements in judgments written before modern methods of
communication were developed or even thought of must be read in
the light of the known circumstances under which they were written.
(at 530)

I have come to the conclusion that there are fundamental and
common-sense principles which govern the present case. Radio
broadcasts are made for the purpose of being heard. The programme
here in question was put on the air for advertising purposes. It is
to be presumed that those who broadcast over a radio network in
the English language intend that the messages they broadcast will be
heard by large numbers of those who receive radio messages in the
English language. It is no doubt intended by those who broadcast for
advertising purposes that the programme shall be heard by as many
as possible. A radio broadcast is not a unilateral operation. It is the
transmission of a message. (at 535)

I think it a "startling proposition" to say that one may, while
standing south of the border or cruising in an aeroplane south of the

border, through the medium of modern sound amplification, utter defamatory matter which is heard in a Province in Canada north of the border, and not be said to have published a slander in the Province in which it is heard and understood. I cannot see what difference it makes whether the person is made to understand by means of written word, sound-waves or ether-waves in so far as the matter of proof of publication is concerned. The tort consists of making a third person understand actionable defamatory matter. (at 537)

[20] The decision in *Pindling, supra*, extended the principle to deal with a defamation action about what was broadcast on a television show originating in the United States but seen in Ontario. The principle was extended to defamatory statements published on the Internet by the decision of the Ontario Court of Appeal in *Barrick, supra* where Blair J.A. stated on behalf of the majority:

> The standard factors to consider in determining damages for defamation are summarized by Cory J. in *Hill* [*v. Church of Scientology of Toronto*, [1955] 2 S.C.R. 1130] at p. 1203. They include the plaintiff's position and standing, the nature and seriousness of the defamatory statements, the mode and extent of publication, the absence or refusal of any retraction or apology, the whole conduct and motive of the defendant from publication through judgment, and any evidence of aggravating or mitigating circumstances.
>
> In the Internet context, these factors must be examined in the light of what one judge has characterized as the "ubiquity, universality and utility" of that medium. In *Dow Jones & Company Inc. v. Gutnick*, [2002] HCA 56 (10 December 2002), that same judge — Kirby J., of the High Court of Australia — portrayed the Internet in these terms, at para. 80:
>
> > The Internet is essentially a decentralized, self-maintained telecommunications network. It is made up of inter-linking small networks from all parts of the world. It is ubiquitous, borderless, global and ambient in its nature. Hence the term "cyberspace" ... is a word that recognizes that the interrelationships created by the Internet exist outside conventional geographic boundaries and comprise a single interconnected body of data, potentially amounting to a single body of knowledge. The Internet is accessible in virtually all places on Earth where access can be obtained either by wire connection or by wireless (including satellite) links. Effectively, the only

constraint on access to the Internet is possession of the means of securing connection to a telecommunications system and possession of the basic hardware.

Thus, of the criteria mentioned above, the mode and extent of publication is particularly relevant in the Internet context, and must be considered carefully. Communication via the Internet is instantaneous, seamless, interactive, blunt, borderless and far-reaching. It is also impersonal, and the anonymous nature of such communications may itself create a greater risk that the defamatory remarks are believed: see *Vaquero Energy Ltd. v. Weir*, 2004 ABQB 68 (CanLII), [2004] A.J. No. 84, 2004 ABQB 68, at para. 17. (at pp. 431–2)

It is true that in the modern era defamatory material may be communicated broadly and rapidly via other media as well. The international distribution of newspapers, syndicated wire services, facsimile transmissions, radio and satellite television broadcasting are but some examples. Nevertheless, Internet defamation is distinguished from its less pervasive cousins, in terms of its potential to damage the reputation of individuals and corporations, by the features described above, especially its interactive nature, its potential for being taken at face value, and its absolute and immediate worldwide ubiquity and accessibility. The mode and extent of publication is therefore a particularly significant consideration in assessing damages in Internet defamation cases. (at p. 433)

[29] Defamation is a tort. The tortious act took place in British Columbia when Mr. Russell accessed the Column on the website while he was within British Columbia. Publication within British Columbia took place at that time as the tort of defamation occurs where the words are heard or read: *Berezovsky v. Michaels et al* [2000] 2 All E.R. 986 (H.L.); *Dow Jones & Co. v. Gutnick*, [2002] H.C.A. 56; and *Wiebe v. Bouchard* [2005] B.C.J. (Q.L.) No. 73 (B.C.S.C.). By publishing on its website a matter which was of interest to people in British Columbia whether or not they were hockey fans, I am satisfied that it was foreseeable that the Column would be picked up by the media in British Columbia given the publicity surrounding the incident at the March 8, 2004 game and the prominence of Mr. Burke within British Columbia. The incident took place in British Columbia. The witnesses to what might have been said by Mr. Burke prior to and during the game all reside in British Columbia. I am satisfied that Mr. Burke has met the onus of establishing jurisdictional facts sufficient to establish a real and substantial

connection within British Columbia to the cause of action. Accordingly, I find that *jurisdiction simpliciter* has been established.

Dow Jones & Co. Inc. v. Gutnick, [2002] HCA 56 at para. 44:

> In defamation, the same considerations that require rejection of locating the tort by reference only to the publisher's conduct, lead to the conclusion that, ordinarily, defamation is to be located at the place where the damage to reputation occurs. Ordinarily that will be where the material which is alleged to be defamatory is available in comprehensible form assuming, of course, that the person defamed has in that place a reputation which is thereby damaged. It is only when the material is in comprehensible form that the damage to reputation is done and it is damage to reputation which is the principal focus of defamation, not any quality of the defendant's conduct. *In the case of material on the World Wide Web, it is not available in comprehensible form until downloaded on to the computer of a person who has used a web browser to pull the material from the web server. It is where that person downloads the material that the damage to reputation may be done. Ordinarily then, that will be the place where the tort of defamation is committed* [emphasis added].

4) Publication and Communication to a Third Party

Publication in defamation law requires communication to a third party.

Roger D. McConchie and David A. Potts provide a discussion of the principle of communication to a third party in *Canadian Libel and Slander Actions* (Toronto: Irwin Law, 2004) at 257–58:

a) An Essential Element
Proof of publication by the defendant to a third party is an essential element in an action for defamation and the burden of proving this element rests on the plaintiff.

> *Gaskin v. Retail Credit Co.*, [1965] S.C.R. 297 per Ritchie J. at 1.
> *Arnott v. College of Physicians and Surgeons of Saskatchewan*, [1954] S.C.R. 538 per Locke J. at 555.
> *Dickhoff v. Armadale Communications* (1993), 108 D.L.R. (4th) 464, per Lane J.A. at 469 (Sask. C.A.).
> *Pressler v. Lethbridge* (2000), 86 B.C.L.R. (3d) 257, per Southin J.A. at para. 53 (C.A.).

b) Publication Requires Communication
There is a distinction between publication and simply creating or uttering defamatory expression. Publication requires an act on the part of the defendant which communicates the defamatory expression to a third party.

McNichol v. Grandy, [1931] S.C.R. 696, where Anglin C.J.C. states at 699:

> The material part of the cause of action in dispute is not the uttering, but the publication, of the language used (*Hebditch v. MacIlwaince* [1894] 2 Q.B. 54, at 58, 61, 64, *O'Keefe v. Walsh* [1903] 2 Ir. R. 681, at 706).

and at the same page approves the following statement from Clement Gatley, *Gatley on Libel and Slander*, 2d ed. (London: Sweet & Maxwell, 1929) at 92:

> . . . publication can be effected by any act on the part of the defendant which conveys the defamatory meaning of the matter to the person to whom it is communicated.

Newson (Chief Provincial Firearms Officer for B.C.) v. Kexco Publishing Co. (1995), 17 B.C.L.R. (3d) 176 per Lambert J.A. at para. 21 (C.A.):

> But publication for the purposes of libel means communication, not creation of the text for the purposes of printing.

Pullman v. Hill & Co., [1891] 1 Q.B. 524 per Lord Esher M.R. at 527:

> What is the meaning of 'publication'? The making known the defamatory matter after it has been written to some person other than the person of whom it is written.

5) Re-Publication

As stated in Roger D. McConchie and David A. Potts in *Canadian Libel and Slander Actions* (Toronto: Irwin Law, 2004) at 270, "Every publication of a libel is a separate tort and each re-publisher is answerable to the plaintiff in damages for his own act of publication."

> *King v. Lewis & Ors*, [2004] EWHC 168 at para. 16
> *Berezovsky v. Michaels*, [2000] UKHL 25 at paras. 6–7, Lord Steyn
> *Basse v. Toronto Star Newspaper Ltd.*, (1983), 44 O.R. (2d) 164 at 165, Montgomery J., citing Patrick Milmo QC, W.V.H. Rogers, Richard Parkes QC, Professor Clive Walker and Godwin Busuttil, eds., *Gatley on Libel and Slander*, 11th ed. (London: Sweet & Maxwell, 2008) at paras. 6.1 and 6.32

6) Upon Proof of Publication

1. A presumption arises that the words are false;

> *Hodgson v. Canadian Newspapers Co.* (1998), O.R. (3d) 235 (S.C.J.)
> *Jerome v. Anderson*, [1964] S.C.R. 291
> *Adam v. Ward*, [1917] A.C. 309 at 318

2. a presumption arises that the words were published maliciously; and

Mack v. North Hill News Ltd. (1964), 44 D.L.R. (2d) 147 at 154
Mitchell v. Victorian Daily Times, [1944] 2 D.L.R. 239

3. a presumption arises that the plaintiff has suffered damage appears. Damages are "at large" in libel actions, meaning that the court is entitled to make a subjective assessment without requiring proof of specific financial loss.

King v. Lewis & Ors, [2004] EWHC 168 at para. 17 (QB)
Hill v. Church of Scientology of Toronto, [1995] 2 S.C.R. 1130 at para. 164
Cassell & Co. Ltd. v. Broome et al., [1972] 1 All E.R. 801 (H.L.)
Julian Porter and David A. Potts, *Canadian Libel Practice* (Toronto: Butterworths, 1986) at 453

7) Defamation a Joint and Several Liability Tort

Defamation is a joint and several liability tort.

Hill v. Church of Scientology of Toronto, [1995] 2 S.C.R. 1130 at para. 176, Cory J.

8) Actionability in other Jurisdictions

It is well established that defamatory statements originating in one jurisdiction are actionable in another jurisdiction where the statements are published or re-published and where the reputation of a plaintiff is said to have been damaged.

Burke v. NYP Holdings Inc., [2005] B.C.J. No. 1993 at paras. 18–21

This general principle regarding publication and re-publication continues to apply as technology moves from radio broadcasts to television broadcasts to Internet broadcasts.

On radio broadcasts:

Jenner v. Sun Oil Company Limited., [1952] 2 D.L.R. 256 (Ont. H.C.)

On television broadcasts:

Pindling v. NBC, [1984] O.J. No. 3417

On Internet publications:

Burke v. NYP Holdings Inc., [2005] B.C.J. No. 1993 at paras. 18–21
King v. Lewis & Ors, [2004] EWHC 168 at para. 16 (QB)
Barrick Gold Corp. v Blanchard & Company, [2003] O.J. No. 5817
Harrods v. Dow Jones and Company, [2003] EWHC 1162 (QB)

Imagis Technologies v. Red Herring Communications Inc., 2003 BCSC 366
Berezovsky v. Michael, [2000] UKHL 25

See also *Dow Jones & Co. Inc. v. Gutnick*, [2002] HCA 56 at para. 198, Callinan, J.:

> As Hedigan J (the motion court judge) held, the torts of libel and slander
> are committed when and where comprehension of the defamatory matter
> occurs. The rules have been universally applied to publications by spoken
> word, in writing, on television, by radio transmission, over the telephone or
> over the Internet. In *Browne v Dunn* the House of Lords held that there was
> no publication of a defamatory petition to a person (Mrs Cook) who had
> signed but not read the petition.

9) Capacity of the Internet to Cause Greater Damage

An individual or corporation, by publishing the defamatory statements on
the Internet chooses a medium capable of causing greater damage to the
reputation of a plaintiff. See *Barrick Gold Corp. v. Lopehandia*, 2004 CanLII
12938 at para. 34 (ON C.A.), Blair J.A.:

> Internet defamation is distinguished from its less pervasive cousins, in terms
> of its potential to damage the reputation of individuals and corporations, by
> the features described above, especially its interactive nature, its potential
> for being taken at face value, and its absolute and immediate worldwide ubi-
> quity and accessibility.

10) Plaintiff's Substantial Reputation

When a plaintiff has a substantial reputation in a jurisdiction he is entitled
to sue in that jurisdiction. See the statement of the Court in *King v. Lewis &
Ors*, [2004] EWHC 168 at para. 20:

> Sixthly, the law regards it as giving a "significant dimension" *to a case if the
> relevant claimant has a reputation to protect specifically in England. Also,
> where it is sought to protect a reputation within England and Wales, the courts
> of this jurisdiction would appear to be the natural forum for achieving vindi-
> cation and assessing compensation* [emphasis added].

See also *King v. Lewis & Ors*, [2004] EWHC 168 at paras. 23–24; and *Harrods Ltd. v. Dow Jones & Company Inc.*, [2003] EWHC 1162.

In *Burke v. NYP Holdings Inc.*, [2005] B.C.J. No. 1993, the Court found at
para. 36:

I accept that Mr. Burke has an interest in having his defamation claim heard in the jurisdiction where he resides as British Columbia Court is best able to assess *reputational damage*. In this regard, I adopt the statement of Lord Nolan in *Berezovsky, supra*:

> Standards of *conduct and of tolerance in such matters vary widely from country* to country. This case is *solely concerned with the plaintiffs' reputations in England*. They seek to have their reputations judged by English standards. The Court of Appeal thought that for this purpose England was the natural forum, and I agree with them. *I do not follow the relevance of the judge's remark that the article has "no connection with anything which has occurred in this country." A businessman or politician takes his reputation with him wherever he goes, irrespective of the place where he has acquired it.* (at p. 998) [emphasis added]

Schapira v. Ahronson & Ors, [1997] EWCA Civ 1303 at paras. 7 and 16
Harrods v. Dow Jones and Company, [2003] EWHC 1162 at para. 36
Black v. Breeden, 2010 ONCA 547 at paras. 36–37
Berezovsky v. Michael, [2000] UKHL 25 paras. 6 and 9

D. JURISDICTION

The first appellate decision on Internet defamation to discuss jurisdictional claims under the *Van Breda* principles is the Ontario Court of Appeal's decision in *Black v. Breeden*, 2010 ONCA 547. The Court of Appeal dismissed the defendant's motion to stay proceedings on jurisdictional grounds. The court discussed the facts of the case as follows at paras. 12–13:

> Black brought these libel actions between February 2004 and March 2005. Two of the actions include a claim for conspiracy to injure. Although the actions initially claimed damages to Black's reputation world-wide, the actions are now restricted to publication in Ontario and to damages to his reputation in Ontario. Black has undertaken not to bring any libel action for publication of the statements in these actions in any other jurisdiction.
>
> The libel suits relate to items posted on the Hollinger International website, including press releases about the Special Committee investigation and the legal disputes that followed; the report of the Special Committee; and a summary of the findings of the Special Committee and related risks in the company's annual securities law form. Hollinger International's website was

accessible in Canada. The press releases provided media, explicitly including Canadian media, with contact information.

1) The Test for Assumed Jurisdiction: *Van Breda*

The Court of Appeal discussed the *Van Breda* principles in relation to the case at paras. 20–25:

> In *Van Breda,* this court reviewed the *Muscutt* test and modified and refined the test to provide for clarity and ease of application (paras. 70, 83 and 109). Sharpe J.A. noted the importance of maintaining the distinction between legal jurisdiction *simpliciter,* an inquiry that does not turn upon a comparison with the strength of the connection with another potentially available jurisdiction, and the discretionary test for *forum non conveniens* (paras. 82 and 109).
>
> Sharpe J.A. identified the core of the real and substantial connection test as the connection that the plaintiff's claim has to the forum and the connection of the defendant to the forum. The remaining considerations or principles should not be treated as independent factors but as analytical tools to assist the court in assessing the significance of the connections between the forum, the claim and the defendant (paras. 84 and 109).
>
> Sharpe J.A. determined that as a first stage, a real and substantial connection is presumed to exist for the purposes of assuming jurisdiction against a foreign defendant, if the case falls within one of the connections set out in the rule for service outside Ontario, r. 17.02 of the *Rules of Civil Procedure,* excepting subrules (h) (damages sustained in Ontario) and (o) (a necessary or proper party) (paras. 72 and 109).
>
> If a real and substantial connection is presumed to exist, the defendant bears the burden of showing that a real and substantial connection does not exist in the specific circumstances of the case. Where no presumption is established, the burden falls on the plaintiff to show that the real and substantial connection test is met. At this second stage, the core of the analysis rests upon the connection between Ontario and the plaintiff's claim and the defendant, respectively (para. 109).
>
> The consideration of the fairness of assuming or refusing jurisdiction, is not a free-standing factor capable of trumping weak connections, but rather is an analytic tool to assess the relevance, quality and strength of the connections between the forum, the plaintiff's claim and the defendant (paras. 96–98 and 109).
>
> The involvement of other parties to the suit is relevant only in cases where it is asserted as a possible (not a presumptive) connecting factor that may

justify jurisdiction (paras. 102 and 109). The court's willingness to recognize and enforce an extra-provincial judgment against an Ontario defendant rendered on the same jurisdictional basis is not a separate factor but remains as a general and overarching principle that disciplines the assumption of jurisdiction over extra-provincial defendants (paras. 103 and 109). The inter-provincial or international nature of the case, comity and the standards of jurisdiction, recognition and enforcement prevailing elsewhere, are general principles of private international law that bear upon the interpretation and application of the real and substantial connection test (paras. 106–109).

Is there a presumption of real and substantive connection on the ground that the case falls within a connection specified in rule 17.02? The Court summarized their analysis as follows at paras. 32–33:

> Black submits that a real and substantial connection is presumed to exist because the claim falls under r. 17.02(g). The motion judge, although not performing the analysis described in *Van Breda*, found that the alleged tort was committed in Ontario. I see no basis to interfere with this conclusion.
>
> The motion judge rejected the defendants' characterization of the claims as being about the governance of a U.S. company in accordance with U.S. law. He stated that, properly characterized, the claims were for defamation committed and damages sustained in Ontario. On the law of defamation, the motion judge explained at para. 35:
>
>> The case law is clear that the heart of a libel action is publication. The tort of defamation is committed where the publication takes place. Publication occurs when the words are heard, read or downloaded. The statements in question may well have been made in the U.S. by the directors or advisors of a U.S. company, but they were published or republished in Ontario and they are alleged to have caused injury in Ontario. The connection between the subject matter of the actions and Ontario is thus significant. [Footnotes omitted.]

2) Characterization of the Claim

One of the first issues to be considered is the characterization of the claim. There have been disputes in other jurisdictional motions concerning defamation cases about the nature of the subject matter or characterizations of the claim. In several decisions, a court has held that it had jurisdiction when the libel was published in its jurisdiction, even though the defendant claimed that statements "related exclusively" to events in another jurisdiction.

Lewis & Ors v. King, [2004] EWHC 168 (HCJ)
Reuben v. Time Inc., [2003] EWHC 1430 (HCJ)
Berezovsky v. Michaels, [2000] UKHL 25 (HL)
Schapira v. Ahronson & Ors, [1997] EWCA Civ 1303
Pindling v. National Broadcasting Corp. et al., [1984] O.J. No. 3417

The Court in *Research in Motion Ltd. v. Visto Corp.*, [2008] O.J. No. 3671 at paras. 85–87 (S.C.J.) discussed this issue:

> Counsel for the defendants submits this factor pertains to the subject-matter of the claim, saying the issues raised do not relate to Ontario as the statements were made in the United States or the United Kingdom by United States citizens regarding a United States patent infringement lawsuit. *With respect, I disagree with this restrictive approach. A generous approach to assumed jurisdiction involves consideration of the connection between the forum and the plaintiff within the framework of the subject matter or damage sustained and the jurisdiction*: see *Morguard*, supra, at para. 42; and *Muscott*, supra, at paras. 77–80. Mere residence, however, is not determinative.
>
>   . . . .
>
> Consideration of the subject matter or damage sustained focuses on the place of the alleged tort. The impugned statements were made in the United States and the United Kingdom *but were disseminated in Ontario by direct contact with the media or by the internet.* [Emphasis added].

In *Barrick Gold Corp. v. Blanchard and Co.*, [2003] O.J. No. 5817 (S.C.J.), Nordheimer J. addressed this factor in connection with statements originating elsewhere. At paragraph 41, he said:

> In my view, the plaintiff has established that there is a real and substantial connection between its claim and Ontario. While the allegedly libellous statements were made in many places, they were clearly made in Ontario. If the tort of defamation consists both of the making and the receipt of a libellous statement, and I conclude that it does, then the tort was committed in Ontario. As admitted by the defendants, the press releases were published in Ontario. I am satisfied on the evidence before me that the notices were sent to persons in Ontario. The websites are accessible in Ontario and, as I shall discuss further below, the damage to reputation only occurs when the offending material is downloaded from the website onto a computer in Ontario and then read by a person in Ontario. Lastly, there were re-publications of the allegedly defamatory statements in Ontario. All of this occurs in the context of a plaintiff which is resident in Ontario and its reputations, if it was libelled, would be damaged in Ontario.

See also *Black v. Breeden*, 2010 ONCA 547 at paras. 48–51

3) The Defendants' Internet-specific Arguments

The defendants raised two Internet-specific arguments in the Court of Appeal in *Black v. Breeden*, 2010 ONCA 547 at paras. 34–38 that were rejected by the Court of Appeal. The arguments and the Court of Appeal's response are contained in Chapter 6, in the section titled "Should Internet-specific Principles Be Adopted?"

4) Had the Defendants Rebutted the Presumption of a Real and Substantial Connection?

The Court commented at para. 46 in *Black v. Breeden*, 2010 ONCA 547, on the connection between the plaintiff's claim and the forum:

> As noted by the defendants, it is clear from *Van Breda* that the inquiry is focussed on whether there is a connection with the plaintiff's claim and Ontario. As such, the focus on the plaintiff's ties to the forum should focus only on ties that are relevant to the plaintiff's claim or the subject matter of the suit.

It is clear from *Van Breda et al. v. Village Resorts Limited*, 2010 ONCA 84, that the inquiry is focused on whether there is a connection with the plaintiff's claim in Ontario. As such, the forum should focus only on ties that are relevant to the plaintiff's claim or the subject matter of the suit. At paras. 47–51, the Court in *Black v. Breeden*, 2010 ONCA 547 found as follows:

> The defendants submit that even if the alleged defamation was committed in Ontario, republication in Ontario and damage to reputation in Ontario are not significant connections in the context of Internet libel and in the context of the subject matter of this case. Thus, the claims, the defendants submit, properly characterized, do not involve a substantial and real connection to Ontario. It is their position that the motion judge erred in dismissing this characterization of the claims and looking at the wrong factors.
>
> It is true that the underlying factual context of the claims involves significant connections to the United States. The subject-matter of the claim and the facts underlying the action are important considerations in determining whether there is a real and substantial connection between the plaintiff's claim and the jurisdiction. Of course, it may be that there is another jurisdiction with an even more substantial connection than Ontario. However, this court cautioned in *Van Breda* that the test for assuming jurisdiction does not

turn upon a comparison with the strength of the connection with another potentially available jurisdiction.

In this case, the damages also clearly arise in Ontario. In *Van Breda*, Sharpe J.A. noted that it is clear from the *Muscutt* quintet that there are many situations where damages sustained in Ontario will not serve as a reliable indicator of a real and substantial connection. As such, subrule 17.02(h) (damages sustained in Ontario) does not have a presumptive effect. However, also in *Van Breda*, the fact that damages were suffered within the jurisdiction was accepted as a significant connection and relevant factor: see also *Muscutt* at para. 81 and *Leufkens v. Alba Tours International Inc.* 2002 CanLII 44958 (ON C.A.), (2002), 60 O.R. (3d) 84 (C.A.), at para. 24. Thus, while it may not be sufficient to give rise to a presumption, I am nonetheless satisfied that "damages sustained in Ontario" is an added connection between Black's claim and Ontario.

In my opinion, the facts relevant to Black's claim relating to publication in Ontario and the damage to Black's Ontario reputation form a significant connection between Black's claims and Ontario.

Accordingly, in all these circumstances, I would not interfere with the motion judge's finding that there was a real and substantial connection between Black's claim and Ontario.

5) The Connection with the Plaintiff's Claim and the Forum (*Muscutt* Test)

See *Van Breda* at paras. 84–88.

A Court has jurisdiction over claims based on publications in that jurisdiction, on the defendants' websites, and the re-publication of the defendant's statements in that jurisdiction. See *Barrick Gold Corp. v. Blanchard and Co.*, [2003] O.J. No. 5817 at para. 41 (S.C.J.):

> In my view, the plaintiff has established that there is a real and substantial connection between its claim and Ontario. While the allegedly libellous statements were made in many places, they were clearly made in Ontario. *If the tort of defamation consists both of the making and the receipt of a libellous statement, and I conclude that it does, then the tort was committed in Ontario.* As admitted by the defendants, the press releases were published in Ontario. I am satisfied on the evidence before me that the notices were sent to persons in Ontario. The websites are accessible in Ontario and, as I shall discuss further below, the damage to reputation only occurs when the offending material is downloaded from the website onto a computer in On-

tario and then read by a person in Ontario. Lastly, there were re-publications of the allegedly defamatory statements in Ontario. All of this occurs in the context of a plaintiff which is resident in Ontario and its reputation, if it was libelled, would be damaged in Ontario [emphasis added].

In *Dow Jones & Co. Inc. v. Gutnick*, [2002] HCA 56, the Court stated at paras. 25–26:

> The tort of defamation, at least as understood in Australia, focuses upon publications causing damage to reputation. It is a tort of strict liability, in the sense that a defendant may be liable even though no injury to reputation was intended and the defendant acted with reasonable care . . . . "It is the publication, not the composition of a libel, which is the actionable wrong."
>
> Harm to reputation is done when a defamatory publication is comprehended by the reader, the listener, or the observer. Until then, no harm is done by it. This being so it would be wrong to treat publication as if it were a unilateral act on the part of the publisher alone. It is not. It is a bilateral act — in which the publisher makes it available and a third party has it available for his or her comprehension.

In *Berezovsky v. Michael*, [2000] UKHL 25, the Court stated at 8: "The jurisdiction in which a tort has been committed is *prima facie* the natural forum for the determination of the dispute."

See similar statements in the following cases:

Burke v. NYP Holdings Inc., [2005] B.C.J. No. 1993
Trizec Properties, Inc. v. Citigroup Global Markets Canada, Inc., [2004] O.J. No. 323
King v. Lewis & Ors, [2004] EWHC 168
Harrods v. Dow Jones and Company, [2003] EWHC 1162
Imagis Technologies v. Red Herring Communications Inc., 2003 BCSC 366
Reuben v. Time Inc., [2003] EWHC 1430
Pindling v. NBC, [1984] O.J. No. 3417
Barrick Gold Corp v. Blanchard and Company, [2003] O.J. No. 5817
Jenner v. Sun Oil Co. Ltd., [1952] 2 D.L.R. 526 (Ont. H.C.)

In *Bangoura v. Washington Post*, 2005 CanLII 32906 (ON C.A.), the Ontario Court of Appeal overturned a decision of a motions court judge, which dismissed an application to stay proceedings. The court provided very detailed reasons, which will be referred to throughout the balance of this chapter in the appropriate sections. Concerning the connection between the forum and the plaintiff's claim the Court of Appeal stated at paras. 22–23:

The connection between Ontario and Mr. Bangoura's claim is minimal at best. In fact, there was no connection with Ontario until more than three years after the publication of the articles in question. In *Muscutt*, Sharpe J.A. raised this very issue at para. 79 of his reasons:

> On the other hand, if the plaintiff lacks a significant connection with the forum, the case for assuming jurisdiction on the basis of damage sustained within the jurisdiction is weaker. If the connection is tenuous, courts should be wary of assuming jurisdiction. Mere residence in the jurisdiction does not constitute a sufficient basis for assuming jurisdiction. See V. Black, "Territorial Jurisdiction Based on the Plaintiff's Residence: *Dennis v. Salvation Army Grace General Hospital Board*" 1997 CanLII 9872 (NS C.A.), (1997), 14 C.P.C. (4th) 207 at p. 232, 156 N.S.R. (2d) 372 (C.A.), where the author writes:
>
> > Permitting a plaintiff to assume a new residence and sue a defendant there in respect of events that occurred elsewhere seems to be harsh to defendants, and this is particularly so when those events comprise a completed tort.
> >
> > . . .
> >
> > Even if the connection is significant, however, the case for assuming jurisdiction is proportional to the degree of damage sustained within the jurisdiction. It is difficult to justify assuming jurisdiction against an out-of-province defendant unless the plaintiff has suffered significant damage within the jurisdiction.

In an affidavit filed by Mr. Bangoura, he deposed:

> As a result of the continued action of the Washington Post, I have sustained damages in Ontario and elsewhere in that my opportunities for economic advancement in my profession have been adversely affected.

No details are provided. The distribution of the articles was minimal. Only Mr. Bangoura's lawyer accessed the two articles on the *Washington Post* Internet database. Whatever damages were suffered by Mr. Bangoura's losing his job with the UN, more than three years before he took up residence in Ontario, are not damages suffered in Ontario. In my view, there is no evidence that Mr. Bangoura has suffered significant damages within Ontario.

6) The Impact of the Plaintiff Limiting Libel Actions to One Jurisdiction and Damage to His Reputation in One Jurisdiction

The courts have considered the situation when the plaintiff has undertaken to sue only in one jurisdiction and is limited to claim damage in that jurisdiction. In *Dow Jones & Co. Inc. v. Gutnick*, [2002] HCA 56 the Court found at para. 48:

> As has been noted earlier, Mr. Gutnick has sought to confine his claim in the *Supreme Court of Victoria to the damage he alleges was caused to his reputation in Victoria as a consequence of the publication that occurred in that State.* The place of commission of the tort for which Mr. Gutnick sues is then readily located as Victoria. That is where the damage to his reputation of which he complains in this action is alleged to have occurred for it is there that the publications of which he complains were comprehensible by readers. It is his reputation in that State, and only that State, which he seeks to vindicate. It follows, of course, that substantive issues arising in the action would fall to be determined according to the law of Victoria. *But it also follows that Mr. Gutnick's claim was thereafter a claim for damages for a tort committed in Victoria, not a claim for damages for a tort committed outside the jurisdiction.* There is no reason to conclude that the primary judge erred in the exercise of his discretion to refuse to stay the proceeding [emphasis added].

See similar statements in the following cases:

Black v. Breeden, 2010 ONCA 547 at paras. 12, 63, 84
King v. Lewis & Ors, [2004] EWHC 168 at para. 18, Eady J.
Harrods v. Dow Jones and Company, [2003] EWHC 1162 at para. 5
Reuben v. Time Inc., [2003] EWHC 1430 at para. 48
Dow Jones & Co. Inc. v. Gutnick, [2002] HCA 56 at para. 65, Gaudron J., at para. 124,
    Kirby J., and at para. 202, Callinan J.
Berezovsky v. Michaels, [2001] 1 W.L.R. 1004 at 1032, Lord Hope

7) The Connection between the Defendant and the Forum

In *Black v. Breeden*, 2010 ONCA 547 at paras. 55–59, the Court of Appeal pointed to Sharpe J.A.'s indication that physical presence or activity by the defendants within the jurisdiction is not always required:

> In *Van Breda* at para. 89, Sharpe J.A. noted that physical presence or activity by the defendants within the jurisdiction is not always required as set out in *Moran v. Pyle National (Canada) Ltd.*, 1973 CanLII 192 (S.C.C.), [1975] 1 S.C.R. 393. Sharpe J.A. cautioned that in the situation where the wrongful

act and injury both occur outside the jurisdiction and the plaintiff returns home, the fact that it was foreseeable that the plaintiff would return home and continue to suffer consequential damages, is not alone sufficient to make the defendant subject to the plaintiff's home jurisdiction under the *Moran* principle (para. 91).

In my view, the motion judge's analogy to the approach in product liability cases, as found in *Moran* was appropriate in the circumstances of this case. In *Moran*, Dickson J. noted at p. 409:

By tendering his products in the market place directly or through normal distributive channels, a manufacturer ought to assume the burden of defending those products wherever they cause harm as long as the forum into which the manufacturer is taken is one that he reasonably ought to have had in his contemplation when he so tendered his goods.

As noted by the motion judge, this approach has been mirrored in Internet defamation cases. In *Barrick Gold Corp. v. Blanchard and Co.*, 2003 CanLII 64238, 9 B.L.R. (4th) 316 (Ont. S.C.J.), Nordheimer J. stated at para. 44:

If a person issues a statement and places that statement in a normal distribution channel designed for media attention and publication, a person ought to assume the burden of defending those statements, wherever they may damage the reputation of the target of those statements and thereby cause the target harm, as long as that harm occurred in a place that the originator of the statements ought reasonably to have had in . . . contemplation when the statements were issued.

While the defendants suggest it is unfair to make foreign defendants defend themselves in a jurisdiction to which the statements were not directed, in fact, as indicated above, there is clear evidence in this case that the press releases were directed to Canadian media.

In all these circumstances, I agree with the motion judge's conclusion that there was a connection between the defendants and the forum.

In *Bangoura v. Washington Post*, 2005 CanLII 32906 at paras. 24–25 (ON C.A.), the court found the following:

The motion judge concluded that the defendants had no connection to Ontario, but observed at para. 22(2) that the *Washington Post* is a major newspaper which is "often spoken of in the same breath as the *New York Times* and the *London Telegraph*." He concluded that "the defendants should have reasonably foreseen that the story would follow the plaintiff wherever he resided."

I agree with the submissions of counsel for the appellants that there is no significant connection between the *Washington Post* defendants and Ontario. I cannot agree with the motion judge when he concluded that the appellants "should have reasonably foreseen that the story would follow the plaintiff wherever he resided." It was not reasonably foreseeable in January 1997 that Mr. Bangoura would end up as a resident of Ontario three years later. To hold otherwise would mean that a defendant could be sued almost anywhere in the world based upon where a plaintiff may decide to establish his or her residence long after the publication of the defamation.

8) Unfairness to the Defendants in Assuming Jurisdiction

This factor and factor nine (unfairness to the plaintiff in not assuming jurisdiction) are collapsed in *Van Breda* at paras. 97–98:

> First, *Muscutt* factors 3 and 4 should be collapsed into one and the fairness of assuming or refusing jurisdiction should be considered together.
>
> Second, consideration of fairness should not be seen as a separate inquiry unrelated to the core of the test, the connection between the forum, the plaintiff's claim and the defendant. Consideration of fairness should rather serve as an analytic tool to assess the relevance, quality and strength of those connections, whether they amount to a real and substantial connection, and whether assuming jurisdiction accords with the principles of order and fairness.

See also the following statements of the court in *Black v. Breeden*, 2009 CanLII 14041 at paras. 61–63 (ON S.C.), on unfairness to Black in not assuming jurisdiction:

> I agree with the plaintiff that if he was forced to sue for libel in New York or Illinois, he would be deprived of the presumptions of falsity, damages and malice. It is indisputable that the law of libel in Ontario is more favorable to plaintiffs than that in the U.S. But, to repeat the point made earlier about loss of juridical advantage and unfairness, the former, by itself, does not necessarily result in the latter, unless there is more to the story. And here, because these are libel actions, there is more to the story.
>
> In my view, it would be unfair to prevent Mr. Black from bringing the libel suits in Ontario, not because of the loss of juridical advantage if he was forced to litigate in the U.S., but because Ontario is where his reputation was

established. Ontario is where he still has many friends and family. Ontario is the place where the defamatory statements were published and republished and where the alleged damage occurred. By suing in Ontario, he is trying to vindicate his reputation in a jurisdiction that is obviously very important to him.

As Brown noted in his text on defamation law: "When the action sounds in defamation and will be tried by a jury, it is important to ensure that the person defamed be tried by a jury in the community where his or her reputation has been established." To deny the plaintiff this right or at least this opportunity in a libel action, would in my view be unfair. [Footnotes omitted].

Further, see the statements of the Court of Appeal in *Black v. Breeden*, 2010 ONCA 547, at paras. 65–67, on unfairness to the defendants in assuming jurisdiction:

In my opinion, there is no unfairness to hold the defendants accountable for the accuracy of statements that were widely disseminated over the Internet and specifically directed to Canadian media. Some activities by their very nature involve a sufficient risk of harm to parties outside the forum in which they originate that any unfairness in assuming jurisdiction is mitigated or eliminated: see *Muscutt* at para 86. In *Barrick Gold Corp. v. Lopehandia*, 2004 CanLII 12938 (ON C.A.), (2004), 71 O.R. (3d) 416 (C.A.), at para. 1, Blair J.A. quoted Matthew Collins, *The Law of Defamation and the Internet* (Oxford University Press, 2001), at para 24.02, that concomitant with the powerful possibilities of Internet, "the Internet is also potentially a medium of virtually limitless international defamation."

I agree with the motion judge that there is no unfairness in requiring the defendants — sophisticated businessmen who targeted the Canadian media and who reasonably foresaw the possibility that their conduct in posting the statements on the Internet would cause damage to Black's reputation in Ontario — to defend defamation actions brought in Ontario, where both the tort and the damages occurred.

In all these circumstances, I agree with the motion judge's conclusion that fairness supports the assumption of jurisdiction. I conclude there is a real and substantial connection between the forum and Black's claims and the forum and the defendants.

See also *Barrick Gold Corp. v. Blanchard and Co.*, 2003 CanLII 64238 (ON S.C.)
Burke v. NYP Holdings Inc., [2005] B.C.J. No. 1993
Trizec Properties Inc. v. Citigroup Global Markets Inc., [2004] O.J. No. 323
Imagis Technologies v. Red Herring Communications Inc., 2003 BCSC 366

The Court of Appeal in *Bangoura v. Washington Post*, 2005 CanLII 32906 (ON C.A.), held that it would be unfair to the defendant if the action proceeded. See paras. 26–27:

> In respect of this factor, the motion judge said at para. 22(3):
>
> > While the personal defendants have no connection to Ontario, the *Post* is a newspaper with an international profile, and its writers influence viewpoints throughout the English-speaking world. I would be surprised if it were not insured for damages for libel or defamation anywhere in the world, and if it is not, then it should be.
>
> There is no evidence in the record in respect of the *Washington Post*'s insurance coverage.

9) Unfairness to the Plaintiff in Not Assuming Jurisdiction

As indicated previously, this factor has collapsed under the *Van Breda* test. See paras. 57 and 98 of *Van Breda et al. v. Village Resorts Limited*, 2010 ONCA 84. See the comments of the Court in *Barrick Gold Corp. v. Blanchard & Co*, [2003] O.J. No. 5817 at para. 36:

> I should mention at this juncture that there is one issue on which the parties agree. They have each filed expert affidavit evidence which establishes that Ontario is a much more favourable jurisdiction for the Plaintiff's claim and Louisiana is a much more favourable jurisdiction for the Defendants' defence given the significant differences between the libel laws of the two jurisdictions.

See similar statements in the following cases.

Black v. Breeden, 2009 CanLII 14041 at paras. 60–63 (ON S.C.)
Research in Motion Ltd. v. Visto Corp., [2008] O.J. No. 3671 at para. 107, Gordon J.
Burke v. NYP Holdings Inc., [2005] B.C.J. No. 1993 at para. 37
Trizec Properties Inc. v. Citigroup Global Markets Inc., [2004] O.J. No. 323 at paras. 43–45
Imagis Technologies v. Red Herring Communications Inc., 2003 BCSC 366 at paras. 25–26, Pitfield, J.
Pindling v. NBC, [1984] O.J. No. 3417 at para. 36

The Supreme Court of Canada has rejected importing the US First Amendment standards into Canadian defamation law as stated in *Hill v. Church of Scientology of Toronto*, [1995] 2 S.C.R. 1130 at para. 173, Cory J.:

> The *New York Times v. Sullivan* decision [the United States Supreme Court ruled that the presumptions of falsity and malice were eradicated, and the

onus was on the plaintiff to prove that, at the time the defamatory statements were made, the defendant either knew them to be false or was reckless as to whether they were or not] has been criticized by judges and academic writers in the United States and elsewhere. It has not been followed in the United Kingdom or Australia. I can see no reason for adopting it in Canada in an action between private litigants. The law of defamation is essentially aimed at the prohibition of the publication of injurious false statements. It is the means by which the individual may protect his or her character, personality and, perhaps, identity. I simply cannot see that the law of defamation is unduly restrictive or inhibiting. Surely it is not requiring too much of individuals that they ascertain the truth of the allegations they publish. The law of defamation provides for the defences of fair comment and of qualified privilege in appropriate cases. Those who publish statements should assume a reasonable level of responsibility.

The Court of Appeal in *Black v. Breeden*, 2010 ONCA 547 at paras. 62–63, commented on the analysis for jurisdiction:

> In para. 101 of *Van Breda*, this court cautioned that the analysis for jurisdiction *simpliciter* "must not anticipate, incorporate or replicate consideration of the matters that pertain to the *forum non conveniens* test". The issue of juridical advantage ought not therefore to be considered in this analysis.
>
> However, because Black's claims relate to statements published in Ontario and his suits are limited to damages to his reputation in Ontario, I agree that it would be unfair to deprive him of a trial before the community in which his reputation has been damaged. Members of the community in which the reputation is harmed are in the best position to assess damages for defamation: see *Hill v. Church of Scientology of Toronto*, 1995 CanLII 59 (S.C.C.), [1995] 2 S.C.R. 1130, at pp. 1196–1197.

On the other hand, the Court of Appeal held at para. 29 in *Bangoura v. Washington Post*, 2005 CanLII 32906 (ON C.A.):

> Although unfairness to the plaintiff in not assuming jurisdiction might often be a powerful factor within a *Muscutt* analysis, it must be remembered that the plaintiff had no connection with Ontario until more than three years after the publication of the articles in question. While in *Muscutt*, Sharpe J.A. found at para. 88 that "the principles of order and fairness should be considered in relation to the plaintiff as well as the defendant," he followed by adverting to *Morguard*, *supra*, at p. 1108, in which La Forest J. held that this factor comes into play only where there is otherwise a real and substantial

connection with the action. If the plaintiff's evidence does not support such a connection elsewhere within the *Muscutt* analysis, it becomes increasingly difficult to accord weight to this factor.

10) The Involvement of Other Parties

In *Van Breda v. Village Resorts Limited*, 2010 ONCA 84, the court commented on the involvement of other parties at paras. 102–4:

> The involvement of other parties to the suit is not, as *Muscutt* suggests, a factor that needs to be routinely considered in all cases. It remains relevant to the real and substantial connection test, but only in cases where it is asserted as a possible (not a presumptive) connecting factor that may justify assuming jurisdiction. In addition, at the *forum non conveniens* stage, the avoidance of a multiplicity of proceedings remains one of the factors to be considered.

11) The Court's Willingness to Recognize and Enforce an Extraprovincial Judgment Rendered on the Same Jurisdictional Basis

This factor is no longer in the *Van Breda* factors. See para. 108 in *Van Breda v. Village Resorts Limited*, 2010 ONCA 84:

> Accordingly, while I would no longer list comity and the standards of jurisdiction, recognition and enforcement prevailing elsewhere as one of several items on a multi-factor list having more or less equal weight with the other factors, I would maintain these legal principles as relevant to the assessment of real and substantial connection.

The Court of Appeal in *Bangoura v. Washington Post*, 2005 CanLII 32906 at paras. 33–34 (ON C.A.), discussed this consideration:

> Sharpe J.A. in *Leufkens* cautioned that if an Ontario court assumes jurisdiction against a foreign defendant, it would require Ontario courts to enforce foreign judgments pronounced on the same jurisdictional basis against Ontario defendants. Although *Leufkens* involved a lawsuit by an Ontario plaintiff against a Swiss travel company for injuries suffered in Costa Rica, the principle raised by Sharpe J.A. at para. 33 of his judgment is apt:
>
> > When assessing the real and substantial connection test and the principles of order and fairness, it is important to consider the in-

terests of potential Ontario defendants as well as those of Ontario plaintiffs. In light of *Morguard* and *Hunt* [v. *T & N plc*, [1993] 4 S.C.R. 289], finding that the real and substantial connection test has been met would require Ontario courts to enforce foreign judgments rendered on the same jurisdictional basis against Ontario defendants who offer tourism services to visitors of this province. In my view, we should not adopt such a rule, since it would impose an unreasonable burden on providers of tourism services in Ontario. To take the example mentioned during oral argument, it would seem harsh to require an Algonquin Park canoe rental operator to litigate the claim of an injured Japanese tourist in Tokyo. Although negligent operators should certainly be held to account for their negligence, if they confine their activities to Ontario, they are entitled to expect that claims will be litigated in the courts of this province.

Admittedly, while the facts in *Leufkens* are more "confined" than they could ever be in litigation involving articles published on the Internet, it must be remembered that on the evidence presented before the motion judge, the articles did not reach significantly into Ontario. As I have mentioned, Mr. Bangoura's lawyer was the only person in Ontario to access the two articles on the *Washington Post* Internet database. While other articles published on the Internet may proliferate well beyond their original target audiences into other jurisdictions, the fact scenario before me falls far closer to the situation described in *Leufkens*. If the cautionary warning of Sharpe J.A. is not taken into account, it could lead to Ontario publishers and broadcasters being sued anywhere in the world with the prospect that the Ontario courts would be obliged to enforce foreign judgments obtained against them.

12) Whether the Case is Interprovincial or International in Nature

See *Van Breda v. Village Resorts Limited*, 2010 ONCA 84 at para. 106.

In *Black v. Breeden*, 2010 ONCA 547 (CanLII) the Court of Appeal found at para. 72:

In *Muscutt*, the Court of Appeal noted that the assumption of jurisdiction is more clearly justified in interprovincial cases than in international cases and that courts should be more cautious assuming jurisdiction in international cases.

See also *Bangoura v. Washington Post*, 2005 CanLII 32906 at para. 35 (ON C.A.)

13) Recognition and Enforcement of Ontario Judgment Elsewhere

This factor is not part of the real and substantial test. *Van Breda v. Village Resorts Limited*, 2010 ONCA 84 at para. 106

Black v. Breeden, 2010 ONCA 547 (CanLII)

Several courts in Canada have held that there is no certainty that courts in the US would not recognize or enforce an Ontario judgment for libel, for example, that might be obtained if Ontario assumes jurisdiction. The likelihood of US Courts recognizing a libel judgment from Ontario or BC may well turn on what facts and conclusions the Ontario or British Columbia court finds in reaching its judgment.

Nordheirmer J. in *Barrick Gold Corp. v. Blanchard & Co.*, [2003] O.J. No. 5817 held at para. 39:

> In terms of the eighth factor, the Defendants submit that there is no prospect that any court in the United States would recognize and enforce any judgment that might be obtained in this action if Ontario assumes jurisdiction. They premise that submission on the very different legal principles that apply to libel cases between the two countries. While I accept the defendants may well be correct in their position, the correctness of their position is not a certainty. *I agree with the plaintiff's position that the likelihood of the courts in the United States recognizing a judgment from this court may well turn on what facts and conclusions this court will find in reaching that judgment* [emphasis added].

In *Black v. Breeden*, 2009 CanLII 14041 (ON S.C.) the Motions Court Judge held at para. 74, referring decision of the Court of Appeal in *Bangoura v. Washington Post*, 2005 CanLII 32906 (ON C.A.):

> . . . For my part, I prefer (and I may well be bound by) Justice Armstrong's much more pragmatic assessment in the *Washington Post* decision: "The reality is that American courts will not enforce foreign libel judgments that are contrary to the actual malice rule." This is, for me, the more realistic prognosis. [Footnotes omitted.]

There may be a value to a plaintiff obtaining a judgment in the jurisdiction, even if she does not reside in that jurisdiction as Justice Nordheimer held. See, for example, the statement of the Court in *Barrick Gold Corp. v. Blanchard & Co.*, [2003] O.J. No. 5817 at para. 40:

> In any event, this factor alone is not determinative. There may be a real value to the Plaintiff obtaining a judgment in its favour in Ontario even if it can-

not be enforced in the Defendants' home jurisdiction. It is recognized in defamation cases that the vindication of one's reputation is as important as any monetary award of damages that might be obtained. For its purposes, Barrick may be quite content with a declaration by a court in Ontario that the statements made by are untrue even if it cannot recover any damages that might be awarded to it as a consequence.

See similar statements in the following cases: *Trizec Properties Inc. v. Citigroup Global Markets Inc.*, [2004] O.J. No. 323 at para. 51; *Imagis Technologies v. Red Herring Communications Inc.*, 2003 BCSC 366 at para. 35:

> Regardless, where it is alleged that a defamatory statement was published in British Columbia and a plaintiff has a reputation to protect in the province, the plaintiff is at liberty to decide whether it wishes to pursue judgment in this jurisdiction in order to have the benefit of a finding in its favour, whether or not any monetary damages may be recovered as a consequence of that judgment. Frequently, financial compensation is but one benefit to be derived by a plaintiff from judgment in a defamation action.

> *Research in Motion Ltd. v. Visto Corp.*, [2008] O.J. No. 3671 at paras. 124–25 (S.C.J.)
> *Metropolitan International Schools Ltd. v. Design Technica Corp. et al.*, [2001]
>   EWHC 1765 QB at para. 116

The Court of Appeal in *Bangoura v. Washington Post*, 2005 CanLII 32906 at paras. 36–41 (ON C.A.) found that the courts in the US would decline to recognize and enforce an Ontario libel judgment:

> In considering this factor, the motion judge referred to *New York Times Co. v. Sullivan*, 376 U.S. 254 (1964), a judgment of the United States Supreme Court, and *Hill v. Church of Scientology*, 1995 CanLII 59 (S.C.C.), [1995] 2 S.C.R. 1130, a judgment of the Supreme Court of Canada. In *New York Times v. Sullivan*, the United States Supreme Court held that public officials could only succeed in a defamation claim where they could establish that the defamatory statement was made "with knowledge that it was false or with reckless disregard of whether it was false or not." See *New York Times v. Sullivan* at p. 280.

> In *Hill v. Scientology*, the Supreme Court of Canada refused to adopt the so-called actual malice rule in *New York Times v. Sullivan*. Counsel for the *Washington Post* had filed on the return of the motion a legal opinion from Lee Levine, a defamation lawyer in Washington, D.C., who stated:

> In the circumstances you posit — i.e., a foreign libel judgment that could not be rendered in the first instance by a court bound by *New York Times Co. v. Sullivan* and its progeny — it is my opinion that a District of Columbia

court would deem such a judgment to be repugnant to the public policy of the District and of the United States and would therefore decline to recognize or enforce it.

. . .

Courts in the District of Columbia and in other American jurisdictions have uniformly held that libel judgments rendered in foreign courts where the law does not comport with the principle set forth in *New York Times Co. v. Sullivan* and its progeny are repugnant to the public policy of those jurisdictions and must therefore be denied recognition.

The motion judge concluded at para. 23:

> Frankly, I see the unwillingness of an American court to enforce a Canadian libel judgment as an unfortunate expression of lack of comity. This should not be allowed to have an impact on Canadian values. The *Washington Post* defendants' home jurisdiction's unwillingness to enforce such an order is not determinative of whether the court should assume jurisdiction. See *Wilson v. Servier Canada Inc.*, 2000 CanLII 22407 (ON S.C.), (2000), 50 O.R. (3d) 219 (Ont. Sup. Ct.) . . .

The motion judge's conclusion does not take into account that the rule in *New York Times v. Sullivan* is rooted in the guarantees of freedom of speech and of the press under the First Amendment of the U.S. Constitution. In any event, the reality is that American courts will not enforce foreign libel judgments that are based on the application of legal principles that are contrary to the actual malice rule. Although the Supreme Court of Canada has rejected the rule for perfectly valid reasons, it is, in my view, not correct to say that the American courts' unwillingness to enforce a Canadian libel judgment is "an unfortunate expression of lack of comity". Canada and the U.S. have simply taken different approaches to a complex area of the law, based upon different policy considerations related to freedom of speech and the protection of individual reputations.

The Supreme Court of Canada has recognized that Canadian courts may refuse to enforce a judgment of a foreign court which is deemed to be contrary to the Canadian concept of justice. In *Beals v. Saldanha, supra*, Major J., writing for the majority, said at para. 71:

> The third and final defence is that of public policy. This defence prevents the enforcement of a foreign judgment which is contrary to the Canadian concept of justice. The public policy defence turns on whether the foreign law is contrary to our view of basic morality. As stated in Castel and Walker, *supra*, at p. 14–28:

> ... the traditional public policy defence appears to be directed at the
> concept of repugnant laws and not repugnant facts.

Given the centrality of freedom of speech to the United States Constitution, it could be argued that an American court's refusal to recognize a Canadian judgment based on principles divergent from *New York Times v. Sullivan* would fall into the category of repugnant law rather than repugnant fact.

The Court of Appeal held that the judgment of the High Court of Australia in *Dow Jones & Co. Inc. v. Gutnick* (2002), 210 C.L.R. 575 (H.C.A.) did not apply to this case.

The Court of Appeal in *Bangoura v. Washington Post* felt that, as there was no jurisdiction, there was no need to consider the forum convenience factors.

E. APPROPRIATE FORUM (*FORUM NON CONVENIENS*)

1) Introduction

In *Van Breda v. Village Resorts Limited*, 2010 ONCA 84 at 48–49, the Court of Appeal stated the following:

> We pointed out, at paras. 42-43, the importance of distinguishing the real and substantial connection test from the *forum non conveniens* doctrine:
>
> While the real and substantial connection test is a legal rule, the *forum non conveniens* test is discretionary. The real and substantial connection test involves a fact-specific inquiry, but the test ultimately rests upon legal principles of general application. The question is whether the forum can assume jurisdiction over the claims of plaintiffs in general against defendants in general given the sort of relationship between the case, the parties and the forum. By contrast, the *forum non conveniens* test is a discretionary test that focuses upon the particular facts of the parties and the case. The question is whether the forum should assert jurisdiction at the suit of this particular plaintiff against this particular defendant.
>
> At para. 41, we described the different list of factors used to assess a claim of *forum non conveniens*:
>
> > Courts have developed a list of several factors that may be considered in determining the most appropriate forum for the action, including the following:
> > * the location of the majority of the parties
> > * the location of key witnesses and evidence

- contractual provisions that specify applicable law or accord jurisdiction
- the avoidance of a multiplicity of proceedings
- the applicable law and its weight in comparison to the factual
  questions to be decided
- geographical factors suggesting the natural forum
- whether declining jurisdiction would deprive the plaintiff of a
  legitimate juridical advantage available in the domestic court

2) Decisions on *Forum Non Conveniens* are Exercises of Judicial Discretions

The court in *Black v. Breeden*, 2010 ONCA 547 found at paras. 77–78 and 80:

> Decisions on *forum non conveniens* are exercises of judicial discretion. As
> Laskin J.A. explained in *Young v. Tyco International of Canada Ltd.* 2008
> ONCA 709 (CanLII), (2008), 92 O.R. (3d) 161 (C.A.), at para. 27:
>
>> On appeal, the usual principle of deference to discretionary decision
>> applies: an appeal court should intervene only if the motion judge
>> errs in principle, misapprehends or fails to take account of material
>> evidence, or reaches an unreasonable decision.
>
> I would not interfere with the motion judge's rejection of the submission that
> the action should be stayed on grounds of *forum non conveniens*.
>
> . . .
>
> The motion judge correctly set out the relevant factors. He conclud-
> ed that Ontario is a convenient and appropriate forum, and that neither
> New York, Illinois, nor any other American jurisdiction, is clearly more
> appropriate.

3) Various Locations of Parties

At para. 81, the Court of Appeal in *Black v. Breeden*, 2010 ONCA 547, stated:

> He considered that given the various locations of the parties, no single juris-
> diction was home to the majority of the parties. Although nine of the eleven
> parties were located in the United States, they were spread across six juris-
> dictions. No matter where the trial was held, most parties would have to
> travel to attend. I am not persuaded that he erred in principle in finding this
> factor to be neutral.

4) Applicable Law

In *Black v. Breeden*, the Court of Appeal held at paras. 83–84:

> The motion judge acknowledged that the main focus at trial would most likely be the truth of the statements. He considered that the defendants' emphasis on the relevance of American securities law and corporate law was overstated. He considered that although the factual questions related to the truth or falsity of the statements, the applicable libel law would be Ontario law. Thus, he was persuaded that this factor favoured Black's choice of forum.
>
> The motion judge recognized that there was a risk of inconsistent findings relating to some portion of the factual issues. He noted, however, that none of the litigation dealt with the issue of damage to Black's reputation in Ontario. He found that there was no risk of inconsistent verdicts given that there were no parallel proceedings in the U.S. and because Black had undertaken not to bring any libel actions in any other jurisdiction. Even if the motion judge ought to have taken a broader view of the potential for inconsistent court decisions, including the risk of inconsistent findings relating to the truth of the statements, it is clear that there already were a multiplicity of proceedings, in a multiplicity of jurisdictions.

See the statement of the court in *Black v. Breeden*, 2009 CanLII 14041 (ON S.C.) at paras. 92 and 94:

> . . . The applicable law is the libel law of Ontario, because the tort was committed and the injuries were sustained in Ontario.
>
> In short, the plaintiff that the applicable law will be Ontario libel law. Even if most of the factual questions that will have to be decided relate to the truth or falsity of the statements contained in the impugned press releases, this evidence will be presented and assessed in accordance with the requirements of Ontario law. I therefore conclude that Factor C favours the plaintiff.

See also *Barrick Gold Corp v. Blanchard & Co.*, [2003] O.J. No. 5817 at para. 63.

5) Juridical Advantage

In *Black v. Breeden*, the Court found at para. 85:

> Finally, the motion judge considered that the loss of juridical advantage, if jurisdiction was declined and Black was required to bring his libel actions in the U.S., strongly favoured Black. The parties agreed that in the U.S., the Canadian common law presumptions of falsity, injury and malice would

not be available and, as a public figure, he would be required to prove actual malice. This was conceded to be a significant juridical disadvantage. The motion judge concluded that, having established a real and substantial connection with Ontario, it was perfectly legitimate for Black to sue in this jurisdiction and take advantage of its laws.

6) Forum Shopping Allegations

A defendant may allege forum shopping as in *Black v. Breeden*. The Court of Appeal did not accept this allegation. The Ontario Court of Appeal affirmed the findings of the motions judge on this point in *Black v. Breeden*, 2010 ONCA 547 at paras. 86–88:

> I agree with the motion judge that it is not appropriate to label it forum shopping or libel tourism if the party has a real and substantial connection with the forum: see *Amchem Products Inc. v. British Columbia (Workers' Compensation Board)*, 1993 CanLII 124 (S.C.C.), [1993] 1 S.C.R. 897, at p. 920. Further, even if the judgment is not enforceable in the United States, it is enforceable in Ontario, and there is also value in the vindication of a defamation judgment regardless of the ability to collect damages.
>
> Given the significance of the loss of juridical advantage to Black, I am not persuaded that the motion judge erred in the exercise of his discretion.
>
> I am not persuaded that it was unreasonable to conclude that neither New York nor Chicago were clearly a more appropriate forum for these actions than Ontario. While this certainly was not a clear cut case, it was a discretionary decision and I see no error in principle that would justify interference.

7) Convenience of Witnesses

Convenience of the witness is not a factor in *Van Breda* under jurisdiction, but is considered under *forum non conveniens*.

See the findings of the Court in *Imagis Technologies v. Red Herring Communications Inc.*, 2003 BCSC 366 at para. 27:

> To the extent the convenience of witnesses is a factor in the consideration of this application, once again, British Columbia is the favoured jurisdiction. The fact of publication will be proved by witnesses in British Columbia. Imagis will be obliged to call witnesses resident in British Columbia to prove loss or damage in the event it is able to persuade the court that the statements complained of were defamatory. While it is true that the defendants will be

obliged to attend any trial in British Columbia, that is a consequence that naturally flows from their choice to carry on a portion of their business in this province.

The issue of convenience of witnesses as a factor in deciding the *forum conveniens* has diminished in importance with advances in technology. See, for example, *Reuben v. Time Inc.*, [2003] EWHC 1430 at para. 59 (QB):

> In my judgment such problems are likely to prove illusory rather than real. *The use of the video-link can now surmount most problems. Many witnesses who may be reluctant to come to London are likely to be willing to give evidence by video link . . . .*

See also: *Black v. Breeden*, 2010 ONCA 547 at para. 82 (CanLII)
Research in Motion Ltd. v. Visto Corp., [2008] O.J. No. 3671 at para. 19
Canada (Attorney General) v. Yasinski, [2006] B.C.J. No. 1093

F. POTENTIAL ABUSE OF PROCESS ARGUMENT IN JURISDICTIONAL MOTIONS

In UK, the courts have recently held in jurisdictional motions, that a libel action may be struck out or stayed as an abuse of process where the evidence is that the extent of publication within the jurisdiction is very small or there is no realistic prospect of achieving vindication in any event.

Carrie v. Tolkien, [2009] EWHC 29 (QB)
Lonzim Plc & Ors v. Sprague, [2009] EWHC 2838 (QB)
Atlantis World Group of Companies NV & Anor v. Gruppo Editoriale L'Espresso SPA, [2008] EWHC 1323 (QB)
Amoudi v. Brisard & Anor, [2006] EWHC 1062
Bin Mahfouz & Ors v. Ehrenfeld & Anor, [2005] EWHC 1156
Dow Jones & Co. Inc. v. Jameel, [2005] EWCA Civ 75

This principle was first enunciated in *Dow Jones & Co. Inc. v. Jameel*, [2005] EWCA Civ 75 by the Court of Appeal. The abuse of process argument is discussed in greater detail in Chapter 11. Canadian lawyers and judges might be interested in this particular argument. It has not been raised so far in Canadian jurisdictional motions. It might be a further discretionary factor on the question of *forum non conveniens*.

CHAPTER 10: Disclosure of the Identity of an Anonymous Author

A. PRIOR TO COMMENCING PROCEEDINGS

Many individuals post their defamatory messages anonymously on the Internet. One of the most common problems the plaintiff faces in a cyberlibel action is tracing and determining the identity and address of the defendant prior to commencing proceedings.

1) How Anonymity Is Achieved

Internet users can attempt to have and often achieve anonymity by
- opening an account with a fake name, or pseudonym;
- posting their defamatory publications from Internet cafés; or
- using some website that hosts companies, which allows them to establish and maintain websites without being required to disclose their true names or address.

See Matthew Collins, *The Law of Defamation and the Internet*, 2d ed. (New York: Oxford University Press, 2005) at 79–80

2) How Anonymity Is Lost

Despite the appearance of impenetrable anonymity, it may, in fact, be harder to hide on the Internet than it is imagined:

1. Every computer connected to the Internet "has a unique numeric address." That numeric address is attached to a particular computer.

See Matthew Collins, *The Law of Defamation and the Internet*, 2d ed. (New York: Oxford University Press, 2005) at 80

b) In the case of Internet users who gain access to the Internet through a commercial Internet Service Provider (ISP), the ISP will usually have the technical ability to monitor and determine how each of its subscribers uses the Internet and to trace individual communications back to the originating computer.

> See Matthew Collins, *The Law of Defamation and the Internet*, 2d ed. (New York: Oxford University Press, 2005) at 78–79

c) For Internet users who send messages via an employer's computer system, the tracing is even easier.

> See Matthew Collins, *The Law of Defamation and the Internet*, 2d ed. (New York: Oxford University Press, 2005) at 78–79

There is some limited protection against invasion of privacy in various legislation, such as:

- *Personal Information Protection and Electronic Documents Act*, S.C. 2000, c.5 [*PIPEDA*]
- *The Data Protection Act 1998* (U.K.), 1998, c. 29

In the Canadian context, the Canadian Association of Internet Providers (CAIP), for example, self-regulates the disclosure of user identity on the Internet through its "Privacy Code" and "Code of Conduct."

> See CAIP, "Privacy Code" (7 November 2000), online: www.cata.ca/files/PDF/caip/ CAIP_Privacy_Code.pdf and CAIP, "Code of Conduct," online: www.cata.ca/ files/PDF/caip/CAIP_Code_of_Conduct.pdf

3) Personal Observations

a) Process

Generally, the process of obtaining the identity of anonymous defendants is as follows:

1. Plaintiff's counsel will write to the ISP identifying the defamatory statement and the Uniform Resource Locator (URL), and request that the ISP disclose the identity to the authorities, and the defamatory information is removed.
2. The ISP will either agree to remove the material and provide the information requested, or remove the material and indicate they will provide the names upon receipt of a court order.

Note that the ISP will not generally oppose the motion, but they will not consent to the motion. In theory, the ISP may refuse, but in practice, I have not seen a refusal. Generally the next step will be for plaintiff's counsel to bring a motion seeking an order for the ISP to disclose the names and addresses of the authors of the defamatory statements. The remedies used are summarized below.

b) Factors to Consider Before Launching a Motion to Obtain the Identity of the Defendant

Before launching such a motion, with all the attendant costs, the following factors may be worth considering:

1. What is your objective?
   - To have the words removed?
   - To sue the author?
2. Why do you care about the identity of the author as long as the statements are removed? Simply ask the ISP to remove the statement. Generally speaking, they will be cooperative and will remove it if the statement is patently defamatory. Normally, the ISP does not want to become embroiled in a libel action in which they have no interest and no knowledge of the truth or falsity of the statements.
3. Does the ISP actually know the true identity of the author? If not, are you willing to incur the cost of conducting further investigations? There is a good likelihood that you will receive bogus names and addresses identifying the author, such as, the Vatican, Buckingham Palace, and the White House.
4. Do you have any idea if the authors reside within the jurisdiction?
5. Is the ISP within the jurisdiction?
6. If the authors do not live within the jurisdiction, or even if they do, sometimes they will simply migrate to another ISP outside of the jurisdiction. They may migrate to a jurisdiction where it is difficult to obtain a court order, either through distance or different rules and laws.
7. Finally, by bringing this motion, you may be creating larger problems for your client.

   The request for disclosure of the name of the author may blossom into a story on its own, both online and in the traditional media. Recently, a Canadian model brought such a motion in a New York court to compel the disclosure of the names of the persons who had been posting defamatory messages about her. Initially the Court allowed the author to oppose the motion on an anonymous basis through counsel. The Court then ordered disclosure of the name. The Court's decisions and its reasons were posted in cyberspace where they reside indefinitely. Moreover, the motion was analyzed by both the online and offline media quite extensively. When "*Cohen v. Google blogger decision*" was searched in Google on 31 August 2010, for example, about 38,800 search results appeared in 0.25 seconds. These discussions remain on the Internet indefinitely.

4) Balancing Interests

In *York University v. Bell Canada Enterprises*, 2009 CanLII 46447 at para. 30 (ON S.C.) the court said:

> The Court is required to balance the benefit to the applicant of revealing the desired information against the prejudice to the alleged wrongdoer in releasing the information. At this stage, the Court may consider the nature of the information sought, the degree of confidentiality accorded to the information by the party against whom the order is sought, and the degree to which the requested order curtails the use to which the information can be put: *Isofoton S.A. v. Toronto Dominion Bank,* above.

> See also *Totalise v. Motley Fool,* [2001] EMLR 29 (QBD); *Irwin Toy Ltd. v. Doe,* [2000] O.J. No. 3318 (S.C.J.); *Sheffield Wednesday Football Club Ltd. & Ors v. Hargreaves,* [2007] EWHC 2375 (QB)

5) Reasonable Expectation of Privacy

There is a reasonable expectation of privacy in subscribers' information, names, and addresses.

Irwin Toy Ltd. v. Doe, [2000] O.J. No. 3318 (S.C.J.) at paras. 10–11:

> Implicit in the passage of information through the internet by utilization of an alias or pseudonym is the mutual understanding that, to some degree, the identity of the source will be concealed. Some internet service providers inform the users of their services that they will safeguard their privacy and/ or conceal their identity and, apparently, they even go so far as to have their privacy policies reviewed and audited for compliance. Generally speaking, it is understood that a person's internet protocol address will not be disclosed. Apparently, some internet service providers require their customers to agree that they will not transmit messages that are defamatory or libellous in exchange for the internet service to take reasonable measures to protect the privacy of the originator of the information.

> In keeping with the protocol or etiquette developed in the usage of the internet, some degree of privacy or confidentiality with respect to the identity of the internet protocol address of the originator of a message has significant

safety value and is in keeping with what should be perceived as being good public policy. As far as I am aware, there is no duty or obligation upon the internet service provider to voluntarily disclose the identity of an internet protocol address, or to provide that information upon request.

York University v. Bell Canada Enterprises, 2009 CanLII 46447 at para. 27 (ON S.C.):

Bell and Rogers have information about the identity of the customers who purchased the internet services that were used by the computers from which the communications were sent. In this case, there is no other practicable source. Professor Noble, who was identified in the anonymous e-mail, has failed to respond to inquiries.

See also *R. v. Cuttell*, 2009 ONCJ 471 — Criminal Law
BMG Canada Inc v. Doe, 2005 FCA 193 — Intellectual Property

6) The Right to Privacy Is Not Absolute

York University v. Bell Canada Enterprises, 2009 CanLII 46447 at paras. 31–36:

[Two large ISPs in Canada] have privacy policies that indicate to their customers that their right to privacy is not absolute. For example, Bell's policy states in part:

> While our general policy is not to provide personal information to any party outside of the Bell Companies, there are certain limited circumstances under which it is necessary for us to do so. When we do provide personal information to third parties, we provide only that information that is required under the particular circumstances.
>
> . . .
>
> We may also provide personal information to Law enforcement agencies and Emergency services in emergency situations or where required by statute or court order.

As well, both internet providers have service agreements with their customers, which the customers consent to by accessing and using the service. The service agreements limit the customers' expectations of privacy. For example, Bell the service agreement provides:

> 2. Conditional Use of the Service. You are solely responsible for all access to the Service through your account. By accessing and using the Service or otherwise agreeing to be bound by the terms and con-

ditions of the Service Agreement, you agree to the terms and conditions contained in this Service Agreement.

. . .

17. User Information; Other Information. . . . you agree that Your Service Provider reserves the right from time to time to monitor the Service electronically, monitor or investigate the content of your use of Your Service Provider's networks, including without limitation bandwith consumption, and to disclose any information necessary to satisfy any laws, regulations or other governmental request from any applicable jurisdiction, or as necessary to operate the Service or to protect itself or others.

In addition, Bell's service agreement contains Bell's Acceptable Use Policy, which states:

You are prohibited from using the Service for activities that include, but are not limited to:

- . . . Harassing users or groups in any way including but not limited to defaming, abusing, stalking, threatening or otherwise violating the legal rights of others. . . .
- Transmitting, posting, receiving, retrieving, storing or otherwise reproducing, distributing or providing access to any program or information constituting or encouraging conduct that would constitute a criminal offence or give rise to civil liability. Violating or breaching any applicable laws and/or regulations.

A Bell customer can reasonably contemplate, therefore, that his or her identity may be disclosed by order of the court in the event he or she engages in unlawful, abusive or tortious activity.

Rogers' customers' use of its services are governed by the Rogers Terms of Service and the Rogers Acceptable Use Policy which are substantially the same as the Bell policies.

Additionally, s. 7(3)(c) of the *Personal Information Protection and Electronic Documents Act*, S.C. 2000, c. 5 ("PIPEDA") authorizes the disclosure of such information by an organization, such as a service provider, without its customer's consent pursuant to a court order:

7(3) For the purpose of clause 4.3 of Schedule 1, and despite the note that accompanies that clause, an organization may disclose personal information without the knowledge or consent of the individual only if the disclosure is . . .

(c) required to comply with a subpoena or warrant issued or an order made by a court, person or body with jurisdiction to compel the production of information, or to comply with rules of court relating to the production of records[.]

7) Should Notice Be Given to the Anonymous Publisher?

The law in Canada and the UK is unsettled as to whether:

- the courts should require that defendants be given notice of and an opportunity to oppose motions to compel the disclosure of their identities by third parties such as websites and ISPs.

    See "Protecting Internet Anonymity — The Case for Providing Notice to Anonymous Defendants in Defamation Cases" (9 November 2009), online: http://defamation.lawblog.wordpress.com

- the plaintiff or the ISP is obliged to give notice. As a matter of practice in Ontario the motions to compel disclosure are usually heard by the courts on an *ex parte* basis.

a) Canada

Two decisions in Canada have commented on this issue. In *York University v. Bell Canada Enterprises*, 2009 CanLII 46447 (ON S.C.) the plaintiff, York University, sought and obtained a pre-action discovery by way of an equitable bill of discovery known as the Norwich Pharmacal Order. This order required the ISP to disclose information necessary for the plaintiff to determine the identity of the anonymous author of allegedly defamatory emails and web postings. Justice Strathy discussed the issue of notice at para. 24:

> It may be appropriate in a given case to require that the unknown publisher of the offending material be given notice of the proceedings. It does not appear to have been done as a matter of course in other Norwich Order cases and I did not consider it necessary to do so in this case.

The Divisional Court in *Warman v. Fournier et al.*, 2010 ONSC 2126 also discussed the question of giving notice to a John Doe defendant at para. 43:

> Finally, as Strathy J. noted in *York University*, there may be circumstances in which it is appropriate that notice of a motion for disclosure be given to a John Doe defendant. *The case law suggests that any such determination is to be made on a case-by-case basis, and we agree.* In a defamation action, little would generally be added by such a step, because any defences that might be raised are not relevant to a determination as to whether a *prima facie* case has

been made out. For such purpose, a plaintiff is required to establish only the elements of defamation within its control. However, in other cases a John Doe defendant may have compelling reasons for wishing to remain anonymous that are not immediately obvious, such as a risk to personal safety, and such grounds could not be put before the court absent notice [emphasis added].

b) The UK

In the English decision *Totalise plc v The Motley Fool*, [2001] EWCA Civ 1897, an order was granted by the High Court that compelled the website operator to reveal the identity of an anonymous defendant that had posted allegedly defamatory statements about the plaintiff. The case was appealed on the issue of costs. The Court of Appeal noted in *obiter* as follows at para. 26 regarding the issue of notice:

> It is difficult to see how the court can carry out this task [i.e. whether to grant the requested order] if what it is refereeing is a contest between two parties, neither of whom is the person most concerned, the data subject; one of whom is the data subject's prospective antagonist; and the other of whom knows the data subject's identity, has undertaken to keep it confidential so far as the law permits, and would like to get out of the cross-fire as rapidly and as cheaply as possible. However the website operator can, where appropriate, tell the user what is going on and to offer to pass on in writing to the claimant and the court any worthwhile reason the user wants to put forward for not having his or her identity disclosed. Further, the court could require that to be done before making an order. Doing so will enable the court to do what is required of it with slightly more confidence that it is respecting the law laid down in more than one statute by Parliament and doing no injustice to a third party, in particular not violating his convention rights.

> Discussed in "Protecting Internet Anonymity — The Case for Providing Notice to Anonymous Defendants in Defamation Cases" (9 November 2009), online: http://defamationlawblog.wordpress.com

In a the case of *Sheffield Wednesday Football Club Ltd v. Hargreaves*, [2007] EWHC 2375 (QB), the Court considered the *Totalise* case and decided at para. 9 ". . . that this was a case where I should require that the website users [i.e., the anonymous defendants] be contacted before making an order."

c) The US

In the US, courts require plaintiffs to give notice to an anonymous defendant. The leading case is *Dendrite International, Inc. v. John Doe No. 3, 775*

A.2d 756 (N.J. App. Div. 2001). In this decision the New Jersey appellate court set forth several requirements that the plaintiffs had to fulfill before a court would order disclosure, including requiring the defendant to make efforts to notify the anonymous defendant that they are the subject of an application for an order to disclose their identity so that the defendants have an opportunity to respond. The Court stated as follows at para. 5:

> We hold that when such an application is made, the trial court should first require the plaintiff to undertake efforts to notify the anonymous posters that they are the subject of a subpoena or application for an order of disclosure, and withhold action to afford the fictitiously-named defendants a reasonable opportunity to file and serve opposition to the application. These notification efforts should include posting a message of notification of the identity discovery request to the anonymous user on the ISP's pertinent message board.
>
> Discussed in "Protecting Internet Anonymity — The Case for Providing Notice to Anonymous Defendants in Defamation Cases" (9 November 2009), online: http://defamation lawblog.wordpress.com

The plaintiff was required to give the anonymous defendant notice in the following cases.

> *Cohen v. Google, Inc.,* 25 Misc.3d 945, 887 N.Y.S.2d 424 (NY Cty. Aug. 17, 2009)
> *Solers, Inc. v. Doe,* 977 A.2d 941 (D.C. 2009)
> *Krinsky v. Doe 6,* 72 Cal. Rptr. 3d 231 (Ct. App. 2008)
> *Mobilisa, Inc. v. Doe 1,* 170 P.3d 712 (Ariz. Ct. App. 2007)
> *Doe No. 1 v. Cahill,* 884 A.2d 451 (Del. 2005);
> *Swartz v. Does* ("*Swartz*") Sixth Circuit Court for Davidson County, Tenn., No. 08C-431 (2009)

d) Arguments in Favour of Mandatory Notice

The arguments in favour of mandatory notice are usefully summarized in "Protecting Internet Anonymity — The Case for Providing Notice to Anonymous Defendants in Defamation Cases" (9 November 2009), online: http://defamation lawblog.wordpress.com:

> Yet, imposing the burden of notice on plaintiffs may have some notable benefits. Unlike the approach advocated in *Totalise* wherein third parties would directly notify anonymous defendants, plaintiffs under the Dendrite approach generally have no choice but to provide indirect notice by posting in a publicly accessible forum. The public nature of a plaintiff's notice will expose the matter to the oxygen of publicity and may affect the extent of

the plaintiff's reputational harm, depending on the context. In some cases, public scrutiny might result in further reputational harm if the public perceives the plaintiff to be unjustifiably attempting to silence the anonymous defendant. In other cases, however, public scrutiny might serve to alleviate the existing reputational harm by calling into question the veracity of the statements. Third parties might even be persuaded to mount a defence against a plaintiff's application in cases where there is significant public support in favour of an anonymous defendant but they lack the resources to defend their anonymity.

. . .

[T]he California appellate court in *Krinsky* rejected the notion of requiring a plaintiff to provide notice where a third party had already voluntarily done so:

> When ISPs and message-board sponsors (such as Yahoo!) themselves notify the defendant that disclosure of his or her identity is sought, notification by the plaintiff should not be necessary.

e) Arguments Against Mandatory Notice

In my opinion the courts should have the discretion to order or refuse to order the ISP, the plaintiff, or both to give notice to an anonymous defendant. It should not be a mandatory requirement but rather made on a case-by-case basis as proposed in *Warman v. Fournier et al.*, [2010] ONSC 2126 (CanLII) at para. 43. The following considerations support this view:

1. Canadian courts should be cautious about uncritically applying American jurisprudence concerning giving notice to anonymous defendants. Anonymous speech is protected in the US under the First Amendment. It is unclear whether anonymous speech enjoys the same level of protection under the *Charter of Rights and Freedoms*. Privacy interests are, however, recognized by the *Charter*. In *Warman v. Fournier et al.*, 2010 ONSC 2126 the Court held at para. 17:

> Of particular relevance to the present proceeding, there is also some support in the case law for the proposition that the removal of an individual's right to remain anonymous may constitute an unjustified breach of freedom of expression: see *Canada (Elections Canada) v. National Citizen's Coalition*, [2003] O.J. No. 3420 at paras. 20-21 (O.C.J.). That is the law in the United States, where the right to publish anonymously is a well established aspect of freedom of speech protected by the First Amendment: see, for example, *McIntyre v. Ohio Elections Commission*, 514 U.S. 334 at paras. 3-4 (1995). The

Supreme Court of Canada has also made it clear that freedom of expression must be given consideration in defamation claims and that, in the context of a defamation claim, giving proper weight to the value of freedom of expression on matters of public interest requires a broadening of the defences available in respect of the communication of facts it is in the public's interest to know: see *Grant v. Torstar Corp.*, 2009 SCC 61.

> See a case discussing the different approaches to defamation law between the US and Canada in *Coates v. The Citizen* (1988), 44 C.C.L.T. 286 (N.S.S.C.). See also *Dow Jones & Co. Inc. v. Gutnick*, [2002] HCA 56 at paras. 188–90, discussing the different approaches to defamation law among Australia, England, and the US.

2. A British Columbia Court has criticized defendants for publishing attacks anonymously. See Fraser J. in *Henry v. Stockhouse Media Corp.*, [1999] B.C.J. No. 3202 at paras. 8 and 13 (S.C.):

> I accept the high and stringent tests which the authorities lay down as to the granting of this kind of injunction. As to granting an injunction on an ex parte basis, the key is that the defendants are afforded no opportunity to say that the statements complained of are true. What has led me to the conclusion that the injunction should go is that the statements complained of are anonymous. Whoever WaveyDavey is, he or she feels free to throw around accusations of the most serious kind behind the cowardly screen of an alias. It seems to me that in these circumstances, the concern for the protection of free speech is lessened [emphasis added].
>
> . . .
>
> However, I consider it inappropriate to grant an injunction which will endure until trial, with the right in the defendants and the anonymous writers only to apply to set aside the injunction. It is my view that the injunction should be for as brief a period of time as is reasonable, with an obligation on the part of the plaintiffs to apply for the injunction to be extended.

3. Protection for the anonymous defendant already exists.
    *   There are obligations on counsel on all *ex parte* applications to make full disclosure of the facts and law. See rules 37.07(2), (3), (4), and 39.01(6) of the *Rules of Civil Procedure* of Ontario and cases cited therein.
    *   There appears to be an obligation on the plaintiff to prove a *prima facie* case. According to *Warman v. Fournier*, 2010 ONSC 2126 at paras. 40–42 the plaintiff must prove:
        a) That there has been publication
        b) That the words are capable of being defamatory
        c) That the words refer to the plaintiff

- The courts were cognizant of this requirement in both *York University v. Bell Canada Enterprises*, 2009 CanLII 46447 (ON S.C.) and *Irwin Toy Ltd. v. Doe*, [2000] O.J. No. 3318 (S.C.J.)

4. The courts are able to refuse the order on the balance of the claim on the basis that the claim is not *bona fide* or does not have a *prima facie* basis.
5. The court is able to order notice to be given by the plaintiff or third party.
6. The defendants are ultimately entitled to strike out the statement of claim as disclosing no cause of action or as an abuse of process. See Chapter 11, below.
7. Making notice mandatory simply increases the costs relating to the actual motion, the motion materials, and appeals. It can add to delays from six months up to a year, which is inconsistent with *Rules of Civil Procedure*. See for example rules 1.04(1) and 1.04(1.1) of the Ontario *Rules of Civil Procedure*.
8. There is no reason in principle that an extra layer of protection should be given to defendants who attack persons anonymously rather than those who identify themselves.
9. There is no reason in principle why defendants, in action pertaining to defamation on the Internet, should have further procedural rights.
10. In these circumstances, defendants are deemed to know that they have no reasonable expectation of privacy. For example, as indicated in *York University v. Bell Canada Enterprises*, 2009 CanLII 46447, the defendants signed an agreement in which they acknowledged their limited expectation of privacy.
11. If notice is considered to be mandatory, the rules should be amended to set forth the circumstances when the courts will order notice.
12. The reputational interests of the plaintiff need to be respected. Delay caused by the imposition of further procedural obligations on the plaintiff can result in irreparable damage to the plaintiff's reputation on the Internet.

8) Remedies in Canada and the UK

a) *Norwich Pharmacal* Order

i) *Canada*

One of the most common remedies for a plaintiff is to obtain a *Norwich Pharmacal* Order. This is a pre-action discovery in order to identify a defendant by way of an equitable bill of discovery.

York University v. Bell Canada Enterprises, 2009 CanLII 46447 at paras. 12–13 and 30 (ON S.C.):

The Norwich Order

A plaintiff or potential plaintiff may seek pre-action discovery in order to identify a defendant by way of an equitable bill of discovery known as a "*Norwich* order." In *Norwich Pharmacal Co. v. Commissioners of Customs & Excise*, above, the case that gave its name to the order, Norwich Pharmacal was the owner of a patent that it claimed was being infringed by the illicit import of a product manufactured abroad. It brought an action against the Customs and Excise Commissioners seeking disclosure of the names and addresses of the importers. The House of Lords held that where a person becomes involved in the tortious acts of others, even innocently, that person has a duty to give full information to the injured party, by way of discovery, to disclose the identity of the wrongdoer.

On August 21, 2009, the Court of Appeal for Ontario released its decision in *GEA Group AG v. Ventra Group Co.* 2009 ONCA 619 (CanLII), 2009 ONCA 619 (*GEA Group*), which conducted an extensive review of the Canadian cases in which *Norwich* orders have been granted and discussed "the circumstances in which this extraordinary discretionary relief may be obtained in Ontario" (at para 1). The Court of Appeal agreed with earlier authorities that the following factors govern the determination of whether to grant a *Norwich* order:

(a) whether the applicant has provided evidence sufficient to raise a valid, *bona fide* or reasonable claim;

(b) whether the applicant has established a relationship with the third party from whom the information is sought, such that it establishes that the third party is somehow involved in the acts complained of;

(c) whether the third party is the only practicable source of the information available;

(d) whether the third party can be indemnified for costs to which the third party may be exposed because of the disclosure; and

(e) whether the interests of justice favour obtaining the disclosure.

See: *Glaxo Wellcome plc v. Canada (Minister of National Revenue)*, 1998 CanLII 9071, [1998] 4 F.C. 439 (C.A.), leave to appeal refused, [1998] S.C.C.A. No. 422

Alberta (Treasury Branches) v. Leahy, 2000 ABQB 575, 270 A.R. 1, aff'd 2002 ABCA 101, 303 A.R. 63, leave to appeal refused, [2002] S.C.C.A. No. 235

Straka v. Humber River Regional Hospital, 2000 CanLII 16979, 51 O.R. (3d) 1 (C.A.)

Meuwissen (Litigation Guardian of) v. Strathroy Middlesex General Hospital (2006), 40 C.P.C. (6th) 6

Isofoton S.A. v. Toronto Dominion Bank, 2007 CanLII 14626, 85 O.R. (3d) 780 (S.C.J.)

The Court is required to balance the benefit to the applicant of revealing the desired information against the prejudice to the alleged wrongdoer in releasing the information. At this stage, the Court may consider the nature of the information sought, the degree of confidentiality accorded to the information by the party against whom the order is sought, and the degree to which the requested order curtails the use to which the information can be put: *Isofoton S.A. v. Toronto Dominion Bank*.

In the *York University v. Bell Canada Enterprises* decision, the judge indicated his reasons for granting an order requiring the ISPs to disclose the names of the individual authors at para. 39:

> In summary, in this case, I was satisfied that:
> (a) the plaintiff had established a *prima facie* case of defamation and the claim appeared to be reasonable and made in good faith;
> (b) the defendants Bell and Rogers, although innocent of any wrongdoing, were implicated in the alleged defamation because their services were used for publication;
> (c) reasonable efforts had been made, with no success, to obtain the information from the only known potential source;
> (d) the costs of compliance were nominal and had been met;
> (e) without the information sought, the plaintiff would be without a remedy;
> (f) the internet service customer(s) who published the communications could not have a reasonable expectation of privacy in relation to the use of the internet for the purpose of publishing defamatory statements; and
> (g) the disclosure of the information was for the limited purpose of enabling the plaintiff to commence litigation, if so advised.

ii) The UK

In the UK, Norwich Pharmacal Orders have been made against ISPs. See the summary in *York University v. Bell Canada Enterprises*, 2009 CanLII 46447 at paras. 20–21:

> In the United Kingdom, *Norwich* orders have been made against service providers and website publishers: see David Price, *Defamation Law, Procedure and Practice*, 3rd ed., (London: Sweet & Maxwell, 2004) at para 35–114, referring to an unreported decision in *Scoot v. Interactive Investor International;* and *Totalise v. Motley Fool Ltd.*, [2001] EMLR 29 (Q.B.D.), varied with respect to costs, [2003] 2 All E.R. 872 (C.A.). In the latter case, Owen, J., granted a *Norwich* order, stating:
>
> > I am mindful of the fact that both defendants have a policy of confidentiality with regard to personal information relating to those

using its websites and do not wish to deviate from that policy. But the claimant argues that it simply wants the author of the [web discussion board postings] to take responsibility for his actions, and that, when balancing the interests of the parties, the respect for an protection of the privacy of those who chose to air their views in the most public of fora must take second place to the obligation imposed upon those who become involved in the tortious acts of others to assist the party injured by those acts.

I have no hesitation in finding that the balance weighs heavily in favour of granting the relief sought. To find otherwise would be to give the clearest indication to those who wish to defame that they can do so with impunity behind the screen of anonymity made possible by the use of web sites on the internet.

The lower court decision in *Totalise v. Motley Fool Ltd.* was appealed to the Court of Appeal on the question of costs. In the course of its reasons, the Court of Appeal suggested that the protection of the privacy rights of the underlying service subscriber was an important consideration, particularly in light in the *Contempt of Court Act 1981*, 1981, c. 49 and the *Human Rights Act 1998*, 1998, c. 42. The Court of Appeal indicated that it might be difficult to do a privacy analysis in the context of a dispute where the plaintiff wanted the information and the service provider or website operator simply wanted "to get out of the crossfire as rapidly and cheaply as possible." (at para 26.) It suggested that in an appropriate case the website operator could notify the user of the proceedings and inform the claimant and the court of any reason put forward by the user for not wishing to have his or her identity disclosed. Further, the court could make notification of the user a condition-precedent to the making of the order.

A Norwich Pharamacal Order against an ISP who owns and operates a website was refused in part in *Sheffield Wednesday Football Club Ltd. & Ors v. Hargreaves*, [2007] EWHC 2375 (QB).

In this case, there was no live issue between the parties as to the content or the propriety of the order sought (see para. 8). The Court held at paras. 9–10 that even if the conditions of the Norwich Pharamacal Order were satisfied, the Court had the discretion of whether or not to make the order.

However, I must satisfy myself that the order sought is indeed a proper order to make. The proposed order will, if granted, disclose to the Claimants the identities, or at least the e-mail addresses, of users of the Defendant's website who must have expected, given their use of anonymous pseudonyms, that their privacy would be respected. As the Court of Appeal observed in

Totalise PLC v The Motley Fool Ltd [2002] EWCA Civ 365, [2002] 1 WLR 2450 at paragraph 25, in a case where the proposed order will result in the identification of website users who expected their identities to be kept hidden, the court must be careful not to make an order which unjustifiably invades the right of an individual to respect for his private life, especially when that individual is in the nature of things not before the court. Equally, it is clear that no order should be made for the disclosure of the identity of a data subject, whether under the Norwich Pharmacal doctrine or otherwise, unless the court has first considered whether the disclosure is warranted having regard to the rights and freedoms or the legitimate interests of the data subject (see paragraph 6 of schedule 2 of the *Data Protection Act 1998*). As the Court of Appeal pointed out (at paragraph 26 of the judgment) it is difficult for the court to carry out this task if it is refereeing a contest between two parties neither of whom is the person most concerned, that is to say the data subject. This is not a case, as I understand it, where the website operator has informed the relevant website users of what is going on or offered to pass to the court any particular reason why the users should not want their identities revealed. It did not seem to me that this was a case where I should require that the website users be contacted before making an order.

The jurisdiction to make such an order was first established by the case of *Norwich Pharmacal v Customs & Excise Commissioners* [1974] AC 133. Lord Reid described the principle as follows (p175):

> . . . if through no fault of his own a person gets mixed up in the tortious acts of others so as to facilitate their wrongdoing, he may incur no personal liability but he comes under a duty to assist the person who has been wronged by giving him information and disclosing the identity of the wrongdoers. I do not think that it matters whether he became so mixed up by voluntary action on his part or because it was his duty to do what he did. It may be that if this causes him expense the person seeking the information ought to reimburse him. But justice requires that he should co-operate in righting the wrong if he unwittingly facilitated its perpetration.

At para. 27, the Court stated that a judge might refuse disclosure of the identity of the alleged wrongdoer, whose attacks, though legally defamatory, are obviously designed merely to insult and therefore do not carry a realistic risk of doing the claimant quantifiable harm. The Court held that some of the postings were trivial and stated at para. 17:

it seems to me that some of the postings which concern the claimants order on the trivial and I do not think it would be right to make an order for the disclosure of the identities of users who posted messages which are barely defamatory or a little more abusive or likely to be understood as jokes. That to me it seems would be disproportionate and unjustifiable intrusive.

b) Discoveries of Non-parties with Leave/Production of Non-party Document with Leave

The rules of civil procedure of most provinces provide mechanisms whereby a plaintiff can ask the court to order a non-party to produce documents or information under certain circumstances. In Ontario, the plaintiff sues a John or Jane Doe defendant and brings a motion under rule 30.10 or 31.20.

See rules 30.10 and 31.10 of the Ontario *Rules of Civil Procedure*, R.R.O. 1990, Reg. 194.

Irwin Toy Ltd. v. Doe, [2000] O.J. No. 3318 at paras. 1 and 7–8 (S.C.J.), Wilkins J.:

> The moving party plaintiff brings this motion for an order pursuant to Rules 30.10 and 31.10 of the *Rules of Civil Procedure*. The plaintiffs are respectively a corporation and the president of the corporation. They have commenced action against a phantom *"nom de guerre"* John Doe, seeking damages for defamation in respect of an individual plaintiff and breach of confidence and conversion with respect to the corporate plaintiff and punitive damages in respect of both plaintiffs.
>
> In the case at bar, the internet service provider has been given notice of this motion. The internet service provider has closed the account of the customer in question, and there is no evidence before me that it had any knowledge of the alleged conduct of its customer.
>
> Although the internet service provider does not oppose this application, it is my view that it is important to comment on this form of motion as it is anticipated that the courts will be seeing motions of this nature on a more frequent basis, as members of the public become curious to determine the true identity of the originator of messages, and/or information passed through the internet, or posted on "notice boards" or disclosed in "chat rooms" therein.

The judge ordered the ISP to disclose the names of the writers at paras. 14–20:

> On the facts of the case at bar the moving parties, in my view, meet all of the tests necessary to obtain the information in the possession of iPrimus Canada

identifying the subscriber with the internet protocol address 216.200.145.35. To date, the moving parties have been unable to obtain information as to the identity of "Joe Doe" which is clearly information to which they would be entitled on any examination on discovery from "Joe Doe," who will be the very person they wish to examine. In addition, it would be unfair to require the moving party to attempt to proceed without having the opportunity of identifying the true defendant.

In my view there would be no unfairness to iPrimus Canada to oblige them to disclose the identity of the specific internet protocol address subscriber by way of answering a written interrogatory containing the name, address or other identification information that would be available in their electronic records.

Ordinarily, under Rule 31.10, the moving party must satisfy the court that they have been unable to obtain the information from other persons whom the moving party is entitled to examine for discovery. In something so fundamental as the proper identification of the true defendant in circumstances such as the case at bar, one has difficulty imagining how the moving parties could ever make that identification by any other means than disclosure from the internet service provider.

Rule 31.10 contemplates that the moving party will demonstrate that there is reason to believe that the person sought to be examined has information relevant to a material issue in the action. Presumably, the true identity and appropriate address for service for a defendant could arguably always be something of such importance as to require its disclosure. Such disclosure, however, in my view, should not be automatic upon the issuance of the Statement of Claim. If such were to be the case, the fact of the anonymity of the internet could be shattered for the price of the issuance of a spurious Statement of Claim and the benefits obtained by the anonymity lost in inappropriate circumstances.

In the circumstances of the case at bar, the moving party has demonstrated on the affidavit material filed before me that it has a *prima facie* case as against Joe Doe in respect to the allegations of claim made in the Statement of Claim. In my view, that is the appropriate test for the court to apply in determining whether or not to order a non-party internet service provider to disclose the identity of an internet protocol address.

The law in Ontario respecting the liability of an internet service provider for the actions of its customer is not clear. It would be unjust and expensive to require a plaintiff to commence a potentially losing law suit just to obtain the identity of the real tortfeasor from the service provider.

The moving party shall therefore be entitled to their order as requested and the internet service provider, iPrimus Canada, is directed to provide that information to the plaintiffs.

c) Other Means of Ascertaining the Name of the Author

The UK case *Takenaka (UK) Ltd & Anor v. Frankl*, [2001] EWCA Civ 348 involved various email messages that were defamatory of the plaintiffs and had been sent under the false name "christinarealtor" using a Hotmail address. The plaintiffs engaged in months of expensive litigation involving motions against various ISPs and Hotmail. The plaintiffs were able to locate the defendant as the likely author of the email messages. The defendant denied writing the emails. "Parties agreed to submit a computer to which the Defendant had had access to, a court appointed, jointly instructed expert for examination."

This was an expert produced report, which concluded on the balance of probability that the defendant had sent the email messages. See *Takenaka (UK) Ltd & Anor v. Frankl*, [2001] EWCA Civ 348 at para. 7.

> Referred to in Matthew Collins, *The Law of Defamation and the Internet*, 2d edition (New York: Oxford University Press, 2005) at 83

Applicants in an Australian case sought and obtained an order that the defendant appear before the Court for the purpose of being examined regarding the identity of the author of a defamatory statement as well as an order that the defendant give discovery of documents relating to the authors identity. *Resolute Ltd. v. Warnos*, [2000] WASC 35.

In the case of *Vaquero Energy v. Weir et al.*, [2004] A.J. No. 84 (Q.B.), the plaintiff introduced expert evidence which convinced the trial judge that the defendant had published the defamatory emails. The defendant denied publishing the statements and testified as such in court. The following is the Court's discussion at paras. 6–8, 10, and 12–13 of the tracing process, the evidence given, and the cross-examination. The discussion is included here because of the practical value for counsel engaged in similar cases:

> [6] The IP addresses were traced to Interface, an Internet provider in Toronto. Their records showed that 66.59.140.3 was assigned to a router which then hosted several companies. One of those companies was Currah Capital. That same router IP address was changed to 66.199.157.129. In July, Interface assigned a set of IP addresses to Currah Capital. Mr. Koppes, the representative of Interface testified that he specifically recalled manually installing 66.199.159.34 on the laptop computer of Mr. Weir at the offices of Currah

Capital. He said that to do so, he was given the laptop and Mr. Weir's password for the computer.

[7] George Sidor was qualified as an expert in computer forensics and the workings of the Internet. He explained that an IP address — Internet Protocol — is somewhat like a telephone number. The IP number will identify where information sent through the Internet network came from. IP addresses are assigned to users. If the IP address and the date and time that an email is sent is known, the computer that sent it can be traced. If the IP address comes from a router, then you need further information to trace the message back to the individual computer.

[8] Mr. Weir testified saying that he did not send the postings. Mr. Weir is a business consultant. He shares office space with Currah Capital. The office has an open concept so that, except for the accountant's computer which is kept in a locked room, the three other people who work there have access to each others computers. He says that they use whatever computer is available. He said that those employees all had stock holdings in Westminster or Vaquero and would have lost money on the stock during the consolidation process. He also said that he did not have in-depth knowledge of the oil and gas industry.

. . .

[10] Mr. Weir called Dr. Thomas Keenan who was qualified as an expert in computer forensics and the workings of the Internet. Dr. Keenan gave evidence about the practice of spoofing which is the theft by one person of another person's IP address. He said that it could be done one of two ways. If the thief had access to the computer, in a few seconds, the thief could determine the IP address and then use it on his computer. The other way would be to install a Trojan. Dr. Keenan said that learning the technique to obtain the IP address was not difficult. Prior to his testimony, he did a Google search of 'spoofing' and found many sites which explained how to spoof. In cross-examination, he said that because of IP address theft, police are relying less on IP address to determine e-mail senders and more on other evidence.

The Court came to the conclusion that Mr. Weir had sent the emails at paras. 12–13:

[12] The second issue is whether it was Mr. Weir who sent the emails. The plaintiffs say that they have proven on a balance of probabilities that it was Mr. Weir. They point to the fact that most of the alec6 e-mails are directly traceable to Mr. Weir's computer. That then leads to a reasonable conclusion that the other e-mails which were sent through a router connected to Cur-

rah Capital among other companies were also sent by Mr. Weir since he was working in the Currah Capital offices. Mr. Weir knew about Vaquero and showed more than a passing interest in the company. The e-mails stopped on the day that Mr. Weir was served with the Statement of Claim. They argue that Mr. Weir's suggestion that someone spoofed his IP address does not make sense. There were three different IP addresses from which these postings emanated. It would require either the installation of a Trojan or the same person re-attending at Mr. Weir's office to get the IP addresses as they were changed by Interface. Mr. Weir argues that it is possible that his IP address was spoofed or that someone else working in the office used his computer to make the postings.

[13] I am satisfied that the postings were done by Mr. Weir. There is no evidence that a Trojan had been installed. I agree that it is highly unlikely that a thief would know when the IP address changed so as to know when to re-enter the Currah offices and obtain the new IP address. Mr. Weir made much of the fact that the Plaintiffs had originally planned to apply to have his computer seized for evidence but then never did. If the computer would have proven exculpatory, it was open to Mr. Weir to offer it as proof. This is not to suggest that there was any burden on Mr. Weir to disprove the allegations. That burden, of course, stayed with the Plaintiffs. There is no doubt that most of the alec6 postings came from Mr. Weir's computer and it is clear that those are of the same type and style of the napo9 postings. Accordingly, I am satisfied that all of the postings were made by Mr. Weir.

B. DURING THE COURSE OF PROCEEDINGS

The Ontario Divisional Court in *Warman v. Fournier et al.*, 2010 ONSC 2126, reversing *Warman v. Wilkins-Fournier*, 2009 CanLII 14054 (ON S.C.), made an important decision regarding the disclosure of the identities of anonymous parties during the course of libel proceedings, in contrast to disclosure prior to the institution of libel proceedings. The Court summarized the appeal at issue at para. 1:

> The appellants, Constance Wilkins-Fournier and Mark Fournier (the "Appellants"), appeal an order of Kershman J. dated March 23, 2009 ordering the Appellants to provide a further and better Affidavit of Documents to the respondent Richard Warman (the "Respondent") listing all documents in their possession relating to the identities of the defendant John Does 1-8 in the action, including their e-mail addresses and the internet protocol ("IP") addresses used by them when making the specific postings identified in the

Respondent's statement of claim. The issue in the proceeding is whether such disclosure is automatic if the Respondent is able to demonstrate relevance and an absence of protection under one of the traditional categories of privilege or whether the Court must also consider the interests of privacy and freedom of expression of the John Doe defendants and, if so, in what manner.

This is the first appellate decision in Canada on this issue, and since it covers so many important substantive procedural issues, as well as containing a lucid statement of the law, the bulk of the reasons are reproduced (paras. 14–35 and 38–42, note treatment of important differences at 38–42), even to the extent of the duplication of some of the statements of law in other parts of this section.

1) Analysis of the Applicable Law

[14] The legal issue arising in this proceeding is whether there are *Charter* values that the Court must take into account in considering the Respondent's request for disclosure and, if so, the manner in which the Court is to balance such *Charter* protected interests against the public interest in promoting the administration of justice by providing the Respondent with full access to the information which will enable him to pursue his defamation action against the alleged wrongdoers.

2) Are *Charter* Values Engaged by the Respondent's Request for Disclosure?

[15] In this case, it is clear that both the right of freedom of expression, guaranteed by section 2(b) of the *Charter,* as well as privacy interests that are also recognized by the *Charter,* are engaged.

[16] As expressed by the Supreme Court, freedom of expression is among the most fundamental of rights possessed by Canadians: see *R. v. Sharpe,* 2001 SCC 2 (CanLII), [2001] 1 S.C.R. 45 at para. 21. The values underlying the right to free expression include individual self-fulfillment, finding the truth through the open exchange of ideas, and the political disclosure fundamental to democracy: see *R. v. Sharpe* at para. 23.

[17] Of particular relevance to the present proceeding, there is also some support in the case law for the proposition that the removal of an individual's right to remain anonymous may constitute an unjustified breach of freedom of expression: see *Canada (Elections Canada) v. National Citizen's Coalition,* [2003] O.J. No. 3420 at paras. 20–21 (O.C.J.). That is the law in the United States, where the right to publish anonymously is a well established aspect

of freedom of speech protected by the First Amendment: see, for example, *McIntyre v. Ohio Elections Commission*, 514 U.S. 334 at paras. 3–4 (1995). The Supreme Court of Canada has also made it clear that freedom of expression must be given consideration in defamation claims and that, in the context of a defamation claim, giving proper weight to the value of freedom of expression on matters of public interest requires a broadening of the defences available in respect of the communication of facts it is in the public's interest to know: see *Grant v. Torstar Corp.*, 2009 S.C.C. 61.

[18] At the same time, the Supreme Court has also recognized that privacy has been accorded constitutional protection: see *Hill v. Church of Scientology of Toronto*, 1995 CanLII 59 (S.C.C.), [1995] 2 S.C.R. 1130 at para. 21. In *R. v. Tessling*, 2004 SCC 67 (CanLII), [2004] 3 S.C.R. 432 at para. 24, the Supreme Court referred to personal, territorial and informational privacy as separate but often overlapping categories. Informational privacy is defined in *R. v. Tessling* at para. 23 as the claim of individuals, groups or institutions to determine for themselves when, how and to what extent information about them is communicated. It involves protection of the "biographical core of personal information" according to Sopinka J. in *Plant* at p. 293. The courts have developed a test to determine whether, in any particular case, there is a reasonable expectation of privacy based on the context of the disclosure and the totality of the circumstances: see *R. v. Cuttell*, [2009] O.J. No. 4053 at paras. 14–16 (O.C.J.), citing *Plant* at p. 293.

[19] Privacy interests arise for consideration in the present case in favour of both the plaintiff and the John Doe defendants. As the Supreme Court ruled in *Hill*, the good reputation of an individual is intimately connected to his right to privacy, and thus the right to privacy of the plaintiff may be affected by the allegedly libelous postings. At the same time, the John Doe defendants who made the allegedly libelous postings arguably had a reasonable expectation of privacy, having expressly elected to remain anonymous when they did so.

[20] In *Irwin Toy Ltd.*, which arose in the context of a defamation action, Wilkins J. suggested at para. 11 that, in keeping with the protocol or etiquette developed in the usage of the internet, some degree of confidentiality regarding identifiers of the originator of a message, "has significant safety value and is in keeping with what should be perceived as being good public policy." His statement is consistent with an implicit understanding of citizens that, to some degree at least, their identities will be protected when they use the internet anonymously. In *Cuttell* at para. 27, the court also held that there was a reasonable expectation of privacy in a party's subscriber information which linked the party's identity to internet usage.

[21] The Appellants submit that the Respondent's request for disclosure raises a concern for informational privacy because the disclosure sought would not only permit identification of the John Doe defendants but would also provide the Respondent with the means to assemble a complete informational profile of each defendant based on other use of the internet in respect of which the defendants would have a legitimate expectation of privacy.

3) Role of the Court of Where *Charter* Values are Engaged

[22] While the *Charter* does not apply to strictly private litigation between litigants not invoking state action, the Divisional Court has held that, because the *Rules of Civil Procedure* have the force of a statute, they must be interpreted in a manner consistent with *Charter* rights and values: see *D.P. v. Wagg*, [2002] O.J. No. 3808 at paras. 65–66 (Div. Ct.). In that case, the court held that whenever one party to a civil suit invokes or relies upon government action (in that case, the *Rules of Civil Procedure*, as enforced by the machinery of the administration of justice) to produce what amounts to the infringement of another party's *Charter* rights, *Charter* values are invoked.

On appeal, Rosenberg J.A., speaking for the Court, was prepared to assume, for purposes of that case, that *Charter* values should inform the discovery process: *D.P. v. Wagg*, 2004 CanLII 39048 (ON C.A.), (2004), 71 O.R. (3d) 229 at para. 61. However, the appeal was ultimately decided on the principle that the Superior Court has inherent jurisdiction to control the discovery and production process under the *Rules of Civil Procedure* to ensure that important state and other third party interests, including *Charter* interests, are protected, even if the particular documents do not, strictly speaking, fall within a recognized category of privilege: see para. 28.

4) Manner in Which Courts Address the Need to Take *Charter* Rights into Consideration in Relation to a Request for Disclosure

[24] In circumstances where *Charter* rights are engaged and therefore courts are required to take such interests into consideration in determining whether to order disclosure, the case law indicates that the *Charter* protected interests are balanced against the public interest in disclosure in the context of the administration of justice by a combination of (1) a requirement of an evidentiary threshold, (2) fulfillment of conditions establishing the necessity of the disclosure sought, and (3) an express weighing of the competing interests in the particular circumstances of the litigation. In order to prevent the abusive use of the litigation process, disclosure cannot be automatic where

Charter interests are engaged. On the other hand, to prevent the abusive use of the internet, disclosure also cannot be unreasonably withheld even if *Charter* interests are engaged.

[25] There is no case law that specifically addresses the relevant considerations to be taken into account by a Court on a motion *for an order that a defendant make disclosure under Rule 30.06 in an on-going action*. However, there is ample authority in the analogous circumstances of proceedings taken against third parties to obtain the identities of prospective defendants [emphasis added].

[26] In civil litigation, the courts have developed the equitable remedy of "pre-action discovery" to permit a plaintiff to discover the identity of a proposed defendant. The remedy has most recently been upheld by the Ontario Court of Appeal in *GEA Group AG v. Flex-N-Gate Corporation* (2009), 96 O.R. (3d) 481 at paras. 40–54, which confirmed the principles originally set out in *Norwich Pharmacal Co. v. Comrs. of Customs and Excise*, [1974] A.C. 133 (H.L.).

[27] The fundamental premise of *Norwich Pharmacal* is that, where privacy interests are involved, disclosure is not automatic even if the plaintiff establishes relevance and the absence of any of the traditional categories of privilege. *Norwich Pharmacal* requires the court to go on to consider five factors including: (1) whether the plaintiff has provided evidence sufficient to raise a valid, *bona fide* or reasonable claim; (2) whether the third party is the only practicable source of the information available; and (3) whether the interests of justice favour obtaining the disclosure: see *Glaxo Wellcome PLC v. Canada (Minister of National Revenue)*, 1998 CanLII 9071 (F.C.A.), [1998] 4 F.C. 439 (F.C.A.).

[28] An important point, reaffirmed by the Ontario Court of Appeal in *GEA*, is that, being an equitable remedy, the principles in *Norwich Pharmacal* are to be applied flexibly and will vary as the particular circumstances of each case require. In this connection, we note that, while there may be some uncertainty as to whether the House of Lords required the plaintiff to satisfy a *bona fide* standard or a *prima facie* standard in *Norwich Pharmacal*, that issue is now resolved on a case-by-case basis. We will return to this issue later.

[29] The principle in *Norwich Pharmacal* was applied by the Federal Court of Appeal in *BMG Canada Inc. v. John Doe* 2005 CAF 193 (CanLII), [2005] 4 F.C.R. 81 at paras. 39–41 (F.C.A.) ("BMG"), aff'g 2004 FC 488 (CanLII), [2004] 3 F.C.R. 241 (F.C.) in the context of an application for disclosure by ISPs of customer information in order to identify anonymous internet users who were sharing music files on the internet. *BMG* illustrates that a court must have regard to the privacy interests of anonymous users of the internet before granting a *Norwich Pharmacal* order, even where the issue involved pertains to property

rights and does not engage the interest of freedom of expression. In that decision, disclosure was sought under Rule 238(1) of the *Federal Court Rules, 1998,* SOR/98-106, which contemplate leave of the Court to examine for discovery a non-party to an action having relevant information. The Federal Court of Appeal upheld the order of the motions judge denying such disclosure.

[30] In doing so, the Federal Court of Appeal expressly stated that the proceeding could have been brought either under Rule 238 or by invoking the common law principles in *Norwich Pharmacal* and that, in either case, the same principles — the principles in *Norwich Pharmacal* — would be applicable because the same issues were at stake. The Federal Court of Appeal held that the following factors governed determination of whether to grant the order:

(1) the applicant must establish a *bona fide* claim against the unknown alleged wrongdoer;

(2) the third party against whom discovery is sought must be in some way connected to or involved in the misconduct;

(3) the third party must be the only practical source of the information available to the applicant;

(4) the third party must be reasonably compensated for expenses and legal costs arising out of compliance with the discovery order; and

(5) the public interest in favour of disclosure must outweigh the legitimate privacy interests.

[31] The earlier decision in *Irwin Toy* also involved a motion for disclosure from ISPs, but in the context of a defamation action. Wilkins J. held that Rule 30.10 and Rule 31.10 of the *Rules of Civil Procedure,* which in the case of Rule 31.10 is similar to Federal Rule 238, could be used to compel production from an ISP of the identity of a subscriber for whom the plaintiffs had obtained the IP address. While Wilkins J. did not expressly adopt the principles in *Norwich Pharmacal,* he did, in substance, consider the factors enumerated in that decision and addressed in *BMG.* In particular, Wilkins J. expressly considered whether the applicant had demonstrated on the affidavit evidence a *prima facie* case of defamation against the John Doe defendant in that action.

5) Application of the Relevant Principles to the Present Proceeding

[32] The principles applied in *BMG* and *Irwin Toy* are equally applicable in the present circumstances. There is no meaningful basis for distinguishing the circumstances or the issue before the Court. The same issues are at stake and the same principles articulated in *Norwich Pharmacal* are applicable. While it is correct that *BMG* and *Irwin Toy* address disclosure from third

parties, for which leave of the Court was required, whereas the case at bar concerns disclosure from a party defendant, this is not a meaningful distinction for present purposes. As has been pointed out, a third party can be made a defendant for the price of issuing a statement of claim. Moreover, the fact that the motion engages the important *Charter* value of freedom of expression, as well as the right to privacy, heightens the need to have regard to considerations beyond the traditional concerns of relevance and privilege.

[33] Further, neither the operation of the deemed undertaking rule in Rule 30.1, which is itself grounded in a concern for privacy, nor the requirement in Rule 76.03 for very broad documentary disclosure is sufficient, in the present circumstances, to displace the requirement to take the *Charter* values into consideration. In particular, the deemed undertaking rule is insufficient to address the potential for abuse of the *Rules of Civil Procedure*. If disclosure were automatic, a plaintiff with no legitimate claim could misuse the *Rules of Civil Procedure* by commencing an unmeritorious action for the sole purpose of revealing the identity of anonymous internet commentators, with a view to stifling such commentators and deterring others from speaking out on controversial issues. For this reason, the commencement of a defamation claim does not trump freedom of expression or the right to privacy.

[34] Given the circumstances in this action, the motions judge was therefore required to have regard to the following considerations: (1) whether the unknown alleged wrongdoer could have a reasonable expectation of anonymity in the particular circumstances; (2) whether the Respondent has established a *prima facie* case against the unknown alleged wrongdoer and is acting in good faith; (3) whether the Respondent has taken reasonable steps to identify the anonymous party and has been unable to do so; and (4) whether the public interests favouring disclosure outweigh the legitimate interests of freedom of expression and right to privacy of the persons sought to be identified if the disclosure is ordered.

[35] Although, as mentioned, there is no case directly on point, these principles emerge from the decisions referred to above. They are also consistent with the decisions of the Superior Court of Justice in *Irwin Toy* and in *York University v. Bell Canada Enterprises*, [2009] O.J. No. 3689, which was released after the decision of the motions judge. We note that an English court reached a similar conclusion in *Sheffield Wednesday Football Club Ltd. and others v. Hargreaves*, [2007] EWHC 2375 (Q.B.).

. . .

[38] We note that there are several important differences between the factors that, in our view, should have been considered by the motion judge in

this proceeding, and the factors outlined by the Federal Court of Appeal in *BMG*. These differences reflect the fact that the Court's inherent jurisdiction to control its procedures, and its equitable jurisdiction, are applied flexibly to meet the particular circumstances of each case. Two differences, in particular, require elaboration.

[39] First, in the present circumstances, the Court need not consider either the second or the fourth requirements in *BMG*, which apply only to third party respondents. These are not appropriate requirements where disclosure is sought against a co-defendant who has established and administers a website on which the allegedly defamatory statements were posted.

[40] Second, and more significantly, as in *Irwin Toy Ltd.*, and *York University*, a *prima facie* standard, rather than merely a *bona fide* standard, is appropriate, for two reasons.

[41] In para. 34 of *BMG*, the Federal Court of Appeal expressed the concern that, in that case, imposition of a *prima facie* case standard would effectively strip an applicant of a remedy because the plaintiff could not know the actual case it wished to assert against the defendants until it knew not only their identities but also the nature of their involvement in the file-sharing activities. Because the present proceeding is a defamation action, that concern does not arise. Unlike *BMG*, the Respondent knows the details of precisely what was done by each of the unknown alleged wrongdoers.

[42] In addition, because this proceeding engages a freedom of expression interest, as well as a privacy interest, a more robust standard is required to address the chilling effect on freedom of expression that will result from disclosure. It is also consistent with the recent pronouncements of the Supreme Court that establish the relative weight that must be accorded the interest in freedom of expression. In the circumstances of a website promoting political discussion, the possibility of a defence of fair comment reinforces the need to establish the elements of defamation on a *prima facie* basis in order to have due consideration to the interest in freedom of expression. On the other hand, there is no compelling public interest in allowing someone to libel and destroy the reputation of another, while hiding behind a cloak of anonymity. The requirement to demonstrate a *prima facie* case of defamation furthers the objective of establishing an appropriate balance between the public interest in favour of disclosure and legitimate interests of privacy and freedom of expression.

See also the decision of the Court in *G & G v. Wikimedia Foundation Inc*, [2009] EWHC 3148 (QB) where the disclosure of names in a potential blackmail case were ordered.

CHAPTER 11: Internet Libel Actions Stayed as an Abuse of Process in the UK

A. INTRODUCTION

In the UK the courts have recently held that a libel action may be struck out or stayed as an abuse of process where the extent of publication within the jurisdiction is very small or there is no realistic prospect of achieving vindication in any event. This argument is discussed in some detail for Canadian lawyers and judges because it is applicable to Internet libel actions in Canada.

> *Dow Jones & Co. Inc. v. Jameel*, [2005] EWCA Civ 75 quoted in *Mardas v. New York Times and Anor*, [2008] EWHC 3135 at para. 35 (QB); *Lonzim Plc & Ors v. Sprague*, [2009] EWHC 2838 (QB)

See, for example, further decisions discussing the abuse of process argument:

> *Budu v. The British Broadcasting Corporation*, [2010] EWHC 616 (QB)
>
> *Kaschke v. Gray & Anor*, [2010] EWHC 1907 (QB)
>
> *Khader v. Aziz & Ors*, [2010] EWCA Civ 716
>
> *Smith v. ADVFN Plc & Ors*, [2010] EWCA Civ 657
>
> *Carrie v. Tolkien*, [2009] EWHC 29 (QB)
>
> *Lonzim Plc & Ors v. Sprague*, [2009] EWHC 2838 (QB)
>
> *Atlantis World Group of Companies NV & Anor v. Gruppo Editoriale L'Espresso SPA*, [2008] EWHC 1323 (QB)
>
> *Ewing v. News International Ltd & Ors*, [2008] EWHC 1390 (QB)
>
> *Smith v. ADVFN Plc & Ors*, [2008] EWHC 1797 (QB)
>
> *Amoudi v. Brisard & Anor*, [2006] EWHC 1062 (QB)
>
> *Bunt v. Tilley & Ors*, [2006] EWHC 407 (QB)
>
> *Bin Mahfouz & Ors v. Ehrenfeld & Anor*, [2005] EWHC 1156 (QB)

B. STATEMENT OF THE PRINCIPLES

The Court of Appeal in *Dow Jones & Co. Inc. v. Jameel*, [2005] EWCA Civ 75 set out the applicable principles at paras. 40, 54–56, 66, and 69–70 as cited in para. 18 of *Lonzim Plc & Ors v. Sprague*, [2009] EWHC 2838 (QB):

> We accept that in the rare case where a claimant brings an action for defamation in circumstances where his reputation has suffered no or minimal actual damage, this may constitute an interference with freedom of expression that is not necessary for the protection of the claimant's reputation. In such circumstances the appropriate remedy for the defendant may well be to challenge the claimant's resort to English jurisdiction or to seek to strike out the action as an abuse of process. We are shortly to consider such an application. An alternative remedy may lie in the application of costs sanctions.
>
> . . .
>
> Mr. Price's submissions amount, so it seems to us, to asserting that Dow Jones' failure to challenge English jurisdiction estops them from relying at this stage on arguments that could have been advanced in support of such a challenge. We do not accept this. An abuse of process is of concern not merely to the parties but to the court. It is no longer the role of the court simply to provide a level playing-field and to referee whatever game the parties choose to play upon it. The court is concerned to ensure that judicial and court resources are appropriately and proportionately used in accordance with the requirements of justice. If Dow Jones have caused potential prejudice to the claimant by failing to raise the points now pursued at the proper time, it does not follow that the court must permit this action to continue. The court has other means of dealing with such prejudice. For instance, appropriate costs orders can compensate for legal costs unnecessarily incurred and relief can be made conditional on Dow Jones undertaking not to raise a limitation defence if proceedings are now commenced in another jurisdiction.
>
> There have been two recent developments which have rendered the court more ready to entertain a submission that pursuit of a libel action is an abuse of process. The first is the introduction of the new Civil Procedure Rules. Pursuit of the overriding objective requires an approach by the court to litigation that is both more flexible and more pro-active. The second is the coming into effect of the *Human Rights Act*. Section 6 requires the court, as a public authority, to administer the law in a manner which is compatible with Convention rights, insofar as it is possible to do so. Keeping a proper balance between the Article 10 right of freedom of expression and the protection of individual reputation must, so it seems to us, require the court to bring to a stop as an

abuse of process defamation proceedings that are not serving the legitimate purpose of protecting the claimant's reputation, which includes compensating the claimant only if that reputation has been unlawfully damaged.

We do not believe that *Brunswick v Harmer*, [1849] 14 QB 185 could today have survived an application to strike out for abuse of process. The Duke himself procured the republication to his agent of an article published many years before for the sole purpose of bringing legal proceedings that would not be met by a plea of limitation. If his agent read the article he is unlikely to have thought the Duke much, if any, the worse for it and, to the extent that he did, the Duke brought this on his own head. He acquired a technical cause of action but we would today condemn the entire exercise as an abuse of process

. . .

So far as concerns the issue currently under consideration there is no conflict between the view of Lord Hoffmann and the view of the majority. This action falls to be considered as relating exclusively to an independent tort, or series of torts, in this country. It is thus not legitimate for the claimant to seek to justify the pursuit of these proceedings by praying in aid the effect that they may have in vindicating him in relation to the wider publication.

. . .

If the claimant succeeds in this action and is awarded a small amount of damages, it can perhaps be said that he will have achieved vindication for the damage done to his reputation in this country, but both the damage and the vindication will be minimal. The cost of the exercise will have been out of all proportion to what has been achieved. The game will not merely not have been worth the candle, it will not have been worth the wick.

If we were considering an application to set aside permission to serve these proceedings out of the jurisdiction we would allow that application on the basis that the five publications that had taken place in this jurisdiction did not, individually or collectively, amount to a real and substantial tort. Jurisdiction is no longer in issue, but, subject to the effect of the claim for an injunction that we have yet to consider, we consider for precisely the same reason that it would not be right to permit this action to proceed. It would be an abuse of process to continue to commit the resources of the English court, including substantial judge and possibly jury time, to an action where so little is now seen to be at stake. Normally where a small claim is brought, it will be dealt with by a proportionate small claims procedure. Such a course is not available in an action for defamation where, although the claim is small, the issues are complex and subject to special procedure under the CPR.

C. JURISDICTION WILL BE EXERCISED RARELY

The jurisdiction of the court to strike out a libel claim for abuse of process will only be exercised in relatively rare cases.

> *Baturina v. Times Newspapers Ltd.,* [2010] EWHC 696 (QB)
> *Mardas v. New York Times and Anor,* [2008] EWHC 3135 (QB)
> *Steinberg v. Pritchard Englefield,* [2005] EWCA Civ 288

D. TIMING OF THE MOTION

A motion for abuse of process is more commonly brought before trial. However, motions to strike out a claim for abuse of process can be brought at trial.

> *Atlantis World Group of Companies NV & Anor v. Gruppo Editoriale L'Espresso
> SPA,* [2008] EWHC 1323 at para. 56 (QB)

E. DEVELOPMENT OF THE CONCEPT OF ABUSE OF PROCESS IN DOMESTIC LIBEL ACTIONS

Shellenberg v. BBC, [2000] E.M.L.R. 296 is referred to at para. 57 of *Dow Jones & Co. Inc. v. Jameel,* [2005] EWCA Civ 75:

> In *Schellenberg v BBC* [2000] EMLR 296 the claimant had settled defamation actions against the *Guardian* and the *Sunday Times* on disadvantageous terms, when it seemed likely that he was about to lose. He then pressed on with this almost identical action against the BBC. Eady J struck this out as an abuse of process. He rejected the submission that he should not do so as this would deprive the claimant of his "constitutional right" to trial by jury.

This occurs when there "is no realistic prospect of a trial yielding any tangible or legitimate advantage such as to out weigh the disadvantages for the parties in terms of expense and the wider public in terms of court resources."

> See *Schellenberg v. BBC,* [2000] E.M.L.R. 296; *Dow Jones & Co. Inc. v. Jameel,* [2005]
> EWCA Civ 75 at para. 57; *Bunt v. Tilley,* [2006] EWAC 407 at para. 78

This statement is adopted in *Bunt v. Tilley,* [2006] EWHC 407 at para. 78. See also *Schellenberg v. BBC,* [2000] E.M.L.R. 296; *Wallace v. Valentine,* [2003] E.M.L.R. 175.

F. APPLICATION OF THE CONCEPT OF ABUSE OF PROCESS TO INTERNET LIBEL ACTIONS

In *Dow Jones & Co. Inc. v. Jameel*, [2005] EWCA Civ. 75 at para. 49, the Court held that Internet publication can raise the potential problem of abuse of process.

> Where there is a worldwide publication of an allegedly defamatory article, whether in hard copy form or on the internet, difficult issues of jurisdiction may occur. Where the claim is governed by the Brussels and Lugano Conventions and the Judgments Regulation (Council Regulation 44/2001 of December 22 2000) a claim for all publications can be brought in the jurisdiction where the defendant is established or individually in each member state where publication has taken place in respect only of the publication within that member state: *Shevill v Presse Alliance* [1995] 2 AC 18. If the latter alternative is adopted, English jurisdiction in respect of the publication in England cannot be challenged on the ground that England is not the most convenient forum. Where the Conventions do not apply, a claimant can obtain permission to serve a foreign publisher out of the jurisdiction in respect of a publication in England, pursuant to CPR 6.20(8). In those circumstances the claim will be limited to the publications within the jurisdiction. Furthermore, the defendant can apply to have service set aside on the ground that there is an alternative jurisdiction "in which the case may be tried more suitably for the interests of all the parties and for the ends of justice": *The Spiliada* [1987] AC 470.

A number of Internet libel cases have been dismissed as an abuse of process.

> *Khader v. Aziz & Ors*, [2009] EWHC 2027
> *Lonzim Plc & Ors v. Sprague*, [2009] EWHC 2838
> *Noorani v. Calver*, [2009] EWHC 561 (QB)
> *P. Corrie v. Tokien*, [2009] EWHC 29
> *Williams v. MGN Limited*, [2009] EWHC 3150
> *Crossley v. Wallace*, [2008] EWHC 2846 (QB)
> *Ewing v. News International Ltd.*, [2008] EWHC 1390 (QB)
> *Bunt v. Tilley*, [2006] EWHC 407 at para. 78

In *Lonzim Plc & Ors v. Sprague*, [2009] EWHC 2838 at para. 47 (QB), the action was dismissed because there was minimal publication in the jurisdiction and there was no evidence of a substantial tort being committed within the jurisdiction. The Court held "[a]ssuming that there was minimal publication within this jurisdiction, there is no prospect of an award of damages greater than a very modest sum, and no prospect of an injunction being granted. The costs and the court resources that would be required to achieve this would be disproportionate."

G. GROUPS OF CASES

While it is difficult to insert cases into categories, as several cases were dismissed for a number of reasons, the following general groupings may be of some assistance to lawyers:

1) Dismissed for Abuse of Process for Limited Publications

Carrie v. Tolkien, [2009] EWHC 29 at para. 19 (QB)
Atlantis World Group of Companies NV & Anor v. Gruppo Editoriale L'Espresso SPA, [2008] EWHC 1323 (QB)

2) Dismissed for Abuse of Process for Little Likelihood of Success

See *Lonzim Plc & Ors v. Sprague,* [2009] EWHC 2838 at paras. 6 and 34 (QB):

> The application of Mr Sprague is not to set aside the order of the Master, but (in brief) for summary judgment under CPR r 24, on the ground that the Claimants have no real prospect of success in establishing any significant publication within this jurisdiction of the words complained of, and for the proceedings to be struck out under CPR r 3.4 as an abuse of the process of the court.
>
> . . . .
>
> If the expression of such views is to give rise to a slander action, there must be reasonable grounds for bringing that action. It is the duty of the court to bring to an end proceedings that are not serving the legitimate purpose of defamation proceedings, which is to protect the claimant's reputation. I have no hesitation in categorising this part of the claim as an abuse of the process of the court. The claim is vexatious.

3) Dismissed as Forum Shopping

See *Atlantis World Group of Companies NV & Anor v. Gruppo Editoriale L'Espresso SPA*, [2008] EWHC 1323 at para. 57 (QB):

> In my judgment the instant case does amount to an abuse of the process. I say that for two broad reasons. Firstly, the case bears all the hallmarks of forum-shopping. Notwithstanding the incorporation of Geoligale in England, this is in essence a claim against an Italian magazine with a miniscule circulation

within the jurisdiction. Furthermore the Claimants' place of business was at all material times in Rome and any damage caused by the publication of the Espresso article complained of was sustained in Italy.

4) The Cost of the Exercise as Out of Proportion with What Had Been Achieved; Disproportionate Use of Resources; "the Game Is Not Worth the Candle"[1]

The Court found in *Lonzim Plc & Ors v. Sprague*, [2009] EWHC 2838 at para. 47 (QB):

> Assuming that there was minimal publication within this jurisdiction, there is no prospect of an award of damages greater than a very modest sum, and no prospect of an injunction being granted. The costs and court resources that would be required to achieve this would be disproportionate.

5) Improper Purpose

The Court stated in *Kaschke v. Osler*, [2010] EWHC 1075 at paras. 14–15 and 25–26 (QB):

> It is suggested by Mr Dougans that there is nothing of substance to be gained from these proceedings by way of giving Ms Kaschke any greater vindication of her reputation, if such was needed, than that already obtained three years ago by the publication of her response on 26 May 2007. He submits that, in all the circumstances, the case falls within the doctrine explained by the Court of Appeal in *Jameel (Yousef) v Dow Jones & Co Inc* [2005] QB 946. It is said that there is no realistic prospect of a trial of these issues yielding any tangible or legitimate advantage, such as to outweigh the disadvantages for the parties in terms of expense, and the wider public in terms of court resources, and that "the game is not worth the candle."
>
> Following the right of reply, it appears that Ms Kaschke did not resurrect her complaint about Mr Osler's posting until 28 March 2008 (i.e. after a lapse of ten months). Although Ms Kaschke is not prepared to admit that she posted the Spiegel article, or exactly what she herself posted in relation to it on her website, the evidence of Mr Osler seems clear enough. His article

---

1   This expression can be found in a number of cases including *Schellenberg v. BBC*, [2000] EMLR 296; *Atlantis World Group of Companies NV & Anor v. Gruppo Editoriale L'Espresso SPA*, [2008] EWHC 1323 at paras. 57–58 (QB); *Kaschke v. Osler*, [2010] EWHC 1075 at paras. 14.

derived from her posting rather than from his own independent research or some other posting.

. . . .

It is necessary, therefore, to try and assess what a jury would make of the alleged injury to Ms Kaschke's reputation against the background I have described. If the jury came to the conclusion that none of the defences raised could succeed, I cannot imagine that the damages would be other than very modest. I would take the view that any such award would be out of all proportion to the time and money spent on this litigation and, in particular, to the cost of a two-week jury trial.

In the circumstances, I have come to the conclusion that this is indeed one of those unusual cases in which the doctrine of abuse of process, as discussed by the Court of Appeal in Jameel, should be applied.

See also, *Lonzim Plc & Ors v. Sprague*, [2009] EWHC 2838.

6) Not Dismissed as an Abuse of Process

In *Mardas v. New York Times and Anor*, [2008] EWHC 3135 (QB) the Court held that the action was not an abuse of process for the following reasons:

1) There was a considerable dispute over the extent of publication of hard copies and therefore the Court held at paras. at 15, 25–26, and 30–31 that it was inappropriate to make a finding of fact on incomplete evidence:

> What matters is whether there has been a real and substantial tort within the jurisdiction (or, at this stage, arguably so). *This cannot depend upon a numbers game, with the court fixing an arbitrary minimum according to the facts of the case.* In *Shevill v Presse Alliance* [1996] AC 959, it was thought that there had been a total of some 250 copies of the French newspaper published within the jurisdiction, of which only five were in Yorkshire where Ms Shevill lived and was most likely to be known. She was permitted to seek her remedies here [emphasis added].
>
> . . .
>
> I am quite satisfied that it was inappropriate for a finding of fact to be made on the scale of publication on the basis of incomplete evidence. It is a matter which should be left to trial. Furthermore, and in any event, even if the publications were confined to the defendant's figure, there was no basis for concluding that there was no real and substantial tort.
>
> The Claimant's legal advisers also take issue with the method of calculating the access to the article via the website. They argue, for example, that

another method of calculation should have been adopted which would result in a possible total of 313 hits on the article within the United Kingdom. This would have involved calculating the percentage of visitors to the website from the United Kingdom accessing the music section as a fraction of the percentage of all visitors who accessed that section. I cannot possibly, at this stage, conclude that that is the right way or the only way of making the necessary calculation. What is apparent, however, is that this cannot be determined until trial, if necessary with the assistance of expert evidence.

. . .

The Claimant does not accept, either, that the estimate of 27 hits on the article via the *International Herald Tribune* website can be relied upon. Evidence from Mr Schattenberg was served on his advisers very shortly before the hearing, so that there was no opportunity to investigate or deal with the material in time. It is again hard to resist the submission that the matter cannot properly be resolved at least until disclosure has taken place.

The *International Herald Tribune* argues that ". . . there is no necessity to put the Defendants to these costs when the simple answer appears to be that a few dozen people have accessed the article on the IHT website to this date." A few dozen is enough to found a cause of action here, although the damages would be likely to be modest.

2) There is an irrebuttable presumption in English law that the publication of a defamatory article causes damage to the reputation of the person defamed (at para. 27). See para. 12:

> It was held in the *Jameel* case, cited above, that there was nothing incompatible in this presumption with the values enshrined in Article 10 of the European Convention on Human Rights and Fundamental Freedoms. Accordingly, it will only be in rare cases that it is appropriate to strike out an action as an abuse on the ground that the claimant"s reputation has suffered only minimal damage and/or that there has been no real and substantial tort within the jurisdiction: see e.g. the remarks of Sedley LJ in *Steinberg v Pritchard Englefield* [2005] EWCA Civ 288.

3) It is rarely appropriate to strike out an action as abuse on the grounds that the claimant's reputation has suffered only minimal damage and/or that there was no real, substantial tort within the jurisdiction (see para. 40).

See the remarks of Sedley L.J. in *Steinberg v. Pritchard Engelfied*, [2005] EWCA Civ 288

4) As the Court found in *Mardas v. New York Times and Anor*, [2008] EWHC 3135 (Q.B.) at para. 13:

It is necessary to remember that both generally and in its application to specific cases the law of defamation is concerned to strike a balance between freedom of information, on the one hand, and the protection of the honour and reputations of individual citizens on the other hand. The right to protect reputation is expressly recognised in Article 10(2). Furthermore, it is increasingly being recognised in the Strasbourg jurisprudence that the right to protect one's honour and reputation is to be treated as falling within the protection of Article 8: see e.g. *Radio France v France* (2005), 40 EHRR 29 and *Pfeifer v Austria*, (App. No. 12556/03), 15 November 2007, at paras. 35 and 38. It is thus obvious that care must be taken on applications of this kind not to deprive a litigant too readily of his Article 6 right of unimpeded access to the courts in pursuit of his remedies.

5) The articles complained of in the case remained on the defendants' websites. See paras. 16–17:

The article complained of in the present case has remained on the Defendants' respective websites to this very day. That fact naturally gives rise at least to a possible inference that there has been a continuing, albeit modest, readership. My attention was drawn in this context to the remarks of Lord Phillips MR (as he then was) in *Loutchansky v Times Newspapers Ltd*, [2002] QB 783, 817D at [72]:

"... If the defendants were exposed to liability ... they had only themselves to blame for persisting in retaining the offending articles on their website without qualifying these in any way."

It is also pertinent to have in mind the remarks of Callinan J in the High Court of Australia in *Gutnick v Dow Jones*, [2002] HCA 56 at [181] and [192] to the following effect:

"A publisher, particularly one carrying on the business of publishing, does not act to put matter on the Internet in order for it to reach a small target. It is its ubiquity which is one of the main attractions to users of it. And any person who gains access to the Internet does so by taking an initiative to gain access to it in a manner analogous to the purchase or other acquisition of a newspaper, in order to read it."

...

"If a publisher publishes in a multiplicity of jurisdictions it should understand, and must accept, that it runs the risk of liability in those jurisdictions in which the publication is not lawful and inflicts damage."

This approach has also been adopted in a number of the decisions in this jurisdiction and, in particular, by the Court of Appeal in *King v Lewis*, [2005] EMLR 45 at [29].

6) The attitude of the defendant is relevant. In this case the defendant had pleaded justification and the plaintiff pleaded that they ought to have the opportunity to be able to respond. See para. 18:

> In judging in any given case whether there has been a real and substantial tort, in respect of which a particular claimant should be allowed to seek his remedies by way of vindication, it may sometimes be relevant to consider the attitude taken by the relevant defendant. In the present case, Mr Browne places reliance upon the fact that in the *International Herald Tribune* action a defence has been entered which seeks to justify the proposition that the Claimant is a "charlatan." He argues that it is singularly inappropriate to strike out an action once a plea of that kind has been put on the record. The Claimant should have a chance to meet it. It is a relevant consideration in determining whether there is any purpose to be served in his pursuing vindication (a point addressed by the Court of Appeal in the *Jameel* case).

> See also *Mardas v. New York Times and Anor*, [2008] EWHC 3135 at para. 26 (QB).

7) The costs of the proceedings and/or the use of judicial resources did not preclude a trial. The Court responded to the Master's concern about the costs involved in the litigation. See paras. 33–35 (QB):

> More generally, I can also understand the Master's dismay at the cost and effort likely to be involved in a full scale trial of the issues in this case. As he pointed out, the events took place a long time ago and with the passage of time there may be difficulties in obtaining the evidence that would be required for a definitive outcome. The fact remains, however, that allegations of charlatanism and of lying cannot be dismissed as trivial. Moreover, even if defamatory allegations do relate to events of long ago, that cannot be a ground in itself for refusing access to justice: see e.g. *Polanski v Condé Nast Publications Ltd.* [2005] 1 WLR 637, HL. The author clearly thought the allegations to be of topical interest to the readers.

> As to the Master's other concerns, Mr Browne invited my attention to the comments of Thomas LJ in *Aldi Stores Ltd v WSB Group Plc* [2007] EWCA Civ 1260 at [24]:

> > I do not see how the mere fact that this action may require a trial and hence take up judicial time (which could have been saved if Aldi had

exercised its right to bring an action in a different way) can make the action impermissible. If an action can be properly brought, it is the duty of the state to provide the necessary resources; the litigant cannot be denied the right to bring a claim (for which he in any event pays under the system which operates in England and Wales) on the basis that he could have acted differently and so made more efficient use of the court's resources . . . . The problems which have arisen in this case should have been dealt with through case management.

It is plainly desirable that some sensible accommodation should be reached, so as to avoid a time-consuming and expensive trial, but that is in the hands of the parties. I am satisfied that the circumstances here cannot be characterised as an abuse of process: nor can it be said that it is appropriate to come to a conclusion on the merits of the litigation, at this early stage, on the basis that a jury would be perverse to resolve the contested issues of fact in the Claimant's favour or to find that he has been defamed.

8) It is irrelevant as a matter of English law that other persons have made similar allegations about the plaintiff. See para. 36:

Reliance is placed by the author, in recently introduced evidence, upon the fact that others have made similar allegations in the past in, for example, "authoritative" biographies and autobiographies. While I can understand his frustration, if this is so, it is irrelevant as a matter of English law, since it would not be admissible either on liability or in mitigation of damages: *Associated Newspapers Ltd v Dingle*, [1964] AC 371, 395 (Lord Radcliffe), 405–6 (Lord Cohen), 410 (Lord Denning), 416–7 (Lord Morris).

9) The plaintiff in this case cannot be characterized as forum shopping. See para. 38:

There can be little doubt that if Mr Mardas succeeds in establishing that he has been libelled here, and a real and substantial tort thus committed within the jurisdiction, he is entitled to bring proceedings: see e.g. *Berezovsky v Michaels*, [2000] 1 WLR 1004 and *Shevill v Presse Alliance*, cited above. Thus, although it is fashionable to rail against "libel tourism," there is no reason in law why the courts of England and Wales should decline jurisdiction. Although the Claimant is now resident in Greece (within the European Union), he is well known in this jurisdiction and lived here, I understand, from 1963 to 1996. Also, he has two children who live here and have British nationality. There is no artificiality about seeking to protect his reputation within this country, as he has done in other litigation (apparently relating to different allegations) in the past. I, like Sir Charles Gray, do not believe that this can be characterised as a case of forum shopping.

10) It does not matter that the plaintiff has not sued in the US or France over allegations where there is wider publication. See para. 39:

> The Defendant's advisers state, accurately, that he has not sued either in the United States or in France over these allegations, where there was wider circulation, but that is beside the point. English law permits him to claim whatever is appropriate compensation and vindication in respect of the smaller local publication here. The approach has long been to recognise that where a tort has been committed the appropriate forum will usually be that of the jurisdiction where it took place. What he cannot do is to claim damages here in respect of (say) publications in the United States.

See also *Baturina v. Times Newspapers Ltd.*, [2010] EWHC 696 (QB); *Polanski v. Conde Nast*, [2005] UKHL 10

The Court in *Sir Stelios Haji-Ioannou v. Mark Dixon Regus Group Plc & Anor*, [2009] EWHC 178 (QB), CIW refused to stay an action permanently for abuse of process at paras. 30–31, 34, and 36, but agreed to a limited stay of proceedings to facilitate settlement negotiations at paras. 43–44.

PART III: Remedies

CHAPTER 12: Damages in Cyberlibel

A. GENERAL PRINCIPLES

General damages in libel are designed to compensate plaintiffs for the damage to their reputations and to vindicate their good names. They include damages for the actual monetary consequences of the attitude adopted by other persons toward the plaintiff as a result of the defamatory publication, as well as damages for distress, hurt, and humiliation caused to the plaintiff.

Hill v. Church of Scientology of Toronto, [1995] 2 S.C.R. 1130 at 1205

Damages for libel are "at large" in the sense that there is a presumption of damage on proof of publication and there is no cap on general damages as for other personal injury claims.

Leenen v. CBC (2000), 48 O.R. (3d) 656 at para. 205 (S.C.J.), aff'd (2001), 54 O.R. (3d) 612 (C.A.)
Munro v. Toronto Sun Publishing Corp. (1982), 21 C.C.L.T. 261 at 296 (Ont. H.C.)

The Supreme Court of Canada in *Hill v. Church of Scientology of Toronto* stated that each libel case is unique, that there is no formula for determining damages, and that reliance on previous cases is of limited value.

Hill v. Church of Scientology of Toronto, [1995] 2 S.C.R. 1130, 126 D.L.R. (4th) 129

See Chapter 30 on damages in Roger D. McConchie and David A. Potts, *Canadian Libel and Slander Actions* (Toronto: Irwin Law, 2004) for a more detailed examination of the subject of damages in libel.

B. FACTORS TO BE CONSIDERED IN AWARDING GENERAL DAMAGES

When awarding general damages, a list of the factors taken into account by the courts were enumerated in *Leenen v. Canadian Broadcasting Corp.* (2000), 48 O.R. (3d) 656 at para. 205 (S.C.J.), aff'd (2001), 54 O.R. (3d) 612 (C.A.), leave to appeal to S.C.C. refused, [2001] S.C.C.A. No. 432, Cunningham J., cited in Roger D. McConchie and David A. Potts, *Canadian Libel and Slander Actions* (Toronto: Irwin Law, 2004) at pages 850–51:

a) the seriousness of the defamatory statement;
b) the identity of the accuser;
c) the breadth of distribution of the publication of the libel;
d) republication of the libel;
e) the failure to give the audience both sides of the picture and not presenting a balanced review;
f) the desire to increase one's professional reputation or to increase ratings of a particular program;
g) the conduct of the defendant and defendant's counsel through to the end of trial;
h) the absence or refusal of any retraction or apology; and
i) the failure to establish a plea of justification.

The phrase "at large" was discussed by Lord Hailsham in *Cassell & Co. v. Broome*, [1972] 1 All E.R. 801 at 824 (H.L.), cited in Roger D. McConchie and David A. Potts, *Canadian Libel and Slander Actions* (Toronto: Irwin Law, 2004) at page 850:

> This is why it is not necessarily fair to compare awards of damages in this field with damages for personal injuries. Quite obviously, the award must include factors for injury to the feelings, the anxiety and uncertainty undergone in the litigation, the absence of apology, or the reaffirmation of the truth of the matters complained of, or the malice of the defendant. The bad conduct of the plaintiff himself may also enter into the matter, where he has provoked the libel, or where perhaps he has libelled the defendant in reply. What is awarded is thus a figure which cannot be arrived at by any purely objective computation. This is what is meant when the damages in defamation are described as being "at large." In a sense, too, these damages are of their nature punitive or exemplary in the loose sense in which the terms were used before 1964, because they inflict an added burden on the defendant proportionate to his conduct, just as they can be reduced if the defendant has behaved

well — as for instance by a handsome apology — or the plaintiff badly, as for instance by provoking the defendant, or defaming him in return. In all such cases it must be appropriate to say with Lord Esher MR in *Praed v. Graham*:

> . . . in actions of libel . . . the jury in assessing damages are entitled to look at the whole conduct of the defendant [I would personally add "and of the plaintiff"] from the time the libel was published down to the time they give their verdict. They may consider what his conduct has been before action, after action, and in court during the trial.

His Lordship discussed the concept further at page 826:

> The expression "at large" should be used in general to cover all cases where awards of damages may include elements for loss of reputation, injured feelings, bad or good conduct by either party, or punishment, and where in consequence no precise limit can be set in extent. It would be convenient if, as the appellants' counsel did at the hearing, it could be extended to include damages for pain and suffering or loss of amenity. Lord Devlin uses the term in this sense in *Rookes v. Barnard*, when he defines the phrase as meaning all cases where "the award is not limited to the pecuniary loss that can be specifically proved." But I suspect that he was there guilty of a neologism. If I am wrong, it is a convenient use and should be repeated.

Compensatory damages are not confined in their scope to pecuniary losses.

> [Defamation] actions involve a money award which may put the plaintiff in a purely financial sense in a much stronger position than he was before the wrong. Not merely can he recover the estimated sum of his past and future losses, but, in case the libel, driven underground, emerges from its lurking place at some future date, he must be able to point to a sum awarded by a jury sufficient to convince a bystander of the baselessness of the charge.

Cassell & Co. v. Broome, [1972] 1 All E.R. 801 at 824 (H.L.); cited with approval in
  Vogel v. C.B.C. (1982), 21 C.C.L.T. 105 at 206 (B.C.S.C.)

The jury should also take into account "the sad truth that no apology, retraction or withdrawal can ever be guaranteed completely to undo the harm it has done or the hurt it has caused."

Ley v. Hamilton (1935), 153 L.T. 384 at 386 (H.L.); quoted by Lord Diplock in *Broome
  v. Cassell & Co.*, [1972] A.C. 1027 at 1125 (H.C.)

Lord Justice Greene in *Rook v. Fairrie.* [1941] 1 K.B. 507 at 515, 516 (C.A.) said as follows: ". . . in a libel action the damages awarded are, for the most part and often entirely, without any real connection with any pecuniary loss at all."

The plaintiff must be able to point to a sum awarded by a jury as sufficient to convince a bystander of the baselessness of the charge.

See *Cassell & Co. v. Broome*, [1972] 1 All E.R. 801 at 824 (H.L.), Lord Hailsham L.C.
Vogel v. C.B.C. (1982), 21 C.C.L.T. 105 at 206 (B.C.S.C.)

C. AGGRAVATED DAMAGES

Aggravated damages would be ordered in circumstances where the conduct of the defendant or his counsel is particularly high-handed, thereby increasing the plaintiff's humiliation or anxiety arising from the defamatory statement.

Hill v. Church of Scientology of Toronto, [1995] 2 S.C.R. 1130

In order for aggravated damages to be awarded in Canada there must be a finding that the defendant was motivated by actual malice, which increased the injury to the plaintiff either by spreading the damage to the plaintiff's reputation or by increasing the mental distress and humiliation of the plaintiff. "Malice may be established by extrinsic evidence that derived from the libel statement itself and the circumstances of the publication or surrounding circumstances which demonstrate that the defendant was motivated by an unjustifiable intention to injure the plaintiff."

Hill v. Church of Scientology of Toronto, [1995] 2 S.C.R. 1130 at para. 190
See c. 30 on damages in Roger D. McConchie & David A. Potts, *Canadian Libel and Slander Actions* (Toronto: Irwin Law, 2004)

D. PUNITIVE DAMAGES

Punitive damages are not at large.

Whiten v. Pilot Insurance Co. (2002), 209 D.L.R. (4th) 257 at para. 133 (S.C.C.)

At common law, punitive damages are awarded only in rare and exceptional cases. Specifically, in situations where the defendant's conduct is so malicious, oppressive, and high-handed that it offends the court's sense of decency.

Hill v. Church of Scientology of Toronto, [1995] 2 S.C.R. 1130 at 1208, Cory J.:

Punitive damages bear no relation to what the plaintiff should receive by way of compensation. Their aim is not to compensate the plaintiff, but rather to punish the defendant. It is the means by which the jury or judge expresses outrage at the egregious conduct of the defendant. They are of the nature of a fine, which is meant to act as a deterrent to the defendant and to others from acting in this manner.

As stated in *Hill v. Church of Scientology of Toronto,* [1995] 2 S.C.R. 1130 at paras. 197–98, punitive damages are only to be awarded in those circumstances:

> . . . where the combined award of general and aggravated damages would be insufficient to achieve the goal of punishment and deterrence . . . . Unlike compensatory damages, punitive damages are not at large. Consequently, courts have a much greater scope and discretion on appeal. The appellate review should be based upon the court's estimation as to whether punitive damages serve a rational purpose. In other words, was the misconduct of the plaintiff so outrageous that punitive damages were rationally required to act as deterrence.

The subject of punitive damages was exhaustively reviewed by the Supreme Court of Canada in *Whiten v. Pilot Insurance Co.* (2002), 209 D.L.R. (4th) 257 (S.C.C.), where the Court upheld a jury award of $1,000,000 in punitive damages against an insurance company for its bad faith in contesting coverage on a fire insurance policy, reversing the Ontario Court of Appeal which had reduced the punitive damages award to $100,000.

> See c. 30 on damages in Roger D. McConchie and David A. Potts, *Canadian Libel and Slander Actions* (Toronto: Irwin Law, 2004) and in particular pp. 851–55.

E. PUNITIVE DAMAGES AWARDED IN CYBERLIBEL CASES

A very thorough discussion of punitive damages and their application to a cyberlibel case is found in *Barrick Gold Corp v. Lopehandia,* 2005 CanLII 12938 at paras. 54–65 (ON C.A.):

> The motions judge dismissed Barrick's claim for punitive damages on several grounds. Relying on the decision of the Supreme Court of Canada in *McElroy v. Cowper-Smith,* 1967 CanLII 70 (S.C.C.), [1967] S.C.R. 425, she decided that "the emotional and unreasoned tenor of [Mr. Lopehandia's] messages" was such that "no reasonable business person or investor would take him seriously," thus mitigating the claim for punitive damages. In addition, she held that there was no evidence of real vulnerability on the part of Barrick, which she viewed as "the powerful party here," and that this was not a case

of Mr. Lopehandia abusing power. Finally, the motions judge concluded that her compensatory award, including costs, would be a sufficient deterrent to prevent the repetition of his conduct.

The key principles regarding punitive damages, of which the motions judge was aware, are outlined below. As discussed below, however, she erred in dismissing the claim in my view.

Appellate courts have greater scope and discretion in reviewing awards for punitive damages than is the case for awards of general or compensatory damages. Appellate review is based upon the court's estimation as to whether the punitive damages serve a rational purpose. See *Hill v. Church of Scientology of Toronto, supra,* at 1208–9; *Whiten v. Pilot Insurance Co.* 2002 SCC 18 (CanLII), (2002), 209 D.L.R. (4th) 257 at 288–89 (S.C.C.).

Justice Cory described punitive damages in the following fashion in *Hill* at 1208:

> Punitive damages may be awarded in situations where the defendant's misconduct is so malicious, oppressive and high-handed that it offends the court's sense of decency. Punitive damages bear no relation to what the plaintiff should receive by way of compensation. Their aim is not to compensate the plaintiff, but rather to punish the defendant. It is the means by which the jury or judge expresses its outrage at the egregious conduct of the defendant. They are in the nature of a fine which is meant to act as a deterrent to the defendant and to others from acting in this manner. It is important to emphasize that punitive damages should only be awarded in those circumstances where the combined award of general and aggravated damages would be insufficient to achieve the goal of punishment and deterrence.

In *Whiten,* at 288–89, Binnie J. reviewed comparative principles regarding punitive damages in various common law jurisdictions, and outlined a number of factors that he found to be "consistent with Canadian practice and precedent." The following observation is particularly apt to the present circumstances:

> . . . [T]here is a substantial consensus that coincides with Lord Pratt C.J.'s view in 1763 that the general objectives of punitive damages are punishment (in the sense of retribution), deterrence of the wrongdoer and others, and denunciation (or, as Cory J. put it in *Hill, supra,* at para. 196, they are "the means by which the jury or judge expresses its outrage at the egregious conduct"). . . .
>
> . . . [A]ll jurisdictions seek to promote rationality. In directing itself to the punitive damages, the court should relate the facts of the particular case

to the underlying purposes of punitive damages and ask itself how, in particular, an award would further one or other of the objectives of the law, and what is the lowest award that would serve the purpose, i.e., because any higher award would be irrational. . . .

. . . [T]he governing rule for quantum is *proportionality*. The overall award, that is to say compensatory damages plus punitive damages plus any other punishment related to the same misconduct, should be rationally related to the objectives for which the punitive damages are awarded (retribution, deterrence and denunciation). Thus, there is broad support for the "if, but only if" test formulated, as mentioned, in *Rookes, supra,* and affirmed here in *Hill, supra* [emphasis in original].

With these principles in mind, I am satisfied that the motions judge erred in failing make an award of punitive damages for the reasons that follow. First, her reliance on the decision of the Supreme Court of Canada in *McElroy v. Cowper-Smith* was misplaced in the circumstances, and was influenced again by her flawed conclusion that the repeated libels of Mr. Lopehandia would not be taken seriously by readers. *McElroy* involved a single defamatory letter circulated to three clergymen and several religious organizations. The defendant was known to be temporarily unstable and given to making unreasoned and extravagant statements about the plaintiffs (who were a lawyer and an insurance executive). Although the majority of the Court recognized the serious damage that can be done to the reputation of a professional person from allegations of misconduct and dishonesty, and that punitive damages may be warranted in some such circumstances, they concluded that reasonable business people — the plaintiffs' clientele — would not likely be affected in their dealings with the plaintiffs "by statements coming from the source which they did in this case." Since the libel had not been published to business people, but only to clergymen and religious organizations who were very familiar with both the plaintiffs and defendant, punitive damages were not warranted in the circumstances.

Such is not the case here. Mr. Lopehandia is not known to the unlimited numbers of persons who may have viewed his avalanche of defamatory postings on the Internet. He holds himself out to be a person of substance, knowledgeable in matters relating to the mining industry in Chile, where Barrick's Pascua Lama Project is located, and a representative of many Chilean mining families and other affected persons worldwide. On the evidence referred to earlier, it is apparent that various individuals and organizations, and at least one regulatory agency, were taking his libelous campaign seriously. In my view, *McElroy* does not assist on the question of punitive damages in this case.

Secondly, while vulnerability is a factor to be considered by the court in assessing punitive damages — see *Whiten* at pages 300–1 — the motions judge misread that factor in the context of this case, in my respectful opinion. Barrick is not "the powerful party" in the context of the Internet. The impact of the Internet is to neutralize whatever "power" Barrick may have had, in terms of a communication battle with Mr. Lopehandia. In reality it is Barrick that is vulnerable to publications of this nature, and Mr. Lopehandia who is abusing his power. The Internet is one of the most powerful tools of communications ever invented and, as the Collins text cited at the outset of these reasons indicates, it is "potentially a medium of virtually limitless international defamation."

Thirdly, the motions judge's conclusion that her compensatory award would operate as a deterrent to Mr. Lopehandia's repeated publications is inconsistent with her own observation that "he has not done so." She found that, in spite of her judgment, "Mr. Lopehandia will continue to make defamatory statements." With respect, an award of general damages in the amount of $15,000 is insufficient to fulfill the dual role of compensation plus punishment and deterrence in the circumstances of this case.

Finally, punitive damages are simply required in a case such as this, in my view. Mr. Lopehandia's conduct is malicious and high handed. It is unremitting and tenacious. It involves defamatory publications that are vicious, spiteful, wide-ranging in substance, and world-wide in scope. They involve the very type of misconduct that — in the words of Cory J. in *Hill* at 1208 — is "so malicious, oppressive and high-handed that it offends the court's sense of decency," calling for an award of punitive damages as a "means by which the jury or judge expresses its outrage at the egregious conduct of the defendant." While it is always important to balance freedom of expression and the interests of individuals and corporations in preserving their reputations, and while it is important not to inhibit the free exchange of information and ideas on the Internet by damage awards that are overly stifling, defendants such as Mr. Lopehandia must know that courts will not countenance the use of the Internet (or any other medium) for purposes of a defamatory campaign of the type engaged in here.

I would therefore set aside the decision of the motions judge not to award punitive damages in favour of the appellant.

Punitive damages were awarded in the following cyberlibel cases:

Hunter Dickinson Inc. v. Butler, 2010 BCSC 939
National Bank of Canada v. Weir 2010 QCCS 402 at paras. 57–58
Fuda v. Conn, 2009 CanLII 1140 (ON S.C.)

Sanchez-Pontigon v. Manalansan-Lord, 2009 CanLII 28216 (ON S.C.)

Griffin v. Sullivan, 2008 BCSC 827

Lane v. Board of School Trustees of School District 68 (Nanaimo-Ladysmith), 2006
    BCSC 129

Loh v. Yang, 2006 BCSC 1131

Newman et al. v. Halstead et al., 2006 BCSC 65

WeGo Kayaking Ltd. et al. v. Sewid et al., 2006 BCSC 334

Ager v. Canjex Publishing d.b.a. Canada Stockwatch, 2005 BCCA 467

Vaquero Energy v. Weir, 2004 ABQB 68

Ager v. Canjex Publishing Ltd., 2003 BCSC 891

Reichmann v. Berlin, [2002] O.J. No. 2732

Southam Inc. v. Chelekis, 2000 BCCA 112

Southam Inc. v. Chelekis, 1998 CanLII 5436 (BC S.C.)

F. FACTORS CONSIDERED BY THE COURTS IN AWARDING DAMAGES IN CYBERLIBEL ACTIONS

1) General Considerations Concerning Internet Defamation

Barrick Gold Corp. v. Lopehandia, 2004 CanLII 12938, 71 O.R. (3d) 416 at paras. 28–34 (C.A.):

> Is there something about defamation on the Internet—"cyber libel," as it is sometimes called—that distinguishes it, for purposes of damages, from defamation in another medium? My response to that question is "Yes."
>
> The standard factors to consider in determining damages for defamation are summarized by Cory J. in *Hill* at p. 1203. They include the plaintiff's position and standing, the nature and seriousness of the defamatory statements, the mode and extent of publication, the absence or refusal of any retraction or apology, the whole conduct and motive of the defendant from publication through judgment, and any evidence of aggravating or mitigating circumstances.
>
> In the Internet context, these factors must be examined in the light of what one judge has characterized as the "ubiquity, universality and utility" of that medium. In *Dow Jones & Company Inc. v. Gutnick* [2002] HCA 56 (10 December 2002), that same judge—Kirby J., of the High Court of Australia—portrayed the Internet in these terms, at para. 80:
>
>> The Internet is essentially a decentralized, self-maintained telecommunications network. It is made up of inter-linking small networks from all parts of the world. *It is ubiquitous, borderless, global and ambient in its nature. Hence the term "cyberspace." This is a word*

that recognizes that the interrelationships created by the Internet exist outside conventional geographic boundaries and comprise a single interconnected body of data, potentially amounting to a single body of knowledge. The Internet is accessible in virtually all places on Earth where access can be obtained either by wire connection or by wireless (including satellite) links. *Effectively, the only constraint on access to the Internet is possession of the means of securing connection to a telecommunications system and possession of the basic hardware* [emphasis added]. [Footnotes omitted.]

Thus, of the criteria mentioned above, the mode and extent of publication is particularly relevant in the Internet context, and must be considered carefully. Communication via the Internet is instantaneous, seamless, inter-active, blunt, borderless and far-reaching. It is also impersonal, and the anonymous nature of such communications may itself create a greater risk that the defamatory remarks are believed: see *Vaquero Energy Ltd. v. Weir,* [2004] A.J. No. 84 (Alta. Q.B.) at para. 17.

These characteristics create challenges in the libel context. Traditional approaches attuned to "the real world" may not respond adequately to the realities of the Internet world. How does the law protect reputation without unduly overriding such free wheeling public discourse? Lyrissa Barnett Lidsky discusses this conundrum in her article, "Silencing John Doe: Defamation and Discourse in Cyberspace" (2000) 49 Duke L.J. 855 at pp. 862–865:

Internet communications lack this formal distance. Because communication can occur almost instantaneously, participants in online discussions place a premium on speed. Indeed, in many fora, speed takes precedence over all other values, including not just accuracy but even grammar, spelling, and punctuation. Hyperbole and exaggeration are common, and "venting" is at least as common as careful and considered argumentation. The fact that many Internet speakers employ online pseudonyms tends to heighten this sense that "anything goes," and some commentators have likened cyberspace to a frontier society free from the conventions and constraints that limit discourse in the real world. While this view is undoubtedly overstated, certainly the immediacy and informality of Internet communications may be central to its widespread appeal.

Although Internet communications may have the ephemeral qualities of gossip with regard to accuracy, they are communicated through a medium more pervasive than print, and for this reason they have tremendous power to harm reputation. Once a message enters cyber-space, millions of people worldwide can gain access to it. Even if the message is posted in a discussion forum frequented by only a handful of people, any one of them can republish the message by printing it or, as is more likely, by forwarding it instantly to a different discussion forum. And if the message is sufficiently provocative, it may be repub-lished again and again. *The extraordinary capacity of the Internet to replicate almost endlessly any defamatory message lends credence to the notion that "the truth rarely catches up with a lie."* The problem for libel law, then, is how to protect reputation without squelching the poten-tial of the Internet as a medium of public discourse [emphasis added].

These characteristics differentiate the publication of defamatory material on the Internet from publication in the more traditional forms of media, in my opinion.

It is true that in the modern era defamatory material may be communicat-ed broadly and rapidly via other media as well. The international distribution of newspapers, syndicated wire services, facsimile transmissions, and radio and satellite television broadcasting are but some examples. Nevertheless, In-ternet defamation is distinguished from its less pervasive cousins, in terms of its potential to damage the reputation of individuals and corporations, by the features described above, especially its interactive nature, its potential for be-ing taken at face value, and its absolute and immediate worldwide ubiquity and accessibility. The mode and extent of publication is therefore a particularly significant consideration in assessing damages in Internet defamation cases.

The following decisions relied upon and referred to *Barrick Gold Corp. v. Lopehandia*, 2004 CanLII 12938 (ON C.A.).

> *Hunter Dickinson Inc. v. Butler*, 2010 BCSC 939 at para. 45
> *Henderson v. Pearlman*, 2009 CanLII 43641 (ON S.C)
> *Sanchez-Pontigon v. Manalenson-Lord*, 2009 CanLII 1128216 at paras. 54–55
> *Inform Cycle Ltd. v. Draper*, 2008 ABQB 309 CanLII at para. 30
> *Disney Enterprises Inc. v. Click Enterprises Inc.*, 2006 CanLII 10213 at para. 1 (ON S.C.)
> *Second Cup Ltd. v. Eftoda*, 2006 CanLII 26174 (ON S.C.) at para. 43
> *Canada (Human Rights Commission) v. Winnicki*, 2005 FC 1493, [2006] 3 F.C.R. 446
> *Ross v. Holley*, [2004] O.J. No. 4643 at paras. 7, 8, and 11

2) The Choice of the Internet as a Medium for Publication of Defamatory Material

The choice of the Internet as the medium for publication of defamatory ma-terial may be an important factor in determining the extent of compensatory damages. In *Barrick Gold Corp. v. Lopehandia*, 2004 CanLII 12938 (ON C.A.), the Court stated at para. 34:

> Internet defamation is distinguished from its less pervasive cousins in terms of its potential to damages the reputation of individuals and corporations by . . . its interactive nature, its potential for being taken at face value and its absolute and immediate worldwide ubiquity and accessibility.

The Internet has greater potential to damage the reputation of individuals and corporations as a result of these features than do its less pervasive cousins.

See also *Vaquero Energy Ltd. v. Weir*, [2004] A.J. No. 84 at para. 17
Sanchez-Pontigon v. Manalansan-Lord, 2009 CanLII 28216 at para. 56 (ON S.C.)

3) Language Use and Impact

Barrick Gold Corp. v. Lopehandia, 2004 CanLII 12938 at paras. 37–43 (ON C.A.):

> The motions judge's conclusion that a reasonable reader was unlikely to take what Mr. Lopehandia said seriously, because of its emotional and intemperate nature and because of his use of capitals and pronunciation, lies at the heart of her finding that the defamatory messages did not cause any serious damage to Barrick's business reputation. In my view it is a finding of fact, or an inference drawn from the facts, that is not supported by the evidence.
>
> The notion that Mr. Lopehandia's Internet dialogue style — a style that may not be taken seriously in a traditional medium such as a newspaper — may undermine the credibility of his message has some appeal to those of us who are accustomed to the traditional media. However, as I have noted, the Internet is not a traditional medium of communication. Its nature and manner of presentation are evolving, and there is nothing in the record to indicate that people did not take Mr. Lopehandia's postings seriously. In fact, the uncontradicted evidence is to the contrary.
>
> For instance, several individuals took the messages seriously enough to contact Barrick by e-mail themselves. On October 25, 2001, Monique Lafleche of The Mining Association of Canada forwarded a Lopehandia message to alert Barrick to the situation. On February 18, 2002, an individual named Jim Versa referred Barrick to two websites where postings could be found. One of these websites, www.goldhaven.com, contained a defamatory posting by Mr. Lopehandia and a response posting from *another individual* referring Mr. Lopehandia to a different website where he could "relate his experience with the crooks at Medinah [Minerals]." Barrick received a number

of communications from John Hartley, one of its shareholders, stating that as a shareholder he was extremely upset that Barrick had not taken action against Mr. Lopehandia . . . .

There is evidence as well that the Toronto Stock Exchange contacted Barrick during 2002 to enquire about Mr. Lopehandia's defamatory statements. An inquiry of that nature from a regulatory agency governing a public company is not to be taken lightly.

In addition to the specific communications referred to, the evidence of Mr. Garver, the Executive Vice-President and General Counsel of the appellant, is that "Barrick continues to receive complaints and inquiries from concerned shareholders, analysts and other members of the public as a direct result of the Lopehandia defamatory postings."

Finally, the record shows that many users of the message boards and bulletin boards have responded to and replied to Mr. Lopehandia's messages. Some invited and encouraged him to go to other websites with his message, thus expanding the scope of the campaign of libel against Barrick, and wishing him well: "may you find your mark," said one of them.

These various communications demonstrate that individuals with a variety of interests in Barrick, and one major regulatory agency, were genuinely concerned about what Mr. Lopehandia had to say. There was no evidence to the contrary. In those circumstances, I find the motions judge's conclusion that people were unlikely to take Mr. Lopehandia's messages seriously, to be contrary to the evidence.

A reasonable person would likely have taken the statements seriously because they were made in a book published on the Internet. See *Sanchez-Pontigon v. Manalansan-Lord*, 2009 CanLII 28216 at para. 50 (ON S.C.).

4) The Extent of Publication of Defamatory Statements on the Internet Is Considered to be a Factor That Aggravates Damages

The extent of publication is a particularly significant consideration in assessing damages in Internet defamation cases.

Ross v. Holley, [2004] O.J. No. 4643 at para. 11

The countervailing feature is the mode and extent of publication of the defamatory statements by the defendant in the case at bar. Cyber-libel takes a number of forms. I would not attempt to catalogue them here, but suffice it to say that there is a palpable difference between a posting on a popular website which may experience millions of "hits" on an ongoing basis and thus give rise to the existence of millions of publishees, and the sending of an e-mail to all of the publisher's acquaintances, even with the exhortation to pass the e-mail on to others as was the case here. Clearly, the use of e-mail is far more powerful than the sending out of a multiple of hard copy letters defaming the plaintiff, but on the other hand, the e-mail medium is far less powerful than a posting on a website that has, as its initial audience, a substantially wider reach and therefore an exponentially greater potential for re-dissemination.

Sanchez-Pontigon v. Manalansan-Lord, 2009 CanLII 28216 (ON S.C.) at para. 53

Inform Cycle v. Draper, 2008 ABQB 369 at para. 32

Barrick Gold v. Lopehandia, 2004 CanLII 12938 (ON C.A.), 71 O.R. (3d) 416 at para. 30

Vaquero Energy Ltd. v. Weir, [2004] A.J. No. 84 (Q.B.)

Reichmann v. Berlin, [2002] O.J. No. 2732

5) No Retraction or Apology Given

Barrick Gold v. Lopehandia, 2004 CanLII 12938 at paras. 49–51 (ON C.A.):

> ... when considering the question of general or compensatory damages, the motions judge did not take into account Mr. Lopehandia's refusal to retract or apologize. She correctly recognized that, while corporations are entitled, without proof of damage, to compensatory damages representing the amount necessary to vindicate the company's business reputation, they cannot receive compensation for injured feelings — and therefore are not entitled to aggravated damages. She also held, properly, that a corporation is entitled to recover more than nominal damages but that compensatory damages may be lower for a corporation than damages received by an individual (who is entitled to receive compensation both for injury to reputation and for injury to feelings): *Walker v. CFTO, supra*, at 113–114. However, there is a caveat to the latter principle. It is to be found in the following passage from Carter-Ruck on *Libel and Slander, supra* at p. 197 (quoted with approval from the 3d ed. by Robins J.A. in *Walker, supra* at 113–114):
>
>> Limited companies, and other corporations, may also be awarded general damages for libel or slander, without adducing evidence of specific loss. However, it is submitted that in practice, in the absence of proof of special damage, or at least of a general loss of business, a limited company is unlikely to be entitled to a really substantial award of damages. As was made clear by Lord Reid in *Lewes v. Daily Telegraph Ltd.*, 'A company cannot be injured in its feelings; it can only be injured in its pocket. Its reputation can be injured by a libel

but that injury must sound in money.' . . . *That there is an entitlement to general damages which are more than nominal damages is certain, but the amount likely to be awarded to a corporation may be small in commercial terms, <u>unless the defendant's refusal to retract or apologize makes it possible to argue that the only way in which the reputation of the company can be vindicated in the eyes of the world is by way of a really substantial award of damages</u>* [emphasis added].

The motions judge acknowledged the repetition of the defamatory statements by Mr. Lopehandia and that "normally, repetition of the libelous statements would increase the damages." However, she discounted the impact of the repetitious statements on the basis of her conclusion that they were unlikely to be taken seriously. She held that a large award of damages was not necessary to vindicate the plaintiff's reputation.

Repetition, however, is only one factor to be considered in determining what award of damages is required to vindicate a plaintiff's reputation. Mr. Lopehandia's clear refusal to retract his statements, or to apologize for them — and, indeed, his dogged pursuit of the libelous campaign even after commencement of the proceedings — is an aggravating factor in this case, and a different factor than the repetition of the libel. The motions judge found that Mr. Lopehandia would likely continue his defamatory statements. Had she considered the lack of retraction and apology, along with repetition, in the context of determining whether "a really substantial award of damages" was required to vindicate Barrick's reputation in the circumstances, she might well have come to a different conclusion than she did.

See also the following Internet libel cases where the refusal to apologize had an impact on the amount of damages awarded:

Hunter Dickinson Inc. v. Butler, 2010 BCSC 939
National Bank of Canada c. Weir, 2010 QCCS 402
Buckle v. Caswell, 2009 SKQB 363
Fuda v. Conn, 2009 CanLII 1140 (ON S.C.)
Henderson v. Pearlman, 2009 CanLII 43641 (ON S.C.)
Griffin v. Sullivan, 2008 BCSC 827
Manno v. Henry, 2008 BCSC 738
Warman v. Grosvenor, 2008 CanLII 57728 (ON S.C.)
Newman et al. v. Halstead et al., 2006 BCSC 65
WeGo Kayaking Ltd. et al. v. Sewid et al., 2006 BCSC 334
Vaquero Energy v. Weir, 2004 ABQB 68

6) Statements Remain on the Internet

The fact that the statements remain accessible on the Internet is an aggravating factor.

Sanchez-Pontigon v. Manalansan-Lord, 2009 CanLII 28216 (ON S.C.)

7) Frequent Re-publication

Griffin v. Sullivan, 2008 BCSC 827 at para. 97–98:

> The defendant published the defamatory statements not only on the ASH website, but on other news groups and internet websites. The countless repetitions of these postings and the "links" to these postings are so vast as to stagger the mind. As stated by the majority in *Barrick Gold Corp. v. Lopehandia*, 2004 CanLII 12938 (ON C.A.), (2004) 71 O.R. (3d) 416 (at paragraph 1):
>
>> The internet . . . enables individuals . . . to communicate with a potentially vast global audience. It is a medium which does not respect geographical boundaries . . . the internet is also potentially a medium of virtually limitless international defamation.
>
> The extent, frequency and repetition of the publication of the defamatory statements in this case is a serious aggravating factor.

Referred to in *Fuda v. Conn*, 2009 CanLII 1140 (ON S.C.)

8) The Defamatory Remarks against Officers, Directors, and Employees

Barrick Gold v. Lopehandia, 2004 CanLII 12938 at paras. 46–48 (ON C.A.):

> [46] . . . the motions judge erred in dismissing the defamatory statements against the officers, directors and employees of Barrick as irrelevant to her determination of damages respecting Barrick. At paragraph 32 of her reasons she stated:
>
>> In assessing the plaintiff's damages, I have only considered the damage to the corporation's reputation. While the affidavit of Mr. Garver and the factum speak of the libel to Barrick and its officers, directors and employees, the only party to this action is Barrick. *Therefore, any defamatory statements regarding any of the officers, directors or employees which have caused damage to their reputations are irrelevant to the calculation of damages in this case.* If their reputations have

been damaged, it is for them to pursue their own actions [emphasis added].

[47] However, a significant element in Mr. Lopehandia's defamatory campaign against Barrick consisted of lengthy attacks on the integrity and *bona fides* of its various officers, directors and employees. A corporation can only act through such individuals. False and defamatory statements concerning the people who are responsible for supervising and conducting the affairs of the corporation — particularly a public corporation such as Barrick — must inevitably affect the business reputation of the corporation, as well as that of the individuals. The authors of P.F. Carter-Ruck and H.N.A. Starte, *Carter-Ruck On Libel and Slander*, 5th ed. (Butterworths: London, 1997), at 197–198, state:

> It is probable that a statement which reflects upon the honesty of the directors of a company, which is calculated by the imputations to which it gives rise to lead third parties no longer to deal with the company, would also entitle the company to seek substantial damages.

[48] I agree. Here, Mr. Lopehandia's campaign was admittedly designed to embarrass Barrick and to influence people to stop dealing with the company. A substantial part of the campaign consisted of the defamatory comments directed at the officers, directors and employees of Barrick for that purpose. While it is true that these individuals would have had to commence their own actions if they wished to recover damages for injury to their own personal reputations, these statements were relevant to the injury to Barrick's reputation. Had the motions judge thought about them in that context, she might well have been persuaded to award substantially higher general damages.

9) The Internet Context

Barrick Gold v. Lopehandia, 2004 CanLII 12938, 71 O.R. (3d) 416 at paras. 44–45 (C.A.):

> . . . the motions judge failed to appreciate, and in my opinion misjudged, the true extent of Mr. Lopehandia's target audience and the nature of the potential impact of the libel in the context of the Internet. She was alive to the fact that Mr. Lopehandia "[had] the ability, through the Internet, to spread his message around the world to those who take the time to search out and read what he posts" and indeed that he had "posted messages on many, many occasions." However, her decision not to take the defamation seriously led her to cease her analysis of the Internet factor at that point. She failed to

take into account the distinctive capacity of the Internet to cause instantaneous, and irreparable, damage to the business reputation of an individual or corporation by reason of its interactive and globally all-pervasive nature and the characteristics of Internet communications outlined in paragraphs 28–33 above.

Had the motions judge taken these characteristics of the Internet more fully into account, she might well have recognized Barrick's exposure to substantial damages to its reputation by reason of the medium through which the Lopehandia message was conveyed.

It was found in *Sanchez-Pontigon v. Manalansan-Lord*, 2009 CanLII 28216 (ON S.C.) at para. 56 that a reasonable person would likely take seriously statements published in a book that was in turn distributed on the Internet.

10) Long-Term Impact of Cyberlibel on Reputation

The long-term impact of cyberlibel on reputations has been very clearly described in two English cases and a law review article by Richard Peltz entitled "Fifteen Minutes of Infamy: Privileged Reporting and the Problem of Perpetual Reputational Harm" (2008) 34 *Ohio Northern University Law Review* 717.

Mr. Justice Tugendhat in *Clarke t/a Elumina Iberica UK v. Bain and Anor*, [2008] EWHC 2636 at paras. 54–56:

> In addressing issues of proportionality, the following must be borne in mind. Defamation actions are not primarily about recovering money damages, but about vindication of a claimant's reputation. If a successful libel claimant recovers, say, £30,000, that figure does not represent the measure of his success. In many cases, after paying his irrecoverable costs, he will be out of pocket if he recovers that amount as damages. That does not mean the litigation is not worthwhile. A claimant wrongly accused of some serious fault, such as malpractice or dishonesty in business, may well suffer very large unquantifiable loss if he does not recover his reputation. The value of the verdict in his favour is expected to consist substantially in the future loss that it is hoped will be avoided by the vindication. Where, as here, the publication complained of is on an Internet news service, a verdict in his favour may provide him with a means of persuading the publishers of an archive to edit it.
>
> The long term effect of a libel has commonly been be expressed in metaphorical terms, such as "the propensity to percolate through underground passages and contaminate hidden springs" (e.g. *Slipper v BBC* [1991] 1 QB 283, 300). The position today can be expressed more strongly, as it was in a article published in *The Guardian* (by Siobhain Butterworth, on 20 October 2008):

"The consequences of putting information . . . into the public domain are more far-reaching in a world where things you say are linked to, easily passed around and can pop up if [the subject's] name is put into a search engine by, for example, a prospective employer. The web makes a lie of the old cliche that today's newspaper pages are tomorrow's fish and chip wrapping. Nowadays, . . . the things . . . in a newspaper are more like tattoos — they can be extremely difficult to get rid of.

The web is an easily searchable repository of everything published online, which makes it a very unforgiving medium. The problem is not that things can't be removed easily, but that news organisations are inherently resistant to un-publishing. Should a newspaper website agree to un-publish on request? The answer to that question depends on what you think a newspaper's archive is for, and whether you think it matters if there are holes where articles used to be.

The established view is that a newspaper's online archive is a historical record and that there is therefore a strong public interest in maintaining its wholeness, unless deletions or amendments are strictly necessary.

Saying yes to all requests for the removal of material that causes the people concerned distress or hinders their employment prospects would be easier, but it's a solution that, over time, will leave a patchy and unreliable record of what was published. It also means abandoning conventional thinking about the importance of the integrity of the archive.

A less extreme solution . . . is to replace a real name with a pseudonym and add a footnote explaining that the change has been made. It's not ideal, but it's preferable to re-writing history completely by deleting an article, blog post or letter and pretending that it didn't exist."

The same judge made similar remarks in *Flood v. Times Newspapers Ltd.*, [2009] EWHC 2375 at para. 233:

Whether or not the scale of a website publication, and any resulting damage, is likely to be modest compared with that of the original publication, will depend on the facts of each case. But the judgment in *Loutchansky* was delivered eight years ago, in 2001. Since then the use of the internet, and in particular of internet search engines has increased. What has also increased is the amount of material on the internet. In 2001 there were relatively few years of back numbers of newspapers available on the internet. Since then each year's publications have been added. In most cases, as time passes, the original print publication will become increasingly difficult to access, and would be forgotten. But the website publication will remain, and in some cases (where the fame of a person has increased) it may even be viewed with increasing frequency. So a person's reputation may be "damaged forever" in the words of Lord Nicholls in *Reynolds* at p201 cited in para 207 above. As I remarked in another case, quoting from an article by a well known media lawyer, what is to be found on the internet may become like a tattoo (*Clarke (t/a Elumina Iberica UK) v. Bain & Anor,* [2008] EWHC 2636 (QB) para 55). Some actual and prospective employers, and teachers, make checks on people by carrying out internet searches. An old defamatory publication may permanently blight a person's prospects. This may be so, even in those cases where the allegation has been authoritatively refuted, but the refutation is either not on the internet, or, where it is on the internet, its authority is not apparent, or is not credited, on the footing that there is no smoke without fire.

The indelible reputational stain in cyberspace even when the individuals were completely exonerated was graphically sketched by Richard Peltz in "Fifteen Minutes of Infamy: Privileged Reporting and the Problem of Perpetual Reputational Harm" (2008) 34 *Ohio Northern University Law Review* 717 at 718–19:

> A review of the top-ten Google results in the Finnerty-Seligmann search does indicate that something is amiss. The eighth search result in the list reports, "Nifong jailed," and Finnerty and Seligmann "declared innocent earlier this year by state prosecutors." But that outcome is not indicated by any of the other nine of top-ten search results, one of which invites users to play, "You're the Jury—Guilty or Not Guilty?" News of the exoneration— while it can be found by follow-up searches on the web sites of Dilby, Findlaw, and Fox—is not indicated anywhere on the top three web pages responsive to the search.
>
> Imagine you are a harried hiring coordinator working for Big X Corporation. Before you sits a stack of 600 resumes, and your job today is to winnow the field by eliminating persons of dubious character. Your tool is Google, today "a commonplace part of hiring (and firing)." A candidate apparently under indictment for rape, sexual assault, and kidnapping is unlikely to make the cut. Applicants Finnerty and Seligmann will probably not get the benefit of careful reading and follow-up searches concerning their charges. Maybe they will get the benefit of your general knowledge about the news. But another applicant, a later-exonerated defendant who once made

small-time news for a charge reported from the police blotter, will not have the advantage of your general knowledge.

Finnerty and Seligmann, then, have been injured in their reputations as well as in their persons through wrongful detention. They will continue to be injured in untold ways; they will not even be cognizant of the ways in which they likely will be injured. Revelation of the prosecutor's misconduct in their extraordinary case has rendered the City of Durham vulnerable to a liability claim; at the time of this writing, Evans, Finnerty, and Seligmann have sued the City for $30 million. But the men have not sued the news media, Dilby, Findlaw, Fox, or any other outlet, for perpetuating recitation of the charges and the injuries that follow.

Meanwhile the reputational injuries to these men are perpetuated and compounded by unusual properties of new technology, such as longevity. Where yesterday's news, before the Internet, faded into obscurity on archival tapes and yellowing paper, the Internet never forgets. The news of 2006 remains at the fingertips of the user of 2008, of 2009, and of 2020. Will the top three responsive web pages to a search in 2048 again reveal only the breaking news of Finnerty's and Seligmann's arrests, or will news of their later exoneration rise to the top? Distressingly, the marvelous flexibility that makes the Internet a medium superior to paper—e.g., the ease of hyperlinking to related content and the ability to correct and update content virtually instantaneously at nominal cost—is not apparently being exploited now. Whereas a newspaper morgue search would readily cross-reference the initial charge and later exoneration of a criminal defendant before the electronic era, the broad range of sources available online are not so readily indexed and cross-referenced.

A chart of cyberlibel damage awards can be found in the reference material at the end of this book.

CHAPTER 13: Injunctions in Cyberlibel

A. RELUCTANCE OF COURTS TO GRANT INTERLOCUTORY INJUNCTIONS IN LIBEL ACTIONS

The courts are generally reluctant to grant interlocutory injunctions in libel actions unless the statement is clearly defamatory and there is no defence of truth or privilege.

Rapp v. McLelland & Stewart (1981), 34 O.R. (2d) 452 at para. 459:

> The guiding principle then is, that the injunction should only issue where the words complained of are so manifestly defamatory that any jury verdict to the contrary would be considered perverse by the Court of Appeal. To put it another way, where it is impossible to say that a reasonably jury must inevitably find the words defamatory, the injunction should not issue.

See also *Canada Metal Co. Ltd. v. CBC* (1974), 3 O.R. (2d) 1, aff'd 7 O.R. (2d) 261; *Meier v. CBC* (1981), 19 C.P.C. 315; *Doe v. CBC* (1994), 86 B.C.L.R. (2d) 202; *Canada (Human Rights Commission) v. Canadian Liberty Net*, [1998] 1 S.C.R. 626; *Campbell v. Cartmell*, [1999] O.J. No. 35, where an injunction was granted for an Internet libel; *Bonnard v. Perryman* [1981] 2 Ch. 269

B. GENERAL PRINCIPLES

The principles of interlocutory injunctive relief for defamation cases were stated very clearly in paras. 14–16 of Murray J.'s reasons in *Beidas v. Pichler*, 2008 CanLII 26255 (ON S.C.D.C.). This case involved the publication of statements on the Internet.

First, it is appropriate to consider the general principles applicable in a case such as the one before this Court. In *Rapp et al. v. McClelland & Stewart*

Ltd. et al. (1982), 34 O.R. (2d) 452, Griffiths J. described generally the requirements for an injunction in a case of defamation at p. 455:

> In this jurisdiction, unless both parties are prepared to waive the
> requirement, a libel action must be tried by a jury and while the
> presiding trial judge has the duty to determine whether in law the
> words complained of are capable of being defamatory of the plaintiff
> it is the exclusive function of the jury to determine whether they
> are, under all the circumstances, in fact defamatory. The words to
> be defamatory must be false and the jury must be satisfied that the
> words in their natural or innuendo meaning tend to lower the plain-
> tiff in the estimate of right-thinking members of society generally or
> cause her to be shunned or avoided or exposed to hatred, contempt
> or ridicule.
>
> As the learned author *Gatley on Libel and Slander*, 7th ed. (1974),
> observes at pp. 23–24:

> > It will be seen that it is not possible to say that any particular
> > imputation is defamatory, regardless of the circumstances of
> > its publication. Whether or not it is so will vary with time,
> > place and the state of public opinion. In any case, whether or
> > not any imputation is defamatory is not a matter of law, but a
> > matter of fact for the jury, and no other jury will be bound to
> > reach the same decision. It is similarly a matter of fact wheth-
> > er any words convey the defamatory imputation alleged, and
> > this may depend to a great extent on the circumstances and
> > context of a particular publication.
> >
> > . . .

In *Rosemond Estates Inc. et al. v. Levy et al.*, 65 O.R. (3d) 79, [2003] O.J. No.
1748, Spence J. stated: "that the court should be particularly cautious about
granting an injunction where the issue concerns defamation is clear from
the decision in *Rapp v. McClelland & Stewart Ltd.* reflex, (1981), 34 O.R. (2d)
452, 128 D.L.R. (3d) 650 (S.C.) per Griffiths J. at p. 455 O.R.

In his treatise *Injunctions and Specific Performance* (2nd ed. 1992 (looseleaf)), Robert Sharpe says the following, at paras. 5.40–5.70 (pp. 5.2–5.4):

> There is a significant public interest in the free and uncensored circu-
> lation of information and the important principle of freedom of the
> press to be safeguarded.
>
> . . .

> The well-established rule is that an interlocutory injunction will not be granted where the defendant indicates an intention to justify [i.e., prove the truth of] the statements complained of, unless the plaintiff is able to satisfy the court at the interlocutory stage that the words are both clearly defamatory and impossible to justify ... it seems clear that the rule is unaffected by the *American Cyanamid* case and that the balance of convenience is not a factor.

Further discussion about injunctions in libel and slander actions can be found in Roger D. McConchie and David A. Potts, *Canadian Libel and Slander Actions* (Toronto: Irwin Law, 2004) c. 5.

See *Henderson v. Pearlman*, 2009 CanLII 43641 at para. 53 (ON S.C.):

> I adopt the reasoning of Himel J. in *Campbell v. Cartemell*, [1999] O.J. No. 3553 (S.C.J.), who held that:
>
> > [w]hile it is important to recognize the principle of free speech and to allow the expression of opinion in our democratic society, the restriction in advance of words spoken or written is justified to prevent any further damage to the plaintiffs' reputations (at para. 60).

C. INTERLOCUTORY INJUNCTIONS INVOLVING CYBERLIBEL

In *Beidas v. Pichler*, (2008) 294 D.L.R. (4th) 310, 238 O.A.C. 103 at paras. 20–23, the Divisional Court allowed an appeal from an order granting an interlocutory injunction involving statements on the Internet.

> First, there was no affidavit evidence before Justice Himel from either Beidas or Pallister and therefore no evidence of irreparable harm from these two plaintiffs. No injunctive relief should have been granted to Beidas or Pallister for this reason.
>
> Secondly, no undertaking as to damages was given by the plaintiffs and no order of the court exempted them from this requirement. See Rule 40.03.
>
> Thirdly, both Beidas and Pallister refused to be examined prior to the return of the motion for interlocutory relief. In the face of such refusal, no injunctive relief should have been granted to the plaintiffs Beidas or Pallister.

Fourthly, the scope of the injunctive relief granted by Justice Himel was too broad for the following reasons:

1. Orders were too broad and unnecessarily impaired the freedom of speech and expression of the defendant (paras. 42–46, Murray J.).

2. The fact that the alleged defamatory expression was published on the Internet did not justify an order that broad (paras. 47–50, Murray J.).
3. Any injunctions cannot be granted to restrict non-defamatory speech on the Internet (paras. 53–54, Murray J.).

An excellent summary of the historical development of the law of prior restraint can be found in *Greene v. Associated Newspapers*, [2009] EWCA Civ 1462. This decision confirms the application of *Bonnard v. Perryman*, [1891] 2 Ch. 269 in defamation actions.

Injunctions were granted in:

CNR v. Google Inc., 2010 ONSC 3121 at para. 33
Takefman c. Bier, 2010 QCCA 486
Henderson v. Pearlman, 2009 CanLII 43641 at para. 50 (ON S.C.)
Canada (Human Rights Commission) v. Winnicki, 2005 FC 1493 at para. 15

Injunctions were refused in:

Bell Canada v. Rogers Communications Inc., 2009 CanLII 39481 (ON S.C.)
Desroches v. Klein, 2009 QCCS 40 at para. 36
Beidas v. Pichler (2008), 294 D.L.R. (4th) 310, 238 O.A.C. 103
Wyeth-Ayerst Canada Inc. v. Phaneuf, [2002] R.J.Q. 949

D. ANONYMOUS SPEECH AND INTERLOCUTORY INJUNCTIONS

It has been held that a concern for freedom of speech is lessened where the allegedly defamatory statements are anonymous postings on Internet sites. A British Columbia court granted an *ex parte* interim injunction requiring the defendant to "forthwith remove the messages written and published on its Internet site" as identified in the motion.

Henry v. Stockhouse Media Corp., [1999] B.C.J. No. 3202 at paras. 8 and 13 (S.C.), Fraser J.:

> I accept the high and stringent tests which the authorities lay down as to the granting of this kind of injunction. As to granting an injunction on an ex parte basis, the key is that the defendants are afforded no opportunity to say that the statements complained of are true. What has led me to the conclusion that the injunction should go is that the statements complained of are anonymous. Whoever WaveyDavey is, he or she feels free to throw around accusations of the most serious kind behind the cowardly screen of an alias. It seems to me that in these circumstances, the concern for the protection of free speech is lessened

. . .

However, I consider it inappropriate to grant an injunction which will endure until trial, with the right in the defendants and the anonymous writers only to apply to set aside the injunction. It is my view that the injunction should be for as brief a period of time as is reasonable, with an obligation on the part of the plaintiffs to apply for the injunction to be extended.

E. CREATIVE COMPROMISE

A creative compromise was adopted by a judge hearing an application for an interlocutory injunction regarding statements published on the Internet in *McLeod (Maslak Mcleod Gallery) v. Sinclair*, 2008 CanLII 67901 at paras. 36–41 (ON S.C.):

> In the circumstances, on their face, the comments and observations of the defendant are defamatory. However, he has not had an opportunity to fully respond and his right to freedom of expression must be borne in mind.
>
> In the circumstances, at this early stage, both sides have a claim to protection.
>
> There is, it seems to me, a way in which a balance can be achieved which recognizes the two principle concerns.
>
> The accusations, opinions and allegations of the defendant are on the website. They are in the public domain. They can be accessed by anyone.
>
> Similarly, the proceedings in this Court are public. However, the court records are not as easily available. If the two perspectives were readily available in the same place, the rights of both sides would obtain a measure of recognition while this matter moves to a more comprehensive and complete proceeding.
>
> Accordingly, I order: The website can remain up pending further order of this Court, but only on the following terms:
>
>> Each and every page which suggests that any distributor, gallery or individual owner who possesses, has owned, or possessed in the past or has sold or is now selling a painting or other work of art attributed to Norval Morriseau, or any page that opines that any work attributed to Norval Morriseau is a fraud, forgery, counterfeit, stolen or in any other way is not authentic or genuine shall have placed on it a label 4 inches by 3 inches in dimension. The label will have a white background, be easily-read with clear wording using a Times New Roman font stating:

The opinions expressed on this website and on this page are those of Ritchie 'Stardreamer' Sinclair and of no other person. These opinions are alleged to be defamatory and are the subject of an action in the Superior Court of Ontario.

In the upper right-hand corner of each label shall be the Ontario Superior Court File Number for this action.

The defendant must post the Notices referred to herein no later than midnight on December 8, 2008, failing which the defendant must remove the website, morriseau.com, from public display until such time as all of the Notices referred to herein are posted

F. PERMANENT INJUNCTIONS IN CYBERLIBEL CASES

Permanent injunctions were granted in the following cyberlibel cases:

Hunter Dickinson Inc. v. Butler, 2010 BCSC 939
National Bank v. Lowell Weir, 2010 QCCS 402 at para. 30
Henderson v. Pearlman, 2009 CanLII 43641 at paras. 48–53 (ON S.C.)
Griffin v. Sullivan, 2008 BCSC 827 at paras. 104 and 119–27
Manson v. Moffet, 2008 CanLII 19789 (ON S.C.)
Ottawa-Carleton District School Board v. Scharf, 2007 CanLII 31571 (ON S.C.)
Newman v. Halstead, 2006 BCSC 65 at paras. 297–301
Barrick Gold Corp. v. Lopehandia, 2004 CanLII 12938 (ON C.A.)

G. EXTRATERRITORIAL APPLICATION OF INJUNCTIONS

The court may refuse to grant the injunction because it is not enforceable in the jurisdiction.

In *Macquarrie Bank Limited & Anor v. Berg,* [1999] NSWSC 526, the New South Wales Supreme Court refused an *ex parte* injunction by the plaintiff bank to enjoin the defendant from publishing defamatory material on the Internet. The judge held that any injunction would likely be ineffective against the defendant, who was living in the US and it was not known if he would return to New South Wales (NSW). The judge also expressed another concern about the potential extraterritorial applications at the injunction at paras. 12–14:

... It is reasonably plain, I think, that once published on the Internet, material is transmitted anywhere in the world that has an Internet connection. It may be received by anybody, anywhere, having the appropriate facilities. Senior counsel [for Macquarrie Bank] conceded that, to make the order as initially sought, would have the effect of restraining publication of all the material presently contained on the Website to any place in the world. Recognizing the difficulties associated with orders of such breadth, he sought to narrow the claim by limiting the order sought to publication of dissemination "within NSW." The limitation, however, is ineffective. Senior counsel acknowledged that he was aware of no means by which material, once published on the Internet, could be excluded from transmission to or receipt in any geographical area. Once published on the Internet, material can be received anywhere, and it does not lie within the competence of the publisher to restrict the reach of the publication . . . .

The consequence is that, if I were to make the order sought (and the defendant were to obey it) he would be restrained from publishing anywhere in the world via the medium of the Internet.

The difficulties are obvious. An injunction to restrain defamation in NSW is designed to ensure compliance with the laws of NSW, and to protect the rights of plaintiffs, as those rights are defined by the law of NSW. Such an injunction is not designed to superimpose the law of NSW relating to defamation on every other state, territory and country of the world. Yet that would be the effect of an order restraining publication on the Internet . . . . For this reason alone, I would refuse the order sought.

In another case, the Ontario Court of Appeal in *Barrick Gold Corp v. Lopehandia*, 2005 CanLII 12938, discussed the concern about the enforceability of an injunction granted by an Ontario Court against a defendant normally resident in British Columbia. The Court recognized that in some circumstances, the courts will permit service of claims outside the jurisdiction seeking to prevent publications in the jurisdiction of libellous material originally outside the jurisdiction. They considered that *Barrick Gold Corp v. Lopehandia* was one of those cases at paras. 73–78:

> The more troubling point respecting the claim for injunctive relief is the *in personam* nature of the remedy, the marginal presence of the defendant in the jurisdiction, and the concerns about enforceability of such an order. The motions judge was correct to be worried about this. Courts have traditionally been reluctant to grant injunctive relief against defendants who are outside the jurisdiction. The reason for this is explained by Robert J. Sharpe in his text, *Injunctions and Specific Performance*, Looseleaf Edition (Toronto: Canada Law Book, November 2002) at 1-54 to 1-55:
>
> > Claims for injunctions against foreign parties present jurisdictional constraints which are not encountered in the case of claims for money judgments. In the case of a money claim, the courts need not limit

assumed jurisdiction to cases where enforceability is ensured. Equity, however, acts *in personam* and the effectiveness of an equitable decree depends upon the control which may be exercised over the person of the defendant. If the defendant is physically present, it will be possible to require him or her to do, or permit, acts outside the jurisdiction. The courts have, however, conscientiously avoided making orders which cannot be enforced. The result is that the courts are reluctant to grant injunctions against parties not within the jurisdiction and the practical import of rules permitting service *ex juris* in respect of injunction claims is necessarily limited. Rules of court are typically limited to cases where it is sought to restrain the defendant from doing anything *within the jurisdiction*. As a practical matter the defendant "who is doing anything within the jurisdiction" will usually be physically present within the jurisdiction to allow ordinary service [emphasis in original].

As the motions judge noted, however, courts do in some circumstances permit service of claims outside the jurisdiction seeking to prevent publication in the jurisdiction of libelous material originating outside the jurisdiction: see Sharpe, *supra*, at 1-55; *Tozier and Wife v. Hawkins* (1885), 15 Q.B. 680. This is one such case, in my view. Moreover, it is also a case where there is a sufficient connection, actual and potential, between the parties and Ontario to justify the granting of a permanent injunction as sought. Not only is there a real and substantial connection between Barrick and Ontario, but there is a connection between the publication of the libel by Mr. Lopehandia and Ontario as well.

Mr. Lopehandia is ordinarily resident in British Columbia, but there is no way to determine from where his postings originate. They could as easily be initiated in an Internet café in downtown Toronto or anywhere else in the world, as in his offices in Vancouver. Given the manner in which the Internet works, it is not possible to know whether the posting of one of Mr. Lopehandia's messages on one of the bulletin boards in question, or the receipt of that message by someone accessing the bulletin board, traveled by way of a server in Ontario to or from the message board. It may have, however. The highly transmissible nature of the tortious misconduct at issue here is a factor to be addressed in considering whether a permanent injunction should be granted. The courts are faced with a dilemma. On the one hand, they can throw up their collective hands in despair, taking the view that enforcement against such ephemeral transmissions around the world is ineffective, and concluding therefore that only the jurisdiction where the originator of the communication may happen to be found can enjoin the offending conduct.

On the other hand, they can at least protect against the impugned conduct re-occurring in their own jurisdiction. In this respect, I agree with the following observation of Kirby J. in *Dow Jones* at para. 115:

> Any suggestion that there can be no effective remedy for the tort of defamation (or other civil wrongs) committed by the use of the Internet (or that such wrongs must simply be tolerated as the price to be paid for the advantages of the medium) is self-evidently unacceptable.

Here, at least one of the bulletin boards utilized by Mr. Lopehandia for the dissemination of his campaign against Barrick is operated by Yahoo Canada Inc. in Toronto. The posting of messages on that board constitutes at least an act done by the defendant that affects Barrick's reputation, goodwill, and personal property in Ontario, and arguably constitutes an act done by him in Ontario. The courts in Ontario must have jurisdiction to restrain such conduct. Even if an injunction may only be enforced in this Province against Mr. Lopehandia if he enters the Province personally, there are two reasons why the injunction may nonetheless be effective. The first is that it will operate to prevent Yahoo from continuing to post the defamatory messages: *Mc-Millan Bloedel Ltd. v. Simpson*, 1996 CanLII 165 (S.C.C.), [1996] 2 S.C.R. 1048; *Attorney-General v. Times Newspapers Ltd.*, [1991] 1 A.C. 191 (H.L.). Secondly, it may be enforceable in British Columbia, where Mr. Lopehandia resides: *Morguard Investments Ltd. v. De Savoye*, 1990 CanLII 29 (S.C.C.), [1990] 3 S.C.R. 1077; J.-G. Castel and Janet Walker, *Canadian Conflict of Laws*, 5th ed. (looseleaf) (Markham, ON: Butterworths, 2004) at 14–31.

Barrick's shares trade on the Toronto Stock Exchange. It is an Ontario corporation with its head offices and employees, and a business reputation, here. Indeed, the protection and vindication of that reputation in Ontario is what gives rise to the court's mandate in cases of this nature. These factors point to a real and substantial connection between Barrick and Ontario rather than to a jurisdictional link with the defendant. However, they suggest that if the appellant were to take an injunction granted by this Court to British Columbia — where Mr. Lopehandia does have a physical presence — and seek to enforce it there, in this "post-*Morguard* era," the order might be enforced against him by the courts of that Province. The argument for enforcement would be based upon the principles of order and fairness and upon what Professor Hogg has referred to as "an implicit full faith and credit rule in the Constitution of Canada" as a result of the Supreme Court of Canada's decision in *Morguard*: see P.W. Hogg, *Constitutional Law of Canada*, looseleaf ed., vol 1 (Carswell: Toronto, 1998), s. 13.5 at 13-20 to 13-21; *Morguard, supra; Muscutt et al. v. Cour-*

celles et al. 2002 CanLII 44957 (ON C.A.), (2002), 60 O.R. (3d) 20 (C.A.); Edward Mazey, "The Enforcement of Labour Orders outside the Jurisdiction of Origin" (2002), 59 U.T. Fac. L. Rev 25, at 37–38. It is not for this court to usurp the role of the courts in another province, of course. However, the British Columbia Court of Appeal has held in two relatively recent cases that jurisdiction based upon the "real and substantial connection" test may be satisfied where the province asserting jurisdiction has a real and substantial connection with the subject matter of the litigation or the cause of action asserted: *Pacific International Securities Inc. v. Drake Capital Securities Inc.*, 2000 BCCA 632 (CanLII), (2000), 194 D.L.R. (4th) 716 (B.C.C.A.) at 722; *Cook v. Pardcel, Mauro, Hultin & Spaanstra, P.C.*, 1997 CanLII 4091 (BC C.A.), (1997), 143 D.L.R. (4th) 213 (B.C.C.A.) at 219; see also *Braintech, Inc. v. Kostiuk*, 1999 BCCA 169 (CanLII), (1999), 171 D.L.R. (4th) 46 (B.C.C.A.). Such is the case here.

I would set aside the decision of the motions judge in this regard and grant a permanent injunction as requested, restraining the defendants from disseminating, posting on the Internet or publishing further defamatory statements concerning Barrick or its officers, directors or employees.

See also *National Bank of Canada c. Weir*, 2010 QCCS 402 for granting a permanent injunction

H. ORDERS IN INJUNCTIONS IN CYBERLIBEL

An important feature of injunctions in cyberlibel cases is the scope and content of the orders granted. The orders illustrate some of the peculiar problems raised by cyberlibel.

1) The Breadth and Scope of Injunctive Relief

The Divisional Court in *Beidas v. Pichler*, 2008 CanLII 26255 at para. 23 (Div. Ct.) held that the order granted by the Motions Court judge was too broad to be sustained:

> ... [T]he scope of the injunctive relief granted by Justice Himel was too broad for the following reasons:
> 1. Orders were too broad and unnecessarily impaired the freedom of speech and expression of the defendant (paras. 42–46, Murray J.)
> 2. The fact that the alleged defamatory expression was published on the Internet did not justify an order that broad (paras. 47–50, Murray J.)
> 3. Any injunctions cannot be granted to restrict non-defamatory speech on the Internet. (paras. 53–54, Murray J.)

The Quebec Court of Appeal in *Takefman c. Bier*, 2010 QCCA 486 overturned the order on the grounds that it was too broad at paras. 20–22 and 24–25:

First there is no justification for a restriction on e-mails or other means of communication between the appellant and third parties, including his liability insurer, for the purposes of preparing his defence to the respondents' action and to initiate his own civil action against them or other persons, as pointed out by my colleague Rochon, J.A. in the judgment authorizing the appeal. The same can be said of written communications with the Syndic du Barreau, the Bar Review Committee and the Bar Discipline Committee in connection with complaints against the respondent Elliot Bier or Mr. Adessky, or with the proper authorities in connection with a criminal complaint.

Second it infringes upon the appellant's freedom of speech by preventing him from expressing, in writing, any comment whatsoever about the respondents. One may well consider that the appellant has abused his freedom of expression by disclosing aspects of the private life of respondents with regard to matters that are not of public interest in any way and that constitute a clear violation of the respondent's right to privacy guaranteed by s. 4 of the *Quebec Charter of Human Rights and Freedoms* and recognized at art. 35 and 36 of the *Civil Code of Quebec*. However, the order also prevents the expression of commentary with regard to the financial services provided by the respondents, which may be of public interest.

In *Champagne, supra*, further to allegations made by a radio host that teachers at the college gave marks in exchange for sexual favours, an interlocutory injunction enjoined that radio host to refrain from defaming, ridiculing and libelling, directly or indirectly, the college and its staff. The injunction was set aside by our Court. In his reasons, Justice Rothman wrote:

But until these issues have been determined, I do not see how the courts can restrain abusive comments, in advance and before they are made, without risking the suppression of legitimate comment. (*Picard v. Johnson & Higgins Willis Faber Ltée* 1987 CanLII 891 (QC C.A.), [1988] R.J.Q. 235, 239).

It is true that the terms of the injunction would only enjoin comments that defame, ridicule or falsely accuse the college, but these terms do very little beyond what the law already does to separate acceptable comment from defamation. All the injunction does is indicate to the potential offender that, for any future breaches, he will be liable to sanctions for contempt in addition to damages. Since the future comments are unknown, this is likely to have a numbingly chilling effect on the expression of any future opinions about the administration of the college. (The situation would, of course, be different if we were dealing with the risk of future publication of a clearly defamatory document, the contents of which were known.).

. . .

The common law authorities in Canada and the U.K. have suggested the guiding principle that interlocutory injunctions should only be granted to restrain in advance written or spoken words in the rarest and clearest of cases — where the words are so manifestly defamatory and impossible to justify that an action in defamation would almost certainly succeed. Given the value we place on freedom of expression, particularly in matters of public interest, that guiding principle has much to recommend it. . . .

These principles were approved by the Supreme Court of Canada in *Canada (HRC) v. Canadian Liberty Net*, 1998 CanLII 818 (S.C.C.), [1998] 1 S.C.R. 626, at p. 667–669, and they are applicable here. Although there is a need to issue an order to restrain the appellant's vicious attacks on the private life of the respondents, the nature of which makes this case an extremely rare example of scavenging of information in matters where there is no public interest, these principles dictate that the second order be restricted to comments and statements concerning the respondents' private life.

Finally, it is well settled that safeguard orders should only be issued for a limited period of time (*Natrel Inc. c. F. Berardini Inc.*, [1995] R.D.J. 383, J.E. 95-584 (C.A.)).

A slightly different approach to the concern raised by the Divisional Court in *Beidas v. Pichler* can be seen in the decision of *Newman et al. v. Halstead et al.*, 2006 BCSC 65 at para. 300(3). In the order the Court prohibited the publication of "any statements" referring to the plaintiff:

Susan Pearl Halstead shall not publish, or cause to be published, or otherwise disseminate or distribute in any manner whatsoever, whether by way of the Internet or otherwise, any statements or other communications which refer to any of the plaintiffs by name, by depiction, or by description.

With great respect, this term is too broad for the following reasons:

1. It prohibits the defendant from publishing non-defamatory speech.
2. It is inconsistent with *Rapp v. McLelland & Stewart* (1981), 34 O.R. (2d) 452 at para. 459 as it prohibits statements that do not meet the *Rapp v. McLelland* test.

3. It turns the court and the plaintiff into perpetual censors of the defendant's right to freedom of speech.

2) Orders Prohibiting the Defendant from Contacting the Plaintiff

Griffin v. Sullivan, 2008 BCSC 827 at para. 124:

> The injunction will also include a term that the defendant be restrained from
> contacting or communicating with the plaintiff, directly or indirectly in any
> way or by any method. In ordering this term (which is broader than the term
> requested in the statement of claim) I rely on the evidence presented and on
> the inherent jurisdiction of this court.

3) Further Relief in Case of Breach

Several decisions have provided the plaintiffs the ability to apply to the court
for further relief in case of a breach by the defendant.
  Griffin v. Sullivan, 2008 BCSC 827 at paras. 125–26:

> In the event that the plaintiff believes that the defendant is in breach of this
> order by failing to remove existing postings on the internet for which he is
> responsible, then, in addition to any other remedy that may be available, the
> plaintiff will have liberty to apply for an order requiring any person or com-
> pany within the jurisdiction of the court who has notice of this order, to remove
> such postings from the part or parts of the internet within their control.
>
> The plaintiff will also have liberty to apply to expand or otherwise change
> the terms of this order on the ground that it has failed or is failing to achieve
> one or more of its purposes.

See *Newman v. Halstead*, 2006 BCSC 65 at para. 300(5)

4) Orders Applying to Pseudonyms Adopted by the Defendant

The use of pseudonyms is common on the Internet. The Court in *Griffin v.
Sullivan*, 2008 BCSC 827, dealt with this problem as follows at paras. 119–23:

> Notwithstanding Mr. Sullivan's strenuous opposition to this claim, in my
> opinion a permanent injunction is not only justified but required in this
> case. In light of his conduct over the past three and one-half years, it cannot
> be assumed that Mr. Sullivan will cease all efforts to publish new defamatory
> material or re-publish old defamatory material, about Mr. Griffin. Nor can
> Mr. Sullivan be trusted to make every possible effort to remove defamatory

material about the plaintiff which he is responsible for publishing, and which still remains on the internet by his own admission.

In my view, the wording of the injunction must be very broad, having regard to Mr. Sullivan's propensity for using many different identities, nick names and internet addresses. There is also evidence that he has used "anonymous re-mailers," which is a device for posting a message on the internet that cannot be traced back to the original sender. Mr. Sullivan raised the objection that if the injunction purports to prohibit the use of anonymous re-mailing, he might get blamed for something that he did not do. The defendant further protests that some of the people who support him in his campaign against the plaintiff may have published or will in the future publish defamatory material about the plaintiff for which he will be blamed. The existence of these risks cannot be denied, but I think they are risks to which the defendant must be subjected. The law of civil contempt requires proof beyond a reasonable doubt, and I think this will provide sufficient protection to Mr. Sullivan from wrongful accusations.

Accordingly, I order that the defendant, by himself, his agents, servants or otherwise be restrained from publishing, or causing to be published, on the internet or by any other method or medium, any defamatory statement referring in any way to the plaintiff, whether by name, pseudonym, address, photograph or other means of identity. The order will prohibit the defendant from publishing or causing to be published any such statement in his own name, in the name of any nick names, pseudonyms, or aliases that he now uses, has used, or may use in the future. The defendant is further prohibited from publishing or causing to be published any such statement about the plaintiff, anonymously, or in the name of another person.

It is my intent that the order will prohibit Mr. Sullivan from using the device or technique of "anonymous re-mailing" to publish or republish any defamatory statement of or concerning the plaintiff.

There will also be a mandatory injunction requiring the defendant to make all reasonable efforts to remove from the internet, the entirety of any and all of the internet postings that he has published or caused to be published, and which refer to "Robert Griffin," "Griffin," "Magnus Pym," "Pym" or "Pymmy" within 60 days of today's date.

See also *Hunter Dickinson Inc. v. Butler,* 2010 BCSC 939

5) Orders in the "Nature of Mandamus"

The Court in *Ottawa-Carleton District School Board v. Scharf,* 2007 CanLII 31571, made the following order at para. 30:

As well, the plaintiffs will have judgment against the defendants for the following:

(a) An order in the nature of mandamus requiring the defendants to remove all defamatory material from any website over which they have control including, but not limited to the documents described as "transcript" pages 1 to 7 and "court order."

(b) An interim and permanent injunction preventing the defendants from republishing defamatory statements about the plaintiffs on any website or in any other medium or otherwise communicating or publishing false and defamatory statements about the plaintiffs.

(c) An order in the nature of mandamus requiring the defendants to issue a public retraction of the "News Release" entitled "Teach Me I Can Learn" such retraction to be published at the defendants' expense in the *Ottawa Sun* and the *Ottawa Citizen* newspapers within 60 days of the date of this judgment.

(d) An order in the nature of mandamus requiring the defendants to issue a public apology to the plaintiffs such apology to be published at the defendants' expense in the *Ottawa Sun* and the *Ottawa Citizen* newspapers within 60 days of the date of this judgment.

a) Observations about this Decision

1. A separate school board was entitled to sue for libel: *Windsor Catholic Separate School Board v. Southam Inc.* (1985), 46 O.R. (2d) 231. However, it is arguable that school boards are now prohibited from doing so by s. 2(b) of the *Charter of Rights and Freedoms*. The courts in Ontario and British Columbia have held that government bodies such as municipalities cannot sue for libel. It is questionable whether school boards are now not in the same category. See *Montague (Township) v. Page* (2006), 79 O.R. (3d) 515; *Halton Hills (Township) v. Kerouac*, 2006 CanLII 12970, 80 O.R. (3d) 577 (S.C.J.); *Dixon v. Powell River (City)*, 2009 BCSC 406.

2. Paragraphs (c) and (d) should, with great respect, be applied with caution. The general rule is that the court cannot order a retraction or an apology in defamation actions unless they are simply repeating a consent agreement.

See *Hunger Project v. Council Mind Abuse (COMA) Inc.* (1995), 22 O.R. (3d) 29 and *contra*, without any discussions of the authorities, *Kelly v. Low* (2000), 257 A.R. 279 (Q.B).

6) Defendants Must Remove Existing Defamatory Statements from the Internet

The defendants in the following cases were ordered to remove existing defamatory statements from the Internet:

Canadian National Railway Company v. Google Inc., 2010 ONSC 3121
Griffin v. Sullivan, 2008 BCSC 827 at para. 123
Ottawa-Carleton District School Board v. Scharf, 2007 CanLII 31571 at para. 30

The Court held that the plaintiff must remove objectionable statements about the defendant:

Griffin v. Sullivan, 2008 BCSC 827 at para. 127 (CanLII)

7) Specificity of Orders

In several decisions the courts will enjoin the publication of specific defamatory statements as in:

Henderson v. Pearlman, 2009 CanLII 43641 at paras. 49 and 52 (ON S.C.)
Newman v. Halstead, 2006 BCSC 65 at para. 300, term 1 and 2

The degree of specificity in the order varies. For example, several decisions grant an injunction restraining the defendants from disseminating, posting on the Internet, or publishing further defamatory statements concerning the plaintiffs without specifying precise examples of such statements.

Barrick Gold Corp. v. Lopehandia, 2004 CanLII 12938 at para. 78 (ON C.A.):

> I would set aside the decision of the motions judge in this regard and grant a permanent injunction as requested, restraining the defendants from disseminating, posting on the Internet or publishing further defamatory statements concerning Barrick or its officers, directors or employees.

National Bank of Canada c. Weir, 2010 QCCS 402
Griffin v. Sullivan, 2008 BCSC 827 at para. 121
Ottawa-Carleton District School Board v. Scharf, 2007 CanLII 31571 at paras. 30(a) and (b) (ON S.C.)

8) The Defendant's Prior and Present Conduct Requires a Permanent Injunction

In several cases, the courts determined that the defendant's conduct required that a permanent injunction to be granted.

Griffin v. Sullivan 2008 BCSC 827 at para. 119:

Notwithstanding Mr. Sullivan's strenuous opposition to this claim, in my opinion a permanent injunction is not only justified but required in this case. In light of his conduct over the past three and one-half years, it cannot be assumed that Mr. Sullivan will cease all efforts to publish new defamatory material or re-publish old defamatory material, about Mr. Griffin. Nor can Mr. Sullivan be trusted to make every possible effort to remove defamatory material about the plaintiff which he is responsible for publishing, and which still remains on the internet by his own admission.

a) Conduct of the Defendant

Henderson v. Pearlman, 2009 CanLII 43641 at paras. 51–52 (ON S.C.):

> This is an exceptional case which calls for the extraordinary relief of an injunction. The defendants have attempted to avoid service, attempted to move the proceedings to Florida and, when unsuccessful, refused to participate in any way in these proceedings.
>
> The defendants have never taken any step to remove the postings from their website.
>
> I am satisfied that on a balance of probabilities, a permanent injunction should be granted to prohibit the defendants from continuing to post these comments. They are clearly defamatory and there is no evidence that the defendants have ever, including until the present time, taken any steps to remove the postings from their website.

b) Where the Defendant Claims to be Judgment-proof

See *Newman v. Halstead* 2006 BCSC 65 at para. 297; *Griffin v. Sullivan* 2008 BCSC 827 at para. 119.

I. PERSONAL OBSERVATIONS ON POTENTIAL PROBLEMS OF INTERLOCUTORY INJUNCTIONS FOR CYBERLIBEL

Aside from the legal obstacles to obtaining an interlocutory injunction to stop publication of cyberlibel and to remove cyberlibel from the Internet, the following issues might be considered:

1. The motion will likely be heard in open court, thereby allowing the media and other observers access to the motion records and the opportunity, particularly but not exclusively, for the press to report on the judicial process with near immunity.

2. The motion will provide a virtually immune platform for the defendant to expand upon and justify the statement originally complained of.
3. The motion materials may be indefinitely re-published throughout the Internet with commentary. To make matters worse, the re-publication and commentary will be archived and perpetually accessible by anyone with a few clicks of a mouse.
4. If the injunction is granted, the plaintiff will have to enforce the order. The defendant may not appear in court. See *Newman v. Hallstead*, 2006 BCSC 65 at para. 297; *Henderson v. Pearlman*, 2009 CanLII 43641 (ON S.C.).
5. Even after the injunction is granted, the whole process may backfire. For example, the defendant may be located in another jurisdiction that will not enforce the injunction and therefore the defendant can, in effect, continue to spew abuse at the plaintiff with impunity. The example below illustrates that possibility.

On 4 June 1997, an *ex parte* application of the Nottingham City Council to the English High Court of Justice granted an injunction against the defendant Hebditch, which required him to remove hypertext links on his website to mirror sites in Belgium and the US and prohibited him from disseminating a confidential report describing how social workers in the Nottingham Department of Social Services allegedly induced a group of abused children to indulge in hysterical fantasies of satanic rights relating to the case histories of the children. When the notice of the injunction was served to Hebditch by email, Nottingham's solicitor requested that Hebditch supply the plaintiff with a postal address to which the writ of summons injunction material could be delivered. On 16 June 1997, Nottingham's lawyer received an email from Peter Junger who owned a website in Cleveland, Ohio. He refused to accede to a demand by Nottingham's lawyer that unless the report was removed from the website forthwith, the Nottingham County Council would issue court proceedings, including injunction proceedings, or take any action as may be appropriate. Mr. Junger's lengthy refusal reads in part:

> My inclination to ignore your threat was naturally strengthened by the realization that, should you actually succeed in getting injunctive relief in the United Kingdom, that injunction would be quite unenforceable here in the United States. But I confess that I found your threats irritating enough that I began to think that I should comply with your demand — publicly. I have little difficulty in imagining the

headlines that would have resulted had I taken such a course of action: "English Prosecutor Forces US Law Professor to Suppress Report on Satanic Social Workers'" or "Satanic Coverup Spreads to US." Although, mind you, the actual headlines that you have already earned for yourself, like Private Eye's "Satanic Abuse Special" or Salon Magazine's "U.K. tries to censor the Internet — An embarrassing report about a bungled satanic abuse investigation brings out the British blue pencil brigade," have already made it clear that your efforts to suppress the truth about what happened at Broxtowe have not had quite the result that you and your client desired. After all, no one would have mirrored the Broxtowe report at their sites on the World Wide Web had you not sought to enjoin its original publication. One would have thought that you would have learned that lesson by now. There are at least a dozen Web sites where the report is mirrored, not one of which would have existed if you had not sought to suppress its original publication on the Web. And at my site alone, the report has already been retrieved more than 2,500 times. For those of us who are opposed to governmental censorship of information on the World Wide Web, this reaction is gratifying. I doubt that it is so for your client.

See Roger McConchie, Canadian Corporate Counsel Association, 11th Annual Meeting (23–24 August 1999) at 38, para. 10.17

1) Injunctions for Injurious Falsehood

An application for an injunction for injurious falsehood is not governed by the same special rules as an application for an injunction for defamation. The differences in the rules was discussed in the recent Australian decision *Beechwood Homes (NSW) Pty Ltd. v. Camenzuli*, [2010] NSWSC 521 at paras. 9–12:

> *Swimsure (Laboratories) Pty Ltd v McDonald*, [1979] 2 NSWLR 796 involved the publication of statements that the plaintiff's pool cleaning product was not suitable for its purpose. No question of free speech or liberty of the press was present. In that case Hunt J said this at 801 as follows:
>
> > It is difficult, if not impossible, to see how these concepts of free speech and discussion and the liberty of the press can be involved in the ordinary slander of goods action. The conflict in defamation action between the plaintiff's right to his unblemished reputation, and the defendant's right publicly to discuss all matters of public interest simply does not arise in an action for slander of goods. The issue is

not whether the defendant, in disparaging the plaintiff's goods, had a right or privilege to do so, but rather whether he has done so maliciously and whether, in doing so, he has caused actual damage to the plaintiff.

In framing its action as one for slander of goods, so far as the matter complained of consists of a disparagement of its product in this case, the plaintiff is not avoiding an action for defamation, and the special exception to the 'balance of convenience' rule in granting interlocutory injunctions. No such action is fairly open to the plaintiff in relation to that disparagement, although clearly it has an arguable case in defamation so far as its own conduct is also disparaged. An injunction limited to the disparagement of the plaintiff's goods does not, in my opinion, have the effect of an injunction which the Court would not grant in defamation. There is, as I have said, no question of free speech and discussion and no question of the liberty of the press involved.

In *Palmer Bruyn & Parker Pty Ltd v Parsons* [2001] HCA 69; (2001) 208 CLR 388 at 58, Gummow J said this:

> Whilst the same factual matrix may found actions in both defamation and injurious falsehood, there are important distinctions between them. In *Joyce v Sengupta*, Sir Donald Nicholls V-C said:
>
>> The remedy provided by the law for words which injure a person's reputation is defamation. Words may also injure a person without damaging his reputation. An example would be a claim that the seller of goods or land is not the true owner. Another example would be a false assertion that a person has closed down his business. Such claims would not necessarily damage the reputation of those concerned. The remedy provided for this is malicious falsehood, sometimes called injurious falsehood or trade libel. This cause of action embraces particular types of malicious falsehood such as slander of title and slander of goods, but it is not confined to those headings.
>
> It is for the plaintiff in injurious falsehood to establish falsity, malice and special damage, burdens not imposed upon the plaintiff by defamation. *On the other hand, the inhibition upon the use of the injunction to restrain further publication of defamatory material does not*

apply to injurious falsehood; a rationale for the distinction is said to be that the latter tort protects proprietary and commercial rather than personal interests. (emphasis added)

In *Australand Holdings Ltd v Transparency & Accountability Council Incorporated*, [2008] NSWSC 669, McCallum J granted a final injunction concerning a threatened publication disparaging of a building company, without referring to any need to consider issues of freedom of speech or special considerations applicable to the exercise of discretion in the circumstances.

A plaintiff cannot avoid the special rules for injunctions simply by framing his case in the tort of injurious falsehood.

See *Beechwood Homes (NSW) Pty Ltd. v. Camenzuli,* [2010] NSWSC 521 at para. 12

CHAPTER 14: Take Down Notices

A. INTRODUCTION

The law of defamation at common law and in statutes encourages the resolution of defamation actions through apologies, retractions, corrections, and statements of contradiction and explanation. Apologies can mitigate or even eliminate certain types of damages if made in compliance with the relevant statutes. Conversely a refusal to apologize or retract can aggravate damages or even contribute to the imposition of punitive damages. The subject of retractions and apologies are covered in detail in Roger D. McConchie and David A. Potts, *Canadian Libel and Slander Actions* (Toronto: Irwin Law, 2004), Chapter 9, pp. 161–206. Consequently, the law will not be repeated here.

The Internet is well-suited to resolving disputes through retractions and apologies. It is possible to tailor the online retraction to exactly the same audience and even a broader audience than the original statement.

B. TAKE DOWN NOTICES IN SOUTH AFRICA AND THE UK

Take down notices are particularly valuable. Regrettably, they have not yet been incorporated into Canadian law. South Africa and the UK have legislation relating to take down notices.

1) South Africa

The take down notification section of South Africa's *Electronic Communications and Transactions Act 2002*, No. 25 of 2002, s. 77 states as follows:

(1) For the purposes of this Chapter, a notification of unlawful activity must be in writing, must be addressed by the complainant to the service provider or its designated agent and must include —

(a) the full names and address of the complainant;

(b) the written or electronic signature of the complainant;

(c) identification of the right that has allegedly been infringed;

(d) identification of the material or activity that is claimed to be the subject of unlawful activity;

(e) the remedial action required to be taken by the service provider in respect of the complaint;

(f) telephonic and electronic contact details, if any, of the complainant;

(g) a statement that the complainant is acting in good faith;

(h) a statement by the complainant that the information in the take-down notification is to his or her knowledge true and correct; and

(2) Any person who lodges a notification of unlawful activity with a service provider knowing that it materially misrepresents the facts is liable for damages for wrongful take-down.

(3) A service provider is not liable for wrongful take-down in response to a notification.

2) The UK

The *Electronic Commerce (EC Directives) Regulations 2002*, SI 2002/2013 states as follows:

Notice for the purposes of actual knowledge

22. In determining whether a service provider has actual knowledge for the purposes of regulations 18(b)(v) and 19(a)(i), a court shall take into account all matters which appear to it in the particular circumstances to be relevant and, among other things, shall have regard to —

(a) whether a service provider has received a notice through a means of contact made available in accordance with regulation 6(1)(c), and

(b) the extent to which any notice includes —

    (i)   the full name and address of the sender of the notice;

    (ii) details of the location of the information in question; and

    (iii) details of the unlawful nature of the activity or information in question.

C. GENERAL ADVICE

The general advice applicable to apologies is applicable to online apologies:

1. The apology should be full and frank. It should not be ironic or equivocal. This will, generally, simply aggravate damages or, at best, not mitigate them.
2. Do not repeat the original libel.
3. It is important not to defame a third party in the apology.
4. The apologies should be connected to the original online article, unless that article has been taken down. If it has been taken down, the apology should be prominently featured and should be connected to the same page, the same search engine, or the same results page, so that it can be easily replicated.

PART IV: Cause of Action and Defences

CHAPTER 15: Publication and Hyperlinks

A. BASIC PRINCIPLES

See Roger D. McConchie and David A. Potts in *Canadian Libel and Slander Actions* (Toronto: Irwin Law, 2004) at 257–58:

1) An Essential Element

Proof of publication by the defendant to a third party is an essential element in an action for defamation and the burden of proving this element rests on the plaintiff.

> *Gaskin v. Retail Credit Co.*, [1965] S.C.R. 297 per Ritchie J.
> *Arnott v. College of Physicians and Surgeons of Saskatchewan*, [1954] S.C.R. 538 per Locke J. at 555.
> *Dickhoff v. Armadale Communications* (1993), 108 D.L.R. (4th) 464, per Lane J.A. at 469 (Sask. C.A.).
> *Pressler v. Lethbridge* (2000), 86 B.C.L.R. (3d) 257, per Southin J.A. at para. 53 (C.A.).

2) Publication Requires Communication to a Third Party

There is a distinction between publication and simply creating or uttering defamatory expression. Publication requires an act on the part of the defendant which communicates the defamatory expression to a third party.

> *McNichol v. Grandy*, [1931] S.C.R. 696, where Anglin C.J.C. states at 699:

> The material part of the cause of action in dispute is not the uttering, but the publication, of the language used (*Hebditch v. MacIlwaince* [1894] 2 Q.B. 54, at 58, 61, 64, *O'Keefe v. Walsh* [1903] 2 Ir. R. 681, at 706).

Newson (Chief Provincial Firearms Officer for B.C.) v. Kexco Publishing Co. (1995), 17 B.C.L.R. (3d) 176 per Lambert J.A. at para. 21 (C.A.):

But publication for the purposes of libel means communication, not creation of the text for the purposes of printing.

Pullman v. Hill & Co., [1891] 1 Q.B. 524 per Lord Esher M.R. at 527:

What is the meaning of 'publication'? The making known the defamatory matter after it has been written to some person other than the person of whom it is written.

3)   Each Publication is a Separate Tort

Every publication of a libel is a separate tort and each re-publisher is answerable to the plaintiff in damages for his own act of publication.

King v. Lewis & Others, [2004] E.W.H.C. 168 at para. 16

Basse v. Toronto Star Newspaper Ltd. (1983), 44 O.R. (2d) 164, per Montgomery J., at 165 citing Clement Gatley and Philip Simon Coleman Lewis, *Gatley on Libel and Slander* 8th ed., (London: Sweet & Maxwell, 1981) paras. 261 and 266

Berezovsky v. Michaels, [2000] U.K.H.L. 25 at paras. 6–7, per Steyn L.J.

1)   When and Where does Publication Occur?

Publication occurs where the defamatory words are published in the sense of being heard, read, or downloaded. See *Dow Jones & Co. Inc. v. Gutnick*, [2002] HCA 56 at paras. 25–27, Gleeson. C.J., Gummow and Hayne J.J.:

The tort of defamation, at least as understood in Australia, focuses upon publications causing damage to reputation. It is a tort of strict liability, in the sense that a defendant may be liable even though no injury to reputation was intended and the defendant acted with reasonable care. Yet a publication made in the ordinary course of a business such as that of bookseller or news vendor, which the defendant shows to have been made in circumstances where the defendant did not know or suspect and, using reasonable diligence, would not have known or suspected was defamatory, will be held not to amount to publication of a libel. There is, nonetheless, obvious force in pointing to the need for the publisher to be able to identify, in advance, by what law of defamation the publication may be judged. But it is a tort concerned with damage to reputation and it is that damage which founds the cause of action. Perhaps, as Pollock said in 1887, the law went "wrong from the beginning in making the damage and not the insult the cause of action" for slander but it is now too late to deny that damage by publication is the focus of the law. *"It is the publication, not the composition of a libel, which is the actionable wrong."* [Emphasis added.]

Harm to reputation is done when a defamatory publication is compre-
hended by the reader, the listener, or the observer. Until then, no harm is done
by it. This being so it would be wrong to treat publication as if it were a uni-
lateral act on the part of the publisher alone. It is not. It is a bilateral act — in
which the publisher makes it available and a third party has it available for his
or her comprehension [emphasis added].

The bilateral nature of publication underpins the long-established common law rule that every communication of defamatory matter founds a separate cause of action. That rule has found reflection from time to time in
various ways in State legislation and it would be a large step now to depart
from it. [Footnotes omitted.]

In the same case, see Callinan J. at para. 184: "*The most important event so*
far as defamation is concerned is the infliction of the damage, and that occurs
at the place (or the places) where the defamation is comprehended" [emphasis
added]. See also *Imagis Technologies v. Red Herring Communications Inc.*,
2003 BCSC 366 at para. 16.

In British Columbia, the Court in *Imagis Technologies v. Red Herring*
Communications Inc., 2003 BCSC 366 found at paras. 22–24:

The cause of action on which Imagis sues arose in British Columbia. "Red Herring" was distributed and sold in British Columbia. The allegedly defamatory
statements therein were repeated and republished by the *Vancouver Sun* newspaper, a Vancouver publication known as *Stockwatch*, and by the *National*
Post, another Canadian newspaper circulated in British Columbia. *The fact*
of publication in British Columbia means that if the published statements were
defamatory, there is a cause of action on which to proceed in British Columbia,
notwithstanding that separate causes of action may have arisen in other juris-
dictions by virtue of publication in those jurisdictions [emphasis added].

If the statements were defamatory, Imagis may have sustained loss or
damage in British Columbia, a factor that favours an action being pursued
in this court. The evidence on this application indicates that Imagis has a
reputation with customers as well as regulatory and financial institutions in
the province. While it may also have a reputation with customers and financial or regulatory institutions in other jurisdictions, there is no evidence to
suggest that such other reputations are disproportionately more significant
than its reputation in British Columbia.

The fact of publication in British Columbia and the claim that Imagis suf-
fered damage here favour British Columbia as the forum conveniens [empha-
sis added].

An Ontario Court found in *Barrick Gold Corp. v. Blanchard & Co.*, [2003] O.J. No. 5817 (S.C.J.) at paras. 41 and 63:

> In my view, the plaintiff has established that there is a real and substantial connection between its claim and Ontario. While the allegedly libellous statements were made in many places, they were clearly made in Ontario. *If the tort of defamation consists both of the making and the receipt of a libellous statement, and I conclude that it does, then the tort was committed in Ontario.* As admitted by the defendants, the press releases were published in Ontario. I am satisfied on the evidence before me that the notices were sent to persons in Ontario. *The websites are accessible in Ontario* and, as I shall discuss further below, *the damage to reputation only occurs when the offending material is downloaded from the website onto a computer in Ontario and then read by a person in Ontario. Lastly, there were re-publications of the allegedly defamatory statements in Ontario. All of this occurs in the context of a plaintiff which is resident in Ontario and its reputation, if it was libelled, would be damaged in Ontario* [emphasis added].
>
> . . .
>
> In this case, of course, factors (i) and (ii) must be read as the location where the tort occurred and the law applicable to the tort. For the reasons I have already *enunciated above, I believe that, if the tort of defamation occurred, in the circumstances of this case it occurred in Ontario.* The law applicable to the determination of whether the tort occurred is therefore the law of Ontario. These factors therefore favour Ontario [emphasis added].

The Court in *Lewis & Ors v. King*, [2004] EWCA Civ 1329 at para. 2, stated:

> The libels alleged consist in two texts stored on websites based in California. In the ordinary way they can be, and have been, downloaded here. *It is common ground that by the law of England the tort of libel is committed where publication takes place, and each publication generates a separate cause of action. The parties also accept that a text on the Internet is published at the place where it is downloaded. Accordingly there is no contest but that subject to any defences on the merits the respondent has been libeled in this jurisdiction* [emphasis added].

In *Burke v. NYP Holdings Inc.*, [2005] B.C.J. No. 1993 (S.C.), the Court held at paras. 18–20 that:

> It is well established that public comments originating in another jurisdiction are actionable in a jurisdiction where the comments are published and where the reputation of a plaintiff is said to have been damaged: *Jenner v. Sun Oil Co.*

Ltd. et al, [1952] 2 D.L.R. 526 (Ont. S.C.); *Chinese Centre of Vancouver et al v. Holt et al* (1978), 87 C.L.R. (3d) 744 (B.C.S.C.); *Pindling v. National Broadcasting Corp. et al* (1985), 49 O.R. (2d) 58 (Ont. H.C.J.); and *Barrick Gold Corporation v. Lopehandia* 2004 CanLII 12938 (ON C.A.), (2005), 71 O.R. (3d) 416 (Ont. C.A.). There has been a steady expansion of that general principle regarding publication and republication as technology moves from radio broadcasts to television broadcasts to internet broadcasts to website broadcasts.

Jenner, supra, dealt with an Ontario defamation action against New York State defendants for alleged defamatory material broadcast by radio in New York with the broadcast being heard in Ontario. In holding that the action could be maintained in Ontario, McRuer C.J.H.C. stated:

> This is a case where it is necessary for Judges and lawyers to realize that statements in judgments written before modern methods of communication were developed or even thought of must be read in the light of the known circumstances under which they were written. (at p. 530)
>
> I have come to the conclusion that there are fundamental and common-sense principles which govern the present case. Radio broadcasts are made for the purpose of being heard. The programme here in question was put on the air for advertising purposes. It is to be presumed that those who broadcast over a radio network in the English language intend that the messages they broadcast will be heard by large numbers of those who receive radio messages in the English language. It is no doubt intended by those who broadcast for advertising purposes that the programme shall be heard by as many as possible. A radio broadcast is not a unilateral operation. It is the transmission of a message. (at p. 535)
>
> I think it a "startling proposition" to say that one may, while standing south of the border or cruising in an aeroplane south of the border, through the medium of modern sound amplification, utter defamatory matter which is heard in a Province in Canada north of the border, and not be said to have published a slander in the Province in which it is heard and understood. I cannot see what difference it makes whether the person is made to understand by means of written word, sound-waves or ether-waves in so far as the matter of proof of publication is concerned. The tort consists of making a third person understand actionable defamatory matter. (at p. 537)

The decision in *Pindling, supra,* extended the principle to deal with a defamation action about what was broadcast on a television show originating in the

United States but seen in Ontario. The principle was extended to defamatory statements published on the Internet by the decision of the Ontario Court of Appeal in *Barrick, supra* where Blair J.A. stated on behalf of the majority:

> The standard factors to consider in determining damages for defama-
> tion are summarized by Cory J. in *Hill* [v. *Church of Scientology of To-
> ronto*, [1955] 2 S.C.R. 1130] at p. 1203 S.C.R. They include the plaintiff's
> position and standing, the nature and seriousness of the defamatory
> statements, the mode and extent of publication, the absence or re-
> fusal of any retraction or apology, the whole conduct and motive of
> the defendant from publication through judgment, and any evidence
> of aggravating or mitigating circumstances.
>
> In the Internet context, these factors must be examined in the
> light of what one judge has characterized as the "ubiquity, universality
> and utility" of that medium. In *Dow Jones & Company Inc. v. Gutnick*,
> [2002] HCA 56 . . . , that same judge — Kirby J., of the High Court of
> Australia — portrayed the Internet in these terms, at para. 80:

> > The Internet is essentially a decentralized, self-maintained
> > telecommunications network. It is made up of inter-linking
> > small networks from all parts of the world. It is ubiquitous,
> > borderless, global and ambient in its nature. Hence the
> > term "cyberspace." . . . [It] is a word that recognizes that the
> > interrelationships created by the Internet exist outside con-
> > ventional geographic boundaries and comprise a single inter-
> > connected body of data, potentially amounting to a single
> > body of knowledge. The Internet is accessible in virtually all
> > places on Earth where access can be obtained either by wire
> > connection or by wireless (including satellite) links. Effective-
> > ly, the only constraint on access to the Internet is possession
> > of the means of securing connection to a telecommunications
> > system and possession of the basic hardware.

> Thus, of the criteria mentioned above, the mode and extent of pub-
> lication is particularly relevant in the Internet context, and must be
> considered carefully. Communication via the Internet is instantan-
> eous, seamless, interactive, blunt, borderless and far-reaching. It is
> also impersonal, and the anonymous nature of such communica-
> tions may itself create a greater risk that the defamatory remarks are
> believed: see *Vaquero Energy Ltd. v. Weir*, 2004 ABQB 68 (CanLII),
> [2004] A.J. No. 84, 2004 ABQB 68, at para. 17. (at pp. 431–2)

It is true that in the modern era defamatory material may be communicated broadly and rapidly via other media as well. The international distribution of newspapers, syndicated wire services, facsimile transmissions, radio and satellite television broadcasting are but some examples. Nevertheless, Internet defamation is distinguished from its less pervasive cousins, in terms of its potential to damage the reputation of individuals and corporations, by the features described above, especially its interactive nature, its potential for being taken at face value, and its absolute and immediate worldwide ubiquity and accessibility. The mode and extent of publication is therefore a particularly significant consideration in assessing damages in Internet defamation cases. (at p. 433)

Gutnick v. Dow Jones, [2002] HCA 56 at para 44:

In defamation, the same considerations that require rejection of locating the tort by reference only to the publisher's conduct, lead to the conclusion that, ordinarily, defamation is to be located at the place where the damage to reputation occurs. Ordinarily that will be where the material which is alleged to be defamatory is available in comprehensible form assuming, of course, that the person defamed has in that place a reputation which is thereby damaged. It is only when the material is in comprehensible form that the damage to reputation is done and it is damage to reputation which is the principal focus of defamation, not any quality of the defendant's conduct. *In the case of material on the World Wide Web, it is not available in comprehensible form until downloaded on to the computer of a person who has used a web browser to pull the material from the web server. It is where that person downloads the material that the damage to reputation may be done. Ordinarily then, that will be the place where the tort of defamation is committed* [emphasis added].

See also paras. 25–28 and see *Burke v. New York Post Holdings Inc.*, [2005] B.C.J. No. 1993 (S.C.).

2) Upon Proof of Publication

Upon proof of publication:

1. A presumption arises that the words are false;

Hodgson v. Canadian Newspapers Co. (1998), O.R. (3d) 235 (S.C.J.)
Jerome v. Anderson, [1964] S.C.R. 291
Adam v. Ward, [1917] A.C. 309 at 318

2. A presumption arises that the words were published maliciously; and

> *Mack v. North Hill News Ltd.* (1964), 44 D.L.R. (2d) 147 at 154
> *Mitchell v. Victorian Daily Times*, [1944] 2 D.L.R. 239

3. A presumption that the plaintiff has suffered damage appears. Damages are at large in libel actions, meaning that the court is entitled to make a subjective assessment without requiring proof of specific financial loss.

> *Lewis & Ors v. King*, [2004] EWHC 168 at para. 17
> *Hill v. Church of Scientology of Toronto*, [1995] 2 S.C.R. 1130 at para. 164
> *Cassell & Co. Ltd. v. Broome et al.*, [1972] 1 All E.R. 801 (H.L.)
> Julian Porter and David A. Potts, *Canadian Libel Practice* (Toronto: Butterworths, 1986) at 453

3) Defamation is a Joint and Several Liability Tort

Hill v. Church of Scientology of Toronto, [1995] 2 S.C.R. 1130 at para. 176, Cory J.

4) Publication in Multiple Jurisdictions

It is well-established that defamatory statements originating in one jurisdiction are actionable in another jurisdiction where the statements are published or re-published and where the reputation of a Plaintiff is said to have been damaged.

> *Burke v. New York Post Holdings Inc.*, [2005] B.C.J. No. 1993 at paras. 18–21

This general principle regarding publication and re-publication continues to apply as technology has moves from radio broadcasts to television broadcasts to Internet broadcasts:

1. radio broadcasts;

> See *Jenner v. Sun Oil Company Limited*, [1952] 2 D.L.R. 256 (Ont. H.C.)

2. television broadcasts; and

> See *Pindling v. NBC* (1985), 49 O.R. (2d) 58 (H.C.J.)

3. Internet broadcasts.

> *Burke v. New York Post Holdings Inc.*, 2005 BCSC 1287
> *Lewis & Ors v. King*, [2004] EWHC 168
> *Barrick Gold Corp. v. Blanchard & Co.*, 2003 CanLII 64238 (ON S.C.)
> *Harrods v. Dow Jones and Company*, [2003] EWHC 1162 (QB)
> *Imagis Technologies v. Red Herring Communications Inc.*, 2003 BCSC 366
> *Berezovsky v. Michael*, [2000] UKHL 25

See also *Dow Jones & Co. Inc. v. Gutnick*, [2002] HCA 56 at para. 198, Callinan, J.:

> ... the torts of libel and slander are committed when and where comprehension of the defamatory matter occurs. The rules have been universally applied to publications by spoken word, in writing, on television, by radio transmission, over the telephone or over the Internet. In *Browne v Dunn* the House of Lords held that there was no publication of a defamatory petition to a person (Mrs Cook) who had signed but not read the petition. [Footnotes omitted.]

B. NO PRESUMPTION OF PUBLICATION ON THE INTERNET IN CANADIAN LAW

1) Statutory Presumptions

Presumptions of publication in relation to newspapers and broadcasts are expressly provided for in sections 2 and 12(2) of the *Libel and Slander Act*, R.S.B.C. 1996, c. 263, which provide:

> 2 Defamatory words in a broadcast are deemed to be published and to constitute libel.
>
> . . .
>
> 12(2) The production of a printed copy of a newspaper is proof, in the absence of evidence to the contrary, of the publication of the printed copy and of the truth of the statements mentioned in subsection (1).

See *Crookes v. Newton*, 2009 BCCA 392 at para. 32

The *Ontario Libel and Slander Act*, R.S.O. 1990, c. L.12 provides a similar presumption in slightly different language:

> 2 Defamatory words in a newspaper or in a broadcast shall be deemed to be published and to constitute libel.
>
> . . .
>
> 8(2) The production of a printed copy of a newspaper is admissible in evidence as proof, in the absence of evidence to the contrary, of the publication of the printed copy and of the truth of the statements mentioned in subsection (1).

2) No Statutory Presumption for Publication on the Internet

There is no such statutory provision providing for presumed publication of communications distributed through the Internet. *Crookes v. Newton*, 2009

BCCA 392 at para. 33:

> There is no such statutory provision providing for presumed publication of communications distributed through the Internet. Nor was the judge persuaded that he should extend the presumption of publication to Internet communications, and, in particular, to the impugned articles accessible by the hyperlinks contained in Mr. Newton's article.

A very succinct, yet comprehensive, statement of the development of the law on the issue of the absence of a presumption of publication on the Internet is found in the dissenting decision in *Crookes v. Newton* at paras. 31–44.

As stated by Justice Prowse at para. 36 of *Crookes v. Newton* the issue of presumption of publication on the Internet was first raised in Canada in BC in *Crookes v. Holloway*:

> ... *Crookes v. Holloway*, 2007 BCSC 1325 (CanLII), 2007 BCSC 1325, 75 B.C.L.R. (4th) 316, aff'd in *Crookes v. Yahoo! Inc.*, 2008 BCCA 165 (CanLII), 2008 BCCA 165 (*sub nom. Crookes v. Holloway*), 77 B.C.L.R. (4th) 201 [*Holloway*]. [In that case], Mr. Crookes argued that there should be a presumption of publication in British Columbia with respect to alleged defamatory material found on the Yahoo Inc.! site. The trial judge in *Holloway* rejected that submission and dismissed the action for want of jurisdiction. [The Court of Appeal] upheld the decision [of the trial judge]. [Regarding] Mr. Crookes' argument that there should be a presumption of publication, Mr. Justice Lowry, speaking for the Court, stated, at para. 6 of the decision:
>
> > [6] In *Wiebe* [*v. Bouchard*, 2005 BCSC 47, 46 B.C.L.R. (4th) 278] significance was attached to the fact the libellous statements were posted on the internet nationwide as well as being made available in the main public library in Victoria. But they were posted on a Government of Canada website and, as was noted, were made available to everyone in the country who had a computer. By contrast, the statements that are the subject of Mr. Crookes' action were posted on a website with restricted access that was not available to the public. The basis for any presumption that might be said to have been recognized in *Wiebe* does not exist here. *I do not consider the mere fact a statement was posted on a website with the kind of restricted access there was in this case supports the presumption it was read by anyone in British Columbia* [Emphasis added.]

The question was examined again in *Crookes v. Newton*. In that case, at para. 31, the Court said "the principal argument of Mr. Crookes at trial was

that the trial judge should apply a *presumption* of publication of the hyperlinked articles by analogy with statements made in newspapers or broadcast
to the general public" [emphasis in original].

The trial judge concluded there was no presumption on the facts and
relied on the previous decision of *Crookes v. Halloway,* 2007 BCSC 1325, affirmed 2008 BCCA 165.

The plaintiff in *Crookes v. Newton* appealed to the British Columbia Court
of Appeal. The appellant argued that the presumption of publication existed
in this case because, unlike the *Crookes v. Holloway* decision, where the website had restricted access, Mr. Newton's site had unrestricted access.

See *Crookes v. Newton,* 2009 BCCA 392 at para. 38

The Court of Appeal confined its decision to the facts and distinguished
between a presumption of publication on the original article and a presumption of publication with respect to the hyperlinked website and articles. Justice Prowse found at paras. 39–40 that this fact did not assist the appellant:

> Given the apparent lack of difficulty in establishing the number of times
> the primary site was accessed in this case, I do not see how it furthers Mr.
> Crookes' case for him to say that Mr. Newton's p2pnet site has world-wide
> accessibility (except to distinguish the case from *Holloway*). It may have
> world-wide accessibility, but it is an accepted fact that it had been accessed
> 1,788 times. It follows that the links to those articles on p2pnet have been
> accessed no more than 1,788 times. *In any event, the critical question is not
> whether there is a presumption of publication of Mr. Newton's article, but
> whether there is a presumption of publication with respect to the hyperlinked
> websites and articles.*
>
> There are undoubtedly world-wide sites dealing with topics which are of
> no interest to anyone except the author. There are others which are probably
> viewed millions of times each day. It may be that in the latter case, a pre-
> sumption of publication could arise with respect to a particular site. *A pre-
> sumption of publication of articles hyperlinked to such a site, however, would
> still be one-step (or one click) removed* [emphasis added].

Ultimately, Prowse J. upheld, with the agreement of the majority (see
para. 78), the decision of the trial judge at paras. 41–42:

> I agree with the trial judge that there is no sound basis for finding a pre-
> sumption of publication of the hyperlinked articles in this case. None of the
> authorities relied on by Mr. Crookes provides a persuasive basis for such a
> presumption. Assuming there may be compelling reasons for a presumption

of publication with respect to materials distributed on the Internet, and, in particular, with respect to hyperlinked materials (and this Court is not in a position based on the evidence in this case to make such a determination), that is a matter which may more readily be determined by the Legislature, rather than by the courts in the first instance. Courts are restricted to the record before them which, in many cases, does not permit the appropriate weighing of values and interests which should be taken into account when a change in the law such as this is advocated. The continuing evolution of the Internet is a phenomenon which raises many complex questions with far-reaching implications on an international scale. I would be loathe to venture into this area without a better compass than has been provided in this case.

In the result, I agree with the trial judge that there is no presumption of publication of hyperlinked articles; that is, there is no presumption that a reader who accesses an internet source containing hyperlinks also accessed the articles found at the hyperlinked source. Nor do I find any persuasive basis for creating such a presumption on the facts of this case.

Finally, Prowse, J. held at para. 43 that:

> ... the trial judge referred to an English authority, *Amoudi v. Brisard*, [2006] EWHC 1062, All E.R. 294 (Q.B.), which, in turn, referred to *Jameel v. Dow Jones*, [2005] EWCA Civ. 75, as supportive of his conclusion that there is no presumed publication of material distributed on the Internet .... I agree with Mr. Newton that, whether or not the trial judge erred in making that statement, he was correct in finding that those authorities support the proposition that, in England, there is no presumption of publication (substantial or otherwise) with respect to Internet publications.

The UK cases will be discussed below in section C.

An Ontario Superior Court of Justice decision made some observations on the question of publication on the Internet in *Manson v. Moffett*, 2008 CanLII 19789 at para. 8 (ON S.C.):

> Apart from the plaintiff's right to rely on the presumption of facts in their favour, the plaintiff is, in my view, upon any reasonable review and analysis of the present circumstances, entitled to judgment in its favour; for the following reasons:
>
> (1) By any reasonable definition, anything disseminated on the internet is intended for consumption by a wide audience and easily meets any reasonable definition of "publication." Indeed, the very concept of a "world-wide web" invites no other reasonable interpretation ....

3) Personal Observations

The decision in *Manson v. Moffett*, 2008 CanLII 19789 (ON S.C.), in my opinion, should be viewed cautiously and restricted to its facts for the following reasons:

1. This was a summary judgment based on a default judgment wherein the defendant did not appear. See Rule 19 under the *Ontario Rules of Civil Procedure.*

2. There appears to be, in this case, a presumption of publication by virtue of r. 19.02(1) which states as follows:

   CONSEQUENCES OF NOTING DEFAULT

   19.02 (1) A defendant who has been noted in default,

   (a) is deemed to admit the truth of all allegations of fact made in the statement of claim. . .

3. There was no evidence of the introduction of evidence as to publication in this case.

4. There was no discussion or examination of the bilateral concept of defamation as stated in *Crookes v. Newton*, 2009 BCCA 392 at para. 24:

   It is trite law that defamation cannot be found without publication. Publication is defined in the following extract from Raymond Brown, *The Law of Defamation in Canada*, 2d ed. Looseleaf (Scarborough: Carswell, 1994), vol. 1, at 7-4, 7-5:

   > Publication is a term of art meaning the communication of defamatory matter to a third person." It is a bilateral act by which the publisher makes available to a reader, listener or observer in a comprehensible form the defamatory information. Therefore, the defamatory remarks, about which the plaintiff complains, must be shown to have been published to a third person, that is, they must have been communicated to some person other than the one defamed, even if that involves only a single individual . . . [Footnotes omitted.]

5. There was no mention of the discussion of proof of publication found in Patrick Milmo QC, W.V.H. Rogers, Richard Parkes QC, Professor Clive Walker and Godwin Busuttil (eds.), *Gatley on Libel and Slander*, 11th edition (London: Sweet & Maxwell, 2003) ("Gatley") or the UK decisions about the absence of the presumption of publication on the Internet,

which were rendered prior to the publication of that edition (November 2008) See *Amoudi v. Brisard*, [2006] EWHC 1062 (QB).

C. NO PRESUMPTION OF PUBLICATION ON THE INTERNET IN THE UK

1) Introduction

The UK does not have a legislative presumption of publication for newspapers and broadcasts as do BC and Ontario.

> BC *Libel and Slander Act*, R.S.B.C. 1996, c. 263, ss.2 and 12(2)
>
> Ontario *Libel and Slander Act*, R.S.O. 1990, c. L.12, ss.2 and s. 8

In the UK, the question of the presumption of publication arises often in the following situations during motions to dismiss for abuse of process:

1. There is evidence of only limited publication.

   > *Atlantis World Group of Companies NV & Anor v. Gruppo Editoriale L'Espresso SPA*, [2008] EWHC 1323 (QB)

2. The action is dismissed where the court finds that there is little likelihood of success even though there is no reference to the amount of publication.

   > *Bunt v. Tilley* [2006] EWHC 407 at paras. 77–78 (QB)

3. There is limited publication as well as other factors such as little likelihood of success.

   > *Atlantis World Group of Companies NV & Anor v. Gruppo Editoriale L'Espresso SPA*, [2008] EWHC 1323 (QB)
   >
   > *Carrie v. Tolkien* [2009] EWHC 29 (QB)
   >
   > *Lonzim PLC and Ors v. Sprague*, [2009] EWHC 2838 (QB)

In other cases the courts have refused to dismiss the actions for abuse of process simply on the basis of a limited number of publications holding that some situations are important enough to proceed regardless of the limited number of publications.

> See *Mardas v New York Times Company & Anor*, [2008] EWHC 3135 at para. 15 (QB)
>
> *Carrie v. Tolkien*, [2009] EWHC 29 at para. 20 (QB) as *obiter*

2) The Abuse of Process Principle

While a full chapter is devoted to the principle of abuse of process elsewhere in this book, it is important enough to be included here as well.

The Court in *Jameel v. Dow Jones*, [2005] QB 946 summarized the law relating to the abuse of process principle as follows at paras. 40, 54–56, 66, 69–70:

> We accept that in the rare case where a claimant brings an action for defamation in circumstances where his reputation has suffered no or minimal actual damage, this may constitute an interference with freedom of expression that is not necessary for the protection of the claimant's reputation. In such circumstances the appropriate remedy for the defendant may well be to challenge the claimant's resort to English jurisdiction or to seek to strike out the action as an abuse of process. We are shortly to consider such an application.
>
> . . .
>
> An abuse of process is of concern not merely to the parties but to the court. It is no longer the role of the court simply to provide a level playing field and to referee whatever game the parties choose to play upon it. The court is concerned to ensure that judicial and court resources are appropriately and proportionately used in accordance with the requirements of justice.
>
> There have been two recent developments which have rendered the court more ready to entertain a submission that pursuit of a libel action is an abuse of process. The first is the introduction of the new Civil Procedure Rules. Pursuit of the overriding objective requires an approach by the court to litigation that is both more flexible and more proactive. The second is the coming into effect of the *Human Rights Act 1998*. Section 6 requires the court, as a public authority, to administer the law in a manner which is compatible with Convention rights, in so far as it is possible to do so. Keeping a proper balance between the article 10 right of freedom of expression and the protection of individual reputation must, so it seems to us, require the court to bring to a stop as an abuse of process defamation proceedings that are not serving the legitimate purpose of protecting the claimant's reputation, which includes compensating the claimant only if that reputation has been unlawfully damaged.
>
> We do not believe that *Duke of Brunswick v. Harmer* 14 QB 185 could today have survived an application to strike out for abuse of process. The Duke himself procured the republication to his agent of an article published many

years before for the sole purpose of bringing legal proceedings that would not be met by a plea of limitation. If his agent read the article he is unlikely to have thought the Duke much, if any, the worse for it and, to the extent that he did, the Duke brought this on his own head. He acquired a technical cause of action but we would today condemn the entire exercise as an abuse of process

. . .

It is . . . not legitimate for the claimant to seek to justify the pursuit of these proceedings by praying in aid the effect that they may have in vindicating him in relation to the wider publication

. . .

If the claimant succeeds in this action and is awarded a small amount of damages, it can perhaps be said that he will have achieved vindication for the damage done to his reputation in this country, but both the damage and the vindication will be minimal. The cost of the exercise will have been out of all proportion to what has been achieved. *The game will not merely not have been worth the candle, it will not have been worth the wick* [emphasis added].

If we were considering an application to set aside permission to serve these proceedings out of the jurisdiction we would allow that application on the basis that the five publications that had taken place in this jurisdiction did not, individually or collectively, amount to a real and substantial tort. Jurisdiction is no longer in issue, but, subject to the effect of the claim for an injunction that we have yet to consider, we consider for precisely the same reason that it would not be right to permit this action to proceed. It would be an abuse of process to continue to commit the resources of the English court, including substantial judge and possibly jury time, to an action where so little is now seen to be at stake. Normally where a small claim is brought, it will be dealt with by a proportionate small claims procedure. Such a course is not available in an action for defamation where, although the claim is small, the issues are complex and subject to special procedure under the CPR.

Cited, for example, in *Lonzim Plc & Ors v. Sprague*, [2009] EWHC 2838 at para. 18 (QB), Tugendhat J.

3) No Presumption of Publication and Substantial Publication on the Internet

The principle of no presumption of substantial publication on the Internet was established in the decision of *Amoudi v. Brisard & Anor*, [2006] EWHC

1062 (QB). The judgment stated the questions to be disposed of in the first two paragraphs:

> This application raises the question whether and, if so, in what circumstances it is open to a claimant complaining of an item on an Internet website open to general access to rely on a presumption that substantial publication of that item has taken place within the jurisdiction of the court. The Claimant, Mr Mohammed Hussein Al Amoudi, contends that there is such a presumption, albeit a rebuttable one. The Defendants, M. Jean Charles Brisard and JCB Consulting International SARL, maintain that no such presumption exists, rebuttable or otherwise. Their case is that the Claimant must prove publication in the ordinary way.
>
> In the event that the Claimant is successful on that question, I am asked to strike out or in the alternative to give summary judgment in favour of the Claimant in relation to those parts of the Defence which deny that there was publication on the website within the jurisdiction.

The Court summarized the arguments for the plaintiff at paras. 21–23 and the arguments for the defendants at paras. 24–27. The discussion and conclusion at paras. 28–37 merit inclusion because of the detailed examination of presumptions and the explanation for the basis of his conclusion.

> It is clear from the terms of the Application Notice, as well as from the skeleton argument of the Claimant, that the preliminary ruling sought by the Claimant is that there is a *presumption* that the words complained of were published via the Internet to a substantial but unquantifiable number of readers in the jurisdiction of the Court. However, it became apparent during the course of the oral hearing that there was disagreement between the parties as to the difference, if any, between a presumption (in this case a rebuttable presumption) on the one hand and an inference. The uncertainty was highlighted by the heavy reliance placed by the Claimant on *Steinberg*, in which case Sedley LJ described the inference of publication as being "irresistible."
>
> The current (16th) edition of *Phipson on Evidence* describes the relevance of presumptions at paragraph 6-16 in these terms:

> > Certain presumptions of fact and law are recognised by the courts. Presumptions may be rebuttable or irrebuttable. Where a presumption operates, the court may or must draw a certain conclusion. On most occasions this will be in the absence of evidence in rebuttal, thus assisting the party who bears the burden of proof on that issue.

The effect of a presumption may be to require less evidence than would otherwise be necessary, or to make it unnecessary to call any evidence at all. Some presumptions are irrebuttable, in that the court is bound to draw a certain conclusion, whether or not there is evidence to contrary effect; in such circumstances evidence in rebuttal will be inadmissible.

The editors then deal at paragraph 6-17 with the different types of presumption as follows:

(a) *Rebuttable presumptions of law*: where a rebuttable presumption of law applies in favour of a party, on the proof or admission of one fact, another fact is to be presumed. Once the presumption applies, the persuasive or evidential burden (as the case may be) is on the other party to disprove the presumed fact.

(b) *Irrebuttable presumptions of law*: where an irrebuttable presumption of law applies, on proof or admission of a basic fact, another fact will be presumed and the other party is barred from calling any evidence in rebuttal . . .

(c) *Presumptions of fact*: presumptions of fact are invariably rebuttable. Where a presumption of fact applies, on the proof or admission of a fact, another fact *may* be presumed. But unlike rebuttable presumptions of law, presumptions of fact do not shift the persuasive or evidential burden. Strictly speaking, the term 'presumption of fact' is a misnomer. It describes the readiness of the court to draw certain repeated inferences as a result of common human experience.

Those paragraphs appear to me to make clear that the presumption for which the Claimant contends in his Application Notice *and in his skeleton argument is a rebuttable presumption of law*. That is to be distinguished from a presumption of fact, which label is described in *Phipson* as "a misnomer" and which is in my view more appropriately described as an inference which the tribunal of fact may, depending on the circumstances, draw as a result of common human experience [emphasis added].

The question which I therefore have to decide is whether the Claimant is right to say that there is a rebuttable presumption of law, in the sense which I have indicated, that the publication on the Internet of the two items complained of was to a substantial but unquantifiable number of people within the jurisdiction.

As to that the general rule, as stated by the editors of the current edition of *Gatley*, at paragraphs 6.1 and 32.5, is that the claimant bears the burden of proving that the words complained of were read or seen by a third party. From that proposition it would appear to follow that, in the case of an Internet libel, it would be for the claimant to prove that the material in question was accessed and downloaded. This is what the editors of *Gatley* suggest at paragraph 32.7. I do not accept that *Fullam* is authority for any contrary proposition; it decides no more than that for the purpose of *pleading* publication in a case where the claimant relies on an innuendo meaning, it is sufficient for the claimant to assert that the publication was to a substantial but unquantifiable number of readers possessing the knowledge of extrinsic facts necessary for them to understand the words in their innuendo meaning.

It is well known (and juries are routinely so directed) that some facts are capable of direct proof, whereas others may properly be proved by inference. Thus publication of the items complained of in the present case to a particular individual could be proved by calling that individual to say that he or she accessed the items and downloaded them within the jurisdiction. A wider publication may be proved by establishing a platform of facts from which the tribunal of fact could properly infer that substantial publication within the jurisdiction has taken place. As I read the observations made (*obiter*) by Sedley LJ when refusing an application for permission to appeal in *Steinberg*, he was simply saying that on the facts of that case the inference that a substantial number of people would have accessed Mr Steinberg's letter was irresistible. He was not in my view suggesting that there was any presumption to that effect.

Contrary to the submission of the Claimant, I consider that my decision in *Loutchansky* is in point. The facts in that case were that the claimant was complaining of the posting on the website of *The Times* of an article defamatory of the claimant which had been published in the newspaper. The evidence showed that a large number of visits had been paid to the website but there was no direct evidence how many of these visitors, if any, accessed the article complained of. In my judgment I said this:

> 14. In the present case, whilst it is not pleaded [counsel for the claimant] contends that the evidence is that 12.5 million direct visits are paid to *The Times*' website each month. He therefore submits that it can safely be assumed that a number of those visits would have been paid in order to gain access to the particular article about the Claimant, which is complained of in this action. [He] further draws

attention to the publicity and promotional material put out by the Defendants advertising the existence of their website and the facility with which access to it can be obtained. [Counsel for the defendants], however, contends that, for a number of reasons, the basis for any such inference of publication having taken place is simply not made out. He points out that the two articles complained of had been placed online on the date when they were published, namely September and October 1999 respectively. The complained made by the Claimant, in respect of those publications, is confined to a period commencing on February 21, 2000. [He] suggests that the articles, being respectively five and six months' old, are unlikely to have been visited so long after their original publication. He also draws attention to the fact that the name of the Claimant was misspelled in the original articles, so that the search engine would not have enabled a person to type in the word "Loutchansky," and so gain access to the articles complained of. For these and other reasons which I need not recite, [counsel for the Defendants] submits that it cannot be presumed, merely because the article was available on the website, that anyone would in fact have read it after February 21, 2000. Moreover, he contends that this is a situation where it is incumbent on a claimant to prove affirmatively that publication took place, and that the court should not permit a claimant to establish publication on the basis of mere inference. Speaking for myself, I understand the force of many of [counsel for the Defendant's] observations. However, it appears to me that proof of publication in a defamation action is no different from proof of a number of other propositions that may fall to be established in the course of such an action. It is possible for publication, as for other propositions, to be established by inviting a tribunal to draw inference from the platform of facts. That, as it appears to me, is what [counsel for the Claimant] is inviting the tribunal in the present case to do.

I consider that the law in *Gatley*, albeit ante-dating website publications over the Internet, accurately sets out the applicable principles. I accept that a publication may be established as a matter of inference if the underlying facts justify the inference being drawn.

. . .

What I said in my judgment in *Loutchansky* appears to me to be consistent with what is now to be found in the section of *Gatley* dealing with proof of publication under the heading "Inferences" at paragraph 32.6. I believe it is also consistent with what Dr Matthew Collins says at paragraph 5.04 of *The Law of Defamation and the Internet* (2nd Edition):

> Proof that Internet communications have been published is therefore not usually a difficult task. Every e-mail message which has been received and seen by a recipient, other than the person defamed, who is capable of understanding it, has been published. So too is every message posted on a bulletin board and every web page which is accessible to computer users, if it can be proved that any third person capable of understanding it has displayed and seen the message or web page on a computer screen. The claimant bears the burden of proof. That burden will generally be discharged by proving that at least one person, other than the claimant, saw, read or heard the communication. In the case of generally accessible web pages and bulletin boards with many subscribers, it may be inferred that publication has occurred.

I think that further assistance on the question which I have to decide can be derived from *Jameel v. Dow Jones Inc.* That was another claim in respect of a libel on a Saudi businessman in respect of an article published on an internet website which was said on behalf of the claimant to be available to between five and ten thousand subscribers within the jurisdiction. The claimant in that case invited the inference to be drawn that a substantial number of readers of the main article would have read the page to which the hyperlink led. The defendant publishers adduced evidence that only five subscribers within the jurisdiction had been able to access the alleged libel via the hyperlink. Of those five, three were members of the claimant's "camp." The Court of Appeal struck out the claim as an abuse of process on the ground that the extent of the publication within the jurisdiction was minimal and did not amount to a real and substantial tort. It appears to me to be of some significance that there was no suggestion made on behalf of the claimant in the context of that case that he could rely on any presumption of publication. The fact that the Court of Appeal struck out the claim provides some support for the view that an argument in favour of the existence of a presumption of publication would not have found favour with the court.

For the above reasons I am unable to accept that under English law a claimant in a libel action on an Internet publication is entitled to rely on a presumption of law that there has been substantial publication [emphasis added].

4) The *Amoudi* Principle Was Used Interchangeably in "No Publication" Cases and "No Substantial Publication" Cases

The decision in *Amoudi v. Brisard & Anor,* [2006] EWHC 1062 (QB), appears to be used interchangeably, in cases involving "no substantial publication" and cases involving "no publication" with no discussion of the difference between the two situations.

For cases involving no substantial publication see the following:
- *Carrie v. Tolkien,* [2009] EWHC 29 at para. 17 (QB)
- *Ewing v. News International Ltd. & Ors,* [2008] EWHC 1390 at para. 101 (QB)
- *Brady v. Norman,* [2008] EWHC 2481 at para. 23 (QB)
- *Trumm v. Norman,* [2008] EWHC 1116 (QB)

For cases involving no publication see the following:
- *Hughes v. Risbridger & Anor,* [2009] EWHC 3244 (QB)
- *Lonzim PLC and Ors v. Sprague,* [2009] EWHC 2838 at para. 19 (QB)
- *Metropolitan International Schools Ltd. (t/a Skillstrain and/or Train-2game) v. Designtechnica Corp (t/a Digital Trends) & Ors,* [2009] EWHC 1765 at para. 33 (QB)

D. INTERNET PUBLICATION DECISIONS PRIOR TO *CROOKES v. NEWTON*

1) *Carter v. B.C. Federation of Foster Parents*

The British Columbia Court of Appeal in *Carter v. B.C. Federation of Foster Parents,* 2005 BCCA 398, held that there is no publication merely because a person places a URL that refers to a defamatory article in a newsletter. The trial judge in *Carter v. B.C. Federation of Foster Parents Association,* 2004 BCSC 137 at para. 51, held there was no publication.

> On the evidence before me, there is nothing in the network newsletter to suggest a defamatory comment if a reader of the network newsletter did not more than read the newsletter. In order to read the alleged defamatory comments, it was necessary to go to the Bopeep Forum. The address of the Bopeep Forum was listed in the Network newsletter. This comment was contained among a myriad of other unobjectionable comments posted on that site (i.e. the Bopeep Forum).

The Court of Appeal upheld the trial judge and dismissed the appeal holding as follows at paras. 12–13:

> In my opinion, the factual situation here is closer to the situation found to exist in the New York cases of *MacFadden v. Anthony*, 117 N.Y.S.2d 520 (Sup. Ct. 1952) and *Klein v. Biben*, 296 N.Y. 638 (Ct. App. 1946), referred to by the trial judge, where the courts held reference to an article containing defamatory comment without repetition of the comment itself should not be found to be a republication of such defamatory comment.
>
> Unlike the situation found in the *Tacket* case, there was here no element of control by the Federation over the Bopeep Forum and the facts of the instant case are quite distinguishable from the situation found to exist in the *Hird* case. In *Hird*, the defendant took active steps to draw the attention of persons to the defamatory placard. I should say that the defendant there was taking active steps to publish to the world the defamatory material contained on the placard. I do not believe the circumstances extant there can be successfully analogized to the instant case. I take note of the fact that this was a reference in a printed newsletter to a website and I would limit the effect of this case to that factual situation. Whether a different result should obtain concerning an internet website that makes reference to another website I would leave for decision when that factual circumstance arises. In the result, I am not persuaded that the learned trial judge made any error in his assessment of this aspect of the matter and I would dismiss the appeal on this issue concerning the Bopeep Forum.

The Court of Appeal held overruling the trial judge at paras. 14–20 that the single publication rule does not apply in BC. This subject is discussed in Chapter 8, section C(8).

Finally, the Court of Appeal held at para. 21: "it was not open for the trial judge to conclude that the defence of innocent dissemination could be successfully made out of the state of the facts here."

2) *Crookes v. Yahoo!*

In *Crookes v. Yahoo!*, 2007 BCSC 1325, 75 B.C.L.R. (4th) 316, Stromberg-Stein J. dismissed the action at para. 30 because there was no proof of publication:

> Publication is an essential element for an action in defamation. In this case, the pleadings are deficient as there is no pleading alleging the purported defamatory postings were published in British Columbia; that is, communicated to a third person: *Braintech Inc. v. Kostiuk*, 1999 BCCA 169 (CanLII),

[1999] B.C.J. No. 622, 1999 BCCA 169. There is no evidence anyone read the material in British Columbia and there is no basis for this court to draw that inference.

The plaintiff appealed to the British Columbia Court of Appeal in *Crookes v. Yahoo!*, 2007 BCSC 1325.

The question on appeal was whether libellous statements posted on the Internet, but subject to limited access, can be presumed to have been published in this jurisdiction such as to constitute the commission of a tort there. The Court of Appeal dismissed the appeal. At paras. 6–8 of *Crookes v. Yahoo!*, 2008 BCCA 165, Lowry J.A. stated:

> In *Wiebe* significance was attached to the fact the libellous statements were posted on the internet nationwide as well as being made available in the main public library in Victoria. But they were posted on a Government of Canada website and, as was noted, were made available to everyone in the country who had a computer. By contrast, the statements that are the subject of Mr. Crookes' action were posted on a website with restricted access that was not available to the public. The basis for any presumption that might be said to have been recognized in *Wiebe* does not exist here. I do not consider the mere fact a statement was posted on a website with the kind of restricted access there was in this case supports the presumption it was read by anyone in British Columbia.
>
> Mr. Crookes also contends the judge erred in holding Yahoo had, without tendering any evidence in support, demonstrated there was no publication in British Columbia. But in my view, the judge reached no such conclusion. She observed Mr. Crookes pleaded case was deficient and no evidence had been adduced on the application that the statements had been read in this province, or that would permit an inference to that effect to be drawn. She held there was no basis to find the proceeding concerned a tort committed in British Columbia such that the court was without jurisdiction.
>
> It follows that I see no error in the judge's dismissal of the action against Yahoo and I would dismiss the appeal.

3) *Crookes v. Pilling*

The British Columbia Supreme Court in *Crookes v. Pilling*, 2007 BCSC 630 dismissed the plaintiff's claim holding at para. 13 that the defendant was not a publisher of the defamatory statements:

I find on the basis of what I have outlined that there is insufficient evidence to support the allegation that the defendant was "at all material times," that is on the alleged dates of publication, a "publisher or member of the OP steering committee."

The plaintiff appealed and the appeal was heard as *Crookes v. De Simone*, 2007 BCCA 515. In that appeal, Mr. Justice Smith upheld the decision of a trial judge dismissing an action because the plaintiff failed to prove publication as follows at paras. 27–28:

> The trial judge weighed the admissible evidence and concluded that the appellants' evidence was not sufficient to prove that the respondent published the alleged libel. That is a finding of fact that was open to him on the evidence before him, and I can see no basis that would justify our interference.
>
> Accordingly, since the trial judge did not err, in my view, in reaching his conclusion that the appellants failed to prove that the respondent published the libel, there is no need to consider the second ground of appeal.

E. PUBLICATION AND HYPERLINKS

1) The Distinction between the Automatic/Embedded Hyperlinks and the User-Activated Hyperlinks

Hyperlinks are discussed in Chapter 5, section B(8). In this section, the distinction between automatic/embedded hyperlinks and user-activated hyperlinks is examined through, in particular, the decision of the British Columbia Court of Appeal in *Crookes v. Newton*, 2009 BCCA 392.

The Copyright Board of Canada decision *SOCAN Statement of Royalties, Public Performance of Musical Works 1996, 1997, 1998 (Tariff 22, Internet) (Re)* (1999), 1 C.P.R. (4th) 417, and the decision of the Supreme Court of Canada in *Society of Composers, Authors and Music Publishers of Canada v. Canadian Association of Internet Providers*, 2004 SCC 45, [2004] 2 S.C.R. 427, explained this distinction very clearly. As noted by the Copyright Board of Canada in the above-mentioned decision:

> Understanding the legal issues arising from the use of hyperlinks requires considering the nature and operation of these links. We will also look at some Canadian business arrangements in which hyperlinks are used to make content available to end users, and consider how persons responsible for linked sites can be located.

a) Nature and operation of hyperlinks [automatic or user activated]

Any page on a Web site may contain one or more hyperlinks to pages on the same or other Web sites, located on the same or different servers from the one that hosts the linking site. The files at the other site normally are under the control of another entity. However, hyperlinks may be made either with or without a business relationship with the owners of the sites to which links are made.

Hyperlinks can be *automatic links* or *user-activated*. A link is *automatic when a code is embedded in the Web page which instructs the browser, upon obtaining access to the first site, to automatically download a file from the second site.* The information from the second site is pulled without the need for further action on the part of the user. *A link is user-activated when the user must click the mouse button over the hyperlink in order to obtain access to the information from the second site.* If the linked files are located on another server, the user's browser makes a direct connection to the second server. The user-activated hyperlink may be made to the home page or a subpage located on the second site, in which case, the end user may have to take further action to access a particular file at that site. The link may also be made directly to a specific file, in which case the user will receive the content represented by that file without the need for further action [emphasis added].

In *Society of Composers, Authors and Music Publishers of Canada v. Canadian Association of Internet Providers*, 2004 SCC 45, [2004] 2 S.C.R. 427, Binnie, J. stated at para. 25:

> The Board was also required to consider the potential copyright infringement of "hyperlinks," particularly when the link is automatic. Automatic links employ an embedded code in the Web page that automatically instructs the browser, upon obtaining access to the first site, to download a file from a second site. The user does not need to do anything but visit the initial site before information from the second site is "pulled." *A different legal issue may arise where the user must take action, such as to click the mouse button over the hyperlink, in order to obtain access to the information from the second site* [emphasis added].

This distinction is of fundamental importance in the discussion of the hyperlinks and publication of the defamatory statements on the Internet through hyperlinks.

See also online: www.w3.org/DesignIssues/LinkLaw
www.w3.org/DesignIssues/LinkMyths

2) *Crookes v. Newton*

In *Crookes v. Newton*, 2009 BCCA 392, the plaintiff, Crookes, sued several parties alleging that he had been defamed in a number of articles which appeared on two different websites. Crookes also sued the defendant Newton, the owner of a third website (Free Speech site located at www.2pnet.net) for linking to these allegedly defamatory articles. Newton had published an article on his website in which he commented on the state of the defamation laws in Canada and, in particular, made reference to Crookes's defamation suit, including providing links to the websites that contained allegedly defamatory content.

a) Summary of Findings

First, all three judges agreed at para. 42 that there is no presumption of publication for hyperlinked articles:

> In the result, I agree with the trial judge that there is no presumption of publication of hyperlinked articles; that is, there is no presumption that a reader who accesses an internet source containing hyperlinks also accessed the articles found at the hyperlinked source. Nor do I find any persuasive basis for creating such a presumption on the facts of this case.

Second, all three judges found at para. 78 that, ". . . the mere fact that Mr. Newton hyperlinked the impugned sites does not make him a publisher of the material found at the hyperlinked sites" (also see para. 58 of the minority).

Third, the majority disagreed with the minority that the trial judge erred in failing to infer publication to at least one party (see para. 79).

Fourth, the majority did not agree that the article by Mr. Newton contained words of encouragement or an invitation to a person accessing Mr. Newton's site. As a result, they dismissed the appeal at para. 79.

Fifth, the majority held that as the request to remove the defamatory statement was not considered by the judge and the finding of facts were not contained in the reasons for judgment to support a discussion of that issue (see para. 94 for the comments of the majority and para. 76 for those of the minority).

Justice Saunders, for the majority, delivered pithy, brilliant reasons at paras. 80–93, which are reproduced here in full:

> There are two aspects to the publication element of the tort of defamation. The first, relating to the defendant as publisher, concerns the act of promulgating the impugned item. The second, relating to the third party receiver of the impugned item, concerns the receipt of that item by a person within the

court's jurisdiction. (I refer to the issue of jurisdiction because publication, to be actionable, must be within this jurisdiction, and publication of internet material occurs where the words are read: *King v. Lewis*, [2005] E.M.L.R. 45, C.A.; *Gutnick v. Dow Jones,* [2002] H.C.A. 56.) In my respectful view, the reasons for judgment of my learned colleague mix these issues as one.

The first of these two aspects is whether, by creating the hyperlinks in question, Mr. Newton can be seen to have promulgated a writing or message that is defamatory of the appellant. A near case was considered by this Court in *Carter v. B.C. Federation of Foster Parents Assn.*, 2005 BCCA 398 (CanLII), 2005 BCCA 398, 42 B.C.L.R. (4th) 1. The issue in *Carter* was whether the defendant, in publishing a web address at which the allegedly defamatory material was contained, had re-published that material. Mr. Justice Hall, for this Court, in holding it did not, said [at para. 12]:

> In my opinion, the factual situation here is closer to the situation found to exist in the New York cases of *MacFadden v. Anthony*, 117 N.Y.S. (2d) 520 (Sup. Ct. 1952) and *Klein v. Biben*, 296 N.Y. 638 (Ct. App. 1946), referred to by the trial judge, where the courts held reference to an article containing defamatory comment without repetition of the comment itself should not be found to be a republication of such defamatory comment.

While the circumstances of *Carter* differ from those before us, there is, in my view, no substantial difference between providing a web address and a mere hyperlink. Whether the hyperlink is a web address, as is often the case, or a more specific reference, both require a decision on the part of the reader to access another website, and both require the reader to take a distinct action, in the one case typing in a web address and in the other case clicking on the hyperlink. In other words, there is a barrier between the accessed article and the hyperlinked site that must be bridged, not by the publisher, but by the reader. The essence of following a hyperlink is to leave the website one was at to enter a different and independent website.

Nor am I persuaded that in this era of rapidly changing technology we should assume access from a mere web address mentioned in an article will require any more effort than from a hyperlink. It is easy to contemplate a program whereby a click of a computer mouse engages a program on the reader's computer that effects the same result as a hyperlink. In other words, I agree with my colleague's conclusion at para. 58:

> I agree with the trial judge that the reasoning of this Court in *Carter* supports Mr. Newton's position that the mere fact he hyperlinked the

impugned sites does not make him a publisher of the material found at the hyperlinked sites.

I agree, as well, that the circumstances of a case may add more so as to demonstrate that a particular hyperlink is an invitation or encouragement to view the impugned site, or adoption of all or a portion of its contents. For example, in *Hird v. Wood* (1894), 38 S.J. 234 (C.A.), referred to in *Carter*, evidence of the defendant pointing to a placard with content was held to be sufficient evidence of publication to go to a jury. So a statement to the effect "N is described at [hyper link]" may itself incorporate a libel so as to be defamatory.

In the case before us, the judge held concerning the context of the hyperlinks [at paras. 32–33]:

> In the present case, although hyperlinks referred the reader to articles now claimed by the plaintiffs to be defamatory, the plaintiffs agree that the defendant did not publish any defamatory content on the p2pnet website itself. The defendant did not reproduce any of the disputed content from the linked articles on p2pnet and did not make any comment on the nature of the linked articles. In these circumstances, a reader of the p2pnet website who did not click on the hyperlinks provided would not have any knowledge of the allegedly defamatory content.
>
> As the Court of Appeal observed in *Carter*, citing the proposition of the New York cases *MacFadden v. Anthony* and *Kline v. Biben*, "reference to an article containing defamatory content without repetition of the comment itself should not be found to be a republication of such defamatory content".

In these observations, in my view, the judge was entirely correct.

My colleague considers that the judge did not fully explore the context of the hyperlinks in determining Mr. Newton had not participated in publishing the impugned articles. In her view the fact Mr. Newton's article containing the hyperlinks deals with free speech and defamation, and the fact it refers to lawsuits involving Mr. Crookes, serve "as words of encouragement, or an invitation," to look further.

For clarity, the article on Mr. Newton's website under the headline "Free Speech in Canada" said:

> Under new developments, thanks to the lawsuit, I've just met Michael Pilling, who runs OpenPolitics.ca. Based in Toronto, he, too, is being sued for defamation. This time by politician Wayne Crookes.

With respect, I see no encouragement or invitation from the fact the discussion concerns free speech and defamation. Nor, in my view, can reference to Mr. Crookes' litigation reasonably have that effect. Those factors, at a minimum, alert the reader to the potential for untrue content or disputed commentary. They fall far short of a statement of approbation, or adoption, and appear to me to be most comparable to a footnote for a reader, or a card index in a library. It is not, as was suggested is sometimes the way in the recent case *Metropolitan Schools v. Google Inc.*, [2009] E.W.H.C. 1765 (Q.B.), a snippet from the article or a snippet produced by a search engine.

On these considerations I conclude Mr. Newton was not a publisher because of his hyperlinks to the offensive article.

The second aspect of publication is whether it can be inferred a person accessed the impugned articles by way of the hyperlinks. My colleague would conclude, from the fact of 1,788 "hits" of Mr. Newton's article that at least one person within this jurisdiction, did so.

In my view, the approach taken by my colleague to the effect that from the number of persons accessing Mr. Newton's website it may be inferred that a person in this jurisdiction accessed the impugned articles by clicking on them, does not sustain scrutiny. In the context of internet life, we have no way to assess the volume of "hits" here compared to the norm, the usual behaviour of internet readers or "surfers," or the jurisdiction in which they reside. *The conclusion drawn by my colleague is, with respect, tantamount to a presumption that in the case of a website accessed to any significant extent, there has been communication of the offensive material. This is contrary to her conclusion on the issue of presumption, and one with which I do not agree. The conclusion effectively reduces the element of publication to the role of the publisher without consideration of the receipt of the impugned material. There may be cases in which more is known supporting such an inference, but such is not the case here where all that is before us is the bald number of hits. In my view there is an insufficient basis upon which to make such an inference, and the inference drawn cannot co-exist with the reasons for judgment on the matter of a presumption* [emphasis added]

Last, the appellant complains that Mr. Newton did not remove the hyperlinks when asked to do so. This is not a question considered by the judge, and findings of fact are not contained in the reasons for judgment to support a discussion of that interesting issue. But for my conclusion on the question of drawing an inference that a person clicked on the hyperlink, I would allow the appeal and remit this question to the trial court for determination. However, in view of my conclusion on the question of inference, I would dismiss the appeal.

Mr. Crookes appealed to the Supreme Court of Canada and the appeal was heard in December 2010.

b) Limits on the Decision of *Hird v. Wood*

The decision of the English Court of Appeal in *Hird v. Wood* (1894), 38 S.J. 234, was referred to and relied upon in both *Carter v. B.C. Federation of Foster Parents Assn.*, 2005 BCCA 398, and *Crookes v. Newton*, 2009 BCCA 392.

In *Carter v. B.C. Federation of Foster Parents Association* the BC Court of Appeal referred to *Hird v. Wood* as follows at paras. 53–54:

> . . . Additionally, liability has been found where a defendant wilfully directed others to defamatory statements when he neither authored nor authorized their publication on premises not controlled by him. See *Hird v. Wood* (1894), 38 S.J. 234 (C.A).
>
> Common to each of these two lines of authorities is that the defendant had knowledge of the defamatory words and it lay within his power to remove the offending words and he failed to do so or he directed others to the words.

The Court Appeal in *Crookes v. Newton*, 2009 BCCA 392 at para. 57 quoted para. 10 of the trial judge's decision:

> . . . The appellant argues, making special reference to the case of *Hird v. Wood* (1894), 38 S.J. 234 (C.A), that the respondent Federation should have been found liable for referring recipients of the Network newsletter to the website where the offensive comments could be found. The *Hird* case concerned an application for a new trial of a libel action. The plaintiff appellant owned a number of cottages in a village and lived in one of the cottages. A new business was set up by boilermakers near to the cottages and the plaintiff obtained an injunction to restrain the carrying on of the business in such a way as to be injurious to his property and as a result the boilermakers' business terminated. Certain individuals in the neighbourhood were displeased by this result and decided to take up a subscription for the persons whose business had been terminated. On a public occasion, a placard was set up containing a notice that subscriptions might be donated to the former owners of the business "who have been ruined in their business and their living taken away by the animosity of one man." I take it from the report of the case that it was common ground that the one man referred to was the plaintiff appellant. Throughout *the first trial* there was no evidence as to who wrote the words on the placard or who erected it, but it was *proven that the defendant took up a position near* to the placard and remained there pointing at the placard

with his hand and attracted attention of passers-by to the placard. At the first trial, the presiding judge held that there was no evidence of publication and directed a verdict for the defendant [emphasis added].

Unlike the situation found in the *Tacket* case, there was here no element of control by the Federation over the Bopeep Forum and the facts of the instant case are quite distinguishable from the situation found to exist in the *Hird* case. *In Hird, the defendant took active steps to draw the attention of persons to the defamatory placard. I should say that the defendant there was taking active steps to publish to the world the defamatory material contained on the placard.* I do not believe the circumstances extant there can be successfully analogized to the instant case. I take note of the fact that this was a reference in a printed newsletter to a website and I would limit the effect of this case to that factual situation. Whether a different result should obtain concerning an internet website that makes reference to another website I would leave for decision when that factual circumstance arises. In the result, I am not persuaded that the learned trial judge made any error in his assessment of this aspect of the matter and I would dismiss the appeal on this issue concerning the Bopeep Forum. [Emphasis added].

At para. 84 of *Crookes v. Newton*, 2009 BCCA 392, the Court held:

I agree, as well, that the circumstances of a case may add more so as to demonstrate that a particular hyperlink is an invitation or encouragement to view the impugned site, or adoption of all or a portion of its contents. For example, in *Hird v. Wood* (1894), 38 S.J. 234 (C.A.), referred to in *Carter*, evidence of the defendant pointing to a placard with content was held to be sufficient evidence of publication to go to a jury. So a statement to the effect "N is described at [hyper link]" may itself incorporate a libel so as to be defamatory.

i)   Observations

- The complete decision of the Court of Appeal in *Hird v. Wood* is as follows:

    The Court (Lord Esher MR, Lopes & Davey L JJ) held that there was evidence of publication which ought to have been left to the jury and accordingly ordered a new trial.

- The decision is limited as authority for that proposition
- This decision of *Hird v. Wood* is not, with respect, authority for the proposition, as stated in the British Columbia Court of Appeal in *Carter v. B.C. Federation of Foster Parents Assn.*, 2005 BCCA 398 at para 9:

additionally liability has been found where a defendant wilfully directed others to defamatory statements when he neither authored nor authorized their publication on premises not controlled by them.

- The reader should be cautious about relying upon the "facts" of the decision. It is difficult to ascertain because of the nature of the report whether the "facts" referred to are findings of fact made by the trial judge or merely the observations of the person reporting the decision for the solicitors journal.
- In any event, the conduct referred to in *Hird v. Wood* is more comparable to an adoption, a repetition, or an inclusion of a defamatory statement than an encouragement or invitation.

c) Personal Observations about the *Crookes v. Newton* Decision

i) No Express Discussion about Type of Hyperlink in this Case
While there was no express discussion as to whether the hyperlinks in this case were automatic/imbedded hyperlinks or use-activated links, it is possible to infer from the reasons of the trial judge and the Court of Appeal in *Crookes v. Newton* that the hyperlink in this case was user-activated link and not an automatic embedded link from remarks made both by the trial judge and the Court of Appeal.

The trial judge in *Crookes v. Newton*, 2008 BCSC 1424, said this at para. 32, ". . . a reader of the P2PNET website who did not click on the hyperlinks provided would not have had any knowledge of the allegedly defamatory content.

Justice Saunders in the Court of Appeal held as follows at paras. 82–83:

> While the circumstances of *Carter* differ from those before us, there is, in my view, no substantial difference between providing a web address and a mere hyperlink. Whether the hyperlink is a web address, as is often the case, or a more specific reference, both require a decision on the part of the reader to access another website, and both require the reader to take a distinct action, in the one case typing in a web address and in the other case clicking on the hyperlink. In other words, there is a barrier between the accessed article and the hyperlinked site that must be bridged, not by the publisher, but by the reader. The essence of following a hyperlink is to leave the website one was at to enter a different and independent website.
>
> Nor am I persuaded that in this era of rapidly changing technology we should assume access from a mere web address mentioned in an article will require any more effort than from a hyperlink. It is easy to contemplate a program whereby a click of a computer mouse engages a program on the

reader's computer that effects the same result as a hyperlink. In other words, I agree with my colleague's conclusion at para. 58:

> I agree with the trial judge that the reasoning of this Court in *Carter* supports Mr. Newton's position that the mere fact he hyperlinked the impugned sites does not make him a publisher of the material found at the hyperlinked sites.

ii) Terminological Confusion

Confusing terminology has caused confusion in the law. It is submitted that a hyperlink is not truly a "link" unless it is an embedded/automatic hyperlink. If the hyperlink is a user-activated hyperlink, it is like a gate, a footnote, or a hinge. In these situations the reader is required to take some action. If she does nothing then there is no activation of the hyperlink, there is no downloading, and, therefore, there is no publication.

See *Crookes v. Newton*, 2009 BCCA 392 at paras. 82–83

In other words:

1. Unless the hyperlink is automatic, the word "link" is a misleading term. It incorrectly suggests an automatic connection without any actions by another person.
2. The word hyperlink incorrectly describes how the technology of a user-activated hyperlink functions.
3. The user-activated hyperlink is simply a navigational device that must be activated by the person viewing the link. It allows the person, if he wishes, to view or visit another website or another page within a website.
4. The person viewing the link must actively click on the navigational device. It is not a link on its face, as the word implies. The viewer is required to activate the link. It is more correct to call the link a "doorway," "gateway," or "access button."

iii) Proposed Summary of Principles of Law about Publication and Hyperlinks

The following is an attempt to summarize some principles of law relating to publication and hyperlinks:

1. The insertion in an article of a hyperlink to a defamatory statement in another website does not constitute publication of that defamatory statement unless:

a. The hyperlink is embedded such that the link opens to the target website automatically, without any activation by the reader; or

b. There is a repetition/republication of the defamation in the article quite apart from the hyperlink; or

c. The hyperlink is worded so as to adopt or reproduce the defamation in the target website: as for example:

    i. "click here for the sordid truth about . . .";

    ii. "click here to learn more about the mischief caused by X";

    iii. "visit Wall Streets Wall of Shame for the real story behind X's rise to power and wealth";

    iv. "click here to learn why X was called "Hitler's Apprentice.""

d. Unless the legislature expressly extends to the publication of statements on the Internet, the existing presumption of publication is applicable to print and television media.[1] The legislature should not extend the presumption of publication to statements on the internet without a thorough and wide-ranging examination of the social, cultural, and economic impact of such legislation upon thousands, if not millions, of individuals and corporations.

2. The ease or facility of the actions required to be taken by the reader to obtain access to the linked defamatory statement should not dictate whether liability for publication is imposed on the author of the original statement.

3. Express repetition/re-publication or incorporation of the defamatory statement should not be confused with an invitation or encouragement to view the defamatory statement through activations of the hyperlink.

4. It is arguable that the references to "encouragement" or "invitation" are *obiter* the decision of BC Court of Appeal in *Crookes v. Newton* on whether the insertion of hyperlinks constituted publication.

5. It is arguable that references to "encouragement" and "invitation" are irrelevant to the question of whether the insertion of a link to a defamatory statement in an article constitutes publication of the linked article. This question will be discussed in the next section.

d) Encouragement and Invitation

The British Columbia Court of Appeal and the trial judge in *Crookes v. Newton*, 2009 BCCA 392 discussed the impact of words of "invitation or en-

---

1   See British Columbia *Libel and Slander Act*, R.S.B.C. 1996, c. 263, and Ontario *Libel and Slander Act*, R.S.O. 1990, c. L. 12.

couragement" on the question of publication on the Internet by URL and hyperlink.

In *Crookes v. Wikimedia Foundation Inc.*, 2008 BCSC 1424 , the trial judge said at para. 34:

> I do not wish to be misunderstood. It is not my decision that hyperlinking can never make a person liable for the contents of the remote site. *For example, if Mr. Newton had written "the truth about Wayne Crookes is found here" and "here" is hyperlinked to the specific defamatory words*, this might lead to a different conclusion [emphasis added].

In the Court of Appeal, Prowse, J., in her minority decision in *Crookes v. Newton*, 2009 BCCA 392, held at paras. 59–60:

> I also agree with the trial judge, however, that hyperlinking may, in some cases amount to publication by the person creating the link. If it is apparent from the context in which the hyperlink is used that it is being used merely as a bibliographical or similarly limited reference to an original source, without in any way *actively encouraging or recommending* to the readers that they access that source, then, following *Carter*, I accept that this would not amount to publication [emphasis added].
>
> It is not sufficient, however, for the creator of a hyperlink to simply depose that he intended the link to be in the nature of a "footnote" in order to avoid liability for publication. While the trial judge appears to have limited the footnote analogy to a footnote which simply provides a source reference (similar to a citation to a legal source utilized regularly by judges), many authors use footnotes (and citations) in a much more expansive way. For that reason, I would not accept the footnote analogy to be a complete answer to the question of whether a hyperlink constitutes publication. More significant factors would include the prominence of the hyperlink, *any words of invitation or recommendation to the reader associated with the hyperlink*, the nature of the materials which it is suggested may be found at the hyperlink (for example, if the hyperlink obviously refers to a scandalous, or obscene publication), the apparent significance of the hyperlink in relation to the article as a whole, and a host of other factors dependant on the facts of a particular case [emphasis added].

The majority, through Saunders, J., discussed the encouragement and invitation issue at paras. 84 and 87–89 as follows:

> I agree, as well, that the circumstances of a case may add more so as to demonstrate that a particular *hyperlink is an invitation or encouragement to view*

the impugned site, or adoption of all or a portion of its contents. For example, in *Hird v. Wood* (1894), 38 S.J. 234 (C.A.), referred to in *Carter*, evidence of the defendant pointing to a placard with content was held to be sufficient evidence of publication to go to a jury. So a statement to the effect "N is described at [hyperlink]" may itself incorporate a libel so as to be defamatory [emphasis added].

> . . . .

My colleague considers that the judge did not fully explore the context of the hyperlinks in determining Mr. Newton had not participated in publishing the impugned articles. In her view the fact Mr. Newton's article containing the hyperlinks deals with free speech and defamation, and the fact it refers to lawsuits *involving Mr. Crookes, serve "as words of encouragement, or an invitation,"* to look further [emphasis added].

For clarity, the article on Mr. Newton's website under the headline "Free Speech in Canada" said:

> Under new developments, thanks to the lawsuit, I've just met Michael Pilling, who runs OpenPolitics.ca. Based in Toronto, he, too, is being sued for defamation. This time by politician Wayne Crookes.

With respect, I see no encouragement or invitation from the fact the discussion concerns free speech and defamation. Nor, in my view, can reference to Mr. Crookes' litigation reasonably have that effect. Those factors, at a minimum, alert the reader to the potential for untrue content or disputed commentary. They fall far short of a *statement of approbation, or adoption, and appear to me to be most comparable to a footnote for a reader, or a card index in a library.* It is not, as was suggested is sometimes the way in the recent case *Metropolitan Schools v. Google Inc.,* [2009] E.W.H.C. 1765 (Q.B.), a snippet from the article or a snippet produced by a search engine [emphasis added].

As stated earlier, it is arguable that the references to "encouragement and invitation" are irrelevant to the question of whether insertion of a hyperlink to a defamatory statement in an article constitutes publication of the linked article.

i) Personal Observations about "Encouragement and Invitations"
There are several observations that arise from this particular line of reasoning:

1. There is a need to distinguish between approbation, adoption, re-publication, or repetition on the one hand, and encouragement and invitation on the other hand.

2. It appears to be inconsistent with the principle in publication, which is that publication must be bilateral, and that without being read, seen, or downloaded, there is no publication.

3. It appears that the encouragement argument appears to be inconsistent with the technology of a user-activated website link. Once again, words of invitation or encouragement cannot transform a *user-activated* hyperlink into an automatic or embedded hyperlink.

4. The invitation arguments appear to encourage form over substance. Which statements would cross the line? Which ones would not?

5. The invitation and encouragement argument appears unfair as it treats the prudent the same as the reckless. A person who only publishes the hyperlink is treated in the same way as the person who publishes the defamatory words.

6. It is submitted that regardless of how enthusiastic or vigorous the invitation, encouragement, or exhortation is, if somebody does not actually access the hyperlink, there is no downloading and therefore there is no publication.

CHAPTER 16: Forms of Defamatory Meaning

A. THE THREE BASIC FORMS OF DEFAMATORY EXPRESSION

The following is extracted from Roger D. McConchie and David A. Potts, *Canadian Libel and Slander Actions* (Irwin Law, 2004) at 290–92:

> The caselaw suggests that defamatory imputations arise in one of three ways:
>
> i) The literal meaning: for example, where the plaintiff has been called a thief or a murderer it is not necessary to go beyond the words themselves. This is called the "natural and ordinary" meaning in the case authorities.
>
> ii) An inferential meaning: Here the sting of the defamation lies not so much in the expression itself as in the meaning that the ordinary person, without special knowledge, will infer from it. This meaning is a matter of impression. This is also called a "natural and ordinary meaning." It is also sometimes referred to as "popular" or "false" innuendo. A discussion of the nature of inferential meanings is contained in the judgment of Lord Reid in *Lewis* v. *Daily Telegraph Ltd.*, [1963] 2 All E.R. 151 at 154–55 (H.L.):
>
>> What the ordinary man would infer without special knowledge has generally been called the natural and ordinary meaning of the words. But that expression is rather misleading in that it conceals the fact that there are two elements in it. Sometimes it is not necessary to go beyond the words themselves as where the plaintiff has been called a thief or a murderer. But more often the sting is not so much in the words themselves as in what the ordinary man will infer from them and that is also regarded as part of their natural and ordinary meaning. Here there would be nothing libelous in saying that an inquiry

into the appellants' affairs was proceeding: the inquiry might be by a statistician or other expert. The sting is in inferences drawn from the fact that it is the fraud squad which is making the inquiry. What those inferences should be is ultimately a question for the jury but the trial judge has an important duty to perform.

. . .

In this case it is, I think, sufficient to put the test this way. Ordinary men and women have different temperaments and outlooks. Some are unusually suspicious and some are unusually naïve. One must try to envisage people between these two extremes and see what is the most damaging meaning that they would put on the words in question . . . What the ordinary man not avid for scandal, would read into the words complained of must be a matter of impression.

iii) A "legal innuendo": This is where an ostensibly innocent expression may convey a defamatory meaning by virtue of extrinsic facts known to specific people or classes of people exposed to that expression. This is also referred to in the case law as a "true innuendo."

Pressler v. Lethbridge (2000), 86 B.C.L.R. (3d) 257 at para. 36 (C.A.)

Hodgson v. Canadian Newspapers Co. (1998), 39 O.R. (3d) 235 at 250–51 (Gen. Div.), varied on appeal as to damages (2000), 49 O.R. (3d) 161 (C.A.)

See also chapter 13 "Defamatory Meaning" and chapter 23 "Pleadings" in Roger D. McConchie and David A. Potts, *Canadian Libel and Slander Actions* (Toronto: Irwin Law, 2004)

The decision of the Ontario Court of Appeal in *Barrick Gold Corp. v. Lopehandia*, 2004 CanLII 12938 (ON C.A.), discusses some of the characteristics of the Internet for the purpose of damages at paras. 28 and 30–38. However, it is submitted that these comments are also applicable to the question of defamatory meanings:

Is there something about defamation on the Internet — "cyber libel," as it is sometimes called — that distinguishes it, for purposes of damages, from defamation in another medium? My response to that question is "Yes."

. . .

In the Internet context, these factors [the standard factors to consider in determining damages for defamation] must be examined in the light of what one judge has characterized as the "ubiquity, universality and utility" of that medium. In *Dow Jones & Company Inc. v. Gutnick* [2002] HCA 56 (10 December 2002), that same judge — Kirby J., of the High Court of Australia — portrayed the Internet in these terms, at para. 80:

The Internet is essentially a decentralized, self-maintained telecommunications network. It is made up of inter-linking small networks from all parts of the world. *It is ubiquitous, borderless, global and ambient in its nature. Hence the term "cyberspace." This is a word that recognizes that the interrelationships created by the Internet exist outside conventional geographic boundaries and comprise a single interconnected body of data, potentially amounting to a single body of knowledge.* The Internet is accessible in virtually all places on Earth where access can be obtained either by wire connection or by wireless (including satellite) links. *Effectively, the only constraint on access to the Internet is possession of the means of securing connection to a telecommunications system and possession of the basic hardware.* [Emphasis added, footnotes omitted.]

Thus, of the criteria mentioned above, the mode and extent of publication is particularly relevant in the Internet context, and must be considered carefully. Communication via the Internet is instantaneous, seamless, inter-active, blunt, borderless and far-reaching. *It is also impersonal, and the anonymous nature of such communications may itself create a greater risk that the defamatory remarks are believed*: see *Vaquero Energy Ltd. v. Weir*, [2004] A.J. No. 84 (Alta. Q.B.) at para. 17 [emphasis added].

These characteristics create challenges in the libel context. Traditional approaches attuned to "the real world" may not respond adequately to the realities of the Internet world. How does the law protect reputation without unduly overriding such free wheeling public discourse? Lyrissa Barnett Lidsky discusses this conundrum in her article, "Silencing John Doe: Defamation and Discourse in Cyberspace," (2000) 49 Duke L.J. 855 at pp. 862–865:

Internet communications lack this formal distance. Because communication can occur almost instantaneously, participants in online discussions place a premium on speed. Indeed, in many fora, speed takes precedence over all other values, including not just accuracy but even grammar, spelling, and punctuation. Hyperbole and exaggeration are common, and "venting" is at least as common as careful and considered argumentation. The fact that many Internet speakers employ online pseudonyms tends to heighten this sense that "anything goes," and some commentators have likened cyberspace to a frontier society free from the conventions and constraints that limit discourse in the real world. While this view is undoubtedly overstated, certainly the immediacy and informality of Internet communications may be central to its widespread appeal.

> *Although Internet communications may have the ephemeral qualities of gossip with regard to accuracy, they are communicated through a medium more pervasive than print, and for this reason they have tremendous power to harm reputation.* Once a message enters cyberspace, millions of people worldwide can gain access to it. Even if the message is posted in a discussion forum frequented by only a handful of people, any one of them can republish the message by printing it or, as is more likely, by forwarding it instantly to a different discussion forum. And if the message is sufficiently provocative, it may be republished again and again. *The extraordinary capacity of the Internet to replicate almost endlessly any defamatory message lends credence to the notion that "the truth rarely catches up with a lie."* The problem for libel law, then, is how to protect reputation without squelching the potential of the Internet as a medium of public discourse [emphasis added].

These characteristics differentiate the publication of defamatory material on the Internet from publication in the more traditional forms of media, in my opinion.

It is true that in the modern era defamatory material may be communicated broadly and rapidly via other media as well. The international distribution of newspapers, syndicated wire services, facsimile transmissions, radio and satellite television broadcasting are but some examples. Nevertheless, Internet defamation is distinguished from its less pervasive cousins, in terms of its potential to damage the reputation of individuals and corporations, by the features described above, especially its interactive nature, *its potential for being taken at face value,* and its absolute and immediate worldwide ubiquity and accessibility. The mode and extent of publication is therefore a particularly significant consideration in assessing damages in Internet defamation cases.

The motions judge's conclusion that a reasonable reader was unlikely to take what Mr. Lopehandia said seriously, because of its emotional and intemperate nature and because of his use of capitals and pronunciation, lies at the heart of her finding that the defamatory messages did not cause any serious damage to Barrick's business reputation. In my view it is a finding of fact, or an inference drawn from the facts, that is not supported by the evidence.

The notion that Mr. Lopehandia's Internet dialogue style — a style that may not be taken seriously in a traditional medium such as a newspaper — may undermine the credibility of his message has some appeal to those of us who are accustomed to the traditional media. However, as I have noted, the Internet is not a traditional medium of communication. Its nature and manner of presentation are evolving, and there is nothing in the record to indicate that people did not take Mr. Lopehandia's postings seriously. In fact, the uncontradicted evidence is to the contrary.

B. CONTEXT AND MODE OF PUBLICATION

The English Court of Appeal in *Charleston v. Newsgroup Newspapers*, [1985] 2 A.C.C. 65 at paras. 70–71, cited in *Islam Expo Ltd. v. The Spectator (1828) Ltd. & Anor*, [2010] EWHC 2011 at para. 8 stated:

> In order to determine the natural and ordinary meaning of the words, of which the plaintiff complains, it is necessary to take into account both the context in which the words were used, and the mode of publication. A plaintiff cannot select an isolated passage in an article and complain of that alone, if other parts of the article throw a different light on that passage. The publication must be considered as a whole, even if the plaintiff only complains of selected passage.

On 30 July 2010 the English High Court in *Islam Expo Ltd. v. The Spectator (1828) Ltd. & Anor*, [2010] EWHC 2011 (QB), though discussing whether the words published on the Internet were capable of being understood to refer to the plaintiff at paras. 6–13, referred to the law relating to defamatory meaning:

> The issue in this case is whether the words complained of are capable of referring to the Claimant. But the principles to be applied are the same as those to be applied where the issue is whether the words complained of are capable of bearing a defamatory meaning. They have most recently been set out by the Court of Appeal in *Jeynes v. News Magazines Limited*, [2008] EWCA Civ 130 at para 14. It is the submission of counsel for the Defendant that the words complained of are incapable of being understood to refer to the Claimant, and especially so when read in the proper context of the underlying hyperlinked documentation.
>
> The words complained of include four hyperlinks. These are marked in the usual way on a website by being in a different coloured typeface. The links are as follows: (1) "Demos," (2) "Harry's Place points out," (3) "Debate" and (4) "Seminar."
>
> It is a principle of law most recently defined in *Charleston v. Newsgroup Newspapers Limited*, [1985] 2 AC 65, 70–71, that in order to determine the

meaning of words complained of it is necessary to take into account the context in which the words were used and the mode of publication. Thus a claimant cannot select an isolated passage in an article and complain of that alone if other parts of the article throw a different light on that passage.

That principle has been established by a number of authorities all of which relate to printed publications. In a printed publication the text may be broken up and parts given more emphasis than others. Some parts may be on one page and a continuation of the same text may appear on a subsequent page.

[Defendant counsel] submits that the *text on web pages*, to which a reader of the words complained of will be directed *if the reader clicks on the hyper-link, is to be treated as parts of the words complained of for the purposes of determining what the words complained of mean.* [Emphasis Added]

. . . The effect of hyperlinks in the context of a dispute about meaning or reference was briefly mentioned by Eady J *in Ali v Associated Newspapers Limited*, [2010] EWHC 100 at para. 28. It is a question that has also been considered in a number of authorities in British Columbia.

. . .

In this case, as in many libel actions brought on internet publications, the extent of publication is very much in issue. A claimant must prove, not only that a prospective reader accessed the relevant website, but also that that reader read the words complained of.

The judge adopted the approach proposed by the defendants' counsel but held that the words were capable of referring to the plaintiff.

Justice Eady in *Ali v. Associated Newspapers Ltd.*, [2010] EWHC 100 (QB), heard a motion relating to the meaning of the words, arising out of a statement that was published in the *Daily Mail* and also on the corresponding publication's website (and website article). He observed at para. 28:

One point that was briefly addressed in the course of submissions was that of the hyperlink. It was said that it is so far undecided in the authorities whether, as a matter of generality, any material to which attention is drawn in a blog by this means should be taken to be incorporated as part of the blog itself. I suspect that a general rule of thumb is unlikely to be adopted. Much will depend on the circumstances of the particular case. What I wish to make clear, however, is that for present purposes I proceed on the assumption that the *Irish Times* interview is not to be treated as an integral part of the Claimant's blog.

The Court rejected the submission that, as a matter of generality, any material to which attention is drawn in a blog should be taken to be incorporated as part of the blog itself.

In *Kermode v. Fairfax Media Publications Pty. Ltd.*, [2009] NSWSC 1263 the Supreme Court of New South Wales held that it was not appropriate to treat a series of linked sites as one package for defamation purposes. A similar determination was made in the decision of the Full Court of the Supreme Court of Western Australia in *The Buddhist Society of Western Australia v. Bristile*, [2000] WASCA 210. In that case, a majority of the Court rejected an argument that separate files on an Internet site that were linked to one another should be regarded as one item for the purposes of the law of defamation.

1) Audiovisual Defamatory Meaning

Since many cyberlibel attacks are multimedia in nature, further assistance in determining the defamatory meaning in cyberlibel actions can be found in the law discussing audiovisual defamation.

> See David Potts and Carol Matthews, "Procedural Concerns in Broadcast Libel" (1988) 10 *Advocates' Quarterly* 29
>
> See generally Roger D. McConchie and David A. Potts, *Canadian Libel and Slander Actions* (Toronto: Irwin Law, 2004) at 548–57

A television broadcast may be defamatory by virtue of the overall impression created by the words and images in the broadcast, even if the words and narrative themselves, taken alone, are not false or defamatory. See the statement of the Court in *Colour Your World Corp. v. Canadian Broadcasting Corporation* (1998), 38 O.R. (3d) 97 at para. 17 (C.A.), cited in *Leenan v. Canadian Broadcasting Corporation* (2000), 48 O.R. (3d) 656 at 45 (S.C.J.), aff'd (2001), 54 O.R. (3d) 612 (C.A.), leave to appeal to S.C.C. denied, [2001] S.C.C.A. No. 432:

> There is no doubt that the audio-visual dimension of a television broadcast can transform the impression one might otherwise get from a statement. Features such as voice intonation, visual background, facial expression, and gesture are brought into unique play, all of which can accompany the articulated facts to dramatic effect. Because of these distinguishing factors, the overall impression of the broadcast, in addition to the accuracy of the statements, is relevant.
>
> *Colour Your World Corp. v. Canadian Broadcasting Corporation* (1998), 38 O.R. (3d) 97 at 106, paras. d–g (C.A.), leave to appeal to S.C.C. dismissed, [1998] S.C.C.A. No. 170

In *Vogel v. C.B.C.*, [1982] 3 W.W.R. 97 at 155 (B.C.S.C.) Esson J., as he then was, held as follows:

I have made many references to the impression conveyed to viewers. This is a matter which must be considered in assessing television programs, which, by reason of their transitory nature, tend to leave the audience with an impression rather than a firm understanding of what was said. Images, facial expressions, tones of voice, symbols and the dramatic effect which can be achieved by juxtaposition of segments may be more important than the meaning derived from careful reading of the words of the script. Television is different from the printed word. The interested reader can reread and analyze. The emphasis in considering the defamatory impact of say, a newspaper story must therefore be upon the words used. Libel by television is, in this respect, more like slander. In slander cases, regard may be had to such things as gestures and intonations.

Finally, in *Pressler v. Lethbridge* (2000), 86 B.C.L.R. (3d) 257 at para. 36 (C.A.), the court held that:

The visual and auditory components of a television broadcast do not render the words used irrelevant. When determining how a reasonable viewer might perceive the meaning of a broadcast, one must look not only to image, sound, and sequence; one must also look to the actual words used. A broadcast must be considered as a whole to determine whether it has a defamatory sting.

CHAPTER 17: Reference to the Plaintiff

A. INTRODUCTION

It is an essential element of a cause of action for defamation that the words complained of should be published "of the plaintiff." If the words are not so published, a plaintiff cannot have any right to ask that the defendant should be held responsible to him.

Knupffer v. London Express Newspaper Ltd., [1974] 1 AC 116 at 118 cited in Roger D. McConchie and David A. Potts, *Canadian Libel and Slander Actions* (Toronto: Irwin Law, 2004) at 234

Bai v. Sing Tao Daily Ltd., [2003] O.J. No. 917 at para. 10 (C.A.), McMurtry C.J.O., leave to appeal to S.C.C. denied, [2003] S.C.C.A. No. 354

Butler v. Southam Inc. (2001), 197 N.S.R. (2d) 97 at para. 29 (C.A.), Cromwell J.A.

Grant v. Cormier-Grant (2001), 56 O.R. (3d) 215 at para. 19 (C.A.), Borins J.A.

Booth v. British Columbia Television Broadcasting System (1982), 139 D.L.R. (3d) 88 at 92 (B.C.C.A.), Lambert J.A.

Arnott v. College of Physicians and Surgeons of Saskatchewan, [1954] S.C.R. 538 at 554, Kellock J.

B. A TWO-PART TEST

To establish this element of the cause of action, the plaintiff must satisfy a two-part test as stated in *Knupffer v. London Express Newspaper Ltd.*, [1944] 1 A.C. 116 at 121, by Viscount Simon.

1. As a question of law, can the expression be regarded as capable referring to the plaintiff?
2. As a question of fact, does the article in fact lead reasonable people who know that plaintiff to the conclusion that it does refer to him?

For further details about the law relating to identification of the plaintiff, see Roger D. McConchie and David A. Potts, *Canadian Libel and Slander Actions* (Toronto: Irwin Law, 2004) c. 13.

On 30 July 2010 the English High Court in *Islam Expo Limited v. The Spectator (1828) Ltd.*, [2010] EWHC 2011 at paras. 6–11 (QB), discussed whether the words published on the Internet were capable of being understood to refer to the plaintiff. An application was brought by the defendants to strike out the claim.

> The issue in this case is whether the words complained of are capable of referring to the Claimant. But the principles to be applied are the same as those to be applied where the issue is whether the words complained of are capable of bearing a defamatory meaning. They have most recently been set out by the Court of Appeal in *Jeynes v. News Magazines Limited* [2008] EWCA Civ 130 at para 14. It is the submission of counsel for the Defendant that the words complained of are incapable of being understood to refer to the Claimant, and especially so when read in the proper context of the underlying hyperlinked documentation.
>
> The words complained of include four hyperlinks. These are marked in the usual way on a website by being in a different coloured typeface. The links are as follows: (1) "Demos," (2) "Harry's Place points out," (3) "Debate" and (4) "Seminar."
>
> It is a principle of law most recently defined in *Charleston v. Newsgroup Newspapers Limited*, [1985] 2 AC 65, 70–71, that in order to determine the meaning of words complained of it is necessary to take into account the context in which the words were used and the mode of publication. Thus a claimant cannot select an isolated passage in an article and complain of that alone if other parts of the article throw a different light on that passage.
>
> That principle has been established by a number of authorities all of which relate to printed publications. In a printed publication the text may be broken up and parts given more emphasis than others. Some parts may be on one page and a continuation of the same text may appear on a subsequent page.
>
> . . .
>
> [Defendant counsel] submits that the *text on web pages*, to which a reader of the words complained of will be directed *if the reader clicks on the hyperlink, is to be treated as parts of the words complained of for the purposes of determining what the words complained of mean* [emphasis added].

Justice Tugendhat made the technologically obvious but legally important finding that it was necessary for a reader "to click on the hyperlink" to reach the context (see paras. 16, 19, and 20). He decided to approach the application on the basis contended for by defendants' counsel. However, he concluded that the words complained of were capable of referring to the plaintiff.[1] At paras. 21 and 22 Justice Tugendhat concluded:

> I remind myself that amongst the principles listed in *Jeynes*, the governing principle is reasonableness, and over elaborate analysis is best avoided. *The hypothetical reader in this case is the hypothetical person who has access to the words complained of.*
>
> I had little hesitation in reaching *the conclusion that the words complained of were capable of referring* to the Claimant [as a matter of law]. The words "Islam Expo" may well be the name both of the Claimant corporation, and of the events which the Claimant corporation organises from time to time. But the fact is that the words "Islam Expo" appear in the relatively short words complained of. A tribunal of fact which decided that those words referred to the Claimant corporation could not be characterised as perverse.

---

1   See also *Ali v. Associated Newspapers Limited*, [2010] EWHC 100 at para. 28 (QB), Eady J., for a brief discussion of the effect of hyperlinks in the context of a dispute about defamatory meaning.

PART V: Defences

CHAPTER 18: Defence of Innocent Dissemination at Common Law

A. INTRODUCTION

The defence of innocent dissemination is very important because of the pivotal role of intermediaries in cyberlibel. In fact in many cases, aside from the defence of no publication, the defence of innocent dissemination may be the only defence available to intermediaries.

B. INNOCENT DISSEMINATION

See Roger D. McConchie and David A. Potts, *Canadian Libel and Slander Actions* (Toronto: Irwin Law, 2004), Chapter 14 at 282–83.

A defendant may be able to rely on the common law defence of innocent dissemination. In certain circumstances, a defendant will be held not to have published the defamatory expression if:

1. it was disseminated in the ordinary course of business;
2. the defendant was innocent of any knowledge of the libel contained in the work the defendant disseminated;
3. there was nothing in the work or the circumstances under which it came to the defendant or was disseminated by the defendant that ought to have led the defendant to suppose that it contained a libel; and
4. when the work was disseminated by the defendant, it was not by any negligence on the defendant's part that the defendant did not know that it contained the libel.

Vizetelly v. Mudie's Select Library Limited, [1900] 2 Q.B. 170 (C.A.), per Rom L.

Slack v. Ad-Rite Associates Ltd. (1998), 79 O.T.C. 46, per Fedak J. at paras. 17–22 (Gen. Div.), citing *Vizetelly v. Mudie's Select Library Limited*, [1900] 2 Q.B. 170 (C.A.)

Hays v. Weiland (1918), 42 O.L.R. 637, per Hodgins J.A. at para. 35 (C.A.) ["Innocence in circulating libelous matter may entirely absolve the person publishing if he shews that he was not negligent"], citing *Vizetelly v. Mudie's Select Library Limited*, [1900] 2 Q.B. 170; *Smith v. Streatfeild*, [1913] 3 K.B. 764; *Haynes v. De-Beck* (1914), 31 T.L.R. 115.

The burden of proving the facts essential to this defence rest on the defendant.

Menear v. Miguna (1997), 33 O.R. (3d) 223 at 223 (Ont. C.A.)
Slack v. Ad-Rite Associates Ltd. (1998), 79 O.T.C. 46, per Fedak J. at para 22

C. DISCUSSION OF THE WORD "LIBEL" AS DISTINCT FROM "DEFAMATORY"

1) Introduction

There is heated debate in England about the meaning of the word "libel." An understanding of the word is central to the defence of innocent dissemination because, as Lord Denning MR found in *Goldsmith v. Sperrings*, [1977] 1 WLR 478 at 487, this defence could not fail unless the defendant knew that the disseminated defamatory material contained a libel of the plaintiff that could not be justified or excused. That is, the defendant could hold no liability unless she was positively aware that any defence of liability would fail. Proponents of an alternative view contend that there can be no liability unless it is shown, simply, that the material in question contained defamatory matter.

2) Majority view

In *Metropolitan International Schools Ltd. (t/a Skillstrain and/or Train2game) v. Designtechnica Corp (t/a Digital Trends) & Ors*, [2009] EWHC 1765 at para. 69 (Q.B.), Justice Eady held that the interpretation by Lord Denning MR creates more problems than it solves.

A good deal of steam seems to have been generated by this hearing in the Court of Appeal, as Scarman and Bridge LJJ expressed their disagreement with the Master of the Rolls in unusually strong terms: see e.g. the observations of Bridge LJ at p598C-F. Mr White is quite right to emphasise that the remarks were *obiter*, since one of the reasons for their strong disagreement was that the point in question had not been argued properly before the court. At all events, the remarks of Bridge LJ in the particular context of innocent dissemination, at p505A-B, were as follows:

The legal background, with which all parties to the settlements must be taken to have been familiar, is that any disseminator of defamatory matter is liable to the party to be defamed, subject to the defence of innocent dissemination. To establish this it is for him to show that he did not in fact know that the publication contained defamatory matter and that he had no reason to believe that it was likely to contain defamatory matter . . . .

Mr White invites me to take the same view of the defence of innocent dissemination as that of Lord Denning MR and to hold that his client would not be liable unless it could be shown that he was positively aware that any defence would fail. There is no other support for that view of the law available. It depends entirely on adopting the reasoning of Lord Denning MR. I should do so, says Mr White, because the common law is obviously uncertain and I should err on the side of protecting his client's Article 10 rights (and, for that matter, the rights of those who use search engines). I have considerable difficulty with doing so, however, because it seems to me that the defence of innocent dissemination as interpreted by Lord Denning MR throws up more problems than it is likely to solve. How could someone hoping to avail himself of the defence know that a defence of justification was bound to fail, save in the simplest of cases? How is he/she to approach the (often controversial and uncertain) question of meaning? How much legal knowledge is to be attributed to him/her in arriving at these conclusions? What of a possible *Reynolds* defence?

D. FURTHER ELEMENTS OF THE DEFENCE

Roger D. McConchie and David A. Potts, *Canadian Libel and Slander Actions* (Toronto: Irwin Law, 2004) observe at 283–84:

The rationale for the defence of innocent dissemination is that distributors do not have an opportunity to review the contents of all material that passes through their hands.

> *Slack v. Ad-Rite Associates Ltd.* (1998), 79 O.T.C. 46 at para. 17, citing *Goldsmith v. Sperrings Ltd.*, [1977] 1 W.L.R. 478 (C.A.).

Other persons in the chain of distribution of defamatory expression who do only mechanical or menial acts may also be able to establish this defence.

> *Slack v. Ad-Rite Associates Ltd.*, (1998), 79 O.T.C. 46 at para. 17, citing *Lobay v. Workers and Farmers Publishing Association Ltd.*, [1939] 2 D.L.R. 272 (Man. Q.B.).

A defendant does not satisfy the onus merely by stating that he did not have actual knowledge of the contents of the publication. A defendant who had an opportunity to read the libelous publication (but did not) and who thought it "might" be libellous does not establish this defence.

Slack v. Ad-Rite Associates Ltd., (1998), 79 O.T.C. 46 at para. 22:

> To object on these grounds "goes for nothing," and would be an ex-
> cuse for "all sorts of infamy," as Lord Mansfield observed in the case
> of *Anon.* (1774), Lofft. 544, 98 E.R. 791. It would be a licence for char-
> acter assassination.

The identity of the person to whom a libel was published is relevant to the defence of innocent dissemination. The intent and knowledge of the printer, when delivering copies of a libelous publication, is an element of considerable weight in determining whether she was an innocent printer or a participant in an attack. The name of the recipient to whom copies were given may be illuminating and indicate the purpose known to the printer.

Hays v. Weiland, [1918] 42 O.L.R. 637, per Hodgins J.A. at paras. 34–35 (S.C.
(A.D.)), referring to *Vizetelly v. Mudie's Select Library Limited*, [1900] 2 Q.B.
170 (C.A.), *Smith v. Streatfeild*, [1913] 3 K.B. 764, *Haynes v. DeBeck* (1914), 31
T.L.R. 115.

It has recently been doubted a printer who merely prints a book and de-livers it to its author, and does not participate in their distribution, can be considered a publisher. The decision, pronounced on a summary dismissal of a libel action, was reversed on appeal on the grounds that there was evi-dence on which a jury could find there was publication. That evidence was not specified in the appeal judgment.

Menear v. Miguna (1996,) 30 O.R. (3d) 602, per J.B. Wright J. at 605 (Gen. Div.),
rev'd (1997), 33 O.R. (3d) 223 at 223 (C.A.).

It has been suggested that a book printer receiving defamatory content in an electronic form should not be held liable simply by virtue of being the printer, in light of changing technology which makes it unnecessary for the printer or any of its employees to actually review the content word by word. Electronic transmission of text from the editor to the printer may result in a situation where the printer does not read the manuscript, has no editing function, and is not aware of the allegedly libellous statements.

Menear v. Miguna, ibid. at 223, citing *Vizetelly v. Mudie's Select Library Ltd.*,
[1900] 2 Q.B. 170 (C.A.).

E. APPLICATION OF THE DEFENCE TO INTERNET LIBEL CASES

The British Columbia Court of Appeal in *Carter v. Foster Parents Association*, 2005 BCCA 398, [2005] B.C.J. 1720, overturned a trial judge's decision that held that the defence of innocent dissemination applied in an Internet libel case. The Court held at para. 21:

> Taylor J. went on to find that in any event the activity of the defendant respondent amounted to innocent dissemination, but this is a difficult defence to maintain as illustrated by the judgment in *Vizetelly v. Mudie's Select Library, Limited*, [1900] 2 Q.B. 170 (C.A.). Romer L.J. pointed out in that case at 180 the heavy burden lying upon a defendant to demonstrate that the publication occurred without negligence on his part. On the evidence in this case, it is difficult to see how it can be successfully argued by the defendant Federation that the continuing publication occurred without negligence on its part. Here the Federation did not take effective steps to remove the offending comment and there seems to have been no proper follow up to see that necessary action had been taken. I do not therefore consider it was open on the evidence for the trial judge to conclude that a defence of innocent dissemination could be successfully made out on the state of facts here.

The Supreme Court of British Columbia refused to strike out a defence of innocent dissemination as it was not plainly obvious that the defence would fail, however.

See *Hemming v. Newton*, 2006 BCSC 1748 at paras. 13–14

The common law defence of innocent dissemination as it applies to Internet libel cases has been discussed in *Bunt v. Tilley & Ors*, [2006] EWHC 407 (Q.B.) (10 March 2006) and *Metropolitan International School Limited v. DesignTechnica Corporation et al.*, [2009] EWHC 1765 (QB).

1) Section 1 of the UK *Defamation Act*

Section 1 of the UK's *Defamation Act 1996* (U.K.), 1996, c. 31 states in part:

1. Responsibility for publication
   (1) In defamation proceedings a person has a defence if he shows that—
      (a) he was not the author, editor or publisher of the statement complained of,
      (b) he took reasonable care in relation to its publication, and

(c) he did not know, and had no reason to believe, that what he did caused or contributed to the publication of a defamatory statement.

. . .

(3) A person shall not be considered the author, editor or publisher of a statement if he is only involved—

(a) in printing, producing, distributing or selling printed material containing the statement;

(b) in processing, making copies of, distributing, exhibiting or selling a film or sound recording (as defined in Part I of the *Copyright, Designs and Patents Act 1988*) containing the statement;

(c) in processing, making copies of, distributing or selling any electronic medium in or on which the statement is recorded, or in operating or providing any equipment, system or service by means of which the statement is retrieved, copied, distributed or made available in electronic form;

(d) as the broadcaster of a live programme containing the statement in circumstances in which he has no effective control over the maker of the statement;

(e) as the operator of or provider of access to a communications system by means of which the statement is transmitted, or made available, by a person over whom he has no effective control.

In a case not within paragraphs (a) to (e) the court may have regard to those provisions by way of analogy in deciding whether a person is to be considered the author, editor or publisher of a statement.

This section was discussed in *Godfrey v. Demon Internet*, where the court held that the defence did not apply because the defendant was a publisher. It was discussed in *Bunt v. Tilley & Ors*, [2006] EWHC 407 (QB), where the court held that as the defendant was not a publisher, there is no need to raise the application of the defence. A similar decision was concluded in the *Metropolitan International Schools Limited v. DesgnTechnica Corporation et al.*, [2009] EWHC 1765. These decisions and the application of section 1 of the *Defamation Act* are discussed in greater detail in Chapter 21.

In England, the defence was raised on behalf of Internet Service Providers (ISPs). The court in *Metropolitan International Schools Ltd. (t/a Skillstrain and/or Train2game) v. Designtechnica Corp. (t/a Digital Trends) & Ors*, [2009] EWHC 1765 (QB), found:

1. The defence of innocent dissemination was not abolished by section 1 of the *Defamation Act 1996* since (at para. 70):

> It is a somewhat curious situation in that I am being asked, 13 years after the common law defence was, at least, superseded, to determine how it should have been construed in its heyday. Nevertheless, it is right that I should state my conclusion on both the issues now raised. I am prepared to find that the defence was not actually abolished in 1996 (albeit no doubt effectively superseded). I have come to that conclusion because the statute does not say that the common law defence is indeed abolished (as, for example, it was made clear when the tort of detinue was abolished in 1977). In the event, however, it makes very little difference and does not assist Mr White's argument. It would almost certainly not be available to a defendant who has had it drawn to his attention that the words are defamatory or, at least, arguably so. To that extent, the common law defence is much more closely in line with the statutory defence introduced in s. 1 of the 1996 Act. Indeed, it is quite likely, if Lord Mackay had thought that there was a significant difference between the scope of the common law defence and that of the proposed statutory one he was commending to Parliament, that the government would have addressed the question directly and decided either to retain the distinctions or to abolish them expressly.

2. There is no need to consider the application of the common law defence of innocent dissemination, section 1 of the *Defamation Act 1996*, or the Electronic Commerce (EC Directive), because Google was not considered to be a publisher at common law at paras. 64, 80, 113, and 124):

> Against this background, including the steps so far taken by the Third Defendant to block the identified URLs, I believe it is unrealistic to attribute responsibility for publication to the Third Defendant, whether on the basis of authorship or acquiescence. There is no doubt room for debate as to what further blocking steps it would be open for it to take, or how effective they might be, but that does not seem to me to affect my overall conclusion on liability. This decision is quite independent of any defence provided by s.1(1) of the 1996 Act, since if a person is not properly to be categorised as the publisher at common law, there is no need of a defence: see e.g. *Bunt v Tilley* at [37].
>
> . . .

There is no need to address the possible defence under s. 1 of the 1996 Act in the light of my finding in the Third Defendant's favour on primary liability. If, however, it should correctly be considered as a "publisher," contrary to my conclusion, it is difficult to see how it would then qualify under s.1(1)(a).

. . .

I prefer to reach my conclusion by reference to straightforward common law principles, albeit adapted to the new environment of the Internet, and in particular I attach importance to the absence of knowledge on the part of the Third Defendant in relation to the offending material prior to the Claimant's complaint and, moreover, the absence of any conduct on its part thereafter which could properly be characterised as authorisation or acquiescence in continuing publication. There may have been delays in the "take down" procedure (whether for technical or other reasons), but even while the attempt is being made to block access to any specific URL, it is impossible to characterise the state of mind of any relevant employee as amounting to authorisation, approval or acquiescence.

. . .

In conclusion, therefore, there are two reasons which in my judgment justify setting aside the Master's order. First, I do not consider that on the evidence before me the Third Defendant can be regarded as a publisher of the words complained of, whether before or after notification. Accordingly, on the evidence before me, I can conclude that the Claimant would have "no reasonable prospect of success." Secondly, I regard the misrepresentations and omissions, as to the nature of the cause of action relied upon, as sufficiently serious to justify setting aside the Master's order in any event.

See also, *Bunt v. Tilley & Ors*, [2006] EWHC 407 (Q.B.) at paras. 36–37:

In all the circumstances I am quite prepared to hold that there is no realistic prospect of the Claimant being able to establish that any of the corporate Defendants, in any meaningful sense, knowingly participated in the relevant publications. His own pleaded case is defective in this respect in any event. More generally, I am also prepared to hold as a matter of law that an ISP which performs no more than a passive role in facilitating postings on the internet cannot be deemed to be a publisher at common law. I would not accept the Claimant's proposition that this issue "can only be settled by a trial," since it is a question of law which can be determined without resolving contested issues of fact.

I would not, in the absence of any binding authority, attribute liability at common law to a telephone company or other passive medium of communication, such as an ISP. It is not analogous to someone in the position of a distributor, who might at common law need to prove the absence of negligence: see *Gatley on Libel and Slander* (10th edn) at para. 6–18. There a defence is needed because the person is regarded as having "published." By contrast, persons who truly fulfil no more than the role of a passive medium for communication cannot be characterised as publishers: thus they do not need a defence.

CHAPTER 19: The Defence of Qualified Privilege

A. ELEMENTS OF THE DEFENCE AT COMMON LAW

See Roger D. McConchie and David A. Potts, *Canadian Libel and Slander Actions* (Toronto: Irwin Law, 2004) at 364–66:

B. QUALIFIED PRIVILEGE AT COMMON LAW

1) The Elements of the Defence: Duty and Interest

This defence applies to an occasion where the defendant has (i) an interest or (ii) a duty — legal, social, or moral — to communicate the defamatory expression and its recipients have a corresponding duty or interest to receive that communication.

> *Pressler v. Lethbridge* (2000), 86 B.C.L.R. (3d) 257, per Southin J.A. at 295 (C.A.).
> *Haight-Smith v. Neden* (2002), 211 D.L.R. (4th) 370, per Levine J.A. for the court at 383 (B.C.C.A.), citing Lord Atkinson in *Adam v. Ward*, [1917] A.C. 309 at 334 (H.L.) and *Mcloughlin v. Kutasy*, [1979] 2 S.C.R. 311 at 321.
> *Stopforth v. Goyer* (1979), 97 D.L.R. (3d) 369, per Jessop J.A. at 372 (Ont. C.A.), adopting the description of the defence contained in *Halsbury's Laws of England*, 3d ed., vol. 24 (London: Butterworths, 1952–64) at 56–57.

Reciprocity of duty and interest between the communicator and the recipient is essential to this defence.

> *Sapiro v. Leader Publishing Co.*, [1926] 3 D.L.R. 68, per Lamont J.A. for the court at 68–69 (Sask. C.A.), citing *Adam v. Ward*, [1917] A.C. 309 (H.L.).

The burden is on the defendant to prove each of the elements of the defence.

Although a communication occurred on an occasion of qualified privilege, the protection of this defence is lost if:

i) the plaintiff proves that the dominant motive for publishing the defamatory expression is actual or express malice; or

ii) the limits of the duty or interest have been exceeded. This occurs when:

    a. the speaker includes anything which is not relevant or pertinent, or in other words, not reasonably appropriate in the circumstances existing on the occasion when the information is given;

    b. the manner and extent of communication is excessive.

> *Hill v. Church of Scientology of Toronto*, [1995] 2 S.C.R. 1130, per Cory J. at 1189–90.
>
> *Botiuk v. Toronto Free Press*, [1995] 3 S.C.R. 29 at 29–30, per Cory J. (La Forest, L'Heureux-Dubé, Gonthier, McLachlin and Iacobucci JJ. concurring).
>
> *Wade and Wells Co. v. Laing* (1957), 11 D.L.R. (2d) 276 at 279, 282–83 (B.C.C.A.), Per Sheppard J.A. (Sidney Smith J.A. concurring), citing *Clark v. Molyneux* (1877), 3 Q.B.D. 237 at 247.
>
> *Kelsie v. Canada (Attorney General)*, [2003] N.J. No. 232, 2003 NLSCTD 139 per Barry J. at para. 33.

The burden of proving actual or express malice rests on the plaintiff.

> *Netupsky v. Craig*, [1973] S.C.R. 55 per Ritchie J. for the court at 61–63.
>
> *McLoughlin v. Kutasy*, [1979] 2 S.C.R. 311 at 324–25.

2) Foundation in Public Policy

The defence of qualified privilege is intended to serve "the general interests of society" and "the common convenience and welfare of society" rather than the interests of individuals or a class.

> *Halls v. Mitchell*, [1928] S.C.R. 125 at 147, per Duff J. (Anglin C.J.C., Mignault, and Lamont JJ. concurring).
>
> *Sapiro v. Leader Publishing Co. Ltd.*, above, at 70.

Macintosh v. Dun, [1908] A.C. 390 (P.C.) per Lord Macnaghten at 398 and 399, citing *Toogood v. Spyring* (1834), 1 C.M. & R. 181 at 193 where Parke B. stated:

> If fairly warranted by any reasonable occasion or exigency, and honestly made, such communications [injurious to the character of another] are protected for the common convenience and welfare of society, and the law has not restricted the right to make them within any narrow limits.

Macintosh v. Dun, above, and *Toogood v. Spyring*, above were expressly approved by Duff J., writing for the majority of the Supreme Court of Canada in *Halls v. Mitchell*, above, at 132–33:

The defamatory statement is . . . only protected when it is fairly warranted by some reasonable occasion or exigency, and when it is fairly made in discharge of some public or private duty, or in the conduct of the defendant's own affairs in matters in which his interests are concerned. The privilege rests not upon the interests of the persons entitled to invoke it, but upon the general interests of society, and protects only communications "fairly made" in the legitimate defence of a person's own interests, or plainly made under a sense of duty, such as would be recognized by "people of ordinary intelligence and moral principles."

B. REPLY TO AN ATTACK

A potential application of the defence of qualified privilege in cyberlibel is the reply-to-an-attack version of qualified privilege.

See Roger D. McConchie and David A. Potts, *Canadian Libel and Slander Actions* (Toronto: Irwin Law, 2004) at 373:

Where an individual or corporation is subject to a defamatory attack, communication, responding to the attack is made on occasion of qualified privilege. Such responses are considered to be essential to protect one's own interest and reputation in the interest of those on behalf of whom the writer is writing.

Botiuk v. Toronto Free Press, [1995] 3 S.C.R. 3 per Cory J. at 31, para. 86

Netupsky v. Craig (1972), [1973] S.C.R. 55, 28 D.L.R. (3d) 742 at 746, Ritchie J. for the Court, approving the reasons of Schroeder J.A. (14 D.L.R. (3d) 387 at 407 (Ont. C.A.)), where he stated:

A more apposite and firmer basis for the privilege arises from the fact that the statements were made in the conduct of the defendants' own affairs in a manner in which their own interest was concerned. More specifically, they were replying to an unfair and unwarranted attack upon their professional integrity and competence which they were justified in repelling by a denial and explanation. This forms a more substantial and relevant foundation for the privilege, and entitles the defendants to considerably wider latitude than does the basis upon which the learned trial judge rested it.

Douglas v. Tucker, [1952] 1 S.C.R. 275 per Cartwright J. at 286, citing *Adam v. Ward*, [1917] A.C. 309 (H.L.)

Mallett v. Clarke (1968), 70 D.L.R. (2d) 67, per Gould J. at 72 (B.C.S.C.) (defendant principal of institute had duty to answer serious allegations made by the plaintiff, an expelled student, to journalists who contacted the defendant for comment)

O'Malley v. O'Callaghan (1992), 4 W.W.R. 81 at 91–92 (Alta. Q.B.) (personal dispute between plaintiff pro-life spokesperson and defendant newspaper publisher over news coverage and editorial policy of newspaper on the abortion issue. Defendant held entitled to respond to attacks on his newspaper)

1) Was the Reply Restricted to a Specific Audience?

See Roger D. McConchie and David A. Potts, *Canadian Libel and Slander Actions* (Toronto: Irwin Law, 2004) at 373–74:

> When determining whether the necessary reciprocity exists between the speaker and the listener, the court will consider whether the defamatory communication was restricted to a specific audience to which the defendant has a duty of information.
>
> In *Upton v. Better Business Bureau of Mainland of B.C.* (1980), 114 D.L.R. (3d) 750 (B.C.S.C.), Gould J. held at 755 that a nonprofit society, incorporated for the purpose, *inter alia*, of "promoting honesty, truthfulness, and reliability in merchandising and advertising of all kinds" and discouraging "fraudulent and deceptive methods in business," published its monthly bulletin to members and to associate Better Business Bureaus across the country on an occasion of qualified privilege. "I hold that it is in the public interest that information from such an institution should be available and that pursuant to its objects the Bureau is under duty to supply such information."
>
> If a publication is given a wider circulation than intended, and that did not occur by reason of any negligence on the part of the defendant, the fact of that wider circulation is not a breach of the privilege.
>
> *Gallant v. West*, [1955] 4 D.L.R. 209, per Walsh C.J. at 217 (Nfld. S.C.).

2) Was the Reply Responsive to the Attack?

See Roger D. McConchie and David A. Potts, *Canadian Libel and Slander Actions* (Toronto: Irwin Law, 2004) at 374–75:

> The response should be in keeping with, and responsive to the original attack, and normally should be made in the same forum. In answering an attack, a person must not make countercharges or unnecessary imputations on the private life of the attacker which are wholly unconnected with the attack and irrelevant to the victim's vindication. The privilege extends only so far

as to enable the victim to repel the charges brought against him, and not to bring fresh accusations against his adversary.

Douglas v. Tucker, above, at 286:

> In my view the appellant was entitled to reply to such a charge and his reply would be protected by qualified privilege, but I think it clear that this protection would be lost if in making his reply the appellant went beyond matters that were reasonably germane to him. It is for the judge alone to rule as a matter of law not only whether the occasion is privileged but also whether the defendant published something beyond what was germane and reasonably appropriate to the occasion so that the privilege does not extend thereto.

O'Malley v. O' Callaghan (1992), 89 D.L.R. (4th) 577, per Mason J. at 587 (Alta Q.B.), citing Philip Lewis, *Gatley on Libel and Slander*, 8th ed. (London: Sweet & Maxwell, 1981) at 218:

> [A] person whose character has been attacked is entitled to answer such attack, and any defamatory statements he may make about the person who attacked him will be privileged, provided they are published *bona fide* and are fairly relevant to the accusations made.

Bennett v. Stupich (1981), 30 B.C.L.R. 57, per Mackoff J. at 62–63 (S.C.) [plea of qualified privilege that defamatory words were written by the defendant in defence of his own reputation and the reputation of other opposition members of the legislature rejected by the court on the basis of a finding of fact "there was here . . . not a word in defence of his reputation or that of the other N.D.P. M.L.A.s . . . The defamatory words of the defendant answer nothing, they only attack."].

3) Was the Reply Made in the Same Forum?

See Roger D. McConchie and David A. Potts, *Canadian Libel and Slander Actions* (Toronto: Irwin Law, 2004) at 375–76:

> Therefore where the original attack is made in the news media, the person attacked may respond in kind in the same or similar news media. The fact that the news media employed by the defendant may have a larger audience or circulation does not destroy the privilege, nor does the fact the defendant employed vigorous language.

> *Mallett v. Clarke* (1968), 70 D.L.R. (2d) 67 (B.C.S.C.).
> *Ward v. Clark*, [2002] 2 W.W.R. 238 per Esson J.A. at paras. 28–29 (B.C.C.A.).

Falk v. Smith, [1941] O.R. 17 at 19, per McFarland J. at 20 (C.A.).
Adam v. Ward, [1917] A.C. 309, per Lord Atkinson at 343 (H.L.) [Defendant, secretary to the Army Council, sent the press a copy of his letter to a General who had been attacked in Parliament by the plaintiff. The letter was published in the British and foreign press.]:

> It would be a disgrace and injury to the Service if a man, publicly accused of the shameful breach of duty of which General Scobell was accused, was allowed to continue in command of a brigade in the Army unless and until he had been cleared of the accusation made against him. Every subject, therefore, who had an interest in the Army had an interest in being by a public communication informed of General Scobell's acquital. But I go further. I think it may be laid down as a general proposition that where a man, through the medium of Hansard's reports of the proceedings in Parliament, publishes to the world vile slanders of a civil, naval or military servant of the Crown in relation to the discharge by that servant of the duties of his office he selects the world as his audience, and that it is the duty of the heads of the service to which the servant belongs, if on investigation they find the imputation against him groundless, to publish his vindication to the same audience to which his traducer has addressed himself.

Ward v. Clark, above, at 252.

4) Does the Language Used Vitiate the Privilege?

See Roger D. McConchie and David A. Potts, *Canadian Libel and Slander Actions* (Toronto: Irwin Law, 2004) at 376:

> An exaggeration or extreme statement could be evidence of malice, but absent proof of malice, it does not defeat the privilege. A defendant may be protected, even if his language is violent or excessively strong.

> > *Netupsky v. Craig*, [1973] S.C.R. 55 at 61–62, citing *Adam v. Ward*, [1917] A.C. 309 (H.L.).
> > *McLoughlin v. Kutasy*, [1979] 2 S.C.R. 311 at 323.

> There is a distinction between disproportionate language, which does not destroy the privilege, and language which is not germane and reasonably appropriate to the occasion, which does.
> > *Ward v. Clark*, [2002] 2 W.W.R. 238 at 257–60:

> > The law does not require either blandness, or accuracy as a condition of successfully invoking qualified privilege . . . The phrase "germane

and reasonably appropriate to the occasion" is derived from the reasons of Cartwright J. (later C.J.C.) in *Tucker v. Douglas* [(1951),[1952] 1 S.C.R. 275 (S.C.C.)]. In using those words, Cartwright J. was not considering whether the statement was bland, or factually correct . . .

Nothing said by Mr. Clark to the *Sun* reporter was unconnected with the matters in controversy. Mr. Clark believed on reasonable grounds that Mr. Ward was "feeding misinformation" on the fast ferry issue. He knew Mr. Ward to be a disgruntled bidder. So it was germane and reasonably appropriate for him to suggest that as explaining why Ward would feed misinformation. It may not have been true, it may have been hurtful but it was germane and reasonably appropriate to the occasion . . . . If a defamatory response meets that test, the law allows much leeway in the language used.

See also *Botiuk v. Toronto Free Press*, [1995] 3 S.C.R. 3, Cory J. at paras. 81 and 86

C. APPLICATION OF THE DEFENCE OF QUALIFIED PRIVILEGE TO CYBERLIBEL CLAIMS

The defence of qualified privilege has thus far had mixed success as a defence to cyberlibel claims. The decision of the motions court in *Porter v. Robinson Sheppard Shapiro et al.* (2004), 71 O.R. (3d) 547, held that the defence of qualified privilege applied to publication of words on the Internet. The Ontario Court of Appeal in *Porter v. Robinson Sheppard*, (2005) 73 O.R. (3d) 560, overturned the decision on other grounds at para. 2: "With respect to the defence of qualified privilege, we are of the opinion that the evidentiary basis before the motions judge was not sufficient to resolve that question at this early stage of the litigation."

As discussed in Roger D. McConchie and David A. Potts, *Canadian Libel and Slander Actions* (Toronto: Irwin Law, 2004) at 374, the British Columbia Supreme Court rejected a defence of qualified privilege raised by a union regarding a publication on its website that attacked a competing union. The defendant argued that the statement was aimed only at its own members who would have had an interest in receiving union news. In this case, the defendant did not restrict access to the portion of the website where the defamatory statements were posted. Other parts of the website were password restricted and accessible only to members. The Court concluded that any privilege was therefore defeated by excessive re-publication. Justice Rice stated at para. 31,

It is not that the internet and use of a website is to be discouraged, but if statements are to be made, which are admittedly defamatory and there is a risk of numbers of interested persons seeing it, that can be excessive and will be if restrictions are available but disregarded.

See *Christian Labour Association v. Retail Whole Sale Union* 2003 BCSC 2000

The defence of qualified privilege was also dismissed in *Mudford v. Smith*, 2009 CanLII 55718 at para. 51 (ON S.C.) and *McQudiq v. Harbour Financial Inc.*, 2009 ABQB 678 at paras. 86, 92, and 101

A similar decision was reached in Australia when the court held that there was no qualified privilege for statements on the Internet, as the recipients of the matters complained of did not have an interest in having information on the subjects reported. Neither the statutory defence of qualified privilege in New South Wales applied nor the common law defence; see *Restifa v. Pallotta*, [2009] NSWSC 958.

Two decisions in England held that the words were not published on an occasion of qualified privilege. In the decision of *Trumm v. Norman*, [2008] EWHC 116 (QB), the Court held that the publications to persons others than members of the union were not published on occasions of qualified privilege. That is, because the publications occurred on a website accessible to any member of the public, the defence of qualified privilege could not apply. At paras. 43–46, the Court said:

> So far as members of the union are concerned, it is common ground that the defence applies to communications to them. It does not matter whether Mr Norman is properly to be regarded as owing a duty to members of the union to make this communication, or sharing a common interest with them. The position in relation to non members is different. It may be that in relation to some of the non members there may also be the reciprocal duty or interest that exists in relation to the members, for example publication to legal advisers, other advisers, and former or retired members. I do not need to consider the position of such publishees, because there are other publishees, most notably journalists, and people who are simply interested subscribers to *Loco Journal*, to whom no duty or can be said to be due, and who do not share a common or reciprocal interest in the affairs of ASLEF. Their interest is no more than any ordinary member of the public. Publication to the members of the public may be protected by qualified privilege as set out in *Reynolds v. Times Newspapers Limited*, [2001] 2 AC 127. But no *Reynolds* defence is available, or has been raised in this case.
>
> There may be, in some instances, cases where the General Secretary of a Union needs to communicate with all the members of the union, but has no means of doing so without, at the same time, and incidentally, communicat-

ing with non members. In such a case Mr Davies accepted that the publication to non-members may be on an occasion of qualified privilege. He referred to examples of such cases given in *Gatley on Libel & Slander* 10th Edition para 14–75. But he submitted that whether that be so or not (and I express no view upon it), in the present case Mr Norman could have communicated only to members of the union had he wished, and, as he said in evidence, he chose to communicate to others. Moreover the publication on the ASLEF website was a publication accessible to any member of the public.

Mr Crystal referred to an occasion when Mr Trumm accepts that he took from an officer of ASLEF the confidential draft of a report into its financial affairs, and gave a copy, not only to the British Transport Police, but also to the Mail on Sunday newspaper. Mr Crystal submitted that it is not consistent for Mr Trumm now to complain of publication by Mr Norman to all the world of the words complained of. In my judgment this is no more than a forensic point in relation to liability. It does not relieve Mr Norman of establishing, if he can, a defence of qualified privilege. But it does have relevance to damages, considered below.

In my judgment it is clear that qualified privilege cannot be relied upon as a defence to publications to journalists and other subscribers to, or publishees of, *Loco Journal*, who cannot be shown to have any interest in the affairs of ASLEF over and above that of any ordinary member of the public. I do not need to consider the position of each of the publishees of the 200 copies separately. It is plain that there was publication of up about 100 copies to persons who had no material interest in the affairs of the union over and above that of any ordinary member of the public. There is no defence of qualified privilege available in respect of publication to such persons.

See also *Sean Brady v. Keith Norman* [2008] EWHC 2481 at para. 17 (Q.B.) for a similar conclusion

The defence of qualified privilege was successfully applied in *Shavluk v. Green Party of Canada*, 2010 BCSC 804 at paras. 81, 82, and 93:

However, a more recent line of cases can be seen to have expanded the scope of the defence in cases of wide dissemination of matters of true public interest, see for example *Stopforth v. Goyer* (1979), 23 O.R. (2d) 696, 97 D.L.R. (3d) 369 (C.A.); *Parlett v. Robinson*, 1986 CanLII 929 (BC C.A.), (1986), 5 B.C.L.R. (2d) 26 (C.A.), leave to appeal ref'd [1986] S.C.C.A. No. 322.; *Ward, supra*; and *Campbell v. Jones*, 2002 NSCA 128 . . . , 220 D.L.R. (4th) 201.

In the present case, at the time of the publication of the press release giving rise to this litigation, a federal election was imminent. The Green Party had announced the candidacy of Mr. Shavluk with a press release. The decision to remove the endorsement of the party leader from the candidate was in my view a matter about which the public at large had an interest. Accordingly, I find that the occasion was one of qualified privilege. Moreover, I find that neither of the defamatory publications at issue exceeded the scope of the privilege.

. . .

In the result, I am satisfied that the defendants have made out the defence of qualified privilege.

Rubin v. Ross, 2010 SKQB 249 also held that the defence of qualified privilege applied

CHAPTER 20: Defence of Responsible Communication on Matters of Public Interest

A. INTRODUCTION

The Supreme Court of Canada created a new defence called responsible communication on matters of public interest.

> See *Grant v. Torstar Corp.*, 2009 SCC 61 at para. 96
> *Cusson v. Quan (Ottawa Citizen) et al.*, 2009 SCC 62

The defence in Canada "should be viewed as a new defence, leaving the traditional defence of qualified privilege intact."

> See *Grant v. Torstar Corp.*, 2009 SCC 61 at para. 95

The defence is available to anyone who publishes materials of public interest on any medium. See *Grant v. Torstar Corp.*, 2009 SCC 61 at paras. 96–97:

> A second preliminary question is what the new defence should be called. In arguments before us, the defence was referred to as the responsible journalism test. This has the value of capturing the essence of the defence in succinct style. However, the traditional media are rapidly being complemented by new ways of communicating on matters of public interest, *many of them online*, which do not involve journalists. These new disseminators of news and information should, absent good reasons for exclusion, be subject to the same laws as established media outlets. I agree with *Lord Hoffmann that the new defence is "available to anyone who publishes material of public interest in any medium"*: Jameel, at para. 54 [emphasis added].
>
> *A review of recent defamation case law suggests that many actions now concern blog postings and other online media which are potentially both more ephemeral and more ubiquitous than traditional print media. While estab-*

lished journalistic standards provide a useful guide by which to evaluate the conduct of journalists and non-journalists alike, *the applicable standards will necessarily evolve to keep pace with the norms of new communications media.* For this reason, it is more accurate to *refer to the new defence as responsible communication on matters of public interest* [emphasis added].

B. BASES FOR THE NEW DEFENCE

The Supreme Court of Canada decided that there were two bases for broadening the defences available to public communications, such as the press, in reporting matters of fact.

1) Argument Based on Principle

The Court held that the law should be changed as a matter of principle at para. 65 in *Grant v. Torstar Corp.*, 2009 SCC 61:

> Having considered the arguments on both sides of the debate from the perspective of principle, I conclude that the current law with respect to statements that are reliable and important to public debate does not give adequate weight to the constitutional value of free expression. While the law must protect reputation, the level of protection currently accorded by the law — in effect a regime of strict liability — is not justifiable. The law of defamation currently accords no protection for statements on matters of public interest published to the world at large if they cannot, for whatever reason, be proven to be true. But such communications advance both free expression rationales mentioned above — democratic discourse and truth-finding — and therefore require some protection within the law of defamation. When proper weight is given to the constitutional value of free expression on matters of public interest, the balance tips in favour of broadening the defences available to those who communicate facts it is in the public's interest to know.

2) Argument Based on the Jurisprudence

The Supreme Court of Canada reviewed the jurisprudence of the common law democracies of Australia, New Zealand, South Africa, the UK, and the US (see *Grant v. Torstar Corp.*, 2009 SCC 61 at paras. 66–84). As a result of the review, the Supreme Court reached the following conclusion at paras. 85–86:

> A number of countries with common law traditions comparable to those of Canada have moved in recent years to modify the law of defamation to

provide greater protection for communications on matters of public interest. These developments confront us with a range of possibilities. The traditional common law defence of qualified privilege, which offered no protection in respect of publications to the world at large, situates itself at one end of the spectrum of possible alternatives. At the other end is the American approach of protecting all statements about public figures, unless the plaintiff can show malice. Between these two extremes lies the option of a defence that would allow publishers to escape liability if they can establish that they acted responsibly in attempting to verify the information on a matter of public interest. This middle road is the path chosen by courts in Australia, New Zealand, South Africa and the United Kingdom.

In my view, the third option, buttressed by the argument from *Charter* principles advanced earlier, represents a reasonable and proportionate response to the need to protect reputation while sustaining the public exchange of information that is vital to modern Canadian society.

C. ELEMENTS OF THE DEFENCE

The Supreme Court of Canada set out the elements of the defence as follows in *Grant v. Torstar Corp.*, 2009 SCC 61 at para. 126:

> The defence of public interest responsible communication is assessed with reference to the broad thrust of the publication in question. It will apply where:
> A. The publication is on a matter of public interest and:
> B. The publisher was diligent in trying to verify the allegation, having regard to:
>   (a) the seriousness of the allegation;
>   (b) the public importance of the matter;
>   (c) the urgency of the matter;
>   (d) the status and reliability of the source;
>   (e) whether the plaintiff's side of the story was sought and accurately reported;
>   (f) whether the inclusion of the defamatory statement was justifiable;
>   (g) whether the defamatory statement's public interest lay in the fact that it was made rather than its truth ("reportage"); and
>   (h) any other relevant circumstances.

Regarding the public interest, the Court noted:

1. The judge must consider the subject matter of the publication as a whole (para. 101);
2. Public interest is not synonymous with what interests the public (para. 102);

3. While the authorities do not offer a single test, nor a static list of topics falling within the public interest, guidance may be found in the cases on fair comment and section 2(b) of the *Canadian Charter of Rights and Freedoms* (para. 103); and
4. Public interest is not confined to publications on government and political matters as in Australia and New Zealand. "The public has a genuine stake in knowing about many matters ranging from science and the arts to the environment, religion and morality" (para. 106).

D. THE ROLE OF JUDGE AND JURY

The role of the judge and jury in the responsible communications defence was succinctly set forth in para. 128 of *Grant v. Torstar Corp.*, 2009 SCC 61:

> The judge decides whether the statement relates to a matter of public interest. If public interest is shown, the jury decides whether on the evidence the defence is established, having regard to all the relevant factors, including the justification for including defamatory statements in the article.

E. APPLICATION OF THE DEFENCE TO DEFAMATION ON THE INTERNET

The Supreme Court of Canada expressly recognized the application of the defence of responsible communications on matters of public interest to defamation on the Internet.

1) The Defence Applies to Online Communications

Grant v. Torstar Corp., 2009 SCC 61 at paras. 96–97:

> A second preliminary question is what the new defence should be called. In arguments before us, the defence was referred to as the responsible journalism test. This has the value of capturing the essence of the defence in succinct style.
>
> A review of recent defamation case law suggests that many actions now concern blog postings and other online media which are potentially both more ephemeral and more ubiquitous than traditional print media. While established journalistic standards provide a useful guide by which to evaluate the conduct of journalists and non-journalists alike, the applicable standards will necessarily evolve to keep pace with the norms of new communications media. For this reason, it is more accurate to refer to the new defence as responsible communication on matters of public interest.

2) The Status and Reliability of the Source

Grant v. Torstar Corp., 2009 SCC 61 at para. 114 :

> Some sources of information are more worthy of belief than others. The less trustworthy the source, the greater the need to use other sources to verify the allegations. This applies as much to documentary sources as to people; for example, an "interim progress report" of an internal inquiry has been found to be an insufficiently authoritative source in the circumstances: *Miller v. Associated Newspapers Ltd.*, [2005] EWHC 557 (Q.B.) (BAILII). Consistent with the logic of the repetition rule, the fact that someone has already published a defamatory statement does not give another person licence to repeat it. *As already explained, this principle is especially vital when defamatory statements can be reproduced electronically with the speed of a few keystrokes.* At the same time, the fact that the defendant's source had an axe to grind does not necessarily deprive the defendant of protection, provided other reasonable steps were taken [emphasis added].

3) The Repetition Rule

The repetition rule is particularly important in the age of the Internet, when defamatory material can spread from one website to another at great speed. *Grant v. Torstar Corp.*, 2009 SCC 61 at para. 119:

> The "repetition rule" holds that repeating a libel has the same legal consequences as originating it. This rule reflects the law's concern that one should not be able to freely publish a scurrilous libel simply by purporting to attribute the allegation to someone else. The law will not protect a defendant who is "willing to wound, and yet afraid to strike": *"Truth" (N.Z.) Ltd. v. Holloway*, [1960] 1 W.L.R. 997 (P.C.), at p. 1001, per Lord Denning. In sum, the repetition rule preserves the accountability of media and other reporting on matters of public interest. The "bald retailing of libels" is not in the public interest: *Charman, per* Sedley LJ., at para. 91. *Maintaining the repetition rule is particularly important in the age of the internet, when defamatory material can spread from one website to another at great speed* [emphasis added].

4) The Standard to be Applied

The standard by which the trier of fact will decide whether the defence is established is set forth in para. 128 of *Grant v. Torstar Corp.*, 2009 SCC 61.

> The judge decides whether the statement relates to a matter of public interest. If public interest is shown, the jury decides whether on the evidence the

defence is established, having regard to all the relevant factors, including the justification for including defamatory statements in the article.

This question will need to be fleshed out by later decisions.

The Supreme Court of Canada has provided the following guidance in *Grant v. Torstar Corp.* at para. 97:

> While established journalistic standards provide a useful guide by which to evaluate the conduct of journalists and non-journalists alike, the applicable standards will necessarily evolve to keep pace with the norms of new communications media.

As noted above, the Supreme Court held that the new defence applies to anyone who publishes material of public interest in any medium.

See *Grant v. Torstar Corp.*, at para. 96

The following questions, at a minimum, emerge:

1. Do established journalistic standards exist?
2. If so, what are they?
3. Do they vary from print to television journalism?
4. Are they peculiar to journalists?
5. Are the standards that have been articulated simply standards of reasonableness and fairness that should apply to everyone?
6. Should different standards apply to online writers and, if so, what are they?

See Matthew Nied, "*Grant v. Torstar* and the Defence of Responsible Communication: Implications for Bloggers and Users of Other Online Media" Defamation Law Blog (25 January 2010), online: http://defamationlawblog.wordpress.com

As can be seen, the Supreme Court has kept these questions open through its flexible statement. In my opinion, the Court should not attempt to establish different standards for journalists and non-journalists because:

- it will be difficult if not impossible to define who is and is not a journalist and when a journalist ceases being a journalist or a non-journalist becomes a journalist;
- the standards that the triers of fact apply should reflect the principles articulated in the *Grant v. Torstar Corp.* decision;
- the factors listed should apply to all defendants;
- no defendant should be given a greater or lesser license to libel; and
- reputation interests should not be jeopardized or sacrificed merely because of the utilization of a different technology.

F. APPLICATION OF THE DEFENCE TO ONLINE COMMUNICATIONS

The defence of responsible communication in the public interest was applied and accepted in *Shavluk v. Green Party of Canada*, 2010 BCSC 804 at paras. 94, 97–102:

> The defence of responsible communication on a matter of public interest was articulated in the decision of the Supreme Court of Canada in *Grant*. There are two elements to this defence. The publication must be on a matter of public interest and the defendant must show that the publication was responsible in that he was diligent in trying to verify the allegations. Unlike the defence of qualified privilege, the issue of whether the publication is in the public interest is concerned with the nature of the statement and not the nature of the occasion.
>
> . . .
>
> On the first element (public interest), I am satisfied that the publications at issue were in relation to a matter of public interest. The suitability of a candidate for public office during a federal election is clearly such a matter.
>
> With respect to the factors in relation to whether the communication was responsible, the allegation was serious hence requiring an elevated level of diligence. However, in assessing diligence, the circumstances in which this matter arose are important. The defendants learned of the post when approached by the press who intended to publish an article and were seeking a response. Mr. Shavluk was notified immediately, his views were sought. The matter was urgent and the timetable was not in the control of the defendants. In the circumstances, I am satisfied that there was urgency and that the defendants exercised reasonable diligence.
>
> The status and reliability of the source are not at issue since the actual post giving rise to the issue was reviewed and Mr. Shavluk's response sought.
>
> Neither the press release nor the September 16 interview included either the text at issue or Mr. Shavluk's explanation that he was repeating the views of others. However, this must be balanced against the fact that the purpose of each was not to report on the issue but to set out the position of the Party with respect to the issue.
>
> With respect to the issue of the inclusion of the defamatory statement, Mr. Shavluk has submitted that it was not necessary for the Party to have given any reason for the decision, in other words, that it was unnecessary for the statement to be included. However, in my view, such a response would not be realistic in the circumstances. It was appropriate for the reasons to be given

for the revocation of support for Mr. Shavluk's candidacy and it was also important to clarify that the Party distanced itself from anti-Semitic views.

In all the circumstances, I am satisfied that both statements were protected by the defence of responsible communication.

The defence was rejected in two cases.

Rubin v. Ross, 2010 SKQB 249 at para. 91:

"In my view, the case of *Grant v. Torstar Corp.* is not applicable to this situation. This is not a case of a broad-based media seeking the protection of the defence granted under that decision."

Hunter v. Chandler, 2010 BCSC 729 at para. 145–46:

Moreover, Mr. Chandler did not disclose the facts that formed the basis of his concern; nor did he state that he had a concern. Instead, he stated that Mr. Hunter was in a conflict of interest. He stated that Mayor Daly had recommended Mr. Hunter without disclosing, implying that Mayor Daly knew of a conflict that ought to have been disclosed. He did not disclose that Mayor Daly was of the view that there was no conflict of interest, nor did he disclose that that view was shared by Mr. Chad.

In the result, although the subject was one of public interest, the communication was not responsible, and accordingly, the defence is not available to Mr. Chandler.

G. THE *REYNOLDS* DEFENCE APPLIED TO ONLINE VERSIONS OF PRINT PUBLICATION

An English Court held that the public interest defence (*Reynolds* defence) applies to online versions of the print publication. If the print publication is protected, then the online version is protected.

See *Flood v. Times News Papers*, [2009] EWHC 2375 at paras. 249, 251, and 255

H. DEFENCE BASED ON CIRCUMSTANCES EXISTING AT THE TIME OF THE WEBSITE PUBLICATION COMPLAINT

Flood v. Times News Papers, [2009] EWHC 2375 at paras. 225 and 233:

[W]here a defendant defends a website publication on the basis of the Reynolds public interest privilege, he must do so by reference to the circumstances that existed at the time the website publication was complained of.

He cannot simply rely upon the circumstances that prevailed at the time of the original publication, that is to say, the circumstances at the time when the words were first published in any form.

. . .

Whether or not the scale of a website publication, and any resulting damage, is likely to be modest compared with that of the original publication, will depend on the facts of each case. *But the judgment in* Loutchansky *was delivered eight years ago, in 2001. Since then the use of the internet, and in particular of internet search engines has increased. What has also increased is the amount of material on the internet.* In 2001 there were relatively few years of back numbers of newspapers available on the internet. Since then each year's publications have been added. In most cases, as time passes, the original print publication will become increasingly difficult to access, and would be forgotten. But the website publication will remain, and in some cases (where the *fame of a person* has increased) it may *even be viewed with increasing frequency. So a person's reputation may be "damaged forever"* in the words of Lord Nicholls in Reynolds at p201 cited in para 207 above. As I remarked in another case, quoting from an article by a well known media lawyer, *what is to be found on the internet may become like a tattoo (Clarke (t/a Elumina Iberica UK) v Bain & Anor* [2008] EWHC 2636 (QB) para 55). Some actual and prospective employers, and teachers, make checks on people by carrying out internet searches. *An old defamatory publication may permanently blight a person's prospects. This may be so, even in those cases where the allegation has been authoritatively refuted, but the refutation is either not on the internet, or, where it is on the internet, its authority is not apparent, or is not credited, on the footing that there is no smoke without fire* [emphasis added].

I.   APPLICATION OF THE PUBLIC INTEREST DEFENCE ON WEBSITES WITH MULTIPLE PAGES

Many websites have multiple pages. Where the separate pages are considered to be separate publications the defendant must plead separate defences to each separate publication comprising the website. The Supreme Court of Western Australia held that the Australian version of the public interest defence (called the *Lange* defence) did not apply to the whole website as a matter of law because one of the statements had nothing to do with the discussion of political government matters as required by the *Lange* defence.

Buddhist Society of Western Australia Inc. v. Bristile Ltd., [2000] WASCA 210

PART VI: Internet-specific Subjects

CHAPTER 21: Internet Intermediaries

A. INTRODUCTION: A SUBJECT OF SOME COMPLEXITY

Intermediaries are one of the pivotal and defining features of the Internet and cyberlibel. "Every Internet communication, whatever its form, passes through a number of intermediate computer systems as a series of IP datagrams en route from one computer to another."[1] The importance of their role and the necessity for some regulation of intermediaries has resulted in the passage of legislation throughout the world,[2] as well as a torrent of commentary, academic and otherwise, online and offline about the liability, exemptions, classification, and roles of intermediaries.[3] Their role in economic and social terms has been examined recently at length in a report published by the Organisation for Economic Co-operation and Development (OECD) in April, 2010.[4]

The role, function, liability, and exemptions of intermediaries are subjects not entirely devoid of complexity for the following reasons.

---

1   Matthew Collins, *The Law of Defamation on the Internet*, 2d ed. (Oxford: Oxford University Press, 2005) at 181, para. 14.01.
2   US *Communications Decency Act*, 1996, 47 U.S.C. s. 230; UK *Defamation Act*, 1996, c.31, s. 1; *Electronic Commerce (EC Directive) Regulations, (2002)*, SI 2002/2013; Australia *Broadcasting Services Act*, 1992, 110, s. 91(1); and Directive 2000/31/EC of the European Parliament and of the Council (Directive on electronic commerce).
3   When the phrase "Internet intermediary liability" was typed into Google Scholar on 5 October 2010, 14,900 articles and cases bubbled up from cyberspace.
4   Karine Perset, "The Economic and Social Role of Internet Intermediaries," *OECD Digital Economy Papers*, No. 171 (2010), online at www.oecd.org/dataoecd/49/4/44949023.pdf; Graham Smith, *Internet Law and Regulation*, 4th ed. (London: Sweet Maxwell, 2007); Matthew Collins, *The Law of Defamation and the Internet*, (Oxford: Oxford University Press, 2001). See also: Patrick Milmo QC, *et al.*, eds., *Gatley on Libel and Slander*, 10th edition (London: Sweet & Maxwell, 2008).

1) Interchangeable Terminology

Different names are interchangeably used for the same concepts. Examples include (carriers/conduits, content hosts/hosts/websites, and exemptions/safe harbours). Further, the way these individual terms are employed creates regrettable confusion, as in, for example, the insertion of the adjective "mere" before the word "conduit," which leaves the impression there is a distinction between a "mere conduit" and a "conduit." See also *Kaschke v. Gray & Anor*, [2010] EWHC 690 at para. 75 for use of the words "storage" and "mere storage."

> See regulation 17 of *Electronic Commerce (EC Directive) Regulations, (2002)* SI
> 2002/2013 (U.K.)

To add to the confusion, section 1 of the UK's *Defamation Act 1996*, c. 31 (UK) defines "publisher" differently from a publisher in a defamation action as Justice Eady explains in *Metropolitan International Schools Ltd. (t/a Skillstrain and/or Train2game) v. Designtechnica Corp (t/a Digital Trends) & Ors*, [2009] EWHC 1765 at paras. 71–73 (QB):

> ... s.1(1) of the *Defamation Act 1996* states:
>
> "In defamation proceedings a person has a defence if he shows that —
> (a) he was not the author, editor or publisher of the statement complained of,
> (b) he took reasonable care in relation to its publication, and
> (c) he did not know, and had no reason to believe, that what he did caused or contributed to the publication of a defamatory statement."

There is some confusion about the terminology in this part of the statute because, whereas in most places the notion of "publication" corresponds with the general usage in the law of defamation, "publisher" is defined in s.1(2) to mean "a commercial publisher, that is, a person whose business is issuing material to the public, or a section of the public, who issues material containing the statement in the course of that business". The different usage is recognised in s.17(1) of the Act, which is the interpretation section.

This dual usage of "publisher" in the Act is apt to cause particular confusion in the present context. [Google] would appear to be a business which issues material to the public, or a section of the public. Yet the common law test of whether [Google] published the words complained of is not necessarily the same as that under the statute of whether it "issues material containing the statement in the course of that business".

2) Multiple Roles of Website Operators

An Internet Service Provider (ISP) website operator can manage a website that has different functions at the same time. Some functions attract liability while others are exempt from liability. Consequently, it is necessary to analyze the roles separately.

> See *Society of Composers, Authors and Music Publishers of Canada v. Canadian Assn. of Internet Providers*, 2004 SCC 45 at para. 111
>
> *Kaschke v. Gray & Anor*, [2010] EWHC 690 (QB)

3) Timing of the Publication

The timing of the publication of the defamatory statement injects a further element of complexity into the process. Different liabilities can arise, depending on whether the statement was published prior to or after notification by the complainant. This usually leads to a further set of questions about the timeliness and sufficiency of notice and the impact of responding or not responding to the notice.

4) ISP Liability Conundrum

A central and enduring conundrum involving Internet intermediary liabilities still vexes ISPs and the courts. On the one hand, an ISP who does nothing and allows defamatory content to flow directly through will not generally incur any liability because they will be categorized as a "mere conduit" or "carrier." On the other hand, an ISP who, with the best of intentions, monitors and moderates its website, removing defamatory or objectionable content, may incur liability or at the very least be deprived of the safe harbour/exemption provisions in the *Electronic Commerce (EC Directive) Regulations 2002.*

Fifteen years ago in the US case of *Stratton Oakmont, Inc. v. Prodigy Services Company*, [1995] WL 323710 (N.Y. Sup. Ct. 1995), an ISP was held to be liable for moderating editorial content. The uproar that this decision evoked was a catalyst, if not a direct cause, for the enactment of section 230 of the *Communications Decency Act of 1996*, 47 U.S.C.A. (*CDA*), which largely insulates an ISP in the US from liability for the publication of defamatory statements by an author on its website. See, for example, *Zeran v. American Online Inc.* 958 F.Supp. 1124 at 1131, 1134 (Ed. Va. 1997).

The *Electronic Commerce (EC Directive) Regulations 2002* enacted in UK, and in different forms throughout the European Union, adopted a slightly different approach involving the creation of exempt and non-exempt categories and take down provisions for defamatory statements upon notification. It appears that one of the objectives of the Directives was to encourage self-regulation and self-moderation. The decision of *Kaschke v. Gray & Anor*, [2010] EWHC 690 (QB) demonstrates how difficult it is to create a nuanced and balanced solution to this problem.

5) No Uniform Global Legislation

No uniform global legislation exists to regulate ISPs. There are different approaches among different jurisdictions. The US provides absolute immunity to ISPs pursuant to section 230 of the *CDA*. Australia, many Continental European countries, South Africa, and the UK all provide immunity in certain situations through legislation. Canada has no legislation regulating the liability of ISPs for defamation.

> See Mark A. Lemley, "Rationalizing Internet Safe Harbors," (2007–8) 6 *J. on Tele-comm. & High Tech. L.* 101

6) "Technology First" Approach

Confusion is likely to increase as some scholars analyze and discuss intermediaries as a discrete legal concept applying, for example, to privacy, intellectual property, defamation, consumer law, and even criminal law. This "technology first" approach already exists in the study and analysis of hyperlinks,[5] search engines,[6] and social networking sites.[7]

B. FUNCTIONS OF INTERNET INTERMEDIARIES

Internet intermediaries have different functions. Generally, intermediaries perform one of three functions in regard to a particular communication. Assuming there is a continuum or spectrum of functions relating to Internet communications, content hosts are at one end with caching in the middle and mere conduits at the other end.

1) Content Hosts

As stated by Matthew Collins in his book *The Law of Defamation and the Internet*, 2d ed. (Oxford: Oxford University Press, 2005) at 181, para. 14.02:

---

5   Mark Sableman, "Link Law Revisited: Internet Linking Law at Five Years" (2001) 16 Berkeley Tech. L.J. 1273.

6   James Grimmelmann, "Structure of Search Engine Law" (2007) 93 Iowa L. Rev. 1.

7   James Grimmelmann, "Saving Facebook" (2009) 94 Iowa L. Rev. 1137.

Intermediaries may be 'content hosts': the operators of computer systems on which Internet content, such as web pages and bulletin board postings, is stored. Content hosts play a part every time the content stored on their computer systems is displayed on the screen of an Internet user, anywhere in the world, because they are the primary storage site for that content.

See Regulation 19, Content Hosting

2) Caching

Next, on the continuum is "caching." The editors of *Gatley* describe caching as "a halfway house between mere transmission and "hosting." See *Gately on Libel and Slander* (11th ed.) at 6.30. Matthew Collins describes "caching" as follows in *The Law of Defamation and the Internet*, 2d ed. (Oxford: Oxford University Press, 2005) at 182, para. 14.04:

> The next function which intermediaries might perform is to "cache" Internet content: this is, to store particular content on a temporary basis on their computer systems for the purpose of making the transmission of that information to Internet users more efficient. Intermediaries who "cache" information are not the same as "content hosts," because they are not the primary storage site for that information. Nor are they the same as "mere conduits," because they store particular Internet content for a period longer than is necessary for its transmission to a particular recipient.

See Regulation 18 on Caching in the *Electronic Commerce (E.C.Directives) Regulations 2002*, SI 2002/2013

A full discussion of caching, and how it functioned in 2006, can be found in *Bunt v. Tilley & Ors*, [2006] EWHC 407 at para. 53 (QB). See also *Society of Composers, Authors and Music Publishers of Canada v. Canadian Assn. of Internet Providers* [2004] SCC 45 at paras. 114–19.

3) Mere Conduits

At the other end of the spectrum is the concept of "mere conduits" or "carriers." Matthew Collins defines this concept in *The Law of Defamation and the Internet*, 2d ed. (Oxford: Oxford University Press, 2005) at 181–82, para. 14.03:

> At the other end of the spectrum, intermediaries may be "mere conduits" in respect of a particular communication: the operators of computer systems through which communications happen to pass on their route from

one computer to another. These intermediaries are perhaps most analogous to the operators of telecommunications networks: they facilitate the communications of others by operating the equipment by means of which the constituent signals are carried. They do not store the signals on their computer systems for any period longer than is necessary for their transmission to a particular recipient.

See *Electronic Commerce (EC Directive) Regulations* 2002, SI 2002/2013, s. 17, "Mere Conduits"

C. CHALLENGES AND OPPORTUNITIES FOR CANADIAN LAWYERS AND JUDGES WHEN FACED WITH DEFAMATION CLAIMS INVOLVING INTERNET INTERMEDIARIES

Canadian lawyers and judges have some challenges and opportunities at this particular time. Unlike for example Australia, South Africa, the US, the UK, or countries in the EU, there is no legislation in Canada that defines, categorizes, and describes the liability exemptions of Canadian intermediaries in defamation claims involving Internet intermediaries. Furthermore, there is no caselaw discussing the application of defamation law to these concepts, other than a decision of the Supreme Court of Canada discussing the role of ISPs in the context of copyright. Despite these gaps, there are at least three sources of guidance for Canadian lawyers and judges.

The first area of guidance is the Supreme Court of Canada decision *Society of Composers, Authors and Music Publishers of Canada v. Canadian Assn. of Internet Providers*, 2004 SCC 45, [2004] 2 S.C.R. 427, arising out of an appeal from the Copyright Board of Canada. It contains a discussion about the role and liability of the Internet intermediaries when performing certain functions. This decision, though it concerns the *Copyright Act*, R.S.C. 1985, c. C-42, is invaluable and the relevant sections are presented below for the use of lawyers and judges when faced with questions about the liability of Internet intermediaries.

Second, there are several UK decisions that discuss the liability of intermediaries in different circumstances.

Kaschke v. Gray & Anor, [2010] EWHC 690 (QB)
Metropolitan International Schools Ltd. (t/a Skillstrain and/or Train2game) v. Designtechnica Corp (t/a Digital Trends) & Ors, [2009] EWHC 1765 (QB)
Bunt v. Tilley & Ors, [2006] EWHC 407 (QB)
Godfrey v. Demon Internet Limited, [1999] EWHC 244 (QB)

Third, the common law of defamation, particularly the law on publication and innocent dissemination, provides guidance and is discussed in separate sections.

D. SUPREME COURT OF CANADA DECISION IN *SOCIETY OF COMPOSERS, AUTHORS AND MUSIC PUBLISHERS OF CANADA v. CANADIAN ASSN. OF INTERNET PROVIDERS*

The decision in *Society of Composers, Authors and Music Publishers of Canada v. Canadian Assn. of Internet Providers*, 2004 SCC 45, though discussing the *Copyright Act*, R.S.C. 1985, c. C-42, has some very useful discussions that are relevant to intermediaries in defamation actions in at least three areas:

1. The section 24(1) *Copyright Act* exemption may have its roots in the common law defence of innocent dissemination.
2. The liability of an intermediary should be determined by its functions in the particular situation in question.
3. Caching as a section 24(1) *Copyright Act* exemption.

1) Innocent Dissemination

The Supreme Court of Canada considered that section 2.4(1)(b) of the *Copyright Act*, R.S.C. 1985, c. C-42, perhaps has its roots perhaps in the defence of innocent dissemination. Binnie J., in *Society of Composers, Authors and Music Publishers of Canada v. Canadian Assn. of Internet Providers*, 2004 SCC 45, [2004] 2 S.C.R. 427 at para 89, held:

> Section 2.4(1)(*b*) is not a loophole but an important element of the balance struck by the statutory copyright scheme. *It finds its roots, perhaps, in the defence of innocent dissemination sometimes available to bookstores, libraries, news vendors, and the like who, generally speaking, have no actual knowledge of an alleged libel, are aware of no circumstances to put them on notice to suspect a libel, and committed no negligence in failing to find out about the libel*; see *Menear v. Miguna*, 1996 CanLII 8214 (ON S.C.), (1996), 30 O.R. (3d) 602 (Gen. Div.), rev'd on other grounds 1997 CanLII 4432 (ON C.A.), (1997), 33 O.R. (3d) 223 (C.A.); *Newton v. City of Vancouver* (1932), 46 B.C.R. 67 (S.C.); *Sun Life Assurance Co. of Canada v. W. H. Smith & Son, Ltd.*, [1933] All E.R. Rep. 432 (C.A.). See generally R. E. Brown, *The Law of Defamation in Canada* (2nd ed. (loose-leaf)), vol. 1, at § 7.12(6) [emphasis added].

2) Different Roles/Functions of Intermediaries

The necessity of examining the different roles of the intermediary in a particular fact situation has been discussed by the Copyright Board and the Supreme Court of Canada. In *Society of Composers, Authors and Music Publishers of Canada v. Canadian Assn. of Internet Providers*, 2004 SCC 45, [2004] 2 S.C.R. 427, the Supreme Court, in the context of the *Copyright Act*, R.S.C. 1985, c. C-42, stated as follows at paras. 102 and 111:

> Of course *an Internet Service Provider in Canada can play a number of roles.*
> In addition to its function *as an intermediary, it may as well act as a content*
> *provider, or create embedded links which automatically precipitate a telecom-*
> *munication of copyrighted music from another source.* In such cases, copy-
> right liability may attach to the added functions. The protection provided
> by s. 2.4(1)(*b*) *relates to a protected function*, not to *all* of the activities of a
> particular Internet Service Provider [emphasis added].
>
> Shorn of its misreading of the *CAB 1994* case, the Board was correct in its
> general conclusion on this point, which for ease of reference I set out again
> (at p. 453):

> > In the end, each transmission must be looked at individually *to deter-*
> > *mine whether* in that case, an intermediary merely acts as a *conduit*
> > *for communications by other persons*, or whether it is acting as some-
> > thing more.

The Copyright Board in *SOCAN Statement of Royalties, Public Perform-*
ance of Musical Works 1996, 1997, 1998 (Tariff 22, Internet) (Re) (1999), 1 C.P.R.
(4th) 417 at 419–420 stated:

> *Internet intermediaries cannot always claim the benefit of paragraph 2.4(1)(b)*
> The liability of an entity participating in any *Internet transmission must be*
> *assessed as a function of the role the entity plays in that transmission*, and
> *not as a function of what it generally does over the Internet.* Consequently,
> Internet intermediaries can rely on paragraph 2.4(1)(*b*) of the *Act* only with
> respect to communications in which they limit themselves to acting as inter-
> mediaries. In some cases, as a result of business relationships or other fac-
> tors, intermediaries will act in concert with others in a different manner.
> Such is the case where an ISP posts content, associates itself with others to
> offer content, creates embedded links or moderates a newsgroup. In these
> cases, these entities are no longer acting as intermediaries; their liability will
> be assessed according to the general rules dealing with copyright liability.
> The same will hold true where an ISP creates a cache for reasons other that

improving system performance, modifies the contents of the cached material or interferes with any means of obtaining information as to the number of "hits" or "accesses" to the cached material.

Thus, entities whose routers handle only some of the transmitted packets will always be able to argue that they do not handle a substantial part of the work. By contrast, attempts at relying on notions of volition or causation to avoid liability will be met with the same scepticism as in other situations, as there is no "prerequisite of knowledge of the existence of the violated copyright or that the action in question amounts to infringement. Infringement is the single act of doing something which 'only the owner of the copyright has the right to do" [emphasis added, footnotes removed].

a) Similar Comments by English Judges

A similar observation about the importance of identifying the service or function of an intermediary in a particular case was made in a UK case examining the liability of an ISP. See the comments of Stadlen, J. in *Kaschke v. Gray & Anor*, [2010] EWHC 690 at para. 86 (QB):

> The evidence summarized above illustrates why it is *potentially important to identify with precision the information society service referred to in Regulation 19*. See further discussions of the different functions of ISPs in the Irish and English decisions cited in *Kaschke v. Gray & Anor*, [2010] EWHC 690 (QB) [emphasis added].

3) The Use of Caches

In *Society of Composers, Authors and Music Publishers of Canada v. Canadian Assn. of Internet Providers*, 2004 SCC 45, [2004] 2 S.C.R. 427 at paras. 114–19, Binnie J. held:

> Parliament has decided that there is a public interest in encouraging intermediaries who make telecommunications possible to expand and improve their operations without the threat of copyright infringement. To impose copyright liability on intermediaries would obviously chill that expansion and development, as the history of caching demonstrates. In the early years of the Internet, as the Board found, its usefulness for the transmission of musical works was limited by "the relatively high bandwidth required to transmit audio files" (p. 426). This technical limitation was addressed in part by using "caches." As the Board noted, at p. 433: "Caching reduces the cost for the delivery of data by allowing the use of lower bandwidth than would otherwise be necessary." The velocity of new technical developments in the computer

industry, and the rapidly declining cost to the consumer, is legendary. Professor Takach has unearthed the startling statistic that if the automobile industry was able to achieve the same performance-price improvements as has the computer chip industry, a car today would cost under five dollars and would get 250, 000 miles to the gallon of gasoline: see Takach, *supra*, at p. 21. Section 2.4(1)(*b*) reflects Parliament's priority that this entrepreneurial push is to continue despite any incidental effects on copyright owners.

In the Board's view, the means "necessary" under s. 2.4(1)(*b*) were means that were content neutral and were necessary to maximize the economy and cost-effectiveness of the Internet "conduit." That interpretation, it seems to me, best promotes "the public interest in the encouragement and dissemination of works of the arts and intellect" (*Théberge, supra*, at para. 30) without depriving copyright owners of their legitimate entitlement. The creation of a "cache" copy, after all, is a serendipitous consequence of improvements in Internet technology, is content neutral, and in light of s. 2.4(1)(*b*) of the Act ought not to have any *legal* bearing on the communication between the content provider and the end user.

As noted earlier, SOCAN successfully relied on the "exigencies of the Internet" to defeat the appellants' argument that they did not communicate a "musical work" but simply packets of data that may or may not arrive in the correct sequence. It is somewhat inconsistent, it seems to me, for SOCAN then to deny the appellants the benefit of a similar "exigencies" argument. "Caching" is dictated by the need to deliver faster and more economic service, and should not, when undertaken only for such technical reasons, attract copyright liability.

A comparable result has been reached under the U.S. *Digital Millennium Copyright Act*, which in part codified the result in *Religious Technology Center v. Netcom On-line Communication Services, Inc.*, 907 F.Supp. 1361 (N.D. Cal. 1995), where it was observed, at pp. 1369–70:

> These parties, who are liable under plaintiffs' theory, do no more than operate or implement a system that is essential if Usenet messages are to be widely distributed. There is no need to construe the Act to make all of these parties infringers. Although copyright is a strict liability statute, there should still be some element of volition or causation which is lacking where a defendant's system is merely used to create a copy by a third party.

See also Melville B. Nimmer, *Nimmer on Copyright*, vol. 3, looseleaf ed. (New York: Matthew Bender, 1997–) at 12B-13.

The European *E-Commerce Directive* mandates member states to exempt ISPs from copyright liability for caching (art. 13(1)) (Para 118, From SCC SOCAN decision of J Binnie).

The Copyright Board's view that caching comes within the shelter of s. 2.4(1) is correct, and I would restore the Board's conclusion in that regard.

E. JUDICIAL DECISIONS ON THE LIABILITY OF INTERMEDIARIES IN DEFAMATION ACTIONS

Several UK decisions discuss the liability of intermediaries in various circumstances.

1) *Godfrey v. Demon Internet*

In *Godfrey v. Demon Internet*, [1999] EWHC 244 (QB), the Court held that the ISP was a publisher and therefore could not rely upon section 1 of the *Defamation Act 1996*. This case was discussed in *Bunt v. Tilley & Ors*, [2006] EWHC 407 at paras. 11–14 (QB), Eady J.:

> . . . In that case, the Defendant was an ISP, which had received and stored a defamatory article on its news server which had been posted by an unknown person via another ISP. Mr Godfrey informed Demon of the defamatory nature of the article and requested its removal from their news server. It remained available, however, until its automatic expiry. In his statement of claim Mr Godfrey made it clear that he was confining his claim for damages to the period after January 1997, when the Defendant had knowledge that the posting was defamatory. The Defendant relied upon s.1(1) of the *Defamation Act 1996*, arguing that it was not the publisher of the statement in question; that it had taken reasonable care; and that it did not know, and had no reason to believe, that it had caused or contributed to the publication of a defamatory statement. Mr Godfrey applied to strike out that part of the defence as unsustainable.
>
> Morland J granted the application, holding on the particular facts that the Defendant was not merely a passive owner of an electronic device through which postings were transmitted. It had actively chosen to receive and store the news group exchanges containing the posting, and it could be accessed by its subscribers. It was within its power to obliterate the posting, as indeed later happened. Once the Defendant knew of the defamatory content and took the decision not to remove it from its news server, it was no longer able to satisfy the requirements of s. 1(1)(b) that reasonable care had been taken, or of s. l(1)(c) that it did not know, and it had no reason to believe, that what

it did caused or contributed to the publication. The learned Judge considered a number of authorities and at p208H-209A concluded:

> In my judgment the defendants, whenever they transmit and whenever there is transmitted from the storage of their news server a defamatory posting, publish that posting to any subscriber to their ISP who accesses the newsgroup containing that posting. Thus every time one of the defendants' customers accesses soc.culture.thai and sees that posting defamatory of the plaintiff there is a publication to that customer.

Reference was also made to certain cases from the United States, namely *Anderson v. New York Telephone Co* (1974) 35 NY 2d 746 ("the telephone company's role is merely passive . . ."); *Cubby Inc v. CompuServe Inc* (1991) 776 FS Supp 135 ("The computer service company was a mere 'distributor' which could not be held liable 'absent showing that it knew or had reason to know of defamation'"); *Stratton Oakmont Inc v. Prodigy Services Co* (1995) 23 Media L Rep 1794 ("Prodigy has uniquely arrogated to itself the role of determining what is proper for its members to post and read on its bulletin boards . . . . Prodigy is a publisher rather than a distributor . . ."); *Zeran v. America Online Inc* (1997) 129 F 3d 327 (concerned with a statutory federal immunity); and *Lunney v. Prodigy Services Co* (1998) 250 AD 2d 230. This latter case was perhaps closest in its background circumstances to the facts of *Godfrey v. Demon Internet.* "Some infantile practical joker" sent an e-mail to a boy scout leader, which falsely gave the impression that it came from Alex G Lunney, "a prospective eagle scout." He complained of that as well as two bulletin board messages posted with the help of Prodigy's service.

Morland J made clear, however, that he found these of little assistance because of the fundamental differences in the approach to the law of defamation between the courts of England and those of the United States.

2) *Bunt v. Tilley & Ors*

In *Bunt v. Tilley & Ors*, [2006] EWHC 407 (QB), the Court found that, in contrast to the *Godfrey v. Demon Internet* decision, there was no liability for an ISP that had truly fulfilled no more than a passive role as owner of an electronic device through which defamatory postings were transmitted (see para. 14). This decision was cited with approval in *Silberberg v. The Builders Collective of Australia*, [2007] FCA 1512 at paras. 31–32.

The first question to be determined is whether there was publication. Justice Eady decided there was no publication, in this case. See his discussion at paras. 15–18 and 21–25:

Publication is a question of fact, and it must depend on the circumstances of each case whether or not publication has taken place: see e.g. *Byrne v. Deane*, [1937] 1 KB 818, 837–838, *per* Greene LJ. The analogies that were held to be inappropriate in *Godfrey v. Demon Internet* might yet be upheld where the facts do not disclose onward transmission with knowledge of the defamatory content. As Dr Collins observes, *op. cit.*, at para. 15.43 [emphasis added]:

> "Mere conduit intermediaries who carry particular Internet communications from one computer to another . . . are analogous to postal services and telephone carriers in the sense that they facilitate communications, without playing any part in the creation or preparation of their content, and almost always without actual knowledge of the content."

Such an approach would tend to suggest that at common law such intermediaries should not be regarded as responsible for publication. Indeed, that is consistent with the approach in *Lunney* where the New York Court of Appeals drew an analogy between an ISP and a telephone company "which one neither wants nor expects to superintend the content of his subscriber's conversations."

It is necessary, on the other hand, to bear in mind that Morland J in *Godfrey*, while acknowledging the factual similarity to the circumstances in the *Lunney* case, nonetheless took the view that it represented an approach to the law which was not consistent with English authority. It was held that Prodigy was not responsible in law for the e-mail or the defamatory bulletin board postings, one of the reasons being that "Prodigy did not publish the statement." Morland J was of opinion that "at English common law Prodigy would clearly have been the publisher" of the message: see p. 212G.

Dr Collins tentatively concludes:

> "In view of Morland J's *obiter dictum* in *Godfrey v. Demon Internet Ltd* and the authorities concerning postal services and telephone carriers discussed above, mere conduit Internet intermediaries are nonetheless probably publishers of the material which passes though their computer systems. Their liability in defamation law will depend on whether they can rely on a defence, the most important of which are the defences for intermediaries . . . ."

In this context, he had in mind the provisions of s. 1 of the *Defamation Act 1996*, the *Electronic Commerce (EC Directive) Regulations 2002*, the common law defence of innocent dissemination, and statutory defences applying in Australia.

Despite this cautious approach, I was invited by counsel in the present case to conclude that the corporate Defendants should not be regarded as responsible according to common law principles for the publication of the relevant postings, the factual situation before me being significantly different from that confronting Morland J.

. . .

In determining responsibility for publication in the context of the law of defamation, it seems to me to be important to focus on what the person did, or failed to do, in the chain of communication. It is clear that the state of a defendant's knowledge can be an important factor. If a person knowingly permits another to communicate information which is defamatory, when there would be an opportunity to prevent the publication, there would seem to be no reason in principle why liability should not accrue. So too, if the true position were that the applicants had been (in the Claimant's words) responsible for "corporate sponsorship and approval of their illegal activities."

I have little doubt, however, that to impose legal responsibility upon anyone under the common law for the publication of words it is essential to demonstrate a degree of awareness or at least an assumption of general responsibility, such as has long been recognized in the context of editorial responsibility. As Lord Morris commented in *McLeod v. St. Aubyn*, [1899] AC 549, 562:

> "A printer and publisher intends to publish, and so intending cannot plead as a justification that he did not know the contents. The appellant in this case never intended to publish."

In that case the relevant publication consisted in handing over an unread copy of a newspaper for return the following day. It was held that there was no sufficient degree of awareness or intention to impose legal responsibility for that "publication."

Of course, to be liable for a defamatory publication it is not always necessary to be aware of the defamatory content, still less of its legal significance. Editors and publishers are often fixed with responsibility notwithstanding such lack of knowledge. On the other hand, for a person to be held responsible there must be knowing involvement in the process of publication of the relevant words. It is not enough that a person merely plays a passive instrumental role in the process. (See also in this context *Emmens v Pottle* (1885) 16 QBD 354, 357, Lord Esher MR.)

. . . A submission was made to me that public policy requires that an ISP who merely facilitates internet publications should not be held responsible as a "publisher," and that it would be desirable for ISPs to be protected in the same way that statutory immunity has been provided for, in respect of all proceedings in tort, by the *Postal Services Act 2000*. I am concerned here not with questions of public policy so much as whether or not any of the relevant Defendants in this case could be said to have been liable for publication in accordance with established common law principles. Nonetheless, in seeking to determine that question, I should have regard to the European Convention on Human Rights and Fundamental Freedoms and relevant Strasbourg jurisprudence, especially that relating to Articles 8 and 10.

One of the factors I have to consider is whether knowledge has been notified to any of the corporate Defendants in such a way as to render the ISP in question responsible for publication from that moment onwards (even assuming "innocence" up to that point). This is a question which I shall have to consider in the context of some of the other defences raised, but it is plainly relevant also to this threshold argument on common law publication.

At para. 36 of *Bunt v. Tilley & Ors*, [2006] EWHC 407 (QB) Eady J. held that there is no liability for an ISP performing a passive role:

> In all the circumstances I am quite prepared to hold that there is no realistic prospect of the Claimant being able to establish that any of the corporate Defendants, in any meaningful sense, knowingly participated in the relevant publications. His own pleaded case is defective in this respect in any event. *More generally, I am also prepared to hold as a matter of law that an ISP which performs no more than a passive role in facilitating postings on the internet cannot be deemed to be a publisher at common law* [emphasis added].

Justice Eady held at para. 37 that there is also no liability for a telephone company:

> I would not, in the absence of any binding authority, attribute liability at common law to a telephone company or other passive medium of communication, such as an ISP. It is not analogous to someone in the position of a distributor, who might at common law need to prove the absence of negligence: see *Gatley on Libel and Slander* (10th ed.) at para. 6–18. There a defence is needed because the person is regarded as having "published." By contrast, persons who truly fulfil no more than the role of a passive medium for communication cannot be characterised as publishers: thus they do not need a defence.

a) Discussion of the Balance of the Decision in *Bunt v. Tilley & Ors*

The balance of the decision which is arguably *obiter* discussed alternative arguments raised by the defendants. The following areas were covered:

1. Several questions were considered under the *Electronic Commerce (EC Directive) Regulations 2002*
   - Are the defendants "intermediary service providers"?
   - Are the defendants "mere conduits," as defined by Regulation 17, exempt from liability?
   - Are the defendants able to avail themselves of the "caching" as outlined in Regulation 18?
2. The application of section 1 of the *Defamation Act* 1996 (c. 31)
3. The application of the notice provisions under *Electronic Commerce (EC Directive) Regulations 2002*.

On the one hand, a detailed understanding of the *Electronic Commerce (EC Directive) Regulations 2002*, their application to particular defendants, and their relationship with section 1 of the UK *Defamation Act 1996* may appear to be of limited value to Canadian lawyers and judges unless the federal government and/or the provinces enact similar legislation. On the other hand, the concepts examined in the balance of the judgment: (1) notice to intermediaries, (2) ISPs, (3) hosting, (4) mere conduits, and (5) caching are of relevance to Canadian lawyers wrestling with cyberlibel problems involving intermediary liability for defamation. Consequently, portions of the balance of the reasons will be included not primarily to explain the conclusions reached in the *Bunt v. Tilley & Ors* decision but to assist Canadian lawyers in understanding the policy considerations behind the *Electronic Commerce (EC Directive) Regulations 2002*, the objectives and interpretations of the regulations, and how a caching works in practice. Notice to intermediaries has been discussed in a separate previous section.

i)   Intermediary Service Providers/ISPs

Justice Eady at paragraph 38, 40, and 41 considered the question of whether the defendants in *Bunt v. Tilley & Ors* were intermediary service providers at paras. 38 and 40–41:

> For the sake of completeness, it is now necessary to address the alternative arguments raised by the applicants. I turn first to the *Electronic Commerce (EC Directive) Regulations 2002*, which came into force in August of that year. They define the circumstances in which internet intermediaries should be held accountable for material which is hosted, cached, or carried by them but which they did not create. The protection which these regulations afford is not confined to the publication of defamatory material. They embrace other illegal material, such as child pornography or the infringement of intellectual property rights.

The effect of the regulations is to implement within this jurisdiction the Directive on Electronic Commerce, issued on 8 June 2000: Directive 2000/311EC of the European Parliament and Council. It was made clear in the recitals that one of the objectives was to remove "existing and emerging disparities in Member States' legislation and case law concerning liability of service providers acting as intermediaries," because it was necessary to avoid their preventing the smooth functioning of the internal market — in particular by impairing the development of cross-border services and producing distortions of competition: see Recital 40. There is recognition that service providers may be obliged on occasion to act in order to prevent or stop unlawful activities. It was plainly thought desirable that the position should be made as clear as possible.

The relevant provisions apply to "information society services." That is an important consideration in the present case, because the Claimant contends that these corporate Defendants are not able to avail themselves of such protection. I must therefore have regard to the definition in Regulation 2(1) which incorporates Article 2(a) of the Directive. This, in turn, incorporates the definition in Directive 98/34/EC. An "information society service" connotes:

> "any service normally provided for remuneration, at a distance, by electronic means and at the individual request of a recipient of services."

It is observed by Dr Collins, in *Law of Defamation and the Internet, op cit,* at para. 17.03 that:

> "Commercial Internet intermediaries, such as ISPs, bulletin board operators, and web hosting services will usually satisfy this definition."

It is certainly the case of these applicants that they each satisfy those requirements.

Justice Eady concluded that the defendants were intermediary service providers at para. 45:

> At all events, it is clear to me from the evidence that these Defendants do indeed fall within the relevant definition. Of course that is challenged by the Claimant, but the facts which lead to that conclusion are themselves uncontroversial. I am thus unable to accept his submission that ". . . the Directive in question most certainly does NOT apply to the business relationship that exists between the three corporate Defendants and the three individual

Defendants." I need to turn next to Regulations 17 and 18, upon which AOL and Tiscali [the defendants] both place reliance.

ii) Mere Conduits

Justice Eady discussed the concept of "mere conduits" in regulation 17(1) of the *Electronic Commerce (EC Directive) Regulations* at para. 46:

> Regulation 17(1), which is concerned with the concept of "mere conduits" provides as follows:
>
> (1) Where an information society service is provided which consists of the transmission in a communication network of information provided by a recipient of the service or the provision of access to a communication network, the service provider (if he otherwise would) shall not be liable for damages or for any other pecuniary remedy or for any criminal sanction as a result of that transmission where the service provider —
>   (a) did not initiate the transmission;
>   (b) did not select the receiver of the transmission; and
>   (c) did not select or modify the information contained III the transmission.

The matter of bulletin board postings and webpages concludes that regulation 17 will usually apply to Internet intermediaries who operate computer systems through which bulletin board postings and webpages happen to pass on route from one computer to another. See Eady J. at para. 50:

> Dr Collins also addresses (at para. 17.09) the matter of bulletin board postings and web pages, and concludes that Regulation 17 will usually apply to internet intermediaries who operate computer systems through which particular bulletin board postings and web pages happen to pass en route from one computer to another. This is subject to the proviso that the intermediary does not store the constituent IP datagrams for any period longer than is reasonably necessary for the transmission. Dr Collins suggests that, in order to attract the protection of Regulation 17, an intermediary would need to configure its computer system to delete any copies of the relevant datagrams immediately after receiving an acknowledgment that they have been received by the intended recipient. Should the datagrams be stored for a longer period, the intermediary would be likely to be deemed to have "cached" or "hosted" them.

At paragraph 47 of *Bunt v. Tilley & Ors*, [2006] EWHC 407 (QB), Eady J. held that the defendants, AOL, Tiscali, and British Telecom, were "mere conduits."

It is further provided by Regulation 17(2) that acts of transmission and of provision of access, for the purposes of Regulation 17(1), would include the automatic, intermediate and transient storage of the information transmitted where it takes place for the sole purpose of carrying out the transmission in the communication network, and provided that the information is not stored for any period longer than is reasonably necessary for the transmission. That again is a point raised by Mr Bunt in the present proceedings. He submits that the material, or some of it, is cached for too long a period for it to be characterised as "reasonably necessary." It is appropriate for this to be judged in the light of the automatic system put in place and the objective it is intended to achieve. The evidence is set out in some detail below.

iii) Caching

Justice Eady discussed the concept of caching in: *Bunt v. Tilley & Ors*, [2006] EWHC 407 at paras. 48–49 (QB):

> Regulation 18 is concerned with caching:
>
> > Where an information society service is provided which consists of the transmission in a communication network of information provided by a recipient of the service, the service provider (if he otherwise would) shall not be liable for damages or for any other pecuniary remedy or for any criminal sanction as result of that transmission where—
> >
> > (a) the information is the subject of automatic, intermediate and temporary storage where that storage is for the sole purpose of making more efficient onward transmission of the information to other recipients of the service upon their request, and
> >
> > (b) the service provider—
> >
> > > (i) does not modify the information;
> > >
> > > (ii) complies with conditions of access to the information;
> > >
> > > (iii) complies with any rules regarding the updating of the information, specified in a manner widely recognised and used by industry;
> > >
> > > (iv) does not interfere with the lawful use of technology, widely recognised and used by industry, to obtain data on the use of the information; and
> > >
> > > (v) acts expeditiously to remove or to disable access to the information he has stored upon obtaining actual knowledge of the fact that the information at the initial source of the transmission has been removed from the network, or access to it has

been disabled, or that a court or an administrative authority
has ordered such removal or disablement

The commentary in *Gatley* at para. 6.28 is helpful:

"The protection is therefore aimed at transient messages, such as
email or at more permanent material which simply passes through the
defendant's system for purposes of access and not at material which is
stored by the defendant for significant periods. The knowledge of the
defendant is irrelevant, so he is not liable (in contrast to s. l of the *Defamation Act 1996*) for failing to take steps to prevent access to another
site which he is aware carries defamatory material. However, the provision does not confer immunity against the grant of an injunction."

The learned editors mention (in footnote 21) a possible qualification with
regard to web-based e-mail, which is normally stored on the provider's server
until deleted by the customer. This qualification has been developed further
by Dr Collins, *op cit*, at para. 17.08:

"The position is likely to be different for intermediaries who operate web-
based e-mail services, such as MSN Hotmail. Such services store e-mail
messages sent to their subscribers on their servers on a more permanent
basis, so that the messages can be viewed by subscribers from any computer, located anywhere in the world. Rather than being deleted automatically from the intermediary's server upon initial transmission to a
subscriber, e-mail messages on web-based e-mail services are usually deleted from the intermediary's server only at the request of the subscriber.
As messages sent to web-based email services are not stored only on an
'intermediate' or 'transient' basis, and are frequently stored for a period
longer than is reasonably necessary for their transmission, regulation 17
is unlikely to apply. Intermediaries operating these services are probably
'hosts,' rather than 'mere conduits,' of messages received by subscribers."

Para. 51 of the case explains the purpose of regulation 18:

The purpose of Regulation 18 is to protect internet intermediaries in
respect of material for which they are not the primary host but which
they store temporarily on their computer systems for the purpose of
enabling the efficient availability of internet material. Many ISPs and
other intermediaries regularly cache, or temporarily store, commonly
accessed web pages on their computer systems, so that those pages
will be more quickly accessible to their subscribers. This is described

by the learned editors of *Gatley* (at para. 6.29) as a "sort of half way house between mere transmission and 'hosting.'"

b) Expert Evidence Explaining the Process of Caching by AOL in 2006

The process of caching was explained in detail by a witness for AOL in *Bunt v. Tilley & Ors.* His evidence was not contradicted and was accepted by the Court at para. 53:

> The process was explained in evidence before me by Mr Nigel Hearth the Director of Technical Operations for AOL. In his witness statement of 10 February 2006 the matter is described as follows:
>
> > 4. When explaining in this statement how the practice of caching works I refer particularly to the practices of AOL in this area, although the practice of caching, and the way this is done (as explained below), is in effect ubiquitous amongst internet service providers.
> >
> > 5. The ability to view web pages quickly is an attractive attribute for users of the internet. The enormous volume of requests for web pages generated by internet users has led to the development of technical solutions by network providers and internet service providers to enable more efficient transmission of that information across the internet.
> >
> > 6. Caching is one such solution. It is a technical process which enables internet providers, such as AOL, to speed up the delivery of web pages to internet users by making a temporary copy of a web page that is requested by a user. When a subsequent request is made for the same page, the user can be provided with that content from the local 'cached' copy made by the internet service provider, rather than having to go back to the original web site which is the source of that page. This process enables the more efficient onward transmission of web pages to internet users.
> >
> > 7. A web cache (including AOL's) is not a copy of the internet — that is neither the purpose of a web cache, nor would it be commercially or technically feasible. In order for web caches not to have to expand in memory size indefinitely the actual content in a web cache is designed to be overwritten in accordance with automatic defined rules ensuring that (i) cached content is up to date and (ii) cached content which is not being searched for (or has been removed or altered) is overwritten.
> >
> > 8. For ease of reference, I shall use a specific example, that of the pages of Google Groups, located at http://groups.google.co.uk/group/uk.loca1.london ("Google Groups London").

9. Google Groups London is provided by Google and the content forming that page is hosted by Google i.e. that content sits on computers controlled by Google. A popular site such as google.co.uk may easily have more than several hundred thousand visitors per day. When a person using an AOL Member Account connected to the internet via the AOL UK Propriety Service (an "AOL User") navigates to Google Groups London, a request is sent form that user's personal computer, via AOL, to the Google computer hosting Google Groups London. The requested page is then sent back to the AOL User, via their AOL connection.

10. When Google computers receive high volumes of requests within short time periods, delivery of the relevant Google Groups London page may be affected and a queue may form for the relevant Google computers to become free to respond to an individual's request. The Google computers may simply become too busy.

11. To help alleviate this problem, AOL in common with all major internet service providers, uses a so-called 'web cache' to make the onward transmission of information of content such as Google Groups London more efficient to users of AOL when they request such information.

12. AOL's web cache consists of a computer system which sits between (in this case) Google's computers, on which the Google Groups London page is stored, and the home computers of individuals wishing to view Google Groups London.

13. The AOL web cache in effect watches requests for web pages made by individuals and then saves copies of the responses from Google's computers. If there is a subsequent request for the Google Groups London page from an AOL User then that request is fulfilled by delivery of the Google Groups London page from the AOL web cache, rather than via the original location on Google computers.

13.1 As the request for the Google Groups London page is delivered from the AOL web cache, rather than the Google servers, it takes less time for AOL to retrieve the images and text on the Google Groups London page and display it to the AOL User wishing to view it.

13.2 The mechanism of storage by the AOL web cache is completely automatic. Providers of web sites set automated 'rules' or conditions specifying; (1) whether a page may be cached; (2) if it may be cached, at what time that cached material should expire; and (3) whether the cache computers should revalidate with the original source web site as to whether a page sitting on AOL's web cache has been updated or deleted. These rules are embedded in instructions which exist 'behind' web pages and the rules are applied by, and are readable by, web browser software in accordance with industry standards. This ensures that users of the internet reach the most up to date versions of web pages available. By way of example, for frequently updated pages like the BBC's news home page (located at http://news. bbc.co.uk), the instructions behind that particular page will dictate that the page should not be cached. Each time that page is requested, those instructions state that it should be retrieved from the original source, not from a cached copy.

13.3 By contrast, the messages hosted by Google Groups London contain instructions that allow caching but require that a web cache should revalidate the content with the original source for each subsequent request. So, if a particular message is cached, before the cache displays that content to a subsequent user requesting that page, the cache will check with Google as to whether that page has subsequently been removed or deleted.

13.4 This entire process is entirely automatic and the only reason for it is to make the transmission of web pages more efficient. AOL does not modify the information contained on web pages in any way. AOL complies with any conditions embedded in such pages regarding access to the information (for example by preventing the caching of pages which contain instructions for them not to be cached) and does not interfere in any way with the lawful use of technology widely used by the industry to obtain data on the use of information (for example tracking how many times a source page has been accessed).

13.5 The storage of such material on AOL's web cache is temporary — permanent storage would be inherently contradictory to the purpose and aim of the AOL web cache, which is to enable more efficient transmission of information to internet users.

13.6 It is core to the function of AOL's web caches and similar caches used by other internet service providers that they do not modify the content of the information they transmit.

13.7 The material will appear in AOL's web cache once the AOL user has requested it if the instructions in the source page permit this. AOL's web cache can only hold a limited amount of information. It will subsequently be overwritten when either:

(a) no AOL users request the Google Groups London page within a specified period (AOL sets this period at 7 days). Thereafter the Google Groups London page will be labelled by AOL's web cache as ready for deletion from the cache (such pages are described as ('Expired')), and will be overwritten, as newer requests for other web pages trigger the storage of those pages in AOL's web cache — this mechanism effectively 'recycles' AOL's web cache memory by overwriting; or

(b) the source material is altered after it is stored in the cache to use my example, if Google altered the content on the Google Groups London page, or removed it entirely, then that content would be labelled for deletion as soon as another AOL User requested that page. Prior to displaying that page to the AOL User, the AOL cache would revalidate the page with Google (in accordance with the automatic rules), find that the source page had changed or been removed and therefore label the Google Groups London page in the AOL web cache as Expired, leading to the overwriting of that page in the manner described above.

(c) Where access t6 [sic] the pages has been disabled or where a court or an administrative authority has ordered the source to remove or disable the content, and they had done so. Those pages stored in AOL caches would not be further displayed to an end user and would eventually be overwritten as the web cache stored other 'fresh' web pages.

3) *Metropolitan International Schools Ltd. (t/a Skillstrain and/or Train2game) v. Designtechnica Corp. (t/a Digital Trends) & Ors*

In this case the Court held that Google was not a publisher of the statements that appeared on the search engine results page *before* notice was given by the plaintiff. Moreover, the Court held that on the evidence in this case Google was not a publisher even *after* notice was given. The Court left open the situations where a search engine could be found to be a publisher after notice. This decision is discussed in greater detail in Chapter 22.

4) *Kaschke v. Gray & Anor*

The decision in *Kaschke v. Gray & Anor,* [2010] EWHC 690 (QB), discusses the applicability of exemptions contained in Regulation 19 (hosting) of the *Electronic Commerce (EC Directive) Regulations 2002* to a user-generated website, as well as the risks of moderating a user generated website. Justice Stadlen held at para. 18:

> The Electronic Commerce (EC Directive) Regulations 2002 are derived from EC Directive 2000/31/EC ("The E-Commerce Directive"). Regulations 17, 18 and 19, which exclude liability in certain circumstances resulting from respectively mere conduit, caching and hosting reflect Articles 12, 13 and 14 respectively of the E-Commerce Directive. [Hereinafter referred to as E-Commerce Directive]

This case revolved around a blog post on a website, Labourhome.org, which claimed the plaintiff had been arrested on suspicion of being a member of a terrorist group. The website operator's defence was that, though he ran the site, he did not edit or review the articles. Therefore his lawyer argued that should qualify under the exemptions of the *Electronic Commerce (EC Directive) Regulations 2002*, in particular, Regulation 19.

The defendant brought a motion regulating that the plaintiff's action should be struck out. The defendant's motion was dismissed before the Master and the defendant appealed to the High Court. Justice Stadlen dismissed the appeal. The essential question to be answered was whether the defendant, as an intermediary service provider, did no more than store the information or no more than facilitate the transmission of the information. See paras. 31–32 (QB).

The precise grounds of appeal, at para. 40, were as follows [bracketed headings have been added to facilitate reading]:

[Storage of Information]

(i)   Is there a realistic prospect that Mr Hilton may fail at trial to prove that he is entitled to invoke Regulation 19 (even if he could satisfy the conditions in Regulation 19(a) and (b))? Put another way is there a realistic prospect that Mr Hilton may fail to prove at trial that if he is otherwise liable as alleged in the particulars of claim that liability would be a result of the provision by him of an information society service consisting of the storage of information provided by a recipient of the service?

[Actual Knowledge]

(ii) If the answer to (i) is no, is there a realistic prospect that Mr Hilton may fail to prove at trial that he neither (a) had actual knowledge of unlawful activity or information nor (b) was aware of factual circumstances from which it would have been apparent to him that that activity or information was unlawful?

[Expedited Removal after Notice]

(iii) If the answer to (i) is no, but the answer to (ii) is yes is there a realistic prospect that Mr Hilton may fail to prove that on obtaining such knowledge or awareness he acted expeditiously to remove or to disable access to the information?

[Acting under authority or control]

(iv) If the answer to (i) is no and the answer to either (ii) or (iii) is no, is there a realistic prospect that Mr Hilton may fail at trial to prove that Mr Gray, the recipient of the service was not acting under his authority or control?

a) Rulings

1. The Court clarified that the operation of a chatroom qualifies as an information society service (ISS) under the *Electronic Commerce (EC Directive) 2002*, thereby allowing the chatroom to take advantage of the exemptions of liability under the Directive.

2. The Court ruled that the moderation of one part of a website does not prevent other areas of the same site from being exempt from liability. Consequently, if a website includes a mix of user-generated content in some parts, which are exempt, and there is another part of the content that is non-exempt, the defendant website operator can still avail themselves of the exemptions under the *E-Commerce Directives* for the user-generated parts. In other words, the Court held that the fact that one area of the site was moderated does not prevent other areas of the same site from having exemption from liability. See paras. 58, 68, and 75, where the Court referred to a decision of the Irish High Court in *Mulvaney v. Betfair* [2009] IENC 133 and an unreported English decision *Imram Karim v. Newsquest Media Group* dated 27 October 2009:

> *Betfair* can of course be of no more than persuasive authority and was concerned with construing and applying a regulation framed in different terms to Regulation 19. It is also the case that Clarke J did not explicitly address or purport to answer the question with which I am currently concerned. However subject to those reservations it seems to me that Betfair provides support for a number of propositions. First there is no reason in principle why the operation of a chat room should be incapable of falling within the definition of the provision of an information society service consisting of the storage of information. Thus in principle there is no reason why it should not be an activity intended to be protected by Article 14 of the E-Commerce Directive and eligible for the exclusion of liability conferred by Regulation 19.

Second it is not necessarily a bar to entitlement to the protection conferred by Regulation 19 (which Member States were intended to provide by Article 14) that the provider of an information society service consisting of storage of information is also engaged in an activity on the same website which is either not an information society service or if it is which does not consist of the storage of information. In Betfair it was accepted that no betting activity took place through the chat room and that the chat room was maintained and run through a separate section of Betfair's website which did not include what was described as betting functionality.

. . .

It seems to me that *Imran Karim* supports the proposition which is also supported by *Betfair* that if an information society service is provided which consists of the storage of information provided by a recipient of the service and the service provider would otherwise be liable for damages as a result of that storage, he is not precluded from invoking the exclusion of liability conferred by Regulation 19 by the mere fact that in addition he also provides some other service, even an information society service, which does not consist of the storage of information

. . .

For all these reasons in my judgment when considering in a particular case whether a defendant is entitled to the immunity conferred by Regulation 19 (subject to satisfying the extra conditions) the question to be asked is whether the information society service provided by the defendant in respect of the information containing the defamatory words which would otherwise give rise to liability consists only of and is limited to storage of that information. If the answer to that question is that it does consist only of storage of the information, Regulation 19 immunity is potentially available even if it would not be available in respect of other information also stored by the defendant in respect of which the service provided by the defendant goes beyond mere storage.

3. The Court determined that the availability of the Regulation 19 defence depends on what is being done with the specific information in question (see para. 70). This principle and its applications to specific pieces of information is clearly stated in para. 86:

The evidence summarised above illustrates why it is potentially important to identify with precision the information society service referred to in Regulation 19. It is in my view clear that if the relevant information society service was the website as a whole or the homepage it would not fall within the definition of consisting only of the storage of information. Accordingly Regulation 19 immunity would not be available to Mr Hilton. Similarly if the relevant information society service was the hosting of all blogs posted on web pages made available by Mr Hilton on his website it again seems to me at least arguable that that also would not fall within the definition of consisting only of the storage of information. In his first witness statement Mr Hilton stated in terms that where a blog is promoted by him he may check the piece for spelling and grammar and make corrections. That in my view arguably goes beyond mere storage of information. The fact that Mr Hilton on a few occasions removed blog posts on grounds of bad language, political provocation or offensiveness falling short of defamation again in my view makes it at least arguable that the service provided in respect of those individual blog posts and also in respect of the general service consisting of making available webpages on his website for such blogs to be posted consisted of more than mere storage.

4. The Court reviewed various activities and held that they went beyond mere storage. The Court held at para. 77 that, in effect, intervention of any sort, at any time, whether prior to or post moderation for offensive conduct or merely correcting the grammar or spelling takes the service beyond mere storage and outside the exemption:

> It is clear from Mr Hilton's own witness statements that he exercised some editorial control on parts of the website and in particular on the homepage. It is quite clear from his evidence that his involvement in the website as a whole and in particular in the homepage went beyond the mere storage of information. Thus for example he tried to secure articles from high profile authors, wrote articles himself for placing on the website and carried out other tasks such as conducting polls and interviews to be placed on the website. The homepage had a segment headed "Recommended" and one headed "Recent Blogs" as well as a more prominent segment headed "Top Entries." As soon as an individual blog post was written and appeared on its own webpage, its title together with the "username" of the person who wrote it and a link to the full text of the post appeared at the top of the "Recent Blogs" segment on the homepage. That segment contained links to the last 15 posts placed by members. That was a completely automatic process requiring no intervention from Mr Hilton and over which he had no influence. See also at paras. 78–85.

5. The defendants' lawyer argued that the defendant should not lose the protection of the Regulation 19 exemption for his post moderation conduct

i.e. checking messages after they appear and removing any that he found to be offensive. To deny the defendant of that protection would provide operators of websites which host blogs an incentive not to monitor their sites with a review to removing offensive material. This, the defendants submitted, would be contrary to the policy in Regulation 19 of encouraging the expeditious removal of information whose storage is unlawful. Justice Stadlen was unconvinced by this argument but decided that he did not have to answer that point (paras. 87–88).

6. Finally, the Court held that whether or not Gray, the individual posting the statement, was acting under the authority or control of the website owner was also a question which might remove the website owner's right to an exemption. This was another issue which required a full trial to decide (para. 105).

b) Several Issues are Left Unclear

The decision in *Kaschke v. Gray & Anor*, [2010] EWHC 690, left several issues uncertain:

1. What is editorial control or editorial involvement and does this include correction of spelling mistakes, grammar, or syntax?[8]
2. Does the approval of one comment hold the ISS liable for any future unmoderated comments by this person? In this case, does any moderation result in a liability? What happens where some of the comments are moderated and others are not?
3. The exemptions, appear to have been developed in order to encourage ISPs to self-regulate and to encourage them to remove defamatory or offensive materials on their own. It is arguable that this decision will have the opposite effect. It encourages blog owners to purposely avoid any manner of moderating, otherwise they risk liability. This is the problem that was addressed years before in *Stratton Oakmont, Inc. v. Prodigy Services Co.*, 1995 WL 323710 (N.Y. Sup. Ct. 1995), in the US. The decision of the Court imposing liability on the ISP was instrumental in Congress

---

8   Outlaw.com: High Court ruling serves as a warning against any moderation of user comments, 8 April 2010; Laidlaw.eu, *Kaschke v. Gray and Hilton*, 20 April 2010.

   Lexology.com: *Kaschke v Gray*, [2010] EWHC 690 (QB): online blogs and the hosting safe harbor, 28 May 2010.

   Mablaw.com: High Court reinforces dangers of moderating comments on website but website *may* be OK if it does not moderate the actual post complained about — *Kaschke v. Gray and Hilton*, High Court, 13 April 2010.

enacting section 230 of the *CDA*, which provides for near immunity for ISPs, in the US.

c) Limits of the Applicability of the Decision to Canadian Lawyers and Judges

There are two obvious limits on the applicability of this decision, even on a persuasive basis to Canadian lawyers and judges:

1. There is no comparable legislation in Canada governing defamation for ISPs;
2. It is important to recognize the particular procedural basis of this decision. It was an appeal to a High Court judge from a decision of the Master dismissing an application to strike out the plaintiff's statement of claim.

d) Value of Decision for Canadian Lawyers and Judges

Despite these limitations, this decision has value for Canadian lawyers and judges:

1. Canadians have no legislation and no decisions at all on these questions of intermediary liability for defamation. Therefore, there is no guidance other than this decision.
2. The sequence of the analysis is instructive.
3. The decision illustrates the importance of recognizing and specifying with precision the information society service referred to in the particular case.
4. It is submitted that the essential question in *Kaschke* will likely be the essential question in the Canadian situation — that is, whether the defendant, as a service provider, did no more than merely store the information or no more than facilitate the transmitting of the information (see para. 33).

CHAPTER 22: Search Engines

A. BACKGROUND

James Grimmelmann has provided a useful description of search engines and their connection to emerging cyberlaw:

> Search engines are the new linchpins of the Internet. A large and growing fraction of the Internet's large and growing volume of traffic flows through them. They are librarians, bringing order to the chaotic online accumulation of human knowledge and creativity. They are messengers, creating new information flows and reorienting others. They are critics, wielding the power to elevate content to prominence or consign it to obscurity. They are inventors, devising new technologies and business models in their relentless drive to better describe complex online realities. And they are spies, asked to carry out investigations with dispatch and discretion.
>
> Lawyers and the law have taken notice of search engines. Governments around the world are casting an increasingly skeptical eye on search engines, questioning whether their actions have always been in the interests of society. More and more parties are presenting themselves at the courthouse door with plausible stories of how they have been injured by search engines.[1]

---

1 James Grimmelmann, "The Structure of Search Engine Law" (2007) 93:1 Iowa L. Rev. 1 at 1. There is a great deal of information about search engine law and search engines.

    1. An excellent website exists at www.linksandlaw.com. This is an encyclopedic source of decisions primarily dealing with intellectual property involving search engines and hyperlinks.

    2. On the history of information retrieval and search engines see for example: John Battelle, *The Search: How Google and Its Rivals Rewrote the Rules of Business and Transformed our Culture*, (London: Penguin Books, 2005) at 203– 8; Amy N.

Web search engines operate websites that "generate and maintain extensive databases of Internet addresses and content in an easily searchable format . . . . Search engines index information and content in an automated fashion, based on sophisticated algorithms."[2] Web portals, as distinct from search engines, typically provide the user with additional services such as news, email, etc., and therefore often integrate many aspects of a company's Web-based business on one site.[3] Search engines create a database of Web content by scanning millions of Web documents for content through automated programs variously known as "bots," "crawlers," or "spiders." These programs automatically and continuously make requests on servers, storing content and, depending on the type of program, scanning part or all of an online document, including its metadata. As the documents are scanned for content, the search engine spider will index the content it finds, imposing predetermined categories in order to facilitate storage and, later, retrieval of the data.[4] Typically, such indexing will be automated though in some cases ongoing human involvement in the process is used.[5]

A user with a query she wishes to satisfy through the Internet will open her preferred Web search engine interface, enter her preferred search terms, and request the search. At this point the chosen search engine will hunt its database, automatically matching the search terms with its indexed content with the object of returning the most relevant Web data. There are two main types of queries that a search engine database may be designed to accept, though most, in fact, will accept both types of query to some degree: Boolean and non-Boolean.[6]

> The three basic functions of the Boolean system include the functional operators AND, OR and NOT. By these three commands, terms can be used to characterize a given set of documents.

Lanville and Carl D. Meyer, *Google's PageRank and Beyond: The Science of Search Engine Rankings* (Woodstock: Princeton University Press, 2006) at 1–5, 6–8, 9–10, 11–12; Randall Stross *Planet Google*, (New York: Free Press, 2008); Ken Auletta, *Googled: The End of the World As We Know It* (New York: Penguin Books, 2009).

2   Karine Perset, "The Economic and Social Role of Internet Intermediaries," *OECD Digital Economy Papers*, No. 171 (2010) at 12 online at www.oecd.org/dataoecd/49/4/44949023.pdf.

3   *Ibid.*

4   Ned Fielden and Lucy Kuntz, *Search Engines Handbook* (Jefferson, NC: McFarland & Company, 2002) at 13–25. Note that, as mentioned at 26, Google will actually "cache" webpages.

5   Karine Perset, "The Economic and Social Role of Internet Intermediaries," above note 2 at 12.

6   Ned Fielden and Lucy Kuntz, *Search Engines Handbook* above note 4 at 29.

Besides the reputation developed over their relatively long tradition in computer circles, Boolean systems have the advantage of being relatively easy to program and quite fast. Their drawbacks include the use of rather inflexible syntax when constructing a query, and an irritating capacity to either return sets with nothing . . . or a huge quantity of unordered and often quite unuseful documents.[7]

. . .

Several varieties of non-Boolean systems are currently in use. They generally attempt to treat queries in the same manner as the documents themselves, trying to make best matches between the two.

Among other features, they employ "natural language processing" allowing queries that do not have to be constructed under the fixed (and sometimes awkward) Boolean formulas.[8]

Search results will be returned according to relevance as determined by the search engine designer/design team. Some of the factors that may be involved in determining relevance could include: number of occurrences; occurrences per document size; proximity; where the term searched is found; page popularity; and term rarity.[9]

As James Grimmelmann notes, individual search engines may differ in their function and the role they fill for users:

Some search engines themselves provide content to users. Where providers create their own search engines, the process of providing results and the process of providing the content itself may merge. A successful search on Wikipedia, for example, simply returns the desired Wikipedia entry directly. Independent search engines sometimes also provide content to users. They may cache content, storing copies to make it easier for users to receive it quickly, or archive content, enabling users to receive it even when the original provider cannot be reached. They may also allow users to preview content, offering smaller (e.g. thumbnails for pictures) or excerpted versions of it. At the extreme end of this trend, search engines become true middlemen, simply purchasing the content from willing sellers and retailing it to users.[10]

---

7   *Ibid.* at 31.
8   *Ibid.* at 31–32.
9   *Ibid.* at 33–34.
10   Grimmelmann, above note 1 at 8.

B. SEARCH ENGINE RESULTS PAGES

Search engine results pages (SERPs)[11] are the outputs produced by search engines after a user enters a query. Typically, SERPs consist of a list of entries, each composed, at a minimum, of a hyperlink to where the matched source appears on the web, a brief passage of text showing the search terms matched in the result presented, and the URL of the result.[12] Many search engines offer more refined search options that will return pages classified as images, blogs, academic articles, or news, for example. An individual search engine will return a list of ranked, hyperlinked results within the parameters chosen by the user according to the constraints of that search engine's own proprietary algorithm. Such algorithms will normally take into account the text on individual webpages, the number of hyperlinks to the page, its centrality, and the popularity or prestige of the page,[13] among many other things.[14] This information is gathered through the use of crawler or spider programs that comb online content and index it. When a query is made through the search engine its unique algorithm is applied to the indexed content and, almost instantaneously, an SERP is generated. In a process known as search engine optimization (SEO) many companies or third-party agencies will study SERPs and algorithms of individual search engines to learn how to maximize the ranking of their online content within a given search engine.[15] This process has become of escalating importance to companies as consumers increasingly look to do business online because studies have shown that users of search engines rarely investigate beyond the initial few results returned.[16]

While SERPs consist mostly of a list of the typical type of search results (discussed above) known as "organic" results, they will also contain links, presented similarly, that are paid for by advertisers. These results are often (as in the case of Google) given a prominent placement on the page and are

---

11 Kerry Dye, "Website Abuse for Search Engine Optimisation" (2008) 3 *Network Security* 4; and see generally, Ravi Kumar Jain Bandamutha, "Search Engines: Trends and Technology" in Ravi Kumar Jain Bandamutha, ed., *Dynamics of Search Engines: An Introduction* (Hyderabad, India: Icfai Press, 2007), c. 1.

12 Nadine Hochstetter and Dirk Lewandowski, "What Users See — Structures in Search Engine Results Pages" (2009) 179 *Information Sciences* 1796–1812.

13 Bing Liu, *Web Data Mining: Exploring Hyperlinks, Contents, and Usage Data* (Berlin: Springer, 2007) at 241–43.

14 "Google's success is largely attributed to its hyperlink-based ranking algorithm called PageRank . . . ." See *ibid.* at 9.

15 Kerry Dye, "Website Abuse for Search Engine Optimisation" (2008) 3 *Network Security* 4.

16 Nadine Hochstetter and Dirk Lewandowski, "What Users See — Structures in Search Engine Results Pages" (2009) 179 *Information Sciences* 1796 at 1797.

designated under "sponsored links" in a small typeface;[17] such hyperlinks are termed "sponsored" links.

An understanding of SERPs is important in cyberlibel proceedings for several reasons. First, they should assist lawyers in deciding whether they should take any action. It may not be worthwhile in taking proceedings if the offensive articles are buried at page fifteen of the SERPs when you go Google the potential plaintiff's name. Second, lawyers may wish to retain information technology, specialists to attempt to move the offensive statements to a lower SERP — for example, from page one to page fifteen. Third, it is important that apologies are placed on the first page of the SERP.

C. LIABILITY OF SEARCH ENGINES BEFORE AND AFTER NOTIFICATION BY THE PLAINTIFF

There are no decisions in Canada at present about search engine liability in defamation cases. The English case *Metropolitan International Schools Limited (t/a Skillstrain and/or Train2game) v. Designtechnica Corp. (t/a Digital Trends) & Ors*, [2009] EWHC 1765 (QB) [*MIS*], is an important (and so far the only) decision in England, Canada and Australia that discusses in detail the question of liability of the search engine before and after notification by the plaintiff on a potentially defamatory statement thrown up by the search engine.

The plaintiff, Metropolitan International Schools Limited (MIS) is a provider of adult distance learning courses in the design and development of computer games. MIS trades under the name "Train2Game." Between 1992 and 2004 it traded under the name "Scheidegger MIS."

MIS brought an action in the High Court against Google Inc. ("Google"), Google UK Limited, and a US company, Designtechnica Corporation trading as Digital Trends. MIS alleged that comments about MIS posted on forums on a Digital Trends website were defamatory. It also claimed that Google was liable as a publisher for an excerpt from the forums which appeared in a Google search engine result (called a "snipett").

The allegedly defamatory comments on Digital Trends' forums were, amongst other things, that MIS courses were nothing more than a scam intended to deceive honest people. MIS claimed that when entering the search term "Train2Game" in Google.co.uk and Google.com, the third and fourth

---

17 *Ibid.*

highest search result included the snippet of text "Train2Game new SCAM for Sheidegger." MIS claimed that this snippet was defamatory.[18]

Google was sued on that snippet, thrown up by the search engine rather than any publications occurring on the first defendant's statement contained on the original website publication.

The questions to be answered were: Can this operator of a search engine be liable for publication of a defamatory statement (a) before notification by the plaintiff? (b) after notification by the plaintiff?

In this case Justice Eady found:

1. That the search engine could not be held liable as a publisher before notification.
2. That, in this particular case, there was no liability after notification.
3. It is arguable that Justice Eady limited his decision to the facts of this case,[19] and that he consequently left open the possibility that in certain cases a search might be exposed to liability after notification.

---

18 Swan Turton Solicitors, "eBulletin: Google not Liable for Defamatory Search Engine Results: *Metropolitan International Schools Limited v. Google Inc. and Others*" (19 August 2009), online: www.swanturton.com/ebulletins/archive/GoogleNotLiable.aspx.

19 See *Metropolitan International Schools Limited (t/a Skillstrain and/or Train2game) v. Designtechnica Corp. (t/a Digital Trends) & Ors*, [2009] EWHC 1765 (QB):

> 57 *In this case the evidence shows that Google has taken* steps to ensure that certain identified URLs are blocked, in the sense that when web-crawling takes place, the content of such URLs will not be displayed in response to Google searches carried out on Google .co.uk. This has now happened in relation to the "scam" material on many occasions. But I am told that the Third Defendant needs to have specific URLs identified and is not in a position to put in place a more effective block on the specific words complained of without, at the same time, blocking a huge amount of other material which might contain some of the individual words comprising the offending snippet.

> 64 *Against this background, including the steps so far taken by the Third Defendant to* block the identified URLs, I believe it is unrealistic to attribute responsibility for publication to the Third Defendant, whether on the basis of authorship or acquiescence. There is no doubt room for debate as to what further blocking steps it would be open for it to take, or how effective they might be, but that does not seem to me to affect my overall conclusion on liability. This decision is quite independent of any defence provided by s.1(1) of the 1996 Act, since if a person is not properly to be categorised as the publisher at common law, there is no need of a defence: see e.g. *Bunt v Tilley* at [37].

> 124 ... I do not consider that *on the evidence before me the Third Defendant can be regarded as a publisher of the words complained of,* whether before or after notification. Accordingly, on the evidence before me, I can conclude that the Claimant

1) Relevance of the *MIS* Decision to Canadian Lawyers and Judges

Aside from being at present the only decision in England, Australia, or Canada discussing search engine liability in detail, *MIS* is a valuable decision for Canadian lawyers and judges for several reasons:

1. It contains a discussion of the question of liability of search engines based on common law principles, which is as applicable in Canada as in the United Kingdom.
2. The reasons provide a clear examination and statement of these principles and their application to the question of search engine liability.
3. A very clear discussion, albeit possibly *in obiter*, of the application of the common law defence of innocent dissemination (section 1 of the UK *Defamation Act* and Regulations 17, 18, and 19 of the *Electronic Commerce (EC Directive) Regulations*) is contained in the decision. Obviously, while the legislation is not binding or even technically persuasive in the absence of any legislation in Canada about liability for defamation, the decision does provide some useful guidance.
4. There is an extremely useful summary of legislation and decisions in other jurisdictions in the European Union and the United States on the liability of search engines.
5. The reasons incorporate counsel's arguments for both parties.
6. There is a clear exposition of the evidence about how this search engine functioned at the time of the decision.

2) Expert Evidence about how Search Engines Operated in this Case

Justice Eady summarized the evidence introduced about how search engines operate at some length at paras. 9–14 of the decision:

> Because it is so central to the issues now before the court, it is necessary for me to summarise the evidence explaining how search engines work. This again derives primarily from Mr Jaron Lewis, although it is a subject also covered in expert evidence introduced by the Claimant from Dr David Sharp.
>
> The Internet comprises web pages containing information and each page has a unique address (the "URL"). The page will appear when the URL is

---

would have "no reasonable prospect of success". Secondly, I regard the misrepresentations and omissions, as to the nature of the cause of action relied upon, as sufficiently serious to justify setting aside the Master's order in any event [emphasis added]

typed into an Internet browser. Each website address ends with a "top level domain," which is a series of letters often denoting the country in which the website is registered. Thus, many websites which are accessed in the United Kingdom will end with the ".uk" domain. Google operates search engines for all the major "country code top level domains" ("ccTLDs"). The principal reason why this is done is to enable Google searches to provide appropriate results for local users. It was explained, by way of example, that a search on the word "bank" would yield different results on www.google.co.uk from those appearing on www.google.ca (where primarily Canadian banks would appear).

It would be impossible for Google to search every page available on the web in real time and then deliver a result in a time frame acceptable to users. What happens is that Google compiles an index of pages from the web and it is this index which is examined during the search process. Although it is well known, it is necessary to emphasise that the index is compiled and updated purely automatically (i.e. with no human input). The process is generally referred to as "crawling" or "the web crawl."

When a search is carried out, it will yield a list of pages which are determined (automatically) as being relevant to the query. The technology ranks the pages in order of "perceived" relevance — again without human intervention. The search results that are displayed in response to any given query must depend on the successful delivery of crawling, indexing and ranking. Content on the Internet is constantly being crawled and re-crawled and the index updated.

Obviously Google has no control over the search terms entered by users of the search engine or of the material which is placed on the web by its users.

The complaint in these proceedings against the First Defendant relates to information appearing on one of its web bulletin boards posted by third parties. Needless to say, the Second and Third Defendants have no control over the First Defendant or over what appears on its bulletin boards.

See also *Budu v. The British Broadcasting Corporation*, [2010] EWHC 616 (QB) adopting the description of search engines at para. 13

3) Can the Operator of a Search Engine be Liable for Publication Prior to Notice?

Google argued that it is not, as a matter of law, liable for publication prior to notice.

1. Google is not responsible for anything appearing on DesignTechnica's corporation website. The defendants submit that Google is not responsible as a matter of law for the content of the "snippet" complained of as produced by Google's own search engine.

2. Google submits that the test for publication in this context is whether the relevant Internet intermediary was knowingly involved in the publication of the relevant words. (See, for example, *Bunt v Tilley & Ors*, [2006] EWHC 407 (QB), cited at paras. 22 and 23.)

Justice Eady held on the issue of publication at paras. 48–51 of *MIS* as follows:

> I turn to what seems to me to be the central point in the present application; namely, *whether the Third Defendant [Google Inc.] is to be regarded as a publisher of the words complained of at all.* The matter is so far undecided in any judicial authority and the statutory wording of the 1996 Act does nothing to assist. It is necessary to see how the relatively recent concept of a search engine can be made to fit into the traditional legal framework (unless and until specific legislation is introduced in this jurisdiction). [Emphasis added].
>
> It has been recognised, at common law, that for a person to be fixed with responsibility for publishing defamatory words, there needs to be present a mental element. I summarised the position in *Bunt v. Tilley* at 21–23:
>
>> In determining responsibility for publication in the context of the law of defamation, it seems to me to be important to focus on what the person did, or failed to do, in the chain of communication. It is clear that the state of a defendant's knowledge can be an important factor. If a person knowingly permits another to communicate information which is defamatory, when there would be an opportunity to prevent the publication, there would seem to be no reason in principle why liability should not accrue. So too, if the true position were that the applicants had been (in the claimant's words) responsible for 'corporate sponsorship and approval of their illegal activities.'
>>
>> I have little doubt, however, that to impose legal responsibility upon anyone under the common law for the publication of words it is essential to demonstrate a degree of awareness or at least an assumption of general responsibility, such as has long been recognised in the context of editorial responsibility. As Lord Morris commented in *McLeod v. St Aubyn*, [1899] AC 549, 562: 'A printer and publisher intends to publish, and so intending cannot plead as a justification

that he did not know the contents. The appellant in this case never intended to publish.' In that case the relevant publication consisted in handing over an unread copy of a newspaper for return the following day. It was held that there was no sufficient degree of awareness or intention to impose legal responsibility for that 'publication.'

Of course, to be liable for a defamatory publication it is not always necessary to be aware of the defamatory content, still less of its legal significance. Editors and publishers are often fixed with responsibility notwithstanding such lack of knowledge. On the other hand, for a person to be held responsible there must be knowing involvement in the process of publication of the relevant words. It is not enough that a person merely plays a passive instrumental role in the process. (See also in this context *Emmens v. Pottle* (1885), 16 QBD 354, 357, *per* Lord Esher MR.)

The passage to which I referred in *Emmens v. Pottle* concerned defendants who were said by the Master of the Rolls to have been *prima facie* liable, on the basis that they had handed to other people the newspaper in which there was a libel on the plaintiff. His Lordship continued:

I am inclined to think that this called upon the defendants to shew some circumstances which absolved them from liability, not by way of privilege, but facts which shew that they did not publish the libel. We must consider what the position of the defendants was. The proprietor of a newspaper, who publishes the paper by his servants, is the publisher of it, and he is liable for the acts of his servants. The printer of the paper prints it by his servants, and therefore he is liable for a libel contained in it. But the defendants did not compose the libel on the plaintiff, they did not write it or print it; they only disseminated that which contained the libel. The question is whether, as such disseminators, they published the libel? If they had known what was in the papers, whether they were paid for circulating it or not, they would have published the libel, and would have been liable for so doing. That, I think, cannot be doubted. But here, upon the findings of the jury, we must take it that the defendants did not know that the paper contained a libel. I am not prepared to say that it would be sufficient for them to show that they did not know of the particular libel. But the findings of the jury make it clear that the defendants did not publish the libel. Taking the view of the jury to be right, that the defendants did not know that the paper was likely to contain a libel, and, still more, that they ought not to have known this, which must mean, that they ought not to have known it, having used reasonable care — the case is reduced to this, that the defendants were innocent disseminators of a thing which they were not bound to know was likely to contain a libel. That being so, I think the defendants are not liable for the libel. If they were liable, the result would be that every common carrier who carries a newspaper which contains a libel would be liable for it, even if the paper were one of which every man in England would say that it was not likely to contain a libel. To my mind the mere statement of such a result shews that the proposition from which it flows is unreasonable and unjust. The question does not depend on any statute, but on the common law, and, in my opinion, any proposition the result of which would be to shew that the Common Law of England is wholly unreasonable and unjust, cannot be part of the Common Law of England.

When a search is carried out by a web user via the Google search engine it is clear, from what I have said already about its function, that there is no human input from the Third Defendant. None of its officers or employees takes any part in the search. It is performed automatically in accordance with computer programmes.

When a snippet is thrown up on the user's screen in response to his search, it points him in the direction of an entry somewhere on the Web that corresponds, to a greater or lesser extent, to the search terms he has typed in. It is for him to access or not, as he chooses. It is fundamentally important to have in mind that [Google Inc.] has no role to play in formulating the search terms. Accordingly, it could not prevent the snippet appearing in response to the user's request unless it has taken some positive step in advance. *There being no input from [Google Inc.], therefore, on the scenario I have so far posited, it cannot be characterised as a publisher at common law. It has not authorised or caused the snippet to appear on the user's screen in any meaningful sense. It has merely, by the provision of its search service, played the role of a facilitator* [emphasis added].

4) Can the Operator of this Search Engine be Liable for Publication After Notice?

In the *MIS* case it would appear that the judge found that Google, in this case, was not liable after notification for the following reasons:

- The search engine was regarded as different than other intermediaries, in particular a website host. (See para. 55.)

- It was considered technologically impossible to remove the defamatory content as requested by the plaintiff. (See para. 59.)
- Google took steps to remove the defamatory content. The judge held that Google used their best efforts in this case, and did not just ignore the request to remove the defamatory content. (See paras. 57, 62, and 64.)
- Google could not be found liable on the basis of authorization, approval or acquiescence while Google was making efforts to achieve a "take down" in relation to a particular URL. (See para. 58.)
- The plaintiff had an available remedy against the author of the defamatory statement. (See para. 63.)

Justice Eady discussed Google's potential liability after notification at paras. 54–58, 62–64, and 114:

The next question is whether the legal position is, or should be, *any different once* [Google Inc.] has *been informed of the defamatory content of a "snippet" thrown up by the search engine.* In the circumstances before Morland J, in *Godfrey v. Demon Internet,* the acquisition of knowledge was clearly regarded as critical. That is largely because the law recognises that a person can become liable for the publication of a libel by acquiescence; that is to say, by permitting publication to continue when he or she has the power to prevent it. As. *If this is not done, then there may be liability on the basis of authorisation or acquiescence* [emphasis added].

A search engine, however, is a different kind of Internet intermediary. It is not possible to draw a complete analogy with a website host. One cannot merely press a button to ensure that the offending words will never reappear on a Google search snippet: there is no control over the search terms typed in by future users. If the words are thrown up in response to a future search, it would by no means follow that [Google Inc.] has authorised or acquiesced in that process [emphasis added].

There are some steps that [Google Inc.] can take and they have been explored in evidence in the context of what has been described as its "take down" policy. There is a degree of international recognition that the operators of search engines should put in place such a system (which could obviously either be on a voluntary basis or put upon a statutory footing) to take account of legitimate complaints about legally objectionable material. It is by no means easy to arrive at an overall conclusion that is satisfactory from all points of view. In particular, the material may be objectionable under the domestic law of one jurisdiction while being regarded as legitimate in others.

In this case, the evidence shows that Google has taken steps to ensure that certain identified URLs are blocked, in the sense that when web-crawling takes place, the content of such URLs will not be displayed in response to Google searches carried out on Google.co.uk. This has now happened in relation to the "scam" material on many occasions. But I am told that [Google Inc.] needs to have specific URLs identified and is not in a position to put in place a more effective block on the specific words complained of without, at the same time, blocking a huge amount of other material which might contain some of the individual words comprising the offending snippet.

It may well be that [Google Inc.'s] "notice and take down" procedure has not operated as rapidly as [the Plaintiff] would wish, but it does not follow as a matter of law that between notification and "take down" the Google becomes or remains liable as a publisher of the offending material. *While efforts are being made to achieve a "take down" in relation to a particular URL, it is hardly possible to fix [Google Inc.] with liability on the basis of authorisation, approval or acquiescence.*

. . .

Thus, [Google's counsel submits], it is practically impossible, and certainly disproportionate, to expect [Google Inc.] to embark on a wild goose chase in order to determine where the words complained of, or some of them, might from time to time "pop up" on the Web.

On the other hand, the evidence suggests that it would be possible for the First Defendant to alter the code on its own website, either for the purpose of ensuring that the offending search results are not picked up by search engines generally or, of course, to remove the snippet from its own website. It is submitted, accordingly, that if the Claimant is to have an effective remedy it must lie against the First Defendant. For the reasons identified, an injunction against [Google Inc.] would be a hopelessly inadequate substitute.

Against this background, including the steps so far taken by [Google Inc.] to block the identified URLs, I believe it is unrealistic to attribute responsibility for publication to [Google Inc.], whether on the basis of authorship or acquiescence. There is no doubt room for debate as to what further blocking steps it would be open for it to take, or how effective they might be, but that does not seem to me to affect my overall conclusion on liability. This decision is quite independent of any defence provided by s. 1(1) of the 1996 Act, since if a person is not properly to be categorised as the publisher at common law, there is no need of a defence: see e.g. *Bunt v. Tilley* at 37 [emphasis added].

. . .

I prefer to reach my conclusion by reference to straightforward common law principles, albeit adapted to the new environment of the Internet, and in particular I attach importance to the absence of knowledge on the part of [Google Inc.] in relation to the offending material prior to the Claimant's complaint and, moreover, the absence of any conduct on its part thereafter which could properly be characterised as authorisation or acquiescence in continuing publication. There may have been delays in the "take down" procedure (whether for technical or other reasons), but even while the attempt is being made to block access to any specific URL, *it is impossible to characterise the state of mind of any relevant employee as amounting to authorisation, approval or acquiescence* [emphasis added].

5) Unresolved Issues

1. It is submitted this decision is limited to the facts and evidence in this case. See paras 57, 64, and 124 of the reasons.
2. Justice Eady at paras. 54 and 55 discusses the differences between a website operator and a search engine. He leaves open the possibility that a search engine who receives notification of a specific defamatory URL and completely ignores the notification may be exposed to liability if Google has the ability to remove the defamatory URL.
3. Is liability imposed on the search engine as soon as notice is received or is there a grace period? While not prescribing any particular period of time, Justice Eady held at para. 58 that, "while efforts are being made to achieve a 'takedown' in relation to a particular URL, it is hardly possible [Google] with liability on the basis of authorizations, approval or acquiesence."

6) Application of this Decision in Canada

Though not binding, the decision is very persuasive authority to support the position that prior to receiving notice a search engine is not liable for the publication of the snippets thrown up by the search engine.

The persuasive authority of the decision in situations after receipt of notice will be contingent on the similarity between the facts in Canadian cases and the facts in *MIS*.

It is submitted that the decision about Google's liability regarding the publication of the snippet should be limited to the evidence introduced in this case about the operations at the search engine in 2006.

A search engine's liability after notification by the plaintiff of the existence of a defamatory URL may be influenced by at least:

- The sufficiency including the precision of the notice of the complaint received by the search engine operator.
- The technological ability of the search engine to respond to the complaint.
- The timeliness of the response by the search engine operator.
- The efforts made by the search engine operator to block the URL that is the subject of the complaint.

7) *Obiter* Discussions

The balance of the decision appears to be *obiter* involving an analysis and discussion about the common law defence of innocent dissemination, the statutory version of the defence in section 1 of the *Defamation* Act, UK. Regulations 17, 18, and 19 under the *Electronic Commerce (EC Directive) Regulations 2002* governing search engines, and finally an examination of European and American laws governing search engine liability.

a) Innocent Dissemination at Common Law

After holding that the common law defence of innocent dissemination was not actually abolished by the passage of section 1 of the *Defamation Act*, Eady J. held that the common law defence would not be available to Google who was a defendant who had their attention drawn to the the fact that the words were defamatory or at least arguably so. See paras. 65, 67, and 70 of *MIS*.

b) The Statutory Defence in the *Defamation Act of 1996*

Google's counsel turned next to the provisions of section 1(1) of the *Defamation Act*, 1996:

> In defamation proceedings a person has a defence if he shows that—
> (a) he was not the author, editor or publisher of the statement complained of,
> (b) he took reasonable care in relation to its publication, and
> (c) he did not know, and had no reason to believe, that what he did caused or contributed to the publication of a defamatory statement."

Justice Eady held at para. 80:

> There is no need to address the possible defence under s.1 of the 1996 Act in the light of my finding in [Google Inc.'s] favour on primary liability. If, however, it should correctly be considered as a "publisher," contrary to my conclusion, it is difficult to see how it would then qualify under s. 1(1)(a).

The judge commented upon the confusing use of the word "publisher" in the statute.[20]

c) The Potential Application of the *Electronic Commerce (EC Directive) Regulations 2002*

Justice Eady held at para 81:

> [Google's counsel] placed reliance also upon the Electronic Commerce (EC Directive) Regulations 2002 (SI 2002 No 2013). As the title suggests, these regulations were enacted by Parliament in order to give effect to the European directive of 8 June 2000. This is concerned with certain aspects of what are called "information society services" within the internal market. The principal objective is to contribute towards the proper functioning of internal markets by ensuring the free movement of information society services between member states.

Justice Eady then referred to and examined Regulations 17, 18, and 19. Regulation 17 refers to mere conduit; Regulation 18 refers to caching; and Regulation 19 refers to hosting. After he reviewed these regulations he concluded at para. 96:

> The important questions would appear to be (a) whether the Third Defendant needs a defence under these Regulations at all (i.e. whether it was a publisher) and (b) whether, if it does, it would qualify as 'hosting.'

---

20 *MIS* at paras. 71–73.

> 71 . . . There is some confusion about the terminology in this part of the statute because, whereas in most places the notion of "publication" corresponds with the general usage in the law of defamation, "publisher" is defined in s.1(2) to mean "a commercial publisher, that is, a person whose business is issuing material to the public, or a section of the public, who issues material containing the statement in the course of that business". The different usage is recognised in s.17(1) of the Act, which is the interpretation section.

> 72 The relevant "statement complained of" against the Third Defendant is, of course, the "snippet" thrown up by the search engine rather than any publication occurring on the First Defendant's website. It is only the First Defendant itself which is sued in respect of the original website publication.

> 73 This dual usage of "publisher" in the Act is apt to cause particular confusion in the present context. The Third Defendant would appear to be a business which issues material to the public, or a section of the public. Yet the common law test of whether the Third Defendant published the words complained of is not necessarily the same as that under the statute of whether it "issues material containing the statement in the course of that business".

d) European Search Engine Legislation and Caselaw

Justice Eady then referred to and reviewed legislation and caselaw about search engine liability in Europe. A number of European countries had offered a measure of extended preparation through legislation to search engine services, including Liechtenstein (para. 98), Austria (paras. 89 and 99), Spain (para. 100), Portugal (para. 101), Hungary (para. 102), Bulgaria (para. 104), and Romania (para 105). The courts in several European countries refused to hold Google or its local representative liable for the secondary act of publishing words originating from third parties. See *MIS* at para. 106, para. 107 (Switzerland), para. 108 (France), para. 109 (Spain), and paras. 110–11 (the Netherlands).

Google's counsel made the following submissions based on the European legislation and caselaw about search engine liability:

1. That search engines, as with other intermediaries, have features which are unique and require extended protection.
2. It would be unnecessary and disproportionate to oppose a condition that the defence of section 1 should only be available if the Internet intermediary does not have notice of a complaint of a defamatory statement. (This would be a different approach than that of Morland J. in relation to the ISP in *Godfrey v. Demon Internet Limited* [1999] EWHC 244 (QB)).
3. To adopt any other interpretation in a UK Court would undermine the policy of the European Commission as identified in the *Electronic Commerce (EC Directive) Regulations 2002*.
4. It would be inconsistent with the *EC Directive*, would cause disadvantages for UK businesses domestically, and would be "inconsistent with the objective of an open and free internal market" (*MIS* para. 111). As can be seen this is an example of a conflict between electronic commerce interests and reputational interests.

Justice Eady declined to accept these submissions and held at paras. 113–14 as follows:

> I prefer to reach my conclusion by reference to straightforward common law principles, albeit adapted to the new environment of the Internet, and in particular I attach importance to the absence of knowledge on the part of [Google Inc.] in relation to the offending material prior to the Claimant's complaint and, moreover, the absence of any conduct on its part thereafter which could properly be characterised as authorisation or acquiescence in continuing publication. There may have been delays in the "take down" procedure (whether for technical or other reasons), but even while the attempt

is being made to block access to any specific URL, it is impossible to characterise the state of mind of any relevant employee as amounting to authorisation, approval or acquiescence.

I believe that my conclusion, although it is an attempt to apply common law principles, is not likely to give rise to any inconsistency with the way that matters are approached in other European jurisdictions or with an open and free internal market.

e) The US Position

Justice Eady, after reviewing section 230 of the *Communications Decency Act* (*CDA*) and the subsequent decision (see reference to cases in *MIS* at paras. 117–18), which on public policy grounds give protection to Internet intermediaries, including the operation of search engines, found that neither the *CDA* nor the caselaw directly influenced his decisions in this case.[21]

---

21 A Court in Pennsylvania held that Google was protected by s. 230 of the *CDA. Parker v. Google, Inc.*, 422 F. Supp. 2d 492 (E.D. Pa. 2006) at 13.

> In this case, there is no doubt that Google qualifies as an "interactive computer service" and not an "information content provider." Thus, it is eligible for immunity under § 230. In each instance raised by Plaintiff's tort claims, Google either archived, cached, or simply provided access to content that was created by a third party. The defamatory statements in USENET postings and on the "Ray-FAQ website" were created by users of USENET and other internet users, as was the information on websites that appears as a result of a search query of Plaintiff's name. It is clear that § 230 was intended to provide immunity for service providers like Google on exactly the claims Plaintiff raises here. See *Green*, 318 F.3d at 471 (finding § 230 immunity proscribes liability on claims of defamation and general negligence); *Carafano*, 339 F.3d at 1125 (§ 230 affords immunity from suit on claims of invasion of privacy, misappropriation of the right of publicity, defamation, and negligence); *Ben Ezra, Weinstein, & Co. v. Am. Online, Inc.*, 206 F.3d 980, 986 (10th Cir.2000) (§ 230 immunity bars claims for defamation and negligence); *Zeran v. America Online, Inc.*, 129 F.3d 327 (4th Cir.1997) (§ 230 bars claim for negligence alleging that service provider unreasonably delayed in removing defamatory messages posted by third parties). Accordingly, we conclude that under § 230 of the *CDA*, Google cannot be held liable for the claims of defamation, invasion of privacy, and negligence alleged here.

CHAPTER 23: User-Generated Content — Web 2.0 and Online Social Networks

A. INTRODUCTION

Due to the rapidly changing character of web-based digital technology, this section may become obsolete in the near future. It is nonetheless important to explore the character and implications of the currently available technology, which continuously evolves to facilitate the production of user-generated content through varied web-based channels and within increasingly diverse digital environments.

B. WEB 2.0

The now ubiquitous term "Web 2.0" refers to the second generation of the Web and was first defined by Tim O'Reilly in an industry newsletter:

> Web 2.0 is the network as platform, spanning all connected devices; Web 2.0 applications are those that make the most of the intrinsic advantages of that platform: delivering software as a continually-updated service that gets better the more people use it, consuming and remixing data from multiple sources, including individual users, while providing their own data and services in a form that allows remixing by others, creating network effects through an "architecture of participation," and going beyond the page metaphor of Web 1.0 to deliver rich user experiences.[1]

Although there is an argument that Web 2.0 is not at all a shift to second generation technology, but rather a shift in the cultural interpretation of and

---

1   Tim O'Reilly, Oreillynet.com newsletter (9 September 2005), cited in Ravi Kumar Jain B, ed., *Web 2.0: An Introduction* (Hyderabad, India: The Icfai University Press, 2007) at 11.

approach to the Internet and Web-based technology,[2] it seems evident that the moniker "Web 2.0" at least serves as an "indicator of the changing paradigm in the activities of the web; from being a traditional media to being a social mass media, from publishing to participation; from web as an application to web as a service; from software application as a product to software application as a service."[3] As Web technology has evolved, new applications have emerged that facilitate user-participation in content generation, leveraging collective intelligence through social connections for information production and, consequently, consumption.[4] As such, through Web 2.0 technology users are given more control, not only over what they consume, but also in their ability to potently produce and share content.

C. SOCIAL NETWORK SITES

Social network sites (SNS) are a high profile component of emerging Web 2.0 technology and culture that often facilitate the formation of online social connections. The networked connections that such participant-based sites produce invariably generate vast amounts of data. These sites, and the companies that operate them, create value from the content sharing that takes place between users by using the data produced and exchanged to inform advertising sales and provide data for aggregation, and for sale to third parties, for example.[5] Despite its apparent utility as a catch-all phrase for many similar sites that encourage user content production, employing "SNS" in this manner can miss some important particularities. Boyd and Ellison provide a useful definition with which to clarify the terminology:

> as web-based services that allow individuals to (1) construct a public or semi-public profile within a bounded system, (2) articulate a list of other users with whom they share a connection, and (3) view and traverse their list of

2   See, for example, Marcus Leaning, *The Internet, Power and Society* (Oxford: Chandos Publishing, 2009) at 45–46.

3   Ravi Kumar Jain B, ed., *Web 2.0: An Introduction* (Hyderabad, India: The Icfai University Press, 2007) at 7.

4   See, for example, Ravi Kumar Jain B, ed., *Web 2.0: An Introduction* (Hyderabad, India: The Icfai University Press, 2007) at 8; Nicole S. Cohen, "The Valorization of Surveillance: Towards a Political Economy of Facebook" (2008) 22:1 *Democratic Communiqué* 5 at 10–16; Kurt Voelker, "Web 2.0 Introduction: The First Appearance of Web 2.0" in Ravi Kumar Jain B, ed., *Web 2.0: An Introduction* (Hyderabad, India: The Icfai University Press, 2007) at 18–19.

5   See, for example, Nicole S. Cohen, "The Valorization of Surveillance: Towards a Political Economy of Facebook" (2008) 22:1 *Democratic Communiqué* 5 at 6.

connections and those made by others within the system. The nature and nomenclature of these connections may vary from site to site .... We chose not to employ the term "networking" for two reasons: emphasis and scope. "Networking" emphasizes relationship initiation, often between strangers. While networking is possible on these sites, it is not the primary practice on many of them, nor is it what differentiates them from other forms of computer-mediated communication (CMC).[6]

Under this definition, among the most popular SNSs in the world are Facebook, MySpace, and Twitter. Facebook is far and away the largest, claiming the registration of its 500 millionth user on 21 July 2010.[7] MySpace, by contrast, averages between 65 and 70 million unique users worldwide per month.[8] Finally, Twitter claims 190 million users "tweeting" around 65 million times a day.[9]

The worldwide prevalence of SNSs and their structure have initiated scholarly inspection in many areas, including, for example, identity studies and identity performance, network structure and bridges between offline and online social networks, education, and privacy,[10] as well as studies of labour and the political economy of social network sites.[11]

As Web technology and SNSs continues to evolve, so too will the ways in which people interact with that technology and with each other. Continued study from all of these perspectives is necessary to inform a depth of understanding of the changes taking place. As a complement, the law too must contend with the transformative power of this increasingly networked culture in order to ensure the citizen and society remain sufficiently protected and regulated while not unduly inhibiting the innumerable and undeniable benefits of the continued diffusion of the Web.

---

6   D.M. Boyd and N.B. Ellison, "Social Network Sites: Definition, History, and Scholarship" (2007) 13:1 *Journal of Computer-Mediated Communication*, article 11, online: http://jcmc.indiana.edu/vol13/issue1/boyd.ellison.html.

7   See Jenna Wortham, "Facebook Tops 500 Million Users" *The New York Times Online* (21 July 2010), online: www.nytimes.com/2010/07/22/technology/22facebook.html?_r=1&scp=2&sq=facebook&st=cse.

8   "News Corp. Plans MySpace Relaunch, Will Go 'Younger'" *The Sydney Morning Herald* (24 July 2010), online: http://news.smh.com.au/breaking-news-technology/news-corp-plans-myspace-relaunch-will-go-younger-20100724-10p79.html.

9   Erick Schonfeld, "Costolo: Twitter Now has 190 Million Users" *Techcrunch.com* (8 June 2010), online: http://techcrunch.com/2010/06/08/twitter-190-million-users.

10   This partial list is reflected in D.M. Boyd and N.B. Ellison, "Social Network Sites: Definition, History, and Scholarship" (2007) 13:1 *Journal of Computer-Mediated Communication*, article 11, online: http://jcmc.indiana.edu/vol13/issue1/boyd.ellison.html.

11   See, for example, Nicole S. Cohen, "The Valorization of Surveillance: Towards a Political Economy of Facebook" (2008) 22:1 *Democratic Communiqué* 5.

1) Facebook

a) Judicial Discussions in Canada about Facebook

In a 2009 motor vehicle action, the Ontario Superior Court discussed Facebook in *Roman v. Leduc*, 2009 CanLII 6838 at paras. 17–20 (ON S.C.):

> The general evidence described Facebook as a "social website" or, as put by its Terms of Use, "a social utility that connects you with the people around you." As of June, 2008, Facebook had more than 70 million active users. Although originally designed for use by American college students, more than half of Facebook's users now are outside of college, and users over 25 years of age make up its fastest growing demographic.
>
> The site is available for the personal, non-commercial use of its users. Content which users may post on Facebook includes photos, profiles (name, image, likeness), messages, notes, text, information, music, video, advertisements, listing and other content. The sites' "Facebook Principles" indicates that a user may "set up your personal profile, form relationships, send messages, perform searches and queries, form groups, set up events, add applications, and transmit information through various channels."
>
> When a person registers with Facebook, he creates his own profile and privacy settings. Profile information is displayed to people in the networks specified by the user in his privacy settings — e.g. a user may choose to make his private profile information available to others within his school, geographic area, employment network, or to "friends" of "friends." A user can set privacy options that limit access to his profile only to those to whom he grants permission — the so-called "friends" of the user.
>
> Facebook contains several applications. A user can post basic personal information — age, contact information, address, employment, personal facts, relationship status, etc. A user can post Photo Albums; Facebook is the largest photo-sharing application on the Web, with more than 14 million photos uploaded daily. A user can create a "wall," or chat board, where friends can post messages to each other. These postings can be viewed by all friends looking at the webpage, unlike emails which only the recipient can read. A user also can join a Facebook "group," essentially a community based on common interests.[12]

---

12 The following are some useful references on Facebook, Blogs and MySpace:
- E.A. Vander Veer, *Facebook: The Missing Manual,* 1st ed. (Sebastopol, CA: Pogue Press/O'Reilly Media, Inc., 2008)
- Eric Boehlert, *bloggers on the bus* (New York: Free Press, 2009)
- David Kline & Dan Burstein, *blog! how the newest media revolution is changing politics, business and culture* (New York: Squibnocket Partners LLC, 2005)

In *A.B. v. Bragg Communications Inc.*, 2010 NSCA 57, the Court of Appeal in Nova Scotia granted the plaintiff's application to proceed by using initials in a privacy claim arising out of false statements placed on Facebook.

b) Judicial Discussions in the UK about Facebook

In *Applause Store Productions Ltd. & Anor v. Raphael*, [2008] EWHC 1781 (QB), the Court found at para. 2:

- Paul McFedries, *Twitter: Tips, Tricks, and Tweets.* (Indianapolis: Wiley Publishing, 2009)
- David D. Perlmutter, *blog wars* (New York: Oxford University Press, 2008)
- Don Tapscott, & Anthony D. Williams, *Wikinomics: How Mass Collaboration Changes Everything* (New York: Penguin Group, 2006)
- Debbie Weil, *The Corporate Blogging—Absolutely Everything You Need To Know To Get It Right* (New York: Penguin Group, 2006)
- Patricia Sánchez Abril, "Recasting Privacy Torts In A Spaceless World" (2007) 21 *Harvard Journal of Law & Technology* 2, online: http://jolt.law.harvard.edu/articles/pdf/v21/21HarvJLTech001.pdf
- Jason Boulette & Tanya DeMent, "Ethical Considerations For Blog-Related Discovery" (2008) 5 Shidler J.L. Com. & Tech. 1, online: www.lctjournal.washington.edu/Vol5/a01BouletteDeMent.html
- Anthony Ciolli, "Bloggers As Public Figures" (2007) 16 Pub. Int. L. Rev. 255, online: www.bu.edu/law/central/jd/organizations/journals/pilj/vol16no2/documents/16-2CiolliArticle.pdf
- Susan Freiwald, "A Comment on James Grimmelmann's Saving Facebook" (2009) 95 Iowa L. Rev. Bull. 5, online: www.uiowa.edu/~ilr/bulletin/ILRB_95_Freiwald.pdf
- Giles, Martin "A World of Connections" *The Economist*, 30 January 2010
- James Grimmelmann, "Saving Facebook" (2009) 94 Iowa L. Rev. 1137, online: http://lawreview.law.uiowa.edu/journals/ilr/Issue%20PDFs/ILR_94-4_Grimmelmann.pdf
- Matthew J. Hodge, "The Fourth Amendment and Privacy Issues on the 'New' Internet: Facebook.com and MySpace.com" (2006) 31 S.Ill. U.L.J. 95, online: www.law.siu.edu/research/31fallpdf/fourthamendment.pdf
- Robert Sprague, "Rethinking Information Privacy In an Age of Online Transparency" (2009) 25 Hofstra Lab. & Empl, L.J. 395, online: http://law2.hofstra.edu/pdf/Academics/Journals/LaborAndEmploymentLawJournal/labor_vol25no2_Sprague.pdf
- James Tumbridge, "Twitter: who's really there?" (2010) 5 *Journal of Intellectual Property Law & Practice* 116, online: http://jiplp.oxfordjournals.org/cgi/content/abstract/5/2/116?maxtoshow=&hits=10&RESULTFORMAT=1&author1=james+tumbridge&andorexacttitle=and&andorexacttitleabs=and&andorexactfulltext=and&searchid=1&FIRSTINDEX=0&sortspec=relevance&resourcetype=HWCIT
- Joshua N. Azriel, "Social Networking as a Communications Weapon to Harm Victims: Facebook, MySpace, and Twitter Demonstrate a Need to Amend Section 230 of the *Communications Decency Act*" (2009) 26 J. Marshall J. of Computer & Info. L. 415
- Leslie Yalof Garfield, "Birds of a Feather: Libel and Slander in the Age of Twitter" (February 18, 2010). Available at SSRN: http://ssrn.com/abstract=1555062

The case concerns the popular social networking site, Facebook, which was started at Harvard several years ago, spread to university networks on both sides of the Atlantic, migrated from the universities as its users graduated, and has now (as appears from the evidence in this case) become popular with older users in the media and television industries. As Mr Firsht's twin brother Simon explained in his evidence, users create 'profiles' for themselves, in which they may include as much personal information as they wish. Facebook enables them to adjust the privacy settings of their profile so that (for example) they may permit general access or restrict access to those whom they accept as 'friends.' The concept of a 'friend' has a special sense in Facebook, for it includes all those who make a request to be accepted as a friend and whose request is accepted by the user. The 'friends' are listed on the user's profile. Profiles will contain a 'wall' on which those permitted access may post messages which can be read by those who have access to the profile, and will contain links to any 'groups' to which the user belongs. 'Groups' are Facebook pages which may be set up by users, notionally, it appears, as a resource which may be visited by any Facebook user interested in the group's subject matter. Simon Firsht himself started using Facebook in December 2006, and neither at that stage nor during the summer of 2007 did he make any attempt to adjust his privacy settings, so that any fellow member of the London network of Facebook could have accessed his profile.

The judge, at paras. 7 and 68, held:

As I say, there is no dispute that the material complained of as being defamatory of the Claimants is indeed defamatory of them. Or rather, there is no dispute that the material complained of from the words 'Has Mathew Firsht lied to you?' to 'Has he lied to you?' is defamatory of the Claimants. I assume that this concession, made by Mr Pendlebury in his skeleton argument, embraces the first use of the phrase 'Has Mathew Firsht lied to you?' in the false profile, as well as the second use on the group page.

. . .

Given that, on my findings, the Defendant was responsible for creation of the Facebook material complained of, I therefore find for the Second Claimant in so far as his claim relates to misuse of private information (the false profile), and for the First and Second Claimants in so far as their claim is in defamation (essentially the group page).

The judge, after an exhaustive review and discussion of the evidence, found that
- the defendant was responsible for publishing the false profile and statement on the group sections of the site;

- the words contained in the profile were defamatory;
- there was no substantive defence; and
- damages for defamation were £26,000 and damages for tort of misuse of private information were £3,500.

The following factors were considered in the award of damages (see paras. 78–80):

1. The defamatory statements were only available on Facebook for seventeen days after which they were removed by Facebook at the request of the plaintiff.
2. Facebook is a medium in which users regularly search for the names of others they know.

Counsel for the plaintiff argued that the following factors supported an inference of wider publication (at para. 70):

> The extent of publication of the Facebook material was not entirely clear. It was common ground that the defamatory group page was published to Richard Jay, Darren Levy and Carole Davies, and of course Simon Firsht and his girlfriend saw all the material when they discovered it with Mathew Firsht on 4th July 2007. Ms Skinner relies also on the following factors in support of her case that an inference of wider publication to a 'not insubstantial number of people' should be drawn:
>
> > (1) The evidence of Max Kelly, who explained that Facebook does not store data showing how many Facebook users merely viewed the profile or group, but only shows those users who performed some activity in relation to them. I think that Ms Skinner is right to characterise his evidence in that way. He did say that Facebook kept no records which showed how many users accessed either the profile or the group, but he also said that the group was 'accessed' by Richard Jay, Darren Levy and Carole Davies. All 'accessed' the group on 20th June. It is not clear to me what the difference is between 'accessing' a profile or group and merely viewing it, but that there is a difference is clear;
> >
> > (2) The general popularity of Facebook as a social networking tool, not least in the television industry;
> >
> > (3) The fact that the false profile and group were placed on the London network, which then had over 850,000 members, to any of whom they would have been visible. In that connection, Ms Skinner points to the fact that one Clifford White, who had offices at Elstree

Studios, sent an email to the profile less than 30 minutes after it was created, saying that he had just found Mr Firsht on Facebook and wondered if he would be interested in setting up a Facebook club for 'studio residents.'

c) Judicial Discussions in the US about Facebook

In *Finkel v. Facebook, Inc.*, 2009 NY Slip Op 32248 (Sup. Ct. 2009), a case involving defamatory statements on Facebook, the Supreme Court held that the site is an online social network that is open to the public and allows members to communicate with each other via "group pages" and to set up and post contents to "profiles and groups."

The plaintiff was a member of Facebook while attending high school in 2007. The four defendants in this lawsuit were classmates of the plaintiff and also members of Facebook. The plaintiff alleged that the defendants created a group on the website and posted defamatory remarks with negative sexual and medical connotations. Facebook was not actively involved in the creation of the defamatory statements.

After reviewing section 230 of the *Communications Decency Act of 1996* (*CDA*) and the complaint, the Court established that Facebook is entitled to the liability shield conferred by the *CDA* and therefore the Court dismissed this action against Facebook because there was no claim.

2) Twitter

Twitter is a form of communication that allows a person to send 140 character text messages (known as "tweets") to all the people who have chosen to follow them.

> "Twitter is perhaps the simplest and most addictive social media tool of them all, and its unprecedented success has been both unexpected and inspirational. I've been fortunate to be part of that journey, tracking Twitter's growth on behalf of Mashable and posting updates about Twitter and social media to the @mashable Twitter account.
>
>   . . . Once the basic principles of Twitter are understood, the possibilities are almost limitless. In fact, much of the service's appeal comes from its simplicity: write anything you wish in 140-characters or less, and then share it with the world. Is it a chat room? Is it a way to send text messages to a group of friends? Is it a new technology or readings news headlines? Is it the world's simplest social network, a barebones version of MySpace and Facebook? It's all those things and more: Twitter is whatever you make it."

Paul McFedries, *Twitter: Tips, Tricks, and Tweets.* (Indianapolis: Wiley Publishing 2009) (Forward)

While several actions in the US have been brought for defamatory "tweets," they have been dismissed. In *Horizon Group Management, LLC v. Amanda Bonnen,* Cook County, Illinois, No. 2009 L 8675, Horizon Group LLC, a real estate management company, claimed that Amanda Bonnen, one of its former tenants, had libeled Horizon by posting a Twitter message (a tweet) to her friends that said, "You should just come anyway. Who said sleeping in a moldy apartment was bad for you? Horizon realty thinks it's ok." The judge dismissed the lawsuit stating that he felt the original tweet was too vague to meet the strict definition of libel.

See "Judge: Tweet 'lacks context' for court action," McCormick Freedom Projects, 20 January 2010, online: www.freedomproject.us/post-exchange/Article-Judge_dismisses_twitter_defamation_lawsuit.aspx.

See also *Barbara Loe Arthur, Plaintiff, v. Paul A. Offit, M.D., et al., Defendants.* Civil Action No. 01:09-cv-1398, U.S. District Court for the Eastern District of Virginia (10 March 2010)

No Canadian Courts have rendered any decisions in Twitter defamation cases.

3) Wikis

"Wikis are webpages that allow users to contribute and edit content hence making a group contribution (e.g. Wikipedia). Wikis (unlike blogs) have a history function which enables previous versions of edited content to be examined and restored."

George Carlisle and Jackie Scerri, "Web 2.0 and User-Generated Content: Legal Challenges in the New Frontier" (2007) 2 *Journal of Information Law & Technology,* online: www2.warwick.ac.uk/fac/soc/law/elj/jilt/2007_2/george_scerri

Wikis, and Wikipedia in particular, have been sued in cases involving defamation on numerous occasions.

Wikipedia, the open source online encyclopedia which allows users to add to its content, has been involved in a number of situations involving defamation. One recent case involved a professional golfer, Fuzzy Zoeller, who instituted action against the alleged author of an edit to his Wikipedia biography. The edit portrayed Zoeller as a drug addict and alcoholic who abused his family when under the influence of these substances. Another case involved John Seigenthaler Sr., (former assistant to Attorney General Robert Kennedy) whose

Wikipedia biography stated that 'for a brief time, he was thought to have been directly involved in the Kennedy assassinations of both John, and his brother, Bobby. Nothing was ever proven'. Yet in another case Skutt High School in Nebraska, USA, was the victim of malicious entries on Wikipedia when the posting for this school mentioned drug use amongst students, and contained harmful comments about the principal. Finally, in 2006, Mumsnet, a site offering advice and support to pregnant and new mothers, was threatened with legal action by Gina Ford (an author of childcare books) due to discussions about her books on this site, which Ford claimed amounted to defamation. In response, Mumsnet published a statement asking its users not to discuss the author.

George Carlisle and Jackie Scerri, "Web 2.0 and User-Generated Content: Legal Challenges in the New Frontier" (2007) 2 *Journal of Information Law & Technology*, online: www2.warwick.ac.uk/fac/soc/law/elj/jilt/2007_2/george_scerri

4) Blogs

"A blog is a personal webpage where a user/blogger posts content such as opinions, commentaries and personal diary information usually arranged chronologically. Usually visitors to blogs can also comment on blog entries."

George Carlisle and Jackie Scerri, "Web 2.0 and User-Generated Content: Legal Challenges in the New Frontier" (2007) 2 *Journal of Information Law & Technology*, online: www2.warwick.ac.uk/fac/soc/law/elj/jilt/2007_2/george_scerri

The following cases involved publications on blogs:
- *Buckle v. Caswell*, 2009 SKQB 363
- *Shavluk v. Green Party of Canada*, 2010 BCSC 804
- *Canadian National Railway Company v. Google Inc.*, 2010 ONSC 3121
- *McQuaig v. Harbour Financial Inc.*, 2009 ABQB 678
- *National Bank of Canada c. Weir*, 2010 QCCS 402

Justice Eady noted in *Smith v. ADVFN Plc & Ors*, [2008] EWHC 1797 (QB) at para. 108:

I would not suggest for a moment that blogging cannot ever form the basis of a legitimate libel claim.

D. LIBEL ISSUES EMERGING FROM WEB 2.0 TECHNOLOGY

While it is impossible to predict all the various libel issues that will emerge from Web 2.0, and OSNs in particular, it is useful to predict some reasonable questions that may arise.

1. The meaning of the words: does the rule of construction relating to vulgar abuse apply? In other words, will statements that are posted on "walls" be considered under the law of libel or slander?

2. There will be questions about social networking sites' status and liability as intermediaries both before and after receiving notice from the plaintiffs.

3. The defence of qualified privilege will be very important in libel actions involving Facebook and other social networking sites:
   - Questions will be asked to determine whether the statements were published on a privileged occasion for such statements posted on walls, blogs, wikis, etc., and whether they were posted for public or private viewership.
   - Will the privilege be lost because of an unnecessarily wide publication?
   - There will probably have to be questions asked to determine what efforts need to be made to keep statements private on social networking sites, and Web 2.0 more broadly.

4. The defence of responsible communications on matters of public interest will be raised and its limits tested.

5. When considering the quantum of damages lawyers and judges may wish to consider the following items:
   - Will the number of "friends" involved through the site be a factor?
   - What is the relevance if the site serves a business function? Personal function?
   - Will the general credibility of the site have an impact?
   - Will the general impact of the site on the plaintiff's life be considered?
   - How will private and public statements be differentiated?
   - To what extent will the accessibility of the statement on the site be weighted?
   - To what extent will the duration the statement has been posted for be considered?

PART VII: Privacy

CHAPTER 24: Invasion of Privacy/Misuse of Private Information

A. INTRODUCTION

Lord Hoffmann in *Jameel et al. v. Wall Street Journal*, [2002] UKHL 44 at para. 38 held:

> Until very recently, the law of defamation was weighted in favour of claimants and the law of privacy weighted against them. True but trivial intrusions into private life were safe. Reports of investigations by the newspaper into matters of public concern which could be construed as reflecting badly on public figures domestic or foreign were risky. The House attempted to redress the balance in favour of privacy in *Campbell v MGN Ltd* [2004] 2 AC 457 and in favour of greater freedom for the press to publish stories of genuine public interest in *Reynolds v. Times Newspapers Ltd* [2001] 2 AC 127.

Defamation provides no remedy for the disclosure of private facts or private information that is true. This problem repeatedly occurs on the Internet. Here are some examples:

1. One party in a relationship discloses to the public photographs about intimate aspects of that relationship, without the other party's consent.
2. Participants on Facebook provide information to one group who then disclose that information to a wider audience, without a participant's consent.
3. Participants in chat rooms that are accessible by password only disclose information to the world about other participants without their consent.
4. Organizations disclose information in the media without consent.
5. The media publishes confidential information without the consent of an individual.

6. Details of a person's private life on the Internet can become "permanent digital "baggage" even when these details occurred at an earlier stage of a person's life.

> For more examples see Daniel Solove, *The Future of Reputation, Gossip, Rumour and Privacy on the Internet* (New Haven, CT: Yale University Press, 2007) at 10

B. SURVEY OF THE LAW

1) The UK

a) No General Tort of Invasion of Privacy
There is no general tort of invasion of privacy in English law.

> *Campbell v. MGN*, [2004] UKHL 22
> *Wainwright & Anor v. Home Office*, [2003] UKHL 53

b) Misuse of Private Information
English law has developed a tort described now as "misuse of private information."

Lord R. Nicholls in *Campbell v. MGN Ltd.*, [2004] UKHL 22, stated at paras. 11–12 and 14–15:

> In this country, unlike the United States of America, there is no over-arching, all-embracing cause of action for 'invasion of privacy': see *Wainwright v. Home Office* [2003] 3 WLR 1137. But protection of various aspects of privacy is a fast developing area of the law, here and in some other common law jurisdictions. The recent decision of the Court of Appeal of New Zealand in *Hosking v. Runting* (25 March 2004) is an example of this. In this country development of the law has been spurred by enactment of the *Human Rights Act 1998*.
>
> The present case concerns one aspect of invasion of privacy: wrongful disclosure of private information. The case involves the familiar competition between freedom of expression and respect for an individual's privacy. Both are vitally important rights. Neither has precedence over the other. The importance of freedom of expression has been stressed often and eloquently, the importance of privacy less so. But it, too, lies at the heart of liberty in a modern state. A proper degree of privacy is essential for the well-being and development of an individual. And restraints imposed on government to pry into the lives of the citizen go to the essence of a democratic state: see La Forest J in *R v Dymont* [1988] 2 SCR 417, 426.
>
> . . .

This cause of action has now firmly shaken off the limiting constraint of the need for an initial confidential relationship. In doing so it has changed its nature. In this country this development was recognised clearly in the judgment of Lord Goff of Chieveley in *Attorney-General v. Guardian Newspapers Ltd (No 2)* [1990] 1 AC 109, 281. Now the law imposes a 'duty of confidence' whenever a person receives information he knows or ought to know is fairly and reasonably to be regarded as confidential. Even this formulation is awkward. The continuing use of the phrase 'duty of confidence' and the description of the information as 'confidential' is not altogether comfortable. Information about an individual's private life would not, in ordinary usage, be called 'confidential.' The more natural description today is that such information is private. *The essence of the tort is better encapsulated now as misuse of private information* [emphasis added].

In the case of individuals this tort, however labelled, affords respect for one aspect of an individual's privacy. That is the value underlying this cause of action. An individual's privacy can be invaded in ways not involving publication of information. Strip-searches are an example. The extent to which the common law as developed thus far in this country protects other forms of invasion of privacy is not a matter arising in the present case. It does not arise because, although pleaded more widely, Miss Campbell's common law claim was throughout presented in court exclusively on the basis of breach of confidence, that is, the wrongful *publication* by the 'Mirror' of private *information.*

c) Principles of the Tort of Misuse of Private Information

For a detailed discussion of the approach taken by the courts in actions for misuse of private information, see *Mosley v. Newsgroup Newspapers Ltd.,* [2008] EWHC 1777 at paras. 7–15 (QB), Eady J.:

Although the law of "old-fashioned breach of confidence" has been well established for many years, and derives historically from equitable principles, these have been extended in recent years under the stimulus of the *Human Rights Act 1998* and the content of the Convention itself. The law now affords protection to information in respect of which there is a reasonable expectation of privacy, even in circumstances where there is no pre-existing relationship giving rise of itself to an enforceable duty of confidence. That is because the law is concerned to prevent the violation of a citizen's autonomy, dignity and self-esteem. It is not simply a matter of "unaccountable" judges running amok. Parliament enacted the 1998 statute which *requires* these values to be acknowledged and enforced by the courts. In any event, the courts had been increasingly taking them into account because of the need to interpret domestic law consistently with the United Kingdom's international obligations. It will be recalled that the United Kingdom government signed up to the Convention more than 50 years ago.

The relevant values are expressed in Articles 8 and 10 of the Convention, which are in these terms:

Article 8

1. Everyone has the right to respect for his private and family life, his home and his correspondence.

2. There shall be no interference by a public authority with the exercise of this right except such as is in accordance with the law and is necessary in a democratic society in the interests of national security, public safety or the economic well-being of the country, for the prevention of disorder or crime, for the protection of health or morals, or for the protection of the rights and freedoms of others.

Article 10

1. Everyone has the right to freedom of expression. This right shall include freedom to hold opinions and to receive and impart information and ideas without interference by public authority and regardless of frontiers. This article shall not prevent States from requiring the licensing of broadcasting, television or cinema enterprises.

2. The exercise of these freedoms, since it carries with it duties and responsibilities, may be subject to such formalities, conditions, restrictions or penalties as are prescribed by law, and are necessary in a democratic society, in the interests of national security, territorial integrity or public safety, for the protection of health or morals, for the protection of the reputation or rights of others, for preventing the disclosure of information received in confidence, or for maintaining the authority and impartiality of the judiciary.

It was recognised in *Campbell v MGN Ltd* [2004] 2 AC 457 that these values are as much applicable in disputes between individuals, or between an individual and a non-governmental body such as a newspaper, as they are in disputes between individuals and a public authority: see e.g. Lord Nicholls at [17]–[18] and Lord Hoffmann at [50]. Indeed, " . . . in order to find the rules of the English law of breach of confidence we now have to look in the jurisprudence of articles 8 and 10": *per* Buxton LJ in *McKennitt v Ash* [2008] QB 73 at [11].

If the first hurdle can be overcome, by demonstrating a reasonable expectation of privacy, it is now clear that the court is required to carry out the next step of weighing the relevant competing Convention rights in the light of an "intense focus" upon the individual facts of the case: see e.g. *Campbell* and *Re S (A Child)* [2005] 1 AC 593. It was expressly recognised that no one Convention right takes automatic precedence over another. In the present context, for example, it has to be accepted that any rights of free expression, as protected by Article 10, whether on the part of Woman E or the journalists working for the *News of the World*, must no longer be regarded as simply "trumping" any privacy rights that may be established on the part of the Claimant. Language of that kind is no longer used. Nor can it be said, without qualification, that there is a "public interest that the truth should out": cf. *Fraser v Evans* [1969] 1 QB 349, 360F-G, *per* Lord Denning MR.

In order to determine which should take precedence, *in the particular circumstances*, it is necessary to examine the facts closely as revealed in the evidence at trial and to decide whether (assuming a reasonable expectation of privacy to have been established) some countervailing consideration of public interest may be said to justify any intrusion which has taken place. This is integral to what has been called "the new methodology": *Re S (A Child)* at [23].

This modern approach of applying an "intense focus" is thus obviously incompatible with making broad generalisations of the kind to which the media often resorted in the past such as, for example, "Public figures must expect to have less privacy" or "People in positions of responsibility must be seen as 'role models' and set us all an example of how to live upstanding lives." Sometimes factors of this kind may have a legitimate role to play when the "ultimate balancing exercise" comes to be carried out, but generalisations can never be determinative. In every case "it all depends" (i.e. upon what is revealed by the intense focus on the individual circumstances).

The exercise is sometimes still described, in terminology used by Lord Goff in the *Spycatcher* litigation, as determining whether any "limiting principles" come into play: see *Att.-Gen. v Guardian Newspapers (No 2)* [1990] 1 AC 109, 282B-F:

> ... The first limiting principle (which is rather an expression of the scope of the duty) is highly relevant to this appeal. It is that the principle of confidentiality only applies to information to the extent that it is confidential. In particular, once it has entered what is usually called the public domain (which means no more than that the infor-

mation in question is so generally accessible that, in all the circumstances, it cannot be regarded as confidential) then, as a general rule, the principle of confidentiality can have no application to it . . . .

The second limiting principle is that the duty of confidence applies neither to useless information, nor to trivia. There is no need for me to develop this point.

The third limiting principle is of far greater importance. It is that, although the basis of the law's protection of confidence is that there is a public interest that confidences should be preserved and protected by the law, nevertheless that public interest may be outweighed by some other countervailing public interest which favours disclosure. This limitation may apply . . . to all types of confidential information. It is this limiting principle which may require a court to carry out a balancing operation, weighing the public interest in maintaining confidence against a countervailing public interest favouring disclosure.

Embraced within this limiting principle is, of course, the so called defence of iniquity. In origin, this principle was narrowly stated, on the basis that a man cannot be made 'the confidant of a crime or a fraud': see *Gartside v Outram* (1857) 26 LJ Charity 113, 114, *per* Sir William Page Wood V-C. But it is now clear that the principle extends to matters of which disclosure is required in the public interest: see *Beloff v Pressdram Ltd* [1973] 1 All ER 241, 260, *per* Ungoed-Thomas J, and *Lion Laboratories Ltd v Evans* [1985] QB 526, 550, *per* Griffiths LJ. It does not however follow that the public interest will in such cases require disclosure to the media, or to the public by the media. There are cases in which a more limited disclosure is all that is required: see *Francome v Mirror Group Newspapers Ltd* [1984] 1 WLR 892.

This "ultimate balancing test" has been recognised as turning to a large extent upon proportionality: see e.g. Sedley LJ in *Douglas v. Hello! Ltd* [2001] QB 967 at para. 137. The judge will often have to ask whether the intrusion, or perhaps the degree of the intrusion, into the claimant's privacy was proportionate to the public interest supposedly being served by it.

One of the more striking developments over the last few years of judicial analysis, both here and in Strasbourg, is the acknowledgment that the balancing process which has to be carried out by individual judges on the facts before them necessarily involves an evaluation of the use to which the relevant defendant has put, or intends to put, his or her right to freedom of expression. That is inevitable when one is weighing up the *relative* worth of one person's rights against those of another. It has been accepted, for example, in the House of Lords that generally speaking "political speech" would be accorded greater value than gossip or "tittle tattle": see e.g. *Campbell* at para. 148 and also *Jameel (Mohammed) v Wall Street Journal Europe Sprl* [2007] 1 AC 359 at para. 147.

> See also *Mosley v. Newsgroup Newspapers Ltd.,* [2008] EWHC 1777 (QB) for a
> lengthy discussion of the law relating to intrusive nature of photography at
> paras. 16–23.

A further lucid summary of the law is found in *Callaghan v. Independent News and Media Ltd.*, [2009] NIQB 1 at para. 24:

> The propositions of law can be summarized as follows:
>
> (a) **The Human Rights Act.** The Human Rights Act 1998 requires the values enshrined in the European Convention on Human Rights be taken into account. The foundation of the jurisdiction to restrain publicity is now derived from Convention rights under the European Convention on Human Rights see *In Re S (A Child)* [2005] 1 AC 593 at paragraph 23. The relevant values in the actions before me are expressed in Article 2, 3, 8 and 10 of the Convention. The Convention "values are as much applicable in disputes between individuals or between an individual and a non Government body such as a newspaper, as they are in disputes between individuals and a public authority," see paragraph 9 of *Mosley v Newsgroup Newspapers Ltd.*
>
> (b) **Expectation of privacy.** "The law now affords protection to information in respect of which there is a reasonable expectation of privacy, even in circumstances where there is no pre-existing relationship giving rise of itself to an enforceable duty of confidence," see paragraph 7 of *Mosley v. Newsgroup Newspapers Ltd.* The question as to whether there is a reasonable expectation of privacy is an objective question and a question of fact. The reasonable expectation is that of the person who is affected by the publicity. The question was defined by Lord Hope in *Campbell v. MGN* [2004] UKHL at paragraph 99 as follows:
>
> > "The question is what a reasonable person of ordinary sensibilities would feel if she was placed in the same position as the claimant and faced with the same publicity."
>
> The question whether there is a reasonable expectation of privacy "is a broad one, which takes account of all the circumstances of the case. They include the attributes of the claimant, the nature of the activity in which

the claimant was engaged, the place at which it was happening, the nature and purpose of the intrusion, the absence of consent and whether it was known or could be inferred, the effect on the claimant and the circumstances in which and the purposes for which the information came into the hands of the publisher" see *Murray v. Express Newspapers* [2008] EWCA Civ 446 at paragraph 36.

(c) **Balancing exercise.** "If the first hurdle can be overcome, by demonstrating a reasonable expectation of privacy, it is now clear that the court is required to carry out the next step of weighing the competing Convention rights in the light of an 'intense focus upon the individual facts of each case'" see paragraph 10 of *Mosley v. Newsgroup Newspapers Ltd* and see also *Murray v. Big Pictures (UK) Ltd* [2008] EWCA 446 at paragraphs 35–40. The balancing exercise is essentially a question of fact with the weight to be attached to the various considerations being of degree and essentially a matter for the trial judge. In carrying out the balancing exercise of weighing the competing Convention rights no one Convention right takes automatic precedence over another. "In order to determine which should take precedence, *in the particular circumstances*, it is necessary to examine the facts closely as revealed in the evidence at the trial and to decide whether (assuming a reasonable expectation of privacy to have been established) some countervailing consideration of public interest may be said to justify any intrusion which has taken place," see paragraphs 10 and 11 of *Mosley v. Newsgroup Newspapers Ltd*. In carrying out the balancing exercise the justifications for interfering or restricting rights under Articles 8 and 10 must be taken into account. Finally proportionality must be applied to each which is called the ultimate balancing test. The judge will have to ask whether the intrusion, or perhaps the degree of intrusion, into the plaintiff's privacy was proportionate to the public interest supposedly being served by it, see paragraph 14 of *Mosley v. Newsgroup Newspapers Ltd* and paragraph 17 of *Re S* [2005] 1 AC at 595. In weighing up the relative worth of one person's rights against those of another the use to which a person has put or intends to put his or her rights is to be taken into account, see paragraph 15 of *Mosley v. Newsgroup Newspapers Ltd*.

(d) **Section 12 (4) of the Human Rights Act 1998 and the balancing exercise.** The requirement in Section 12(4) of the Human Rights Act 1998 to pay particular regard to Article 10 of the European Convention on Human Rights requires the court to pay particular regard to the rights of others in accordance with Article 10(2) including the rights under Articles 2 and

3 as well as Article 17 which prohibits the abuse of rights, see Sedley LJ in *Douglas v Hello!* [2001] IPT 391 at paragraphs [133]–[134] and see also paragraph [50] of *Venables & Thompson v Newsgroup Newspapers Ltd* [2001] 1 All ER 908. One does not start with the balance tilted in favour of Article 10, see paragraph [82] of *Douglas & Ors v Hello! Ltd & Ors* (No 3) [2005] EWCA Civ 595.

(e) **Photographs.** In carrying out the balancing exercise intensely focussing on the facts in the individual case then if that case involves competing rights under Article 10 to publish a photograph and Article 8 to restrain publication a court should be alive to the potential, depending on the particular facts of each individual case, that "as a means of invading privacy a photograph is particularly intrusive", see *Douglas & Ors v Hello! Ltd & Ors* (No 3) [2006] QB 125 at paragraph [84]. In *Von Hannover v Germany* 40 EHRR 1 at paragraph [59] the European Court of Human Rights remarked: —

> "Although freedom of expression also extends to the publication of photos, this is an area in which the protection of the rights and reputation of others takes on particular importance. The present case does not concern the dissemination of "ideas", but of images containing very personal or even intimate "information" about an individual. Furthermore, photos appearing in the tabloid press are often taken in a climate of continual harassment which induces in the person concerned a very strong sense of intrusion into their private life or even of persecution."

(f) **Article 8 of the Convention**. The terms of Article 8 are

> "1. Everyone has the right to respect for his private and family life, his home and his correspondence.
>
> 2. There shall be no interference by a public authority with the exercise of this right except such as is in accordance with the law and is necessary in a democratic society in the interests of national security, public safety or the economic well-being of the country, for the prevention of disorder or crime, for the protection of health or morals, or for the protection of the rights and freedoms of others."

"The guarantee afforded by Article 8 is primarily intended to ensure the development, without outside interference, of the personality of each individual in his relations with other human beings. There is therefore a zone of interaction of a person with others, even in a public context, which may fall within the scope of 'private life'" see *Von Hannover v. Germany* [2004] ECHR 294 at paragraph 50.

(g) **Article 2 of the Convention.** "The right to life in Article 2 of the European Convention on Human Rights covers not only the negative obligation not to take the life of another person but imposes on contracting states a positive obligation to take certain steps towards the prevention of loss of life at the hands of others than the State. The positive obligation only arises when the risk is "real and immediate". A real risk is one that is objectively verified and an immediate risk is one that is present and continuing. The criterion of a real and immediate risk is one that is not easily satisfied: in other words the threshold is high," see paragraphs 19–20 of *Re Officer L* [2007] UKHL 36. "Furthermore there is a reflection of the principle of proportionality in the level of precautions which the State authorities have to take to avoid being in breach of the positive obligation under Article 2. There has to be a demonstration that the authorities have failed to do all that was reasonably to be expected of them to avoid the risk of life. This brings in the ease or difficulty of taking precautions and the resources available. It has not been definitely settled in the Strasbourg jurisprudence whether countervailing factors relating to the public interest as distinct from the practical difficulty of taking elaborate and far reaching precautions, maybe taken into account in deciding if there has been a breach of the positive obligation under Article 2." Lord Carswell continued in *Re L (An Officer)* at paragraph 21 by stating that — it may be correct in principle to take such factors into account but that he would prefer to reserve his opinion on the point. In this case the first plaintiff contends that there is a real and immediate risk to his life if those in his local community know his "whereabouts" by the publication of an unpixelated photograph. However such knowledge may also come through publication of his name to which the first plaintiff does not object. I consider that in so far as the first plaintiff's case is based on the suggestion that there is a risk to his life then it is necessary for him to establish whether there is an increased risk to his life by virtue of the publication of an unpixelated photograph of him.

(h) **Freedom of expression.** The importance that the Strasbourg Court attaches to freedom of expression is illustrated by passages from the judgment of the court in *Nilsen & Johnsen v. Norman* [1999] 30 EHRR 878 at paragraph 43 and *Observer and Guardian v. UK* [1999] 14 EHRR 152 at paragraph 59. In domestic law that importance was also emphasised, see the summary of the relevant authorities at paragraph 23 of *Thomas v Newsgroup Newspapers Ltd & Anor* [2001] EWCA Civ 1233.

Murray v. Big Pictures (UK) Ltd., [2008] EWCA 446 at paras. 35–40 is a useful discussion about the rights of a child in privacy proceedings (in this case the son of J.K. Rowling, author of Harry Potter series of books).

The court found an invasion of privacy in the following cases:

- *Callaghan v. Independent News and Media Ltd.*, [2009] NIQB 1
- *Mosley v. Newsgroup Newspapers Ltd.*, [2008] EWHC 1777 (QB)
- *Campbell v. MGN*, [2004] UKHL 22
- *Theakston v. MGN Ltd.*, [2002] EWHC 137 (QB)

The court found no invasion of privacy in the following cases:

- *Murray v. Big Picture (UK) Ltd.*, [2008] EWCA 446 (at paras. 35–40 — potential invasion of privacy)
- *John v. Associated Newspapers Ltd*, [2006] EWHC 1611 (QB)

2) New Zealand

In *Hosking and Hosking v. Simon Runting and Anor*, [2004] NZCA 34 at para. 259, Bunting J. of the New Zealand Court of Appeal succinctly summarized the tort of invasion of privacy in New Zealand as follows:

> Holding the balance fairly between plaintiffs and defendants in this field is not likely to be easy. The law should be as simple and easy of application as possible in the interests of those who have to make decisions about what and what not to publish. I would therefore summarise the broad content of the tort of invasion of privacy in these terms. It is actionable as a tort to publish information or material in respect of which the plaintiff has a reasonable expectation of privacy, unless that information or material constitutes a matter of legitimate public concern justifying publication in the public interest. Whether the plaintiff has a reasonable expectation of privacy depends largely on whether publication of the information or material about the plaintiff's private life would in the particular circumstances cause substantial offence to a reasonable person. Whether there is sufficient public concern about the information or material to justify the publication will depend on whether in the circumstances those to whom the publication is made can reasonably be said to have a right to be informed about it.

3) Canada

a) Introduction

The *Canadian Charter of Rights and Freedoms* does not specifically guarantee a right to privacy. However, as stated by the New Zealand Court of Appeal in

Hosking & Hosking v. Simon Runting & Anor, [2004] NZCA 34, there is recognition of the desirability of protection of privacy. The New Zealand Court of Appeal in a survey of the law in the Commonwealth on privacy, succinctly summarizes the Supreme Court of Canada's recognition of the desirability of protection of privacy in *Hosking & Hosking v. Simon Runting & Anor* at paras. 60–64.

b) Statutory Cause of Action

British Columbia, Manitoba, and Saskatchewan have legislation enacting a statutory tort of privacy that provides for civil remedies for violating the privacy of another person.

> See Roger D. McConchie and David A. Potts, *Canadian Libel and Slander Actions* (Toronto: Irwin Law, 2004) 902–5 for further information

c) Canadian Common Law Tort of Invasion of Privacy

i) Is the Claim a Dressed Up Defamation Action?

In Canada one of the first questions defendants generally raise is whether the claim is a dressed up defamation action in which the plaintiff is trying to circumvent the notice and/or limitation requirements or certain defences in libel actions by pleading an action for invasion of privacy.

Canadian courts have not been reluctant to strike claims other than libel at the preliminary stage of proceedings where the claims are for alleged damage to reputation. The courts do so on the basis that the damages allegedly sustained by the plaintiffs stem only from the publication of the statement itself and therefore must be characterized as defamation.

> *Byrne v. Maas*, [2007] O.J. No. 4457
>
> *Bai v. Sing Tao Daily Limited*, [2003] O.J. No. 1917, 226 D.L.R. (4th) 477 (C.A.)
>
> *Trizec Properties Inc. et al. v. CitiGroup Global Markets Inc. et al.*, [2004] O.J. No. 2906 at para. 12
>
> *Fulton v. Globe and Mail*, [1996] A.J. No. 1222, 46 Alta. L.R. (3d) 348
>
> *Lubarevich v. Nurgitz*, [1996] O.J. No. 1457 (Ct. J. Gen. Div.)
>
> *Elliott v. Canadian Broadcasting Corp.* (1993), 16 O.R. (3d) 677 at 689

In *Elliott v. Canadian Broadcasting Corporation* (1993), 16 O.R. (3d) 677, the plaintiff advanced claims for defamation, malicious falsehood, conspiracy, negligence, and breach of fiduciary duty, all based on the publication of a film and book and consequent damages to reputation. Justice Montgomery dismissed all the claims with these words at para. 40:

> In my view, the whole claim rests on the publication of the film and the book. Attempts to find another cause of action inexorably lead back to the alleged

harm and damage to reputation by the words complained of. The so-called subsidiary torts are nothing more or less than defamation.

This passage was quoted with approval by the Court of Appeal in the subsequent case of *Bai v. Sing Tao Daily Ltd.*, [2003] O.J. No. 1917 at para. 21 (C.A.).

In a similar vein, in *Byrne v. Maas*, [2007] O.J. No. 4457, the motions judge struck out various claims at para. 9 on the basis that "where a claim is not framed as defamation but is based on harm to reputation, the courts have concluded that the claims should be struck. A defamation cannot be 'dressed up' as another claim to evade the defences available in a defamation action."

In *St. Elizabeth Home Society v. Hamilton (City)*, [2005] O.J. No. 5369 (S.C.J.), Crane J. dismissed negligence claims after a very long trial on the basis that those claims "merged with the defamation claim" which was statute-barred under the *Libel and Slander Act*, R.S.O. 1990, c. L.12. In doing so, Crane J. accepted the defendants' argument that damages arising from loss of reputation are only recoverable in an action for defamation.

See *Nitsopoulos v. Wong*, 2008 CanLII 45407 (ON S.C.)

d) Recent Recognition of the Tort of Invasion of Privacy

Recently, the Ontario Court in *Somwar v. McDonald's Restaurants of Canada Ltd.*, 2006 CanLII 202 (ON S.C.), held that the "time has come to recognize invasion of privacy as a tort in its own right" at para. 31. At para. 22 Stinson J. stated: "In light of the trial decisions listed in this brief survey of Ontario jurisprudence and the absence of any clear statement on the point by an Ontario appellate court, I conclude that it is not settled law in Ontario that there is no tort of invasion of privacy."

This decision was cited with approval in *Nitsopoulos v. Wong*, 2008 CanLII 45407 at para. 19 (ON S.C.). The judge in that case agreed with the proposition of Stinson J. that "it is not settled law in Ontario that there is no tort of invasion of privacy." The Court cited at para. 20 the statement of claim pleaded in support of their claim for invasion of privacy:

> . . . Wong intruded into their seclusion and private affairs with the full knowledge and consent of the newspaper, breaching their reasonable expectation of privacy within their own home and with respect to their personal information. They claim that as a result of Wong's intrusion and surveillance, they have suffered personal injury which includes harm to their dignity interests, personal autonomy and that they have experienced embarrassment and mental distress. It is clear from the Statement of Claim that at least some of the damages claimed do not depend upon publication or publicity.

The Court stated at paras. 15–16:

> In my view, the plaintiffs' claims based on torts of deceit and invasion of privacy do stand alone and are not subsumed in the law of libel and defamation. In this particular case, the damages claimed in the Statement of Claim are not exclusively damages to reputation. Furthermore, it is not the mere words or the publication that is at issue. The plaintiffs allege Wong's unlawful conduct in gaining entry to their home by deceit resulted in personal harm and damages discrete from, and beyond, harmed reputation or the publication alone. Damages for invasion of privacy and deceit do not necessarily engage damages for loss of reputation. See, for example, *Yonge v. Bella*, 2006 SCC 3, [2006] 1 S.C.R. 108 at para. 55–56. The Supreme Court of Canada clearly rejected the submission that the law of defamation has "cornered the market" on damages for reputational injury.
>
> I therefore reject the *Globe and Mail's* submission that the damages claimed in this case *only* arise as a consequence of the publication, or are limited to reputational harm. The law of libel and slander should not act to bludgeon other meritorious causes of action where they can stand on their own. [Emphasis in the original].

The Court also relied upon and referred to the *Mosley v. News Group Newspapers Limited*, [2008] EWHC 1777 (QB) decision at para. 21:

> In decisions outside of Ontario, public disclosure of embarrassing private facts about a person have resulted in damage awards, even where the facts disclosed are true and not libellous or defamatory. See for example *Max Mosley v. News Group Newspapers Limited* [2008] EWHC 1777 (QB) (U.K.).

C. INJUNCTIONS FOR INVASION OF PRIVACY IN CANADA/ MISUSE OF PRIVATE INFORMATION

The following Canadian decisions have considered applications for injunctions for invasion of privacy, arising out of statements published on the Internet:

- *MacDonnell v. Halifax Herald Ltd.*, 2009 NSCC 187
- *A.T. v. L.T.H.*, 2006 BCSC 1689
- *Friedt v. Landry*, 2006 SKCA 37, (2006), 275 Sask. R. 56
- *P.M.F. v. M.M.L.*, 2006 SKCA 37
- *Interior Healthy Authority et al. v. Sellin et al.*, 2005 BCSC 1819

1) *A.T. v. L.T.H.*

In *A.T. v. L.T.H.*, 2006 BCSC 1689, the British Columbia Supreme Court granted an application for an injunction for invasion of privacy. This case involved a matrimonial dispute, however, the method of analysis submitted is applicable in other privacy cases.

Extracts from this decision are reproduced here for two reasons:

1. The competing interests, the arguments by counsel, and the resolution of the conflict are very clearly examined and stated.
2. These types of application are likely to be frequently brought before the courts as parties in matrimonial disputes resort to the Internet to obtain information support or even funding for their disputes. See paras. 2–8, 10–11 and 13.

The facts are summarized as follows at para. 5:

In the spring of 2006, *M turned to the internet* to try to garner support. She provided information accessible by internet which described the alleged sexual abuse by F, providing both particulars of the alleged abuse and personal details of C, such as her name, photograph, school name and home address. F objected, and applied to court in these divorce proceedings for an injunction restraining *M from publishing certain information in various places including the internet* [emphasis added].

The father's ("F") argument is treated at paras. 10–11:

F argued that an interlocutory injunction is necessary to protect C from predators and to protect her privacy, and argued that the court can and should make such an order under its *parens patriae* jurisdiction. F also argued that the interlocutory injunction he seeks is necessary to protect his own privacy and reputation. He has been found by this court to be innocent of the wrongdoing alleged by M.

F argued that the facts in this case are such that the necessary order must be in the broad terms of the consent interim injunction. That would include restricting publication of anything relating to what I have termed the "Wrongdoing Lawsuit."

The mother's ("M") argument is presented at para. 13:

M argued that the form of order sought by F is too broad, for the following reasons:

(a) it will hamper C's safety, because it will restrict M's ability to appeal to the public for assistance in this case, to pressure for change in the system for similar cases, and to keep the parties involved in this lawsuit in the public eye in the hope that they will as a result behave as well as possible;

(b) it will impair M's freedom of expression, and to the extent that M speaks for her daughter C, will also impair C's freedom of expression;

(c) it will violate the principle that the court system should be open and accessible to the public; and

(d) it will impair M's right to equality before and under the law if restrictions on publication about this case apply only to her rather than generally.

The Court considered that the test from *RJR-Macdonald Inc. v. Canada (Attorney-General)*, [1994] 1 S.C.R. 311, should apply, even though it involved injunctions in a defamation case. The Court did not consider or discuss *Rapp v. McClelland & Stewart Ltd.* (1981), 34 O.R. (2d) 452, or *Bonnard v. Perryman*, [1891] 2 Ch. 269.

See *A.T. v. L.T.H.*, 2006 BCSC 1689 at paras. 15–16:

> The test for an interlocutory injunction is the same as for an interim injunction, and is set out in *B.C. (A.G.) v. Wale*, 1986 CanLII 171 (BC C.A.), (1986), 9 B.C.L.R. (2d) 333 (C.A.), aff'd 1991 CanLII 109 (S.C.C.), [1991] 1 S.C.R. 62, [1991] 2 W.W.R. 568. In that case, McLachlin J.A., as she then was, said as follows at p. 345:
>
> > The traditional test for the granting of an interim injunction in British Columbia is two-pronged. First, the applicant must satisfy the court that there is a fair question to be tried as to the existence of the right which he alleges and a breach thereof, actual or reasonably apprehended. Second, he must establish that the balance of convenience favours the granting of the injunction.
>
> A similar test, although with three parts instead of two, was described by Sopinka and Cory JJ. on behalf of the Supreme Court of Canada in *RJR-Macdonald Inc. v. Canada (Attorney-General)*, 1994 CanLII 117 (S.C.C.), [1994] 1 S.C.R. 311 at p. 334, 111 D.L.R. (4th) 385, as follows:
>
> > First, a preliminary assessment must be made of the merits of the case to ensure that there is a serious question to be tried. Secondly, it must be determined whether the applicant would suffer irreparable harm if the application were refused. Finally, an assessment must be made as to which of the parties would suffer greater harm from the granting or refusal of the remedy pending a decision on the merits.

a) Conflicting Interests

The Court in *A.T. v. L.T.H.*, 2006 BCSC 1689 outlined conflicting interests, which were:

1. The Court's *parens patriae* interest, treated at para. 19:

    > F relies in part on the court's *parens patriae jurisdiction*. The history and scope of the *parens patriae* jurisdiction was discussed by the Supreme Court of Canada in *R. v. Eve*, 1986 CanLII 36 (S.C.C.), [1986] 2 S.C.R. 388 at pp. 425–26, 31 D.L.R. (4th) 1 . . .

2. *Charter* interests generally, which were considered at paras. 20–30:

    > The *Charter* includes the following:
    >
    > 1. The *Canadian Charter of Rights and Freedoms* guarantees the rights and freedoms set out in it subject only to such reasonable limits prescribed by law as can be demonstrably justified in a free and democratic society.
    >
    > 2. Everyone has the following fundamental freedoms:
    >
    > . . .
    >
    > (b) freedom of thought, belief, opinion and expression, including freedom of the press and other media of communication;
    >
    > . . .
    >
    > 7. Everyone has the right to life, liberty and security of the person and the right not to be deprived thereof except in accordance with the principles of fundamental justice.
    >
    > 8. Everyone has the right to be secure against unreasonable search or seizure.
    >
    > . . .
    >
    > 15.(1) Every individual is equal before and under the law and has the right to the equal protection and equal benefit of the law without discrimination and, in particular, without discrimination based on race, national or ethnic origin, colour, religion, sex, age or mental or physical disability.
    >
    > . . .
    >
    > 24.(1) Anyone whose rights or freedoms, as guaranteed by this *Charter*, have been infringed or denied may apply to a court of competent jurisdiction to obtain such remedy as the court considers appropriate and just in the circumstances.
    >
    > . . .
    >
    > 32.(1) This *Charter* applies

(a) to the Parliament and government of Canada in respect of all matters within the authority of Parliament . . . and

(b) to the legislature and government of each province in respect of all matters within the authority of the legislature of each province.

The common law provides that the court has discretion to grant injunctions in appropriate cases. The court must exercise discretion within the boundaries set out by the principles of the *Charter*, as discussed in *Dagenais v. Canadian Broadcasting Corp.*, 1994 CanLII 39 (S.C.C.), [1994] 3 S.C.R. 835 at p. 875, 120 D.L.R. (4th) 12.

In this case, that requires consideration of the right to privacy and the freedom of opinion and expression.

i) Right to Privacy

The right to privacy was discussed by L'Heureux-Dubé J. in *R. v. O'Connor*, 1995 CanLII 51 (S.C.C.), [1995] 4 S.C.R. 411 at paras. 110–19, 130 D.L.R. (4th) 235, as follows:

> This Court has on many occasions recognized the great value of privacy in our society. It has expressed sympathy for the proposition that s. 7 of the *Charter* includes a right to privacy: *Beare, supra*, at p. 412; *B. (R.) v. Children's Aid Society of Metropolitan Toronto*, 1995 CanLII 115 (S.C.C.), [1995] 1 S.C.R. 315, at p. 369, per La Forest J. On numerous other occasions, it has spoken of privacy in terms of s. 8 of the *Charter*: see, e.g., *Hunter v. Southam Inc.*, 1984 CanLII 33 (S.C.C.), [1984] 2 S.C.R. 145; *R. v. Pohoretsky*, 1987 CanLII 62 (S.C.C.), [1987] 1 S.C.R. 945; *R. v. Dyment*, 1988 CanLII 10 (S.C.C.), [1988] 2 S.C.R. 417. On still other occasions, it has underlined the importance of privacy in the common law: *McInerney v. MacDonald*, 1992 CanLII 57 (S.C.C.), [1992] 2 S.C.R. 138, at pp. 148–49; *Hill v. Church of Scientology of Toronto*, 1995 CanLII 59 (S.C.C.), [1995] 2 S.C.R. 1130.
>
> On no occasion has the relationship between "liberty," "security of the person," and essential human dignity been more carefully canvassed by this Court than in the reasons of Wilson J. in *R. v. Morgentaler*, 1988 CanLII 90 (S.C.C.), [1988] 1 S.C.R. 30. In her judgment, she notes that the *Charter* and the right to individual liberty guaranteed therein are tied inextricably to the concept of human dignity. She urges that both "liberty" and "security of the person" are capable of a broad range of meaning and that a purposive interpretation of the *Charter* requires that the right to liberty contained in s. 7 be read to "guarantee[] to every individual a degree of personal autonomy over important decisions intimately affecting their private lives" (p. 171). Concur-

ring on this point with the majority, she notes, as well, that "security of the person" is sufficiently broad to include protection for the psychological integrity of the individual.

Equally relevant, for our purposes, is Lamer J.'s recognition in *Mills, supra*, at p. 920, that the right to security of the person encompasses the right to be protected against psychological trauma. In the context of his discussion of the effects on an individual of unreasonable delay contrary to s. 11(b) of the *Charter*, he noted that such trauma could take the form of

> stigmatization of the accused, loss of privacy, stress and anxiety resulting from a multitude of factors, including possible disruption of family, social life and work, legal costs, uncertainty as to the outcome and sanction.

If the word "complainant" were substituted for the word "accused" in the above extract, I think that we would have an excellent description of the psychological traumas potentially faced by sexual assault complainants. These people must contemplate the threat of disclosing to the very person accused of assaulting them in the first place, and quite possibly in open court, records containing intensely private aspects of their lives, possibly containing thoughts and statements which have never even been shared with the closest of friends or family.

. . . Respect for individual privacy is an essential component of what it means to be "free." As a corollary, the infringement of this right undeniably impinges upon an individual's "liberty" in our free and democratic society.

A similarly broad approach to the notion of liberty has been taken in the United States. . . .[T]he right to privacy was expressly found to reside in the term "liberty" in the Fourteenth Amendment in the landmark case of *Roe v. Wade*, 410 U.S. 113 (1973). In a similar vein, the right to personal privacy has also received recognition in international documents such as Article 17 of the *International Covenant on Civil and Political Rights*, 999 U.N.T.S. 171, Article 12 of the *Universal Declaration of Human Rights*, G.A. Res. 217 A (III), U.N. Doc. A/810, at 71 (1948), and Article 8 of the *European Convention for the Protection of Human Rights and Fundamental Freedoms*, 213 U.N.T.S. 221.

Privacy has traditionally also been protected by the common law, through causes of action such as trespass and defamation. In *Hill, supra*, which dealt with a *Charter* challenge to the common law tort of defamation, Cory J. reiterates the constitutional significance of the right to privacy (at para. 121):

> . . .*reputation is intimately related to the right to privacy which has been accorded constitutional protection. As La Forest J. wrote in R. v.*

Dyment, 1988 CanLII 10 (S.C.C.), [1988] 2 S.C.R. 417, at p. 427, *privacy, including informational privacy, is "(g)rounded in man's physical and moral autonomy" and "is essential for the well-being of the individual."* The publication of defamatory comments constitutes an invasion of the individual's personal privacy and is an affront to that person's dignity. The protection of a person's reputation is indeed worthy of protection in our democratic society and must be carefully balanced against the equally important right of freedom of expression.

. . .

It is apparent, however, that privacy can never be absolute. It must be balanced against legitimate societal needs. This Court has recognized that the essence of such a balancing process lies in assessing *reasonable expectation of privacy*, and balancing that expectation against the necessity of interference from the state: *Hunter, supra*, at pp. 159–60. Evidently, the greater the reasonable expectation of privacy and the more significant the deleterious effects flowing from its breach, the more compelling must be the state objective, and the salutary effects of that objective, in order to justify interference with this right. See *Dagenais, supra*.

In *R. v. Plant*, 1993 CanLII 70 (S.C.C.), [1993] 3 S.C.R. 281, albeit in the context of a discussion of s. 8 of the *Charter*, a majority of this Court identified one context in which the right to privacy would generally arise in respect of documents and records (at p. 293):

> In fostering the underlying values of dignity, integrity and autonomy, it is fitting that s. 8 of the *Charter* should seek to protect a biographical core of personal information which individuals in a free and democratic society would wish to maintain and control from dissemination to the state. *This would include information which tends to reveal intimate details of the lifestyle and personal choices of the individual.*

Although I prefer not to decide today whether this definition is exhaustive of the right to privacy in respect of all manners of documents and records, I am satisfied that the nature of the private records which are the subject matter of this appeal properly brings them within that rubric. Such items may consequently be viewed as disclosing a reasonable expectation of privacy which is worthy of protection under s. 7 of the *Charter*.

The essence of privacy, however, is that once invaded, it can seldom be regained [emphasis Added]. For this reason, it is all the more important for reasonable expectations of privacy to be protected at the point of disclosure. As La Forest J. observed in *Dyment, supra*, at p. 430:

. . . if the privacy of the individual is to be protected, we cannot afford to wait to vindicate it only after it has been violated. This is inherent in the notion of being secure against unreasonable searches and seizures. *Invasions of privacy must be prevented, and where privacy is outweighed by other societal claims, there must be clear rules setting forth the conditions in which it can be violated* [emphasis in last sentence added.]

In the same way that our constitution generally requires that a search be premised upon a pre-authorization which is of a nature and manner that is proportionate to the reasonable expectation of privacy at issue (*Hunter, supra; Thomson Newspapers, supra*), s. 7 of the *Charter* requires a reasonable system of "pre-authorization" to justify court-sanctioned intrusions into the private records of witnesses in legal proceedings. Although it may appear trite to say so, I underline that when a private document or record is revealed and the reasonable expectation of privacy therein is thereby displaced, the invasion is not with respect to the particular document or record in question. Rather, it is an invasion of the dignity and self-worth of the individual, who enjoys the right to privacy as an essential aspect of his or her liberty in a free and democratic society.

ii) Freedom of Expression

The importance of freedom of expression was described by Lamer C.J.C. in *Dagenais* as a paramount value in society at p. 826 as follows:

Like the right of an accused to a fair trial, a fundamental principle of our justice system which is now expressly protected by s. 11(d) of the *Charter*, freedom of expression, including freedom of the press, is now recognized as a paramount value in Canadian society, as demonstrated by its enshrinement as a constitutionally protected right in s. 2(b) of the *Charter*. Section 2(b) guarantees the rights of all Canadians to "freedom of thought, belief, opinion and expression, including freedom of the press and other media of communication." The importance of the s. 2(b) freedoms has been recognized by this Court on numerous occasions (see, for example, *RWDSU v. Dolphin Delivery Ltd.*, 1986 CanLII 5 (S.C.C.), [1986] 2 S.C.R. 573; *Ford v. Quebec (Attorney General)*, 1988 CanLII 19 (S.C.C.), [1988] 2 S.C.R. 712; *Irwin Toy Ltd. v. Quebec (Attorney General)*, 1989 CanLII 87 (S.C.C.), [1989] 1 S.C.R. 927; *Rocket v. Royal College of Dental Surgeons of Ontario*, 1990 CanLII 121 (S.C.C.), [1990] 2 S.C.R. 232; *R. v. Keegstra*, 1990 CanLII 24 (S.C.C.), [1990] 3 S.C.R. 697; and *R. v. Zundel*, 1992 CanLII 75 (S.C.C.), [1992] 2 S.C.R. 731).

The Court engaged in the balancing of the rights and freedoms at paras. 25–30. See also paras. 25–26.

iii) Balancing of Rights & Freedoms

Neither the right to privacy nor the freedom of speech is absolute. There are numerous examples of reasonable limits to rights and freedoms. One example relates to freedom of speech. In *Fraser v. Public Services Staff Relations Board*, 1985 CanLII 14 (S.C.C.), [1985] 2 S.C.R. 455 at 462–63, 23 D.L.R. (4th) 122, Dickson C.J. said for the Court:

> "[F]reedom of speech" is a deep-rooted value in our democratic system of government. It is a principle of our common law constitution, inherited from the United Kingdom by virtue of the preamble to the *Constitution Act, 1867.*
>
> But it is not an absolute value. Probably no values are absolute. All important values must be qualified, and balanced against, other important, and often competing, values. This process of definition, qualification and balancing is as much required with respect to the value of "freedom of speech" as it is for other values.

Dickson C.J. went on to say at 467–68 (cited to S.C.R.):

> [I]t is equally obvious that free speech or expression is not an absolute, unqualified value. Other values must be weighed with it. Sometimes these other values supplement, and build on, the value of speech. But in other situations there is a collision. When that happens the value of speech may be cut back if the competing value is a powerful one .... We also have laws imposing restrictions on the press in the interests of, for example, ensuring a fair trial or protecting the privacy of minors or victims of sexual assaults.

The Court, in *A.T. v. L.T.H.*, 2006 BCSC 1689, concluded as follows:

1. There was a fair question to be tried as to whether the courts should rely on its *parens patriae* jurisdiction or its jurisdiction under the *Family Relations Act* to protect C from being identified as an alleged victim of parental abuse (see paras. 36–37).
2. At paras. 37–38 the Court found:

> Publication of information which identifies C as a victim of abuse, and in particular, of sexual abuse, and more particularly, of sexual abuse by her father, may harm C. Such information may make her the subject of comment, stigma, and embarrassment. That is, of course, one of the policy reasons behind the restriction on publication of the names of complainants in

sexual assault cases contemplated by s. 486.4 of the *Criminal Code*. In up-holding the constitutionality of a publication ban in *Canadian Newspapers Co.*, *supra*, the Supreme Court of Canada considered the need to protect victims of assault from the trauma of widespread publication resulting in embarrassment and humiliation.

Identification of C as a victim of sexual abuse may also make her a potential target for a sexual predator, although that is a more remote possibility than embarrassment.

3. The Court held that there is a fair question to be tried as to whether the publication of information suggesting he abused or neglected C should be restrained on an ongoing basis (see para. 44). In this case the Court, without considering the *Rapp v. McClelland & Stewart Ltd.* (1981), 34 O.R. (2d) 452 test or *Bonnard v. Parryman*, [1891] 2 Ch. 269, concluded at para. 41 that the statement was defamatory.

4. The Court, at paras. 43 and 46–48, held:

> Injunctions restraining anticipated defamation are rare but can be made in appropriate circumstances, such as to prevent irreparable harm by protecting the identity of people alleged to have perpetrated sexual assaults: see *A. v. C. reflex*, (1994), 89 B.C.L.R. (2d) 92 at para. 12, 113 D.L.R. (4th) 726, and *BG v. British Columbia*, 2002 BCSC 1417 (CanLII), (2002), 221 D.L.R. (4th) 75 . . . .
>
> . . .
>
> If the injunction sought is denied, M will likely publish personal details about C and defamatory allegations about F. As a result, the evidence establishes that F and C may suffer irreparable harm to their privacy if the injunction is not granted.
>
> As discussed by L'Heureux-Dubé J. in *O'Connor, supra*, at para. 119, quoted above, the essence of privacy is that once invaded, it can seldom be regained. Similarly, as discussed by Cory J. in *Hill v. Church of Scientology of Toronto*, 1995 CanLII 59 (S.C.C.), [1995] 2 S.C.R. 1130, 126 D.L.R. (4th) 129, quoted above in *O'Connor*, privacy is essential to an individual's well-being, and publication of defamatory comments constitutes an invasion of personal privacy.
>
> Publishing information concerning the allegations of sexual misconduct, which to date have been disproven, would constitute an invasion of C and F's privacy, and the stigma and harm associated with this intrusion would be difficult, if not impossible, to remedy at a later time.

5. The Court concluded at paras. 54–55 that the balance of favours protected C as much as reasonably possible from being identified publicly as being the alleged victim of parental sexual abuse:

With respect to M's freedom of speech, the restraint resulting from an interlocutory injunction will be a reasonable one, in the context of the privacy rights of C and F, so long as M remains able to proceed in court, in dealings with disciplinary bodies having an obligation of confidentiality and with professionals in the child protection system, and in her family relationships.

The balance favours protecting C as much as reasonably possible from being identified publicly as being the alleged victim of parental sexual abuse. The question of what information will lead to that identification is more difficult.

6. At para. 67 the Court found: "The appropriate order in this case must ensure that C is not identified as the alleged victim of parental abuse or neglect and that F is not identified as the alleged perpetrator of abuse or neglect."

The Saskatchewan Court of Appeal in *PMF v. MML*, 2006 SKCA 37, upheld an injunction prohibiting a parent from publishing his child's image or name. The Court had ordered joint custody of the child with very specific parenting provisions. During the course of the custody dispute, the father embarked on a very public campaign claiming his constitutional rights to equal custody, parenting and decision-making with regard to the child were infringed. During this campaign, the child's name and photograph were made public. The mother obtained an order prohibiting the father from using or providing the name or image of the child, and the father appealed. He argued that his constitutional right to freedom of speech was infringed.

The Saskatchewan Court of Appeal held that the restriction of the use of the child's name on the Internet was overly broad for several reasons as explained in para. 8:

> . . . we see the limitation of the use of the child's name on the Internet as an overly broad restriction because such a broad prohibition prevents the father from reasonably using the child's name in purely private communications. It would, for example, prohibit the father from sending pictures of his child to his family and prohibit the parties from e-mailing each other (noting some copies of e-mail were part of the material filed for this appeal.) Such private communications are not reasonably seen as harmful to the child's best interests. We would amend the order to exclude from its scope purely private e-mail communications while continuing to prohibit the use of the name and images or likeness of the child for any public purposes.

2) *Interior Health Authority et al. v. Sellin et al.*

In *Interior Health Authority et al. v. Sellin et al.*, 2005 BCSC 1819, the plaintiffs sought an interlocutory injunction pending a trial with respect to a web video entitled "For the Sake of Seniors" and videotapes from which the web video was created.

The Court dicussed the two different tests applicable for injunctions for defamation and breach of privacy at paras. 5–7:

> It is common ground that the burden on a plaintiff applying for injunctive relief in respect of an alleged defamation *is higher* than the burden under the traditional test as articulated in *RJR-MacDonald Inc. v. Canada*, 1994 CanLII 117 (S.C.C.), [1994] 1 S.C.R. 311. On an application to restrain publication of alleged defamation, the applicant must show that the subject materials are so manifestly defamatory that any jury verdict to the contrary would be considered perverse by a Court of Appeal: see *Compass Group Canada (Health Services) Ltd. v. Hospital Employees' Union*, 2004 BCSC 51, 2004 BCSC 51. It must also be demonstrated that the alleged defamation will likely be repeated or further published. [Emphasis added].
>
> This test requires the court to make a determination, on the evidence before it, that the subject materials are clearly defamatory. However, it is not necessary for the court to speculate on what additional evidence could be available at trial.
>
> In my view, the test has been met. Portions of the web video are so manifestly defamatory that a jury verdict to the contrary would be considered perverse. The circumstances of this case lead to an irresistible inference that the Defendants would publish the web video again if there is no injunction to restrain them.

The Court held at para. 9 that, as

> the injunctive relief in respect of the five videotapes is based not on an allegation of defamation *but on an allegation of breach of privacy* of the three plaintiffs, the traditional test should apply. *RJR-MacDonald Inc. v. Canada*, 1994 CanLII 117 (S.C.C.), [1994] 1 S.C.R. 311 [emphasis added].

At paras. 10–13 the Court stated:

> The traditional test requires the court to consider the following three questions:
> 1. Has the applicant made out a *prima facie* case?
> 2. Will the applicant suffer irreparable harm if the injunction is refused? And
> 3. Does the balance of convenience favour the applicant?
>
> The first two questions must clearly be answered in the affirmative. The individual Plaintiffs have made out a *prima facie* case that the filming of the videotapes and the publication in their present form is an invasion of their privacy. The harm to the individual Plaintiffs will be irreparable if the

injunction is not granted because the videotapes affect their reputation, and there is evidence to the effect that the Defendants do not have the resources to satisfy a judgment against them.

I would also answer the third question in the affirmative except for a concession which counsel for the Defendants makes on behalf of his clients. He acknowledges that the individual Plaintiffs are entitled to some measure of protection in terms of their names, faces and voices being disseminated. If the videotapes are altered so that the identity of the individual Plaintiffs and all other employees of the Overlander Residential Care Facility cannot be ascertained from viewing or listening to the videotapes, their privacy rights will be protected in any further publications. If this is the case, then the balance of convenience will not favour the granting of an injunction. In saying this, I appreciate that the publication of the web video has already disclosed the identity of at least two of the individual Plaintiffs.

3) *MacDonnell v. Halifax Herald Ltd.*

The Supreme Court of Nova Scotia in *MacDonnell v. Halifax Herald Ltd.*, 2009 NSSC 187 rejected an application for an injunction for invasion of privacy. The case summary outlines the case as follows: "A press secretary inadvertently recorded five hours of casual conversation with a federal minister. The recording found its ways into the hands of a reporter. The press secretary started an action and moved for an interim injunction against publishing parts of the recorded conversation." The judge doubted whether the principle of prior restraint applied in cases other than in defamation (see para. 4). The judge applied the usual *RJR MacDonald* test (see para. 2). It rejected the application for an injunction and held that the low threshold for a serious issue was not met. The recorded statements were not made in privacy as they were heard by a driver for the Ministry of Natural Resources.
The judge held at para. 18 that it would be wrong to deprive the press and the public it serves of the information:

> Here is where I see the restriction on prior restraint having some place in laws of invasion of privacy, if such a tort is to emerge. It is wrong to deprive the press, and the public it serves, of remarks made privately, but not confidentially in the sense of trade secrets or privileged communications, after those remarks became available because of poor record keeping or management.

Finally, the Court found at paras. 25–27 that the balance of convenience weighed strongly against an interim injunction and in favour of freedom of the press.

D. REQUEST BY THE PLAINTIFF APPLICANT TO USE PSEUDONYMS

The following case involved an applicant requesting the use of pseudonyms and initials for the purpose of an appeal and for a publication ban.

A.B. v. Bragg Communications Inc., 2010 NSCA 57

A Nova Scotia Court of Appeal judge in chambers held:

An order is granted permitting the appellant and her litigation guardian to provide by way of pseudonym, that is by initials, for the purposes of the appeal;
and an order is granted imposing a publication ban on the actual words in the
fake Facebook profile of the appellant, pending any further order of this court.

This is the first Canadian appellate decision involving issues of privacy and
freedom of the press arising out of a publication ban on statements published
on Facebook.

The facts, quoted from paras. 2–5, are as follows:

A person whose identity is not known to her created a fake Facebook profile of the fifteen year old applicant. The applicant, by her litigation guardian who is her father, applied for permission to proceed by way of initials
for herself and her litigation guardian, for a publication ban concerning the
substance of the allegedly defamatory statements made about her, and for
an order requiring the respondent, Bragg Communications Incorporated, to
provide any information in its possession regarding the identity of the owner
of the IP address used to create that fake profile. Bragg Communications did
not participate in the application. The media respondents opposed the application for a publication ban and the use of initials.

The applicant's application in Supreme Court Chambers was partially
successful. Justice Arthur J. LeBlanc was satisfied that a *prima facie* case of
defamation had been made out, that there was no means other than production of the documents sought by which the required information could be
obtained, and that public interest favouring disclosure of such information
prevailed over freedom of expression and privacy in this case. However, he
denied the confidentiality measures sought by the applicant, namely the use
of initials and a publication ban. His decision is reported as 2010 NSSC 215.
No order has yet issued.

In subsequent oral decisions, the judge stayed the effect of his decision
until the end of the day of June 16, 2010 and then extended that stay until
midnight tonight, June 25, 2010.

The applicant has appealed the Chambers judge's denials of her requests for permission for her and her litigation guardian to proceed by way of initials and for a publication ban. On June 17, 2010 she filed a notice of motion seeking:

(i) an order permitting her and litigation guardian to proceed by way of pseudonym for the purposes of the appeal, pursuant to *Civil Procedure Rule* 90.37(15)(a); and

(ii) an order extending the stay of the judgment below pending the final disposition of the appeal matter pursuant to *Rule* 90.41(2).

The judge identified the conflicting tensions that arise on motions for confidentiality (see paras. 9, 11–15, 17, 18, and 24):

> It is helpful to begin by identifying the tensions which arise on motions for confidentiality in court proceedings. In *Shannex Health Care Mangement Inc. v. Nova Scotia (Attorney General)*, 2005 NSCA 158, 2005 NSCA 158, Bateman, J.A. for this court stated:
>
>> The open court principle is a hallmark of a democratic society. Openness is required in "both the proceedings of the dispute, and in the material that is relevant to its resolution". (*Sierra Club of Canada v. Canada (Minister of Finance)*, 2002 SCC 41, [2002] 2 S.C.R. 522, 2002 SCC 41, at para. 1, per Iacobucci, J.)
>>
>> . . . It is recognized, however, that the principle must sometimes yield to the need for confidentiality (*R. v. Mentuck*, 2001 SCC 76, [2001] 3 S.C.R. 442, 2001 SCC 76 at para. 31). Courts, therefore, retain the discretion to grant confidentiality orders.
>
> . . .
>
> I turn then, to the applicant's motion for permission for the applicant and her litigation guardian to proceed by way of initials for the purposes of the appeal and for a stay of the judgment below or a publication ban pending the final disposition of the appeal.
>
> *Rule* 90.37 the Nova Scotia Rules of Civil Procedure reads in part:
>
>> 90.37 (15) A judge of the Court of Appeal, on motion, may make an order to do any of the following, until the Court of Appeal provides a further order:
>>
>> (a) allow the use of pseudonyms in the pleadings.
>
> In *Sierra Club, supra*, Iacobucci, J. for the Court stated at ¶ 53:
>
>> A confidentiality order . . . should only be granted when:

(a) such an order is necessary in order to prevent a serious risk to an important interest, including a commercial interest,

(b) the context of litigation because reasonably alternative measures will not prevent the risk; and

(c) the salutary effects of the confidentiality order, including the effects on the right of civil litigants to a fair trial, outweigh its deleterious effects, including the effects on the right to free expression, which in this context includes the public interest in open and accessible court proceedings.

These principles were reiterated and applied in *Osif v. The College of Physicians and Surgeons of Nova Scotia*, 2008 NSCA 113, 2008 NSCA 113 which also referred to authorities including *Dagenais v. Canadian Broadcasting Corp.*, 1994 CanLII 39 (S.C.C.), [1994] 3 S.C.R. 835 and *Mentuck, supra.*

The *Dagenais/Mentuck* test, as framed in *Sierra Club, supra* imposes a two-part burden on the applicant. First, she must demonstrate that the confidentiality measures sought are necessary to prevent a serious risk to an important interest where reasonable alternative measures will not prevent it. I accept the applicant's argument that a person's reputation is an important interest. The principles of defamation law, including the presumption of damage and liability for republication, reflect the importance of one's reputation. Individual privacy can also be considered. Although it is not absolute and must be balanced against legitimate societal needs, it is an accepted value in our society, one which the common law has protected through causes of action such as trespass and defamation: *R. v. O'Connor*, 1995 CanLII 51 (S.C.C.), [1995] 4 S.C.R. 411 at ¶ 115 and 117.

According to the applicant, the serious risk to be prevented consists of the risk of further damage to her reputation by republication and of damage to her emotional well-being. In his affidavit evidence, the applicant's father deposed that by his observation, his fifteen year old daughter was "extremely shaken and distressed" by the fact that the Chambers judge's decision would require her name to be publicized in order to obtain the information towards identifying the person who created and published the fake Facebook page. Neither he nor his daughter had expected, nor was prepared for, the national media attention the case has attracted. He also deposed that he was concerned that his daughter would suffer "emotional harm and perhaps other adverse effects on her mental and emotional health if her identify were disclosed along with the defamatory statements as part of this proceeding."

. . .

I am satisfied that the applicant has established that the use of initials is necessary to prevent a serious risk to an important interest where reasonable alternative measures will not prevent it. She has met the first part of the *Sierra Club, supra*, test.

The second part of the burden on the applicant is to show that the benefits of the confidentiality measure outweigh any deleterious effects. The salutary effects of the use of initials are evident. The identity of the minor applicant, and that of her litigation guardian, her father, whose identity could lead to disclosure of the applicant's identity, would be protected. The risk to her mental and emotional health would be reduced, if not eliminated.

. . .

I will grant an order imposing a publication ban on the actual words in the fake Facebook profile of the applicant, pending any further order of this court.

E. INJUNCTIONS FOR MISUSE OF PRIVATE INFORMATION/ INVASION OF PRIVACY IN THE UK

There is a growing body of law in the UK surrounding the application of injunctions to prevent the disclosure of private information.

BKM Ltd v. BBC, [2009] EWHC 3151 (Ch)
Murray v. Big Pictures (UK) Ltd, [2008] EWCA Civ 446
Mosley v. News Group, [2008] EWHC 1777 (QB)
T v. BBC, [2007] EWHC 1683 (QB) at para. 15
Aziz v. Aziz & Ors, [2007] EWCA Civ 712, [2008] 2 All E.R. 501
Browne v. Associated Newspapers Ltd. Rev 1, [2007] EWCA Civ 295
Douglas & Ors v. Hello! Ltd. & Ors, [2007] UKHL 21
Ash & Anor v. McKennit & Ors, [2006] EWCA Civ 1714
Cox & Anor v. MGN Ltd. & Ors, [2006] EWHC 1235 (QB)
Jameel & Ors v. Wall Street Journal Europe Sprl, [2006] UKHL 44
John v. Associated Newspapers Ltd., [2006] EWHC 1611 (QB) at para. 2
Mahmood v. Galloway & Ors, [2006] EWHC 1286 (QB)
Green Corns Ltd. v. CLA Verley Group Ltd. & Anr, [2005] EWHC 958 (QB)
Campbell v. MGN, [2004] UKHL 22
Cream Holdings Ltd. v. Banerjee (House of Lords), [2004] UKHL 44 (HL)
Wainwright & Anor v. Home Office, [2003] UKHL 53
Grupo Torres SA and Ors v. Sheikh Fahad and Ors, [1999] EWHC 300 (Comm)
Mahon v. Rahn & Ors, [1997] EWCA Civ 1770
Attorney General v. Guardian Newspapers (No 2), [1990] 1 A.C. 109 at 286

1) The Restrictions of *Bonnard v. Perryman* do Not Apply

The restrictions on the granting of interim injunctions in defamation cases do not apply to claims for misuse of private information because publication of the information before trial would render a permanent injunction for misuse of private information futile. In other words, *Bonnard v. Perryman*, [1891] 2 Ch. 269 does not apply to prevent the injunctions for disclosure of private information.

> *Terry v. Persons Unknown (Rev 1)*, [2010] EWHC 119 (QB) at para. 124–29
>
> *McKennitt v. Ash*, [2006] EWCA Civ 714, [2007] EMLR 4 at para. 79–80

2) Decisions, Including the Appeal are often Heard in Privacy in the UK

In the UK, many of the applications are heard in private pursuant to civil procedure rules.

> See *Civil Procedure Rules 1998*, S.I. 1998/3132, L.17, r. 39.2(3)(4)
>
> See also *Terry v. Persons Unknown*, [2010] EWHC 119 at paras. 1 and 22
>
> *Aziz v. Aziz*, [2007] EWCA Civ 712
>
> *Douglas & Ors v. Hello! Ltd. & Ors*, [2007] UKHL 21
>
> *T v. BBC*, [2007] EWHC 1683 (QB) at para. 15
>
> *John v. Associated Newspapers Ltd.*, [2006] EWHC 1611 (QB) at para. 2
>
> *McKennitt v. Ash*, [2006] EWCA Civ 714, [2008] QB 73 at 75
>
> *XTY v. Persons Unknown*, [2006] EWHC 2783
>
> *Campbell v. MGN*, [2004] UKHL 22

The judge in *Terry v. Persons Unknown (Rev 1)*, [2010] EWHC 119 (QB) discussed the important reasons for open justice and the conflicting pressures for private hearings for applications for misuse of private information at paras. 106–9.

Ontario, for example, has a similar rule: see section 135 of the *Courts of Justice Act*, R.S.O. 1990, c. C.43, which states as follows:

Public hearings

135. (1) Subject to subsection (2) and rules of court, all court hearings shall be open to the public.

(2) The court may order the public to be excluded from a hearing where the possibility of serious harm or injustice to any person justifies a departure from the general principle that court hearings should be open to the public.

3) Injunctions Granted for the Misuse of Private Information

The courts have granted injunctions for misuse of private information in the following cases:

- *Applause Store Productions Ltd. & Anor v. Raphael*, [2008] EWHC 1781 (QB)
- *Mosley v. News Group Newspapers Ltd.*, [2008] EWHC 2341 (QB)
- *Douglas & Ors v. Hello! Ltd. & Ors*, [2007] UKHL 21

- *T v. The British Broadcasting Corporation (BBC)*, [2007] EWHC 1683 (QB)
- *Browne v. Associated Newspapers Ltd. Rev 1*, [2007] EWCA Civ 295
- *Ash & Anor v. McKennitt & Ors*, [2006] EWCA Civ 1714
- *Green Corns Ltd. v. CLA Verley Group Ltd. & Anor*, [2005] EWHC 958 (QB)
- *Campbell v. MGN Ltd.*, [2004] UKHL 22

4) Partially Granted Injunctions

In the following cases some of the materials have been held to be private and others not private.

- *BKM Ltd. v. British Broadcasting Corporation*, [2009] EWHC 3151 (Ch)
- *John v. MGN Ltd.*, [1995] EWCA Civ 23

5) Refusal to Grant an Injunction

The Court refused to grant an injunction restraining publications in a decision with very thorough reasons in *John v. Associated Newspapers Ltd.*, [2006] EWHC 1611 (QB). Justice Eady held at para. 7: "I am satisfied here that neither of those circumstances arises and therefore the appropriate test for me to apply is the more general one of whether the claimant is more likely than not to succeed at the trial with regard to this remedy of an injunction restraining publication." The Court supported its decision with the following considerations:

1. Expectations of privacy when the photograph and the story did contain information relevant to Elton John's health (at paras. 13–14):

   One of the questions I have to address is whether or not on the evidence before me, it could be said that there is a reasonable expectation of privacy on the part of Sir Elton John in relation to the content of the photograph, that is to say the information conveyed by the photograph.

   In *Campbell v MGN*, as is well known, the material photograph concerned Ms Naomi Campbell emerging from a drug rehabilitation clinic into the street. The *photograph and the story* contained information which *was relevant to her health in general terms*, and more particularly to a course of drug rehabilitation treatment which she was undergoing at the time, in respect of which it was recognised that the publication might have some impact. That was a special factor and it was contrasted, in the words of one of the members of the House of Lords, with a situation where a well-known person is observed or photographed in more casual circumstances "popping out for a pint of milk" [emphasis added].

2. There was no element of harassment (at para. 16):

    > An important factor in *Von Hannover v Germany* (2005) 40 EHRR 1 was the
    > element of harassment, as in the recent case of *Howlett v Holding* [2006] EHWC
    > 41 (QB), where a woman was being followed by a person who had a grudge
    > against her and whom she had sued on more than one occasion for libel. There
    > is nothing here in the evidence before me to disclose a case of harassment.
    > There is no question, either, of anything which discloses a course of conduct (to
    > use the phrase which appears in the *Protection from Harassment Act 1997*).

3. The photographs were not exceptionally intrusive and insensitive (at para.
    19):

    > An unusual case, where photographs in a public street were held to give rise
    > to a claim, was that of *Peck v United Kingdom* (2003) 36 EHRR 41, where Mr
    > Peck had taken the opportunity late at night in Brentwood High Street to
    > attempt suicide without realising that he was being photographed by CCTV
    > cameras. He was not aware of the presence of anyone else. Publishing the
    > photographs of someone attempting to commit suicide is exceptionally in-
    > trusive and insensitive There is nothing here which is remotely comparable
    > to that tragic situation.

4. Interference with the press must be justified (at paras. 8–9):

    > My attention was also drawn to the decision of the Court of Appeal in the
    > case of *A v B Plc* [2003] QB 195 which, although it was handed down only a
    > few years ago, might be thought in certain respects to have been overtaken
    > by later developments. Nevertheless, it is right that it should be accorded
    > consideration and respect. My attention was particularly focused by Mr
    > Warby QC on certain principles upon which he placed particular reliance.
    > The first was this:
    >
    > > Any interference with the press has to be justified because it inevit-
    > > ably has some effect on the ability of the press to perform its role in
    > > society. This is the position irrespective of whether a particular pub-
    > > lication is desirable in the public interest.
    >
    > That, if I may say so with respect, is a general statement of the law which
    > remains valid. In other words, it is not necessary to demonstrate, in the case
    > of a tabloid publication in particular, that the contents of an article or the
    > content of photographs is desirable in the public interest. It may very well be
    > that, in certain circumstances, it will be necessary to focus upon whether or
    > not it is in the public interest to publish material in respect of which there

is a prima facie legitimate expectation of privacy. But that is a consideration which has to be addressed later down the line.

The other proposition which was referred to was this. Regardless of the quality of the material which it is intended to publish, *prima facie* the court should not interfere with its publication. Again, that is a statement of the obvious and a principle which has long applied ever since Blackstone's observations on prior or "previous" restraint: Commentaries (1765), Book IV, pp. 151–2.

5. The strength of the claim for privacy (at para. 10):

Furthermore, guideline (vii) in Lord Woolf's judgment was identified:

> . . . Usually the answer to the question whether there exists a private interest worthy of protection will be obvious. In those cases where the answer is not obvious an answer will often be unnecessary. This is because the weaker the claim for privacy the more likely that the claim for privacy will be outweighed by the claim based on freedom of expression.

6. Is the plaintiff a public figure? (at para. 11)

Finally, reference was made to "guideline (xii)":

> Where an individual is a public figure, he is entitled to have his privacy respected in the appropriate circumstances. The individual, however, should recognise that because of his public position he must expect and accept that his actions will be more closely scrutinised by the media. Even trivial facts relating to a public figure can be of great interest to readers and other observers of the media . . . . Whether you have courted publicity or not, you may be a legitimate subject of public attention.

Justice Eady summarized his reasons for refusing to grant the injunction as follows at para. 20:

> Against that background, and applying the test which I have already identified in *Cream Holdings v Banerjee*, I am not satisfied that the claimant is more likely than not to obtain injunctive relief at trial, in the sense of establishing the threshold requirement that there was a reasonable expectation of privacy in the circumstances in which he found himself, or, alternatively, that if there was such a reasonable expectation, the claimant's Article 8 rights would at trial prevail over the defendant's Article 10 rights. I have no doubt that the article is likely to cause offence and embarrassment to Sir Elton. There is reason to suppose from correspondence, which I need not refer to

in this judgment, that the article is likely to be dismissive and personally offensive. That, however, in this day and age is regarded as quite a distinct matter from coverage which gives rise to a cause of action, whether in breach of confidence or for that matter libel. I must put to one side, as is made clear by the judgment of Lord Woolf in *A v B Plc*, considerations about whether or not the material has any particular worth or quality, and I do so.

6) Relationship between Invasion of Privacy and Defamation

Terry v. Persons Unknown (Rev 1), [2010] EWHC 119 (QB) at para. 96, Tugendhat J.:

> Before leaving the topic of defamation, I note that it is only in limited classes of cases that the law of privacy gives rise to an overlap with the law of defamation. In broad terms the cases may be considered in at least four different groups. The first group of cases, where there is no overlap, is where the information cannot be said to be defamatory (eg *Douglas v. Hello!*, and *Murray*). It is the law of confidence, privacy and harassment that are likely to govern such cases. There is a second group of cases where there is an overlap, but where it is unlikely that it could be said that protection of reputation is the nub of the claim. These are cases where the information would in the past have been said to be defamatory even though it related to matters which were involuntary eg disease. There was always a difficulty in fitting such cases into defamation, but it was done because of the absence of any alternative cause of action. There is a third group of cases where there is an overlap, but no inconsistency. These are cases where the information relates to conduct which is voluntary, and alleged to be seriously unlawful, even if it is personal (eg sexual or financial). The claimant is unlikely to succeed whether at an interim application or (if the allegation is proved) at trial, whether under the law of defamation or the law of privacy. The fourth group of cases, where it may make a difference which law governs, is where the information relates to conduct which is voluntary, discreditable, and personal (eg sexual or financial) but not unlawful (or not seriously so). In defamation, if the defendant can prove one of the libel defences, he will not have to establish any public interest (except in the case of *Reynolds* privilege, where the law does require consideration of the seriousness of the allegation, including from the point of view of the claimant). But if it is the claimant's choice alone that determines that the only cause of action which the court may take into account is misuse of private information, then the defendant cannot succeed unless he establishes that it comes within the public interest exception (or, perhaps, that he believes that it comes within that exception).

See also *Terry v. Persons Unknown (Rev 1)*, [2010] EWHC 119 at paras. 97–105 (QB)

7) Discussion of when Notice Should be Given

In *Terry v. Persons Unknown (Rev 1)*, [2010] EWHC 119 at paras. 112–20 (QB) Tugendhat J. discussed when notice should be given and relied upon the decision of Eady J. in *X v. Persons Unknown*, [2006] EWHC 2873 (QB). Justice Tugendhat's summary is found at para. 112:

> . . . Eady J has considered this point in *X v Persons Unkown*. He said at para. 18:

>> It is not for me to lay down practice directions, but what I can say is that a proper consideration for the Article 10 rights of media publishers, and indeed their rights under Article 6 as well, would require that where a litigant intends to serve a prohibitory injunction upon one or more of them, in reliance on the *Spycatcher* principle, those individual publishers should be given a realistic opportunity to be heard on the appropriateness or otherwise of granting the injunction, and upon the scope of its terms.

>> The point of principle for which Mr Caldecott contends [I interpolate that Mr Caldecott was acting for one of the media defendants] can be encapsulated in the terms of the draft placed before the court for this hearing, which obviously mirrors closely the provisions contained in section 12 of the Human Rights:

>>> A claimant, who applies for an interim order restraining a defendant from publishing allegedly private or confidential information, should give advance notice of the application and of the injunctive relief sought to any non-party on whom the claimant intends to serve the order so as to bind that party by application of the *Spycatcher* principle . . . unless:
>>> (a) The claimant has no reason to believe that the non-party has or may have an existing specific interest in the outcome of the application; or
>>> (b) The claimant is unable to notify the non-party having taken all practicable steps to do so; or
>>> (c) There are compelling reasons why the non-party should not be notified

Justice Tugendhat found none of these reasons existed in this case.

PART VIII: Reference Material

CYBERLIBEL DAMAGE AWARDS GRANTED[*]

Email

Case	Citation	Medium of Publication	G.D.	A.D.	P.D.
Alleslev-Krofchak v. Valcom Limited	2009 CanLII 30446 (ON S.C.)	Email	$100,000	N/A	N/A
Ross v. Holley	[2004] O.J. No. 4643	Email	$75,000	$50,000	N/A
Smith v. Cross	2007 BCSC 1757	Email	$25,000	N/A	$10,000
Vaquero Energy Ltd. v. Weir	2004 ABQB 68, 352 A.R. 191	Email (and messages in chatrooms)	$10,000 (company) $40,000 (individual)	N/A	$25,000 (individual)
Shell v. Cherrier	[2007] O.J. No. 5152	Email	$7,500	N/A	N/A
Lee v. Ng	2007 BCSC 1947, appeal dismissed 2009 BCCA 91	Email	$5,000	N/A	N/A

---

* Damages are stated in Canadian dollars unless otherwise stated. G.D. stands for general damages, A.D. for aggravated damages, and P.D. for punitive damages.

Website

Case	Citation	Medium of Publication	G.D.	A.D.	P.D.
Newman v. Halstead	2006 BCSC 65	Website	$676,000 (divided over 11 plaintiffs: highest individual amount $150,000)	N/A	$50,000 (divided equally over 11 plaintiffs)
Reichmann v. Berlin	[2002] O.J. No. 2732, [2002] O.T.C. 464	Website	$200,000	$50,000 (each def)	$50,000 (each def)
Hunter-Dickinson v. Butler	2010 BCSC 939	Website	$125,000	$75,000	$25,000
Simpson v. Mair	2004 BCSC 754	Website	$100,000	N/A	N/A
Griffin v. Sullivan	2008 BCSC 827	Website	$100,000	$50,000	$4,644.40 special damages $25,000 for invasion of privacy
Abou-Khalil c. Diop	2008 QCCS 1921	Website	$100,000	N/A	$25,000
WeGo Kayaking Ltd. et al. v. Sewid et al.	2007 BCSC 49	Website	$100,000 (WeGo) $150,000 (Northern Lights)	N/A	$2,500 (WeGo) $5,000 (Northern Lights)
Barrick Gold Corp. v. Lopehandia	(2004), 239 D.L.R. (4th) 577	Website	$75,000	N/A	$50,000
McQuaig v. Harbour Financial Inc.	2009 ABQB 678	Financial Statements	$75,000		
Linsley v. Domaille	2009 VCC 554	Website	$70,000 (Australian dollars)		

Case	Citation	Medium of Publication	G.D.	A.D.	P.D.
Fuda v. Conn	2009 CanLII 1140 (ON S.C.)	Website	$50,000	$20,000	N/A
Loh v. Yang	2006 BCSC 1131	Website	$50,000	$25,000	$10,000
Metropolitan International Schools v. Designtechnica Corp. et al.	[2010] EWHC 2411 (QB)	Website	£50,000		
Warman v. Grosvenor	[2008] O.J. No. 4462	Website	$20,000	$10,000	N/A
Warman v. Fromm and Canadian Association for Free Expression Inc.	Ontario Court File No: 04-CV-26550SR, appeal dismissed 2008 ONCA 842, leave to appeal to Supreme Court of Canada denied: 23 March 2009, [2008] SCCA No. 40.	Website	$20,000	$10,000	N/A
Manson v. Moffett	2008 CanLII 19789 (ON S.C.)	Website	$20,000	N/A	N/A
Ottawa-Carleton District School Board v. Scharf	[2007] O.J. No. 3030, aff'd 2008 ONCA 154	Website	$15,000 (each Plaintiff)	N/A	N/A
Henderson v. Pearlman	2009 CanLII 43641 (ON S.C.)	Website	$10,000 (each Plaintiff)	N/A	N/A
Keith-Smith v. Williams	[2006] EWHC 860	Website	£5,000 and £5,000		
Inform Cycle Ltd. v. Draper	2008 ABQB 369	Website	$5,000	N/A	$5,000

Blog

Case	Citation	Medium of Publication	G.D.	A.D.	P.D.
Wade c. Diop	2009 QCCS 350	Blog	$75,000	N/A	$50,000 in punitive damages
Buckle v. Caswell	2009 SKQB 363	Blog	$50,000		
National Bank of Canada v. Weir	2010 QCCS 402	Blog	$20,000		

News/Radio Broadcast Website

Case	Citation	Medium of Publication	G.D.	A.D.	P.D.
Southam Inc. v. Chelekis	2000 BCCA 112	Newspaper electronic broadcasts	$675,000	$100,000	$100,000
Greg v. WIN Television NWS Pty Limited	[2009] NSWC 632	Television station website	$200,000 (Australian dollars)		
Ramsey v. Pacific Press, a Division of Southam Inc.	2000 BCSC 1551	Radio Broadcast/Website	$30,000	N/A	N/A
Lamarre c. Allard	2008 QCCS 5266	News broadcast/Website	$15,000	N/A	N/A

Newspaper Website

Case	Citation	Medium of Publication	G.D.	A.D.	P.D.
Manno v. Henry	2008 BCSC 738	Hard copy publication and online newspaper	$210,000 to five individuals	N/A	N/A
Lavigne v. Chenail	2009 QCCS 2518	Newspaper/website	$50,000 $20,000 (Husband)	N/A	$10,000 exemplary damages $10,000 exemplary damages (Husband)
Sanjh Savera Weekly v. Ajit Newspaper Advertising	[2006] O.J. No. 2464	Newspaper/website	$45,000 $5,000 (to company)	N/A	$15,000 (for individual)
Hansen v. Tilley	2009 BCSC 360	Newspaper Website	$30,000	N/A	N/A
Reaburn v. Langen	2008 BCSC 1342	Newspaper/website	$20,000	N/A	N/A

Online Book/Print Book

Case	Citation	Medium of Publication	G.D.	A.D.	P.D.
Sanchez-Pontigon v. Mandalansan-Lord	2009 CanLII 28216 (ON S.C.)	Online book/Print book	$25,000	$12,500	N/A

Facebook

Case	Citation	Medium of Publication	G.D.	A.D.	P.D.
Applause Store Productions Ltd. & Anor v. Raphael	[2008] EWHC 1781 (QB)	Facebook	£15,000 for individual libel £5,000 for corporation for libel £2,000 for breach of privacy		N/A

CYBERLIBEL INJUNCTIONS

Injunctions Granted

Case	Citation	Medium of Publication
A.T. v. L.T.H.	2006 BCSC 1689	Internet
Barrick Gold Corp. v. Lopehandia	(2004), 239 D.L.R. (4th) 577	Website
Buckle v. Caswell	2009 SKQB 363	Blog
Canadian National Railway Company v. Google Inc.	2010 ONSC 3121	Website
Emerald Passport Inc. v. MacIntosh	2008 BCSC 1289	Website
Griffin v. Sullivan	2008 BCSC 827	Website
Henderson v. Pearlman	2009 CanLII 43641 (ON S.C.)	Internet
Hunter-Dickinson v. Butler	2010 BCSC 939	Website
Koopman v. Rathwell	2006 BCSC 366	Media and Internet
Manson v. Moffett	[2008] O.J. No. 1697	Website
McQuaig v. Harbour Financial Inc.	2009 ABQB 678	Blog
National Bank of Canada v. Weir	2010 QCCS 402	Blog
Newman v. Halstead	2006 BCSC 65	Website
Rawdon (Municipalité de) c. Leblanc (Solo)	2009 QCCS 3151	Website
Warman v. Wilkins-Fournier	[2009] O.J. No. 1305	Website
WeGo Kayaking Ltd. et al. v. Sewid	2007 BCSC 49	Website

Injunctions Denied

Case	Citation	Medium of Publication
Beidas v. Pichler	[2008] O.J. No. 2135, reversing [2007] O.J. No. 3684	Internet
Desroches c. Klein	2009 QCCS 340	Website
Mcleod (c.o.b. Maslak Mcleod Gallery) v. Sinclair	[2008] O.J. No. 5242	Website

CYBERLIBEL JURISDICTIONAL MOTIONS

Case	Citation	Medium of Publication	Result
Bangoura v. The Washington Post	2005 CanLII 46932 (ON C.A.), rev'g (2004), 235 D.L.R. (4th) 564 (S.C.J.), leave to appeal to S.C.C. denied without reasons, 2006 CanLII 4742 (S.C.C.)	Website	Allowed
Banro Corporation v. Éditions Écosociété Inc.	[2009] O.J. No. 733	Website	Dismissed
Black v. Breeden	2009 CanLII 14041 (ON S.C.), 2010 ONCA 547	Website & Media	Dismissed
Guilbert v. Guilleaume	2008 QCCS 3504	Website	Allowed
Research in Motion Ltd. v. Visto Corp.	[2008] O.J. No. 3671	Media and Website	Dismissed
TimberWest Forest Corp. v. United Steel, Paper and Forestry, Rubber Manufacturing, Energy, Allied Industrial and Service Workers International Union	2008 BCSC 388	Video News conference	Dismissed
Vincent v. Forget	2008 QCCS 2466	Website	Allowed
Bains v. Sadhu Singh Hamdard Trust	2007 CanLII 9610 (ON S.C.)	Newspaper website	Dismissed
Barrick Gold Corp. v. Blanchard & Co.	[2003] O.J. No. 5817 (SCJ)	Website	Dismissed
Burke v. NYP Holdings, Inc.	2005 BCSC 1287	Website	Dismissed
Trizec Properties Inc. v. Citigroup Global Markets Inc.	[2004] O.J. No. 323	Website	Dismissed
Wiebe v. Bouchard	2005 BCSC 47	Website	Dismissed

JUDICIAL GLOSSARY OF SELECTED INTERNET TERMS

As was mentioned at the beginning of this book, the judicial glossary has a limited scope and limited purpose. Encyclopedic and comprehensive glossaries of Internet terms can be found in the following resources:

- Barry Sookman, *Computer, Internet and Electronic Commerce Terms: Judicial, Legislative and Technical Definitions* (Toronto: Carswell, 2001)
- www.webopedia.com
- http://en.wikipedia.org/wiki/Glossary_of_Internet-related_terminology
- http://whatis.techtarget.com

This glossary is really a judicial version of the Frequently Asked Questions chapter. No jurisdiction has a monopoly on the best explanations of these terms. For this reason, definitions have been drawn from not only Canada but also Australia, the UK, and the US, as well as some pertinent non-judicial sources. The process for developing the treatment of the list below was as follows: if comprehensive explanations or definitions of a particular topic in Canada existed, I did not proceed any farther. Where comprehensive explanations or definitions were unavailable in Canadian jurisdictions, the discussion of the term is supplemented by Australian, UK, and non-judicial source-material.

BLOG

Canadian Law

R. v. Fenton, 2008 ABQB 251, [2008] A.J. No. 439, 443 A.R. 275, 77 W.C.B. (2d) 629, 92 Alta. L.R. (4th) 125, 2008 CarswellAlta 515, [2008] 11 W.W.R. 743 at para. 3:

Between January 22, 2006 and December 7, 2006 the Respondent visited the Windows Live Spaces website where he maintained a weblog or "blog." A blog can be described as an online journal that is frequently updated and intended for general public consumption. It is a series of entries posted to a single page in reverse chronological order. A blog generally represents the personality of the author or portrays the purpose of the website that hosts the blog. Topics sometimes include brief philosophical musings, commentary on internet and other social issues and links to other sites the author favours, especially those that support a point being made on a post. On the particular blog in question, the Respondent posted material that could be accessed and viewed by anyone on the internet.

R. v. LeBlanc, 2006 NBPC 37, [2006] N.B.J. No. 514, [2006] A.N.-B. no 514, 2006
   NBCP 37, 311 N.B.R. (2d) 224, 72 W.C.B. (2d) 49 at paras. 3 and 4

Australia

Melbourne University Student Union Inc. (in liq) v. Ray, [2006] VSC 205 at para. 3
   (S.C. Vic.):

On 30 January 2006, Mr Cass set up a "blog" (an abbreviation for "weblog") on his website, which is essentially an online diary. Mr Cass has described the website as being dedicated towards a critique of the liquidator's professional conduct. The contents of the website will be considered in detail shortly; suffice to say that they are highly critical of Mr McVeigh's conduct as MUSU liquidator.

CACHE

Canada

Society of Composers, Authors and Music Publishers of Canada v. Canadian Assn. of Internet Providers, 2004 SCC 45, [2004] 2 S.C.R. 427 at para. 23:

A particular issue arose in respect of the appellants' use of "caching." When an end user visits a Web site, the packets of data needed to transmit the requested information will come initially from the host server where the files for this site are stored. As they pass through the hands of an Internet Service Provider, a temporary copy may be made and stored on its server. This is a cache copy. If another user wants to visit this page shortly thereafter, using the same Internet Service Provider, the information may be transmitted to the subsequent user either directly from the Web site or from what is kept in the cache copy. The practice of creating "caches" of data speeds up the transmission and lowers the cost. The subsequent end user may have no idea that it is not getting the information directly from the original Web site. Cache copies are not retained for long periods of time since, if the original files change, users will get out-of-date information. The Internet Service Provider controls the existence and duration of caches on its own facility, although in some circumstances it is open to a content provider to specify no caching, or an end user to program its browser to insist on content from the original Web site.

UK

R. v. Graham Westgarth, R. v. Smith Mike Jayson, [2002] EWCA Crim 683 at para. 16:

The question of *mens rea* was, however, considered by the Divisional Court in Atkins. Like Bowden, that was a case of downloading images from the Internet. Some were deliberately stored by the defendant on one of the computer's directories. Others were stored in the computer's cache, a temporary information store created automatically by an Internet browser programme when accessing a site on the Internet. The defendant was charged with making both the photographs stored in the directory and those stored in the cache. He was also charged with possessing the photographs stored in the cache. The Stipendiary Magistrate was not sure that the defendant had been aware of the operation of the computer's cache, but convicted him of the offence of being in possession, holding that the offence under section 160(1) of the 1988 Act was one of strict liability. He ruled that there was no case to answer in relation to the charges of making, since making required an act of creation, and it was not satisfied by storing or copying a document.

Atkins v. Director Of Public Prosecutions, Goodland v. Director Of Public Prosecutions, [2000] EWHC Admin 302 (8th March, 2000) (H.C.J. — Q.B. Div.)

The internet is a medium to publish and obtain information using computers. A browser programme, for example the Netscape browser, can be used to access the internet. The browser is able to locate servers and in doing so the user is able to download information, or 'documents.' A user can deliberately choose to download or save documents, but it is not commonly known by users that the browser automatically creates a temporary information store, a 'cache,' of recently viewed documents. The reason for this is that when the user revisits the documents the browser may use the locally stored cache, provided that it is not too old and does not need updating, which saves time in fetching the documents . . . . The cache is automatically emptied of documents as it becomes full, but even then it is possible to retrieve information forensically. Expert computer users can access the cache directly . . . . The J Directory does not form part of the cache and must have been created separately.

CRAIGSLIST

US

Chicago Lawyers' Comm. Civ. Rights v. Craigslist, 461 F. Supp. 2d 681 (ND Illinois
    2006) at 4–7:

Craigslist operates a website that allows third-party users to post and read notices for, among other things, housing sale or rental opportunities. (R. 1-1, Pl.'s
Compl. at ¶ 7; R. 13-1, Def.'s Ans. at ¶ 7.) The website, which is accessible at
"chicago.craigslist.org" (among other web addresses), is titled "craigslist: chicago classifieds for jobs, apartments, personals, for sale, services, community:
Non-commercial bulletin board for events, jobs, housing, personal ads and
community discussion." (R. 1-1, Pl.'s Compl. at ¶ 7; R. 13-1, Def.'s Ans. at ¶ 7.)
The website contains a link entitled "post to classifieds" that, if clicked, will
display a webpage located at "post.craigslist.org/chi" and titled "*chicago craigslist >> create posting.*" (R. 1-1, Pl.'s Compl. at ¶ 8; R. 13-1, Def.'s Ans. at ¶ 8.)
That webpage categorizes posts and advertisements and offers the following
links: (1) "job," (2) "gigs," (3) "housing," (4) "for sale/wanted," (5) "resume," (6)
"services offered," (7) "personal/romance," (8) "community," and (9) "event."
The webpage also contains additional links labeled "*log into your account*" and
"*(Apply for Account).*" (R. 1-1, Pl.'s Compl. at ¶ 8; R. 13-1, Def.'s Ans. at ¶ 8.)

    When a user clicks on the website link "housing," the website will display
a page located at "post.craigslist.org/chi/H" that bears the title "*chicago* craigslist > housing > create posting" and contains a line reading "Are you offering
space/housing, or do you need space/housing?" (R. 1-1, Pl.'s Compl. at ¶ 9; R. 13-
1, Def.'s Ans. at ¶ 9.) On this webpage, directly under this quoted text, there are
two links labeled "I am offering housing" and "I need housing" as well as two
other links (at the upper right of the page) labeled "log into your account" and
"(Apply for Account)." (R. 1-1, Pl.'s Compl. at ¶ 9; R. 13-1, Def.'s Ans. at ¶ 9.)

    When a user clicks on the link "I am offering housing," the website dis-
plays a page located at "post.craigslist.org/chi/H?want=n," also titled "*chicago
craigslist* > housing > create posting." (R. 1-1, Pl.'s Compl. at ¶ 10; R. 13-1, Def.'s
Ans. at ¶ 10.) This webpage contains a line reading: "Your ad will expire in 7
days. Please choose a category:" followed by eight categorized links entitled:
(1) "rooms & shares," (2) "apartments for rent," (3) "housing swap," (4) "office
& commercial," (5) "parking & storage," (6) "real estate for sale," (7) "sublets &
temporary," and (8) "vacation rentals," as well as two other links (at the upper
right of the page) labeled "log into your account" and "(Apply for Account)."
(R. 1-1, Pl.'s Compl. at ¶ 10; R. 13-1, Def.'s 685*685 Ans. at ¶ 10.) Accessing any of
these links opens a new webpage making available suggested and "[r]equired"

fields that comprise the content of the post or advertisement. (R. 1-1, Pl.'s Compl. at ¶ 10.) These content fields list rent or price, specific and general location, the title of the advertisement, a contact email address, and a description with the capability to add pictures. (R. 1-1, Pl.'s Compl. at ¶ 10.)

The webpage further offers the option to "anonymize" a contact email address with a newly-assigned and unique email address using the domain name "craigslist.org." (R. 1-1, Pl.'s Compl. at ¶ 10.) When a user clicks on the link "I need housing" the website displays a webpage located at "post.craigslist.org/chi/H?want=y" that bears the title *"chicago craigslist* > housing > posting." This webpage categorizes posts and advertisements under links to the following: (1) "apts wanted," (2) "real estate wanted," (3) "room/share wanted," and (4) "sublet/temp wanted." (R. 1-1, Pl.'s Compl. at ¶ 11; R. 13-1, Def.'s Ans. at ¶ 11.) When a user clicks on these links, the webpage offers the option to anonymize a contact email address and the same suggested and "required" fields appear as when a user clicks on links associated with the "I am offering housing" link. (R. 1-1, Pl.'s Compl. at ¶ 11; R. 13-1, Def.'s Ans. at ¶ 11.) The webpage link titled "log in to your account," opens a webpage titled "craigslist: account log in" that lists an "Email/Flandle" field and a "Password" field so that those with "craigslist accounts" may access their personal accounts, prior postings, responses to such postings, and other information. (R. 1-1, Pl.'s Compl. at ¶ 12; R. 13-1, Def.'s Ans. at ¶ 12.) This sign-in page has a line that reads "need help?" followed by a link that enables a user to send an email to the email address "accounts@craigslist.org." (R. 1-1, Pl.'s Compl. at ¶ 12; R. 13-1, Def.'s Ans. at ¶ 12.) The webpage link titled "Apply for Account," opens a new webpage located at "accounts.craigslistorg/login/signup," titled "craigslist: account signup," that directs individuals to type a five-letter verification word, to provide a contact email address, and to click on a button to "create account" so that prior content and information may be saved and accessed later. (R. 1-1, Pl.'s Compl. at ¶ 13; R. 13-1, Def.'s Ans. at ¶ 13.) When home-seekers are interested in posted sale or rental housing opportunities, they obtain the necessary contact information from content published on Craigslist's website. (R. 1-1, Pl.'s Compl. at ¶ 14.)

CONDUIT

Canada

Canadian Radio-television and Telecommunications Commission (Re), 2010 FCA 178, [2010] F.C.J. No. 849, 322 D.L.R. (4th) 337 at paras. 17–18:

The Coalition submits that the reference question should be answered in the negative. It argues that the definition of "broadcasting undertaking" is to be interpreted in light of the object of the *Broadcasting Act* and it is evident that, by enabling end-users to access "broadcasting" through the Internet, ISPs fall outside of this definition. The definition of "broadcasting undertaking" is not exhaustive. However, unlike distribution and programming undertakings and networks, ISPs do not exercise any control over creating, choosing, or acquiring rights to the content that end-users receive. ISPs play no editorial role nor do they "receive" programs; rather, they simply provide a passive connection through which "programs" may travel. Indeed, the courts have consistently found ISPs to be mere conduits, analogous to telephone lines, and therefore not liable for copyright-infringing or defamatory content that is sent or accessed using their facilities.

As the primary focus of the *Broadcasting Act* is to foster the enrichment of Canada via the broadcasting of programs that promote Canadian artistic creativity, expression and talent, the Coalition is of the view that its interpretation is in line with Parliament's intent. As mere conduits, ISPs have no meaningful role to play in ensuring the attainment of these objectives. Parliament could not have intended to capture undertakings with the characteristics of ISPs. Rather, it is submitted that the function of the ISPs are at the core of the policy objectives of the *Telecommunications Act*.

Society of Composers, Authors and Music Publishers of Canada v. Canadian Assn. of Internet Providers, 2004 SCC 45, [2004] 2 S.C.R. 427 at paras. 32 and 92:

The Board rejected SOCAN's argument that s. 2.4(1)(b) should be narrowly construed as an exemption to copyright liability. The Board held that where an intermediary merely acts as a "conduit for communications by other persons" (p. 453 (emphasis added)), it can claim the benefit of s. 2.4(1)(b). If an intermediary does more than merely act as a conduit (for example if it creates a cache for reasons other than improving system performance or modifies the content of cached material), it may lose the protection. Insofar as the Internet Service Provider furnishes "ancillary" services to a content provider or end user, it could still rely on s. 2.4(1)(b) as a defence to copyright infringement, provided any such "ancillary services" do not amount in themselves to communication or authorization to communicate the work. Creation of an automatic "hyperlink" by a Canadian Internet Service Provider will also attract copyright liability.

. . .

Section 2.4(1)(b) shields from liability the activities associated with providing the means for another to communicate by telecommunication. "The 'means,' as the Board found, '. . . are not limited to routers and other hardware. They include all software connection equipment, connectivity services, hosting and other facilities and services without which such communications would not occur'" (p. 452). I agree. So long as an Internet intermediary does not itself engage in acts that relate to the content of the communication, i.e., whose participation is content neutral, but confines itself to providing "a conduit" for information communicated by others, then it will fall within s. 2.4(1)(b). The appellants support this result on a general theory of "Don't shoot the messenger!"

TELUS Communications Inc. v. Canadian Radio-television and Telecommunications Commission et al. (2004), 2004 FCA 365, [2005] 2 F.C.R. 388, [2004] F.C.J. No. 1808 at para. 1:

LÉTOURNEAU J.A.: — Was Telecom Decision CRTC 2003-54 [Part VII Application by Shaw Communications Inc. Requesting a Proceeding to Consider the Rates for Type B, C and D Conduct Provided by TELUS Communications Inc.] an illegal exercise in retroactive rate setting as contended by the appellant or was it rather, as the respondents, Delta Cable Communications Ltd. (Delta) and the Canadian Cable Television Association (CCTA) submit, simply a restoration of the *status quo ante* with respect to rates applicable to Type B, C and D conduit owned by the appellant? A conduit is a type of support structure designed to house and support the wires and other infrastructures used to deliver cable television, high-speed Internet access and other telecommunications services to subscribers. In a nutshell, a conduit is a "reinforced passage or opening in, on, over or through the ground or watercourses capable of containing communications facilities": see paragraph 12 of the Telecom Decision CRTC 2003-54.

CONTENT ON THE INTERNET

US

ACLU v. Reno, 929 F. Supp. 824 (E.D. Pa. 1996) at paras. 74–81:

The types of content now on the Internet defy easy classification. The entire card catalogue of the Carnegie Library is on-line, together with journals, journal abstracts, popular magazines, and titles of compact discs. The director of the Carnegie Library, Robert Croneberger, testified that on-line services are the emerging trend in libraries generally. Plaintiff Hotwired Ventures LLC organizes its Web site into information regarding travel, news and commentary, arts and entertainment, politics, and types of drinks. Plaintiff America Online, Inc., not only creates chat rooms for a broad variety of topics, but also allows members to create their own chat rooms to suit their own tastes. The ACLU uses an America Online chat room as an unmoderated forum for people to debate civil liberties issues. Plaintiffs' expert, Scott

Bradner, estimated that 15,000 newsgroups exist today, and he described his own interest in a newsgroup devoted solely to Formula 1 racing cars. America Online makes 15,000 bulletin boards available to its subscribers, who post between 200,000 and 250,000 messages each day. Another plaintiffs' expert, Harold Rheingold, participates in "virtual communities" that simulate social interaction. It is no exaggeration to conclude that the content on the Internet is as diverse as human thought.

The Internet is not exclusively, or even primarily, a means of commercial communication. Many commercial entities maintain Web sites to inform potential consumers about their goods and services, or to solicit purchases, but many other Web sites exist solely for the dissemination of non-commercial information. The other forms of Internet communication — e-mail, bulletin boards, newsgroups, and chat rooms — frequently have non-commercial goals. For the economic and technical reasons set forth in the following paragraphs, the Internet is an especially attractive means for not-for-profit entities or public interest groups to reach their desired audiences. There are examples in the parties' stipulation of some of the non-commercial uses that the Internet serves. Plaintiff Human Rights Watch, Inc., offers information on its Internet site regarding reported human rights abuses around the world. Plaintiff National Writers Union provides a forum for writers on issues of concern to them. Plaintiff Stop Prisoner Rape, Inc., posts text, graphics, and statistics regarding the incidence and prevention of rape in prisons. Plaintiff Critical Path AIDS Project, Inc., offers information on safer sex, the transmission of HIV, and the treatment of AIDS.

Such diversity of content on the Internet is possible because the Internet provides an easy and inexpensive way for a speaker to reach a large audience, potentially of millions. The start-up and operating costs entailed by communication on the Internet are significantly lower than those associated with use of other forms of mass communication, such as television, radio, newspapers, and magazines. This enables operation of their own Web sites not only by large companies, such as Microsoft and Time Warner, but also by small, not-for- profit groups, such as Stop Prisoner Rape and Critical Path AIDS Project. The Government's expert, Dr. Dan R. Olsen, agreed that creation of a Web site would cost between $1,000 and $15,000, with monthly operating costs depending on one's goals and the Web site's traffic. Commercial online services such as America Online allow subscribers to create Web pages free of charge. Any Internet user can communicate by posting a message to one of the thousands of newsgroups and bulletin boards or by engaging in an on-line "chat," and thereby reach an audience worldwide that shares an interest in a particular topic.

The ease of communication through the Internet is facilitated by the use of hypertext markup language (HTML), which allows for the creation of "hyperlinks" or "links." HTML enables a user to jump from one source to other related sources by clicking on the link. A link might take the user from Web site to Web site, or to other files within a particular Web site. Similarly, by typing a request into a search engine, a user can retrieve many different sources of content related to the search that the creators of the engine have collected.

Because of the technology underlying the Internet, the statutory term "content provider," which is equivalent to the traditional "speaker," may actually be a hybrid of speakers. Through the use of HTML, for example, Critical Path and Stop Prisoner Rape link their Web sites to several related databases, and a user can immediately jump from the home pages of these organizations to the related databases simply by clicking on a link. America Online creates chat rooms for particular discussions but also allows subscribers to create their own chat rooms. Similarly, a newsgroup gathers postings on a particular topic and distributes them to the newsgroup's subscribers. Users of the Carnegie Library can read on-line versions of Vanity Fair and Playboy, and America Online's subscribers can peruse the New York Times, Boating, and other periodicals. Critical Path, Stop Prisoner Rape, America Online and the Carnegie Library all make available content of other speakers over whom they have little or no editorial control.

Because of the different forms of Internet communication, a user of the Internet may speak or listen interchangeably, blurring the distinction between "speakers" and "listeners" on the Internet. Chat rooms, e-mail, and newsgroups are interactive forms of communication, providing the user with the opportunity both to speak and to listen.

It follows that unlike traditional media, the barriers to entry as a speaker on the Internet do not differ significantly from the barriers to entry as a listener. Once one has entered cyberspace, one may engage in the dialogue that occurs there. In the argot of the medium, the receiver can and does become the content provider, and vice-versa. The Internet is therefore a unique and wholly new medium of worldwide human communication [footnotes omitted.]

CYBERSPACE

US

ACLU v. Reno, 929 F. Supp 824 (E.D. Pa. 1996) at paras. 1–11:

The Internet is not a physical or tangible entity, but rather a giant network which interconnects innumerable smaller groups of linked computer networks. It is thus a network of networks. This is best understood if one considers what a linked group of computers — referred to here as a "network" — is, and what it does. Small networks are now ubiquitous (and are often called "local area networks"). For example, in many United States Courthouses, computers are linked to each other for the purpose of exchanging files and messages (and to share equipment such as printers). These are networks.

Some networks are "closed" networks, not linked to other computers or networks. Many networks, however, are connected to other networks, which are in turn connected to other networks in a manner which permits each computer in any network to communicate with computers on any other network in the system. This global Web of linked networks and computers is referred to as the Internet.

The nature of the Internet is such that it is very difficult, if not impossible, to determine its size at a given moment. It is indisputable, however, that the Internet has experienced extraordinary growth in recent years. In 1981, fewer than 300 computers were linked to the Internet, and by 1989, the number stood at fewer than 90,000 computers. By 1993, over 1,000,000 computers were linked. Today, over 9,400,000 host computers worldwide, of which approximately 60 percent located within the United States, are estimated to be linked to the Internet. This count does not include the personal computers people use to access the Internet using modems. In all, reasonable estimates are that as many as 40 million people around the world can and do access the enormously flexible communication Internet medium. That figure is expected to grow to 200 million Internet users by the year 1999.

Some of the computers and computer networks that make up the Internet are owned by governmental and public institutions, some are owned by non-profit organizations, and some are privately owned. The resulting whole is a decentralized, global medium of communications — or "cyberspace" — that links people, institutions, corporations, and governments around the world. The Internet is an international system. This communications medium allows any of the literally tens of millions of people with access to the Internet to exchange information. These communications can occur almost instantaneously, and can be directed either to specific individuals, to a broader group of people interested in a particular subject, or to the world as a whole.

The Internet had its origins in 1969 as an experimental project of the Advanced Research Project Agency ("ARPA"), and was called ARPANET. This network linked computers and computer networks owned by the military, defense contractors, and university laboratories conducting defense-related research. The network later allowed researchers across the country to access directly and to use extremely powerful supercomputers located at a few key universities and laboratories. As it evolved far beyond its research origins in the United States to encompass universities, corporations, and people around the world, the ARPANET came to be called the "DARPA Internet," and finally just the "Internet."

From its inception, the network was designed to be a decentralized, self-maintaining series of redundant links between computers and computer networks, capable of rapidly transmitting communications without direct human involvement or control, and with the automatic ability to re-route communications if one or more individual links were damaged or otherwise unavailable. Among other goals, this redundant system of linked computers was designed to allow vital research and communications to continue even if portions of the network were damaged, say, in a war.

To achieve this resilient nationwide (and ultimately global) communications medium, the ARPANET encouraged the creation of multiple links to and from each computer (or computer network) on the network. Thus, a computer located in Washington, D.C., might be linked (usually using dedicated telephone lines) to other computers in neighboring states or on the Eastern seaboard. Each of those computers could in turn be linked to other computers, which themselves would be linked to other computers.

A communication sent over this redundant series of linked computers could travel any of a number of routes to its destination. Thus, a message sent from a computer in Washington, D.C., to a computer in Palo Alto, California, might first be sent to a computer in Philadelphia, and then be forwarded to a computer in Pittsburgh, and then to Chicago, Denver, and Salt Lake City, before finally reaching Palo Alto. If the message could not travel along that path (because of military attack, simple technical malfunction, or other reason), the message would automatically (without human intervention or even knowledge) be re-routed, perhaps, from Washington, D.C. to Richmond, and then to Atlanta, New Orleans, Dallas, Albuquerque, Los Angeles, and finally to Palo Alto. This type of transmission, and re-routing, would likely occur in a matter of seconds.

Messages between computers on the Internet do not necessarily travel entirely along the same path. The Internet uses "packet switching" communication protocols that allow individual messages to be subdivided into smaller "packets" that are then sent independently to the destination, and are then automatically reassembled by the receiving computer. While all packets of a given message often travel along the same path to the destination, if computers along the route become overloaded, then packets can be re-routed to less loaded computers.

At the same time that ARPANET was maturing (it subsequently ceased to exist), similar networks developed to link universities, research facilities, businesses, and individuals around the world. These other formal or loose networks included BITNET, CSNET, FIDONET, and USENET. Eventually, each of these networks (many of which overlapped) were themselves linked together, allowing users of any computers linked to any one of the networks to transmit communications to users of computers on other networks. It is this series of linked networks (themselves linking computers and computer networks) that is today commonly known as the Internet.

No single entity — academic, corporate, governmental, or non-profit — administers the Internet. It exists and functions as a result of the fact that hundreds of thousands of separate operators of computers and computer networks independently decided to use common data transfer protocols to exchange communications and information with other computers (which in turn exchange communications and information with still other computers). There is no centralized storage location, control point, or communications channel for the Internet, and it would not be technically feasible for a single entity to control all of the information conveyed on the Internet.

DOMAIN NAMES

Canada

BCAA et al. v. Office and Professional Employees' Int. Union et al., 2001 BCSC 156 at paras. 17–20:

Businesses and people may secure domain names that are usually shorter than Internet Protocol Addresses and have meaning in one or more human languages ("Domain Names"). Domain Names are "mapped" to particular Internet Protocol Addresses so that an internet user can reach a particular computer.

Domain Names have two key components, namely the top level domain name ("TLD") and the second level domain name ("SLD"). The TLD consists of two or three letters located at the far right of any domain name preceded by a decimal point. Examples include ".com", ".net", and ".ca". SLDs must be registered with non-governmental registrars in combination with a particular TLD. For example, a law firm Jones & Company uses the second level domain name "jones" and has registered that SLD with the .ca Domain Registrar resulting in the combined domain name "jones.ca." SLDs must be registered in conjunction with TLDs. Hence, one may register "jones.ca," "jones.com," or "jones.net."

The most important functions of Domain Names are as website addresses and e-mail addresses.

Website addresses are identified by a uniform resource locator ("URL"). Most URL's begin with the letters "www," which represents the World Wide Web. Those three letters are usually added to the SLD and the TLD to form the main portion of a URL. Following the example of the Jones & Company's Domain Name, Jones & Company's URL is www.jones.ca.

Itravel2000.com Inc. (c.o.b. Itravel) v. Fagan, 2001 CanLII 28230, 197 D.L.R. (4th) 760, [2001] O.T.C. 180, 11 C.P.R. (4th) 164, 104 A.C.W.S. (3d) 172 at para. 36 (S.C.J.):

At paragraph 12, the Court describes the use of a domain name as follows:

Every web page has its own web site, which is its address, similar to a telephone number or street address. Every web site on the Internet has an identifier called a "domain name." The domain name often consists of a person's name or a company's name or trademark. For example, Pepsi has a web page with a web site domain name consisting of the company name, Pepsi, and, the "top level" domain designation.

Further, at paragraph 15:

A domain name is the simplest way of locating a web site. It a computer user does not know a domain name, she can use an Internet "search engine." To do this, the user types in a key word search, and the search will locate all of the web sites containing the key word. Such key word searches can yield hundreds of web sites. To make it easier to find their web sites, individuals and companies prefer to have a recognizable domain name.

FACEBOOK

Canada

Wice v. Dominion of Canada General Insurance Co., 2009 CanLII 36310, [2009] O.J. No. 2946, 75 C.C.L.I. (4th) 265, 2009 CarswellOnt 4076 at para. 12 (S.C.J.):

"Facebook" is a social networking site, used by members to communicate information about one's personal life to other members of the Facebook community: *Leduc v. Roman,* [2009] O.J. No. 681 (S.C.J.). The evidence filed in support of the Defendant's motion indicates that the Plaintiff has a Facebook account. His account is one that is "closed" to the public. In other words, not just any Facebook member can view his personal information. Only those that are given access to his profile may view it. Those parties with access are known as "Facebook fri34ends." Mr. Wice has some 110 Facebook friends.

R. v. R.G., 2010 ONSC 2157, [2010] O.J. No. 4001 at para. 47 (S.C.J.):

After her disclosure of the abuse, R.G. sent her a Facebook message. Facebook is a social networking site that facilitates communication and correspondence between friends and acquaintances.

British Columbia Teachers' Federation v. British Columbia (Attorney General), 2009 BCSC 436, [2009] B.C.J. No. 619, [2009] 11 W.W.R. 294, 94 B.C.L.R. (4th) 267, 188 C.R.R. (2d) 143, 2009 CarswellBC 795 at para. 217:

Social networking websites, such as Facebook and Myspace, permit users to establish networks of "friends." Messages can be sent to a user's immediate network; those users can then pass the messages along to other users in their own networks, and so forth exponentially.

US

Finkel v. Facebook, Inc., 2009 NY Slip Op 32248 (N.Y.Sup. Sep 15, 2009) at 1–2:

According to the movant, Facebook is a "social networking" internet website that is open to the public. The website allows members to communicate with each other via "group pages" and to set up and post content to profiles and groups.

Plaintiff in opposition to the motion states that she was a member of the Facebook website while attending high school in January 2007. Four of the defendants in this suit, Michael Dauber, Jeffrey Schwartz, Melinda Danowitz and Leah Herz, were classmates of plaintiff and also members of the Facebook website. The complaint alleges that the four classmates-defendants created a group on the website and posted defamatory statements with negative sexual and medical connotations.

Facebook seeks dismissal based upon the *Communications Decency Act of 1996* (47 USC 230 *et seq*) that provides immunity to interactive computer services from civil liability for defamatory content.

GOOGLE

US

Perfect 10, Inc. v. Amazon. com, Inc., 508 F.3d 1146 (9th Cir. 2007) at 1155–57:

Google's computers, along with millions of others, are connected to networks known collectively as the "Internet." "The Internet is a world-wide network of networks . . . all sharing a common communications technology." *Religious Tech. Ctr. v. Netcom On-Line Commc'n Servs., Inc.,* 923 F.Supp. 1231, 1238 n. 1 (N.D.Cal.1995). Computer owners can provide information stored on their computers to other users connected to the Internet through a medium called a webpage. A webpage consists of text interspersed with instructions written in Hypertext Markup Language ("HTML") that is stored in a computer. No images are stored on a webpage; rather, the HTML instructions on the webpage provide an address for where the images are stored, whether in the webpage publisher's computer or some other computer. In general, webpages are publicly available and can be accessed by computers connected to the Internet through the use of a web browser.

Google operates a search engine, a software program that automatically accesses thousands of websites (collections of webpages) and indexes them within a database stored on Google's computers. When a Google user accesses the Google website and types in a search query, Google's software searches its database for websites responsive to that search query. Google then sends relevant information from its index of websites to the user's computer. Google's search engines can provide results in the form of text, images, or videos.

The Google search engine that provides responses in the form of images is called "Google Image Search." In response to a search query, Google Image Search identifies text in its database responsive to the query and then communicates to users the images associated with the relevant text. Google's software cannot recognize and index the images themselves. Google Image Search provides search results as a webpage of small images called "thumbnails," which are stored in Google's servers. The thumbnail images are reduced, lower-resolution versions of full-sized images stored on third-party computers.

When a user clicks on a thumbnail image, the user's browser program interprets HTML instructions on Google's webpage. These HTML instructions direct the user's browser to cause a rectangular area (a "window") to appear on the user's computer screen. The window has two separate areas of information. The browser fills the top section of the screen with information from the Google webpage, including the thumbnail image and text. The HTML instructions also give the user's browser the address of the website publisher's computer that stores the full-size version of the thumbnail. By following the HTML instructions to access the third-party webpage, the user's browser connects to the website publisher's computer, downloads the full-size image, and makes the image appear at the bottom of the window on the user's screen. Google does not store the images that fill this lower part of the window and does not communicate the images to the user; Google simply provides HTML instructions directing a user's browser to access a third-party website. However, the top part of the window (containing the information from the Google 712*712 webpage) appears to frame and comment on the bottom part of the window. Thus, the user's window appears to be filled with a single integrated presentation of the full-size image, but it is actually an image from a third-party website framed by information from Google's website. The process by which the webpage directs a user's browser to incorporate content from different computers into a single window is referred to as "in-line linking." *Kelly v. Arriba Soft Corp.*, 336 F.3d 811, 816 (9th Cir.2003). The term "framing" refers to the process by which information from one computer appears to frame and annotate the in-line linked content from another computer. *Perfect 10* 416 F.Supp.2d at 833–34.

Google also stores webpage content in its cache. For each cached webpage, Google's cache contains the text of the webpage as it appeared at the time Google indexed the page, but does not store images from the webpage. *Id.* at 833. Google may provide a link to a cached webpage in response to a user's search query. However, Google's cache version of the webpage is not automatically updated when the webpage is revised by its owner. So if the webpage owner updates its webpage to remove the HTML instructions for finding an infringing image, a browser communicating directly with the webpage would not be able to access that image. However, Google's cache copy of the webpage would still have the old HTML instructions for the infringing image. Unless the owner of the computer changed the HTML address of the infringing image, or otherwise rendered the image unavailable, a browser accessing Google's cache copy of the website could still access the image where it is stored on the website publisher's computer. In other words, Google's cache copy could provide a user's browser with valid directions to an infringing image even though the updated webpage no longer includes that infringing image.

In addition to its search engine operations, Google generates revenue through a business program called "AdSense." Under this program, the owner of a website can register with Google to become an AdSense "partner." The website owner then places HTML instructions on its webpages that signal Google's server to place advertising on the webpages that is relevant to the webpages' content. Google's computer program selects the advertising automatically by means of an algorithm. AdSense participants agree to share the revenues that flow from such advertising with Google.

Google also generated revenues through an agreement with Amazon.com that allowed Amazon.com to in-line link to Google's search results. Amazon.com gave its users the impression that Amazon.com was providing search results, but Google communicated the search results directly to Amazon.com's users. Amazon.com routed users' search queries to Google and automatically transmitted Google's responses (i.e., HTML instructions for linking to Google's search results) back to its users.

713*713 Perfect 10 markets and sells copyrighted images of nude models. Among other enterprises, it operates a subscription website on the Internet. Subscribers pay a monthly fee to view Perfect 10 images in a "members' area" of the site. Subscribers must use a password to log into the members' area. Google does not include these password-protected images from the members' area in Google's index or database. Perfect 10 has also licensed Fonestarz Media Limited to sell and distribute Perfect 10 reduced-size copyrighted images for download and use on cell phones.

Some website publishers republish Perfect 10's images on the Internet without authorization. Once this occurs, Google's search engine may automatically index the webpages containing these images and provide thumbnail versions of images in response to user inquiries. When a user clicks on the thumbnail image returned by Google's search engine, the user's browser accesses the third-party webpage and in-line links to the full-sized infringing image stored on the website publisher's computer. This image appears, in its original context, on the lower portion of the window on the user's computer screen framed by information from Google's webpage [footnotes omitted.]

UK

Metropolitan International Schools Ltd. (t/a Skillstrain and/or Train2game) v. Design-technica Corp (t/a Digital Trends) & Ors, [2009] EWHC 1765 at paras. 6–8 (QB):

The Second Defendant, Google UK Ltd, is a subsidiary of the well known US corporation, Google Inc (being incorporated under the laws of Delaware and based in California). Google Inc has been joined as the Third Defendant. Its services can be accessed via the Internet from most countries in the world. It has approximately 20,000 employees and, I understand, made profits in the first quarter of 2009 of £952m. Those services include Internet search, cartography, news aggregation and the hosting of blogs and emails. Its revenue is derived from advertising.

The scale of the operation emerges from the evidence of Mr Jaron Lewis, who is the solicitor for the Second and Third Defendants. There were in

January 2005 approximately 11.5 billion publicly indexable web pages; that is to say, pages which a search engine such as that made available by Google would be able to access. Since then, the number of such pages has increased to approximately 39 billion. This figure is derived from worldwidewebsize.com. As at 31 March of this year, there were approximately 1.59 billion users accessing the Internet. This is based on the most recently available statistics published by InternetWorldStats.com.

The Second Defendant does not operate the Google search engines, as was explained to the Claimant's solicitor before the commencement of these proceedings. According to its defence, served on 9 June 2009, it carries on a sales and marketing business but does not provide online services (as the Claimant alleges). It employs some 600 people, including technical staff, who provide information technology support services to the front-line marketing staff or are software engineers or product managers. It is averred that it does not operate or control any Google branded search engine: moreover, its employees do not have access to any of the technology used to operate and control google.com and google.co.uk, which are owned and operated by the Third Defendant. Despite this, it is alleged in the particulars of claim that the Second Defendant is responsible for the publication of information gathered in response to Google searches. Accordingly it is pleaded on behalf of the Second Defendant that ". . . the Claimant has sued the wrong person and should discontinue its claim or have judgment entered against it."

HOST

Canada

Society of Composers, Authors and Music Publishers of Canada v. Canadian Assn. of Internet Providers, 2004 SCC 45, [2004] 2 S.C.R. 427 paras. 8 and 18:

The Internet is a huge communications facility which consists of a worldwide network of computer networks deployed to communicate information. A "content provider" uploads his or her data, usually in the form of a website, to a host server. The content is then forwarded to a destination computer (the end user). End users and content providers can connect to the Internet with a modem under contract with an Internet Service Provider.

. . .

A content provider may store files on its own computer, but it may also purchase space on a "host server" operated by an Internet Service Provider under commercial arrangements that include storing, making available and transmitting Web site content to end users. Once a musical work or other content has been posted on a host server, it is possible for any person with a computer and an arrangement with an Internet Service Provider to access the work on demand from anywhere in the world via the Internet.

Australia

Trumpet Software Pty Ltd. & Anor v. OzEmail Pty Ltd. & Ors, [1996] FCA 560 at
　para. 5:

In general terms, the Internet consists of a large number of computers throughout the world which are connected to each other, either directly through communication links or indirectly through other computers and communication links. The computers which are directly linked in this way are known as Internet hosts. Some Internet hosts, such as universities or large companies, only allow users within their organisations to connect to the Internet. Other Internet hosts, called Internet Service Providers (ISP), allow members of the public to connect to the Internet through the provider's computer. The individual user connects to the Internet by using a modem in conjunction with his or her computer. The modem provides the user with a telephone dial-in link to the chosen ISP who will usually charge a fee for providing access in this way. OzEmail is an ISP.

UK

Bunt v. Tilley & Ors, [2006] EWHC 407 at para. 9 (QB):

Google Groups London is provided by Google and the content forming that page is hosted by Google i.e. that content sits on computers controlled by Google. A popular site such as google.co.uk may easily have more than several hundred thousand visitors per day. When a person using an AOL Member Account connected to the internet via the AOL UK Propriety Service (an "AOL User") navigates to Google Groups London, a request is sent form that user's personal computer, via AOL, to the Google computer hosting Google Groups London. The requested page is then sent back to the AOL User, via their AOL connection.

INTERNET

Canada

SOCAN Statement of Royalties, Public Performance of Musical Works 1996, 1997, 1998 (Tariff 22, Internet) (Re) (1999), 1 C.P.R. (4th) 417 at p. 441. Adopted by the Supreme Court in *SOCAN v. Canadian Assn. of Internet Providers*, 2004 SCC 45, [2004] 2 S.C.R. 427:

The essence of what the Internet is and what occurs on it can be stated in a few sentences. It is a telecommunications network. Its purpose is to transmit files containing date, including music as that term is commonly understood. In order for a transmission to occur, the following events must take place. First, the file is incorporated to an Internet-accessible server. Second, upon request and at a time chosen by the recipient, the file is broken down into packets and transmitted from the host server to the recipient's service, via one or more routers. Third, the recipient, usually using a computer, can reconstitute and open the file upon reception or save it to open it later; either action involves a reproduction of the file, again as that term is commonly understood.

Barrick Gold Corp. v. Lopehandia, 2004 CanLII 12938 at paras. 28–34 (ON C.A.):

Is there something about defamation on the Internet — "cyber libel," as it is sometimes called — that distinguishes it, for purposes of damages, from defamation in another medium? My response to that question is "Yes."

The standard factors to consider in determining damages for defamation are summarized by Cory J. in *Hill* at p. 1203. They include the plaintiff's position and standing, the nature and seriousness of the defamatory statements, the mode and extent of publication, the absence or refusal of any retraction or apology, the whole conduct and motive of the defendant from publication through judgment, and any evidence of aggravating or mitigating circumstances.

In the Internet context, these factors must be examined in the light of what one judge has characterized as the "ubiquity, universality and utility" of that medium. In *Dow Jones & Company Inc. v. Gutnick* [2002] HCA 56 (10 December 2002), that same judge — Kirby J., of the High Court of Australia — portrayed the Internet in these terms, at para. 80:

The Internet is essentially a decentralized, self-maintained telecommunications network. It is made up of inter-linking small networks from all parts of the world. *It is ubiquitous, borderless, global and ambient in its nature. Hence the term "cyberspace." This is a word that recognizes that the interrelationships created by the Internet exist outside conventional geographic boundaries and comprise a single interconnected body of data, potentially amounting to a single body of knowledge.* The Internet is accessible in virtually all places on Earth where access can be obtained either by wire connection or by wireless (including satellite) links. *Effectively, the only constraint on access to the Internet is possession of the means of securing connection to a telecommunications system and possession of the basic hardware* [emphasis added, footnotes omitted].

Thus, of the criteria mentioned above, the mode and extent of publication is particularly relevant in the Internet context, and must be considered carefully. Communication via the Internet is instantaneous, seamless, interactive, blunt, borderless and far-reaching. It is also impersonal, and the anonymous nature of such communications may itself create a greater risk that the defamatory remarks are believed: see *Vaquero Energy Ltd. v. Weir*, [2004] A.J. No. 84 (Alta. Q.B.) at para. 17.

These characteristics create challenges in the libel context. Traditional approaches attuned to "the real world" may not respond adequately to the realities of the Internet world. How does the law protect reputation without unduly overriding such free wheeling public discourse? Lyrissa Barnett Lidsky discusses this conundrum in her article, "Silencing John Doe: Defamation and Discourse in Cyberspace," (2000) 49 Duke L.J. 855 at pp. 862–865:

> Internet communications lack this formal distance. Because communication can occur almost instantaneously, participants in online discussions place a premium on speed. Indeed, in many fora, speed takes precedence over all other values, including not just accuracy but even grammar, spelling, and punctuation. Hyperbole and exaggeration are common, and "venting" is at least as common as careful and considered argumentation. The fact that many Internet speakers employ online pseudonyms tends to heighten this sense that "anything goes," and some commentators have likened cyberspace to a frontier society free from the conventions and constraints that limit discourse in the real world. While this view is undoubtedly overstated, certainly the immediacy and informality of Internet communications may be central to its widespread appeal.
>
> *Although Internet communications may have the ephemeral qualities of gossip with regard to accuracy, they are communicated through a medium more pervasive than print, and for this reason they have tremendous power to harm reputation.* Once a message enters cyber-

space, millions of people worldwide can gain access to it. Even if the message is posted in a discussion forum frequented by only a handful of people, any one of them can republish the message by printing it or, as is more likely, by forwarding it instantly to a different discussion forum. And if the message is sufficiently provocative, it may be republished again and again. *The extraordinary capacity of the Internet to replicate almost endlessly any defamatory message lends credence to the notion that "the truth rarely catches up with a lie."* The problem for libel law, then, is how to protect reputation without squelching the potential of the Internet as a medium of public discourse [emphasis added].

These characteristics differentiate the publication of defamatory material on the Internet from publication in the more traditional forms of media, in my opinion.

It is true that in the modern era defamatory material may be communicated broadly and rapidly via other media as well. The international distribution of newspapers, syndicated wire services, facsimile transmissions, radio and satellite television broadcasting are but some examples. Nevertheless, Internet defamation is distinguished from its less pervasive cousins, in terms of its potential to damage the reputation of individuals and corporations, by the features described above, especially its interactive nature, its potential for being taken at face value, and its absolute and immediate worldwide ubiquity and accessibility. The mode and extent of publication is therefore a particularly significant consideration in assessing damages in Internet defamation cases.

Pro-C Ltd. v. Computer City, Inc., 1999 CanLII 14926 at paras. 1–3, 6–11, and 13 (ON S.C.):

The Internet, in reality a network of networks, has created a whole new territory independent of conventional geography. The conceptual location of this electronic interactivity available to us through our computers is oft referred to as "cyberspace." Unlike a "real" territory with fixed borders, the Internet is constantly growing and at a phenomenal rate.

The Internet has become an immense mass of information or data. Again, in contrast to a real territory, it is not mapped in the sense of its limits and features being charted. The cartographers of the net are the various directories and search engines, but they are hampered by the sheer immensity and growth rate of the Internet. The search for any "site" is keyword driven.

It is against this backdrop that Computer City, Inc. (Computer City) a Delaware corporation and a subsidiary of the Tandy Corporation launched a new line of personal computers called WINGEN on December 15, 1997.

WINGEN was registered in both the United States and Canada as a trade-mark for computer programs used to generate programs for Windows. The owner of the trade-mark is the plaintiff Pro-C Limited (Pro-C) who also registered the domain name *WINGEN.com*. Pro-C is a Waterloo, Ontario based company which merchandises software for software architects (persons who design software) and provides software consulting. The Computer City launch of its new product line was accompanied by various press releases, advertising in United States based newspapers, in-store advertising, and advertising at the Web site of Computer City (*www.computercity.com*).

. . .

The Internet is a network of networks accessible by computer. It is sometimes referred to as the worldwide web or simply "the web". Its growth to a large extent has been fuelled by the proliferation of computer use. Justice Peck in *Hearst Corp. v. Goldsberger,* U.S. Dist. Lexus 2065 (1997) (United States District Court for the Southern District of New York), at page 2 states that:

> In 1997 over 9.4 million computers, 60% of which are located in the United States, are estimated to be linked to the Internet. This does not count personal computers that people use to access the Internet using modems. Reasonable estimates are that as many as 40 million people around the world can and do access the Internet. That figure is expected to grow to 200 million Internet users by 1999.

The Internet was established approximately 25 years ago as a United States Defence Department project. It allows users to send e-mail documents, pictures and other data to other users. Each user has a domain name or address, which is the functional equivalent of a telephone number or a municipal address.

It is possible to have at a domain name a Web page which is essentially a file of stored data. A Web page can include printed matter, sound, pictures and links to other Web pages.

In an article entitled *Intellectual Property and the Internet in Canada 1998,* Donald Cameron describes a domain name registration process as follows:

> The National Science Foundation was until December 3, 1992 responsible for distributing domain names. On that date an agreement was entered into with a public company Network Solution Inc. (NSI) whereby NSI would act "as the clearing house" for domain names on the Internet. Before registering a new domain name, NSI merely checks to make sure the proposed domain site name is not already

registered as a domain name. As part of the domain name agreement, the applicant must state that to the best of his knowledge "the name does not infringe a trade-mark." [At page 49.]

Mr. Cameron advises that as of 1998 there were 4.8 million domain names registered worldwide increasing by 70,000 weekly.

Since its inception, commercial users on the Internet have grown. Web pages are used by companies to provide details about their organization and products or services. Greater detail is possible than with conventional hard copy advertisements.

. . . .

A helpful analysis of how one searches or "surfs" the Internet is contained in the following description provided by Justice R. Arcara of the United States District Court — Western District of New York in *OBH, Inc. and Columbia Insurance Co. v. Spotlight Magazine Inc. and Claude Tortora,* 86 F.Supp.2nd 176, [2000] U.S. Dist. Lexis 4462, pp. 8-9:

> Using a Web browser, such as Netscape's Navigator or Microsoft's Internet Explorer, an Internet user may navigate the Web—searching for, communicating with, and retrieving information from various web sites. *See Brookfield,* 174 F.3d at 1044 [citations omitted]. A specific web site is most easily located by using its domain name. *See Panavision,* 141 F.3d at 1327. Upon entering a domain name into the web browser, the corresponding web site will quickly appear on the computer screen. Sometimes, however, a user will not know the domain name of the site he or she is looking for, whereupon he or she has two principal options: trying to guess the domain name or seeking the assistance of an Internet "search engine." *Brookfield,* 1743d at 1044.
>
> Oftentimes, an Internet user will begin trying to guess at the domain name, especially if there is an obvious domain name to try. Users often assume, as a rule of thumb, that the domain name of a particular company will be the company name followed by ".com." *See id.* at 1045. For example, if a user wanted information about a Ford automobile, he or she could find such information at "ford.com." Sometimes, a trademark is better known than the company itself, in which case a user may assume that the domain address will be "'trademark'.com." *See id.* (citing *Beverly v. Network solutions, Inc.,* 1998 WL 320829, at 1 (N.D. Cal. June 12, 1998) ("Companies attempt to make the search for their web site as easy as possible. They do so by using a corporate name, trademark or service mark as their web site address.")). For instance, a

user seeking the Kentucky Fried Chicken web site might presume, correctly as it happens, that entering the address *www.KFC.com* will turn up a Kentucky Fried Chicken web site. Guessing domain names, however, is not an exact science. The user who assumes that "'X'.com" will always correspond to the web site of company X or trademark X will sometimes be misled. For example, one looking for information about Delta Airlines might sensibly try "delta.com." However, that domain name turns up a web site for Delta Financial Corporation, an unrelated company (Delta Airlines web site is actually "deltaairlines.com").

An Internet user's second option when he or she does not know the domain name is to utilize an Internet search engine, such as Yahoo, Altavista, or Lycos.

See id. [citations omitted]. When a keyword is entered, the search engine processes it through an index of web sites to generate a list relating to the entered keyword. Each search engine uses its own algorithm to arrange indexed materials in sequence, so the list of web sites that any particular set of keywords will bring up may differ depending on the search engine used. *See id.* [citations omitted].

Search engines look for keywords in places such as domain names, actual text on the web page, and metatags. Metatags are HTML code intended to describe the contents of the web site. There are different types of metatags, including "description" and "keyword" metatags. The description metatags are intended to describe the web site; the keyword metatags, at least in theory, contain keywords relating to the contents of the web site. The more often a term appears in the metatags and in the text of the web page, the more likely it is that the web page will be "hit" in a search for that keyword and the higher, on the list of "hits" the web page will appear.

. . .

Given the current state of search engine technology, that search will often produce a list of hundreds of web sites through which the user must sort in order to find what he or she is looking for. As a result, companies strongly prefer that their domain name be comprised of the company or brand trademark and the suffix ".com".

Sporty's Farm, 2000 WL 124389, at ˙1.

Because a particular domain name can only identify one web site, just as a particular mailing address can only identify one physical location, a company that owns an intuitive domain name owns a potentially valuable asset, as ownership of such a name makes it more likely that users will be able to accurately guess its web site address and visit its corporate web site rather than the web site of a competitor. The value of this intuitive name is magnified by the fact that there is no exhaustive, central listing of Internet domain names equivalent to a telephone book. *See Washington Speakers Bureau,* 33 F. Supp.2d at 499 [citations omitted].

It should also be noted that there are varying degrees of interactivity amongst Web sites or pages. An interactive site will allow the user to exchange information with the host computer. Orders can be placed, paid for by the provision of a credit card number, and a product or services shipped to the address of the purchaser. A passive Web site in contrast merely posts information on the Web page and has no interactive component.

BCAA et al. v. Office and Professional Employees' Int. Union et al., 2001 BCSC 156 at para. 16:

The internet is an international network of computers that communicate with each other according to certain protocols. Every computer participating in the internet is assigned a particular alpha-numerical address that has no other meaning in any human language (an "Internet Protocol Address").

Australia

Dow Jones and Company Inc v. Gutnick, [2002] HCA 56, 210 C.L.R. 575, 194 A.L.R. 433, 77 A.L.J.R. 255 at paras. 14–16 and 78–92:

One witness called by Dow Jones, Dr Clarke, described the Internet as "a telecommunications network that links other telecommunication networks." In his opinion, it is unlike any technology that has preceded it. The key differences identified by Dr Clarke included that the Internet "enables intercommunication using multiple data-formats . . . among an unprecedented number of people using an unprecedented number of devices [and] among people and devices without geographic limitation".

The World Wide Web is but one particular service available over the Internet. It enables a document to be stored in such a way on one computer connected to the Internet that a person using another computer connected to the Internet can request and receive a copy of the document. As Dr Clarke said, the terms conventionally used to refer to the materials that are transmitted in this way are a "document" or a "web page" and a collection of web pages is usually referred to as a "web site." A computer that makes documents available runs software that is referred to as a "web server"; a computer that requests and receives documents runs software that is referred to as a "web browser."

The originator of a document wishing to make it available on the World Wide Web arranges for it to be placed in a storage area managed by a web server. This process is conventionally referred to as "uploading." A person wishing to have access to that document must issue a request to the relevant server nominating the location of the web page identified by its "uniform resource locator (URL)." When the server delivers the document in response to the request the process is conventionally referred to as "downloading."

. . .

The Internet: The history of the Internet, its ubiquity, universality and utility have been described in the reasons of many courts in the United Kingdom, the United States, Canada, Australia and elsewhere. In the expert evidence before the primary judge in this case, there was no relevant dispute about the main features of the Internet and of the World Wide Web specifically. Some additional evidence relevant to those features was placed before this Court, without objection, in support of the application of a number of organisations which were granted leave to intervene. Although the supporting affidavits were not part of the record in the appeal, and cannot be so treated, most of the features of the Internet there described confirm the evidence given at trial. They are, in any case, readily ascertainable from standard works that describe the Internet's basic elements.

It is important to consider these features because they afford the foothold for the appellant's argument that the Internet is such a new and different medium of human communication that it demands a radical reconceptualisation of the applicable common law, specifically with respect to the tort of defamation.

It has been estimated that, by the end of 2002, the number of Internet users will reach 655 million. The number continues to grow exponentially. It is estimated that in some countries, the number of users doubles every six months. The Internet is essentially a decentralised, self-maintained telecommunications network. It is made up of inter-linking small networks from all parts of the world. It is ubiquitous, borderless, global and ambient in its nature. Hence the term "cyberspace." This is a word that recognises that the interrelationships created by the Internet exist outside conventional geographic boundaries and comprise a single interconnected body of data, potentially amounting to a single body of knowledge. The Internet is accessible in virtually all places on Earth where access can be obtained either by wire connection or by wireless (including satellite) links. Effectively, the only constraint on access to the Internet is possession of the means of securing connection to a telecommunications system and possession of the basic hardware.

The World Wide Web: The Web is a forum consisting of millions of individual "sites". Each site contains information provided by, or to, the creator of that site. When a publisher of information and opinion wishes to make its content available on the Web, it commonly does so by creating a "website" and "posting" information to that site. Such a website is a collection of electronic messages maintained on a type of computer known as a "web server." Typically, this is controlled either by the publisher concerned or by a third party contracted by the publisher to provide "web hosting" services.

An Internet user may access the information maintained on a website provided the user knows, or can ascertain, the Internet address of the relevant website. By entering that address into the user's web browser, the user will be directed to that website. Once the user locates the website in this way, the user may be required to take additional steps to access information stored on the web server associated with the website. Thus, to post an article to a website, a publisher must prepare a version in digital (computer readable) format. Such an article becomes part of the digital collection of data known as a web page. Such a web page is transmitted to a web server. It, along with the other web pages, comprises the website.

By posting information on a website, the publisher makes the content available to anyone, anywhere, having access to the Web. However, accessibility will depend on whether there is open access (under which any web user can access the site); subscription access (under which only web users who register, and commonly pay, for the service can secure access); combination access (where only a portion of a site may be accessed after registration and/or payment of a fee) and restricted access (access limited to specified users authorised by the website operator to view the website, eg employees of a particular company).

Difficulty of controlling access: The nature of the Web makes it impossible to ensure with complete effectiveness the isolation of any geographic area on the Earth's surface from access to a particular website. Visitors to a website automatically reveal their Internet Provider ("IP") address. This is a numerical code that identifies every computer that logs onto the Internet. The visitor may also disclose certain information about the type of browser and computer that the visitor uses. The IP addresses of users are generally assigned to them by an Internet Service Provider ("ISP"). The user's IP address will remain the same whenever and wherever the user "surfs" the Web. But some ISPs do not assign a permanent IP address. Instead, they assign a new IP address every time a user logs onto the Web. Because of these features, there is presently no effective way for a website operator to determine, in every case, the geographic origin of the Internet user seeking access to the website.

For similar reasons, with respect to subscription accounts, checking the issuing location of a credit card provided by a user would not afford a universally reliable means of ascertaining the geographic location of a user seeking access to a website. Thus, even assuming that a geographic restriction could be introduced isolating Australia (and hence Victoria) by reference to the origin of the visitor's credit card, a resident of Australia with a credit card issued by a United States bank, would be able to access sites that might be denied to an Australian resident with an Australian credit card, although both users were physically located in Australia.

In addition to these difficulties of controlling access to a website by reference to geographic, national and subnational boundaries, the Internet has recently witnessed a rapid growth of technologies ("anonymising technologies") that enable Internet users to mask their identities (and locations). By reason of these developments, the provision of cost effective, practical and reliable identity verification systems, that could afford a universally reliable recognition of the point of origin of an Internet user, has not emerged. This is why the nature of Internet technology itself makes it virtually impossible, or prohibitively difficult, cumbersome and costly, to prevent the content of a given website from being accessed in specific legal jurisdictions when an Internet user in such jurisdictions seeks to do so. In effect, once information is posted on the Internet, it is usually accessible to all Internet users everywhere in the world. Even if the correct jurisdiction of an Internet user could be ascertained accurately, there is presently no adequate technology that would enable non-subscription content providers to isolate and exclude all access to all users in specified jurisdictions.

These special features of the Internet present peculiar difficulties for the legal regulation of its content and, specifically, for the exclusion of access in defined jurisdictions. Such difficulties may have a bearing on the question of whether a particular jurisdiction has an advantage in regulating content published and accessed on the Internet. This does not mean (and no party before the Court suggested) that the Internet is, or should be, a law-free zone. However, in considering what the law, and specifically the common law of Australia, should say in relation to the contents of the Internet, particularly with respect to allegedly defamatory material on a website, the appellant argued that regard had to be taken of these elementary practical features of the technology.

Novel features of the Web: The crucial attributes, so it was said, include the explosion in the availability of readily accessible information to hundreds of millions of people everywhere, with the consequent enhancement of human knowledge, and the beneficial contribution to human freedom and access to information about the world's peoples and their diverse lives and viewpoints that the Internet makes available, thereby contributing to human understanding. It was argued that the law should generally facilitate and encourage such advances, not attempt to restrict or impede them by inconsistent and ineffective, or only partly effective, interventions, for fear of interrupting the benefit that the Internet has already brought and the greater benefits that its continued expansion promises.

This Court has made reference to the fact that modern development in mass communications and particularly the electronic media may influence the continued relevance or reformulation of established legal principles. The appellant contested the respondent's suggestion that the Internet was merely the latest of many technologies that have enhanced the spread of information. It submitted that the Internet involved a quantum leap of technological capacity and the ubiquitous availability of information that demanded a root and branch revision of some of the earlier legal rules in order to take into account the Internet's special features.

The appellant accepted that it was requesting this Court to take a large step in re-expressing the principles of the common law. However, it argued that the Court should seek a bold solution because of the revolutionary character of the technology that had produced the need to do so. Because the common law adapts even to radically different environments, this Court was asked to be no less bold than the technologists who had invented and developed the Internet. We were reminded of Judge Learned Hand's observation:

> The respect all men feel in some measure for customary law lies deep in their nature; we accept the verdict of the past until the need for change cries out loudly enough to force upon us a choice between the comforts of further inertia and the irksomeness of action.

In *Theophanous v Herald and Weekly Times Limited*, Brennan J, citing these remarks, noticed that some judges "find the call to reform more urgent." In the context of the development of the Internet, the unique features that I have described and the many beneficial advantages which I acknowledge, I am one of those to whom Brennan J referred.

The idea that this Court should solve the present problem by reference to judicial remarks in England in a case, decided more than a hundred and fifty years ago, involving the conduct of the manservant of a Duke, despatched to procure a back issue of a newspaper of minuscule circulation, is not immediately appealing to me. The genius of the common law derives from its capacity to adapt the principles of past decisions, by analogical reasoning, to the resolution of entirely new and unforeseen problems. When the new problem is as novel, complex and global as that presented by the Internet in this appeal, a greater sense of legal imagination may be required than is ordinarily called for. Yet the question remains whether it can be provided, conformably with established law and with the limited functions of a court under the Australian constitution to develop and re-express the law.

US

Reno v. ACLU, 521 U.S. 844 (1997) at paras. 17–24:

The Internet is an international network of interconnected computers. It is the outgrowth of what began in 1969 as a military program called "ARPANET," which was designed to enable computers operated by the military, defense contractors, and universities conducting defense related research to communicate with one another by redundant channels even if some portions of the network were damaged in a war. While the ARPANET no longer exists, it provided an example for the development of a number of civilian networks that, eventually linking with each other, now enable tens of millions of people to communicate with one another and to access vast amounts of information from around the world. The Internet is "a unique and wholly new medium of worldwide human communication."

The Internet has experienced "extraordinary growth." The number of "host" computers — those that store information and relay communications — increased from about 300 in 1981 to approximately 9,400,000 by the time of the trial in 1996. Roughly 60% of these hosts are located in the United States. About 40 million people used the Internet at the time of trial, a number that is expected to mushroom to 200 million by 1999.

Individuals can obtain access to the Internet from many different sources, generally hosts themselves or entities with a host affiliation. Most colleges and universities provide access for their students and faculty; many corporations provide their employees with access through an office network; many communities and local libraries provide free access; and an increasing number of storefront "computer coffee shops" provide access for a small hourly fee. Several major national "online services" such as America Online, CompuServe, the Microsoft Network, and Prodigy offer access to their own extensive proprietary networks as well as a link to the much larger resources of the Internet. These commercial online services had almost 12 million individual subscribers at the time of trial.

Anyone with access to the Internet may take advantage of a wide variety of communication and information retrieval methods. These methods are constantly evolving and difficult to categorize precisely. But, as presently constituted, those most relevant to this case are electronic mail ("e mail"), automatic mailing list services ("mail exploders," sometimes referred to as "listservs"), "newsgroups," "chat rooms," and the "World Wide Web." All of these methods can be used to transmit text; most can transmit sound, pictures, and moving video images. Taken together, these tools constitute a unique medium — known to its users as "cyberspace" — located in no particular geographical location but available to anyone, anywhere in the world, with access to the Internet.

E mail enables an individual to send an electronic message — generally akin to a note or letter — to another individual or to a group of addressees. The message is generally stored electronically, sometimes waiting for the recipient to check her "mailbox" and sometimes making its receipt known through some type of prompt. A mail exploder is a sort of e mail group. Subscribers can send messages to a common e mail address, which then forwards the message to the group's other subscribers. Newsgroups also serve groups of regular participants, but these postings may be read by others as well. There are thousands of such groups, each serving to foster an exchange of information or opinion on a particular topic running the gamut from, say, the music of Wagner to Balkan politics to AIDS prevention to the Chicago Bulls. About 100,000 new messages are posted every day. In most newsgroups, postings are automatically purged at regular intervals. In addition to posting a message that can be read later, two or more individuals wishing to communicate more immediately can enter a chat room to engage in real time dialogue — in other words, by typing messages to one another that appear almost immediately on the others' computer screens. The District Court found that at any given time "tens of thousands of users are engaging in conversations on a huge range of subjects." It is "no exaggeration to conclude that the content on the Internet is as diverse as human thought."

The best known category of communication over the Internet is the World Wide Web, which allows users to search for and retrieve information stored in remote computers, as well as, in some cases, to communicate back to designated sites. In concrete terms, the Web consists of a vast number of documents stored in different computers all over the world. Some of these documents are simply files containing information. However, more elaborate documents, commonly known as Web "pages," are also prevalent. Each has its own address — "rather like a telephone number." Web pages frequently contain information and sometimes allow the viewer to communicate with the page's (or "site's") author. They generally also contain "links" to other documents created by that site's author or to other (generally) related sites. Typically, the links are either blue or underlined text — sometimes images.

Navigating the Web is relatively straightforward. A user may either type the address of a known page or enter one or more keywords into a commercial "search engine" in an effort to locate sites on a subject of interest. A particular Web page may contain the information sought by the "surfer," or, through its links, it may be an avenue to other documents located anywhere on the Internet. Users generally explore a given Web page, or move to another, by clicking a computer "mouse" on one of the page's icons or links. Access to most Web pages is freely available, but some allow access only to those who have purchased the right from a commercial provider. The Web is thus comparable, from the readers' viewpoint, to both a vast library including millions of readily available and indexed publications and a sprawling mall offering goods and services.

From the publishers' point of view, it constitutes a vast platform from which to address and hear from a world wide audience of millions of readers, viewers, researchers, and buyers. Any person or organization with a computer connected to the Internet can "publish" information. Publishers include government agencies, educational institutions, commercial entities, advocacy groups, and individuals. Publishers may either make their material available to the entire pool of Internet users, or confine access to a selected group, such as those willing to pay for the privilege. "No single organization controls any membership in the Web, nor is there any centralized point from which individual Web sites or services can be blocked from the Web." [Footnotes omitted.]

Reno v. ACLU, 521 U.S. 844 (1997) at paras. 91–94:

The Court in *Ginsberg* concluded that the New York law created a constitutionally adequate adult zone simply because, on its face, it denied access only to minors. The Court did not question — and therefore necessarily assumed — that an adult zone, once created, would succeed in preserving adults' access while denying minors' access to the regulated speech. Before today, there was no reason to question this assumption, for the Court has previously only considered laws that operated in the physical world, a world that with two characteristics that make it possible to create "adult zones": geography and identity. See Lessig, Reading the Constitution in Cyberspace,

45 Emory L. J. 869, 886 (1996). A minor can see an adult dance show only if he enters an establishment that provides such entertainment. And should he attempt to do so, the minor will not be able to conceal completely his identity (or, consequently, his age). Thus, the twin characteristics of geography and identity enable the establishment's proprietor to prevent children from entering the establishment, but to let adults inside.

The electronic world is fundamentally different. Because it is no more than the interconnection of electronic pathways, cyberspace allows speakers and listeners to mask their identities. Cyberspace undeniably reflects some form of geography; chat rooms and Web sites, for example, exist at fixed "locations" on the Internet. Since users can transmit and receive messages on the Internet without revealing anything about their identities or ages, see Lessig, *supra*, at 901, however, it is not currently possible to exclude persons from accessing certain messages on the basis of their identity.

Cyberspace differs from the physical world in another basic way: Cyberspace is malleable. Thus, it is possible to construct barriers in cyberspace and use them to screen for identity, making cyberspace more like the physical world and, consequently, more amenable to zoning laws. This transformation of cyberspace is already underway. Lessig, *supra*, at 888–889. *Id.*, at 887 (cyberspace "is moving . . . from a relatively unzoned place to a universe that is extraordinarily well zoned"). Internet speakers (users who post material on the Internet) have begun to zone cyberspace itself through the use of "gateway" technology. Such technology requires Internet users to enter information about themselves — perhaps an adult identification number or a credit card number — before they can access certain areas of cyberspace, 929 F. Supp. 824, 845 (ED Pa. 1996), much like a bouncer checks a person's driver's license before admitting him to a nightclub. Internet users who access information have not attempted to zone cyberspace itself, but have tried to limit their own power to access information in cyberspace, much as a parent controls what her children watch on television by installing a lock box. This user based zoning is accomplished through the use of screening software (such as Cyber Patrol or SurfWatch) or browsers with screening capabilities, both of which search addresses and text for keywords that are associated with "adult" sites and, if the user wishes, blocks access to such sites. *Id.*, at 839–842. The Platform for Internet Content Selection (PICS) project is designed to facilitate user based zoning by encouraging Internet speakers to rate the content of their speech using codes recognized by all screening programs. *Id.*, at 838–839.

Despite this progress, the transformation of cyberspace is not complete. Although gateway technology has been available on the World Wide

Web for some time now, *id.*, at 845; *Shea v. Reno*, 930 F. Supp. 916, 933–934 (SDNY 1996), it is not available to all Web speakers, 929 F. Supp., at 845–846, and is just now becoming technologically feasible for chat rooms and USE-NETnewsgroups, *Brief for Federal Parties* 37–38. Gateway technology is not ubiquitous in cyberspace, and because without it "there is no means of age verification," cyberspace still remains largely unzoned — and unzoneable. 929 F. Supp., at 846; *Shea, supra*, at 934. User based zoning is also in its infancy. For it to be effective, (i) an agreed upon code (or "tag") would have to exist; (ii) screening software or browsers with screening capabilities would have to be able to recognize the "tag"; and (iii) those programs would have to be widely available — and widely used — by Internet users. At present, none of these conditions is true. Screening software "is not in wide use today" and "only a handful of browsers have screening capabilities." *Shea, supra*, at 945–946. There is, moreover, no agreed upon "tag" for those programs to recognize. 929 F. Supp., at 848; *Shea, supra*, at 945.

INTERNET SERVICE PROVIDER (ISP)

Canada

Intranet Technologies Inc. v. NTG International Inc., 1996 CanLII 8193, [1996] O.J. No. 3808, 17 O.T.C. 388, 70 C.P.R. (3d) 172, 66 A.C.W.S. (3d) 950 at para. 5 (S.C.J.):

Mr. Hollister describes the activities of the plaintiff company as follows:

1) It provides ISP (internet service provider) services (that is, it facilitates connectivity and acts as a gateway to the internet for individual and multiple clients);
2) It designs world wide web pages;
3) It has developed and markets in Ontario, an easy to use software package for using the internet, called "Internet in Minutes."

UK

Pitman Training Ltd & Anor v. Nominet UK & Anor, [1997] EWHC Ch 367:

A Service Provider is a company whose business it is to arrange access to the Internet for its customers. A charge is naturally made for this service. The Service Provider can provide the customer with the facilities the customer needs in order to get connected to the Internet. It can obtain for the customer a domain name and e-mail facilities and set up a web site for the customer.

I-Way Ltd & Anor v. World Online Telecom & Ors, [2004] EWHC 244 (Comm) at
   para. 18:

A company which enables customers to access the internet through their
home PCs is known as an "internet service provider" (thus "ISP"). Certain
equipment is required in order to provide such access, primarily modems
and computers. The equipment owned by an ISP which enables customers to
access the internet is referred to collectively as its "platform" or its "server."
Localtel did not own such a platform. In order to provide internet access to
its customers, therefore, Localtel had to conclude an agreement with an ISP
whereby that ISP would make its platform available to Localtel's customers
for the purpose of accessing the internet.

INTERMEDIARY

Canada

*Society of Composers, Authors and Music Publishers of Canada v. Canadian Assn.
   of Internet Providers*, 2004 SCC 45, [2004] 2 S.C.R. 427 at paras. 92, 95, and 98
   (note: the reference to s. 2.4(1)(b) is to the *Copyright Act*, R.S.C. 1985, c. C-42):

Section 2.4(1)(b) shields from liability the activities associated with providing
the means for another to communicate by telecommunication. "The 'means,'
as the Board found, ". . . are not limited to routers and other hardware. They
include all software connection equipment, connectivity services, hosting and
other facilities and services without which such communications would not
occur" (p. 452). I agree. So long as an Internet intermediary does not itself engage
in acts that relate to the content of the communication, i.e., whose participation
is content neutral, but confines itself to providing "a conduit" for information
communicated by others, then it will fall within s. 2.4(1)(b). The appellants
support this result on a general theory of "Don't shoot the messenger!"

   . . .

   This conclusion, as I understand it, is based on the findings of fact by the
Board of what an Internet intermediary, including a host server provider,
actually does. To the extent they act as innocent disseminators, they are protected by s. 2.4(1)(b) of the Act. As the Board put it, at p. 452:

   As long as its role in respect of any given transmission is limited to providing the means necessary to allow data initiated by other persons to be
transmitted over the Internet, and as long as the ancillary services it provides
fall short of involving the act of communicating the work or authorizing its
communication, it should be allowed to claim the exemption.

I agree with this approach. Having properly instructed itself on the law, the Board found as a fact that the "conduit" begins with the host server. No reason has been shown in this application for judicial review to set aside that conclusion.

. . . .

Similarly, the European E-Commerce Directive provides, in clause 42 of its Preamble, that Internet intermediaries are not liable where their actions are confined to

> the technical process of operating and giving access to a communication network over which information made available by third parties is transmitted or temporarily stored, for the sole purpose of making the transmission more efficient; this activity is of a mere technical, automatic and passive nature, which implies that the [Internet intermediary] has neither knowledge of nor control over the information which is transmitted or stored.

HYPERLINK

Canada

Society of Composers, Authors and Music Publishers of Canada v. Canadian Assn. of Internet Providers, 2004 SCC 45, [2004] 2 S.C.R. 427 at para. 25:

The Board was also required to consider the potential copyright infringement of "hyperlinks," particularly when the link is automatic. Automatic links employ an embedded code in the Web page that automatically instructs the browser, upon obtaining access to the first site, to download a file from a second site. The user does not need to do anything but visit the initial site before information from the second site is "pulled." A different legal issue may arise where the user must take action, such as to click the mouse button over the hyperlink, in order to obtain access to the information from the second site.

Dell Computer Corp. v. Union des consommateurs, 2007 SCC 34, [2007] 2 S.C.R. 801 at para. 97:

A Web page may contain many links, each of which leads in turn to a new Web page that may itself contain many more links, and so on. Obviously, it cannot be argued that all these different but interlinked pages constitute a single document, or that the entire Web, as it scrolls down a user's screen, is just one document. However, it is difficult to accept that the need for a single command by the user would be sufficient for a finding that the provision governing external clauses is applicable. Such an interpretation would be inconsistent with the reality of the Internet environment, where no real distinction is made between scrolling through a document and using a hyperlink. Analogously to paper documents, some Web documents contain several pages that can be accessed only by means of hyperlinks, whereas others can be viewed by scrolling down them on the computer's screen. There is no reason to favour one configuration over the other. To determine whether clauses on the Internet are external clauses, therefore, it is necessary to consider another rule that, although not expressly mentioned in art. 1435 C.C.Q., is implied by it.

US

Intermatic Inc. v. Toeppen, 947 F. Supp. 1227 (ND Ill. 1996) at 1232:

A hyperlink is a link from one site on the Internet to a second site on the Internet. "Clicking" on a designated space on the initial page which references the subsequent site by a picture, by some highlighted text or by some other indication will take a person viewing the initial web page to a second page. In addition to their use in indexes, hyperlinks are commonly placed on existing web pages, thus allowing Internet users to move from web page to web page at the click of a button, without having to type in URLs.

Hyperlinks can be and commonly are established without reference to the domain name of the second site. A hyperlink for the Champaign-Urbana map page might be a picture of a map or a statement such as "a map of Champaign-Urbana" or, more simply, "Champaign-Urbana." A hyperlink is not technically related to a domain name and therefore it can be identical to an existing domain name without conflicting with that domain name. For example, were Intermatic to establish an Intermatic home page at http: www. xyz.com, any number of indexes could be employed and hyperlinks could be established to bring up the page through use of the word INTERMATIC.

Tom Hayes, *Jump Point* (New York: McGraw-Hill, 2008) at 109:

The personal computer, mobile phone, and Internet make all the headlines, but I predict hyperlinks will be remembered as among the most culturally significant innovations of our time.

Hyperlinks, or simply links, are navigational elements within electronic documents that take the user from one reference or document to another. This journey from one point to another one can take us in an infinite number of directions in pursuit of a train of thought or the right information. There is an element of discovery and serendipity to the use of links. You never know where the process of exploration will take you: you may be but one click away from adventure.

What are the implications? People of the Western world learn to read left to right, up to down. People in the East are taught to read right to left, down to up. Either way, from our earliest days forward we have been trained to process information sequentially, from start to finish, rudimentary to complex, from A to B to C, and so on. Essentially, we have all been taught to be linear thinkers.

Since the arrival of the hyperlinked internet, people increasingly are becoming nonlinear thinkers. Our brains have been retrained to find information and process it differently than those of the hunt and peck, assembly-line, Dewey Decimal System past. Naturally, this reprogramming shapes and informs our communications, our work, and even our world view. Instead of drilling down a single path, Web users today are more likely to let the information trail lead where it will. And with an array of tools to mark or "tag" their paths, we are prone to set ourselves free to stumble upon new things, new ideas, and never-before-imagined places. And, we are more likely to share our findings with others, as well as take the counsel of our fellow travellers.

Hyperlinks make people less predictable, their behaviour less formulaic and reckonable. And that reality is already shaking up the young Web world. Whereas great fortunes have been amassed by the Yahoo!s and Googles because they brought order to the linear world of Web search, the emphasis is now on discovery, not search.

Discovery is a decidedly nonlinear process. When consumers adopt a discovery mindset, contextual, see-and-say advertising strategies break down. The inline shopper who follows a link to a jewellery offer may be just a few clicks away from buying a car. And as consumers realize the power of discovery, they are more likely to become more elusive and intractable in their behaviour.

And there are broader cultural implications to this nonlinearity as well, such as a greater acceptance of ambiguity and a tolerance for failure. The social acceptability of experimentation and failure, have long been tenets of Silicon Valley culture. Indeed, it would be difficult to imagine any of the iconic brands we know today were it not for the freedom to fail in Silicon Valley and places like it.

Philip M. Parker, *Hyperlink: Webster's Timeline History 1965–2007* (San Diego: Icon Group International, 2009) at 5:

Hyperlink: The term "hyperlink" was coined in 1965 (or possibly 1964) by Theodor Nelson at the start of Project Xanadu. Nelson had been inspired by "As We May Think," a popular essay by Vannevar Bush. In the essay, Bush described a microfilm-based machine in which one could link any two pages of information and then scroll back and forth among pages in a trail as if they were on a single microfilm reel. The closest contemporary analogy would be to build a list of bookmarks to topically related Web pages and then allow the user to scroll forward and backward through the list.

META TAGS

Canada

BCAA et al. v. Office and Professional Employees' Int. Union et al., 2001 BCSC 156 at paras. 32–33:

A meta tag is part of a website not automatically displayed on the user's computer screen in the normal course of viewing a website. A meta tag is put on the website by the website owner to provide key information about the website. Through the use of meta tags, a website creator can describe what is available at that particular site or insert any other information. A meta tag is written in HTML.

When search engines gather information they seek out and obtain the information in the meta tags. Meta tags are used by most search engines and directories to gather information, index a website and match the website to the key words in a user's query. This generates search results corresponding to the user's query. It is common to use meta tags to specify key words that will be matched to key words entered by someone conducting a search.

METHODS TO COMMUNICATE OVER THE INTERNET

US

ACLU v. Reno, 929 F. Supp 824 (ED Pa. 1996) at paras. 22–32:

Once one has access to the Internet, there are a wide variety of different methods of communication and information exchange over the network. These many methods of communication and information retrieval are constantly evolving and are therefore difficult to categorize concisely. The most common methods of communications on the Internet (as well as within the major online services) can be roughly grouped into six categories:

(1) one-to-one messaging (such as "e-mail"),

(2) one-to-many messaging (such as "listserv"),

(3) distributed message databases (such as "USENET newsgroups"),

(4) real time communication (such as "Internet Relay Chat"),

(5) real time remote computer utilization (such as "telnet"), and

(6) remote information retrieval (such as "ftp," "gopher," and the "World Wide Web").

Most of these methods of communication can be used to transmit text, data, computer programs, sound, visual images (i.e., pictures), and moving video images.

One-to-one messaging. One method of communication on the Internet is via electronic mail, or "e-mail," comparable in principle to sending a first class letter. One can address and transmit a message to one or more other people. E-mail on the Internet is not routed through a central control point, and can take many and varying paths to the recipients. Unlike postal mail, simple e-mail generally is not "sealed" or secure, and can be accessed or viewed on intermediate computers between the sender and recipient (unless the message is encrypted).

One-to-many messaging. The Internet also contains automatic mailing list services (such as "listservs"), [also referred to by witnesses as "mail exploders"] that allow communications about particular subjects of interest to a group of people. For example, people can subscribe to a "listserv" mailing list on a particular topic of interest to them. The subscriber can submit messages on the topic to the listserv that are forwarded (via e-mail), either automatically or through a human moderator overseeing the listserv, to anyone who has subscribed to the mailing list. A recipient of such a message can reply to the message and have the reply also distributed to everyone on the mailing list. This service provides the capability to keep abreast of developments or events in a particular subject area. Most listserv-type mailing lists automatically forward all incoming messages to all mailing list subscribers. There are thousands of such mailing list services on the Internet, collectively with hundreds of thousands of subscribers. Users of "open" listservs typically can add or remove their names from the mailing list automatically, with no direct human involvement. Listservs may also be "closed," i.e., only allowing for one's acceptance into the listserv by a human moderator.

Distributed message databases. Similar in function to listservs — but quite different in how communications are transmitted — are distributed message databases such as "USENET newsgroups." User-sponsored newsgroups are among the most popular and widespread applications of Internet services, and cover all imaginable topics of interest to users. Like listservs, newsgroups are open discussions and exchanges on particular topics. Users, however, need not subscribe to the discussion mailing list in advance, but can instead access the database at any time. Some USENET newsgroups are "moderated" but most are open access. For the moderated newsgroups, all messages to the newsgroup are forwarded to one person who can screen them for relevance to the topics under discussion. USENET newsgroups are disseminated using *ad hoc*, peer to peer connections between approximately 200,000 computers (called USENET "servers") around the world. For unmoderated newsgroups, when an individual user with access to a USENET server posts a message to a newsgroup, the message is automatically forwarded to all adjacent USENET servers that furnish access to the newsgroup, and it is then propagated to the servers adjacent to those servers, etc. The messages are temporarily stored on each receiving server, where they are available for review and response by individual users. The messages are automatically and periodically purged from each system after a time to make room for new messages. Responses to messages, like the original messages, are automatically distributed to all other computers receiving the newsgroup or forwarded to a moderator in the case of a moderated newsgroup. The dissemination of messages to USE-NET servers around the world is an automated process that does not require direct human intervention or review.

There are newsgroups on more than fifteen thousand different subjects. In 1994, approximately 70,000 messages were posted to newsgroups each day, and those messages were distributed to the approximately 190,000 computers or computer networks that participate in the USENET newsgroup system. Once the messages reach the approximately 190,000 receiving computers or computer networks, they are available to individual users of those computers or computer networks. Collectively, almost 100,000 new messages (or "articles") are posted to newsgroups each day.

Real time communication. In addition to transmitting messages that can be later read or accessed, individuals on the Internet can engage in an immediate dialog, in "real time," with other people on the Internet. In its simplest forms, "talk" allows one-to-one communications and "Internet Relay Chat" (or IRC) allows two or more to type messages to each other that almost immediately appear on the others' computer screens. IRC is analogous to a telephone party line, using a computer and keyboard rather than a telephone. With IRC, however, at any one time there are thousands of different party lines available, in which collectively tens of thousands of users are engaging in conversations on a huge range of subjects. Moreover, one can create a new party line to discuss a different topic at any time. Some IRC conversations are "moderated" or include "channel operators."

In addition, commercial online services such as America Online, CompuServe, the Microsoft Network, and Prodigy have their own "chat" systems allowing their members to converse.

Real time remote computer utilization. Another method to use information on the Internet is to access and control remote computers in "real time" using "telnet." For example, using telnet, a researcher at a university would be able to use the computing power of a supercomputer located at a different university. A student can use telnet to connect to a remote library to access the library's online card catalog program.

Remote information retrieval. The final major category of communication may be the most well known use of the Internet — the search for and retrieval of information located on remote computers. There are three primary methods to locate and retrieve information on the Internet.

A simple method uses "ftp" (or file transfer protocol) to list the names of computer files available on a remote computer, and to transfer one or more of those files to an individual's local computer.

Another approach uses a program and format named "gopher" to guide an individual's search through the resources available on a remote computer.

MYSPACE

US

Doe v. MySpace, Inc., 528 F.3d 413 (5th Cir. 2008) at 415–16:

MySpace.com is a Web-based social network. Online social networking is the practice of using a Web site or other interactive computer service to expand one's business or social network. Social networking on MySpace.com begins with a member's creation of an online profile that serves as a medium for personal expression, and can contain such items as photographs, videos, and other information about the member that he or she chooses to share with other MySpace.com users. Members have complete discretion regarding the amount and type of information that is included in a personal profile. Members over the age of sixteen can choose the degree of privacy they desire regarding their profile; that is, they determine who among the MySpace.com membership is allowed to view their profile. Once a profile has been created, the member can use it to extend "invitations" to existing friends who are also MySpace.com users and to communicate with those friends online by linking to their profiles, or using e-mail, instant messaging, and blogs, all of which are hosted through the MySpace.com platform.

Members can also meet new people at MySpace.com through user groups focused on common interests such as film, travel, music, or politics. MySpace.com has a browser feature that allows members to search the Web site's membership using criteria such as geographic location or specific interests. MySpace.com members can also become online "friends" with celebrities, musicians, or politicians who have created MySpace.com profiles to publicize their work and to interface with fans and supporters.

MySpace.com membership is free to all who agree to the Terms of Use. To establish a profile, users must represent that they are at least fourteen years of age. The profiles of members who are aged fourteen and fifteen are automatically set to "private" by default, in order to limit the amount of personal information that can be seen on the member's profile by MySpace.com users who are not in their existing friends network and to prevent younger teens from being contacted by users they do not know. Although MySpace. com employs a computer program designed to search for clues that under-age members have lied about their age to create a profile on the Web site, no current technology is foolproof. All members are cautioned regarding the type of information they release to other users on the Web site, including a specific prohibition against posting personal information such as telephone numbers, street addresses, last names, or e-mail addresses. MySpace. com members are also encouraged to report inaccurate, inappropriate, or obscene material to the Web site's administrators.

UK

Dearlove (t/a and Professionally Known as "Diddy") v. Combs (t/a and Professionally Known as "Sean 'Puffy' Combs", "Puffy" and "P.Diddy"), [2007] EWHC 375 at paras. 28–29 (Ch.):

MySpace is something of an online cultural phenomenon. It describes itself as a social networking service that allows members to create personal profiles online in order to find and communicate with old and new friends. Members are able to maintain web-pages accessible by members of the public and which contain photographs, music, videos and text. MySpace is now widely used by artists as a way of promoting and marketing their music following the enormous success of bands launched largely through MySpace, such as the Arctic Monkeys and Lily Allen.

YouTube is in some ways similar to MySpace, but concentrates on allowing users to share and view video footage online. It originally started as a personal video sharing service but, like MySpace, is now used by artists as a way of promoting their recordings and performances. As Mr Calvert accepts, YouTube is a valuable promotional and marketing tool for many current music artists. Indeed, it is one of the fastest growing websites on the Internet. As of July 2006, one hundred million clips were viewed daily on YouTube, with an additional sixty five thousand new videos uploaded every 24 hours. The site has almost 20 million visitors each month. YouTube commands up to 64% of the UK online video market.

SEARCH ENGINES AND SEARCH DIRECTORIES

Canada

BCAA et al. v. Office and Professional Employees' Int. Union et al., 2001 BCSC 156 at paras. 25–31 :

A search engine uses specialised computer programs sometimes called "spiders" or "crawlers" to electronically visit websites, gather relevant data about those websites, and compile and index the information.

Directories only list information about websites that is intentionally entered into the directory. A business may register information about its website with a directory.

To use a directory or search engine, the computer user must access the website of a directory or search engine. There the computer user will find a space in which a search query can be entered, usually one or more key words. When a search is activated using a search engine or a directory, the search engine then compares the words used in the search query with information stored and indexed by the search engine or directory and ranks stored data about web pages according to relevance established by reference to the key words entered in the search. Relevance is determined in various ways, including the frequency matching key words appear on the webpage and the particular location of matching key words on a webpage.

Based upon its own program for ranking websites according to search queries, each search engine and directory will generate the search results, which are a list of websites. These results are displayed. The search engine or directory is programmed to rank websites in order of relevance.

Each listed website is assigned a number ranking and is usually accompanied by descriptive information to describe the contents of the website.

Websites identified in search results include hyperlinks which, when clicked on by the searcher, connect the searcher to the particular website.

Operators of websites usually want to encourage visits to their websites.

One technique is to register a website with search engines and directories. Websites can be registered with a number of different search engines and directories. Another technique commonly used by website operators to encourage visits to their website is to utilize a URL that reflects the identity of the site operator so that internet users can readily locate the site without the use of a search engine or directory.

Private Career Training Institutions Agency v. Vancouver Career College (Burnaby) Inc., 2010 BCSC 765 at paras. 14–26:

Internet search engines collect and store data about websites, including keywords contained in the website and the location of the website. When a user enters a query into a search engine such as Google or Yahoo, the search terms are compared to the website information stored in the search engine. The search engine then produces a list of websites, which are ranked according to relevance, as determined by the search engine.

One way in which a website operator can attempt to increase the traffic to their website is through the use of pay-per-click advertising. The relevant form of pay-per-click advertising in the case at bar is keyword advertising ("Keyword Advertising"). This service allows the website operator to pay search engines for links to their websites to appear as "sponsored links" alongside the search engine's normal or "organic" search results.

In order to use Keyword Advertising, a website operator will create an advertisement which specifies certain keywords to describe their website and set the maximum price they are willing to pay to use those keywords. The keywords then act as a trigger causing the advertisement and the associated link to be displayed. Specifically, when a user enters a search query containing a triggering keyword, the search engine checks to see which advertisement is most relevant and has placed the highest bid for the selected keywords. These advertisements and the associated links are displayed as "sponsored links" in a prominent location among the organic search results. If the user selects one of the sponsored links, that website is charged according to its bid.

The website operator will provide instructions to the search engine as to how much money they want to spend in a particular advertising campaign. Those instructions can be modified daily, depending on the success of the keywords or campaign. Once the maximum amount of money to be spent in a campaign is exhausted, including daily maximums, the online advertisement will stop appearing when the keywords are searched.

Assuming there are funds available in a campaign, all bids on keywords will result in the online advertisement being displayed if those keywords are used in conjunction with an online search. The higher the bid, the higher the placement of the online advertisement. Bids that are not high enough will result in online advertisements that do not appear on the first results page, which is the most desirable placement.

Typically, Keyword Advertising is purchased in a campaign where keywords are grouped around themes aimed at specific marketing goals. For example, an advertising campaign built around "online degrees" could include keywords such as "online," "online degrees," "online education," "online studies," "online training" and "internet training." The idea is to try to predict what terms the searcher will use when looking for a product or service.

The keyword does not need to match the exact search term entered by the internet user in order to trigger the occurrence of a sponsored link. For example, if one bids on the keyword "college" and the user searches "Vancouver colleges", the results could include the sponsored link.

In addition, keywords are not case sensitive, so if a user searches "business," it may trigger the occurrence of a sponsored link where the word "business" was bid on.

The actual online advertisement that appears as a part of Keyword Advertising typically consists of a title, a description and a URL, and have to fit within the following prescribed limits:

- For Google online advertisements, the title line is limited to 25 characters; the two description lines are limited to 35 characters; and the URL is limited to 35 characters;
- For Yahoo online advertisements, the title line is limited to 40 characters; the two description lines are limited to 70 characters; and the URL is limited to 40 characters.

In the context of the present dispute between the parties, it is important to note that the advertisements that are listed in the search results as "sponsored links" do not displace or replace the organic search results that typically appear free of charge when a user conducts an online search. The sponsored links are displayed along with the organic search results and appear either to the right of the organic search results, separated by a vertical line, or above the organic search results, within either a yellow or blue shaded box. In both cases, the sponsored links are clearly designated as such or as "sponsor results."

It is also important to note that the person who has conducted a search and who has chosen to examine a sponsored link can always click on the "back" button on their browser and return to the original search results page to locate other sites of interest.

Website operators will sometimes specify trademarks or operating names of their competitors as triggering keywords, since these terms are often not bid on, even by their rightful owner. If the owner of the trademark or operating name has not specified their trademark or operating name as a triggering keyword in conjunction with Keyword Advertising, or if their bid for these keywords is too low, other advertisements may appear as a sponsored link and can outrank the rightful owner of the trademark or operating name. Again, it is important to remember that the rightful owner of the trademark or operating name will still appear as part of the organic search results; they will simply not be positioned in the "sponsored links" area of those results.

Although some of the materials filed by the Agency complain of VCC Inc.'s possible use of competitors' trademarks in its metatags, the evidence before the Court does not support such a conclusion. On the contrary, VCC Inc. has specifically denied it has ever used the names of competitors or trademarked terms in the title line, description line or URL of its online advertisements, and I accept that as a fact.

BCAA et al. v. Office and Professional Employees' Int. Union et al, 2001 BCSC 156, [2001] B.C.J. No. 151, [2001] 4 W.W.R. 95, 85 B.C.L.R. (3d) 302, 10 C.P.R. (4th) 423, 102 A.C.W.S. (3d) 975, [2001] B.C.T.C. 156 paras. 25–31:

A search engine uses specialized computer programs sometimes called "spiders" or "crawlers" to electronically visit websites, gather relevant data about those websites, and compile and index the information.

Directories only list information about websites that is intentionally entered into the directory. A business may register information about its website with a directory.

To use a directory or search engine, the computer user must access the website of a directory or search engine. There the computer user will find a space in which a search query can be entered, usually one or more key words. When a search is activated using a search engine or a directory, the search engine then compares the words used in the search query with information stored and indexed by the search engine or directory and ranks stored data about web pages according to relevance established by reference to the key words entered in the search. Relevance is determined in various ways, including the frequency matching key words appear on the webpage and the particular location of matching key words on a webpage.

Based upon its own program for ranking websites according to search queries, each search engine and directory will generate the search results, which are a list of websites. These results are displayed. The search engine or directory is programmed to rank websites in order of relevance.

Each listed website is assigned a number ranking and is usually accompanied by descriptive information to describe the contents of the website.

Websites identified in search results include hyperlinks which, when clicked on by the searcher, connect the searcher to the particular website.

Operators of websites usually want to encourage visits to their websites. One technique is to register a website with search engines and directories. Websites can be registered with a number of different search engines and directories. Another technique commonly used by website operators to encourage visits to their website is to utilize a URL that reflects the identity of the site operator so that internet users can readily locate the site without the use of a search engine or directory.

Pro-C Ltd. v. Computer City Inc., 1999 CanLII 14926 at para. 13 (ON S.C.):

A helpful analysis of how one searches or "surfs" the Internet is contained in the following description provided by Justice R. Arcara of the United States District Court — Western District of New York in *OBH, Inc. and Columbia Insurance Company v. Spotlight Magazine Inc. and Claude Tortora*, 86 F.Supp.2nd 176 [2000] U.S. Dist. Lexis 4462. pp. 8–9:

> Using a Web browser, such as Netscape's Navigator or Microsoft's Internet Explorer, an Internet user may navigate the Web — searching for, communicating with, and retrieving information from various web sites. See *Brookfield*, 174 F.3d at 1044 (citations omitted). A specific web site is most easily located by using its domain name. See *Panavision*, 141 F.3d at 1327. Upon entering a domain name into the web browser, the corresponding web site will quickly appear on the computer screen. Sometimes, however, a user will not know the domain name of the site he or she is looking for, whereupon he or she has two principal options: trying to guess the domain name or seeking the assistance of an Internet "search engine." *Brookfield*, 174 F.3d at 1044.
>
> Often times, an Internet user will begin trying to guess at the domain name, especially if there is an obvious domain name to try. Users often assume, as a rule of thumb, that the domain name of a particular company will be the company name followed by ".com." See *id.* at 1045. For example, if a user wanted information about a Ford automobile, he or she could find such information at "ford.com." Sometimes, a trademark is better known than the company itself, in which case a user may assume that the domain address will be "'trademark'.com." See *id.* (citing *Beverly v. Network solutions, Inc.*, 1998 WL 320829, at *1 (N.D. Cal. June 12, 1998) ("Companies attempt to make the search for their

web site as easy as possible. They do so by using a corporate name, trademark or service mark as their web site address.")). For instance, a user seeking the Kentucky Fried Chicken web site might presume, correctly as it happens, that entering the address www.KFC.com will turn up a Kentucky Fried Chicken web site. Guessing domain names, however, is not an exact science. The user who assume that "'X'.com" will always correspond to the web site of company X or trademark X will sometimes be misled. For example, one looking for information about Delta Airlines might sensibly try "delta.com." However, that domain name turns up a web site for Delta Financial Corporation, an unrelated company (Delta Airlines web site is actually "deltaairlines.com").

An Internet user's second option when he or she does not know the domain name is to utilize an Internet search engine, such as Yahoo, Altavista, or Lycos.

See id. (citations omitted). When a keyword is entered, the search engine processes it through an index of web sites to generate a list relating to the entered keyword. Each search engine uses its own algorithm to arrange indexed materials in sequence, so the list of web sites that any particular set of keywords will bring up may differ depending on the search engine used. *See id.* (citations omitted).

Search engines look for keywords in places such as domain names, actual text on the web page, and metatags. Metatags are HTML code intended to describe the contents of the web site. There are different types of metatags, including "description" and "keyword" metatags. The description metatags are intended to describe the web site; the keyword metatags, at least in theory, contain keywords relating to the contents of the web site. The more often a term appears in the metatags and in the text of the web page, the more likely it is that the web page will be "hit" in a search for that keyword and the higher on the list of "hits" the web page will appear.

. . .

Given the current state of search engine technology, that search will often produce a list of hundreds of web sites through which the user must sort in order to find what he or she is looking for. As a result, companies strongly prefer that their domain name be comprised of the company or brand trademark and the suffix ".com."

UK

Metropolitan International Schools Ltd. (t/a Skillstrain and/or Train2game) v.
   Designtechnica Corp (t/a Digital Trends) & Ors, [2009] EWHC 1765 at paras. 5
   and 9–13 (QB):

Internet users who wish to post a comment within a specified thread, or to
commence a new thread, are required to register a username with the website. This will then be published alongside any posted contribution together
with the date and time on which it was made. Anyone may access the forums
and read their contents. So too, the contents are accessible to Internet search
engines.

. . .

Because it is so central to the issues now before the court, it is necessary
for me to summarise the evidence explaining how search engines work. This
again derives primarily from Mr Jaron Lewis, although it is a subject also covered in expert evidence introduced by the Claimant from Dr David Sharp.

The Internet comprises web pages containing information and each page
has a unique address (the "URL"). The page will appear when the URL is typed
into an Internet browser. Each website address ends with a "top level domain",
which is a series of letters often denoting the country in which the website is
registered. Thus, many websites which are accessed in the United Kingdom
will end with the ".uk" domain. Google operates search engines for all the
major "country code top level domains" ("ccTLDs"). The principal reason why
this is done is to enable Google searches to provide appropriate results for local
users. It was explained, by way of example, that a search on the word "bank"
would yield different results on www.google.co.uk from those appearing on
www.google.ca (where primarily Canadian banks would appear).

It would be impossible for Google to search every page available on the
web in real time and then deliver a result in a time frame acceptable to users.
What happens is that Google compiles an index of pages from the web and it
is this index which is examined during the search process. Although it is well
known, it is necessary to emphasise that the index is compiled and updated
purely automatically (i.e. with no human input). The process is generally referred to as "crawling" or the "web crawl."

When a search is carried out, it will yield a list of pages which are determined (automatically) as being relevant to the query. The technology ranks
the pages in order of "perceived" relevance — again without human intervention. The search results that are displayed in response to any given query
must depend on the successful delivery of crawling, indexing and ranking.

Content on the Internet is constantly being crawled and re-crawled and the index updated.

Obviously Google has no control over the search terms entered by users of the search engine or of the material which is placed on the web by its users.

The complaint in these proceedings against the First Defendant relates to information appearing on one of its web bulletin boards posted by third parties. Needless to say, the Second and Third Defendants have no control over the First Defendant or over what appears on its bulletin boards.

US

ACLU v. Reno, 929 F. Supp 824 (ED Pa. 1996) at paras. 12–21:

Individuals have a wide variety of avenues to access cyberspace in general, and the Internet in particular. In terms of physical access, there are two common methods to establish an actual link to the Internet. First, one can use a computer or computer terminal that is directly (and usually permanently) connected to a computer network that is itself directly or indirectly connected to the Internet. Second, one can use a "personal computer" with a "modem" to connect over a telephone line to a larger computer or computer network that is itself directly or indirectly connected to the Internet. As detailed below, both direct and modem connections are made available to people by a wide variety of academic, governmental, or commercial entities.

Students, faculty, researchers, and others affiliated with the vast majority of colleges and universities in the United States can access the Internet through their educational institutions. Such access is often via direct connection using computers located in campus libraries, offices, or computer centers, or may be through telephone access using a modem from a student's or professor's campus or off-campus location. Some colleges and universities install "ports" or outlets for direct network connections in each dormitory room or provide access via computers located in common areas in dormitories. Such access enables students and professors to use information and content provided by the college or university itself, and to use the vast amount of research resources and other information available on the Internet worldwide.

Similarly, Internet resources and access are sufficiently important to many corporations and other employers that those employers link their office computer networks to the Internet and provide employees with direct or modem access to the office network (and thus to the Internet). Such access might be used by, for example, a corporation involved in scientific or medical research or manufacturing to enable corporate employees to exchange information and ideas with academic researchers in their fields.

Those who lack access to the Internet through their schools or employers still have a variety of ways they can access the Internet. Many communities across the country have established "free-nets" or community networks to provide their citizens with a local link to the Internet (and to provide local-oriented content and discussion groups). The first such community network, the Cleveland Free-Net Community Computer System, was established in 1986, and free-nets now exist in scores of communities as diverse as Richmond, Virginia, Tallahassee, Florida, Seattle, Washington, and San Diego, California. Individuals typically can access free-nets at little or no cost via modem connection or by using computers available in community buildings. Free-nets are often operated by a local library, educational institution, or non-profit community group.

Individuals can also access the Internet through many local libraries. Libraries often offer patrons use of computers that are linked to the Internet. In addition, some libraries offer telephone modem access to the libraries' computers, which are themselves connected to the Internet. Increasingly, patrons now use library services and resources without ever physically entering the library itself. Libraries typically provide such direct or modem access at no cost to the individual user.

Individuals can also access the Internet by patronizing an increasing number of storefront "computer coffee shops," where customers — while they drink their coffee — can use computers provided by the shop to access the Internet. Such Internet access is typically provided by the shop for a small hourly fee.

Individuals can also access the Internet through commercial and non-commercial Internet service providers" that typically offer modem telephone access to a computer or computer network linked to the Internet. Many such providers — including the members of plaintiff Commercial Internet Exchange Association — are commercial entities offering Internet access for a monthly or hourly fee. Some Internet service providers, however, are non-profit organizations that offer free or very low cost access to the Internet. For example, the International Internet Association offers free modem access to the Internet upon request. Also, a number of trade or other non-profit associations offer Internet access as a service to members.

Another common way for individuals to access the Internet is through one of the major national commercial "online services" such as America Online, CompuServe, the Microsoft Network, or Prodigy. These online services offer nationwide computer networks (so that subscribers can dial-in to a local telephone number), and the services provide extensive and well organized content within their own proprietary computer networks. In addition to allowing access to the extensive content available within each online service, the services also allow subscribers to link to the much larger resources of the Internet. Full access to the online service (including access to the Internet) can be obtained for modest monthly or hourly fees. The major commercial online services have almost twelve million individual subscribers across the United States.

In addition to using the national commercial online services, individuals can also access the Internet using some (but not all) of the thousands of local dial-in computer services, often called "bulletin board systems" or "BBSs." With an investment of as little as $2,000.00 and the cost of a telephone line, individuals, non-profit organizations, advocacy groups, and businesses can offer their own dial-in computer "bulletin board" service where friends, members, subscribers, or customers can exchange ideas and information. BBSs range from single computers with only one telephone line into the computer (allowing only one user at a time), to single computers with many telephone lines into the computer (allowing multiple simultaneous users), to multiple linked computers each servicing multiple dial-in telephone lines (allowing multiple simultaneous users). Some (but not all) of these BBS systems offer direct or indirect links to the Internet. Some BBS systems charge users a nominal fee for access, while many others are free to the individual users.

Although commercial access to the Internet is growing rapidly, many users of the Internet — such as college students and staff — do not individually pay for access (except to the extent, for example, that the cost of computer services is a component of college tuition). These and other Internet users can access the Internet without paying for such access with a credit card or other form of payment.

James Grimmelmann, "The Structure of Search Engine Law" (2007) 93 *Iowa Law Review* 1 at 7:

A search engine in isolation is useless. It becomes valuable only through its interactions with *content providers* and with *users*. By aggregating its knowledge of what content providers have to offer and organizing that knowledge in a form useful to users, a search engine can match users with appropriate content providers, to the benefit of both. This matching, however, can antagonize *third parties* who would rather that certain connections not be made. (As discussed in more detail below, such third parties include copyright holders, targets of libel, stalker-fearing privacy lovers, and censorious governments.) Visualizing the information flows between search engines and these three groups illustrates how search works.

At its core, search consists of four flows of information:
1. The search engine gathers content.
2. A user queries the search engine.
3. The search engine provides the user with results.

WEBSITES AND THE WORLD WIDE WEB

Canada

BCAA et al. v. Office and Professional Employees' Int. Union et al., 2001 BCSC 156,
[2001] 4 W.W.R. 95, 10 C.P.R. (4th) 423, 85 B.C.L.R. (3d) 302 at paras. 21–24 :

The World Wide Web is comprised of electronic documents called "webpages." Webpages are stored on computers known as "servers." A "website" is a collection of related webpages stored on a single server. A "homepage" is the "front door" of the website.

The programming language used to create the content, design and overall layout of individual webpages is known as "HyperText Markup Language" or "HTML."

Computer programs known as "browsers" are used on a searcher's computers to read HTML information and interact with it. The browsers read the website coding to display designs and text on the user's computer screen.

Internet users can access websites in three main ways. First, if the user knows the URL of a particular site, or is able to guess it and add a convention such as ".com" or ".ca," the user can access the website directly by typing in the URL on the user's browser. Second, the URL can be added to the "bookmarks" stored on the user's browser. Third, a user can locate and access a website through the use of search engines and directories, which are common tools for finding information and websites.

US

ACLU v. Reno, 929 F. Supp 824 (ED Pa. 1996) at paras. 33–48:

A third approach, and fast becoming the most well- known on the Internet, is the "World Wide Web." The Web utilizes a "hypertext" formatting language called hypertext markup language (HTML), and programs that "browse" the Web can display HTML documents containing text, images, sound, animation and moving video. Any HTML document can include links to other types of information or resources, so that while viewing an HTML document that, for example, describes resources available on the Internet, one can "click" using a computer mouse on the description of the resource and be immediately connected to the resource itself. Such "hyperlinks" allow information to be accessed and organized in very flexible ways, and allow people to locate and efficiently view related information even if the information is stored on numerous computers all around the world.

Purpose. The World Wide Web (W3C) was created to serve as the platform for a global, online store of knowledge, containing information from a diversity of sources and accessible to Internet users around the world. Though information on the Web is contained in individual computers, the fact that each of these computers is connected to the Internet through W3C protocols allows all of the information to become part of a single body of knowledge. It is currently the most advanced information system developed on the Internet, and embraces within its data model most information in previous networked information systems such as ftp, gopher, wais, and Usenet.

History. W3C was originally developed at CERN, the European Particle Physics Laboratory, and was initially used to allow information sharing within internationally dispersed teams of researchers and engineers. Originally aimed at the High Energy Physics community, it has spread to other areas and attracted much interest in user support, resource recovery, and many other areas which depend on collaborative and information sharing. The Web has extended beyond the scientific and academic community to include communications by individuals, non-profit organizations, and businesses.

Basic Operation. The World Wide Web is a series of documents stored in different computers all over the Internet. Documents contain information stored in a variety of formats, including text, still images, sounds, and video. An essential element of the Web is that any document has an address (rather like a telephone number). Most Web documents contain "links." These are short sections of text or image which refer to another document. Typically the linked text is blue or underlined when displayed, and when selected by the user, the referenced document is automatically displayed, wherever in the world it actually is stored. Links for example are used to lead from overview documents to more detailed documents, from tables of contents to particular pages, but also as cross-references, footnotes, and new forms of information structure.

Many organizations now have "home pages" on the Web. These are documents which provide a set of links designed to represent the organization, and through links from the home page, guide the user directly or indirectly to information about or relevant to that organization.

As an example of the use of links, if these findings were to be put on a World Wide Web site, its home page might contain links such as those: *THE NATURE OF CYBERSPACE *CREATION OF THE INTERNET AND THE DEVELOPMENT OF CYBERSPACE *HOW PEOPLE ACCESS THE INTERNET *METHODS TO COMMUNICATE OVER THE INTERNET

Each of these links takes the user of the site from the beginning of the Findings to the appropriate section within this Adjudication. Links may also take the user from the original Web site to another Web site on another computer connected to the Internet. These links from one computer to another, from one document to another across the Internet, are what unify the Web into a single body of knowledge, and what makes the Web unique. The Web was designed with a maximum target time to follow a link of one tenth of a second.

Publishing. The World Wide Web exists fundamentally as a platform through which people and organizations can communicate through shared information. When information is made available, it is said to be "published" on the Web. Publishing on the Web simply requires that the "publisher" has a computer connected to the Internet and that the computer is running W3C server software. The computer can be as simple as a small personal computer costing less than $1500 dollars or as complex as a multi-million dollar mainframe computer. Many Web publishers choose instead to lease disk storage space from someone else who has the necessary computer facilities, eliminating the need for actually owning any equipment oneself.

The Web, as a universe of network accessible information, contains a variety of documents prepared with quite varying degrees of care, from the hastily typed idea, to the professionally executed corporate profile. The power of the Web stems from the ability of a link to point to any document, regardless of its status or physical location.

Information to be published on the Web must also be formatted according to the rules of the Web standards. These standardized formats assure that all Web users who want to read the material will be able to view it. Web standards are sophisticated and flexible enough that they have grown to meet the publishing needs of many large corporations, banks, brokerage houses, newspapers and magazines which now publish "online" editions of their material, as well as government agencies, and even courts, which use the Web to disseminate information to the public. At the same time, Web publishing is simple enough that thousands of individual users and small community organizations are using the Web to publish their own personal "home pages," the equivalent of individualized newsletters about that person or organization, which are available to everyone on the Web.

Web publishers have a choice to make their Web sites open to the general pool of all Internet users, or close them, thus making the information accessible only to those with advance authorization. Many publishers choose to keep their sites open to all in order to give their information the widest potential audience. In the event that the publishers choose to maintain restrictions on access, this may be accomplished by assigning specific user names and passwords as a prerequisite to access to the site. Or, in the case of

Web sites maintained for internal use of one organization, access will only be allowed from other computers within that organization's local network.

Searching the Web. A variety of systems have developed that allow users of the Web to search particular information among all of the public sites that are part of the Web. Services such as Yahoo, Magellan, Altavista, Webcrawler, and Lycos are all services known as "search engines" which allow users to search for Web sites that contain certain categories of information, or to search for key words. For example, a Web user looking for the text of Supreme Court opinions would type the words "Supreme Court" into a search engine, and then be presented with a list of World Wide Web sites that contain Supreme Court information. This list would actually be a series of links to those sites. Having searched out a number of sites that might contain the desired information, the user would then follow individual links, browsing through the information on each site, until the desired material is found. For many content providers on the Web, the ability to be found by these search engines is very important.

Common standards. The Web links together disparate information on an ever-growing number of Internet-linked computers by setting common information storage formats (HTML) and a common language for the exchange of Web documents (HTTP). Although the information itself may be in many different formats, and stored on computers which are not otherwise compatible, the basic Web standards provide a basic set of standards which allow communication and exchange of information. Despite the fact that many types of computers are used on the Web, and the fact that many of these machines are otherwise incompatible, those who "publish" information on the Web are able to communicate with those who seek to access information with little difficulty because of these basic technical standards.

A distributed system with no centralized control. Running on tens of thousands of individual computers on the Internet, the Web is what is known as a distributed system. The Web was designed so that organizations with computers containing information can become part of the Web simply by attaching their computers to the Internet and running appropriate World Wide Web software. No single organization controls any membership in the Web, nor is there any single centralized point from which individual Web sites or services can be blocked from the Web. From a user's perspective, it may appear to be a single, integrated system, but in reality it has no centralized control point.

Contrast to closed databases. The Web's open, distributed, decentralized nature stands in sharp contrast to most information systems that have come before it. Private information services such as Westlaw, Lexis/Nexis, and Dialog, have contained large storehouses of knowledge, and can be accessed from the Internet with the appropriate passwords and access software. However, these databases are not linked together into a single whole, as is the World Wide Web.

Success of the Web in research, education, and political activities. The World Wide Web has become so popular because of its open, distributed, and easy-to-use nature. Rather than requiring those who seek information to purchase new software or hardware, and to learn a new kind of system for each new database of information they seek to access, the Web environment makes it easy for users to jump from one set of information to another. By the same token, the open nature of the Web makes it easy for publishers to reach their intended audiences without having to know in advance what kind of computer each potential reader has, and what kind of software they will be using.

ANNOTATED BIBLIOGRAPHY ON
INFORMATION WARFARE

This bibliography does not pretend to be definitive or exhaustive. It is intended, rather, as a starting point for further reading that I have found useful, enjoyable, and applicable to cyberlibel proceedings. Some sections have little or no annotation because of their self-evident application to cyberlibel. Others are discussed or commented on in greater detail, either because the relevance may not be as self-evident or because they were of particular value to me.

This section has several further objectives:

1. to provide the reader with further resources in a number of different disciplines and fields that are in practice are very much interconnected;
2. to explain the applicability and utility of some of these resources; and
3. to provide a catalyst for discussion, reflection, and development of principles, strategies, and tactics for understanding, coping, and succeeding in cyberlibel actions as a form of informational warfare.

A. CRISIS MANAGEMENT

Andert, Stephen and Donald K. Burleson, *Web Stalkers: Protect Yourself from Internet Criminals & Psychopaths* (Kittrell, NC: Rampant Tech-Press, 2005)

Fombrun, Charles J., *Reputation: Realizing Value from the Corporate Image* (Boston: Harvard Business School Press, 1996)

Gottschalk, Jack A., *Crisis Response* (Detroit: Visible Ink Press, 1993)

Irvine, Robert S., *When You Are the Headline: Managing a Major News Story* (Louisville: Harmony House, 1987)

Janal, Daniel S., *Risky Business* (New York: John Wiley & Sons, 1998)

Koenig, Fredrick, *Rumor in the Marketplace* (Dover, MA: Auburn House, 1985)

Mitroff, Ian I., *Crisis Leadership: Planning for the Unthinkable* (Hoboken, NJ: John Wiley & Sons, 2004)

Mitroff, Ian I., *Managing Crises Before They Happen: What Every Executive and Manager Needs to Know about Crisis Management* (New York: Amacom, 2001)

Mitroff, Ian I., Christine M. Pearson, and Katharine L. Harrington, *The Essential Guide to Managing Corporate Crises: A Step-by-Step Handbook for Surviving Major Catastrophes* (New York: Oxford University Press, 1996)

Pauchant, Thierry C. and Ian I. Mitroff, *Transforming the Crisis-Prone Organization* (San Francisco: Jossey-Bass Publishers, 1992)

The textbooks by Ian I. Mitroff are superb and provide extremely valuable insights.

B. "WHAT IF?" HISTORY

Cowley, Robert, ed., *What If? The World's Foremost Military Historians Imagine What Might Have Been* (New York: Berkley Books, 1999)

Cowley, Robert, ed., *What If? Eminent Historians Imagine What Might Have Been* (New York: Berkley Books, 2002)

Cowley, Robert, ed., *What Ifs? Of American History: Eminent Historians Imagine What Might Have Been* (New York: G.P. Putnam's, 2003)

Kantor, MacKinlay, *If the South Had Won the Civil War* (Montreal: Bantam Books, 1961)

Tsouras, Peter G., *Rising Sun Victorious: An Alternate History of the Pacific War* (New York: Presidia Press, 2007)

"What if" or alternative history books are valuable in several ways in planning a response to cyberlibel attacks because:

1. They compel the reader to examine all assumptions and biases;
2. They compel the reader to examine a wide range of contingencies; and
3. They hammer home the lack of inevitability during the course of disputes.

C. INFORMATION WARFARE/CYBERWAR

Arquilla, John and David Ronfeldt, *In Athena's Camp: Preparing for Conflict In The Information Age* (Santa Monica, CA: Rand, 1997)

Arquilla, John and David Ronfeldt, *Networks and Netwars* (Santa Monica, CA: Rand, 2001)

Clarke, Richard A. and Robert K. Knake, *Cyber War: The Next Threat to National Security and What to Do about It* (New York: Ecco, 2010)

Denning, Dorothy E., *Information Warfare and Security* (New York: ACM Press, 1999)

Forno, Richard and Ronald Baklarz, *The Art of Information Warfare: Insight Into The Knowledge Warrior Philosophy* (Dunkirk, MD: Universal, 1999)

Hutchinson, Bill and Matt Warren, *Information Warfare: Corporate Attack and Defence in a Digital World* (Woburn, MA: Butterworth Heinemann, 2001)

Loundy, David J., *Computer Crime, Information Warfare, and Economic Espionage* (Durham, N.C.: Carolina Academic Press, 2003)

Munro, Iain, *Information Warfare: Corporate Attack and Defence in a Digital World* (New York: Routledge Taylor & Francis Group, 2005)

Rattray, Greg, *Strategic Warfare in Cyberspace* (Cambridge, MA: MIT Press, 2001)

Weimann, Gabriel, *Terror on the Internet: The New Arena, The New Challenges* (Washington: United States Institute of Peace, 2006)

As can be seen from the title themselves, these informational warfare and cyberwar titles are generally broken down into three categories:

1. Texts written about information warfare in military conflicts.
2. Texts written about information warfare through information technology (for example, Dorothy Denning's text *Information Warfare and Security*).
3. Texts that attempt to bridge several fields, including information technology, cyberwar, and crisis management (such as Hutchinson and Munro's *Information Warfare: Corporate Attack and Defence in a Digital World*). This last category is probably the most applicable to the issues facing lawyers generally, and defamation lawyers and corporate counsel in particular.

D. RISKS

Ariely, Dan, *Predictably Irrational: The Hidden Forces that Shape Our Decisions* (New York: HarperCollins, 2008)

Barker, Joel Arthur, *Paradigms: The Business of Discovering the Future* (New York: William Morrow and Company, 1992)

Bernstein, Peter L., *Against the Odds: The Remarkable Story of Risk* (New York: John Wiley & Sons, 1996)

Holmes, Andrew, *Smart Risk* (Chicester, UK: Capstone, 2004)

Kaplan, Michael and Ellen Kaplan, *Chances Are . . . Adventures in Probability* (London, UK: Penguin, 2006)

Mamis, Justin, *The Nature of Risk: Stock Market Survival & the Meaning of Life* (Flint Hill, VA: Fraser Publishing, 1999)

Taleb, Nassim Nicholas, *Fooled By Randomness: The Hidden Role of Chance in Life and in the Markets* (New York: Random House, 2001)

Taleb, Nassim Nicholas, *The Black Swan: The Impact of the Highly Improbable*, 2d ed. (New York: Random House, 2007)

E. STRATEGIC STUDIES AND GUERRILLA WARFARE

Asher, Jerry and Eric Hammel, *Duel for the Golan: The 100-Hour Battle That Saved Israel* (New York: William Morrow and Company, 1987)

Boot, Max, *The Savage Wars of Peace: Small Wars and the Rise of American Power* (New York: Basic Books, 2002)

Boot, Max, *War Made New: Technology, Warfare, and the Course of History, 1500 to Today* (London, UK: Penguin, 2006)

Clark, Wesley K., *Waging Modern War: Bosnia, Kosovo, and the Future of Combat* (New York: The Perseus Books Group, 2001)

Cordingly, David, *The Real Master and Commander* (New York: Bloomsbury, 2007)

Davis, Burke, *Jeb Stuart: The Last Cavalier* (New York: Bonanza Books, 1957)

Davis, Burke, *They Called Him Stonewall: The Life Of Lt. General T.J. Jackson, C.S.A.* (New York: Rinehart, 1954)

Earle, Edward Mead, *Makers of Modern Strategy: Military Thought from Machiavelli to Hitler* (New York: Princeton University Press, 1970)

Halter, Ed, *From Sun Tzu to Xbox: War and Videogames* (New York: Thunder's Mouth Press, 2006)

Hart, B.H. Liddell, *The Rommel Papers* (London: Collins, 1953)

Hughes-Wilson, John, *Military Intelligence Blunders* (London: Constable, 1999)

Keegan, John, *Knowledge of the Enemy from Napoleon to Al-Qaeda: Intelligence in War* (Toronto: Key Porter Books, 2003)

Lawrence, T.E., *Lawrence of Arabia: Seven Pillars of Wisdom* (Australia: Penguin, 1962)

Manchester, William, *American Caesar: Douglas MacArthur — 1880–1964* (Toronto: Little, Brown, 1978)

Messenger, Charles, *The Commandos: 1940–1946* (London: William Kimber & Co., 1985)

Owen, David Lloyd, *Providence Their Guide* (London: George G. Harrap & Co., 1980)

Reitz, Deneys, *Commando: A Boer Journal of the Boer War* (London: Faber and Faber, 1929)

Sawyer, Ralph D., *The Seven Military Classics of Ancient China* (New York: Perseus Books, 1993)

Thomas, Emory M., *Bold Dragoon: The Life of J.E.B. Stuart* (New York: First Vintage Books, 1988)

Tzu, Sun, *The Art of War* (New York: Delacorte Press, 1983)

Wert, Jeffry D., *Mosby's Rangers: From the High Tide of the Confederacy to the Last Days at Appomattox: The Story of the Most Famous Command of The Civil War and its Legendary Leader, John S. Mosby* (New York: Simon and Schuster, 1990)

Wills, Brian Steel, *A Battle from the Start: The Life of Nathan Bedford Forrest* (New York: HarperCollins, 1992)

This section could be ten times the size and still not scratch the surface of the questions about strategic studies and guerrilla warfare which I believe are essential to understanding — let alone cultivating success in — the conduct of cyberlibel actions, either for a plaintiff or a defendant. If one is confined to a single text, I would, without a doubt, recommend Sun Tzu, *The Art of War*. The text is over 2,500 years old but is still as relevant today as at the time of its writing. Some of the titles may be more obvious than others contained in this category and may require some explanation.

Wesley Clark's book is very useful as it is an excellent discussion of one of the first instances where cyber warfare and shooting warfare converged. His discussions about the necessity of handling both optics and military considerations are very applicable in engaging in and conducting cyberlibel actions.

William Manchester's biography of Douglas MacArthur provides some interesting insights about MacArthur's Pacific island-hopping campaign. Instead of attacking the most fortified islands and losing hundreds of thousands of soldiers against well-defended positions, MacArthur executed brilliant, amphibious operations and, in many cases, just ignored some of the most heavily defended islands. The insight here that I found applicable for cyberlibel proceedings is that, in many cases, if a plaintiff is facing three or four different defendants at different levels, such as the author, the ISP, and the operator of the search engine, sometimes it is better to proceed against all three at once while other times it is better to proceed against only one. Categorical rules cannot be established but the insights gained from reading this book on MacArthur's Pacific campaign are helpful.

T.E. Lawrence's book, *Seven Pillars of Wisdom,* is also very useful and is discussed in Munro's *Information Warfare: Corporate Attack And Defence in a Digital World* (listed under section C, above). *Seven Pillars of Wisdom* demonstrates the necessity of fluidity — being able to operate very quickly and avoid getting bogged down in particular types of actions. All these considerations, and many more contained in the texts above, are applicable for success in the conduct of cyberlibel proceedings.

TABLE OF CASES

INDEX

online versions of print publication and, 305

Right to reply, 17

Search engines, 9, 39, 41, 43, 44, 48, 50, 53,
    197, 223, 246, 281, 306, 312, 332, 339–56
background, 339–41
Boolean system, 340–41
Canadian legislation on, 458–64
defamatory statements and, 3
    liability of, 22, 56, 58
non-Boolean system, 340–41
notification by plaintiff, liability of
    before and after, 343–56
    grace period, existence of, 352
    *Metropolitan International Schools
    Ltd. (t/a Skillstrain and/or Train-
    2game) v. Designtechnica Corp (t/a
    Digital Trends) & Ors* and, 343–56
    decision application in Canada,
        352–53
    obiter discussions, 353–56
        Defamation Act of 1996,
            statutory defence in,
            353–54
        *Electronic Commerce (EC
        Directive) Regulations
        2002*, potential applica-
        tion of, 354
        European legislation and
            caselaw, 355–56
        innocent dissemination at
            common law, 353
        US position, 356
    operator liability for publication
        after notice, 349–52
        before notice, 346–49
    relevance of to Canadian law-
        yers and judges, 345
    search engine operation meth-
        ods, evidence about in, 345–46
    unresolved issues, 352
search engine results pages (SERPs),
    342–43
snippets, 256, 263, 343, 344
UK legislation on, 464–65
US legislation on, 465–68
web portals vs., 340
website host vs., 350, 352
SERPs, 342–43

Shallow linking, 19
Single publication rule, 57, 61, 67, 71, 83, 84,
    249
    Australia, Canada, and UK rejection of,
        85–87
    description of, 85–87
Snippets, 3, 256, 263, 343, 344, 347, 349, 350,
    351, 352, 354*n*
Social network sites (SNS), 358–66
    blogs, 366
        Australian legislation on, 418–19
        Canadian legislation on, 417–18
    defined, 358–59
    Facebook, 359
        Canadian judicial discussions about,
            360–61
        pseudonym, plaintiff request to use,
            397–400
        qualified privilege, defence of, 367
        UK judicial discussions about, 361–64
        US judicial discussions about, 364
    networking vs., 359
    Twitter, 359, 364–65
    Wikis, 365–66
Spamming, 35
Standards, cyberlibel vs. offline libel litiga-
    tion, 49–51
Statutory report privilege, defence of, 16, 27

Take down notices, 9, 221–23, 286, 311, 350,
    351, 352, 355
    general, 221
    guidelines for, 223
    South African legislation, 221–22
    UK legislation, 222
"Technology first" approach, Internet inter-
    mediaries and, 312
Telephone carriers, 21, 310, 313, 321
Temporal indeterminacy, Internet defama-
    tion and, 46–47
Third parties
    publication and communication to,
        jurisdiction and, 107–8
        essential element, 107
        publication requires communication,
            107–8
True innuendo, defamatory expression, of,
    266
Twitter, 359, 364–65

ABOUT THE AUTHOR

David A. Potts received his BA from Cape Town University, his LLB from Dalhousie and his LLM from Osgoode Law School. He was called to the Ontario Bar in 1979. Since then, he has specialized in libel and slander law and in reputation management for a diverse range of clients. He has served on the Ontario Attorney General's Advisory Committee on the law of defamation, and is a sought-after speaker and writer (CBC, Forbes, *USA Today*, the Canadian and International Bar Associations, The Law Society of Upper Canada, and many others). He is co-author of *Canadian Libel and Slander Actions* (Irwin Law, 2004) with Roger McConchie and *Canadian Libel Practice* (Butterworths, 1985) with Julian Porter, as well as being a contributor to *Cyberlibel in Electronic Commerce — A Practitioner's Guide* (Carswell, 2002)

0 1341 1389506 1

LaVergne, TN USA
04 March 2011

218751LV00005B/2/P

9 781552 212035